KU-540-938

*Peasant Customs and Savage Myths*

# PEASANT CUSTOMS
# AND SAVAGE MYTHS

*SELECTIONS FROM*
*THE BRITISH FOLKLORISTS*

Edited by

RICHARD M. DORSON

VOLUME ONE

LONDON: ROUTLEDGE & KEGAN PAUL

*First published in 1968*
*by Routledge & Kegan Paul Limited*
*Broadway House, 68-74 Carter Lane*
*London E.C.4*

*Printed in Great Britain*
*by Butler & Tanner Limited*
*Frome and London*

© *Copyright Richard M. Dorson 1968*

*No part of this book may be reproduced*
*in any form without permission from*
*the publishers, except for the quotation of*
*brief passages in criticism*

*SBN 7100 2965 9*

CHESHUNT
PUBLIC
LIBRARIES

398·0942

X125595

*To my sister Audre, and to the memory of her late husband, wonderful, witty John Gingold, with whom it all started*

# Acknowledgements

THE OFFICERS AND MEMBERS of The Folk-Lore Society have shown me kindnesses ever since I first made acquaintance with the Society and its splendid library in University College, London, in the summer of 1948. For their favours I thank a succession of presidents: W. L. Hildburgh, Allan Gomme, Peter Opie, Douglas Kennedy, Katharine M. Briggs. The Hon. Editor of *Folklore*, Christina Hole, has generously given me permission to reprint selections from the journals and book publications of the Society. The British Museum and the Cambridge University libraries have proved hospitable and bountiful places in which to work. Oliver and Boyd, Ltd., have granted permission to reprint the selection from Alexander Carmichael's Introduction to *Carmina Gadelica*. My thanks go to Dr. B. W. Andrzejewski for translating the medieval Latin legend of Thomas Hickathrift on page 266.

The present work was begun during the tenure of a John Simon Guggenheim fellowship. I am grateful to Dr. Gordon N. Ray, director of the Guggenheim Memorial Foundation, for his constant encouragement. Indiana University has aided me with an International Studies research grant, derived from the Ford Foundation, and with a research assistant, Shou-hua Yearwood, who has performed tedious tasks cheerfully.

The selections here reprinted follow the original texts and reproduce the authors' forms of citation, often highly at variance with each other. Spellings are inconsistent: 'folklore' is spelled with and without the hyphen or even as two words. Biographical dictionaries, obituary notices, and the resources of the Public Record Office and the British Museum Reading Room furnished inclusive dates for some but not all of the writers on folklore active during the past century.

It is my hope that these volumes will help bring recognition to undeservedly forgotten folklorists who wrote in their spare hours with learning, passion, and excitement.

R.M.D.

# Contents

CONTENTS

## V THE GREAT TEAM: THESES AND VIEWPOINTS

# Introduction

THROUGHOUT THE NINETEENTH CENTURY a host of
talented Victorians wrote vigorously and polemically on the
subject given the name of 'folklore' in 1846. The intellectual
history of this movement is treated in the companion volume
I have written, *The British Folklorists, A History*. Characteristic
essays, rejoinders, addresses, chapters, and prefaces from the
spirited body of literature produced by the British folklorists are
offered in the present work.

The boundaries of the movement can be set between 1813, the
year in which Henry Ellis edited the revised manuscript of John
Brand's *Observations on Popular Antiquities*, to the outbreak of the
first World War in 1914. William John Thoms, who coined 'folklore,' justly called Brand's 'Popular Antiquities' the 'textbook of
the students of our English "Folk Lore".' The science of folklore
marched steadily forward until the dislocation of the Great War,
coincident with the passing of a brilliant generation, interrupted its
progress and fulfilment. As with all chapters of intellectual history,
this one too has its prehistory, dipping back into the seventeenth-
century concern with antiquarian and topographical researches,
and its posthistory up to the present time, marked by occasional
flashes of the old genius. But the heart of the movement lies in the
golden century from 1813 to 1914 when diverse intellectual pursuits
flourished during the Pax Britannica and the physical scope of
Empire afforded special bonuses to the folklorists of Britain.

The groupings of the selections follow closely the chapters of the
history. In order to present selections complete in themselves as well
as representative of their authors' thought, it has sometimes been
necessary to bypass major works, such as Hartland's *The Legend of
Perseus*, Gomme's *Folklore as an Historical Science*, and Nutt's
*Studies on the Legend of the Holy Grail*, in favour of the pithy article.
Fortunately for the anthologist, the Victorian folklorists and

mythologists engaged in continuous debate, challenging, defining and redefining, clarifying and defending cherished theories. These sharp ripostes can often serve better to convey the reasoning of a celestial mythologist, a unilinear evolutionist, an Aryan diffusionist, or a White Archaian racist than a monumental treatise.

The British folklorists were first and foremost men of ideas. Even the antiquaries who first explored the physical and mental relics of the past sought to uncover the pagan roots of extant ceremonies, rather than to amass olden curiosities as a private hobby. Then the philologists, the mythologists, and the anthropologists eagerly pressed into service the newly available materials of folklore in behalf of their systems. The origin and dispersion of the Aryans, the mythopoeic world view of early man, the animistic philosophy of savages, the survivals of primitive belief among peasants—these were the questions enlivening the folklore controversies. Even when the emphasis shifted from the library to the field, Empire collectors in India, Africa, and Australia, travellers in Europe, and Gaelic-speaking fieldworkers in Scotland and Ireland gathered their hoards with mythological or racialist or comparativist ideas in mind.

These then are volumes of theoretical writings. The actual folklore materials of legend, custom, belief, game, and charm appear only as illustrations of an hypothesis or data to score a debating point. Selections have been chosen to illumine the idea of folklore as it emerged in the minds of antiquaries, took wing with the celestial mythologists, came down to earth with the anthropological folk-lorists, was fought over by evolutionists and diffusionists, travelled around the world with British empire-builders and cosmopolites, and finally cleft the Isles at home with separatist emotions. By the time the Great War ended the Pax Britannica, the concepts of folklore had profoundly altered the thinking of civilized man.

# I   The Antiquaries

THE SCIENCE OF FOLKLORE took root in the well-grubbed soil of antiquarian learning. English gentlemen from the reigns of Queen Elizabeth to Queen Victoria professed a love for antiquities, as a respite from humdrum toil, a curiosity to the inquiring mind, and a bond with the past. '. . . every man is naturally an Antiquarian,' wrote Francis Grose, himself one of the most versatile antiquaries of the eighteenth century. The national pride of Englishmen in their country's historical rise and their local affection for shire, village, and manor found a satisfying outlet in the quest for antiquarian remains. While the first antiquaries viewed these remains as physical artifacts in the form of ancient monuments, forts, coins, and costumes, later antiquaries extended the concept to cover mental and spiritual relics of pagan or early Christian times. The antiquary often doubled as traveller, romancer, and artist, associating tragic ballad, heroic legend, and the fairy mythology with crumbled ruin and desolate landscape. A rude and primitive peasantry fitted naturally into the landscape and intrigued the traveller with their superstitious rites and ceremonies. From the mounting interest in these popular antiquities of the common people emerged, in 1846, the idea and the name of 'folklore.'

## [ 1   FRANCIS   GROSE ]

In the introduction to *The Antiquarian Repertory*, a journal he founded and edited from 1775 to 1784, Francis Grose (1731–91) defended the study of antiquities from the charge of dilettantism and enumerated its values as a serious branch of national learning. His statement and the pages of his periodical reveal the earlier conception of antiquities as attached to physical and visual remains and scenes and to the memorials of the great rather than the lowly. The corpulent, Falstaffian bookseller produced a series of volumes

[1]

exhibiting and describing the architectural antiquities of the British Isles, but at the same time he showed interest in the verbal antiquities of dialects and local beliefs, evinced in his *A Classical Dictionary of the Vulgar Tongue* and *A Provincial Glossary*.

Text from *The Antiquarian Repertory*, I (London, 1775). Pages [iii]–viii, 'Introduction.'

It has long been the fafhion to laugh at the ftudy of Antiquities, and to confider it as the idle amufement of a few humdrum, plodding fellows, who wanting genius for nobler ftudies, bufied themfelves in heaping up illegible Manufcripts, mutilated Statues, obliterated Coins, and broken Pipkins; in this the laughers may perhaps have been fomewhat juftified, from the abfurd purfuits of a few Collectors, but at the fame time an argument deduced from the abufe or perverfion of any ftudy, is by no means conclufive againft the ftudy itfelf; and in this particular cafe I truft I fhall be able to prove, that without a competent fund of Antiquarian Learning, no one will ever make a refpectable figure, either as a Divine, a Lawyer, Statefman, Soldier, or even a private Gentleman, and that it is the *fine quâ non* of feveral of the more liberal profeffions, as well as many trades; and is befides a ftudy to which all perfons in particular inftances have a kind of propenfity, every man being, as Logicians exprefs it, '*Quoad hoc*,' an Antiquarian.

Let us begin then with the Divine. His profeffion indifpenfibly obliges him to be an Antiquarian in the moft extenfive fenfe of the word, and to confider this Globe, and all things in it, from their very infancy. The formation of which being fo minutely recorded in the Holy Scriptures, feems to give a fanction to the purfuit. How will he defend the truth of the Prophecies from the cavils of Infidels, how fhew the harmony between the facred and prophane writers, without a thorough knowledge in Hiftory and Chronology; and how are thefe to be acquired but by the ftudy of Ancient Monuments, Statues, Coins, Manufcripts and Cuftoms?

In a more limited view, confidering him as a Member of the national Church. He ought to be minutely acquainted with the Ecclefiaftical Antiquities, which ferve for the foundation of the ceremonials he daily performs, and the veffels, utenfils and garments he conftantly wears and makes ufe of. And in order to be enabled to manage his own property, or that of any Church over which he may prefide, an infight into the Monaftick Hiftory and Terms are abfolutely neceffary. He fhould alfo be enabled to read the ancient charters and deeds of endowment, be converfant in the weights, meafures,

cuftoms and immunities of former times, all which are expreffed
in a language totally unintelligible to a mere claffic Scholar, and are
only to be attained by a courfe of Antiquarian refearches.

That a thorough knowledge of the national Antiquities is indifpenfibly neceffary for every man of the Law, feems fo felf-
evident a propofition, that an attempt at proofs would rather
obfcure than demonftrate it. What is the *Lex non Scripta*, or Common Law, but a feries of ancient cuftoms? Does not the origin of
almoft every writ in ufe depend on fome piece of Ancient Hiftory?
And how can a Judge or Advocate expatiate on the fpirit of any
ftatute, without knowing the hiftory of the manners, cuftoms, and
even vices of the times when it was framed? What, befides a liberal
arrangement of thefe matters, which may be called Legal Antiquities, has made the Commentaries of Judge Blackftone fo uni-
verfally read, and fo juftly admired?

Let us next turn to the Statefman and Legiflator; here we find his
very being depends on the knowledge of Hiftory and Antiquities.
It is not fimply the retaining in the memory of a fucceffion of events,
catalogues of tyrants, plagues, battles and revolutions; but clear
ideas of the laws, cuftoms, opinions, arts, arms and commerce of
the different æras; from thefe he may draw the caufes of the fub-
verfion of kingdoms, popular commotions, or the fpirit that
actuated the feveral Minifters in the treaties of alliances made by
them. This knowledge is to be collected from the confideration
of Ancient Ufages, Arms, Coins, Medals, Utenfils, Buildings and
Infcriptions.

As a Member of either Houfe he ought to know the rules, pre-
cedents and orders of that community, or, in other words, the Par-
liamentary Hiftory and Antiquities. If he is a Peer, his perfonal
attendance in the great ceremonials require him to be mafter of that
part of Antiquarian Knowledge which fettles all forts of precedency.

A general knowledge of Antiquity is profeffionally neceffary to a
Soldier; without it, it will be impoffible he fhould receive the leaft
benefit from the relations of former fieges or battles, in which to
make proper deductions he fhould take into his confideration the
Ancient military buildings, engines, weapons, both offenfive and
defenfive, together with the difcipline of the times. Adequate ideas
of the former can only be gained by a critical examination of
Ancient forts and caftles; and a proper judgment of the latter
formed from public arfenals, Ancient coins, fepulchral monuments,
acts of parliament, illuminated manufcripts and old chronicles.
Owing to too great a neglect of thefe enquiries, few Officers are able
to give a rational account of many of their parade motions and

ceremonials, which though they to them may feem arbitrary, were neverthelefs founded on convenience and neceffity.

To the private Gentleman nothing can be more ornamental than a tincture of this knowledge in general, or more ufeful than an accurate acquaintance with the Antiquities of his country in particular; without it he cannot underftand its hiftory, neither is he qualified ably to ferve as a Member of Parliament or Juftice of the Peace, or even as a Juror; a proper execution of all thefe offices in different degrees requiring an acquaintance with the conftitution, laws and cuftoms of our anceftors, and thefe cannot be obtained but by the perufal of Ancient records, coins and monuments, which at the fame time that they inftruct, ferve to fix in the memory the æra of the different events, and Hiftory of the times in which they were conftructed.

Even as a man of pleafure fome fmattering of this knowledge is required. Would he appear at a mafquerade in any particular old Englifh character, if he has not fome ftandard for the forming of his drefs, he may perfonate King Alfred in the ruff, fhort jacket, fhoulder belt, and quail pipe boots, worn in the reign of Charles the Second.

The profeffors of Architecture, Sculpture or Painting, cannot go on a moment in their refpective profeffions without more than a moderate fhare of Antiquarian Learning. If the firft is employed to conftruct a Gothic ruin in a garden, or is defired to repair an Ancient church or cathedral, without this, he would jumble together the different ftiles of Saxon, Norman and modern Gothic. Or fuppofe the Painter was to reprefent the battle of Haftings, he might perhaps draw the Conqueror in the character of a French Marefchal, his large peruke and drapery waving in the wind, he, ferenely fmiling amidft the flight of burfting bombs, cannon balls and vollies of fmall arms, brandifhing his truncheon in one hand, whilft the other, garnifhed with a laced ruffle, is placed akimbo on his hips. In fhort, to make ufe of their own terms, this deficiency would betray them conftantly into a violation of the *coutume*.

The want of Acquaintance with thefe matters often caufes theatrical heroes and princeffes to fall into manifeft abfurdities. To this we owe the tye wig of a Mark Anthony, and the ample hoop and chafed watch of the beautiful Cleopatra. I will not, however, charge them with the frequent folecifms feen in the furniture of the mimic palaces and apartments, thefe being the works of the fcene painter; but for want of attention to this kind of propriety, I have more than once feen the chamber of a Roman Lady decorated with a harpfichord, whilſt the chimney has been loaded with china joſſes and mandarines, beneath a picture repreſenting the taking of Porto Bello, the battle of Culloden, or ſome other ſimilar Anachroniſms.

I have ſaid that every man is naturally an Antiquarian, and to every ones own breaſt I appeal for a proof. Is he poſſeſſed of an Ancient seat, does he not earneſtly deſire to know its hiſtory and the ſucceſſion of his predeceſſors in that manſion, and if it has been the ſcene of any remarkable tranſaction, does not he read every thing concerning it with particular avidity; and can he refrain enquiring and making himſelf maſter of every circumſtance and place of action; and does not this propenſity even extend to the pariſh or town wherein he lives? Let any one go to Runny Mead, or Boſworth Field, there is not a clown that reſides thereabouts, however rude, but can tell him the ſpot where the Barons aſſembled, and where Richard fell.

In cultivating the ſtudy of Antiquities, care muſt be taken not to fall into an error, to which many have been ſeduced, I mean that of making collections of things which have no other merit than that of being old, or having belonged to ſome eminent perſon, and are not illuſtrative of any point of hiſtory. Such is the Scull of Oliver Cromwell, preſerved in the Aſhmolean Muſcum at Oxford, and pieces of the Royal Oak, hoarded by many loyal old ladies. That Oliver had a ſcull and brains too would have been allowed without this proof; and thoſe who have conſidered the Royal Oak do not, I believe, find it eſſentially different from the wood of a common kitchen table. There may be rather ſtiled Reliques than Pieces of Antiquity, and it is ſuch trumpery that is gibed at by the ridiculers of Antiquity.

Having thus, I hope, pointed out the importance of the ſtudy of Antiquities, let me ſay a word of the following Work.

This Collection is meant as a Repoſitory for fugitive pieces, reſpecting the Hiſtory and Antiquities of this country. In the courſe of it care ſhall be taken to admit only ſuch Views as may be depended on, and have never before been publiſhed, and which, at the ſame time that they pleaſe the eye, ſhall repreſent ſome remains of Antiquity, ſome capital Manſion, or ſtriking Proſpect. The Portraits ſhall introduce to the public acquaintance only ſuch perſons as have figured in ſome eminent ſtation, or been remarkable for their abilities, ſtations, or accidents in life. And the Letter-Preſs ſhall convey either original eſſays, or extracts from books, whoſe price and ſcarcity have rendered them acceſſible only to a few. Any Gentlemen poſſeſſed of Drawings, Coins, or Manuſcripts, with which they would chuſe to oblige the Public, may, by ſending them to the

[5]

Publiſher, have them, if confiſtent with the plan, elegantly executed; and if incompatible or improper, immediately returned.

The cheapneſs and ſingularity of this undertaking will, it is hoped, recommend it to the public favour, to deſerve which neither pains nor expence ſhall be ſpared; and the Editor begs leave to aſſure the Purchaſers, that ſhould he be ſo happy as to meet with ſucceſs, he will, inſtead of flagging, redouble his efforts to pleaſe.

## [2  JOHN  BRAND]

Introducing his *Observations on Popular Antiquities* in 1777, John Brand (1744–1806) stressed the role of tradition, his opening word, and in particular of *oral tradition*, a term he italicized, in preserving the superstitious fancies of the common people. In using this phrase Brand displayed a modern touch, for folklorists today most frequently employ 'oral tradition' as a synonym or explanation for 'folklore.' The clergyman from Newcastle and longtime secretary of the Society of Antiquaries in London had detected a special segment of antiquities, aural rather than visual, intangible and noncorporeal. This was the world of spirits and demons, charms and exorcisms, usages and observances, sharing with material remains the same character of misshapen fragments surviving from a bygone day. Brand viewed these verbal and vulgar antiquities with revulsion as pagan-Popish deviltries, but he reminded his enlightened readers that their ancestors of ten centuries earlier dwelt in darkness. Apart from his brief preface, Brand had little to say in the way of theory; his passion lay in the relentless accumulation of popular and calendrical antiquities enmeshed in printed records, and he communicated his zeal to his countrymen, who found the *Observations* a treasure of reference and stimulus for their own observations.

Text from John Brand, *Observations on Popular Antiquities* [1777]. London: Vernor, Hood, and Sharpe, Poultry; James Cundee, Ivy-Lane; and W. Baynes, Paternoster-Row, 1810. Pages iii–ix, 'The General Preface.'

Tradition has in no Instance so clearly evinced her Faithfulness, as in the transmitting of vulgar Rites and popular Opinions.

Of these, when we are desirous of tracing them backwards to their Origin, many lose themselves in Antiquity.

They have indeed travelled down to us through a long Succession

[6]

of Years, and the greatest part of them, it is not improbable, will be of perpetual Observation: for the generality of Men look back with superstitious Veneration on the Ages of their Forefathers: And Authorities, that are grey with Time, seldom fail of commanding those filial Honours, claimed even by the Appearance of hoary old Age.

Many of these it must be confessed are mutilated, and, as in the Remains of ancient Statuary, the Parts of not a few of them have been awkwardly transposed: they preserve, however, the principal *Traits*, that distinguished them in their origin.

Things, composed of such flimsy Materials as the Fancies of a Multitude, do not seem calculated for a long Duration; yet have these survived Shocks, by which even Empires have been overthrown, and preserved at least some *Form* and *Colour* of Identity, during a Repetition of Changes, both in Religious Opinions, and in the Policy of States.

But the strongest Proof of their remote Antiquity, is, that they have out-lived the general Knowledge of the very Causes that gave rise to them.

The Reader will find in the subsequent pages an union of Endeavours to rescue many of these Causes from Oblivion. If, on the investigation, they appear to any so frivolous as not to have deserved the Pains of the Search, the humble Labourers will avoid Censure, by incurring Contempt.

How trivial soever such an Enquiry may seem to some, yet all must be informed that it is attended with no small share of Difficulty and Toil.

A Passage is to be forced through a Wilderness intricate and entangled: few Vestiges of former Labours can be found to direct us; we must oftentimes trace a tedious retrospective Course; perhaps to return at last weary and unsatisfied, from the making of Researches, fruitless as those of some ancient enthusiastic Traveller, who ranging the barren *African* Sands, had in vain attempted to investigate the hidden Sources of the *Nile*.

Rugged and narrow as this Walk of Study may seem to many, yet *Fancy* (who shares with *Hope* the pleasing Office of brightening a passage through every *Route* of human Endeavour) opens from hence to Prospects, enriched with the choicest Beauties of her magic Creation.

The *prime* Origin of the superstitious Notions and Ceremonies of the People is absolutely unattainable; we despair of ever being able to reach the Fountain Head of Streams which have been running and increasing from the Beginning of Time. All that we aspire to do, is only to trace backwards, as far as possible, the Courses of them on those Charts, that remain, of the distant Countries from whence they were first perceived to flow.

Few, who are desirous of investigating the popular Notions and vulgar Ceremonies in our Nation, can fail of deducing them in their first Direction from the Times when Popery was our established Religion.

We shall not wonder that these were able to survive the Reformation, when we consider, that though our sensible and spirited Forefathers were, upon Conviction, easily induced to forego religious Tenets, which had been weighed in the Balance, and found wanting; yet were *the People* by no means inclined to annihilate the seemingly innocent Ceremonies of their former superstitious Faith.

These, consecrated to the Fancies of Men, by a Usage from Time immemorial, though erazed by public Authority from the *written Word*, were committed as a venerable Deposit to the keeping of *oral Tradition*: like the *Penates* of another *Troy*, recently destroyed, they were religiously brought off, after having been snatched out of the smoking Ruins of Popery.

It is not improbable that, in the Infancy of Protestantism, the continuance of many of these was connived at by the State. For Men, 'who are but Children of a "larger Growth," ' are not weaned all at once, and the Reformation of Manners, and of Religion, is always most surely established, when effected by slow Degrees, and as it were imperceptible Gradations.

Thus also at the first Promulgation of Christianity to the Gentile Nations, through the Force of Conviction they yielded indeed to Truth; yet they could not be persuaded to relinquish many of their Superstitions, which rather than forego them altogether, they chose to blend and incorporate with their new Faith.

Christian, or rather Papal Rome, borrowed her Rites, Notions, and Ceremonies, in the most luxurious Abundance from ancient and Heathen Rome; and much the greater Number of these flaunting Externals, which *Infallibility* has adopted, and used as Feathers to adorn *her Triple Cap*, have been stolen out of the Wings of the *dying Eagle*.

With regard to the Rites, Sports, &c. of the Common People, I am aware that the morose and bigoted Part of Mankind[1] without distinguishing between the right Use and the abuse of such Entertainments, cavil at and malign them. Yet must such be told that Shows and Sports have been countenanced by the best and wisest

[1] I shall quote here the subsequent *curious Thoughts* on this Subject: the Puritans are ridiculed in them. (*Continued at foot of opposite page*)

of States; and though it cannot be denied that they have been sometimes prostituted to the Purposes of Riot and Debauchery, yet were we to reprobate everything that has been thus abused, *Religion* itself could not be retained; perhaps we should be able to keep nothing.

The Common People, confined by daily Labour, seem to require their proper Intervals of Relaxation; perhaps it is of the highest political Utility to encourage Innocent Sports and Games among them. The revival of many of these, would, I think, be highly pertinent at this particular Season, when the general Spread of Luxury and Dissipation threatens more than at any preceding Period to extinguish the Character of our boasted national Bravery. For the Observation of an honest old Writer, Stow, (who tells us, speaking of the May-games, Midsummer-Eve[1] Rejoicings, &c. antiently used in the Streets of London, 'which *open* Pastimes in my Youth being now 'supprest, worse Practices *within Doors* are to be feared)' may be with singular propriety adopted on the most transient Survey of our present popular Manners.

Mr. Bourne, my predecessor in this Walk, has not, from whatever Cause, done Justice to the Subject he undertook to treat of. Far from having the Vanity to think that I have exhausted it, the utmost of my Pretensions is to the Merit of having endeavoured, by making Additions, to improve it. I think him, however, deserving of no Small Share of Praise for his imperfect Attempt, for 'much is due to those, who first broke the Way to knowledge, and left only to their Successors the Task of smoothing it.'

New Lights have arisen since his Time. The English Antique has become a general and fashionable Study; and the Discoveries of the very respectable Society of Antiquaries have rendered the Recesses of Papal and Heathen Antiquities easier of access.

I flatter myself I have turned all these Circumstances in some

---

[1] I call to mind here the pleasing Account **Mr.** Sterne has left us in his Sentimental Journey, of the *Grace-dance* after Supper.—I agree with that amiable Writer in thinking that *Religion* may mix herself in the Dance, and that innocent Cheerfulness is no inconsiderable Part of Devotion; such indeed as cannot fail of being grateful to the *Good Being*,—it is a *silent* but *eloquent* Mode of praising him!

> *These* teach that *Dancing* is a Jezabell,
> And *Barley break* the ready Way to Hell;
> The *Morrice Idols*, *Whitsun-ales* can be
> But prophane Reliques of a Jubilee:
> These in a Zeal t'expresse how much they do
> The *Organs* hate, have silenc'd *Bagpipes* too;
> And harmless *Maypoles* are all rail'd upon,
> As if they were the *Tow'rs of Babylon*.
>
> Randolph's Poems, 1646.

[9]

measure to Advantage. I have gleaned Passages that seemed to throw Light upon the Subject, from a great variety of Volumes, and those written too in several Languages; in the doing of which, if I shall not be found to have deserved the Praise of Judgment, I must at least make Pretensions to the Merit of Industry.

Elegance of Composition will hardly be expected in a Work of this Kind, which stands much less in need of Attic Wit, than of Roman Perseverance and *Dutch* Assiduity.

I shall offer some Discoveries, which are peculiarly my own; for there are Customs yet retained here in the North, of which I am persuaded the learned of the Southern Part of the Island have not heard, which is, perhaps, the sole Cause why they have never before been investigated.

In perusing the subsequent Observations, the candid Reader, who has never before considered this neglected Subject, is requested not to be rash in passing Sentence, but to suspend his Judgment, at least, till he has carefully examined all the Evidence; by which Caution I do not wish to have it understood, that our Determinations are thought to be infallible, or that every Decision here is not amenable to an higher Authority. In the meantime Prejudice may be forwarned, and it will apologize for many seemingly trivial Reasons, assigned for the beginning and transmitting of this or that *Notion*, or *Ceremony*, to reflect, that what may appear foolish to the enlightened Understandings of Men in the *Eighteenth* Century, wore a very different Aspect when viewed through the Gloom that prevailed in the *seventh* or *eighth*.

I should trespass upon the patience of my Reader, were I to enumerate all the Books I have consulted on this Occasion; to which however, I shall take care in their proper Places to refer: but I own myself under particular Obligations to *Durand*'s Ritual of Divine Offices; a Work inimical to every Idea of rational Worship, but to the Enquirer into the Origin of our popular Ceremonies, an invaluable Magazine of the most interesting Intelligence. I would stile this Performance the great *Ceremonial Law* of the Romanists, in Comparison with which the *Mosaic Code* is *barren* of Rights and Ceremonies. We stand amazed on perusing it at the enormous Weight of a new Yoke which *Holy Church* fabricating *with her own hands* has imposed on her servile Devotees.

Yet the Forgers of these Shackles had artfully contrived to make them sit easy, by twisting Flowers around them. Dark as this Picture, drawn by the Pencil of gloomy Superstition, appeared upon *the whole*, yet it was its deep *Shade* contrasted with pleasing *Light*.

The Calendar was crowded with Red-Letter Days, nominally

indeed consecrated to *Saints*; but which, by the encouragement of Idleness and Dissipation of Manners, gave every kind of countenance to SINNERS.

A Profusion of childish Rites, Pageants and Ceremonies diverted the Attention of the People from the consideration of their real State, and kept them in humour, if it did not sometimes make them in love with their slavish Modes of Worship.

To the Credit of our sensible and manly Forefathers, they were among the first who felt the Weight of this new and unnecessary Yoke, and had Spirit enough to throw it off.

I have fortunately in my Possession one of those antient Romish Calendars of singular Curiosity, which contains under the immoveable Feasts and Fasts (I regret much its Silence on the moveable ones) a variety of brief Observations, contributing not a little to the elucidation of many of our popular Customs, and proving them to have been sent over from Rome, with *Bulls, Indulgencies,* and other Baubles, bartered, as it should seem, for our *Peter-pence,* by those who trafficked in spiritual Merchandize from the Continent.

These I shall carefully translate (though in some Places it is extremely difficult to render the very barbarous *Latin,* of which I fear the Critic will think I have transfused the Barbarity, Brevity, and Obscurity into my own *English*) and lay before my Reader, who will at once see and acknowledge their Utility.

A learned Performance, by a Doctor Moresin in the Time of James I and dedicated to that Monarch, is also luckily in my Possession. It is written in Latin, and entitled 'The Origin and Increase of Depravity in Religion'; containing a very masterly Parallel between the Rites, Notions, &c. of *Heathen* and those of *Papal* Rome.

The copious Extracts from this Work, with which I shall adorn the subsequent Pages will be their own Eulogy, and supersede my poor Encomiums.

When I call to remembrance the *Poet of Humanity,*[1] who has transmitted his Name to Immortality, by Reflections written among the little Tomb-stones of the Vulgar, in a Country Church-Yard; I am urged by no false Shame to apologize for the seeming Unimportance of my Subject.

The Antiquities of the Common People cannot be studied without acquiring some useful Knowledge of Mankind. By the chemical Process of Philosophy, even Wisdom may be extracted from the Follies and Superstitions of our Forefathers.

The *People*, of whom Society is chiefly composed, and for whose

[1] The late Mr. Gay.

[11]

good, Superiority of Rank is only a Grant made originally by mutual Concession, is a respectable Subject to every one who is the Friend of Man.

Pride, which, independent of the Idea arising from the Necessity of civil Polity, has portioned out the human *Genus* into such a variety of different and subordinate *Species*, must be compelled to own, that the lowest of these derives itself from an Origin, common to it with the highest of the Kind. The beautiful Sentiment of *Terence*:

'*Homo* sum, *humani* nihil à me alienum puto,'

may be adopted therefore in this Place, to persuade us that nothing can be foreign to our Enquiry, which concerns the smallest of the Vulgar; of those *little ones*, who occupy the lowest Place in the political Arrangement of human Beings.

*Westgate Street, Newcastle,*                                    J. B.
   *Nov. 27, 1776.*

## [3 WALTER SCOTT]

Few figures exerted so commanding an influence on the early antiquaries in England and Scotland as Sir Walter Scott. The Waverley romancer heard, collected, wrote about, and commented in fictional story and scrupulous notes on the stirring ballads and traditions of the Border. He himself veered back and forth between the roles of story-writer and story-recorder. In his novel *The Antiquary* (1816) he showed his appreciation of the species represented by his title character, Jonathan Oldbuck, modelled on an old friend of his youth, whom he placed in a den crammed with bulging bookcases, Roman lamps, tapestries, historical portraits, maps, parchments, ancient British pottery, and antique spurs and buckles. To the quest for antiquities Scott imparted a new fillip, by showing that the collector could on occasion move from the library to the village green and there imbibe the oral tradition discerned by Brand in books and manuscripts. The *Letters on Demonology and Witchcraft* amply prove how knowledgeable and learned was Scott in the printed sources of supernaturalism. Written toward the close of his life, the *Letters* offer the first sustained treatise in English on supernatural beliefs of gentry and peasantry and promptly joined Brand on the shelf of indispensable reference works for the antiquary interested in occult matters. The following selections reveal Sir

Walter's alertness to the mingling of witch and fairy traditions in the folk mind, a point subsequently confirmed by modern folk-lorists.

Text from Walter Scott, *Letters on Demonology and Witchcraft* [1830]. London: George Routledge and Sons, 1884. Pages 120–43, from Letter V.

. . . To return to Thomas the Rhymer, with an account of whose legend I concluded the last letter, it would seem that the example which it afforded of obtaining the gift of prescience, and other supernatural powers, by means of the fairy people, became the common apology of those who attempted to cure diseases, to tell fortunes, to revenge injuries, or to engage in traffic with the invisible world, for the purpose of satisfying their own wishes, curiosity, or revenge, or those of others. Those who practised the petty arts of deception in such mystic cases, being naturally desirous to screen their own impostures, were willing to be supposed to derive from the fairies, or from mortals transported to fairyland the power necessary to effect the displays of art which they pretended to exhibit. A confession of direct communication and league with Satan, though the accused were too frequently compelled by torture to admit and avow such horrors, might, the poor wretches hoped, be avoided by the avowal of a less disgusting intercourse with sublunary spirits, a race which might be described by negatives, being neither angels, devils, nor the souls of deceased men; nor would it, they might flatter themselves, be considered as any criminal alliance, that they held communion with a race not properly hostile to man, and willing, on certain conditions, to be useful and friendly to him. Such an intercourse was certainly far short of the witch's renouncing her salvation, delivering herself personally to the devil, and at once ensuring condemnation in this world, together with the like doom in the next.

Accordingly, the credulous, who, in search of health, knowledge, greatness, or moved by any of the numberless causes for which men seek to look into futurity, were anxious to obtain superhuman assistance, as well as the numbers who had it in view to dupe such willing clients, became both cheated and cheaters, alike anxious to establish the possibility of a harmless process of research into futurity, for laudable, or at least innocent objects, as healing diseases and the like; in short, of the existence of white magic, as it was called, in opposition to that black art exclusively and directly derived from intercourse with Satan. Some endeavoured to predict a

[13]

man's fortune in marriage or his success in life by the aspect of the stars; others pretended to possess spells, by which they could reduce and compel an elementary spirit to enter within a stone, a looking-glass, or some other local place of abode, and confine her there by the power of an especial charm, conjuring her to abide and answer the questions of her master. Of these we shall afterwards say something; but the species of evasion now under our investigation is that of the fanatics or impostors who pretended to draw information from the equivocal spirits called fairies; and the number of instances before us is so great as induces us to believe that the pretence of communicating with Elfland, and not with the actual demon, was the manner in which the persons accused of witchcraft most frequently endeavoured to excuse themselves, or at least to alleviate the charges brought against them of practising sorcery. But the Scottish law did not acquit those who accomplished even praiseworthy actions, such as remarkable cures by mysterious remedies; and the proprietor of a patent medicine who should in those days have attested his having wrought such miracles as we see sometimes advertised, might perhaps have forfeited his life before he established the reputation of his drop, elixir, or pill.

Sometimes the soothsayers, who pretended to act on this information from sublunary spirits, soared to higher matters than the practice of physic, and interfered in the fate of nations. When James I was murdered at Perth in 1437, a Highland woman prophesied the course and purpose of the conspiracy, and had she been listened to, it might have been disconcerted. Being asked her source of knowledge, she answered Hudhart had told her; which might either be the same with Hudkin, a Dutch spirit somewhat similar to Friar Rush or Robin Goodfellow,[1] or with the red-capped demon so powerful in the case of Lord Soulis, and other wizards, to whom the Scots assigned rather more serious influence.

The most special account which I have found of the intercourse between Fairyland and a female professing to have some influence in that court, combined with a strong desire to be useful to the distressed of both sexes, occurs in the early part of a work to which I have been exceedingly obliged in the present and other publications.[2] The details of the evidence, which consists chiefly of the un-

---

[1] Hudkin is a very familiar devil, who will do nobody hurt, except he receive injury, but he cannot abide that, nor yet be mocked. He talketh with men friendly, sometimes visibly, sometimes invisibly. There go as many tales upon this Hudkin in some part of Germany as there did in England on Robin Goodfellow.—'Discourse concerning Devils,' annexed to 'The Discovery of Witchcraft,' by Reginald Scot, book i, chap. 21.

[2] The curious collection of trials, from 'The Criminal Records of Scotland,' now in the

fortunate woman's own concession, are more full than usual, and comprehend some curious particulars. To spare technical repetitions, I must endeavour to select the principal facts in evidence in detail, so far as they bear upon the present subject.

On November 8, 1576, Elizabeth or Bessie Dunlop, spouse to Andro Jak, in Lyne, in the Barony of Dalry, Ayrshire, was accused of sorcery and witchcraft and abuse of the people. Her answers to the interrogatories of the judges or prosecutors ran thus: It being required of her by what art she could tell of lost goods or prophesy the event of illness, she replied that of herself she had no knowledge or science of such matters, but that when questions were asked at her concerning such matters, she was in the habit of applying to one Thome Reid, who died at the battle of Pinkie (September 10, 1547), as he himself affirmed, and who resolved her any questions which she asked at him. This person she described as a respectable elderly-looking man, grey-bearded, and wearing a grey coat, with Lombard sleeves of the auld fashion. A pair of grey breeches and white stockings gartered above the knee, a black bonnet on his head, close behind and plain before, with silken laces drawn through the lips thereof, and a white wand in his hand, completed the description of what we may suppose a respectable-looking man of the province and period. Being demanded concerning her first interview with this mysterious Thome Reid, she gave rather an affecting account of the disasters with which she was then afflicted, and a sense of which perhaps aided to conjure up the imaginary counsellor. She was walking between her own house and the yard of Monkcastle, driving her cows to the common pasture, and making heavy moan with herself, weeping bitterly for her cow that was dead, her husband and child that were sick of the land-ill (some contagious sickness of the time), while she herself was in a very infirm state, having lately borne a child. On this occasion she met Thome Reid for the first time, who saluted her courteously, which she returned. 'Sancta Maria, Bessie!' said the apparition, 'why must thou make such dole and weeping for any earthly thing?' 'Have I not reason for great sorrow,' said she, 'since our property is going to destruction, my husband is on the point of death, my baby will not live, and I am myself at a weak point? Have I not cause to have a sore heart?' 'Bessie,' answered the spirit, 'thou hast displeased God in asking something that thou should not, and I counsel you to amend your fault. I tell thee, thy child shall die ere thou

course of publication, by Robert Pitcairn, Esq., affords so singular a picture of the manners and habits of our ancestors, while yet a semibarbarous people, that it is equally worth the attention of the historian, the antiquary, the philosopher, and the poet.

get home; thy two sheep shall also die; but thy husband shall recover, and be as well and feir as ever he was.' The good woman was something comforted to hear that her husband was to be spared in such her general calamity, but was rather alarmed to see her ghostly counsellor pass from her and disappear through a hole in the garden wall, seemingly too narrow to admit of any living person passing through it. Another time he met her at the Thorn of Dawmstarnik, and showed his ultimate purpose by offering her plenty of everything if she would but deny Christendom and the faith she took at the font-stone. She answered, that rather than do that she would be torn at horses' heels, but that she would be comformable to his advice in less matters. He parted with her in some displeasure. Shortly afterwards he appeared in her own house about noon, which was at the time occupied by her husband and three tailors. But neither Andrew Jak nor the three tailors were sensible of the presence of the phantom warrior who was slain at Pinkie; so that, without attracting their observation, he led out the good-wife to the end of the house near the kiln. Here he showed her a company of eight women and four men. The women were busked in their plaids, and very seemly. The strangers saluted her, and said, 'Welcome, Bessie; wilt thou go with us?' But Bessie was silent, as Thome Reid had previously recommended. After this she saw their lips move, but did not understand what they said; and in a short time they removed from thence with a hideous ugly howling sound, like that of a hurricane. Thome Reid then acquainted her that these were the good wights (fairies) dwelling in the court of Elfland, who came to invite her to go thither with them. Bessie answered that, before she went that road, it would require some consideration. Thome answered, 'Seest thou not me both meat-worth, clothes-worth, and well enough in person?' and engaged she should be easier than ever she was. But she replied, she dwelt with her husband and children, and would not leave them; to which Thome Reid replied, in very ill-humour, that if such were her sentiments, she would get little good of him.

Although they thus disagreed on the principal object of Thome Reid's visits, Bessie Dunlop affirmed he continued to come to her frequently, and assist her with his counsel; and that if any one consulted her about the ailments of human beings or of cattle, or the recovery of things lost and stolen, she was, by the advice of Thome Reid, always able to answer the querists. She was also taught by her (literally ghostly) adviser how to watch the operation of the ointments he gave her, and to presage from them the recovery or death of the patient. She said Thome gave her herbs with his own hand,

[16]

with which she cured John Jack's bairn and Wilson's of the Town-head. She also was helpful to a waiting-woman of the young Lady Stanlie, daughter of the Lady Johnstone, whose disease, according to the opinion of the infallible Thome Reid, was 'a cauld blood that came about her heart,' and frequently caused her to swoon away. For this Thome mixed a remedy as generous as the balm of Gilead itself. It was composed of the most potent ale, concocted with spices and a little white sugar, to be drunk every morning before taking food. For these prescriptions Bessie Dunlop's fee was a peck of meal and some cheese. The young woman recovered. But the poor old Lady Kilbowie could get no help for her leg, which had been crooked for years; for Thome Reid said the marrow of the limb was perished and the blood benumbed, so that she would never recover, and if she sought further assistance, it would be the worse for her. These opinions indicate common sense and prudence at least, whether we consider them as originating with the *umquhile* Thome Reid, or with the culprit whom he patronized. The judgments given in the case of stolen goods were also well chosen; for though they seldom led to recovering the property, they generally alleged such satisfactory reasons for its not being found as effectually to cover the credit of the prophetess. Thus Hugh Scott's cloak could not be returned, because the thieves had gained time to make it into a kirtle. James Jamieson and James Baird would, by her advice, have recovered their plough-irons, which had been stolen, had it not been the will of fate that William Dougal, sheriff's officer, one of the parties searching for them, should accept a bribe of three pounds not to find them. In short, although she lost a lace which Thome Reid gave her out of his own hand, which, tied round women in childbirth, had the power of helping their delivery, Bessie Dunlop's profession of a wise woman seems to have flourished indifferently well till it drew the evil eye of the law upon her.

More minutely pressed upon the subject of her familiar, she said she had never known him while among the living, but was aware that the person so calling himself was one who had in his lifetime, actually been known in middle earth as Thome Reid, officer to the Laird of Blair, and who died at Pinkie. Of this she was made certain, because he sent her on errands to his son, who had succeeded in his office, and to others his relatives, whom he named, and commanded them to amend certain trespasses which he had done while alive, furnishing her with sure tokens by which they should know that it was he who had sent her. One of these errands was somewhat remarkable. She was to remind a neighbour of some particular which she was to recall to his memory by the token that Thome

[17]

Reid and he had set out together to go to the battle which took place on the Black Saturday; that the person to whom the message was sent was inclined rather to move in a different direction, but that Thome Reid heartened him to pursue his journey, and brought him to the Kirk of Dalry, where he bought a parcel of figs, and made a present of them to his companion, tying them in his handkerchief; after which they kept company till they came to the field upon the fatal Black Saturday, as the battle of Pinkie was long called.

Of Thome's other habits, she said that he always behaved with the strictest propriety, only that he pressed her to go to Elfland with him, and took hold of her apron as if to pull her along. Again, she said she had seen him in public places, both in the churchyard at Dalry and on the street of Edinburgh, where he walked about among other people, and handled goods that were exposed to sale, without attracting any notice. She herself did not then speak to him, for it was his command that, upon such occasions, she should never address him unless he spoke first to her. In his theological opinions, Mr. Reid appeared to lean to the Church of Rome, which, indeed, was most indulgent to the fairy folk. He said that the *new law*, *i.e.*, the Reformation, was not good, and that the old faith should return again, but not exactly as it had been before. Being questioned why this visionary sage attached himself to her more than to others, the accused person replied, that when she was confined in childbirth of one of her boys, a stout woman came into her hut, and sat down on a bench by her bed, like a mere earthly gossip; that she demanded a drink, and was accommodated accordingly; and thereafter told the invalid that the child should die, but that her husband, who was then ailing, should recover. This visit seems to have been previous to her meeting Thome Reid near Monkcastle garden, for that worthy explained to her that her stout visitant was Queen of Fairies, and that he had since attended her by the express command of that lady, his queen and mistress. This reminds us of the extreme doting attachment which the Queen of the Fairies is represented to have taken for Dapper in 'The Alchemist.' Thome Reid attended her, it would seem, on being summoned thrice, and appeared to her very often within four years. He often requested her to go with him on his return to Fairyland, and when she refused, he shook his head, and said she would repent it.

If the delicacy of the reader's imagination be a little hurt at imagining the elegant Titania in the disguise of a *stout* woman, a heavy burden for a clumsy bench, drinking what Christopher Sly would have called very sufficient small-beer with a peasant's wife,

[18]

the following description of the fairy host may come more near the idea he has formed of that invisible company:—Bessie Dunlop declared that as she went to tether her nag by the side of Restalrig Loch (Lochend, near the eastern port of Edinburgh), she heard a tremendous sound of a body of riders rushing past her with such a noise as if heaven and earth would come together; that the sound swept past her and seemed to rush into the lake with a hideous rumbling noise. All this while she saw nothing; but Thome Reid showed her that the noise was occasioned by the wights, who were performing one of their cavalcades upon earth.

The intervention of Thome Reid as a partner in her trade of petty sorcery did not avail poor Bessie Dunlop, although his affection to her was apparently entirely platonic—the greatest familiarity on which he ventured was taking hold of her gown as he pressed her to go with him to Elfland. Neither did it avail her that the petty sorcery which she practised was directed to venial or even beneficial purposes. The sad words on the margin of the record, 'Convict and burnt,' sufficiently express the tragic conclusion of a curious tale.

Alison Pearson, in Byrchill, was, May 28, 1588, tried for invocation of the spirits of the devil, especially in the vision of one Mr. William Sympson, her cousin and her mother's brother's son, who she affirmed was a great scholar and doctor of medicine, dealing with charms and abusing the ignorant people. Against this poor woman her own confession, as in the case of Bessie Dunlop, was the principal evidence.

As Bessie Dunlop had Thome Reid, Alison Pearson had also a familiar in the court of Elfland. This was her relative, William Sympson aforesaid, born in Stirling, whose father was king's smith in that town. William had been taken away, she said, by a man of Egypt (a Gipsy), who carried him to Egypt along with him; that he remained there twelve years, and that his father died in the meantime for opening a priest's book and looking upon it. She declared that she had renewed her acquaintance with her kinsman so soon as he returned. She further confessed that one day as she passed through Grange Muir she lay down in a fit of sickness, and that a green man came to her, and said if she would be faithful he might do her good. In reply she charged him, in the name of God and by the law he lived upon, if he came for her soul's good to tell his errand. On this the green man departed. But he afterwards appeared to her with many men and women with him, and against her will she was obliged to pass with them farther than she could tell, with piping mirth, and good cheer; also that she accompanied

[19]

them into Lothian, where she saw puncheons of wine with tasses or drinking-cups. She declared that when she told of these things she was sorely tormented, and received a blow that took away the power of her left side, and left on it an ugly mark which had no feeling. She also confessed that she had seen before sunrise the good neighbours make their salves with pans and fires. Sometimes, she said, they came in such fearful forms as frightened her very much. At other times they spoke her fair, and promised her that she should never want if faithful, but if she told of them and their doings, they threatened to martyr her. She also boasted of her favour with the Queen of Elfland and the good friends she had at that court, notwithstanding that she was sometimes in disgrace there, and had not seen the queen for seven years. She said William Sympson is with the fairies, and that he lets her know when they are coming; and that he taught her what remedies to use, and how to apply them. She declared that when a whirlwind blew the fairies were commonly there, and that her cousin Sympson confessed that every year the tithe of them were taken away to hell. The celebrated Patrick Adamson, an excellent divine and accomplished scholar, created by James VI Archbishop of St. Andrews, swallowed the prescriptions of this poor hypochondriac with good faith and will, eating a stewed fowl, and drinking out at two draughts a quart of claret, medicated with the drugs she recommended. According to the belief of the time, this Alison Pearson transferred the bishop's indisposition from himself to a white palfrey, which died in consequence. There is a very severe libel on him for this and other things unbecoming his order, with which he was charged, and from which we learn that Lethington and Buccleuch were seen by Dame Pearson in the Fairyland.[1] This poor woman's kinsman, Sympson, did not give better shelter to her than Thome Reid had done to her predecessor. The margin of the court-book again bears the melancholy and brief record, '*Convicta et combusta.*'

The two poor women last mentioned are the more to be pitied as, whether enthusiasts or impostors, they practised their supposed art exclusively for the advantage of mankind. The following extraordinary detail involves persons of far higher quality, and who sought to familiars for more baneful purposes.

Katherine Munro, Lady Fowlis, by birth Katherine Ross of Balnagowan, of high rank, both by her own family and that of her husband, who was the fifteenth Baron of Fowlis, and chief of the warlike clan of Munro, had a stepmother's quarrel with Robert Munro, eldest son of her husband, which she gratified by forming a

[1] See *Scottish Poems*, edited by John G. Dalzell, p. 321.

scheme for compassing his death by unlawful arts. Her proposed advantage in this was, that the widow of Robert, when he was thus removed, should marry with her brother, George Ross of Balnagowan; and for this purpose, her sister-in-law, the present Lady Balnagowan, was also to be removed. Lady Fowlis, if the indictment had a syllable of truth, carried on her practices with the least possible disguise. She assembled persons of the lowest order, stamped with an infamous celebrity as witches; and, besides making pictures or models in clay, by which they hoped to bewitch Robert Munro and Lady Balnagowan, they brewed upon one occasion, poison so strong that a page tasting of it immediately took sickness. Another earthen jar (Scotticè *pig*) of the same deleterious liquor was prepared by the Lady Fowlis, and sent with her own nurse for the purpose of administering it to Robert Munro. The messenger having stumbled in the dark, broke the jar, and a rank grass grew on the spot where it fell, which sheep and cattle abhorred to touch; but the nurse, having less sense than the brute beasts, and tasting of the liquor which had been spilled, presently died. What is more to our present purpose, Lady Fowlis made use of the artillery of Elfland in order to destroy her stepson and sister-in-law. Laskie Loncart, one of the assistant hags, produced two of what the common people called elf-arrow heads, being, in fact, the points of flint used for arming the ends of arrow-shafts in the most ancient times, but accounted by the superstitious the weapons by which the fairies were wont to destroy both man and beast. The pictures of the intended victims were then set up at the north end of the apartment, and Christian Ross Malcolmson, an assistant hag, shot two shafts at the image of Lady Balnagowan, and three against the picture of Robert Munro, by which shots they were broken, and Lady Fowlis commanded new figures to be modelled. Many similar acts of witchcraft and of preparing poisons were alleged against Lady Fowlis.

Her son-in-law, Hector Munro, one of his stepmother's prosecutors, was, for reasons of his own, active in a similar conspiracy against the life of his own brother. The rites that he practised were of an uncouth, barbarous, and unusual nature. Hector, being taken ill, consulted on his case some of the witches or soothsayers, to whom this family appears to have been partial. The answer was unanimous that he must die unless the principal man of his blood should suffer death in his stead. It was agreed that the vicarious substitute for Hector must mean George Munro, brother to him by the half-blood (the son of the Katherine Lady Fowlis before commemorated). Hector sent at least seven messengers for this

[21]

young man, refusing to receive any of his other friends till he saw the substitute whom he destined to take his place in the grave. When George at length arrived, Hector, by advice of a notorious witch, called Marion MacIngarach, and of his own foster-mother, Christian Neil Dalyell, received him with peculiar coldness and restraint. He did not speak for the space of an hour, till his brother broke silence and asked, 'How he did?' Hector replied, 'That he was the better George had come to visit him,' and relapsed into silence, which seemed singular when compared with the anxiety he had displayed to see his brother; but it was, it seems, a necessary part of the spell. After midnight the sorceress Marion MacIngarach, the chief priestess or Nicneven of the company, went forth with her accomplices, carrying spades with them. They then proceeded to dig a grave not far from the seaside, upon a piece of land which formed the boundary betwixt two proprietors. The grave was made as nearly as possible to the size of their patient Hector Munro, the earth dug out of the grave being laid aside for the time. After ascertaining that the operation of the charm on George Munro, the destined victim, should be suspended for a time, to avoid suspicion, the conspirators proceeded to work their spell in a singular, impressive, and, I believe, unique manner. The time being January, 1588, the patient, Hector Munro, was borne forth in a pair of blankets, accompanied with all who were entrusted with the secret, who were warned to be strictly silent till the chief sorceress should have received her information from the angel whom they served. Hector Munro was carried to his grave and laid therein, the earth being filled in on him, and the grave secured with stakes as at a real funeral. Marion MacIngarach, the Hecate of the night, then sat down by the grave, while Christian Neil Dalyell, the foster-mother, ran the breadth of about nine ridges distant, leading a boy in her hand, and, coming again to the grave where Hector Munro was interred alive, demanded of the witch which victim she would choose, who replied that she chose Hector to live and George to die in his stead. This form of incantation was thrice repeated ere Mr. Hector was removed from his chilling bed in a January grave and carried home, all remaining mute as before. The consequence of a process which seems ill-adapted to produce the former effect was that Hector Munro recovered, and after the intervention of twelve months George Munro, his brother, died, Hector took the principal witch into high favour, made her keeper of his sheep, and evaded, it is said, to present her to trial when charged at Aberdeen to produce her. Though one or two inferior persons suffered death on account of the sorceries practised in the house of Fowlis, the Lady Katharine

[22]

and her stepson Hector had both the unusual good fortune to be found not guilty. Mr. Pitcairn remarks that the juries, being composed of subordinate persons not suitable to the rank or family of the person tried, has all the appearance of having been packed on purpose for acquittal. It might also, in some interval of good sense, creep into the heads of Hector Munro's assize that the enchantment being performed in January, 1588, and the deceased being only taken ill of his fatal disease in April, 1590, the distance between the events might seem too great to admit the former being regarded as the cause of the latter.[1]

Another instance of the skill of a sorcerer being traced to the instructions of the elves is found in the confession of John Stewart, called a vagabond, but professing skill in palmistry and jugglery, and accused of having assisted Margaret Barclay, or Dein, to sink or cast away a vessel belonging to her own good brother. It being demanded of him by what means he professed himself to have knowledge of things to come, the said John confessed that the space of twenty-six years ago, he being travelling on All-Hallow Even night, between the towns of Monygoif (so spelled) and Clary, in Galway, he met with the King of the Fairies and his company, and that the King of the Fairies gave him a stroke with a white rod over the forehead, which took from him the power of speech and the use of one eye, which he wanted for the space of three years. He declared that the use of speech and eyesight was restored to him by the King of Fairies and his company, on an Hallowe'en night, at the town of Dublin, in Ireland, and that since that time he had joined these people every Saturday at seven o'clock, and remained with them all the night; also, that they met every Hallow-tide, sometimes on Lanark Hill (Tintock, perhaps), sometimes on Kilmaurs Hill, and that he was then taught by them. He pointed out the spot of his forehead on which, he said, the King of the Fairies struck him with a white rod, whereupon the prisoner, being blindfolded, they pricked the spot with a large pin, whereof he expressed no sense or feeling. He made the usual declaration, that he had seen many persons at the Court of Fairy, whose names he rehearsed particularly, and declared that all such persons as are taken away by sudden death go with the King of Elfland. With this man's evidence we have at present no more to do, though we may revert to the execrable proceedings which then took place against this miserable juggler and the poor women who were accused of the same crime. At present it is quoted as another instance of a fortune-teller referring to Elfland as the source of his knowledge.

[1] Pitcairn's *Trials*, vol. i, pp. 191–201.

At Auldearne, a parish and burgh of a barony in the county of Nairne, the epidemic terror of witches seems to have gone very far. The confession of a woman called Isobel Gowdie, of date April, 1662, implicates, as usual, the Court of Fairy, and blends the operations of witchcraft with the facilities afforded by the fairies. These need be the less insisted upon in this place, as the arch-fiend, and not the elves, had the immediate agency in the abominations which she narrates. Yet she had been, she said, in the Dounie Hills, and got meat there from the Queen of Fairies more than she could eat. She added, that the queen is bravely clothed in white linen and in white and brown cloth, that the King of Fairy is a brave man; and there were elf-bulls roaring and *skoilling* at the entrance of their palace, which frightened her much. On another occasion this frank penitent confesses her presence at a rendezvous of witches, Lammas, 1659, where, after they had rambled through the country in different shapes—of cats, hares, and the like—eating, prinking, and wasting the goods of their neighbours into whose houses they could penetrate, they at length came to the Dounie Hills, where the mountain opened to receive them, and they entered a fair big room, as bright as day. At the entrance ramped and roared the large fairy bulls, which always alarmed Isobel Gowdie. These animals are probably the water-bulls, famous both in Scottish and Irish tradition, which are not supposed to be themselves altogether *canny* or safe to have concern with. In their caverns the fairies manufactured those elf-arrow heads with which the witches and they wrought so much evil. The elves and the arch-fiend laboured jointly at this task, the former forming and sharpening the dart from the rough flint, and the latter perfecting and finishing (or, as it is called, *dighting*) it. Then came the sport of the meeting. The witches bestrode either corn-straws, bean-stalks, or rushes, and calling, 'Horse and Hattock, in the Devil's name!' which is the elfin signal for mounting, they flew wherever they listed. If the little whirlwind which accompanies their transportation passed any mortal who neglected to bless himself, all such fell under the witches' power, and they acquired the right of shooting at him. The penitent prisoner gives the names of many whom she and her sisters had so slain, the death for which she was most sorry being that of William Brown, in the Milntown of Mains. A shaft was also aimed at the Reverend Harrie Forbes, a minister who was present at the examination of Isobel, the confessing party. The arrow fell short, and the witch would have taken aim again, but her master forbade her, saying the reverend gentleman's life was not subject to their power. To this strange and very particular confession we shall have occasion to recur when witchcraft is the more immediate subject. What is above narrated marks the manner in which the belief in that crime was blended with the fairy superstition.

To proceed to more modern instances of persons supposed to have fallen under the power of the fairy race, we must not forget the Reverend Robert Kirke, minister of the Gospel, the first translator of the Psalms into Gaelic verse. He was, in the end of the seventeenth century, successively minister of the Highland parishes of Balquidder and Aberfoyle, lying in the most romantic district of Perthshire, and within the Highland line. These beautiful and wild regions, comprehending so many lakes, rocks, sequestered valleys, and dim copsewoods, are not even yet quite abandoned by the fairies, who have resolutely maintained secure footing in a region so well suited for their residence. Indeed, so much was this the case formerly, that Mr. Kirke, while in his latter charge of Aberfoyle, found materials for collecting and compiling his Essay on the 'Subterranean and for the most part Invisible People heretofore going under the name of Elves, Fawnes, and Fairies, or the like.'[1] In this discourse, the author, 'with undoubting mind,' describes the fairy race as a sort of astral spirits, of a kind betwixt humanity and angels—says, that they have children, nurses, marriages, deaths, and burials, like mortals in appearance; that, in some respect, they represent mortal men, and that individual apparitions, or doublemen, are found among them, corresponding with mortals existing on earth. Mr. Kirke accuses them of stealing the milk from the cows, and of carrying away, what is more material, the woman in pregnancy, and new-born children from their nurses. The remedy is easy in both cases. The milk cannot be stolen if the mouth of the calf, before he is permitted to suck, be rubbed with a certain balsam, very easily come by; and the woman in travail is safe if a piece of cold iron is put into the bed. Mr. Kirke accounts for this by informing us that the great northern mines of iron, lying adjacent to the place of eternal punishment, have a savour odious to these 'fascinating creatures.' They have, says the reverend author, what one would not expect, many light toyish books (novels and plays, doubtless), others on Rosycrucian subjects, and of an abstruse mystical character; but they have no Bibles or works of devotion. The essayist fails not to mention the elf-arrow heads, which have

[1] The title continues:—'Among the Low Country Scots, as they are described by those who have the second sight, and now, to occasion farther enquiry, collected and compared by a circumspect enquirer residing among the Scottish-Irish (*i.e.*, the Gael, or Highlanders) in Scotland.' It was printed with the author's name in 1691, and reprinted, Edinburgh, 1815, for Longman & Co.

something of the subtlety of thunderbolts, and can mortally wound the vital parts without breaking the skin. These wounds, he says, he has himself observed in beasts, and felt the fatal lacerations which he could not see.

It was by no means to be supposed that the elves, so jealous and irritable a race as to be incensed against those who spoke of them under their proper names, should be less than mortally offended at the temerity of the reverend author, who had pryed so deeply into their mysteries, for the purpose of giving them to the public. Although, therefore, the learned divine's monument, with his name duly inscribed, is to be seen at the east end of the churchyard at Aberfoyle, yet those acquainted with his real history do not believe that he enjoys the natural repose of the tomb. His successor, the Rev. Dr. Grahame, has informed us of the general belief that, as Mr. Kirke was walking one evening in his night-gown upon a *Dun-shi*, or fairy mount, in the vicinity of the manse or parsonage, behold! he sunk down in what seemed to be a fit of apoplexy, which the unenlightened took for death, while the more understanding knew it to be a swoon produced by the supernatural influence of the people whose precincts he had violated. After the ceremony of a seeming funeral, the form of the Rev. Robert Kirke appeared to a relation, and commanded him to go to Grahame of Duchray, ancestor of the present General Graham Stirling. 'Say to Duchray, who is my cousin as well as your own, that I am not dead, but a captive in Fairyland, and only one chance remains for my liberation. When the posthumous child, of which my wife has been delivered since my disappearance, shall be brought to baptism, I will appear in the room, when, if Duchray shall throw over my head the knife or dirk which he holds in his hand, I may be restored to society; but if this opportunity is neglected, I am lost for ever.' Duchray was apprised of what was to be done. The ceremony took place, and the apparition of Mr. Kirke was visibly seen while they were seated at table; but Grahame of Duchray, in his astonishment, failed to perform the ceremony enjoined, and it is to be feared that Mr. Kirke still 'drees his weird in Fairyland,' the Elfin state declaring to him, as the Ocean to poor Falconer, who perished at sea after having written his popular poem of 'The Shipwreck'—

*'Thou hast proclaimed our power—be thou our prey!'*

Upon this subject the reader may consult a very entertaining little volume, called 'Sketches of Perthshire,'[1] by the Rev. Dr. Grahame of Aberfoyle. The terrible visitation of fairy vengeance

[1] Edinburgh, 1812.

which has lighted upon Mr. Kirke has not intimidated his successor, an excellent man and good antiquary, from affording us some curious information on fairy superstition. He tells us that these capricious elves are chiefly dangerous on a Friday, when, as the day of the Crucifixion, evil spirits have most power, and mentions their displeasure at any one who assumes their accustomed livery of green, a colour fatal to several families in Scotland, to the whole race of the gallant Grahames in particular; insomuch that we have heard that in battle a Grahame is generally shot through the green cheek of his plaid; moreover, that a veteran sportsman of the name, having come by a bad fall, he thought it sufficient to account for it, that he had a piece of green whip-cord to complete the lash of his hunting-whip. I remember, also, that my late amiable friend, James Grahame, author of 'The Sabbath,' would not break through this ancient prejudice of his clan, but had his library table covered with blue or black cloth, rather than use the fated colour commonly employed on such occasions.

To return from the Perthshire fairies, I may quote a story of a nature somewhat similar to that of Mas Robert Kirke. The life of the excellent person who told it was, for the benefit of her friends and the poor, protracted to an unusual duration; so I conceive that this adventure, which took place in her childhood, might happen before the middle of last century. She was residing with some relations near the small seaport town of North Berwick, when the place and its vicinity were alarmed by the following story:—

An industrious man, a weaver in the little town, was married to a beautiful woman, who, after bearing two or three children, was so unfortunate as to die during the birth of a fourth child. The infant was saved, but the mother had expired in convulsions; and as she was much disfigured after death, it became an opinion among her gossips that, from some neglect of those who ought to have watched the sick woman, she must have been carried off by the elves, and this ghastly corpse substituted in the place of the body. The widower paid little attention to these rumours, and, after bitterly lamenting his wife for a year of mourning, began to think on the prudence of forming a new marriage, which, to a poor artisan with so young a family, and without the assistance of a housewife, was almost a matter of necessity. He readily found a neighbour with whose good looks he was satisfied, whilst her character for temper seemed to warrant her good usage of his children. He proposed himself and was accepted, and carried the names of the parties to the clergyman (called, I believe, Mr. Matthew Reid) for the due proclamation of banns. As the man had really loved his late partner,

[27]

it is likely that this proposed decisive alteration of his condition brought back many reflections concerning the period of their union, and with these recalled the extraordinary rumours which were afloat at the time of her decease, so that the whole forced upon him the following lively dream:—As he lay in his bed, awake as he thought, he beheld, at the ghostly hour of midnight, the figure of a female dressed in white, who entered his hut, stood by the side of his bed, and appeared to him the very likeness of his late wife. He conjured her to speak, and with astonishment heard her say, like the minister of Aberfoyle, that she was not dead, but the unwilling captive of the Good Neighbours. Like Mr. Kirke, too, she told him that if all the love which he once had for her was not entirely gone, an opportunity still remained of recovering her, or *winning her back*, as it was usually termed, from the comfortless realms of Elfland. She charged him on a certain day of the ensuing week that he should convene the most respectable housekeepers in the town, with the clergyman at their head, and should disinter the coffin in which she was supposed to have been buried. 'The clergyman is to recite certain prayers, upon which,' said the apparition, 'I will start from the coffin and fly with great speed round the church, and you must have the fleetest runner of the parish (naming a man famed for swiftness) to pursue me, and such a one, the smith, renowned for his strength, to hold me fast after I am overtaken; and in that case I shall, by the prayers of the church, and the efforts of my loving husband and neighbours, again recover my station in human society.' In the morning the poor widower was distressed with the recollection of his dream, but, ashamed and puzzled, took no measures in consequence. A second night, as is not very surprising, the visitation was again repeated. On the third night she appeared with a sorrowful and displeased countenance, upbraided him with want of love and affection, and conjured him, for the last time, to attend to her instructions, which, if he now neglected, she would never have power to visit earth or communicate with him again. In order to convince him there was no delusion, he 'saw in his dream' that she took up the nursling at whose birth she had died, and gave it suck; she spilled also a drop or two of her milk on the poor man's bed-clothes, as if to assure him of the reality of the vision.

The next morning the terrified widower carried a statement of his perplexity to Mr. Matthew Reid, the clergyman. This reverend person, besides being an excellent divine in other respects, was at the same time a man of sagacity, who understood the human passions. He did not attempt to combat the reality of the vision which had thrown his parishioner into this tribulation, but he contended it could be only an illusion of the devil. He explained to the widower that no created being could have the right or power to imprison or detain the soul of a Christian—conjured him not to believe that his wife was otherwise disposed of than according to God's pleasure—assured him that Protestant doctrine utterly denies the existence of any middle state in the world to come—and explained to him that he, as a clergyman of the Church of Scotland, neither could nor dared authorize opening graves or using the intervention of prayer to sanction rites of a suspicious character. The poor man, confounded and perplexed by various feelings, asked his pastor what he should do. 'I will give you my best advice,' said the clergyman. 'Get your new bride's consent to be married tomorrow, or today, if you can; I will take it on me to dispense with the rest of the banns, or proclaim them three times in one day. You will have a new wife, and, if you think of the former, it will be only as of one from whom death has separated you, and for whom you may have thoughts of affection and sorrow, but as a saint in Heaven, and not as a prisoner in Elfland.' The advice was taken, and the perplexed widower had no more visitations from his former spouse.

An instance, perhaps the latest which has been made public, of communication with the Restless People—(a more proper epithet than that of *Daoine Shi*, or Men of Peace, as they are called in Gaelic)—came under Pennant's notice so late as during that observant traveller's tour in 1769. Being perhaps the latest news from the invisible commonwealth, we give the tourist's own words.

'A poor visionary who had been working in his cabbage-garden (in Breadalbane) imagined that he was raised suddenly up into the air, and conveyed over a wall into an adjacent corn-field; that he found himself surrounded by a crowd of men and women, many of whom he knew to have been dead for some years, and who appeared to him skimming over the tops of the unbending corn, and mingling together like bees going to hive; that they spoke an unknown language, and with a hollow sound; that they very roughly pushed him to and fro, but on his uttering the name of God all vanished, but a female sprite, who, seizing him by the shoulder, obliged him to promise an assignation at that very hour that day seven-night; that he then found his hair was all tied in double knots (well known by the name of elf-locks), and that he had almost lost his speech; that he kept his word with the spectre, whom he soon saw floating through the air towards him; that he spoke to her, but she told him she was at that time in too much haste to attend to him, but bid him go away and no harm should befall him, and so the affair rested when I left the country. But it is incredible the mischief these *agri somnia* did in the neighbourhood. The friends and neighbours of the deceased, whom the old dreamer had named, were in the utmost anxiety at finding them in such bad company in the other world; the almost extinct belief of the old idle tales began to gain ground, and the good minister will have many a weary discourse and exhortation before he can eradicate the absurd ideas this idle story has revived.'[1]

It is scarcely necessary to add that this comparatively recent tale is just the counterpart of the story of Bessie Dunlop, Alison Pearson, and of the Irish butler who was so nearly carried off, all of whom found in Elfland some friend, formerly of middle earth, who attached themselves to the child of humanity, and who endeavoured to protect a fellow-mortal against their less philanthropic companions.

These instances may tend to show how the fairy superstition, which, in its general sense of worshipping the *Dii Campestres*, was much the older of the two, came to bear upon and have connexion with that horrid belief in witchcraft which cost so many innocent persons and crazy impostors their lives for the supposed commission of impossible crimes.

# [ 4 HUGH MILLER ]

Among the Scotch men of letters and ideas stimulated by Scott to preserve oral antiquities bound to the landscape, Hugh Miller (1802–56) left his own special mark. The midwife attending his mother in the bleak northern town of Cromarty told her the unusual shape of the baby's head portended an idiot. Hugh grew up to be one of the most eminent Scotsmen of his day, beginning as a stone-cutter but gaining fame as an author, editor, geologist, and religious liberal. He is remembered for such geological writings as *The Old Red Sandstone* and *The Testimony of the Rocks* reconciling science and faith, and for his pamphlets espousing a free church in Scotland. Little heed is given to an early literary endeavour, *Scenes and Legends of the North of Scotland*, first issued in 1835 and reissued in enlarged form in 1850. Titles of this sort are often misleading for the folklorist, but this book lived fully up to title and subtitle, 'The Traditional History of Cromarty,' and memorably recounts the legendary traditions of Cromarty folk, from the battle of Culloden to the escapades of cross-grained characters.

Miller wrote without precise concepts or terms to guide him and

[1] Pennant's *Tour in Scotland*, vol. i, p. 110.

in his opening chapter we see him fumbling for descriptive labels to separate the several classes of folk narrative. He recognized the existence of purely realistic, purely fictional, and mixed veins of storytelling, and of the specialized talents in these veins possessed by individual narrators. These questions of oral style and repertoire have engaged twentieth-century scholars, but the stonemason of Cromarty had to grapple with the phenomena of oral tradition in intellectual isolation.

Text from Hugh Miller, *Scenes and Legends of the North of Scotland*. Edinburgh: Adam and Charles Black, 1835. Pages 3–10.

. . . Old grey-headed men, and especially old women, became my books;—persons whose minds not having been preoccupied by that artificial kind of learning, which is the result of education, had gradually filled, as they passed through life, with the knowledge of what was occurring around them, and with the information derived from people of a similar cast with themselves, who had been born half an age earlier. And it was not long before I at least *thought* I discovered that their narratives had only to be translated into the language of books, to render them as interesting as even the better kind of written stories. They abounded with what I deemed as true delineations of character, as pleasing exhibitions of passion, and as striking instances of the vicissitudes of human affairs—with the vagaries of imaginations as vigorous, and the beliefs of superstitions as wild. Alas! the epitaph of the famous American Printer may now be written over the greater part of the volumes of this my second library; and so unfavourable is the present age to the production of more, that even that wise provision of nature which implants curiosity in the young, while it renders the old communicative, seems abridged of one half its usefulness. For though the young must still learn, the old need not teach;—the press having proved such a supplanter of the past-world schoolmaster, Tradition, as the spinning wheel was in the last age to the distaff and spindle. I cannot look back on much more than twenty years of the past, and yet in that comparatively brief space, I see the stream of tradition rapidly lessening as it flows onward, and displaying, like those rivers of Africa, which lose themselves in the burning sands of the desert, a broader and more powerful volume as I trace it towards its source.

It has often been a subject of regret to me, that this oral knowledge of the past, which I deem so interesting, should be thus suffered to be lost. The meteor, says my motto, if it once fall, cannot be rekindled. Perhaps had I been as conversant five years ago

[31]

with the art of the writer, as with the narratives of my early monitors, no one at this time of day would have to entertain a similar feeling; but I was not so conversant with it, nor am I yet, and the occasion still remains. The Sibyline tomes of tradition are disappearing in this part of the country one by one; and I find, like Selkirk in his island, when the rich fruits of autumn were dropping around him, that if I myself do not preserve them, they must perish. I therefore set myself to the task of storing them up as I best may, and urge as my only apology, the emergency of the case. Not merely do I regard them as the produce of centuries, and like the blossoms of the Aloe, interesting on this account alone, but also as a species of produce, which the harvests of future centuries may fail to supply. True it is, that superstition is a weed indigenous to the human mind, and will spring up in the half cultivated corners of society in every coming generation; but then the superstitions of the future may have little in common with those of the past. True it is, that human nature is intrinsically the same in all ages and all countries; but then it is not so with its ever varying garb of custom and opinion, and never again may it wear this garb in the curious obsolete fashion of a century ago.—Geologists tell us that the earth produced its plants and animals at a time when the very stones of our oldest ruins existed only as mud or sand; but they were certainly not the plants and animals of Linnaeus or Buffon.

The traditions of this part of the country, and of perhaps every other, may be divided into three great classes. Those of the first and simplest class are strictly local; they record real events, and owe their chief interest to their delineations of character. Those of the second are pure inventions. They are formed mostly after a set of models furnished, perhaps, by the later bards, and are common, though varying in different places according to the taste of the several imitators who first introduced them, or the chance alterations they afterwards received, to almost every district of Scotland. The traditions of the third and most complex class are combinations of the two others, with, in some instances, a dash of original invention, and in others, a mixture of that superstitious credulity, which can misconceive as ingeniously as the creative faculty can invent. The value of stories of the first class is generally in proportion to their truth, and there is a simple test by which we may ascertain the degree of credit proper to be attached to them. There is a habit of minute attention almost peculiar to the common people (in no class, at least, is it more perfect than in the commonest), which leads them to take a kind of microscopic survey of every object suited to interest them; and hence their narratives of events

[32]

which have really occurred, are as strikingly faithful in all the minor details, as Dutch paintings. Not a trait of character, not a shade of circumstance is suffered to escape. Nay more,—the *dramatis personœ* of their little histories are almost invariably introduced, to tell their own stories in their own language. And though this be the easiest and lowest style of narrative, yet to invent in this style is so far from being either low or easy, that, with the exception of Shakspeare, and one or two more, I know not any who have excelled in it. Nothing more common than those faithful memories which can record whole conversations, and every attendant circumstance, however minute; nothing less so than that just conception of character and vigour of imagination, which can alone construct a natural dialogue, or depict, with the nice pencil of truth, a scene wholly fictitious. And thus, though any one, even the weakest, can mix up falsehoods with the truths related in this way, not one of a million can make them amalgamate. The iron and clay, to use Bacon's illustration, retain their separate natures, as in the feet of the image, and can as easily be distinguished.

The traditions of the second class, being in most instances only imperfect copies of extravagant and ill-conceived originals, are much less interesting than those of the first; and such of them as are formed on the commoner models, or have already, in some shape or other, been laid before the public, I shall take the liberty of rejecting. A very few of them, however, are of a superior and more local cast, and these I shall preserve. Their merit, such as it is, consists principally in their structure as stories—a merit, I am disposed to think, which, when even at the best, is of no high order. I have observed that there is more of plot and counter plot in our commonest novels, and lowest kind of plays, than in the tales and dramas of our best writers; and what can be more simple than the fables of the Iliad and the Paradise Lost!—From the third class of traditions I trust to derive some of my choicest materials. Like those of the first, they are rich in character and incident, and to what is natural in them and based on fact, there is added, as in Epic poetry, a kind of machinery, supplied either by invention or superstition, or borrowed from the fictions of the bards, or from the old classics. In one or two instances, I have met with little strokes of fiction in them, of a similar character with some of even the finest strokes in the latter, but which seem to be rather coincidences of invention, if I may so express myself, than imitations.—There occurs to me a story of this class which may serve to illustrate my meaning.

In the upper part of the parish of Cromarty there is a singularly

[33]

curious spring, termed Sludach, which suddenly dries up every year
early in summer, and breaks out again at the close of autumn. It
gushes from the bank with an undiminished volume until within a
few hours before it ceases to flow for the season, and bursts forth on
its return in a full stream. And it acquired this peculiar character,
says tradition, sometime in the seventeenth century. On a very
warm day of summer, two farmers employed in the adjacent fields
were approaching the spring in opposite directions, to quench their
thirst. One of them was tacksman of the farm on which the spring
rises, the other tenanted a neighbouring farm. They had lived for
some time previous on no very friendly terms. The tacksman, a
course, rude man, reached the spring first, and taking a hasty
draught, he gathered up a handful of mud, and just as his neighbour came up, flung it into the water. 'Now,' said he, turning away
as he spoke, 'you may drink your fill.' Scarcely had he uttered the
words, however, when the offended stream began to boil like a
caldron, and after bubbling a while among the grass and rushes,
sunk into the ground. Next day at noon, the heap of grey sand
which had been incessantly rising and falling within it, in a little
conical jet, for years before, had become as dry as the dust of the
fields; and the strip of white flowering cresses which skirted either
side of the runnel that had issued from it, lay withering in the sun.
What rendered the matter still more extraordinary, it was found
that a powerful spring had burst out on the opposite side of the
frith, which at this place is nearly five miles in breadth, a few hours
after the Cromarty one had disappeared. The story spread; the
tacksman, rude and coarse as he was, was made unhappy by the
forebodings of his neighbours, who seemed to regard him as one
resting under a curse; and going to an elderly person in an adjoining
parish, much celebrated for his knowledge of the supernatural, he
craved his advice. 'Repair,' said the seer, 'to the old hollow of the
fountain, and, as nearly as you can guess, at the hour in which you
insulted the water, and after clearing it out with a clean linen
towel, lay yourself down beside it, and abide the result.' He did so,
and waited on the bank above the hollow from noon until near
sunset; when the water came rushing up with a noise like the roar of
the sea, scattering the sand for several yards around; and then sub-
siding to its common level, it flowed on as formerly between the
double row of cresses. The spring on the opposite side of the frith
withdrew its waters about the time of the rite of the cleansing, and
they have not since reappeared; while those of Sludach from that
day to the present, are presented, as if in scorn, during the moister
seasons, when no one regards them as valuable, and withheld in the

seasons of drought, when they would be prized. We recognize in this singular tradition a kind of sou or Naiad of the spring, susceptible of offence, and conscious of the attentions paid it; and the passage of the waters beneath the sea reminds us of the river Alpheus sinking at Peloponnesus to rise in Sicily.

Next in degree to the pleasure I have enjoyed in collecting these traditions, is the satisfaction which I have had in contemplating the various cabinets, if I may so speak, in which I found them stored up according to their classes. For I soon discovered that the different sorts of stories were not lodged indiscriminately in every sort of mind,—the people who cherished the narratives of a particular cast, frequently rejecting those of another. I found, for instance, that the traditions of the third class, with all their machinery of wraiths and witches, were most congenial to the female mind; and I think I can now perceive that this was quite in character. Women, taken in the collective, are more poetical, more timid, more credulous than men. If we add to these general traits, one or two that are less so, and a few very common circumstances; if we but add a judgment not naturally vigorous, an imagination more than commonly active, an ignorance of books and of the world, a long cherished belief in the supernatural, a melancholy old age, and a solitary fireside, we have compounded the elements of that terrible poetry which revels among sculls, and coffins, and enchantments, as certainly as Nature did when she moulded the brain of a Shakspeare. The stories of the second class I have almost never found in communion with those of the third, and never heard well told—except as jokes. To tell a story avowedly untrue, and to tell it as a piece of humour, requires a very different cast of mind from that which characterized the melancholy people who were the grand depositories of the darker traditions: they entertained these only because they deemed them mysterious and very awful truths, while they regarded open fictions as worse than foolish. Nor were their own stories better received by a third sort of persons, from whom I have drawn some of my best traditions of the first class, and who were mostly shrewd, sagacious men, who having acquired such a tinge of scepticism as made them ashamed of the beliefs of their weaker neighbours, were yet not so deeply imbued with it as to deem these beliefs mere matters of amusement. They did battle with them both in themselves and the people around them, and found the contest too serious an affair to be laughed at. Now, however (and the circumstance is characteristic), the successors of this order of people venture readily enough on telling a good ghost story, when they but get one to tell. Superstition, so long as it was living superstition, they deemed, like the live tiger in his native woods, a formidable, mischievous thing, fit only to be destroyed; but now that it has perished, they possess themselves of its skin and its claws, and store them up in their cabinets.

## [ 5 THOMAS KEIGHTLEY ]

Mythology joined popular antiquities and oral tradition as a related interest bringing together antiquaries, bookmen, and private scholars in London societies of the 1820's and '30's. In preparing *The Fairy Mythology* in 1828, a work revised and reprinted throughout the century, Thomas Keightley (1789–1872) turned attention from the remote literary mythology of Greek and Roman gods, on which he himself had previously written, to contemporary rustic legends of sprites and goblins. Keightley had contributed some legends from his own childhood memories to the *Fairy Traditions from the South of Ireland*, related by a fellow Anglo-Irishman, Thomas Crofton Croker, in 1828, and thereupon commenced to examine foreign literatures for accounts of similar diminutive beings known to the European peasantry. Intrigued by the resemblances in these traditions, Keightley next focused on the question ever central to folklorists, whether similar tales resulted from borrowing or from independent invention. The product of these musings, *Tales and Popular Fictions* (1834), was the first book in English to demonstrate the widely scattered appearances of folktale plots and incidents. Although Keightley necessarily relied on literary rather than field versions of traditional tales, he well understood the nature of oral storytelling, as the following selection shows.

Text from Thomas Keightley, *Tales and Popular Fictions*. London: Whittaker and Co., 1834. Pages 6–13, Chapter 1, 'Origin of the Work.'

When chance led me to think of writing the Fairy Mythology, I had to read a great quantity of poems, tales, romances, legends, and traditions of various countries and in various languages. I here met such a number of coincidences where there could hardly have been any communication, that I became convinced that the original sameness of the human mind revealed itself as plainly in fiction as in the mechanical arts, or in manners and customs, civil or religious.

Accordingly, in the Preface to that work, I stated how much I had been struck by this similarity, and expressed my dissent from those who supposed nations of common origin to have brought these legends with them at the time of their migration from a common country; and I reminded the reader of the sameness which runs through the thoughts and the actions of man, which wearies us in history, in fiction, and in common life.

Some legends were, I thought, transmitted; others, of independent formation. When in a tale of some length a number of circumstances are the same, and follow in the same order, as in another, I should feel disposed to assert that this is a case of transmission. Brief fictitious circumstances, such as shoes of swiftness and coats of darkness, might, I thought, be independent, and be referred to what I termed the poverty of the human imagination, which, having a limited stock of materials to work on, must of necessity frequently produce similar combinations. A third class of fictions, such as Whittington and his Cat,—a legend to be found (as I shall show,) in more countries than one,—I professed myself unable to dispose of to my own satisfaction: they might be transmitted, they might be independent.

'These,' said I, 'are a few hints on a subject, the full discussion of which would demand a volume.' Little, at the time, did I think that I ever should write a volume on it; but 'thou knowest not what a day may bring forth': the volume is written, and I have only to request that no one will suppose it intended to be a 'full discussion' of the subject. It only claims to be regarded as a development of the principles contained in that Preface, and is designed, by giving a sufficient number of instances of resemblance, to enable the reader to judge for himself on this curious subject. The tales and legends are given at length; for what conviction could I hope to convey to the mind of a reader, by merely telling him that such a tale in the Neapolitan Pentamerone, for instance, resembles a Hindoo legend? or that an episode of the Persian Shah Nameh is founded on the same circumstance with an Irish poem? How many readers would, how many could, examine these different tales and compare them?

I am, certainly, neither so ignorant nor so sanguine, as to reckon on a very extensive class of readers; and if I 'fit audience find though few,' I shall be very well content. The direction taken by what is usually, but incorrectly, termed the 'march of intellect',[1] is such, that all the lighter and more elegant branches of literature seem likely to fall, ere long, into utter neglect. Wild improbable

[1] I say so, because with us *march* is a military term, whereas the *marche* of the French, from whom we have borrowed the phrase, merely denotes progression. *La marche de l'esprit* can hardly be said to be figurative.

[37]

romance, bit-and-scrap knowledge, or political disquisitions, alone have attractions. Never shall I forget the look of mingled pity and contempt with which I was regarded by a gentleman who has written some things on political economy, when I chanced, in his hearing, to speak on the subject of classical mythology. He seemed altogether amazed at my folly in expecting that such puerile fictions could find readers in this enlightened age.

Yet, though thus despised by the narrow-minded and intolerant disciples of utility, popular fiction has attractions for those whose views are more enlarged, and who love to behold Philosophy extending her dominion over all the regions of the human mind. A writer whom I shall frequently quote in the following pages, and who was no mere man of letters, thus expresses himself on the subject.[1] 'Believe me, he who desires to be well acquainted with a people, will not reject their popular stories or local superstitions. Depend upon it, that man is too far advanced into an artificial state of society who is a stranger to the effect which tales and stories like these have upon the feelings of a nation; and his opinions of its character are never likely to be more erroneous, than when in the pride of reason he despises such means of forming his judgement.' Sir Walter Scott[2] says, 'A work of great interest might be compiled on the origin of popular fiction, and the transmission of popular tales from age to age and from country to country. The mythology of one period would then appear to pass into the romance of the next century, and that into the nursery tale of the subsequent ages. Such an investigation, while it went greatly to diminish our ideas of the richness of human invention, would also show that these fictions, however wild and childish, possess such charms for the populace, as enable them to penetrate into countries unconnected by manners and language, and having no apparent intercourse to facilitate the means of transmission.' And long since the illustrious Luther[3] said, 'I would not for any quantity of gold part with the wonderful tales which I have retained from my earliest childhood, or have met with in my progress through life.' Surely then, even though few should be induced to go the same road, I need feel no shame to travel in such society as this, and may let those plod on their weary way, who, knowing but one subject, think it contains all knowledge.

Those words of the great Reformer reveal the true cause of the high degree of pleasure which some minds derive from popular fictions. They bring back the memory of childhood—of those

[1] Sir John Malcolm, *Sketches of Persia*, ii, 92.    [2] Note on the *Lady of the Lake*.
[3] Quoted by Grimm, *Kinder- und Hausmärchen*, iii, 265.

innocent and happy days when, as a Swedish poet most beautifully expresses it, 'the dew of morning lay upon life':[1] they come surrounded by a thousand delightful associations, whose effect, though powerful, is not to be described; for, mellowed by distance, every event and every scene connected with childhood acquires a charm to the eye of memory. It is, I apprehend, only on those who have passed their early days in the country that this principle operates with its entire force. May I, since such is the case with myself, (and it is not totally alien to the matter in hand,)—may I hope for indulgence while I trace the origin of my own fondness for popular fiction?

It was my lot (no unenviable one) to be reared in the country, and near the mountains. In Ireland we are less aristocratic, and mingle more familiarly with the lower orders of the people, than seems to me to be the case here: one cause of this I believe to be nearly the same with that which produces similar affability in the East,[2] and which also operates in the South of Europe. Be this as it may, in consequence of this state of manners, a great companion of my younger days was Johnny Stykes, who, like Guse Gibbie of famous memory, first kept the turkeys, and then, as his years advanced, was promoted to the more important office of minding the cows. Johnny, by the way, though called Stykes, and a good Catholic,[3] knew well that his real name was Sykes,[4] and that he derived his lineage from one of the soldier-saints of the formidable Oliver Cromwell, to whom the lines had fallen in those pleasant places where we dwelt. Often, as memory looks back through the glade of life along which my course has lain, doth her eye rest on the figure of my humble companion, returning in the evening from the stubble with his feathered charge, who go along *yeeping* and leisurely picking their steps, heedless of the *hushing* and bawling of their driver. To any one who should then ask Johnny how many turkeys he had, he would stammer out, 'Three twenties and a ten' or so,—an answer which was always sure to produce a laugh, either on account of his employing *twenty* for *score*, or it may be from the 'march of intellect,' which had taught the peasant to despise his forefathers' simple mode of counting by dozens and scores.

[1] 'In her early dawn, with the "dew of her youth" so fresh upon her. . . .'—*Robert Hall, of the Princess Charlotte*. Was the passage of Scripture here quoted in the mind of the Swede also?

[2] See *Sketches of Persia*, ii, 185, 186.

[3] The lower order of the Irish Catholics are quite proud if they can prove that they have what they call good Protestant blood in their veins. They regard the Protestants as a superior caste.

[4] It is very amusing to observe the corruption of proper names. Among the peasantry of the place of which I write, Archbold had become Aspal, and Hopkins, Hubbuk.

But it was in Johnny's bucolic days that he was favoured most with my society; partly because he was a capital player at *tip-top-castle*, but chiefly because he had not his fellow in the whole country for what is called *shanahas*, or old talk, that is, tales, legends, and traditions, handed down from age to age, and transmitted from mouth to mouth. And let me now fearlessly confess the truth. I have since seen some of Nature's finest scenery, I have conversed with the learned and the ingenious, and have read the master-works of the human mind; and yet I am convinced I have never, at most very rarely, felt a degree of pleasure at all comparable to what I enjoyed, when sitting with Johnny, of a summer's day, beneath a spreading tree, or on the bank of a purling stream, while the cows were feeding around, and the air was filled with the melody of birds, and listening to some wild tale of wonder and enchantment. Much would I give to be able to recollect his tale of The Fair Norah na Vodha and the White Bear of Worroway (Norway), a Beauty-and-Beast kind of story, in which the heroine is pursued by I know not who, and 'when he was on the hill she was in the hollow, and when she was on the hill he was in the hollow'; or another about a princess (for he had all kinds of high personages at command), who was confined in some dismal place all full of *sarpints* and toads and *vifers*.[1] Johnny, too, had a story answering to the Robber-bridegroom in MM. Grimm's collection, in which the lady at the bridal banquet told, as if relating a dream, all that she had seen when she secretly entered the robber's den, and as she proceeded in her narrative, the disguised robber would get up and say,

'Dreams are but *feebles*, and *feebles* are but lies;
By your leave, gentlemen, pray let me by.'

He also knew the Frog-king,[2] and several others in the same collection; and he had tales of fairies without end. Poor Johnny! he grew up, got married, died young (no uncommon fate with the Irish peasant), and lies buried at the ruined church of Tipper; a place to which, in my serious moods, I was wont to repair, to meditate among the—graves, not tombs, for tombs there were none.

[1] Animals nearly as unknown to the Irish peasant as kangaroos and opossums.
[2] This story was also related to me by a woman from Somersetshire. Dr. Leyden heard it in Scotland. My Somerset friend concluded it by saying, 'and I came away.' She could not tell why; but it is, I should suppose, a *formula* signifying that the narrator knows nothing further.

## [ 6  THOMAS  WRIGHT ]

The mythological studies of English antiquaries received a powerful stimulus and a determining influence from the *Deutsche Mythologie* of Jacob Grimm (1st edition 1835, 2nd edition 1844, 3rd edition 1854, 4th edition 1875–8); translated into English by James S. Stallybrass (four vols., 1880–8). This theoretical work from the great collector proved more remarkable even than the *Kinder- und Hausmärchen*, giving order and philosophic meaning to the mass of popular superstitions scattered amongst the peasantry. Using the method of philological examination of word roots, Grimm traced the names of demons extant among the villagers to heathen gods and goddesses. In London, the prolific writer on medieval history, literature, and manners, Thomas Wright (1810–1877), at once recognized the applicability of Grimm's system to the English middle ages when monks and missionaries yet nourished the old heathen notions. In the review essay excerpted below, Wright inserted examples of the dark mythology still visible in English mediaeval manuscripts, noting however that these evidences reflected only the vicious side of demonology feared by the prelates. The innocuous fairy creed did not become visible until the lively chronicles of the twelfth and thirteenth centuries. As Keightley had demonstrated the lateral spread of the fairy mythology across Europe and the East, Wright now illustrated its historical depth at home.

  Text from Thomas Wright, *Essays on Subjects Connected with the Literature, Popular Superstitions, and History of England in the Middle Ages*. Two volumes. London: John Russell Smith, 1846. I, 237–52, from Essay VII, 'On Dr. Grimm's German Mythology.'

  There is no subject of inquiry relating to the history of a people more interesting than its popular mythology and superstitions. In these we trace the early formation of nations, their identity or analogy, their changes, as well as the inner texture of the national character, more deeply than in any other circumstances, even in language itself. It has been brought before us in all its generality by the *Mythologie* of Dr. James Grimm, one of the most admirable books that Germany has ever sent us. An English reader will not be sorry to be made in some degree acquainted with this work, although it is in itself too extensive, and at the same time by far too compact, to allow of our attempting to give an analysis of its

[41]

contents. We will add a few facts from our own desultory researches, which bear on the subject introduced in it.

Christianity was first introduced among the Teutonic tribes about the beginning of the fourth century, when a few missionaries carried it to the banks of the Rhine, and to the Alamanns and Goths. Among the latter people it obtained a permanent establishment during that century, being first adopted by the West-Goths, and afterwards by the East-Goths. The Vandals and the Gepidae followed soon after in their footsteps. The Burgundians, in Gaul, became Christians at the beginning of the fifth century, and the Suevi, in Spain, about fifty years later. At the conclusion of this century and the beginning of the next, the Franks were converted, and they were followed by the Alamanns and the Langobards. In the seventh and eighth centuries followed the conversion of the Bavarians; in the eighth, that of the Frieslanders, the Hessians, and the Thuringians; and towards the ninth, that of the Saxons. In Britain, the Anglo-Saxons had received the Gospel about the conclusion of the sixth and the beginning of the seventh century. In the tenth century the Danes became Christians; at the beginning of the eleventh, the Norwegians; in the second half of the eleventh, the Swedes and the Icelanders. The period of the establishment of Christianity among the Slavic and Hungarian tribes varied from the eighth to the eleventh century. The Lithuanians were not converted till the beginning of the fifteenth; and the Laplanders are scarcely more than half Christians at the present day.

Just as in our island we have districts where the people are much more ignorant than in others, and where the popular superstitions still retain their hold on the peasantry, so was it with the Teutonic tribes in the earlier ages of their Christianity. In the midst of the Christian peoples, there were still districts where the light of the Gospels had not penetrated. Thus in Neustria, the banks of the Loire and the Seine—in Burgundia, the Vosges—in Austrasia, the Ardennes, were inhabited in the sixth and seventh centuries by people who were mere Pagans. Similarly there dwelt pagan tribes towards Friesland and in Flanders, long after the surrounding tribes had been converted. From this circumstance it arises, that among some of the earlier monkish writers we have notices of heathen customs which they had had an opportunity of witnessing, and allusions to articles of the older creed which still in their time survived partially, and which now throw great light on the history of *Teutonic Mythology*.

Moreover, when Christianity was fully established, in their conversion the old pagans had received a new belief, without quitting altogether their old one. There were certain beings of the ancient creed who were worshipped as gods, and with whom the people were only acquainted through their priests; and with these Christianity of course clashed at its first introduction. But there was a much larger class of beings of the popular belief, with whom the people supposed they had a nearer connexion, and whose influence, good or evil, they believed themselves to be daily experiencing; these were, like themselves, works of the Creator,—with passions, too, like themselves, and in whose invisible society they were themselves frequently living. They were substantial beings also, but of a far more refined nature, and infinitely more powerful. They wielded the elements, caused most of the visible convulsions of nature, as well as many of the accidents with which humanity was visited. While Christianity destroyed every where the worship of Woden, the belief in the airy spirits of the popular creed was unimpaired; for, whatever different opinion the monks might entertain of their nature and calling, they found nothing in their own faith which directly proscribed them.

In fact, the popular belief in these things and their effects was so intimately interwoven in the national character, that they held by it like the language, with which, also, they had a strong tie in the multitude of words and names for things and circumstances which called them perpetually to men's minds. The common ceremonies of life at every minute bore allusions to them; things so difficult to eradicate, that now, after so many centuries of successive improvement and refinement, in our salutations, in our eating and drinking, even in our children's games, we are perpetually, though unwittingly, doing the same things which our forefathers did in honour or in fear of the elves and nymphs of the heathen creed.

Many of these ceremonies and customs appeared to the monks, and with reason, to be much more objectionable than others. Some of them bore too pointed an allusion to the worship of the old pagan deities—others were of a degrading nature, or of a mischievous tendency, which was quite at variance even with the lowest estimate of Christianity. Some of these were marked out for public punishment in the laws of the different states; but many more are entered in the penitentiaries and ecclesiastical laws among the crimes to be atoned for by that spiritual punishment which the penitence of the offender was made to inflict upon himself. Hence to us these penitentiaries and laws are the most valuable authorities for the early history of the popular superstitions. The Anglo-Saxon penitentiaries, in particular, are full of curious details of this nature, whether we find them written in the Latin or in the

[43]

vernacular tongue, in both of which they are tolerably abundant. A few specimens may amuse some of our readers, both from their connexion with the subject of which we are speaking, and from the curious manner in which the punishments are doled out. We prefer giving them from inedited sources. In a valuable Penitentiary, printed in a collection of Anglo-Saxon remains not yet published,[1] are, among others, the following notices:—

'If any man destroy another by witchcraft, let him fast seven years; three on bread and water, and, during the other four, three days a week on bread and water.'

'If any one observe lots, or divination; or keep his wake (watch) at any wells, or at any other created things, except at God's church; let him fast three years, the first on bread and water, and the other two, on Wednesdays and Fridays, on bread and water; and the other days let him eat his meat, but without flesh.'[2]

'The same for a woman who useth any witchcraft to her child, or who draws it through the earth at the meeting of roads, because that is great heathenness.'

'If a mouse fall into liquor, let it be taken out, and sprinkle the liquor with holy-water, and, if it be alive, the liquor may be used, but if it be dead, throw the liquor out and cleanse the vessel.'

'He who uses any thing that a dog or mouse has eaten of, or a weasel polluted, if he do it knowingly, let him sing a hundred psalms; and if he know it not, let him sing fifty psalms.'

'He who gives to others the liquor that a mouse or weasel has been drowned in, if he be a layman, let him fast three days; if he be a churchman, let him sing three hundred psalms. And if he did it without his knowledge, but afterwards knew it, let him sing the psalter.'

In a Saxon homily against witchcraft and magic, preserved in the public library of the University of Cambridge, we have several notices of the *heathen* superstitions of our forefathers, at a comparatively short distance of time from their conversion. 'We are ashamed,' says the writer, 'to tell all the scandalous divinations that every man useth through the devil's teaching, either in taking a wife, or in going a journey, or in brewing, or at the asking of something when he begins anything, or when anything is born to him.'[3] And again, 'Some men are so blind, that they bring their

---

[1] By the Record Commission in the volume containing the poetry of the Vercelli MS.
[2] Gyf hwa hlytas oðð̄e hwatunga bega; oðð̄e his wæccean æt ænigum wylle hæbbe, oðð̄e æt ænigre oþre ge-sceafte butan æt Godes cyricean; fæste he III. gear, þæt an on hlafe and on wætere, and þa twa on Wodnes-dagum and Frige-dagum on hlafe and on watere, and þa oðre dagas bruce his metes butan flæsce anum.
[3] Us sceameð to secganne ealle ð̄a sceandlican wiglunga þe ge-hwæs menn drifað,

offerings to immoveable rocks, and also to trees, and to wells, as witches teach, and will not understand how foolishly they do, or how the lifeless stone or the dumb tree may help them, or heal them, when they themselves never stir from the place.'[1] 'Moreover,' he goes on to say, 'many a silly woman goes to the meeting of ways, and draweth her child through the earth, and so gives to the devil both herself and her offspring.'[2] In fact, as the same early writer observes, 'Every one who trusts in divinations either by fowls, or by sneezings, or by horses, or by dogs, he is no Christian, but a notorious apostate.'[3] Among the many Latin penitentialia in the British Museum, there is one which is very full in its enumeration of such offences against 'Christendom,' although it seems that many of them were criminal chiefly when committed by a priest or monk. Amongst other offenders are here enumerated,—

'He who endeavours by any incantation or magic to take away the stores of milk, or honey, or other things belonging to another, and to acquire them himself.

'He who, deceived by the illusion of hobgoblins, believes and confesses that he goes or rides in the company of her whom the foolish peasantry call Herodias or Diana, and with immense multitude, and that he obeys her commands.

'He who prepares with three knives in the company of persons, that they may predestine happiness to children who are going to be born there.

'He who makes his offering to a tree, or to water, or to any thing, except a church.

'They who follow the custom of the pagans in inquiring into the future by magical incantations on the first of January, or begin works on that day, as though they would on that account prosper better the whole year.

'They who make ligatures or incantations and various fascinations with magical charms, and hide them in the grass, or in a tree, or in the path, for the preservation of their cattle.

---

[1] Sume men synd swa ablende þæt hí bringað heora lác to corðfæstum stanum, and eac to treowum, and to wyl-springum, swa swa wiccan tæcað, and nellað understandan hu stuntlice hí doð, oððc hu ðe deade stán oððe þæt dumbe treow him mage ge-helpan, oððc hælc for-gifan, þonne hí sylfe ne a-styriað of þære stowe næfre. (*Ibid.*, fol. 396.)
[2] Eác sume ge-witlease wif farað to wega ge-lætum, and teoð hcora cild þurh ða eorðan, and swa deofle be-tæcað hí sylfe and heora bearn. (*Ibid.*)
[3] Eall swa ge-lice ðe þe ge-lyfð wiglungum oððe be fugelum, oððe be fnórum, oððe be horsum, oððe be hundum, ne bið he na Cristen ac bið for-cuð wiðer-saca. (*Ibid.*, fol. 394.)
þurh deofles lare, oððe on wifunge, oððe on wadunge, oððe on brywlace, oþþe gif hí man hwæs bitt þonne hí hwæt onginnað, oþþe hí hwæt bið accenned. (*MS. Bibl. Pub. Camb.*, Ii, 1, 33, fol. 395.)

'He who places his child on the roof or in a furnace for the recovery of his health, or for this purpose uses any charms, or characters, or magical figment, or any art, unless it be holy prayers, or the liberal art of medicine.

'He who shall say any charm in the collecting of medicinal herbs, except such as the paternoster and the credo.'

Many of the customs alluded to in the foregoing extracts may be traced, under different forms, nearly up to the present day; and none more so than well-worship, some of the ceremonies of which are still performed in different parts of our island. We are tempted to point out two inedited allusions to this latter branch of popular superstition, which we think extremely curious. When the Saxon hero, Hereward, was holding so bravely the marshes of Ely against the Norman Conqueror, he one day repaired in disguise to William's court, and before presenting himself there, passed the night in a cottage in the town where the court was then held. It happened that at the same time there resided in the cottage a noted witch, who was employed by the king to daunt the courage of Hereward's soldiers by her incantations. Being disturbed at midnight by hearing the witch in conversation with his hostess, he followed them into the garden. They repaired to a fountain of water which flowed towards the east, and there he heard them holding converse with the spirit of the fountain.[1] In the following rather humorous song, preserved in a manuscript at Cambridge, written in the earlier part of the fifteenth century, we have an allusion by name to the ceremony of *waking the well*, mentioned before in the Anglo-Saxon Penitentiary.

*I have forsworne hit, whil I life, to wake the well*

> The last tyme I the wel woke,
> Sir Johan caght me with a croke,
> He made me to swere be bel and boke
>         I shuld not tell.
>
> Yet he did me a wel worse turne,
> He layde my hed agayn the burne,[2]
> He gafe my maýdenhed a spurne,
>         And refe my bell.
>
> Sir John came to oure hows to play,
> Fro evensong tyme til light of the day

---

[1] Porro in medio noctis-silentio illas ad fontes aquarum in orientem affluentes juxta [h]ortum domus etam (*sic*) egressas Herwardus percepit. Quas statim secutus est, ubi eas eminus colloquentes audivit, nescio a quo custode fontium responsa et interrogantes et sui expectantes. (*De Gestis Herwardi Saxonis.*)

[2] *Burne*, toward the stream—*refe*, stole—*copious*, came frequently—*schrew*, I curse.

We made as mery as flowres in May,
　　I was so gyled.

Sir John he came to our hows,
He made it wonder copious,
He seyd that I was gracious
　　To beyre a child.

I go with childe, wel I wot;
I schrew the fader that hit gate,
Withowten he fynde hit mylke and pape
　　A long while ey.[1]

If we believe the satirical writings of the reformers, the ceremonies attendant on the popular superstitions had frequently a similar *dénouement* to that which in the present instance followed the *waking of the well.*

Not only were the popular superstitions of our pagan forefathers preserved in their full force, after the introduction of Christianity, from the circumstance of their having considerable influence over the minds of the monks themselves; but the first missionaries, by adopting many of the objects and places of former worship, in the hope of turning more readily the piety of their converts along with them into another direction, and sometimes in the pride of showing how the new religion had seated itself in the very strongholds of idolatry, were the cause of preserving, in the traditions of the people, many legends and articles of former belief, which otherwise would have perished with the objects to which they had been linked. Our extracts have afforded us several proofs how general was the worship of trees; they were looked upon originally as the temple of the object, and not as the object, of worship. Everybody who pays any attention to the subject, knows how commonly, even at the present time, legends and popular traditions of the most grotesque description are connected with trees that are venerable for their age and magnitude. Numerous notices in early writers, the greater part of which will be found collected in Grimm's *Mythologie*, shows us, that in the earlier ages of western paganism such trees were universally the objects of superstitious reverence. When St. Boniface, sometime between the years 725 and 731, and during the reign of Charles Martel, visited the Hessians, he found that, though the greater number of them had embraced the Christian faith, there were still many who followed their old idolatry. Boniface was determined to do all he could to root out heathendom, and, by the

[1] ме. Pub. Lib. Camb., Ff. 5, 48.

advice of the converted Hessians, he resolved on cutting down 'an oak of wonderful magnitude' which stood in a place called Gaesmere (Geismar), and to which their pagan forefathers had given, in their language, a name which signified the *oak of Jupiter* (Thor's Oak?).[1] The work of felling this vast tree was commenced in presence of an immense crowd of spectators, many of them pagans, who believed that their oak would be proof against the power of the axe, and who seemed to regard this trial as a test of the superiority of the one religion over the other. But the oak of Jupiter bowed and fell with a terrible crash, and hundreds of its worshippers became Christians on the spot. Thereupon Boniface, by the advice of his companions, cut up the sacred tree, and with the timber built an oratory on the spot, which he dedicated to Saint Peter. The life of St. Amandus, A.D. 674, speaks of trees dedicated to demons (*arbores quae erant daemonibus dedicatae*).

In like manner, it was a very common thing to place a Christian church on the same spot where had stood a temple dedicated to some one of the German divinities.

Besides these causes of the preservation of traces of the earlier Teutonic mythology, the language itself, in all its dialects and varieties, at every step bears marks of the original creed of the people who spoke it, not only in the names of the different mythic beings and of their habitation and worship, but in multitudes of expressions and terms applied at a later period to other objects and actions, which by their formation show how, at an early period, those objects and actions were connected with the popular culture. These are found more particularly in the names of plants and diseases, and of some animals, and in the apparently unmeaning formulae which, at a much later period, ignorant people used as magical charms. Grimm has given several popular rhymes in vogue among the peasantry of different parts of Germany, in which are found the names of Woden and Irmen. The names of the Teutonic gods are still preserved in those of the days of the week.

The information which these different authorities afford us concerning the early forms of Teutonic mythology, is tolerably copious, but at the same time so unconnected and vague, that it required all the industry and genius of a Grimm to reduce it to order, and to elicit from it the outline and the details of a system. The materials of an early date come chiefly through the hands of those who seized most readily on the terrific and disagreeable points of the popular

---

[1] Quorum consultu atque consilio *arborem* quandam *mirae magnitudinis*, quae *prisco paganorum vocabulo* appellatur *robur Jovis*, in loco qui dicitur Gaesmere. (*Vita Bonfac. ap. Grimm*, p. 44.)

mythology. They do not make us acquainted with the more harmless elves and fairies, although there are sufficient traces of them to take away all doubt of their having formed a part of the creed of our forefathers at this remote period. The elves and dwarfs are frequently alluded to in the legends of the Anglo-Saxon saints; and, though they are much disguised under the name of devils, or rather of hobgoblins, yet there are good reasons for believing that from this period to the time when it becomes more perfectly known to us, in this particular the popular belief had not altered. The *white ladies* are mentioned in the life of Hereward, already quoted, and in such a manner as to leave little doubt on our minds of their having been identical with the fairies of later times.

The latter half of the twelfth century and beginning of the thirteenth was the period when the feudal barons possessed the greatest power. It seems also to have been the age when literature was most patronized, and the writings which it has left us, whether in prose or verse, in Latin or Anglo-Norman (for those were the two languages in which people wrote), show more spirit, elegance, and imagination, than at any other period of the middle ages. The chronicles at this period become far more interesting than they had been before: there is more life and anecdote in them; and, curiously enough, they abound in fairy legends. What makes them still more valuable is, that these legends are evidently given as told by the peasantry, without any, or at least with very little, adventitious colouring. In Gervase of Tilbury, Giraldus Cambrensis, William of Newbury, and Walter Mapes, we have the elves and fairies in all their frolicsome airiness and in all their glory, and we trace them in their dances and gambols by moonlight in their under-ground country, and in their interference in the affairs of men. From this time the documents of the history of popular mythology are more abundant, and appear in multifarious shapes, like the superstitions to which they relate. Strange it is that so many centuries after the abolition of paganism, these superstitions, so intimately grounded upon it, should still keep their hold on people's minds so firmly as from time to time to give even a character to the age. At one time they turned the philosopher into a magician, and led the scholar in wilder vagaries after the philosopher's stone and elixirs than ever Robin Goodfellow put upon the benighted traveller. At a still later period of European history, when education had been much more widely spread, in the great cry against witchcraft, these superstitions drenched England, as well as France and Germany, in torrents of blood. When we see that at that period the learning which had been so widely spread only served to defend the popular belief, we

[49]

shall easily perceive how impossible it was for the primitive missionaries to eradicate it from the minds of their converts.

In the earlier ages of Christianity among the Teutonic people,
the monks supposed that the elves and fairies of the people were
neither more nor less than so many devils, whose business it was to
delude people; so that in transmitting to us the outlines of the
popular legends they give them a colouring of which it is not always
easy to divest them. At later periods, without going so far as to
make them absolutely devils, some of the most intelligent writers
had very curious ideas about their origin. Giraldus tells us of a fairy
who lived some years with a northern bishop as a faithful servant.
Before he left the service of his master, he told him who and what
he was. He said that the elves and fairies were a portion of the
angels who fell with Lucifer from Heaven; but inasmuch as, though
they had been seduced and deluded, they were not so criminal as
their fellows, their sentence had been less severe: they were allowed
to live on the earth, some of them having their peculiar dwelling-
place in the air, others in the waters, some again in trees and
fountains, and many in the caverns of the earth. He confessed, also,
that as Christianity spread, they had much less liberty than formerly. As much of the popular middle-age legends relating to the
fall of the angels was probably rooted on the older mythology, this
story may itself be the shadow of an earlier article of pagan creed
relating to the origin of the elves.

At the same time, as the monks exerted an influence over the
superstitions of the people, in modifying them into apparent
accordance with Christianity, these superstitions were also influencing the latter, and without doubt gave rise to that multiplicity
and multiformity of demoniacal agency which pervades the monkish legends. In their system the whole world was believed to be
peopled with innumerable hordes of devils, who possessed only a
certain degree of power, which they used in tormenting, seducing,
and misleading mankind. Diseases were often the effect of their
malignity, and conflagrations and numerous fatal accidents were
commonly supposed to be brought about by their agency. They
also exerted an influence over the elements, and caused storms,
floods, and even greater convulsions of nature. The monks sometimes invented strange stories to account for the influence which
the devils thus exerted, because they were not aware of the real
source from which they had been adopted. An inedited English
poet of the thirteenth century, after explaining in a popular manner
the nature of thunder and lightning, proceeds to show how it
happens to cause so much mischief. 'When Christ suffered death,'

[50]

says he, 'he bound the devil, and broke down hell-gates in order to let out those who suffered there. His visit was attended with such terrible thunder, that the devils have been afraid of thunder ever since; and if any of them happen to be caught in a storm, they fly, as quick as wind, and kill men and destroy trees, &c., which they meet in their way. This is the reason that people are killed in a storm.'

We give the passage for the sake of its quaintness—

'Ye mowe sigge whan thundre is menging of fur and wete,
Hou is that hit quelleth men by weyes and bi strete,
And smyt adoun grete treow, and doth meni other wonder?
Therefore ic mot you telle more of the cunde of thunder.
Tho oure Loverd an urthe tholede deth, the devel he bond anon,
And debrusede helle gates, with thundre thider he com:
Therefore ever eft afterward wher so develen beo,
Of thundre hi beoth so sore agast that hi nute whoder fleo,
And sleth men bi the wey as hi fleoth, as me may ofte i-seo,
That moche fere hem geve God that he the worse ne beo.'
                                    (*MS. Harl.*, No. 2277, fol. 129.)

As we have just observed, it required all the masterly skill of a Grimm to reduce the scattered and often apparently discordant materials which such authorities have left us for the history of the mythology of the Teutonic tribes, into order and system; to show their analogies and connexions with each other; to snatch facts from beneath the adventitious garb, which time and error had given them; to make ceremonies and superstitions of a later period guide back to the substance of which they are only the shadow. This is what James Grimm has undertaken, and he has done it completely and satisfactorily. His *Deutsche Mythologie* is a storehouse of facts and of discoveries relative to every part of this curious subject.


## [ 7  WILLIAM  JOHN  THOMS ]

By 1846 several currents of interest were converging in the antiquarian societies of London to signal a new field of learning. These mingling interests included the culling of popular antiquities from all kinds of literary records, as Brand had done; the observation of living antiquities in the countryside, encouraged by William Hone in his *Every-Day Book*; and the reconstruction of a heathen mythology from oral and written memorials, in the manner of Grimm.

[51]

One astute antiquary, William John Thoms (1803–1885) perceived the confluence of these inquiries and determined to call dramatic attention to them with an appropriate neologism. His celebrated letter to the *Athenaeum* printed on August 22, 1846, not only proposed 'Folk-Lore' as a name to replace 'Popular Antiquities' but also, with the approval of the editor, announced a design to further the study of folklore. Correspondents would submit items of folklore coming under their personal observation to Ambrose Merton (the pseudonym initially used by Thoms), as a means of preserving these fast vanishing specimens and contributing to an eventual English version of the *Deutsche Mythologie*. Even since 1828 the fairy traditions described by Keightley had melted away, sighed Merton-Thoms in the stock grievance since echoed by all folklorists.

The first four numbers of Ambrose Merton's new department of 'Folk-Lore,' here reproduced, indicate the tactics adopted by Thoms. He planted suggestions and inquiries, commented on contributions, and continually invoked the revered name of Grimm to reinforce the mythological value of the subjects discussed. By the third number he had elicited a splendid communication from 'H.' (Robert Hunt, the first systematic field collector in England, who issued *Popular Romances from the West of England* in 1865) on the Cornish legends of Tregeagle. The *Athenaeum* with its broadly literary format did not prove the most effective vehicle for Thoms' column and he founded *Notes and Queries* in 1849, happily suited to his temperament and taste for the episodic recording of antiquarian and folkloric matters.

Text from *The Athenaeum*, Numbers 982–5, August 22, August 29, September 5, September 12, 1846. Pages 862–3, 886–7, 908–9, 932.

(August 22, 1846, Number 982)

FOLK-LORE

August 12.

Your pages have so often given evidence of the interest which you take in what we in England designate as Popular Antiquities, or Popular Literature (though by-the-bye it is more a Lore than a Literature, and would be most aptly described by a good Saxon compound, Folk-Lore,—*the Lore of the People*)—that I am not without hopes of enlisting your aid in garnering the few ears which are remaining, scattered over that field from which our forefathers might have gathered a goodly crop.

No one who has made the manners, customs, observances, superstitions, ballads, proverbs, &c., of the olden time his study, but must have arrived at two conclusions:—the first, how much that is curious and interesting in these matters is now entirely lost—the second, how much may yet be rescued by timely exertion. What Hone endeavoured to do in his 'Every-Day Book,' &c., the *Athenaeum*, by its wider circulation, may accomplish ten times more effectually—gather together the infinite number of minute facts, illustrative of the subject I have mentioned, which are scattered over the memories of its thousands of readers, and preserve them in its pages, until some James Grimm shall arise who shall do for the Mythology of the British Islands the good service which that profound antiquary and philologist has accomplished for the Mythology of Germany. The present century has scarcely produced a more remarkable book, imperfect as its learned author confesses it to be, than the second edition of the '*Deutsche Mythologie*': and, what is it?—a mass of minute facts, many of which, when separately considered, appear trifling and insignificant,—but, when taken in connexion with the system into which his master-mind has woven them, assume a value that he who first recorded them never dreamed of attributing to them.

How many such facts would one word from you evoke, from the north and from the south—from John o'Groats to the Land's End! How many readers would be glad to show their gratitude for the novelties which you, from week to week, communicate to them, by forwarding to you some record of old Time—some recollection of a now neglected custom—some fading legend, local tradition, or fragmentary ballad!

Nor would such communications be of service to the English antiquary alone. The connexion between the FOLK-LORE of England (remember I claim the honour of introducing the epithet Folk-Lore, as Disraeli does of introducing Father-Land, into the literature of this country) and that of Germany is so intimate that such communications will probably serve to enrich some future edition of Grimm's Mythology.

Let me give you an instance of this connexion.—In one of the chapters of Grimm, he treats very fully of the parts which the Cuckoo plays in Popular Mythology—of the prophetic character with which it has been invested by the voice of the people; and gives many instances of the practice of deriving predictions from the number of times which its song is heard. He also records a popular

[53]

notion, 'that the Cuckoo never sings till he has thrice eaten his fill of cherries.' Now, I have lately been informed of a custom which formerly obtained among children in Yorkshire, that illustrates the fact of a connexion between the Cuckoo and the Cherry,—and that, too, in their prophetic attributes. A friend has communicated to me that children in Yorkshire were formerly (and may be still) accustomed to sing round a cherry-tree the following invocation:—

> Cuckoo, Cherry-tree,
> Come down and tell me
> How many years I have to live.

Each child then shook the tree,—and the number of cherries which fell betokened the years of its future life.

The Nursery Rhyme which I have quoted, is, I am aware, well known. But the manner in which it was applied is not recorded by Hone, Brand, or Ellis:—and is one of those facts, which, trifling in themselves, become of importance when they form links in a great chain—one of those facts which a word from the *Athenaeum* would gather in abundance for the use of future inquirers into that interesting branch of literary antiquities,—our Folk-Lore.

AMBROSE MERTON.

P.S.—It is only honest that I should tell you I have long been contemplating a work upon our '*Folk-Lore*' (under *that title*, mind Messrs. A, B, and C.—so do not try to forestall me);—and I am personally interested in the success of the experiment which I have, in this letter, albeit imperfectly, urged you to undertake.

We have taken some time to weigh the suggestion of our correspondent—desirous to satisfy ourselves that any good of the kind which he proposes could be effected in such space as we are able to spare from the many other demands upon our columns; and having before our eyes the fear of that shower of trivial communication which a notice in conformity with his suggestion is too likely to bring. We have finally decided that, if our antiquarian correspondents be earnest and well-informed, and subject their communications to the condition of having something worthy to communicate, we may—now that the several antiquarian societies have brought their meetings, for the season, to a close—at once add to the amusement of a large body of our readers and be the means of effecting some valuable salvage for the future historian of old customs and feelings, within a compass that shall make no unreasonable encroachment upon our columns. With these views, however, we must announce to our future contributors under the above head, that their communications will be subjected to a careful sifting—both as regards value, authenticity, and novelty; and that they will save both themselves and us much unnecessary trouble if they will refrain from offering any facts or speculations which do not at once *need* recording and deserve it. Brevity will be always a recommendation—where there are others; and great length in any article will, of necessity, exclude it, even where its merits would recommend. The cases will be very rare in which an article should exceed a couple of our columns,—and the exception can be only when the article itself will bear dividing without injury. But notices much shorter will always be more welcome;—and, in fact, extent will be, on all occasions, an important element in our estimate of the admissibility of a communication. We will hint, also, to our correspondents, that we should, in each case, prefer receiving (though we do not make it absolute as a rule,) the confidential communication of the writer's real name and address.

August 29, 1846, Number 983

### FOLK-LORE

Bartholomew Tide.

I do not know that I can better show my gratitude for the insertion in last Saturday's *Athenaeum* of my letter inviting you to receive, and your country readers to furnish, communications on the subject of our 'Folk-Lore,' than by indicating to 'intending' correspondents some points connected with our Popular Mythology and Observances, respecting which new facts and existing traditions might prove of considerable value.

I would observe, in the first place, that, as the Fairy Mythology of England, as preserved to us in the writings of Shakspeare (its best and most beautiful expositor), exhibits a striking intermixture of Celtic and Teutonic elements, all local traditions respecting that mystic race,—whether

Of elves, of hills, brooks, standing lakes, or groves,—

will be useful in developing the influence which such elements respectively exercised upon this poetical branch of our Popular Mythology. And as I agree with Mr. Keightley—no mean authority on such a subject—in opinion 'that the belief in Fairies is by no means extinct in England,—and that in districts, if there be any such, where steam-engines, cotton mills, mail coaches,[1] and similar

[1] This was written, by Mr. Keightley, in 1828; but now, what Chaucer said of the 'elves' may almost be applied to the mails—'But now can no man see non *mails* mo.'

exorcists have not yet penetrated, numerous legends might be collected,'—I am not without hope of seeing many 'a roundel and a fairy song' rescued from destruction through the agency of the *Athenaeum*.

Can no Devonshire correspondent furnish new and untold stories of his native Pixies? Are there no records of a fairy pipe-manufactory to be gathered at Swinborne in Worcestershire?—In the mining and mountainous districts of Derbyshire are all 'such antique fables and such fairy toys' entirely extinct?—If so, is not the neighbourhood of Haddon, or of Hardwicke, or of both, still visited by the coach drawn by headless steeds, driven by a coachman as headless as themselves?—Does not such an equipage still haunt the mansion of Parsloes, in Essex?—and could not some correspondent from that county furnish you with stories of the inhabitants of Coggeshall, to prove them very rivals of the Wise Men of Gotham?—Is the Barguest no longer seen in Yorkshire?—Is 'howdening' altogether obsolete in Kent—and, if so, when was this last trace of a heathen rite performed?—Are the legends of Tregeagle no longer current in Cornwall?—These are all subjects not undeserving attention: and it should be remembered that legends and traditions which are considered trifling, in the localities to which they more immediately relate, assume an interest in the eyes of strangers to whom they are not familiar—and an importance when placed in apposition with cognate materials, by the light which they both receive and furnish from such juxtaposition.

There is another matter, too, on which local information is much to be desired while it is still attainable. I mean the 'Feasts' which are still annually celebrated in the more remote parts of the country; many of which are, doubtless, of very considerable antiquity—even as old as the days of Heathenism. This is a branch of our Popular Antiquities which—to use a happy phrase of Horace Walpole's—has not yet been 'tapped' in England; one which can now be thoroughly and properly investigated only by ascertaining, in each case, the following particulars, among others:—the day on which the Feast is held; the peculiar observances by which it is accompanied, and—which will serve, in some measure, to illustrate the history of the climate in this country, and (strange combination!) the progress of social improvement—the peculiar dishes which are usually introduced on such festivals.

I ought to apologize for thus occupying so much of your space: but, as you have kindly consented, at my request, to open your pages to contributions on the subject of our 'Folk-Lore,' I thought it might be of advantage to point out to correspondents some matters respecting which communications would be both valuable and acceptable.

AMBROSE MERTON.

### The Epithet 'Old Scratch'

Of that huge mass of imperfectly digested materials which may be said to constitute the text book of the students of our English 'Folk-Lore,' Brand's 'Popular Antiquities,' there is no chapter more imperfect, and consequently more unsatisfactory, than that entitled 'Popular Notions concerning the Apparition of the Devil.'

In this chapter,—after some allusion to the names 'Old Nick,' 'Old Harry,' 'Old Scratch,' and 'The Old One,'—Brand observes:— 'The epithet "old" to so many of his titles seems to favour the common opinion, that the Devil can only appear in the shape of an old man.'—It may, however, be doubted whether the epithet 'old' has not, in this case, been derived from the Early Latin Fathers; who frequently use the expression, 'Antiquus hostis,' when speaking of the Enemy of mankind. In this way, the Anglo-Saxon, Caedmon, speaks of 'se ealda deofol,'—'se ealda,' 'the Old Devil,' 'the Old One'; and in North Friesland, the same epithet, 'de ual duivel,' still obtains. *Gammel* Erik (Old Erik) is a title bestowed upon the Devil by the Danes; and in this *Old Erik* we have, probably, the origin of our 'Old Harry.' In the old Norse, 'Kölski'—which signifies both 'senex' and 'diàbolus'—is the epithet by which the 'foul fiend' is usually designated.

Again,—though the epithet 'Scratch' is, by modern usage, exclusively applied to his Satanic Majesty, such was not its original application. In the old High German monuments, mention is made of a small elfish sprite, *Scrat* or *Scrato,*—by Latin writers translated Pilosus; as Waltschrate, or Wood Scrat, is Satyrus. In the 'Vocabularius' of 1482 we find Schretlin (penates), Nacht-schrettele (Ephialtes). The Anglo-Saxon Schritta (Hermaphroditus), and the Old Norse Skratti (malus genius, gigas), are also clearly allied to this elfish Being.

Grimm describes the *Schrat* as resembling in its nature the Latin Faun, and the Greek Satyr,—the 'Sylvanus' of Livy; and the Schratlein as being a domestic spirit more resembling the German Wichtel and Alp. The Schrat is never represented as a female; and differs from the Elf as appearing only singly—not in hosts.

The reader of the third volume of the 'Fairy Legends of the South of Ireland'—which contains a translation of the Brothers Grimm's 'Essay on the Irish Legends'—will, doubtless, remember the very curious old German poem there translated, in which the nature of

[57]

the Schretel or Schrat is fully described. The manner in which the sprite encounters a huge white bear, by whom it is worsted in the contest,—in consequence of which the house is freed from its intrusion,—is told with considerable humour; and will give the reader a satisfactory notion of the malicious spirit who has been despoiled of his name, for the purpose of enriching the abundant nomenclature in which Old Scratch—as the Devil is now improperly designated—already rejoices.

September 5, 1846, Number 984

### FOLK-LORE

### *Medical Superstitions—The Ash-tree*

One important branch of the extensive subject which you have opened under the title of Folk-lore comprises *Medical Superstitions*; —and a curious sub-division of that branch of the subject relates to *trees used superstitiously with a view to the cure of diseases*. An instance of this kind of superstition has lately occurred in a parish in this neighbourhood,—which it may be worth while to record. It is an evidence of the almost ineradicable power of superstition; and, also, of the extraordinarily defective condition of our popular education upon medical subjects.

A poor woman, a native of the parish alluded to, applied, a few weeks ago, to the rector of that parish for permission to pass a sick child through one of his ash-trees. The object was, to cure the child of the disease ordinarily called the rickets:—and the mode in which the operation used to be performed is thus described in White's 'Natural History of Selborne,' and in Sir John Cullum's 'History of Hawsted.' Whilst the tree was young and flexible, its stem was severed longitudinally:—the fissure was kept open, and the child, stripped naked, was passed three times, head foremost, through the aperture. After the operation, the tree was swathed up, and plastered over with loam. It was believed that if the severed parts of the tree re-united, the child and the tree gradually recovered together; if the cleft continued to gape—which could only happen from some great negligence or want of skill—it was thought that the operation had proved ineffectual.

Other descriptions and instances may be found in the *Gentleman's Magazine* for October, 1804,—and in Ellis's 'Brand,' iii. 149–56.

Two points for consideration arise upon this superstition:—

1. Why was the ash the selected tree?—In reply, I would suggest, that diseases not arising from any obvious external cause were anciently supposed to be the result of witchcraft; and that the ash was

universally deemed to be an antidote to sorcery, and a preservative against the arts and the fascination of evil spirits. Pliny describes the ash as 'excellent good, and nothing so sovereign' (I use the translation of Philemon Holland) 'against the poison of serpents; nay, so forcible is their virtue, that a serpent dareth not come near unto the shadow of that tree, . . . you may be sure they will not approach the tree itself by a great way. And this' (he adds) 'I am able to deliver by the experience which I have seen,—that if a man do make a round circle with the leaves thereof, and environ therewith a serpent and fire together within, the serpent will choose rather to go into the fire than to fly from it to the leaves of the ash.' (Book xvi., cap. 12.) Now, there is a mysterious connexion between the superstitions relating to serpents and those respecting witchcraft; but, not to dwell upon that point at the present time, the following is more directly connected with our subject. It is an extract from a scarce volume entitled 'Occult Physick, or the Three Principles in Nature Anatomized by a Philosophical Operation taken from experience. By W.[illiam] W.[illiams], Philosophus; Student in the Celestial Sciences. London. 8vo., 1660.' 'Of the Quick-banc-tree, or Wild Ash.— Take a cluster of Quick-bane-tree berries green, and convey them about the party suspected to be a witch, and then examine her, and she shall confess. Pound the same berries and strain them, and give them to any beast, or man, that is overseen by a witch, or witchcraft, and it helpeth them.' And in Dalyell's 'Darker Superstitions of Scotland' is the following:—'The rowan-tree, or mountain ash, is observed to be frequent in the neighbourhood of those monuments of antiquity commonly called Druidical circles. One stood in every churchyard in Wales, as the yew did in England; and on a certain day of the year, every person wore a cross of the wood. It averted fascination and evil spirits.[1] Nor has it been esteemed less beneficial to cattle here' [i.e., in Scotland] 'for the dairy-maid will not forget to drive them to the shealing, or summer pastures, with a rod of the rowan-tree, which she carefully lays up over the door of the sheal-boothy, or summer-house, and drives them home again with the same.'[2] In England it was held also a preservative; 'upon which account, many are very careful to have a walking-staff of it, and will stick the boughs of it about their beds.' [p. 401].[3]

2. A second point arises upon the 'passing through.' This form of operation was of almost universal use. Children offered to Moloch, 'horrid king!. . . . passed through fire to his grim idol.' The passing through a cleft or aperture in a rock is a medical superstition which

[1] Evelyn's Sylva, cap. xvi, voce Quick-beam.
[2] Johnston's Flora of Berwick, p. 110.       [3] Plot's Staffordshire, ch. vi, sec. 52.

has been found in many countries. It is mentioned in the 'Asiatic Researches' as common in the East. Borlase commemorates it as practised with perforations of Druidical stones in Cornwall. In Scotland, the same superstition assumed another shape. Sick persons were passed through a garland of green woodbine, or 'a heap of green yarn,'—which was afterwards cut in nine pieces and burnt, or buried in the earth. All these various passings-through, a garland, a skein of yarn, a cleft, or an aperture, seem symbolical (as Dalyell has remarked, p. 123) of regeneration,—'a second birth, whereby a living being is ushered into the world free of those impurities and imperfections incorporated with a former life.'

JOHN BRUCE.

Hyde, near Stroud, Gloucestershire.

P.S. It is to be hoped that continental, as well as British, antiquaries will take advantage of the opportunity of mutual communication, upon points relating to our common customs and superstitions, which is offered by your insertion of Mr. Ambrose Merton's papers. It would, also, be very useful if Mr. Merton would give us the substance of Grimm's collections upon any point which may be brought before you. For instance,—what says the illustrious German respecting the passing of children through an ash-tree?

### Tregeagle of Trevordor

The spread of knowledge has banished from most of the recesses of the far west the dreams of superstition; yet there still linger, in parts of the coast of Cornwall, some of those traditionary tales which your correspondent, in common with many of your readers, is desirous of preserving.

Tregeagle being one of those to which he has directed attention, I forward you the more common legend of that malignant spirit; which some years since interested me much,—and which I spared no pains to collect. The story is differently told in the various localities wherein the fiend's name is still in use as the representative of terror; but the principal features of the tradition are in all cases the same.

John Tregeagle—whose arbitrary and tyrannical conduct has secured for his name a most unenviable notoriety—was a magistrate, dwelling at Trevordor, in the parish of St. Breock; in the church of which place is a monument erected to his memory. Trevordor is now a farm house; and was, when I visited it in 1830, in the possession of a farmer of the name of West. The 'old mansion,' as it was called, is now nearly, if not entirely, destroyed; but at that

[60]

period, many rooms, curiously panelled, were to be seen.—But, to the legend.

Carrying his malignity beyond the grave, Tregeagle appeared as a witness, some years after his death, against an old enemy, in the court of Bodmin. At the conclusion of the trial,—which was decided by the evidence of Tregeagle,—and on the breaking up of the court, the spirit remained; and the lawyers discovered that they had no power to remove him. The monks of Bodmin were called in to aid them; but they found that, Tregeagle having voluntarily 'burst his cerements,' they could not again consign his spirit to repose. A never-ending task was, therefore, to be found for him: and it was at length decided that he should be employed to empty the unfathomable Dosmery Pool, with a leaky limpet shell. For a long period he was thus occupied,—subjected to continual torture by the Devil, who visited him every time an east wind prevailed. These torments at length became too severe for the endurance of the Spirit; and Tregeagle fled, pursued by the arch-fiend, to Roach Rocks. There, dashing his head through the windows of the chapel, he escaped from his tormentor; who dared not approach so sacred a spot as that hallowed by the prayers of the holy hermit of St. Roach. The ghastly head of Tregeagle, in the oriel window of the little chapel, was naturally an object of terror; and '*he glares like Tregeagle*' became, and is now, a common expression in this part of Cornwall.

The hermit and priests of Roach now set about devising a fresh employment for Tregeagle:—and, by the aid of sundry exorcisms, they banished him to the hills of blown sand in the neighbourhood of Padstow; where his task was to make trusses of sand, and bind them with ropes twisted out of the same material. Tregeagle was frequently near the accomplishment of his task; but always, when the completion of it was expected, a tempest arose, his sands were blown to distant hills, and the shrieks and howlings of the tortured spirit were heard above the roar of the storm. The people of Padstow were distressed at the frequent recurrence of these dreadful notes; and resolved to procure his removal from their vicinity. This was at length effected by the aid of the Church; and Tregeagle was then doomed, as a Gigantic Spirit, to sweep the sands from the British Channel, round the Land's End, into the Atlantic Ocean;— from which, however, they were as constantly brought back by the prevailing winds and currents.

Tregeagle was often excited to the height of malignity; and over every part of the southern coast of Cornwall we find traces of his deep and dread revenge. The most lasting is the sand-bar which now separates the Looe Lake from the sea. This is stated to have been formerly a beautiful estuary; and Helstone, which stood on its banks, to have been a most thriving sea-port. The sack of sand which Tregeagle placed at the mouth of the estuary deprived Helstone for ever of its trade.

From Looe to the Land's End, there is not a fishing cove in which some tradition of Tregeagle is not to be met with; and everywhere along the coast the low moaning sound which predicates a storm is yet said to be like the groaning of Tregeagle. Amongst the inhabitants of this exposed shore the expression still lives of 'it roars like Tregeagle,'—when describing the deep notes of a tempest echoing in the caverns and clefts of the coast.

One story of Tregeagle relates that this fiend got within his power the heir of an ancient Cornish family,—whom he most cruelly murdered:—and there are many others, in which personal deformity and intellectual weakness are attributed to the influence of this malignant spirit. Frequently, in the fishing coves around the Land's End, I have heard mothers threatening their noisy children that they should be given to Tregeagle if they were not quiet; and, indeed, I believe his name is, now, more frequently employed as the scarecrow of the fishermen's children than in any other way. H.

It is obvious that, in these legends of Tregeagle, tradition has invested the troubled shade of the revengeful magistrate of Trevordor with many of the attributes which in popular Mythology are generally ascribed to the Evil One Himself. The fruitless task of weaving ropes of sand is the duty frequently imposed upon the Devil in the various legends in which he is represented as making compacts with mankind, and being ultimately outwitted by the superior cunning of those whom he has sought to ensnare. To the same Spirit of Evil—or, in some instances, to those Gigantic Spirits who, as Grimm observes in his 'Mythologie,' ofttimes assume his place in tradition—does the popular voice assign all such local changes as that of the separation of the Looe Lake from the Sea,—regardless of the truth, that the sand which did the mischief fell from Time's hour-glass, and was not emptied out of the sack of the great Enemy of mankind.

Further illustrations of Tregeagle's story would probably show that to his unpopularity he is indebted for having transferred to his name Legends which, there is little doubt, existed before his time,—but had, then, for their hero some Cornish giant or spirit whose designation no longer exists. A more terrific picture of hatred extending beyond the grave than that presented by Tregeagle appear-

[62]

ing in a court of justice, as a witness against an ancient enemy, is not to be found in the whole wide range of popular legends.

September 12, 1846, Number 985

### FOLK-LORE

#### Wiltshire Rhymes on the Cuckoo

The lines relating to the cuckoo quoted in Ambrose Merton's first letter are common, I believe, throughout the country. I do not wonder at poets and rhymesters having something to say about this bird. The Wiltshire people used to sing:—

> The cuckoo's a fine bird,
> She sings as she flies;
> She brings us good tidings,
> And tells us no lies.

> She sucks the small birds' eggs
> To make her voice clear;
> And the more she sings 'Cuckoo!'
> The summer draws near.

And again,

> The cuckoo comes in April,
> Stays the month of May,
> Sings a song at Midsummer,
> And then goes away.

P. P.

There is no county in England from which more abundant materials for a History of our Popular Antiquities might be gathered than that of Wilts[hire]. It is obvious, from our correspondent's communication, that the prophetic character of the Cuckoo is still recognized in the popular rhymes of the peasantry: while in Akerman's 'Glossary of Provincial Words and Phrases in Use in Wiltshire' we find the following Chaucerian illustration, under the head 'Dock':—

'A decoction of dock-root called "dock-root tea," is considered an excellent purifier of the blood; and the leaf is supposed to be good for the sting of a nettle. When a child is stung, he plucks a dock-leaf, and laying it on the part affected, sings,—

> Out 'ettle
> In dock,

[63]

Dock shall ha'
A new smock;
'Ettle zhant
Ha' narrun.

Mr Ackerman refers to the following passage in Chaucer's 'Troilus and Cressida,' iv. 460–1,—

And can'st thou play in raket, to and fro,
Nettle in, docke out, now this, now that, Pandare,—

as 'one in which the phrase "Nettle in, docke out," has much puzzled the glossarists.' A passage strikingly similar is to be found in the 'Testament of Love' (p. 482, ed. Urry):—'Ye wete wel Ladie eke (quoth I) that I have not plaid raket, Nettle in, Docke out, and with the weathercocke waved.'

## Passing through Trees, Stones, &c. for the Cure of Diseases

I readily accept the invitation of your correspondent, Mr. Bruce, that I should 'give the readers of the *Athenaeum* the substance of Grimm's collections upon any point which may be brought before them—for instance, what the illustrious German says respecting the passing of children through an ash-tree': and I do so in the hope that the following notes will be accepted by him as an acknowledgment of the interest excited by his able letter,—and by others of your readers as some inducement to forward notices of popular customs and superstitions, which may receive similar annotations.

Grimm, to whom the notion of these 'passings-through' being symbolical of regeneration does not appear to have suggested itself, has, in the first edition of his 'Mythologie,' little more upon the subject than the long and well-known passage from White's 'Selborne,'—and, as a note, the paragraph from Plot's 'Staffordshire,' in which he describes the cruel ceremony of making a nursrow tree or shrew ash. In his second edition, when speaking of the cure of diseased children and cattle by their passing through holes in the earth, hollowed stones, or trees split for the purpose, which ceremonies, he observes, had the virtue of curing or counteracting the effects of enchantment, and operated sympathetically,—he quotes the Anglo-Saxon version of the 'Canones Edgari,' in Thorpe's 'Ancient Laws and Institutes of England,' forbidding 'tree worshipings and stone worshipings and that devil's craft whereby children are drawn through the earth'; and then adds, in illustration, other passages,—as the Interrogation, from Burchard, of Worms:— 'Fecisti quod quaedam mulieres facere solent, illae, dico, qui habent vagientes infantes, effodiunt terram et ex parte *pertusant* eam, et

[64]

*per illud foramen pertrahunt* infantem, et sic dicunt vagientis infantis cessare vagitum,'—this appropriate quotation, from a sermon by St. Eligius, 'Nullus praesumat *lustrationes* facere, nec *herbas incantare: neque pecora per cavam arborem* vel *per terram foratam* transire,'—and the following, from the 'Collection of Superstitions,' which form a supplement to his work:—'Nurses take new-born infants and force them through a hole.'—'If a child will not learn to go alone, let it creep silently, on three Friday mornings, through a bough of a bramble, both ends of which are growing in the earth.' Grimm gives instances of perforated stones, of the nature alluded to, being mentioned in early documents, as 'from thyrelan stane,' in a charter of Aetheluulf, dated in 847, printed in the second volume of Kemble's 'Codex Diplomaticum Ævi Saxonicum'; and supposes such stones to have been substituted occasionally in the place of decayed trees, which had formerly been highly prized. Stones of this kind were sometimes called *nadelöhr* (the eye of a needle); and Paul Hentzner, in his 'Itinerarium,' speaking of one near Friedewald, says, 'Est lapis perforatus in locum arboris olim excavatae in media silva venatoribus ob ferarum silvestrium copiam frequente a Mauritio Hassiae landgravio ad viam positis, per quem pretereunte joci et vexationis gratia *proni perrepere* solent.' He then speaks of this passing-through the tree, earth, or stone, as appearing as if its object was to transfer the sickness or enchantment under which the patient was suffering to the genius of the tree, the earth, &c. In Sweden, the open rounds in boughs of trees which have grown together are called Elf-holes (*elfenlöcher*)—and women in their 'hour of trouble' are drawn through them.

But I am trespassing at too great length upon your columns:—so, with an Anglo-Saxon allusion to the practice, which has escaped the notice of Grimm, I will bring the present communication to an end. It occurs in Aelfric's Homily on the Passion of St. Bartholomew (vol. i. p. 475, of 'The Homilies of the Anglo-Saxon Church'), edited, for the Aelfric Society, by Mr. Thorpe:—'It is not allowed to any Christian man to fetch his health *from any stone, nor from any tree*, unless it be the holy sign of the Rood, nor from any place, unless it be the holy house of God.'

AMBROSE MERTON.

[65]

# II   The Mythologists

WHILE Thoms was patiently accumulating diversified scraps of folklore in *Notes and Queries* for the book on English mythology he would never write, a wholly new perspective on mythological investigations reoriented the subject he had baptized. The unlocking of Sanskrit, the classical language of India, expanded and altered the philological mythology Jacob Grimm had focused on the Teutonic peasant. The new school of comparative mythologists, led by Max Müller and Adalbert Kuhn, continued to employ Grimm's method of tracing deities and demons back to their original character through etymological interpretations of proper names. Certain similarities between the Sanskrit and classical Greek god-names, notably Dyâus and Zeus for the crowning sky god of both pantheons, electrified the German philologists, who now joined India to Europe in one vast Aryan family once sharing a common language, culture, and religion. A probing of these correspondences could, the Sanskritists believed, illuminate the true nature of the gods and heroes of classical antiquity.

As Dyâus-Zeus represented the sky, so did all the other gods and goddesses symbolize some element of the heavens. The new school of comparative mythologists all agreed on the basic premise that the central figures in Greek and Roman myths, and in the fairy tales and local legends descended from the myths, reflected heavenly phenomena. All they disagreed on was the primacy of the celestial elements, whether the sun or the lightning, clouds or thunder, stars or the moon. In 1856 comparative mythology based on heavenly symbolism made its bow in England in Müller's famous essay and swept all the materials of folklore into its orbit. No demurrer was heard until the 1870's, by which time English disciples of the German Sanskritists had greatly enlarged the original domain of celestial mythology to encompass all of the Aryan and Semitic pantheons.

[66]

# [ 1  MAX MÜLLER ]

The oracle of celestial mythology for the Victorians was Friedrich Max Müller (1823–1900) who came from Germany to England in 1846 to translate the Sacred Books of the East from Sanskrit into English and remained there the rest of his life as a distinguished Oxford don. In 1856 he published in *Oxford Essays* an extended treatise on 'Comparative Mythology' which startled and thrilled Victorian intellectuals. Here he elaborated his famous theory of the 'disease of language' to explain the rise of myths through verbal misapprehension and expounded on the strategic value of the Sanskrit Vedas in revealing the root names of the Greek and Roman gods. His new science of comparative mythology grew neatly out of the established subject of comparative philology, wedding the growth of language to the origins of poetry, metaphor, and myth in a series of ingenious and seemingly erudite hypotheses. And all this learning produced so happy and clear a result, ensconcing the sun god at the centre of the tangled myth plots garbled by priests, poets, and peasants in India, Greece, and Germany. The barbarous features of the classic myths and nursery tales were now explained as poetic and metaphoric phrases of man in his mythopoeic stage. For years to come celestial mythologists in England continued to apply the tenets of Müller's famous essay to all kinds of traditions.

Text from Max Müller, *Chips from a German Workshop*. Four volumes. New York: Scribner, Armstrong and Co., 1871–6. From 'Comparative Mythology,' II (1872), 52–126, 139–41.

This earliest period, then, previous to any national separation, is what I call the *mythopoeic* period, for every one of these common Aryan words is, in a certain sense, a myth. These words were all originally appellative; they expressed one out of many attributes, which seemed characteristic of a certain object, and the selection of these attributes and their expression in language, represents a kind of unconscious poetry, which modern languages have lost altogether.

Language has been called fossil poetry. But as the artist does not know that the clay which he is handling contains the remnants of organic life, we do not feel that when we address a father, we call him protector, nor did the Greeks, when using the word δαήρ, brother-in-law, know that this term applied originally only to the younger brothers of the husbands, who stayed at home with the bride while their elder brother was out in the field or the forests. The Sanskrit 'devar' meant originally playmate,—it told its own story,—it was a myth; but in Greek it has dwindled down into a mere name, or a technical term. Yet, even in Greek it is not allowed to form a feminine of δαήρ, as little as we should venture even now to form a masculine of 'daughter.'

Soon, however, languages lose their etymological conscience, and thus we find in Latin, for instance, not only *vidua*, husbandless ('Penelope tam diu vidua viro suo caruit'), but *viduus*, a formation which, if analysed etymologically, is as absurd as the Teutonic 'a widower.' It must be confessed, however, that the old Latin *viduus*,[1] a name of Orcus, who had a temple outside Rome, makes it doubtful whether the Latin *vidua* is really the Sanskrit 'vi-dhavâ,' however great their similarity. At all events we should have to admit that a verb *viduare* was derived from *vidua*, and that afterwards a new adjective was formed with a more general sense, so that *viduus* to a Roman ear meant nothing more than *privatus*.

But, it may be asked, how does the fact, that the Aryan languages possess this treasure of ancient names in common, or even the discovery that all these names had originally an expressive and poetical power, explain the phenomenon of mythological language among all the members of this family? How does it render intelligible that phase of the human mind which gave birth to the extraordinary stories of gods and heroes,—of gorgons and chimaeras,—of things that no human eye had ever seen, and that no human mind in a healthy state could ever have conceived?

Before we can answer this question, we must enter into some more preliminary observations as to the formation of words. Tedious as this may seem, we believe that while engaged in these considerations the mist of mythology will gradually clear away, and enable us to discover behind the floating clouds of the dawn of thought and language, that real nature which mythology has so long veiled and disguised.

All the common Aryan words which we have hitherto examined referred to definite objects. They are all substantives, they express something substantial, something open to sensuous perception. Nor is it in the power of language to express originally anything except objects as nouns, and qualities as verbs. Hence, the only definition we can give of language during that early state is, that it is the conscious expression in sound, of impressions received by all the senses.

To us, abstract nouns are so familiar that we can hardly appre-

[1] Hartung, *Die Religion der Römer*, vol. ii, p. 90.

ciate the difficulty which men experienced in forming them. We can scarcely imagine a language without abstract nouns. There are, however, dialects spoken at the present day which have no abstract nouns, and the more we go back in the history of languages, the smaller we find the number of these useful expressions. As far as language is concerned, an abstract word is nothing but an adjective raised into a substantive; but in thought the conception of a quality as a subject, is a matter of extreme difficulty, and, in strict logical parlance, impossible. If we say, 'I love virtue,' we seldom connect any definite notion with 'virtue.' Virtue is not a being, however unsubstantial; it is nothing individual, personal, active; nothing that could by itself produce an expressible impression on our mind. The word 'virtue' is only a short-hand expression; and when men said for the first time 'I love virtue,' what they meant by it originally was, 'I love all things that become an honest man, that are manly, or virtuous.'

But there are other words, which we hardly call abstract, but which, nevertheless, were so originally, and are so still, in form; I mean in words like 'day' and 'night,' 'spring' and 'winter,' 'dawn' and 'twilight,' 'storm' and 'thunder.' For what do we mean if we speak of day and night, or of spring and winter? We may answer, a season, or any other portion of time. But what is time, in our conceptions? It is nothing substantial, nothing individual; it is a quality raised by language into a substance. Therefore if we say 'the day dawns,' 'the night approaches,' we predicate actions of things that cannot act, we affirm a proposition which, if analysed logically, would have no definable subject.

The same applies to collective words, such as 'sky' and 'earth,' 'dew' and 'rain,'—even to 'rivers' and 'mountains.' For if we say, 'The earth nourishes man,' we do not mean any tangible portion of soil, but the earth, conceived as a whole; nor do we mean by the sky the small horizon which our eye can scan. We imagine something which does not fall under our senses, but whether we call it a whole, a power, or an idea, in speaking of it we change it unawares into something individual.

Now in ancient languages every one of these words had necessarily a termination expressive of gender, and this naturally produced in the mind the corresponding idea of sex, so that these names received not only an individual, but a sexual character. There was no substantive which was not either masculine or feminine; neuters being of later growth, and distinguishable chiefly in the nominative.[1]

[1]'It is with the world, as with each of us in our individual life; for as we leave child-

What must have been the result of this? As long as people thought in language, it was simply impossible to speak of morning or evening, of spring and winter, without giving to these conceptions something of an individual, active, sexual, and at last, personal character. They were either nothings, as they are nothings to our withered thought, or they were something; and then they could not be conceived as mere powers, but as beings powerful. Even in our time, though we have the conception of nature as a power, what do we mean by power, except something powerful? Now, in early language, nature was *Natura*, a mere adjective made substantive; she was the Mother always 'going to bring forth.' Was this not a more definite idea than that which we connect with nature? And let us look to our poets, who still think and feel in language,—that is, who use no word without having really enlivened it in their mind, who do not trifle with language, but use it as a spell to call forth real things, full of light and colour. Can they speak of the sun, or the dawn, or the storms as neutral powers, without doing violence to their feelings? Let us open Wordsworth, and we shall hardly find him use a single abstract term without some life and blood in it:—

### Religion

'Sacred Religion, mother of form and fear,
Dread arbitress of mutable respect,
New rites ordaining when the old are wrecked,
Or cease to please the fickle worshipper.'

### Winter

'Humanity, delighting to behold
A fond reflection of her own decay,
Hath painted Winter like a traveller old,
Propped on a staff, and, through the sullen day,

---

hood and youth behind us, we bid adieu to the vivid impressions things once made upon us, and become colder and more speculative. To a little child, not only are all living creatures endowed with human intelligence, but *everything* is *alive*. In *his* Kosmos, Pussy takes rank with Pa and Ma, in point of intelligence. He beats the chair against which he has knocked his head; and afterwards kisses it in token of renewed friendship, in the full belief, that like himself, it is a moral agent amenable to rewards and punishments. The fire that burns his finger is 'Naughty Fire,' and the stars that shine through his bedroom window are Eyes, like Mamma's, or Pussy's, only brighter.

'The same instinct that prompts the child to *personify* everything remains unchecked in the savage, and grows up with him to manhood. Hence in all simple and early languages, there are but two genders, masculine and feminine. To develop such an idea as that of a *neuter*, requires the slow growth of civilization for its accomplishment. We see the same tendency to class everything as masculine or feminine among even civilized men, if they are uneducated. To a farm labourer, a bundle of hay is "*he*," just as much as is the horse that eats it. He resolutely ignores "*it*," as a pronoun for which there is not the slightest necessity.'—*Printer's Register*, February 6, 1868.

In hooded mantle, limping o'er the plain,
As though his weakness were disturbed by pain:
Or, if a juster fancy should allow
An undisputed symbol of command,
The chosen sceptre is a withered bough,
Infirmly grasped within a palsied hand.
These emblems suit the helpless and forlorn;
But mighty Winter the device shall scorn.
For he it was—dread Winter!—who beset,
Flinging round van and rear his ghastly net,
That host, when from the regions of the Pole
They shrunk, insane Ambition's barren goal,—
That host, as huge and strong as e'er defied
Their God, and placed their trust in human pride!
As fathers prosecute rebellious sons,
He smote the blossoms of their warrior youth;
He called on *Frost's* inexorable tooth
Life to consume in manhood's firmest old. . . .
      And bade the *Snow* their ample backs bestride,
      And to the battle ride.'

So, again, of *Age and the Hours*:—

'*Age!* twine thy brows with fresh spring flowers,
And call a train of laughing *Hours*,
And bid them dance, and bid them sing;
And thou, too, mingle in the ring!'

Now, when writing these lines, Wordsworth could hardly have thought of the classical *Horae*: the conception of dancing Hours came as natural to his mind as to the poets of old.

Or, again, of *Storms and Seasons*:—

'Ye *Storms*, resound the praises of your King!
And ye mild Seasons,—in a sunny clime,
Midway, on some high hill, while father *Time*
Looks on delighted,—meet in festal ring,
And loud and long of Winter's triumph sing!'

We are wont to call this poetical diction, and to make allowance for what seems to us exaggerated language. But to the poet it is no exaggeration, nor was it to the ancient poets of language. Poetry is older than prose, and abstract speech more difficult than the out-pouring of a poet's sympathy with nature. It requires reflection to divest nature of her living expression, to see in the swift-riding clouds nothing but vaporous exhalations, in the frowning mountains masses of stone, and in the lightning electric sparks. Wordsworth feels what he says, when he exclaims,—

'Mountains, and Vales, and Floods, I call on you
To share the passion of a just disdain;'

and when he speaks of 'the last hill that parleys with the setting sun,' this expression came to him as he was communing with nature; it was a thought untranslated as yet into the prose of our traditional and emaciated speech; it was a thought such as the men of old would not have been ashamed of in their common everyday conversation.

There are some poems of this modern ancient which are all mythology, and as we shall have to refer to them hereafter, I shall give one more extract, which to a Hindu and an ancient Greek would have been more intelligible than it is to us:—

'Hail, orient Conqueror of gloomy Night!
Thou that canst shed the bliss of gratitude
On hearts, howe'er insensible or rude;
Whether thy punctual visitations smite
The haughty towers where monarchs dwell,
Or thou, impartial Sun, with presence bright
Cheer'st the low threshold of the peasant's cell!
Not unrejoiced I see thee climb the sky,
In naked splendour, clear from mist and haze,
Or cloud approaching to divert the rays,
Which even in deepest winter testify
   Thy power and majesty,
Dazzling the vision that presumes to gaze.
Well does thine aspect usher in this Day;
As aptly suits therewith that modest pace
   Submitted to the chains
That bind thee to the path which God ordains
   That thou shouldst trace,
Till, with the heavens and earth, thou pass away!
Nor less, the stillness of these frosty plains—
Their utter stillness, and the silent grace
Of yon ethereal summits, white with snow,
(Whose tranquil pomp and spotless purity
   Report of storms gone by
   To us who tread below)—
Do with the service of this day accord.

Divinest object which th' uplifted eye
Of mortal man is suffered to behold;
Thou, who upon these snow-clad Heights has poured
Meek lustre, nor forget'st the humble Vale;
Thou who dost warm Earth's universal mould,
And for thy bounty wert not unadored
   By pious men of old;
Once more, heart-cheering Sun, I bid thee hail!
Bright be thy course to-day,—let not this promise fail!'

Why then, if we ourselves, in speaking of the Sun or the Storms, of Sleep and Death, of Earth and Dawn, connect either no distinct idea at all with these names, or allow them to cast over our mind the fleeting shadows of the poetry of old; why, if we, when speaking with the warmth which is natural to the human heart, call upon the Winds and the Sun, the Ocean and the Sky, as if they would still hear us; why, if plastic thought cannot represent any one of these beings or powers, without giving them, if not a human form, at least human life and human feeling,—why should we wonder at the ancients, with their language throbbing with life and revelling in colour, if instead of the grey outlines of our modern thought, they threw out those living forms of nature, endowed with human powers, nay, with powers more than human, inasmuch as the light of the Sun was brighter than the light of a human eye, and the roaring of the Storms louder than the shouts of the human voice. We may be able to account for the origin of rain and dew, of storm and thunder; yet, to the great majority of mankind, all these things, unless they are mere names, are still what they were to Homer, only perhaps less beautiful, less poetical, less real, and living.

So much for that peculiar difficulty which the human mind experiences in speaking of collective or abstract ideas,—a difficulty which, as we shall see, will explain many of the difficulties of Mythology.

We have now to consider a similar feature of ancient languages,— the auxiliary verbs. They hold the same position among verbs, as abstract nouns among substantives. They are of later origin, and had all originally a more material and expressive character. Our auxiliary verbs have had to pass through a long chain of vicissitudes before they arrived at the withered and lifeless form which fits them so well for the purposes of our abstract prose. *Habere*, which is now used in all the Romance languages simply to express a past tense, 'j'ai aimé,' I loved, was originally, to hold fast, to hold back, as we may see in its derivative, *habenae*, the reins. Thus *tenere*, to hold,

[73]

becomes, in Spanish, an auxiliary verb, that can be used very much in the same manner as *habere*. The Greek ἔχω is the Sanskrit 'sah,' and meant originally, to be strong, to be able, or to can. The Latin *fui*, I was, the Sanskrit 'bhû,' to be, corresponds to the Greek φύω, and there shows still its original and material power of growing, in an intransitive and transitive sense. 'As,' the radical of the Sanskrit 'as-mi,' the Greek ἐμ-μί, the Lithuanian 'as-mi,' I am, had probably the original meaning of breathing, if the Sanskrit 'as-u,' breath, is correctly traced back to that root. *Stare*, to stand, sinks down in the Romance dialects to a mere auxiliary, as in 'j'ai-été,' I have been, *i.e.*, *habeo-statum*, I have stood; 'j'ai-été convaincu,' I have stood convinced; the phonetic change of *statum* into *été* being borne out by the transition of *status* into *état*. The German 'werden,' which is used to form futures and passives, the Gothic 'varth,' points back to the Sanskrit '*vrit*,' the Latin *verto*. 'Will,' again, in 'he will go,' has lost its radical meaning of wishing; and 'shall' used in the same tense, 'I shall go,' hardly betrays, even to the etymologist, its original power of legal or moral obligation. 'Schuld,' however, in German means debt and sin, and 'soll' has there not yet taken a merely temporal signification, the first trace of which may be discovered, however, in the names of the three Teutonic Parcae. These are called 'Vurdh,' 'Verdhandi,' and 'Skuld,'—Past, Present, and Future.[1] But what could be the original conception of a verb which, even in its earliest application, has already the abstract meaning of moral duty or legal obligation? Where could language, which can only draw upon the material world for its nominal and verbal treasures, find something analogous to the abstract idea of he shall pay, or, he ought to yield? Grimm, who has endeavoured to follow the German language into its most secret recesses, proposes an explanation of this verb, which deserves serious consideration, however strange and incredible it may appear at first sight.

*Shall*, and its preterite *should*, have the following forms in Gothic:—

| *Present.* | *Preterite.* |
|---|---|
| Skal | Skulda |
| Skalt | Skuldês |
| Skal | Skulda |
| Skulum | Skuldedum |
| Skuluth | Skuldeduth |
| Skulun | Skuldedun |

In Gothic this verb 'skal,' which seems to be a present, can be

[1] Kuhn, *Zeitschrift für vergleichende Sprachforschung*, vol. iii, p. 449.

proved to be an old perfect, analogous to Greek perfects like οἶδα, which have the form of the perfect but the power of the present. There are several verbs of the same character in the German language, and in English they can be detected by the absence of the *s*, as the termination of the third person singular of the present. 'Skal,' then, according to Grimm, means, 'I owe,' 'I am bound'; but originally it meant 'I have killed.' The chief guilt punished by ancient Teutonic law, was the guilt of manslaughter,—and in many cases it could be atoned for by a fine. Hence, 'skal' meant literally, 'I am guilty,' 'ich bin schuldig'; and afterwards, when this full expression had been ground down into a legal phrase, new expressions became possible, such as I have killed a free man, a serf, *i.e.*, I am guilty of a free man, a serf; and at last, I owe (the fine for having slain) a free man, a serf. In this manner Grimm accounts for the still later and more anomalous expressions, such as he shall pay, *i.e.*, he is guilty to pay ('er ist schuldig zu zahlen'); he shall go, *i.e.*, he must go; and last, I shall withdraw, *i.e.*, I feel bound to withdraw.

A change of meaning like this seems, no doubt, violent and fanciful, but we should feel more inclined to accept it, if we considered how almost every word we use discloses similar changes as soon as we analyse it etymologically, and then follow gradually its historical growth. The general conception of thing is in Wallachian expressed by 'lucru,' the Latin *lucrum*, gain. The French 'chose' was originally *causa*, or *cause*. If we say, 'I am obliged to go,' or 'I am bound to pay,' we forget that the origin of these expressions carries us back to times when men were bound to go, or bound over to pay. *Hoc me fallit* means, in Latin, 'it deceives me,' 'it escapes me.' Afterwards, it took the sense of 'it is removed from me,' I want it, I must have it: and hence, 'il me faut,' I must. Again, *I may* is the Gothic

Mag, maht, mag, magum, maguth, magun;

and its primary signification was, 'I am strong.' Now, this verb also was originally a preterite, and derived from a root which meant, 'to beget,' whence the Gothic 'magus,' son, *i.e.*, begotten, the Scotch 'Mac,' and Gothic 'magath-s,' daughter, the English 'maid.'

In mythological language we must make due allowance for the absence of merely auxiliary words. Every word, whether noun or verb, had still its full original power during the mythopoeic ages. Words were heavy and unwieldy. They said more than they ought to say, and hence, much of the strangeness of the mythological language, which we can only understand by watching the natural growth of speech. Where we speak of the sun following the dawn, the ancient poets could only speak and think of the Sun loving and

[75]

embracing the Dawn. What is with us a sunset, was to them the Sun growing old, decaying, or dying. Our sunrise was to them the Night giving birth to a brilliant child, and in the Spring they really saw the Sun or the Sky embracing the earth with a warm embrace, and showering treasures into the lap of nature. There are many myths in Hesiod, of late origin, where we have only to replace a full verb by an auxiliary, in order to change mythical into logical language. Hesiod calls Nyx (Night) the mother of Moros (Fate), and the dark Kêr (Destruction); of Thanatos (Death), Hypnos (Sleep), and the tribe of the Oneiroi (Dreams). And this her progeny she is said to have borne without a father. Again, she is called the mother of Mômos (Blame), and of the woful Oizys (Woe), and of the Hesperides (Evening Stars), who guard the beautiful golden apples on the other side of the far-famed Okeanos, and the trees that bear fruit. She also bore Nemesis (Vengeance), and Apatê (Fraud), and Philotes (Lust), and the pernicious Geras (Old Age), and the strong-minded Eris (Strife). Now, let us use our modern expressions, such as 'the stars are seen as the night approaches,' 'we sleep,' 'we dream,' 'we die,' 'we run danger during night,' 'nightly revels lead to strife, angry discussions, and woe,' 'many nights bring old age, and at last death,' 'an evil deed concealed at first by the darkness of night will at last be revealed by the day,' 'Night herself will be revenged on the criminal,' and we have translated the language of Hesiod—a language to a great extent understood by the people whom he addressed—into our modern form of thought and speech.[1] All this is hardly mythological language, but rather a poetical and proverbial kind of expression known to all poets, whether modern or ancient, and frequently to be found in the language of common people.

Uranos, in the language of Hesiod, is used as a name for the sky; he is made or born that 'he should be a firm place for the blessed gods.'[2] It is said twice, that Uranos covers everything (v. 127), and that when he brings the night, he is stretched out everywhere, em-

[1] As to Philotes being the Child of Night, Juliet understood what it meant when she said:—

> 'Spread thy close curtain, love-performing Night!
> That unawares eyes may wink; and Romeo
> Leap to these arms, untalked of and unseen!—
> Lovers can see to do their amorous rites
> By their own beauties; or, if Love be blind,
> It best agrees with Night.'

[2] Hesiod, *Theog.* 128:—

> Γαῖα δέ τοι πρῶτον μὲν ἐγείνατο ἶσον ἑαυτῇ
> Οὐρανὸν ἀστερόενθ', ἵνα μιν περὶ πάντα καλύπτοι,
> ὄφρ' εἴη μακάρεσσι θεοῖς ἕδος ἀσφαλὲς αἰεί.

bracing the earth. This sounds almost as if the Greek myth had still preserved a recollection of the etymological power of Uranos. For 'Uranos' is the Sanskrit 'Varuṇa' and this is derived from a root VAR, to cover; 'Varuṇa' being in the Veda also a name of the firmament, but especially connected with the night, and opposed to 'Mitra,' the day. At all events, the name of 'Uranos' retained with the Greek something of its original meaning, which was not the case with names like 'Apollo' or 'Dionysos'; and when we see him called ἀστερόεις, the starry heaven, we can hardly believe, as Mr. Grote says, that to the Greek, 'Uranos, Nyx, Hypnos, and Oneiros (Heaven, Night, Sleep, and Dream) are persons, just as much as Zeus and Apollo.' We need only read a few lines further in Hesiod, in order to see that the progeny of Gaea, of which Uranos is the first, has not yet altogether arrived at that mythological personification or crystallization which makes most of the Olympian gods so difficult and doubtful in their original character. The poet has asked the Muses in the introduction how the gods and the earth were first born, and the rivers and the endless sea, and the bright stars, and the wide heaven above (οὐρανὸς εὐρὺς ὕπερθεν). The whole poem of the 'Theogony' is an answer to this question; and we can hardly doubt therefore that the Greek saw in some of the names that follow, simply poetical conceptions of real objects, such as the earth, and the rivers, and the mountains. Uranos, the first offspring of Gaea, is afterwards raised into a deity,—endowed with human feelings and attributes; but the very next offspring of Gaea, Οὔρεα μακρά, the great Mountains, are even in language represented as neuter, and can therefore hardly claim to be considered as persons like Zeus and Apollo.

Mr. Grote goes too far in insisting on the purely literal meaning of the whole of Greek mythology. Some mythological figures of speech remained in the Greek language to a very late period, and were perfectly understood,—that is to say, they required as little explanation as our expressions of 'the sun sets,' or 'the sun rises.' Mr. Grote feels compelled to admit this, but he declines to draw any further conclusions from it. 'Although some of the attributes and actions ascribed to these persons,' he says, 'are often explicable by allegory, the whole series and system of them never are so: the theorist who adopts this course of explanation finds that, after one or two simple and obvious steps, the path is no longer open, and he is forced to clear a way for himself by gratuitous refinements and conjectures.' Here, then, Mr. Grote admits what he calls allegory as an ingredient of mythology; still he makes no further use of it and leaves the whole of mythology as a riddle, that cannot and

[77]

ought not to be solved, as something irrational—as a past that was never present—declining even to attempt a partial explanation of this important problem in the history of the Greek mind. Πλέον ἥμισυ παντός. Such a want of scientific courage would have put a stop to many systems which have since grown to completeness, but which at first had to make the most timid and uncertain steps. In palaeontological sciences we must learn to be ignorant of certain things; and what Suetonius says of the grammarian, 'boni grammatici est non-nulla etiam nescire,' applies with particular force to the mythologist. It is in vain to attempt to solve the secret of every name, and nobody has expressed this with greater modesty than he who has laid the most lasting foundation of Comparative Mythology. Grimm, in the introduction to his 'German Mythology,' says, without disguise, 'I shall indeed interpret all that I can, but I cannot interpret all that I should like.' But surely Otfried Müller had opened a path into the labyrinth of Greek mythology, which a scholar of Mr. Grote's power and genius might have followed, and which at least he ought to have proved as either right or wrong. How late mythological language was in vogue among the Greeks has been shown by O. Müller (p. 65) in the myth of Kyrene. The Greek town of Kyrene in Libya was founded about Olymp. 37; the ruling race derived its origin from the Minyans, who reigned chiefly in Iolkos, in Southern Thessaly; the foundation of the colony was due to the oracle of Apollo at Pytho. Hence, the myth,—'The heroic maid Kyrene, who lived in Thessaly, is loved by Apollo and carried off to Libya'; while in modern language we should say,—'The town of Kyrene, in Thessaly, sent a colony to Libya, under the auspices of Apollo.' Many more instances might be given, where the mere substitution of a more matter-of-fact verb divests a myth at once of its miraculous appearance.[1]

Kaunos is called the son of Miletos, *i.e.*, Kretan colonists from Miletos had founded the town of Kaunos in Lycia. Again, the myth says that Kaunos fled from Miletos to Lycia, and his sister Byblos was changed, by sorrow over her lost brother, into a fountain. Here Miletos in Ionia, being better known than the Miletos in Kreta, has been brought in by mistake, Byblos being simply a small river near the Ionian Miletos. Again, Pausanias tells us as a matter of history, that Miletos, a beautiful boy, fled from Kreta to Ionia, in order to escape the jealousy of Minos,— the fact being, that Miletos in Ionia was a colony of the Miletos of Kreta, and Minos the most famous king of that island. Again, Marpessa is called the daughter of Evenos, and a myth represents her as carried away by Idas,—Idas

[1] Kanne's *Mythology*, §10, p. xxxii.

being the name of a famous hero of the town of Marpessa. The fact, implied by the myth and confirmed by other evidence, is, that colonists started from the river Evenos, and founded Marpessa in Messina. And here again, the myth adds, that Evenos, after trying in vain to reconquer his daughter from Idas, was changed by sorrow into a river, like Byblos, the sister of Miletos.

If the Hellenes call themselves αὐτόχθονες, we fancy we understand what is meant by this expression. But, if we are informed that πυρρά, the red, was the oldest name of Thessaly, and that Hellen was the son of Pyrrha, Mr. Grote would say that we have here to deal with a myth, and that the Greeks, at least, never doubted that there really was one individual called Pyrrha, and another called Hellen. Now, this may be true with regard to the later Greeks, such as Homer and Hesiod; but was it so—could it have been so originally? Language is always language,—it always meant something originally, and he, whoever it was, who first, instead of calling the Hellenes born of the soil, spoke of Pyrrha, the mother of Hellen, must have meant something intelligible and rational; he could not have meant a friend of his whom he knew by the name of Hellen, and an old lady called Pyrrha; he meant what we mean if we speak of Italy as the mother of Art.

Even in more modern times than those of which Otfried Müller speaks, we find that 'to speak mythologically,' was the fashion among poets and philosophers. Pausanias complains of those 'who genealogize everything, and make Pythis the son of Delphos.' The story of Eros in the 'Phaedros' is called a myth (μῦθος, 254 D; λόγος, 257 B); yet Sokrates says ironically, 'that is one of those which you may believe or not' (τούτοις δὴ ἔξεστι μὲν πείεσθαι, ἔξεστι δὲ μή). Again, when he tells the story of the Egyptian god Theuth, he calls it a 'tradition of old' (ἀκοήν γ' ἔχω λέγειν τῶν προτέρων), but Phaedros knows at once that it is one of Sokrates' own making, and he says to him, 'Sokrates, thou makest easily Egyptian or any other stories, (λόγοι). When Pindar calls Apophasis the daughter of Epimetheus, every Greek understood this mythological language as well as if he had said 'an after-thought leads to an excuse.'[1] Nay, even in Homer, when the lame Litae (Prayers) are said to follow Atê (Mischief),

[1] O. Müller has pointed out how the different parents given to the 'Erinyes' by different poets were suggested by the character which each poet ascribed to them. 'Evidently,' he says, in his *Essay on the Eumenides*, p. 184, 'this genealogy answered better to the views and poetical objects of Aeschylos than one of the current genealogies by which the Erinyes are derived from Skotos and Gaea (Sophokles), Kronos and Eurynome (in a work ascribed to Epimenides), Phorkys (Euphorion), Gaea Eurynome (Istron), Acheron and Night (Eudemos), Hades and Persephone (Orphic hymns), Hades and Styx (Athenodoros and Mnaseas).' See, however, *Ares*, by H. D. Müller, p. 67.

trying to appease her, a Greek understood this language as well as we do, when we say that 'Hell is paved with good intentions.'

When Prayers are called the daughters of Zeus, we are hardly as yet within the sphere of pure mythology. For Zeus was to the Greeks the protector of the suppliants, $Zεὺς$ $ἱκετέσιος$,—and hence Prayers are called his daughters, as we might call Liberty the daughter of England, or Prayer the offspring of the soul.

All these sayings, however, though mythical, are not yet myths. It is the essential character of a true myth that it should no longer be intelligible by a reference to the spoken language. The plastic character of ancient language, which we have traced in the formation of nouns and verbs, is not sufficient to explain how a myth could have lost its expressive power or its life and consciousness. Making due allowance for the difficulty of forming abstract nouns and abstract verbs, we should yet be unable to account for anything beyond allegorical poetry among the nations of antiquity; mythology would still remain a riddle. Here, then, we must call to our aid another powerful ingredient in the formation of ancient speech, for which I find no better name than *Polyonymy* and *Synonymy*.[1] Most nouns, as we have seen before, were originally appellatives or predicates, expressive of what seemed at the time the most characteristic attribute of an object. But as most objects have more than one attribute, and as, under different aspects, one or the other attribute might seem more appropriate to form the name, it happened by necessity that most objects, during the early period of language, had more than one name. In the course of time, the greater portion of these names became useless, and they were mostly replaced in literary dialects by one fixed name, which might be called the proper name of such objects. The more ancient a language, the richer it is in synonyms.

Synonyms, again, if used constantly, must naturally give rise to a number of homonyms. If we may call the sun by fifty names expressive of different qualities, some of these names will be applicable to other objects also, which happen to possess the same quality. These different objects would then be called by the same name—they would become homonyms.

In the Veda, the earth is called 'urvî' (wide), 'prithvî' (broad), 'mahî' (great), and many more names, of which the Nighantu mentions twenty-one. These twenty-one words would be synonyms. But 'urvî' (wide) is not only given as a name of the earth, but also means a river. 'Prithvî' (broad) means not only earth, but sky and dawn.

[1] See the Author's letter to Chevalier Bunsen, *On the Turanian Languages*, p. 35.

'Mahî' (great, strong) is used for cow and speech, as well as for earth. Hence, earth, river, sky, dawn, cow, and speech, would become homonyms. All these names, however, are simple and intelligible. But most of the old terms, thrown out by language at the first burst of youthful poetry, are based on bold metaphors. These metaphors once forgotten, or the meaning of the roots whence the words were derived once dimmed and changed, many of these words would naturally lose their radical as well as their poetical meaning. They would become mere names handed down in the conversation of a family; understood, perhaps, by the grandfather, familiar to the father, but strange to the son, and misunderstood by the grandson. This misunderstanding may arise in various manners. Either the radical meaning of the word is forgotten, and thus what was originally an appellative, or a name, in the etymological sense of the word (*nomen* stands for *gnomen*, 'quo gnoscimus res,' like *natus* for *gnatus*), dwindled down into a mere sound—a name in the modern sense of the word. Thus ζεύς, being originally a name of the sky, like the Sanskrit 'dyáus,' became gradually a proper name, which betrayed its appellative meaning only in a few proverbial expressions, such as Ζεὺς ὕει, or 'sub Jove frigido.'

Frequently it happened that after the true etymological meaning of the word had been forgotten, a new meaning was attached to it by a kind of etymological instinct which exists even in modern languages. Thus, Λυκηγενής, the son of light—Apollo, was changed into a son of Lycia, Δήλιος, the bright one, gave rise to the myth of the birth of Apollo in Delos.

Again, where two names existed for the same object, two persons would spring up out of the two names, and as the same stories could be told of either, they would naturally be represented as brothers and sisters, as parent and child. Thus we find Selene, the moon, side by side with Mene, the moon: Helios (Sûrya), the Sun, and Phoebos (Bhava, a different form of Rudra); and in most of the Greek heroes we can discover humanized forms of Greek gods, with names which, in many instances, were epithets of their divine prototypes. Still more frequently it happened that adjectives connected with a word as applied to one object, were used with the same word even though applied to a different object. What was told of the sea was told of the sky, and the sun once being called a lion or a wolf, was soon endowed with claws and mane, even where the animal metaphor was forgotten. Thus the Sun with his golden rays might be called 'golden-handed,' *hand* being expressed by the same word as *ray*. But when the same epithet was applied to Apollo or Indra, a myth would spring up, as we find it in German and Sanskrit mythology, telling us that Indra lost his hand, and that it was replaced by a hand made of gold.

Here we have some of the keys to mythology, but the manner of handling them can only be learnt from comparative philology. As in French it is difficult to find the radical meaning of many a word, unless we compare it with its corresponding forms in Italian, Spanish, or Provencal; we should find it impossible to discover the origin of many a Greek word, without comparing it with its more or less corrupt relatives in German, Latin, Slavonic, and Sanskrit. Unfortunately we have in this ancient circle of languages nothing corresponding to Latin, by which we can test the more or less original form of a word in French, Italian, and Spanish. Sanskrit is not the mother of Latin and Greek, as Latin is the mother of French and Italian. But although Sanskrit is but one among many sisters, it is, no doubt, the eldest, in so far as it has preserved its words in their most primitive state; and if we once succeed in tracing a Latin and Greek word to its corresponding form in Sanskrit, we are generally able at the same time to account for its formation, and to fix its radical meaning. What should we know of the original meaning of πατήρ, μήτηρ, and θυγάτηρ,[1] if we were reduced to the knowledge of one language like Greek? But as soon as we trace these words to Sanskrit, their primitive power is clearly indicated. O. Müller was one of the first to see and acknowledge that classical philology must surrender all etymological research to comparative philology, and that the origin of Greek words cannot be settled by a mere reference to Greek. This applies with particular force to mythological names. In order to become mythological, it was necessary that the radical meaning of certain names should have been obscured and forgotten in the language to which they belong. Thus what is mythological in one language, is frequently natural and intelligible in another. We say, 'the sun sets,' but in our own Teutonic mythology, a seat or throne is given to the sun on which he sits down, as in Greek 'Eos' is called χρυσόθρονος, or as the modern Greek speaks of the setting sun as ἥλιος Βασιλεύι. We doubt about 'Hekate,' but we understand at once Ἕκατος and Ἑκατήβολος. We hesitate about *Lucina*, but we accept immediately what is a mere contraction of *Lucna*, the Latin *Luna*.

What is commonly called Hindu mythology is of little or no avail for comparative purposes. The stories of Siva, Vishnu, Mahâdeva, Pârvati, Kali, Krishna, etc., are of late growth, indigenous to India,

---

[1] Here is a specimen of Greek etymology, from the *Etymologicum Magnum*:
Θυγάτηρ παρὰ τὸ θύειν καὶ ὁρμᾶν κατὰ γαστρός· ἐκ τοῦ θύω καὶ τοῦ γαστήρ· λέγεται γὸρ τα θήλεα τάχιον κινεῖσθαι ἐν τῇ μήτρῳ.

and full of wild and fanciful conceptions. But while this late mythology of the Purânas and even of the Epic poems, offers no assistance to the comparative mythologist, a whole world of primitive, natural, and intelligible mythology has been preserved to us in the Veda. The mythology of the Veda is to comparative mythology what Sanskrit has been to comparative grammar. There is, fortunately, no system of religion or mythology in the Veda. Names are used in one hymn as appellatives, in another as names of gods. The same god is sometimes represented as supreme, sometimes as equal, sometimes as inferior to others. The whole nature of these so-called gods is still transparent: their first conception, in many cases, clearly perceptible. There are as yet no genealogies, no settled marriages between gods and goddesses. The father is sometimes the son, the brother is the husband, and she who in one hymn is the mother, is in another the wife. As the conceptions of the poet varied, so varied the nature of these gods. Nowhere is the wide distance which separates the ancient poems of India from the most ancient literature of Greece more clearly felt than when we compare the growing myths of the Veda with the full-grown and decayed myths on which the poetry of Homer is founded. The Veda is the real Theogony of the Aryan races, while that of Hesiod is a distorted caricature of the original image. If we want to know whither the human mind, though endowed with the natural consciousness of a divine power, is driven necessarily and inevitably by the irresistible force of language as applied to supernatural and abstract ideas, we must read the Veda; and if we want to tell the Hindus what they are worshipping,—mere names of natural phenomena, gradually obscured, personified, and deified,—we must make them read the Veda. It was a mistake of the early Fathers to treat the heathen gods[1] as demons or evil spirits, and we must take care not to commit the same error with regard to the Hindu gods. Their gods have no more right to any substantive existence than Eos or Hemera,—than Nyx or Apatê. They are masks without an actor,—the creations of man, not his creators; they are *nomina*, not *numina*; names without being, not beings without names.

In some instances, no doubt, it happens that a Greek, or a Latin, or a Teutonic myth, may be explained from the resources which each of these languages still possesses, as there are many words in Greek which can be explained etymologically without any reference

[1] Aristotle has given an opinion of the Greek gods in a passage of the *Metaphysics*. He is attacking the Platonic ideas, and tries to show their contradictory character, calling them αἰσθητὰ ἀίδια, eternal uneternals, *i.e.*, things that cannot have any real existence; as men, he continues, maintain that there are gods, but give them a human form, thus making them really 'immortal mortals,' *i.e.*, nonentities.

to Sanskrit or Gothic. We shall begin with some of these myths, and then proceed to the more difficult, which must receive light from more distant regions, whether from the snowy rocks of Iceland and the songs of the 'Edda,' or from the borders of the 'Seven Rivers,' and the hymns of the Veda.

The rich imagination, the quick perception, the intellectual vivacity, and ever-varying fancy of the Greek nation, make it easy to understand that, after the separation of the Aryan race, no language was richer, no mythology more varied, than that of the Greeks. Words were created with wonderful facility, and were forgotten again with that carelessness which the consciousness of inexhaustible power imparts to men of genius. The creation of every word was originally a poem, embodying a bold metaphor or a bright conception. But like the popular poetry of Greece, these words, if they were adopted by tradition, and lived on in the language of a family, of a city, of a tribe, in the dialects, or in the national speech of Greece, soon forgot the father that had given them birth, or the poet to whom they owed their existence. Their genealogical descent and native character were unknown to the Greeks themselves, and their etymological meaning would have baffled the most ingenious antiquarian. The Greeks, however, cared as little about the etymological individuality of their words as they cared to know the name of every bard that had first sung the 'Aristeia' of Menelaos or Diomedes. One Homer was enough to satisfy their curiosity, and any etymology that explained any part of the meaning of a word was welcome, no historical considerations being ever allowed to interfere with ingenious guesses. It is known how Sokrates changes, on the spur of the moment, Eros into a god of wings, but Homer is quite as ready with etymologies, and they are useful, at least so far as they prove that the real etymology of the names of the gods had been forgotten long before Homer.

We can best enter into the original meaning of a Greek myth when some of the persons who act in it have preserved names intelligible in Greek. When we find the names of Eos, Selene, Helios, or Herse, we have words which tell their own story, and we have a ποῦ στῶ for the rest of the myth. Let us take the beautiful myth of Selene and Endymion. Endymion is the son of Zeus and Kalyke, but he is also the son of Aethlios, a king of Elis, who is himself called a son of Zeus, and whom Endymion is said to have succeeded as king of Elis. This localizes our myth, and shows, at least, that Elis is its birthplace, and that, according to Greek custom, the reigning race of Elis derived its origin from Zeus. The same custom prevailed in India, and gave rise to the two great royal families

[84]

of ancient India,—the so-called Solar and the Lunar races: and Purûravas, of whom more by and by, says of himself,—

'The great king of day
And monarch of the night are my progenitors;
Their grandson I. . . .'

There may, then, have been a king of Elis, Aethlios, and he may have had a son, Endymion; but what the myth tells of Endymion could not have happened to the king of Elis. The myth transfers Endymion to Karia, to Mount Latmos, because it was in the Latmian cave that Selene saw the beautiful sleeper, loved him and lost him. Now about the meaning of Selene, there can be no doubt; but even if tradition had only preserved her other name, Asterodia, we should have had to translate this synonym, as Moon, as 'Wanderer among the stars.' But who is Endymion? It is one of the many names of the sun, but with special reference to the setting or dying sun. It is derived from ἐνδύω, a verb which, in classical Greek, is never used for setting, because the simple verb δύω had become the technical term for sunset. Δυσμαὶ ἡλίου, the setting of the sun, is opposed to ἀνατολαί, the rising. Now, δύω meant originally, to dive into; and expressions like ἠέλιος δ' ἄρ' ἔδυ, the sun dived, presuppose an earlier conception of ἔδυ πόντον, he dived into the sea. Thus Thetis addresses her companions ('Il.' xviii. 140):—

,Ὑμεῖς μὲν νῦν δῦτε θαλάσσχ; ευρέα κόλπον.
'You may now dive into the broad bosom of the sea.'

Other dialects, particularly of maritime nations, have the same expression. In Latin we find,[1] 'Cur mergat seras aequore flammas.' In Old Norse, 'Sol gengr i aegi.' Slavonic nations represent the sun as a woman stepping into her bath in the evening, and rising refreshed and purified in the morning; or they speak of the Sea as the mother of the Sun (the 'apâm napât'), and of the Sun as sinking into her mother's arms at night. We may suppose, therefore, that in some Greek dialect ἐνδύω was used in the same sense; and that from ἐνδύω, ἔνδυμα was formed to express sunset. From this was formed ἐνδυμίων,[2] like οὐρανίων from οὐρανός, and like most of the names of the Greek months. If ἔνδυμα had become the commonly received name for sunset, the myth of Endymion could never have arisen. But the original meaning of Endymion being once forgotten, what was told originally of the setting sun was now

[1] Grimm's *Deutsche Mythologie*, p. 704.
[2] Lauer, in his *System of Greek Mythology*, explains Endymion as the Diver. Gerhard, in his *Greek Mythology*, gives, 'Ἐνδυμίων ὁ ἐν δύμῃῶν.

[85]

told of a name, which, in order to have any meaning, had to be changed into a god or a hero. The setting sun once slept in the Latmian cave, the cave of night—'Latmos' being derived from the same root as 'Leto,' 'Latona,' the night;—but now he sleeps on Mount Latmos, in Karia. Endymion, sinking into eternal sleep after a life of but one day, was once the setting sun, the son of Zeus, the brilliant Sky, and of Kalyke, the covering Night (from καλύπτω); or, according to another saying, of Zeus and Protogeneia, the first-born goddess, or the Dawn, who is always represented, either as the mother, the sister, or the forsaken wife of the Sun. Now he is the son of a king of Elis, probably for no other reason except that it was usual for kings to take names of good omen, connected with the sun, or the moon, or the stars,—in which case a myth, connected with a solar name, would naturally be transferred to its human namesake. In the ancient poetical and proverbial language of Elis, people said 'Selene loves and watches Endymion,' instead of 'it is getting late'; 'Selene embraces Endymion,' instead of 'the sun is setting and the moon is rising'; 'Selene kisses Endymion into sleep,' instead of 'it is night.' These expressions remained long after their meaning had ceased to be understood; and as the human mind is generally as anxious for a reason as ready to invent one, a story arose by common consent, and without any personal effort, that Endymion must have been a young lad loved by a young lady, Selene; and, if children were anxious to know still more there would always be a grandmother happy to tell them that this young Endymion was the son of the Protogeneia,—she half meaning and half not meaning by that name the dawn who gave birth to the sun; or of Kalyke, the dark and covering Night. This name, once touched, would set many chords vibrating; three or four different reasons might be given (as they really were given by ancient poets) why Endymion fell into this everlasting sleep, and if any one of these was alluded to by a popular poet, it became a mythological fact, repeated by later poets; so that Endymion grew at last almost into a type, no longer of the setting sun, but of a handsome boy beloved of a chaste maiden, and therefore a most likely name for a young prince. Many myths have thus been transferred to real persons, by a mere similarity of name, though it must be admitted that there is no historical evidence whatsoever that there ever was a prince of Elis, called by the name of Endymion.

Such is the growth of a legend, originally a mere word, a μῦθος, probably one of those many words which have but a local currency, and lose their value if they are taken to distant places, words useless for the daily interchange of thought, spurious coins in the hands of the many,—yet not thrown away, but preserved as curiosities and ornaments, and deciphered at last by the antiquarian, after the lapse of many centuries. Unfortunately, we do not possess these legends as they passed originally from mouth to mouth in villages or mountain castles,—legends such as Grimm has collected in his 'Mythology,' from the language of the poor people in Germany. We do not know them, as they were told by the older members of a family, who spoke a language half intelligible to themselves and strange to their children, or as the poet of a rising city embodied the traditions of his neighbourhood in a continuous poem, and gave to them their first form and permanence. Unless where Homer has preserved a local myth, all is arranged as a system; with the 'Theogony' as its beginning, the 'Siege of Troy' as its centre, and the 'Return of the Heroes' as its end. But how many parts of Greek mythology are never mentioned by Homer! We then come to Hesiod —a moralist and theologian, and again we find but a small segment of the mythological language of Greece. Thus our chief sources are the ancient chroniclers, who took mythology for history, and used of it only so much as answered their purpose. And not even these are preserved to us, but we only believe that they formed the sources from which later writers, such as Apollodoros and the scholiasts, borrowed their information. The first duty of the mythologist is, therefore, to disentangle this cluster, to remove all that is systematic, and to reduce each myth to its primitive unsystematic form. Much that is unessential has to be cut away altogether, and after the rust is removed, we have to determine first of all, as with ancient coins, the locality, and, if possible, the age, of each myth, by the character of its workmanship; and as we arrange ancient medals into gold, silver, and copper coins, we have to distinguish most carefully between the legends of gods, heroes, and men. If, then, we succeed in deciphering the ancient names and legends of Greek or any other mythology, we learn that the past which stands before our eyes in Greek mythology, has had its present, that there are traces of organic thought in these petrified relics, and that they once formed the surface of the Greek language. The legend of Endymion was present at the time when the people of Elis understood the old saying of the Moon (or Selene) rising under the cover of Night (or in the Latmian cave), to see and admire, in silent love, the beauty of the setting Sun, the sleeper Endymion, the son of Zeus, who had granted to him the double boon of eternal sleep and everlasting youth.

Endymion is not the Sun in the divine character of Phoibos Apollon, but a conception of the Sun in his daily course, as rising early from the womb of Dawn, and after a short and brilliant career, setting in the evening, never to return again to this mortal life. Similar conceptions occur in most mythologies. In Betshuana, an African dialect, 'the sun sets' is expressed by 'the sun dies.'[1] In Aryan mythology the Sun viewed in this light is sometimes represented as divine, yet not immortal; sometimes as living, but sleeping; sometimes as a mortal beloved by a goddess, yet tainted by the fate of humanity. Thus, 'Tithonos,' a name that has been identified with the Sanskrit 'didhynmah'[2] brilliant, expressed originally the idea of the Sun in his daily or yearly character. He also, like Endymion, does not enjoy the full immortality of Zeus and Apollon. Endymion retains his youth, but is doomed to sleep. Tithonos is made immortal, but as Eos forgot to ask for his eternal youth, he pines away as a decrepit old man, in the arms of his ever-youthful wife, who loved him when he was young, and is kind to him in his old age. Other traditions, careless about contradictions, or ready to solve them sometimes by the most atrocious expedients, call Tithonos the son of Eos and Kephalos, as Endymion was the son of Protogeneia, the Dawn; and this very freedom in handling a myth seems to show, that at first, a Greek knew what it meant if Eos was said to leave every morning the bed of Tithonos. As long as this expression was understood, I should say that the myth was present; it was passed when Tithonos had been changed into a son of Laomedon, a brother of Primos, a prince of Troy. Then the saying, that Primos left his bed in the morning, became mythical, and had none but a conventional or traditional meaning. Then, as Tithonos was a prince of Troy, his son, the Ethiopian Memnon, had to take part in the Trojan war. And yet how strange!—even then the old myth seems to float through the dim memory of the poet!— for when Eos weeps for her son, the beautiful Memnon, her tears are called 'morning-dew,'—so that the past may be said to have been still half-present.

As we have mentioned Kephalos as the beloved of Eos, and the father of Tithonos, we may add, that Kephalos also, like Tithonos and Endymion, was one of the many names of the Sun. Kephalos, however, was the rising sun—the head of light,—an expression frequently used of the sun in different mythologies. In the Veda, where the sun is addressed as a horse, the head of the horse is an expression meaning the rising sun. Thus, the poet says (Rv. I. 163, 6), 'I have known through my mind thyself when it was still far—thee, the bird flying up from below the sky; I saw a head with wings,

[1] See Pott, Kuhn's *Zeitschrift*, vol. ii, p. 109.
[2] See Sonne, 'On Charis,' in Kuhn's *Zeitschrift*, vol. x, p. 178

toiling on smooth and dustless paths.' The Teutonic nations speak of the sun as the eye of Wuotan, as Hesiod speaks of—

$$\Pi\acute{\alpha}\nu\tau\alpha\ \emph{i}\delta\grave{\omega}\nu\ \varDelta\iota\grave{o}\varsigma\ \emph{o}\varphi\vartheta\alpha\lambda\mu\grave{o}\varsigma\ \varkappa\alpha\grave{\iota}\ \pi\acute{\alpha}\nu\tau\alpha\ \nu o\acute{\eta}\sigma\alpha\varsigma;$$

and they also call the sun the face of their god.[1] In the Veda, again, the sun is called (I. 115, 1) 'the face of the gods,' or 'the face of Aditi' (I. 113, 19); and it is said that the winds obscure the eye of the sun by showers of rain (V. 59, 5).

A similar idea led the Greeks to form the name of Kephalos; and if Kephalos is called the son of Herse—the Dew,—this patronymic meant the same in mythological language that we should express by the sun rising over dewy fields. What is told of Kephalos is, that he was the husband of Prokris, that he loved her, and that they vowed to be faithful to one another. But Eos also loved Kephalos; she tells her love, and Kephalos, true to Prokris, does not accept it. Eos, who knows her rival, replies, that he might remain faithful to Prokris, till Prokris had broken her vow. Kephalos accepts the challenge, approaches his wife disguised as a stranger, and gains her love. Prokris, discovering her shame, flies to Kreta. Here Diana gives her a dog and a spear, that never miss their aim, and Prokris returns to Kephalos disguised as a huntsman. While hunting with Kephalos, she is asked by him to give him the dog and the spear. She promises to do so only in return for his love, and when he has assented, she discloses herself, and is again accepted by Kephalos. Yet Prokris fears the charms of Eos; and while jealously watching her husband, she is killed by him unintentionally, by the spear that never misses its aim.

Before we can explain this myth, which, however, is told with many variations by Greek and Latin poets, we must dissect it, and reduce it to its constituent elements.

The first is 'Kephalos loves Prokris.' Prokris we must explain by a reference to Sanskrit, where 'prush' and 'prish' mean to sprinkle, and are used chiefly with reference to rain-drops. For instance (Rv. I. 168, 8): 'The lightnings laugh down upon the earth, when the winds shower forth the rain.'

The same root in the Teutonic languages has taken the sense of 'frost'; and Bopp identifies 'prush' with O. H. G. 'frus,' 'frigere.' In Greek we must refer to the same root $\pi\varrho\acute{\omega}\xi$, $\pi\varrho\omega\varkappa\acute{o}\varsigma$, a dew-drop, and also 'Prŏkris,' the dew.[2] Thus, the wife of Kephalos is only a

---

[1] Grimm, *Deutsche Mythologie*, p. 666.

[2] I see no reason to modify this etymology of 'Prokris.' 'Prish' in Sanskrit means to sprinkle, and 'prishita' occurs in the sense of shower, in 'vidyut-stanayitnu prishiteshu,' 'during lightning, thunder, and rain,' *Gobh.* 3, 3, 15, where Professor Roth ingeniously, but without necessity, suspects the original reading to have been

repetition of Herse, her mother,—'Herse,' dew, being derived from Sanskrit 'v*r*ish,'[1] to sprinkle; 'Prokris,' dew, from a Sanskrit root 'prush,' having the same sense. The first part of our myth, therefore, means simply, 'the Sun kisses the Morning Dew.'

The second saying is 'Eos loves Kephalos.' This requires no explanation; it is the old story, repeated a hundred times in Aryan mythology, 'The Dawn loves the Sun.'

The third saying was, 'Prokris is faithful; yet her new lover, though in a different guise, is still the same Kephalos.' This we may interpret as a poetical expression for the rays of the sun being reflected in various colours from the dew-drops,—so that Prokris may be said to be kissed by many lovers; yet they are all the same Kephalos, disguised, but at last recognized.

The last saying was, 'Prokris is killed by Kephalos,' *i.e.*, the dew is absorbed by the sun. Prokris dies for her love to Kephalos, and he must kill her because he loves her. It is the gradual and inevitable absorption of the dew by the glowing rays of the sun which is expressed, with so much truth, by the unerring shaft of Kephalos thrown unintentionally at Prokris hidden in the thicket of the forest.[2]

We have only to put these four sayings together, and every poet will at once tell us the story of the love and jealousy of Kephalos, Prokris, and Eos. If anything was wanted to confirm the solar nature of Kephalos, we might point out how the first meeting of

---

[1] This derivation of ἔρση, dew, from the Sanskrit root 'vrish' has been questioned, because Sanskrit *v* is generally represented in Greek by the digamma, or the spiritus lenis. But in Greek we find both ἔρση and ἔρση, a change of frequent occurrence, though difficult to explain. In the same manner the Greek has ἴστωρ and ἴστωρ from the root 'vid,' ἑστία from a root 'vas'; and the Attic peculiarity of aspirating aspirated initial vowels was well known even to ancient grammarians (Curtius, *Grundtüge*, p. 617). Forms like ἐέρση and ἄερσα clearly prove the former presence of a digamma (Curtius, *Grundzüge*, p. 509).

[2]         'La rugiada
        Pugna col sole.'—Dante, *Purgatorio*, i, 121.

---

'prushita.' 'P*r*ishat,' fem. 'prishatî,' means sprinkled, and is applied to a speckled deer, a speckled cow, a speckled horse. 'Prishata,' too, has the same meaning, but is likewise used in the sense of drops. 'Prush,' a cognate root, means in Sanskrit to sprinkle, and from it we have 'prushva,' the rainy season, and 'prushvâ,' a drop, but more particularly a frozen drop, or frost. Now, it is perfectly true, that the final *sh* of 'prish' or 'prush' is not regularly represented in Greek by a guttural consonant. But we find that in Sanskrit itself the lingual *sh* of this root varies with the palatal *s*, for instance, in 'pris-ni,' speckled; and Professor Curtius has rightly traced the Greek περκ-νός, spotted, back to the same root as the Sanskrit 'pris-ni,' and has clearly established for πρόξ and προκάς, the original meaning of a speckled deer. From the same root, therefore, not only πρώξ, a dew-drop, but προκ-ρίς also may be derived, in the sense of dew or hoar-frost, the derivative syllable being the same as in νεβ-φίς, or ἴδ-ρις, gen. ιος or ιδος.

Kephalos and Prokris takes place on Mount Hymettos, and how Kephalos throws himself afterwards, in despair, into the sea, from the Leukadian mountains. Now, the whole myth belongs to Attika, and here the sun would rise, during the greater part of the year, over Mount Hymettos like a brilliant head. A straight line from this, the most eastern point, to the most western headland of Greece, carries us to the Leukadian promontory,—and here Kephalos might well be said to have drowned his sorrows in the waves of the ocean.

Another magnificent sunset looms in the myth of the death of Herakles. His twofold character as a god and as a hero is acknowledged even by Herodotos; and some of his epithets are sufficient to indicate his solar character, though, perhaps, no name has been made the vehicle of so many mythological and historical, physical and moral stories, as that of Herakles. Names which he shares with Apollo and Zeus are Δαφνηφόρος, ᾽Αλεξίκακος, Μάντις, ᾽Ιδαῖος, ᾽Ολύμπιος, Παγγενέτωρ.

Now, in his last journey, Herakles also, like Kephalos, proceeds from east to west. He is performing his sacrifice to Zeus, on the Kenaeon promontory of Euboea, when Deianeira ('dâsya-narî' = 'dâsa-patnî') sends him the fatal garment. He then throws Lichas into the sea, who is transformed into the Lichadian islands. From thence Herakles crosses over to Trachys, and then to Mount Oeta, where his pile is raised, and the hero is burnt, rising through the clouds to the seat of the immortal gods—himself henceforth immortal and wedded to Hebe, the goddess of youth. The coat which Deianeira sends to the solar hero is an expression frequently used in other mythologies; it is the coat which in the Veda, 'the mothers weave for their bright son,'—the clouds which rise from the waters and surround the sun like a dark raiment. Herakles tries to tear it off; his fierce splendour breaks through the thickening gloom, but fiery mists embrace him, and are mingled with the parting rays of the sun, and the dying hero is seen through the scattered clouds of the sky, tearing his own body to pieces, till at last his bright form is consumed in a general conflagration, his last-beloved being Iole,—perhaps the violet-coloured evening clouds,—a word which, as it reminds us also of ἰός, poison (though the i is long), may perhaps have originated the myth of a poisoned garment.

In these legends the Greek language supplies almost all that is necessary in order to render these strange stories intelligible and rational, though the later Greeks—I mean Homer and Hesiod—had certainly in most cases no suspicion of the original import of their own traditions. But as there are Greek words which find no explanation in Greek, and which, without a reference to Sanskrit and

[91]

the other cognate dialects, would have forever remained to the philologist mere sounds with a conventional meaning, there are also names of gods and heroes inexplicable from a Greek point of view, and which cannot be made to disclose their primitive character, unless confronted with contemporary witnesses from India, Persia, Italy, or Germany. Another myth of the dawn will best explain this:—

'Ahan' in Sanskrit is a name of the day, and is said to stand for 'dahan,' like 'aṣru,' tear, for 'daṣru,' Greek δάϰϱυ. Whether we have to admit an actual loss of this initial $d$, or whether the $d$ is to be considered rather as a secondary letter, by which the root 'ah' was individualized to 'dah,' is a question which does not concern us at present. In Sanskrit we have the root 'dah,' which means to burn, and from which a name of the day might have been formed in the same manner as 'dyu,' day, is formed from 'dyu,' to be brilliant. Nor does it concern us here, whether the Gothic 'daga,' nom. 'dag-s,' day, is the same word or not. According to Grimm's law, 'daha,' in Sanskrit should in Gothic appear as 'taga,' and not as 'daga.' However, there are several spots in which the aspiration affects either the first or the last letter or both. This would give us 'dhah' as a secondary type of 'dah,' and thus remove the apparent irregularity of the Gothic 'daga.'[1] Bopp seems inclined to consider 'daga' and 'daha' identical in origin. Certain it is that the same root from which the Teutonic words for day are formed, has also given rise to the name for dawn. In German we say, 'der Morgen tagt'; and in Old English day was 'dawe'; while to dawn was in Anglo-Saxon 'dagian.' Now, in the Veda, one of the names of the dawn is 'Ahanâ.' It occurs only once (Rv. I. 123, 4):—

'Grihám griham Ahanấ yâti ákkha
Divé dive ádhi nấma dádhânâ
Sísâsanti Dyotanấ sásvat â agât́
A'gram agram ít bhagate vásûnmâ.'

Ahanâ (the dawn) comes near to every house,—she who makes every day to be known.

Dyotanâ (the dawn), the active maiden, comes back for evermore,—she enjoys always the first of all goods.

We have already seen the Dawn in various relations to the Sun, but not yet as the beloved of the Sun, flying before her lover, and destroyed by his embrace. This, however, was a very familiar ex-

[1] This change of aspiration has been fully illustrated, and well explained by Grassmann, in Kuhn's *Zeitschrift*, vol. xii, p. 110.

pression in the old mythological language of the Aryans. The Dawn has died in the arms of the Sun, or the Dawn is flying before the Sun, or the Sun has shattered the car of the Dawn, were expressions meaning simply, the sun has risen, the dawn is gone. Thus, we read in the Rv. IV. 30, in a hymn celebrating the achievements of Indra, the chief solar deity of the Veda:—

> And this strong and manly deed also thou hast performed, O Indra, that thou struckest the daughter of Dyaus (the Dawn), a woman difficult to vanquish.
>
> Yes, even the daughter of Dyaus, the magnified, the Dawn, thou, O Indra, a great hero, hast ground to pieces.
>
> The Dawn rushed off from her crushed car, fearing that Indra, the bull, might strike her.
>
> This her car lay there well ground to pieces; she went far away.

In this case, Indra behaves rather unceremoniously to the daughter of the sky; but, in other places, she is loved by all the bright gods of heaven, not excluding her own father. The Sun, it is said (Rv. I. 115, 2), follows her from behind, as a man follows a woman. 'She, the Dawn, whose cart is drawn by white horses, is carried away in triumph by the two Asvins,' as the Leukippides are carried off by the Dioskuroi.

If now we translate, or rather transliterate, 'Dahanâ' into Greek, Dáphne stands before us, and her whole history is intelligible. Daphne is young and beautiful,—Apollo loves her,—she flies before him, and dies as he embraces her with his brilliant rays. Or, as another poet of the Veda (X. 189) expresses it, 'The Dawn comes near to him,—she expires as soon as he begins to breathe,—the mighty one irradiates the sky.' Any one who has eyes to see and a heart to feel with nature like the poets of old, may still see Daphne and Apollo,— the dawn rushing and trembling through the sky, and fading away at the sudden approach of the bright sun. Thus even in so modern a poet as Swift, the old poetry of nature breaks through when, in his address to Lord Harley on his marriage he writes:—

> 'So the bright Empress of the Morn
> Chose for her spouse a mortal born:
> The Goddess made advances first,
> Else what aspiring hero durst?
> Though like a maiden of fifteen
> She blushes when by mortals seen:

Still blushes, and with haste retires
When Sol pursues her with his fires.'

The metamorphosis of Daphne into a laurel-tree is a continuation
of the myth of peculiarly Greek growth. Daphne, in Greek, meant
no longer the dawn, but it had become the name of the laurel.[1]
Hence the tree Daphne was considered sacred to the lover of
Daphne, the dawn and Daphne herself was fabled to have been
changed into a tree when praying to her mother to protect her from
the violence of Apollo.

Without the help of the Veda, the name of Daphne and the
legend attached to her, would have remained unintelligible, for the
later Sanskrit supplies no key to this name. This shows the value
of the Veda for the purpose of comparative mythology, a science
which, without the Veda, would have remained mere guesswork,
without fixed principles and without a safe basis.[2]

In order to show in how many different ways the same idea may
be expressed mythologically, I have confined myself to the names of
the dawn. The dawn is really one of the richest sources of Aryan
mythology; and another class of legends, embodying the strife
between winter and summer, the return of spring, the revival of
nature, is in most languages but a reflection and amplification of the
more ancient stories telling of the strife between night and day, the
return of the morn, the revival of the whole world. The stories,
again, of solar heroes fighting through a thunder-storm against the
powers of darkness, are borrowed from the same source; and the
cows, so frequently alluded to in the Veda, as carried off by Vritra
and brought back by Indra, are in reality the same bright cows
which the Dawn drives out every morning to their pasture ground;
sometimes the clouds, which, from their heavy udders, send down
refreshing and fertilizing rain or dew upon the parched earth; sometimes the bright days themselves, that seem to step out one by one
from the dark stable of the night, and to be carried off from their
wide pasture by the dark powers of the West. There is no sight in

[1] Professor Curtius admits my explanation of the myth of Daphne as the dawn, but
he says, 'If we could but see why the dawn is changed into a laurel!' I have explained
before the influence of homonymy in the growth of early myths, and this is only
another instance of this influence. The dawn was called δάφνη, the burning, so was
the laurel, as wood that burns easily. Afterward the two, as usual, were supposed to
be one, or to have some connection with each other, for how, the people would say,
could they have the same name? See *Etym. M.*, p. 250, 20, δαυχμόν᾽ εὔκαυστον ξύλον;
Hesych. δαυχμόν᾽ ἔνκαυστον ξίλον δάφνης (1. εὔκαυστον ξύλον δύφνην, Ahrens, *Dial.
Græc.*, ii. 532). Legerlotz, in Kuhn's *Zeitschrift*, vol. vii, p. 292. *Lectures on the Science
of Language*, Second Series, p. 502.
[2] For another development of the same word 'Ahanâ,' leading ultimately to the
myth of Athene, see *Lectures on the Science of Language*, Second Series, p. 502.

nature more elevating than the dawn even to us, whom philosophy would wish to teach that *nil admirari* is the highest wisdom. Yet in ancient times the power of admiring was the greatest blessing bestowed on mankind; and when could man have admired more intensely, when could his heart have been more gladdened and overpowered with joy, than at the approach of—

'the Lord of light,
Of life, of love, and gladness!'

The darkness of night fills the human heart with despondency and awe, and a feeling of fear and anguish sets every nerve trembling. There is man like a forlorn child, fixing his eye with breathless anxiety upon the East, the womb of day, where the light of the world has flamed up so many times before. As the father waits the birth of his child, so the poet watches the dark heaving Night who is to bring forth her bright son, the sun of the day. The doors of heaven seem slowly to open, and what are called the bright flocks of the Dawn step out of the dark stable, returning to their wonted pastures. Who has not seen the gradual advance of this radiant procession,—the heaven like a distant sea tossing its golden waves, —when the first rays shoot forth like brilliant horses racing round the whole course of the horizon,—when the clouds begin to colour up, each shedding her own radiance over her more distant sisters! Not only the east, but the west, and the south, and the north, the whole temple of heaven is illuminated, and the pious worshipper lights in response his own small light on the altar of his hearth, and stammers words which express but faintly the joy that is in nature and in his own throbbing heart:—

'Rise! Our life, our spirit has come back! the darkness is gone, the light approaches!'

If the people of antiquity called these eternal lights of heaven their gods, their bright ones ('deva'), the Dawn was the first-born among all the gods,—Protogeneia,—dearest to man, and always young and fresh. But if not raised to an immortal state, if only admired as a kind being, awakening every morning the children of man, her life would seem to be short. She soon fades away, and dies when the fountain-head of light rises in naked splendour, and sends his first swift glance through the vault of heaven. We cannot realize that sentiment with which the eye of antiquity dwelt on these sights of nature. To us all is law, order, necessity. We calculate the refractory power of the atmosphere, we measure the possible length of the dawn in every climate, and the rising of the sun is to us no greater surprise than the birth of a child. But if we could believe

[95]

again, that there was in the sun a being like our own, that in the dawn there was a soul open to human sympathy,—if we could bring ourselves to look for a moment upon these powers as personal, free, and adorable, how different would be our feelings at the blush of day! That Titanic assurance with which we say, the sun *must* rise, was unknown to the early worshippers of nature, or if they also began to feel the regularity with which the sun and the other stars perform their daily labour, they still thought of free beings kept in temporary servitude, chained for a time, and bound to obey a higher will, but sure to rise, like Herakles, to a higher glory at the end of their labours. It seems to us childish when we read in the Veda such expressions as, 'Will the Sun rise?' 'Will our old friend, the Dawn, come back again?' 'Will the powers of darkness be conquered by the God of light?' And when the Sun rose, they wondered how, but just born, he was so mighty, and strangled, as it were, in his cradle, the serpents of the night. They asked how he could walk along the sky? why there was no dust on his road? why he did not fall backward? But at last they greeted him like the poet of our own time,—

'Hail, orient Conqueror of gloomy Night!'

and the human eye felt that it could not bear the brilliant majesty of him whom they call 'the Life, the Breath, the brilliant Lord and Father.'

Thus sunrise was the revelation of nature, awakening in the human mind that feeling of dependence, of helplessness, of hope, of joy and faith in higher powers, which is the source of all wisdom, the spring of all religion. But if sunrise inspired the first prayers, called forth the first sacrificial flames, sunset was the other time when, again, the heart of man would tremble, and his mind be filled with awful thoughts. The shadows of night approach, the irresistible power of sleep grasps man in the midst of his pleasures, his friends depart, and in his loneliness his thoughts turn again to higher powers. When the day departs, the poet bewails the untimely death of his bright friend, nay, he sees in his short career the likeness of his own life. Perhaps, when he has fallen asleep, his sun may never rise again, and thus the place to which the setting sun withdraws in the far West rises before his mind as the abode where he himself would go after death, where 'his fathers went before him,' and where all the wise and the pious rejoice in a 'new life with Yama and Varuna.' Or he might look upon the sun, not as a short-lived hero, but as young, unchanging, and always the same, while generations after generations of mortal men were passing away. And hence, by

[96]

the mere force of contrast, the first intimation of beings which do not wither and decay—of immortals, of immortality! Then the poet would implore the immortal sun to come again, to vouchsafe to the sleeper a new morning. The god of day would become the god of time, of life and death. Again, the evening twilight, the sister of the dawn, repeating, though with a more sombre light, the wonders of the morning, how many feelings must it have roused in the musing poet—how many poems must it have elicited in the living language of ancient times! Was it the Dawn that came again to give a last embrace to him who had parted from her in the morning? Was she the immortal, the always returning goddess, and he the mortal, the daily dying sun? Or was she the mortal, bidding a last farewell to her immortal lover, burnt, as it were, on the same pile which would consume her, while he would rise to the seat of the gods?

Let us express these simple scenes in ancient language, and we shall find ourselves surrounded on every side by mythology full of contradictions and incongruities, the same being represented as mortal or immortal, as man or woman, as the poetical eye of man shifts its point of view, and gives its own colour to the mysterious play of nature.

One of the myths of the Veda which expresses this correlation of the Dawn and the Sun, this love between the immortal and the mortal, and the identity of the Morning Dawn and the Evening Twilight, is the story of Urvasî and Purûravas. The two names 'Urvasî' and 'Purûravas,' are to the Hindu mere proper names, and even in the Veda their original meaning has almost entirely faded away. There is a dialogue in the Rigveda between Urvasî and Purûravas, where both appear personified in the same manner as in the play of 'Kalidâsa.' The first point, therefore, which we have to prove is that 'Urvasî' was originally an appellation, and meant dawn.

The etymology of 'Urvasî' is difficult. It cannot be derived from 'urva' by means of the suffix 'sa,'[1] because there is no such word as 'urva,' and because derivatives in 'sa,' like 'romasá,' 'yuvasá,' etc., have the accent on the last syllable.[2] I therefore accept the common Indian explanation by which this name is derived from 'uru,' wide (εὐρύ), and a root 'as,' to pervade, and thus compare 'uru-asî' with another frequent epithet of the Dawn, 'urûkî,' the feminine of 'uru-ak,' far-going. It was certainly one of the most

[1] Pânini, V. 2, 100.
[2] Other explanations of 'Urvasî' may be seen in Professor Roth's edition of the Nirukta, and in the Sanskrit Dictionary published by him and Professor Boehtlingk.

striking features, and one by which the Dawn was distinguished from all the other dwellers in the heavens, that she occupies the wide expanse of the sky, and that her horses ride, as it were, with the swiftness of thought round the whole horizon. Hence we find that names beginning with 'uru' in Sanskrit, and with εὐρύ in Greek, are almost invariably old mythological names of the Dawn or the Twilight. The earth also, it is true, claims this epithet, but in different combinations from those which apply to the bright goddess. Names of the Dawn are Euryphaessa, the mother of Helios; Eurykyde or Eurypyle, the daughter of Endymion; Eurymede, the wife of Glaukos; Eurynome; the mother of the Charites; and Eurydike, the wife of Orpheus, whose character as an ancient god will be discussed hereafter. In the Veda the name of Ushas or Eos is hardly ever mentioned without some allusion to her far and wide-spreading splendour; such as 'urviyâ vibhâti,' she shines wide; 'urviyâ vikákshe,' looking far and wide; 'varîyasî,' the widest,[1] whereas the light of the Sun is not represented as wide-stretching, but rather as far-darting.

But there are other indications beside the mere name of Urvasî, which lead us to suppose that she was originally the goddess of the dawn. 'Vasishtha,' though best known as the name of one of the chief poets of the Veda, is the superlative of 'vasu,' bright; and as such also a name of the Sun. Thus it happens that expressions which apply properly to the sun only, were transferred to the ancient poet. He is called the son of Mitra and Varuna, night and day, an expression which has a meaning only with regard to Vasishtha, the sun; and as the sun is frequently called the off-spring of the dawn, Vasishtha, the poet, is said to owe his birth to Urvasî (Rv. VII. 33, 11). The peculiarity of his birth reminds us strongly of the birth of Aphrodite, as told by Hesiod.

Again, we find that in the few passages where the name of Urvasî occurs in the Rig-veda, the same attributes and actions are ascribed to her which usually belong to Ushas, the Dawn.

It is frequently said of Ushas, that she prolongs the life of man, and the same is said of Urvasî (V. 41, 19; X. 95, 10). In one passage (Rv. IV. 2, 18) Urvasî is even used as a plural, in the sense of many

---

[1] The name which approaches nearest to 'Urvasî' in Greek might seem to be 'Europe,' because the palatal s is occasionally represented by a Greek π, as αδυα = ἱπος π. The only difficulty is the long ω in Greek; otherwise Europe, carried away by the white bull ('vrishan,' man, bull, stallion, in the Veda a frequent appellation of the sun, and 'sveta,' white, applied to the same deity), carried away on his back (the sun being frequently represented as behind or below the dawn, see p. 92 and the myth of Eurydike on p. 127); again carried to a distant cave (the gloaming of the evening); and mother of Apollo, the god of daylight, or of Minos (Manu, a mortal Zeus),—all this would well agree with the goddess of the dawn.

dawns or days increasing the life of man, which shows that the appellative power of the word was not yet quite forgotten. Again, she is called 'antarikshaprâ,' filling the air, a usual epithet of the sun, 'brihaddivâ,' with mighty splendour, all indicating the bright presence of the dawn. However, the best proof that 'Urvasî' was the dawn is the legend told of her and of her love to Purûravas, a story that is true only of the Sun and the Dawn. That 'Purûravas' is an appropriate name of a solar hero requires hardly any proof. 'Purûravas' meant the same as πολυδευκής, endowed with much light; for though 'rava' is generally used of sound, yet the root 'ru,' which means originally to cry, is also applied to colour,[1] in the sense of a loud or crying colour, i.e., red (cf. ruber, rufus, Lith. 'rauda,' O. H. G. 'rôt,' 'rudhira,' ἐρυθρός also Sanskrit 'ravi,' sun). Besides, Purûravas calls himself 'Vasishtha,' which, as we know, is a name of the Sun; and if he is called 'Aida,' the son of 'Idâ,' the same name is elsewhere (Rv. III. 29, 3) given to 'Agni,' the fire.

Now the story, in its most ancient form, is found in the Brâhmana of the Yagur-veda. There we read:—

'Urvasî, a kind of fairy, fell in love with Purûravas, the son of Idâ, and when she met him, she said: "Embrace me three times a day, but never against my will, and let me never see you without your royal garments, for this is the manner of women." In this manner she lived with him a long time, and she was with child. Then her former friends, the Gandharvas, said: "This Urvasî has now dwelt a long time among mortals; let us see that she come back." Now, there was a ewe, with two lambs, tied to the couch of Urvasî and Purûravas, and the Gandharvas stole one of them. Urvasî said: "They take away my darling, as if I lived in a land where there is no hero and no man." They stole the second and she upbraided her husband again. Then Purûravas looked and said: "How can that be a land without heroes or men where I am?" And naked, he sprang up; he thought it too long to put on his dress. Then the Gandharvas sent a flash of lightning, and Urvasî saw her husband naked as by daylight. Then she vanished; "I come back," she said—and went. Then he bewailed his vanished love in bitter grief; and went near Kurukshetra. There is a lake there, called 'Anyatahplaksha,' full of lotus flowers, and while the king walked

---

[1] Thus it is said (Rv. VI. 3, 6) the fire cries with light, 'sokishâ rârapîti,' the two Spartan Charites are called Κλητά (κλητά, incluta) and Φαεννά, i.e. Clara, clear shining (see Sonne, in Kuhn's Zeitschrift, vol. x, p. 363). In the Veda the rising sun is said to cry like a new-born child (Rv. IX. 74, 1). Professor Kuhn himself has evidently misunderstood my argument. I do not derive 'ravas' from 'rap,' but I only quote 'rap' as illustrating the close connection between loudness of sound and brightness of light. See also Justi, Orient und Occident, vol. ii, p. 69.

along its border, the fairies were playing there in the water, in the shape of birds. And Urvasî discovered him, and said:—

' "That is the man with whom I dwelt so long." Then her friends said: "Let us appear to him." She agreed, and they appeared before him. Then the king recognized her and said:—

' "Lo! my wife! stay, thou cruel in mind! let us now exchange some words! Our secrets, if they are not told now, will not bring us luck on any later day."

'She replied: "What shall I do with thy speech? I am gone like the first of the dawns. Purûravas, go home again! I am hard to be caught, like the wind."

'He said, in despair: "Then may thy former friend now fall down, never to rise again; may he go far, far away! Maybe he lie down on the threshold of death, and may rabid wolves there devour him!"

'She replied: "Purûravas, do not die! do not fall down! let not evil wolves devour thee! there is no friendship with women, their hearts are the hearts of wolves. When I walked among mortals under a different form—when I dwelt with thee, four nights of the autumn, I ate once a day a small piece of butter—and even now I feel pleasure from it."

'Thus, at last, her heart melted, and she said: "Come to me the last night of the year, and thou shalt be with me for one night, and a son will be born to thee." He went the last night of the year to the golden seats, and while he was alone, he was told to go up, and then they sent Urvasî to him. Then she said: "The Gandharvas will to-morrow grant thee a wish; choose!" He said: "Choose thou for me." She replied: "Say to them, let me be one of you." Early the next morn, the Gandharvas gave him his choice: but when he said "Let me be one of you," they said: "That kind of sacred fire is not yet known among men, by which he could perform a sacrifice, and become one of ourselves." They then initiated Purûravas in the mysteries of a certain sacrifice, and when he had performed it, he became himself one of the Gandharvas.'

This is the simple story, told in the Brâhmana, and it is told there in order to show the importance of a peculiar rite, the rite of kindling the fire by friction, which is represented as the one by which Purûravas obtained immortality.[1] The verses quoted in the story are taken from the Rig-veda, where we find, in the last book, together with many strange relics of popular poetry, a dialogue between

[1] A most interesting and ingenious explanation of this ceremony is given by Professor Kuhn, in his Essay, *Die Herabkunft des Feuers*, p. 79. The application of that ceremony to the old myth of Urvasî and Purûravas belongs clearly to a later age; it is an after-thought that could only arise with people who wished to find a symbolical significance in every act of their traditional ritual.

the two celestial lovers. It consists of seventeen verses, while the author of the Brâhma*n*a knew only fifteen. In one of the verses which he quotes, Urva*s*î says, 'I am gone forever, like the first of the dawns,' which shows a strange glimmering of the old myth in the mind of the poet, and reminds us of the tears which the mother of Memnon shed over the corpse of her son, and which even by later poets are called morning dew. Again in the fourth verse, Urva*s*î addressing herself, says: 'This person (that is to say I), when she was wedded to him, O Dawn! she went to his house, and was embraced by him day and night.' Again, she tells Purûravas that he was created by the gods in order to slay the powers of darkness ('dasyuhatyâya'), a task invariably ascribed to Indra and other solar beings. Even the names of the companions of Urva*s*î point to the dawn, and Purûravas says:—

'When I, the mortal, threw my arms around those flighty immortals, they trembled away from me like a trembling doe, like horses that kick against the cart.'

No goddess is so frequently called the friend of man as the Dawn. 'She goes to every house' (I. 123, 4); 'she thinks of the dwelling of man' (I. 123, 1); 'she does not despise the small or the great' (I. 124, 6); 'she brings wealth' (I. 48, 1); 'she is always the same, immortal, divine' (I. 124, 4; I. 123, 8); 'she does not grow old' (I. 113, 15); 'she is the young goddess, but she makes man grow old' (I. 92, 11). Thus Purûravas called Urva*s*î 'the immortal among the mortals;' and, in his last verse, he addressed his beloved in the following words:—

'I, the brightest Sun, I hold Urva*s*î, her who fills the air (with light), who spreads the sky. May the blessing of thy kind deed be upon thee! Come back, the heart burns me.'

Then the poet says:—

'Thus the gods spake to thee, O son of I*d*â; in order that thou, bound to death, mayest grow to be this (immortal), thy race should worship the gods with oblations! Then thou also wilt rejoice in heaven.'

We must certainly admit, that even in the Veda, the poets were as ignorant of the original meaning of Urva*s*î and Purûravas as Homer was of Tithonos, if not of Eos. To them they were heroes, indefinite beings, men yet not men, gods yet not gods. But to us, though placed at a much greater distance, they disclose their true meaning. As Wordsworth says:—

'Not unrejoiced, I see thee climb the sky
In naked splendour, clear from mist and haze'—

Antiquity spoke of the naked Sun, and of the chaste Dawn hiding her face when she had seen her husband. Yet she says she will come again. And after the Sun has travelled through the world in search of his beloved, when he comes to the threshold of death, and is going to end his solitary life, she appears again in the gloaming, the same as the dawn,—as Eos in Homer begins and ends the day,—and she carries him away to the golden seats of the immortals.[1]

I have selected this myth chiefly in order to show how ancient poetry is only the faint echo of ancient language, and how it was the simple story of nature which inspired the early poet, and held before his mind that deep mirror in which he might see reflected the passions of his own soul. For the heart of man, as long as it knows but its own bitterness, is silent and sullen. It does not tell its love and its loss. There may be a mute poetry in solitary grief, but 'Mnemosyne,' the musing goddess of recollection, is not a muse herself, though she is the mother of the Muses. It is the sympathy with the grief of others which first gives utterance to the poet's grief, and opens the lips of a silent despair. And if his pain was too deep and too sacred, if he could not compare it to the suffering of any other human heart, the ancient poet had still the heart of nature to commune with, and in her silent suffering he saw a noble likeness of what he felt and suffered within himself. When, after a dark night, the light of the day returned, he thought of his own light that would never rise again. When he saw the Sun kissing the Dawn, he dreamt of days and joys gone forever. And when the Dawn trembled, and grew pale, and departed, and when the Sun seemed to look for her, and to lose her the more his brilliant eye sought her, an image would rise in his mind, and he would remember his own fate and yet forget it, while telling in measured words the love and loss of the Sun. Such was the origin of poetry. Nor was the evening without its charms. And when, at the end of a dreary day, the Sun seemed to die away in the far West, still looking for his Eastern bride, and suddenly the heavens opened, and the glorious image of the Dawn rose again, her beauty deepened by a gloaming sadness—would not the poet gaze till the last ray had vanished, and would not the last vanishing ray linger in his heart, and kindle there a hope of another life, where he would find again what he had loved and lost on earth?

> 'There is a radiant, though a short-lived flame,
> That burns for poets in the dawning east;
> And oft my soul has kindled at the same,
> When the captivity of sleep had ceased.'

[1] *Od.* v. 390. ἀλλ' ὅτε δὴ τρίτον ἦμαρ ἐϋπλόκαμος τέλεσ' Ἠώς. For different explanations of this and similar verses, see Völcker, *Über homerische Geographie und Weltkunde*, Hannover, 1830, p. 31.

There is much suffering in nature to those who have eyes for silent grief, and it is this tragedy—the tragedy of nature—which is the life-spring of all the tragedies of the ancient world. The idea of a young hero, whether he is called 'Baldr,' or 'Sigurd,' or 'Sîfrit,' or 'Achilles,' or 'Meleager,' or 'Kephalos,' dying in the fullness of youth, a story so frequently told, localized, and individualized, was first suggested by the Sun, dying in all his youthful vigour, either at the end of a day, conquered by the powers of darkness, or at the end of the sunny season, stung by the thorn of Winter. Again, that fatal spell by which these sunny heroes must leave their first love, become unfaithful to her or she to them, was borrowed from nature. The fate of these solar heroes was inevitable, and it was their lot to die by the hand or by the unwilling treachery of their nearest friends or relatives. The Sun forsakes the Dawn, and dies at the end of the day according to an inexorable fate, and bewailed by the whole of nature. Or the Sun is the Sun of Spring, who woos the Earth, and then forsakes his bride and grows cold, and is killed at last by the thorn of Winter. It is an old story, but it is forever new in the mythology and the legends of the ancient world. Thus Baldr, in the Scandinavian 'Edda,' the divine prototype of Sigurd and Sîfrit, is beloved by the whole world. Gods and men, the whole of nature, all that grows and lives, had sworn to his mother not to hurt the bright hero. The mistletoe alone, that does not grow on the earth, but on trees, had been forgotten, and with it Baldr is killed at the winter solstice:—

> 'So on the floor lay Balder, dead; and round
> Lay thickly strewn, swords, axes, darts, and spears,
> Which all the gods in sport had idly thrown
> At Balder, whom no weapon pierced or clove:
> But in his breast stood fixt the fatal bough
> Of mistletoe, which Lok, the accuser, gave
> To Hoder, and unwitting Hoder threw:
> 'Gainst that alone had Balder's life no charm.'

Thus Isfendiyar, in the Persian epic, cannot be wounded by any weapon, yet it is his fate to be killed by a thorn, which, as an arrow, is thrown into his eye by Rustem. Rustem, again, can only be killed by his brother; Herakles, by the mistaken kindness of his wife; Sîfrit, by the anxious solicitude of Kriemhilt, or by the jealousy of Brunhilt, whom he had forsaken. He is vulnerable in one spot only, like Achilles, and it is there where Hagene (the thorn) strikes him. All these are fragments of solar myths. The whole of nature was divided into two realms—the one dark, cold, wintry, and deathlike, the other bright, warm, vernal, and full of life. Sigurd, as the solar hero is called in the 'Edda,' the descendant of Odin, slays the serpent Fafnir, and conquers the treasure on which Andvari, the dwarf, had pronounced his curse. This is the treasure of the Niflungs or Nibelungs, the treasure of the earth, which the nebulous powers of winter and darkness had carried away like robbers. The vernal sun wins it back, and like Demeter, rich in the possession of her restored daughter, the earth becomes for a time rich with all the treasures of spring.[1] He then, according to the 'Edda,' delivers Brynhild, who had been doomed to a magic sleep after being wounded with a thorn by Odin, but who is now, like the spring after the sleep of winter, brought back to new life by the love of Sigurd. But he, the lord of the treasure ('vasupati'), is driven onward by his fate. He plights his troth to Brynhild, and gives her the fatal ring he had taken from the treasure. But he must leave her, and when he arrives at the castle of Gunnar, Gunnar's wife, Grimhild, makes him forget Brynhild, and he marries her daughter, Gudrun. Already his course begins to decline. He is bound to Gunnar, nay, he must conquer for him his own former bride, Brynhild, whom Gunnar now marries. Gunnar Gjukason seems to signify darkness, and thus we see that the awakening and budding spring is gone, carried away by Gunnar, like Proserpina by Pluto; like Sîtâ by Râvana. Gudrun, the daughter of Grimhild, and sometimes herself called Grimhild, whether the latter name meant summer (cf. 'gharma' in Sanskrit) or, the earth and nature in the latter part of the year, is a sister of the dark Gunnar, and though now married to the bright Sigurd, she belongs herself to the nebulous regions. Gunnar, who has forced Sigurd to yield him Brynhild, is now planning the death of his kinsman, because Brynhild has discovered in Sigurd her former lover, and must have her revenge. Högni dissuades his brother Gunnar from the murder; but at last the third brother Hödr, stabs Sigurd while he is asleep at the winter solstice. Brynhild has always loved him, and when her hero is killed she distributes the treasure, and is burnt, like Nanna, on the same pile with Sigurd, a sword being placed between the two lovers. Gudrun also bewails the death of her husband, but she forgets him, and marries Atli, the brother of Brynhild. Atli now claims the treasure from Gunnar and Högni, by right of his wife, and when they refuse to give it up, he invites them to his home, and makes them pris-

---

[1] Cf. Rig-veda V. 47, 1: 'Prayuñgatî divah eti bruvânâ mahî mâtâ duhituh bodhayantî, âvivâsantî yuvatih manîshâ pitribhyah â sadanc gohuvânâ.' On 'mahî mâtâ' = *Magna Mater*, see Grassmann, in Kuhn's *Zeitschrift*, vol. xvi, p. 169. 'Duhitur bodhayantî,' inquiring for or finding her daughter.

oners. Gunnar still refuses to reveal the spot where the treasure is buried till he sees the heart of Högni, his brother. A heart is brought him, but it quivers, and he says, 'This is not the heart of my brother.' The real heart of Högni is brought at last, and Gunnar says, 'Now I alone know where the treasure lies, and the Rhine shall rather have it than I will give it up to thee. He is then bound by Atli, and thrown among serpents. But even the serpents he charms by playing on the harp with his teeth, till at last one viper crawls up to him, and kills him.

How much has this myth been changed, when we find it again in the poem of the 'Nibelunge' as it was written down at the end of the twelfth century in Germany! All the heroes are Christians, and have been mixed up with historical persons of the fourth, fifth, and sixth centuries. Gunther is localized in Burgundy, where we know that, in 435, a Gundicarius or Gundaharius happened to be a real king, the same who, according to Cassiodorus, was vanquished first by Aetius, and afterwards by the Huns of Attila. Hence Atli, the brother of Brynhild, and the second husband of Gudrun (or Kriemhilt), is identified with Attila, the king of the Huns (453); nay, even the brother of Attila, Bleda, is brought in as Blödelin, the first who attacked the Burgundians, and was killed by Dankwart. Other historical persons were drawn into the vortex of the popular story, persons for whom there is no precedent at all in the 'Edda.' Thus we find in the 'Nibelunge' Dietrich von Bern, who is no other but Theodoric the Great (455–525), who conquered Odoacer in the battle of Ravenna (the famous Rabenschlacht), and lived at Verona, in German, Bern. Irenfried, again, introduced in the poem as the Landgrave of Thuringia, has been discovered to be Hermanfried, the king of Thuringia, married to Amalaberg, the niece of Theodoric. The most extraordinary coincidence, however, is that by which Sigurd, the lover of Brynhild, has been identified with Siegbert, king of Austrasia from 561 to 575, who was actually married to the famous Brunehault, who actually defeated the Huns, and was actually murdered under the most tragical circumstances by Fredegond, the mistress of his brother Chilperic. This coincidence between myth and history is so great, that it has induced some euhemeristic critics to derive the whole legend of the 'Nibelunge' from Austrasian history, and to make the murder of Siegbert by Brunehault the basis of the murder of Sîfrit or Sigurd by Brynhild. Fortunately, it is easier to answer these German than the old Greek euhemerists, for we find in contemporary history that Jornandes, who wrote his history at least twenty years before the death of the Austrasian Siegbert, knew already the daughter of the

[105]

mythic Sigurd, Swanhild, who was born, according to the 'Edda,' after the murder of his father, and afterwards killed by Jörmunrek, whom the poem has again historicized in Hermanricus, a Gothic king of the fourth century.

Let us now apply to the Greek myths what we have learned from the gradual growth of the German myth. There are evidently historical facts round which the myth of Herakles has crystallized, only we cannot substantiate them so clearly as in the myth of the 'Nibelunge,' because we have there no contemporaneous historical documents. Yet as the chief Herakles is represented as belonging to the royal family of Argos, there may have been a Herakles, perhaps the son of a king called Amphitryo, whose descendants, after a temporary exile, reconquered that part of Greece which had formerly been under the sway of Herakles. The traditions of the miraculous birth, of many of his heroic adventures, and of his death, were as little based on historical facts as the legends of Sîfrit. In Herakles killing the Chimaera and similar monsters, we see the reflected image of the Delphian Apollo killing the worm, or of Zeus, the god of the brilliant sky, with whom Herakles shares in common the names of Idaeos, Olympios, and Pangenetor. As the myth of Sigurd and Gunnar throws its last broken rays on the kings of Burgundy, and on Attila and Theodoric, the myth of the solar Herakles was realized in some semi-historical prince of Argos and Nykenae. Herakles may have been the name of the national god of the Heraklidae, and this would explain the enmity of Hêrê, whose worship flourished in Argos before the Dorian immigration. What was formerly told of a god was transferred to Herakles, the leader of the Heraklidae, the worshippers or sons of Herakles, while, at the same time, many local and historical facts connected with the Heraklidae and their leaders may have been worked up with the myth of the divine hero. The idea of Herakles, being as it were, the bond-servant of Eurystheus, is of solar origin—it is the idea of the sun fettered to his work, and toiling for men, his inferiors in strength and virtue.[1] Thus Sîfrit is toiling for Gunther, and even Apollo is for one year the slave of Laomedon—pregnant expressions, necessitated by the absence of more abstract verbs, and familiar even to modern poets:—

'As aptly suits therewith that modest pace
Submitted to the chains

[1] The Peruvian Inca, Yupanqui, denied the pretension of the sun to be the doer of all things, for if he were free, he would go and visit other parts of the heavens where he had never been. 'He is,' said the Inca, 'like a tied beast who goes ever round and round in the same track.' *Garcilaso de la Vega*, part I, viii, 8. Acosta, *Historia del Nuero Orbe*, cap. v. Tylor, *Early History of Mankind*, p. 343. Brinton, *The Myths of the New World*, p. 55.

That bind thee to the path which God ordains
That thou shouldst trace.'

The later growth of epic and tragical poetry may be Greek, or
Indian, or Teutonic; it may take the different colours of the different
skies, the different warmth of the different climes; nay, it may
attract and absorb much that is accidental and historical. But if we
cut into it and analyse it, the blood that runs through all the
ancient poetry is the same blood; it is the ancient mythical speech.
The atmosphere in which the early poetry of the Aryans grew up
was mythological, it was impregnated with something that could
not be resisted by those who breathed in it. It was like the siren
voice of the modern rhyme, which has suggested so many common
ideas to poets writing in a common language.

We know what Greek and Teutonic poets have made of their epic
heroes; let us see now whether the swarthy Hindu has been able to
throw an equally beautiful haze around the names of his mythical
traditions.

The story of the loves of Purûravas and Urvasî has frequently
been told by Hindu poets. We find it in their epic poems, in their
Purânas, and in the Brihatkathâ, the 'Great Story,' a collection of
the popular legends of India. It has suffered many changes, yet even
in Kalidâsa's[1] play, of which I shall give a short abstract, we recognize the distant background, and we may admire the skill with
which this poet has breathed new life and human feeling into the
withered names of a language long forgotten.

The first act opens with a scene in the Himâlaya mountains. The
nymphs of heaven, on returning from an assembly of the gods, have
been attacked, and are mourning over the loss of Urvasî, who has
been carried off by a demon. King Purûravas enters on his chariot,
and on hearing the cause of their grief, hastens to the rescue of the
nymph. He soon returns, after having vanquished the robber, and
restores Urvasî to her heavenly companions. But while he is carrying the nymph back to her friends in his chariot, he falls in love with
her and she with him. He describes how he saw her slowly recovering from her terror:—

'She recovers, though but faintly.
So gently steals the moon upon the night,
Retiring tardily; so peeps the flame
Of coming fires through smoky wreaths; and thus

---

[1] Professor Wilson has given the first and really beautiful translation of this play in
his *Hindu Theatre*. The original was published first at Calcutta, and has since been
reprinted several times. The best edition is that published by Professor Bollensen.

The Ganges slowly clears her troubled wave,
Engulfs the ruin that the crumbling bank
Has hurled across her agitated course,
And flows a clear and stately stream again.'

When they part, Urvasî wishes to turn round once more to see
Purûravas. She pretends that 'a straggling vine has caught her
garland,' and while feigning to disengage herself, she calls one of her
friends to help her. Her friend replies,—

'No easy task, I fear: you seem entangled
Too fast to be set free: but, come what may,
    Depend upon my friendship.'

The eye of the king then meets that of Urvasî, and he exclaims,—

'A thousand thanks, dear plant, to whose kind aid
I owe another instant, and behold
But for a moment, and imperfectly,
Those half-averted charms.'

In the second act we meet the the king at Allahabad, his residence. He walks in the garden of the palace, accompanied by a
Brahman, who acts the part of the gracioso in the Indian drama.
He is the confidential companion of the king, and knows his love for
Urvasî. But he is so afraid of betraying what must remain a secret
to everybody at court, and in particular to the queen, that he hides
himself in a retired temple. There a female servant of the queen
discovers him, and 'as a secret can no more rest in his breast than
morning dew upon the grass,' she soon finds out from him why the
king is so changed since his return from the battle with the demon,
and carries the tale to the queen. In the meantime, the king is in
despair, and pours out his grief,—

'Like one contending with the stream,
And still borne backwards by the current's force.'

But Urvasî also is sighing for Purûravas, and we suddenly see her,
with her friend, descending through the air to meet the king. Both
are at first invisible to him, and listen to the confession of his love.
Then Urvasî writes a verse on a birch-leaf, and lets it fall near the
bower where her beloved reclines. Next, her friend becomes visible;
and, at last, Urvasî herself is introduced to the king. After a few
moments, however, both Urvasî and her friend are called back by a
messenger of the gods, and Purûravas is left alone with his jester.

[108]

He looks for the leaf on which Urva*s*î had first disclosed her love, but it is lost, carried away by the wind:—

> 'Breeze of the south, the friend of love and spring,
> Though from the flower you steal the fragrant down
> To scatter perfume, yet why plunder me
> Of these dear characters, her own fair hand,
> In proof of her affection, traced? Thou knowest,
> The lonely lover that in absence pines,
> Lives on such fond memorials.'

But worse than this, the leaf is picked up by the queen, who comes to look for the king in the garden. There is a scene of matrimonial upbraiding, and, after a while, her majesty goes off in a hurry, like a river in the rainy season. The king is doubly miserable, for though he loves Urva*s*î, he acknowledges a respectful deference for his queen. At last he retires:—

> '''Tis past midday: exhausted by the heat,
> The peacock plunges in the scanty pool
> That feeds the tall tree's root; the drowsy bee
> Sleeps in the hollow chamber of the lotus,
> Darkened with closing petals; on the brink
> Of the new tepid lake the wild duck lurks
> Amongst the sedgy shades; and, even here,
> The parrot from his wiry bower complains,
> And calls for water to allay his thirst.'

At the beginning of the third act we are first informed of what befell Urva*s*î, when she was recalled to Indra's heaven. She had to act before Indra—her part was that of the goddess of beauty, who selects Vish*n*u for her husband. One of the names of Vish*n*u is Puru-shottama, and poor Urva*s*î, when called upon to confess whom she loves, forgetting the part she has to act, says, 'I love Purûravas, instead of 'I love Purushottama.' The author of the play was so much exasperated by this mistake, that he pronounced a curse upon Urva*s*î, that she should lose her divine knowledge. But when the performance was over, Indra observing her as she stood apart, ashamed and disconsolate, called her. The mortal who engrossed her thoughts, he said, had been his friend in the hours of peril; he had aided him in conflict with the enemies of the gods, and was entitled to his acknowledgments. She must, accordingly, repair to the monarch, and remain with him 'till he beholds the offspring she shall bear him.'

A second scene opens, in the garden of the palace. The king has been engaged in the business of the state, and retires as the evening approaches:—

> 'So ends the day, the anxious cares of state
> Have left no interval for private sorrow.
> But how to pass the night? its dreary length
> Affords no promise of relief.'

A messenger arrives from the queen, apprising his majesty that she desires to see him on the terrace of the pavilion. The king obeys—and ascends the crystal steps while the moon is just about to rise, and the east is tinged with red.

> *King.*—''Tis even so; illumined by the rays
> Of his yet unseen orb, the evening gloom
> On either hand retires, and in the mist
> The horizon glows, like a fair face that smiles
> Betwixt the jetty curls on either brow
> In clusters pendulous. I could gaze forever.'

As he is waiting for the queen, his desire for Urvaśî is awakened again:—

> 'In truth, my fond desire
> Becomes more fervid as enjoyment seems
> Remote, and fresh impediments obstruct
> My happiness—like an impetuous torrent,
> That, checked by adverse rocks, awhile delays
> Its course, till high with chafing waters swollen
> It rushes past with aggravated fury.
> As spreads the moon its lustre, so my love
> Grows with advancing night.'

On a sudden Urvaśî enters on a heavenly car, accompanied by her friend. They are invisible again, and listen to the king; but the moment that Urvaśî is about to withdraw her veil, the queen appears. She is dressed in white, without any ornaments; and comes to propitiate her husband, by taking a vow.

> *King.*—'In truth she pleases me. Thus chastely robed
> In modest white, her clustering tresses decked
> With sacred flowers alone, her haughty mien
> Exchanged for meek devotion: thus arrayed
> She moves with heightened charms.
> *Queen.*—'My gracious lord, I would perform a rite,
> Of which you are the object, and must beg you
> Bear with the inconvenience that my presence

May for brief time occasion you.'

*King.*—'You do me wrong; your presence is a favour,
. . . . Yet trust me, it is needless
To wear this tender form, as slight and delicate
As the lithe lotus stem, with rude austerity.
In me behold your slave, whom to propitiate
Claims not your care,—your favour is his happiness.'

*Queen.*—'Not vain my vow, since it already wins me
My lord's complacent speech.'

Then the queen performs her solemn vow; she calls upon the god of the moon—

'Hear, and attest
The sacred promise that I make my husband!
Whatever nymph attract my lord's regard,
And share with him the mutual bonds of love,
I henceforth treat with kindness and complacency.'

'*The Brahman, the confidential friend of the king,* (apart to Purûravas). The culprit that escapes before his hand is cut off determines never to run such a risk again. (*Aloud.*) What then; is his majesty indifferent to your grace?'

*Queen.*—'Wise sir, how think you,—to promote his happiness
I have resigned my own. Does such a purpose
Prove him no longer dear to me?'

*King.*—'I am not what you doubt me; but the power
Abides with you; do with me as you will.
Give me to whom you please, or if you please,
Retain me still your slave.'

*Queen.*—'Be what you list;
My vow is plighted—nor in vain the rite,
If it afford you satisfaction. Come
Hence, girls; 'tis time we take our leave.'

*King.*—'Not so:
So soon to leave me is no mark of favour.'

*Queen.*—'You must excuse me; I may not forego
The duties I have solemnly incurred.'

It does not bring out the character of the king under a very favourable light, that this scene of matrimonial reconciliation, when the queen acts a part which we should hardly expect on an oriental stage, should be followed immediately by the apparition of Urvasî. She has been present, though invisible, during the preceding

[111]

conversation between him and his queen, and she now advances behind the king, and covers his eyes with her hands.

> 'It must be Urva*s*î (the king says);
> No other hand could shed such ecstasy
> Through this emaciate frame. The solar ray
> Wakes not the night's fair blossom; that alone
> Expands when conscious of the moon's dear presence.'[1]

Urva*s*î takes the resignation of the queen in good earnest, and claims the king as granted her by right. Her friend takes leave, and she now remains with Purûravas as his beloved wife.

> *U*rva*î*s—'I lament
>      I caused my lord to suffer pain so long.'
> *King.*—'Nay, say not so! The joy that follows grief
>      Gains richer zest from agony foregone.
>      The traveller who, faint, pursues his track
>      In the fierce day alone can tell how sweet
>      The grateful shelter of the friendly tree.'

The next act is the gem of the whole play, though it is very difficult to imagine how it was performed without a *mise en scène* such as our modern theatres would hardly be able to afford. It is a melo-dramatic intermezzo, very different in style from the rest of the play. It is all in poetry, and in the most perfect and highly elaborate metres. Besides, it is not written in Sanskrit, but in Prâkrit, the *lingua vulgaris* of India, poorer in form, but more melodious in sound than Sanskrit. Some of the verses are like airs to be performed by a chorus, but the stage directions which are given in the MSS. are so technical as to make their exact interpretation extremely difficult.

We first have a chorus of nymphs, deploring the fate of Urva*s*î. She had been living with the king in the groves of a forest, in undisturbed happiness.

> 'Whilst wandering pleasantly along the brink
> Of the Mandâkinî, a nymph of air,
> Who gambolled on its sandy shore, attracted
> The monarch's momentary glance,—and this
> Aroused the jealous wrath of Urva*s*î.

---

[1] This refers to a very well-known legend. There is one lotus which expands its flower at the approach of the sun and closes them during night: while another, the beloved of the moon, expands them during night and closes them during day-time. We have a similar myth of the *daisy*, the Anglo-Saxon 'dæges eâge,' day's eye. Wordsworth's darling.

Thus incensed
She heedlessly forgot the law that bars
All female access from the hateful groves
Of Kârtikeya. Trespassing the bounds
Proscribed, she suffers now the penalty
Of her transgression, and, to a slender vine
Transformed, there pines till time shall set her free.'

Mournful strains are heard in the air—

'Soft voices low sound in the sky,
    Where the nymphs a companion deplore,
And lament, as together they fly,
    The friend they encounter no more.

'So sad and melodious awakes
    The plaint of the swan o'er the stream
Where the red lotus blossoms, as breaks
    On the wave the day's orient beam.

'Amidst the lake where the lotus, shining,
    Its flowers unfold to the sunny beam.
The swan, for her lost companion pining,
    Swims sad and slow o'er the lonely stream.'

The king now enters, his features expressing insanity—his dress disordered. The scene represents a wild forest, clouds gathering overhead, elephants, deer, peacocks, and swans are seen. Here are rocks and waterfalls, lightning and rain. The king first rushes frantically after a cloud which he mistakes for a demon that carried away his bride.

'Hold, treacherous fiend; suspend thy flight—forbear:
Ah! whither wouldst thou bear my beauteous bride?
And now his arrows sting me; thick as hail,
From yonder peak, whose sharp top pierces heaven,
They shower upon me.

[*Rushes forward as to the attack, then pauses, and looks upwards.*]

It is no demon, but a friendly cloud,—
No hostile quiver, but the bow of Indra;
The cooling rain-drops fall, not barbed shafts,—
And I mistake the lightning for my love.'

[113]

These raving strains are interrupted by airs, bewailing the fate of the separated lovers; but it is impossible to give an idea of the real beauty of the whole, without much fuller extracts than we are able to give. The following passages may suffice:—

> 'Ah me! whatever I behold but aggravates
> My woe. These bright and pendulous flowers,
> Surcharged with dew, resemble those dear eyes,
> Glistening with starting tears. How shall I learn
> If she have passed this way?'

He addresses various birds, and asks them whether they have seen his love: the peacock, 'the bird of the dark blue throat and eye of jet,'—the cuckoo, 'whom lovers deem Love's messenger,'—the swans, 'who are sailing northward, and whose elegant gait betrays that they have seen her,'—the '*k*akravâka,' 'a bird who, during the night, is himself separated from his mate,'—but none give answer. Neither he, nor the bees who murmur amidst the petals of the lotus, nor the royal elephant, that reclines with his mate under the kadamba-tree, has seen the lost one.

*King.*—'From his companion he accepts the bough
> Her trunk has snapped from the balm-breathing tree—
> How rich with teeming shoots and juicy fragrance.
> He crushes it.
>
>             Deep on the mountain's breast
> A yawning chasm appears—such shades are ever
> Haunts of the nymphs of air and earth. Perchance,
> My Urvasî now lurks within the grotto,
> In cool seclusion. I will enter.—All
> Is utter darkness. Would the lightning's flash
> Now blaze to guide me—No, the cloud disdains—
> Such is my fate perverse—to shed for me
> Its many-channelled radiance. Be it so.
> I will retire—but first the rock address.

> ### Air.
>
> 'With horny hoofs and a resolute breast,
>      The boar through the thicket stalks;
> He ploughs up the ground, as he plies his quest
>      In the forest's gloomiest walks.

'Say, mountain, whose expansive slope confines
The forest verge,—O tell me, hast thou seen
A nymph, as beauteous as the bride of love,

Mounting, with slender frame, thy steep ascent,
Or, wearied, resting in thy crowning woods?
How! no reply? remote, he hears me not,—
I will approach him nearer.

*Air.*

'From the crystal summits the glistening springs
    Rush down the flowery sides,
And the spirit of heaven delightedly sings,
    As among the peaks he hides.
  Say, mountain so favoured,—have the feet
  Of my fair one pressed this calm retreat?

'Now, by my hopes, he answers! He has seen her:
Where is she?—say. Alas! again deceived.
Alone I hear the echo of my words,
As round the cavern's hollow mouth they roll,
And multiplied return. Ah, Urvasî!
Fatigue has overcome me. I will rest
Upon the borders of this mountain torrent,
And gather vigour from the breeze that gleans
Refreshing coolness from its gelid waves.
Whilst gazing on the stream whose new swoln waters
Yet turbid flow, what strange imaginings
Possess my soul, and fill it with delight.
The rippling wave is like her arching brow;
The fluttering line of storks, her timid tongue;
The foamy spray, her white loose floating robe;
And this meandering course the current tracks,
Her undulating gait. All these recall
My soon-offended love. I must appease her. . . .
I'll back to where my love first disappeared.
Yonder the black deer couchant lies; of him
I will inquire. O, antelope, behold. . . .
How! he averts his gaze, as if disdaining
To hear my suit! Ah no, he, anxious, marks
His doe approach him; tardily she comes,
  Her frolic fawn impeding her advance.'

At last the king finds a gem, of ruddy radiance; it is the gem of union, which, by its mighty spell, should restore Urvasî to her lover. He holds it in his hands, and embraces the vine, which is now transformed into Urvasî. The gem is placed on Urvasî's forehead, and the king and his heavenly queen return to Allahabad.

'Yonder cloud
Shall be our downy car, to waft us swift
And lightly on our way; the lightning's wave
Its glittering banners; and the bow of Indra (the rainbow)
Hangs as its overarching canopy
Of variegated and resplendent hues.'

[*Exeunt on the cloud. Music.*]

The fifth and last act begins with an unlucky incident. A hawk has borne away the ruby of reunion. Orders are sent to shoot the thief, and, after a short pause, a forester brings the jewel and the arrow by which the hawk was killed. An inscription is discovered on the shaft, which states that it belonged to Âyus, the son of Urvaśî and Purûravas. The king is not aware that Urvaśî has ever borne him a son; but while he is still wondering, a female ascetic enters, leading a boy with a bow in his hand. It is Âyus, the son of Urvaśî, whom his mother confided to the pious *K*yavana, who educated him in the forest, and now sends him back to his mother. The king soon recognizes Âyus as his son. Urvaśî also comes to embrace him:—

'Her gaze intent
Is fixed upon him, and her heaving bosom
Has rent its veiling scarf.'

But why has she concealed the birth of this child? and why is she now suddenly bursting into tears? She tells the king herself,—

'When for your love I gladly left the courts
Of heaven, the monarch thus declared his will:
"Go, and be happy with the prince, my friend;
But when he views the son that thou shalt bear him,
Then hitherward direct thy prompt return." . . .
The fated term expires, and to console
His father for my loss, he is restored.
I may no longer tarry.'

*King.*—'The tree that languished in the summer's blaze
Puts forth, reviving, as young rain descends,
Its leafy shoots, when lo! the lightning bursts
Fierce on its top, and fells it to the ground.'

*Urvaśî.*—'But what remains for me? my task on earth
Fulfilled. Once gone, the king will soon forget me.'

*King.*—'Dearest, not so. It is no grateful task
To fear our memory from those we love.
But we must bow to power supreme; do you
Obey your lord; for me, I will resign

[116]

My throne to this my son, and with the deer
Will henceforth mourn amidst the lonely woods.'

Preparations are made for the inauguration of the young king, when a new *deus ex machina* appears—Narada, the messenger of Indra.

*Messenger.*—'May your days be many! King attend:
The mighty Indra, to whom all is known,
By me thus intimates his high commands.
Forego your purpose of ascetic sorrow,
And Urva*s*î shall be through life united
With thee in holy bonds.'

After this all concludes happily. Nymphs descend from heaven with a golden vase containing the water of the heavenly Ganges, a throne, and other paraphernalia, which they arrange. The prince is inaugurated as partner of the empire, and all go together to pay their homage to the queen, who had so generously resigned her rights in favour of Urva*s*î, the heavenly nymph.

Here, then, we have the full flower whose stem we trace through the Purâ*n*as and the Mahâbhârata to the Brâhma*n*as and the Veda, while the seed lies buried deep in that fertile stratum of language from which all the Aryan dialects draw their strength and nourishment. Mr. Carlyle had seen deep into the very heart of mythology when he said, 'Thus, though tradition may have but one root, it grows, like a banian, into a whole overarching labyrinth of trees.' The root of all the stories of Purûravas and Urva*s*î were short proverbial expressions, of which ancient dialects are so fond. Thus: 'Urva*s*î loves Purûravas,' meant 'the sun rises'; 'Urva*s*î sees Purûravas naked,' meant 'the dawn is gone'; 'Urva*s*î finds Purûravas again,' meant 'the sun is setting.' The names of Purûravas and Urva*s*î are of Indian growth, and we cannot expect to find them identically the same in other Aryan dialects. But the same ideas pervade the mythological languages of Greece. There one of the many names of the dawn was Eurydike (p. 102). The name of her husband is, like many Greek words, inexplicable, but Orpheus is the same word as the Sanskrit '*R*ibhu' or 'Arbhu,' which, though it is best known as the name of the three *R*ibhus, was used in the Veda as an epithet of Indra, and a name of the sun. The old story then, was this: 'Eurydike is bitten by a serpent (*i.e.*, by the night), she dies, and descends into the lower regions. Orpheus follows her, and obtains from the gods that his wife should follow him if he promised not to look back. Orpheus promises,—ascends from the dark world below; Eurydike is behind him as he rises, but, drawn by doubt or by love, he looks round; the first ray of the sun glances at the dawn, —and the dawn fades away.' There may have been an old poet of the name of Orpheus,—for old poets delight in solar names; but, whether he existed or not, certain it is, that the story of Orpheus and Eurydike was neither borrowed from a real event, nor invented without provocation. In India also, the myth of the *R*ibhus has taken a local and historical colouring by a mere similarity of names. A man, or a tribe of the name of Bribu (Rv. VI. 45, 31–3),[1] was admitted into the Brahmanic community. They were carpenters, and had evidently rendered material assistance to the family of a Vedic chief, Bharadvâga. As they had no Vaidik gods, the *R*ibhus were made over to them, and many things were ascribed to these gods which originally applied only to the mortal Bribus. These historical realities will never yield to a mythological analysis, while the truly mythological answers at once if we only know how to test it. There is a grammar by which that ancient dialect can be retranslated into the common language of the Aryans. . . .

If Hegel calls the discovery of the common origin of Greek and Sanskrit the discovery of a new world, the same may be said with regard to the common origin of Greek and Sanskrit mythology. The discovery is made, and the science of comparative mythology will soon rise to the same importance as that of comparative philology. I have here explained but a few myths, but they all belong to one small cycle, and many more names might have been added. I may refer those who take an interest in this geology of language to the 'Journal of Comparative Philology,' published by my learned friend, Dr. Kuhn, at Berlin, who, in his periodical, has very properly admitted comparative mythology as an integral part of comparative philology, and who has himself discovered some of the most striking parallelisms between the traditions of the Veda and the mythological names of other Aryan nations. The very 'Hippokentaurs and the Chimaera, the Gorgons and Pegasos, and other monstrous creatures,' have apparently been set right; and though I differ from Dr. Kuhn on several points, and more particularly with regard to the elementary character of the gods, which he, like Lauer, the lamented author of the 'System of Greek Mythology,' seems to me to connect too exclusively with the fleeting phenomena of clouds, and storms, and thunder, while I believe their original conception to have been almost always solar, yet there is much to be learnt from both. Much, no doubt, remains to be done, and even with the assistance of the Veda, the whole of Greek mythology will never be deciphered and translated. But can this be urged as an objection? There are many

[1] This explains the passage in Manu X. 107, and shows how it ought to be corrected.

Greek words of which we cannot find a satisfactory etymology, even by the help of Sanskrit. Are we therefore to say that the whole Greek language has no etymological organization? If we find a rational principle in the formation of but a small portion of Greek words, we are justified in inferring that the same principle which manifests itself in part, governed the organic growth of the whole; and though we cannot explain the etymological origin of all words, we should never say that language had no etymological origin, or that etymology 'treats of a past which was never present.' That the later Greeks, such as Homer and Hesiod, ignored the origin and purport of their myths, I fully admit, but they equally ignored the origin and purport of their words. What applies to etymology, therefore, applies with equal force to mythology. It has been proved by comparative philology that there is nothing irregular in language, and what was formerly considered as irregular in declension and conjugation is now recognized as the most regular and primitive stratum in the formation of grammar. The same, we hope, may be accomplished in mythology, and instead of deriving it, as heretofore, 'ab ingenii humani imbecillitate et a dictionis egestate,' it will obtain its truer solution, 'ab ingenii humani sapientia et a dictionis abundantia.' Mythology is only a dialect, an ancient form of language. Mythology, though chiefly concerned with nature, and here again mostly with those manifestations which bear the character of law, order, power, and wisdom impressed on them, was applicable to all things. Nothing is excluded from mythological expression; neither morals nor philosophy, neither history nor religion, have escaped the spell of that ancient sibyl. But mythology is neither philosophy, nor history, nor religion, nor ethics. It is, if we may use a scholastic expression, a *quale*, not a *quid*—something formal, not something substantial, and, like poetry, sculpture, and painting, applicable to nearly all that the ancient world could admire or adore.

## [ 2  WALTER  K.  KELLY ]

Seven years after Max Müller's essay on 'Comparative Mythology' cast a solar glow over Britain, another German celestial mythologist invaded England, although this time not in person. Adalbert Kuhn's *Der Herabkunst der Feuer* (*The Descent of the Gods*, 1859) so strongly impressed Walter K. Kelly that he summarized much of its content in his *Curiosities of Indo-European Tradition and Folk-Lore* (1836). Kuhn differed from Müller in emphasizing lightning, and the fire it produced, over the sun as the central element in mythic tales. Because Kelly applied Kuhn's thesis to the available English traditions, his book enjoyed wide popularity among Victorian folklorists.

Kelly was an active translator of folkloristic works such as *The Decameron of Boccaccio* (1846) and *The Heptameron of Margaret, Queen of Navarre* (1846), as well as of French, Spanish, and papal histories and Spanish novels. His language skills and taste for lore led him to compile *Proverbs of all Nations compared, explained, and illustrated* (1859) which enjoyed several editions.

Kelly commenced his *Curiosities* with a watered-down abstract of Müller's mythological views but then shifted to the mythic role of Prometheus, the god of lightning and fire who served Kuhn as Herakles and other sun heroes served Müller. Not only oral narratives but also festal observances still maintained by the European peasantry gave evidence of the ancient fire worship. In shafts of lightning from the heavens and the ritual fires of the early Aryans lay the symbols and the keys to Hindu and Greek mythology.

Text from Walter K. Kelly, *Curiosities of Indo-European Tradition and Folk-Lore*. London: Chapman and Hall, 1863. Pages 1–14; 37–57, from chapters 1 and 2.

It is indisputable that the principal races of Europe who are known in history, as well as the high caste Hindoos and the ancient Persians, all belong to the same stock; and that the common ancestors of this Aryan or Indo-European race once dwelt together in the regions of the Upper Oxus, now under the dominion of the khan of Bokhara. The evidence upon which this cardinal fact has been established is of like kind with that which commands our belief in the ascertained truths of geology, and is in no wise inferior to it in fullness, consistency, and force of inductive detail. It is drawn from the analysis and mutual comparison of all the languages of the Indo-Europeans, in which they have unconsciously written the history of their race, just as the earth has written the history of the mutations which its surface has undergone, in the strata which now compose its outer crust.

The Aryans of Europe are the Celts, Greeks, Latins, Germans (Teuton and Scandinavian), Letts and Slaves. The only portions of its soil not possessed by them are those occupied by the Basques, Magyars, Turks, Finns, Laps, and some Ugrian and Tatar tribes of Russia.

[120]

In the act of tracing out the mutual affinities of the Aryan languages it was impossible to overlook the traditional beliefs, rites, and customs which those languages record. Hence the investigation gradually resolved itself into the two allied sciences of Comparative Philology and Comparative Mythology. Both sciences bear testimony to the primitive unity, mental and physical, of the whole Aryan family. Often is the same verbal root found underlying words and groups of words most dissimilar in appearance, and belonging to widely different languages, under circumstances that entirely preclude the hypothesis that it is in any one of them a borrowed possession. It is just the same with a multitude of beliefs and customs which have existed from time immemorial in Greece and in Scandinavia, in the Scottish highlands, the forests of Bohemia, and the steppes of Russia, on the banks of the Shannon, the Rhine, and the Ganges. Take any of them separately, as it appears among a single people, and it will rarely happen that we can penetrate very deeply into its meaning or the causes of its being. We shall even be in danger of too hastily attributing its origin to some arbitrary caprice of ignorance and superstition, just as fossil shells and bones have by some been supposed to have been so formed *ab origine* by a freak of nature. But the mystery clears up more and more as we examine the subject on all sides by the light of kindred phenomena; and in this way we are led on to many surprising and pregnant discoveries of the common elements out of which the mythical traditions of Greece, Italy, and the Northern nations have been severally and independently developed. In this way also the most trivial maxim or practice of modern superstition may become an important link in the chain of human history, taking that term in its most comprehensive sense. For 'popular tradition is tough,' and there are still extant among ourselves and elsewhere items innumerable of an ancient lore, transcending that of the school-master, and now only succumbing at last to the navvy and the steam-engine; a lore which remains unchanged at the core from what it was some thousands of years ago, ere the first Aryan emigrants had turned their steps westwards from their old home in Central Asia. The dog had been domesticated long before that event occurred, yet watch him now when he lies down to sleep. Though his bed be a bare board, or ground as destitute of herbage, he turns himself round and round before he lies down, just as his wild ancestors used to do before him, when they prepared their couch in the long grass of the prairie. With not less tenacity does the popular mind hold fast by the substance of its ancient traditions, and also for the most part with as much unconsciousness of their primary import.

[121]

Previously to the dispersion of the Aryans, their condition, as revealed by the languages of their several branches, was in the main nomadic and patriarchal, yet not without some beginnings of agriculture, and, in proportion thereto, some rudiments of a higher form of social life, some approach to a municipal polity.[1] Their stock of knowledge was what they had gathered for themselves during their passage from the savage state to that in which we here find them. The growth of their vocabulary had kept pace with the progress of their observation and experience, and was in fact an automatic register of that progress. It was a highly figurative vocabulary, for that is a necessary condition of every primitive tongue. In all stages of language, even in that at which it has become 'a dictionary of faded metaphors,' comparison is the ready handmaid of nomenclature. A piece of machinery, for instance, is called a spinning-jenny, because it does the work of a spinning woman. 'To call things which we have never seen before by the name of that which most nearly resembles them, is a practice of every day life. That children at first call all men "father," and all women "mother," is an observation as old as Aristotle. The Romans gave the name of Lucanian ox to the elephant, and camelopardus to the giraffe, just as the New Zealanders are stated to have called horses large dogs. The astonished Caffers gave the name of cloud to the first parasol which they had seen; and similar instances might be adduced almost indefinitely. They prove that it is an instinct, if it be not a necessity, to borrow for the unknown the names already used for things known.'[2]

In this way the primitive Aryans composed their vocabulary of things seen in the sky, and so it became for all succeeding generations an inexhaustible repertory of the raw material of myths, legends and nursery tales. The sun, for instance, was a radiant wheel, or a golden bird, or an eye, an egg, a horse; and it had many other names. At sunrise or sunset, when it appeared to be squatting on the water, it was a frog; and out of this name, at a later period, when the original metaphor was lost sight of, there grew a Sanscrit story, which is found also in German and Gaelic with a change of gender. The Sanscrit version is that 'Bhekî (the frog) was a beautiful girl, and that one day, when sitting near a well, she was discovered by a king, who asked her to be his wife. She consented, on condition that he should never show her a drop of water. One day, being tired, she asked the king for water; the king forgot his promise, brought

[1] Kuhn, *Herabk.*, p. 1, and in Weber's *Ind. Stud.*, i, 321–63.
[2] Farrar, *On the Origin of Language*, p. 119.

[122]

water, and Bhekî disappeared.'[1] That is to say, the sun disappeared when it touched the water.

Clouds, storms, rain, lightning and thunder, were the spectacles that above all others impressed the imagination of the early Aryans, and busied it most in finding terrestrial objects to compare with their ever-varying aspect. The beholders were at home on the earth, and the things of the earth were comparatively familiar to them; even the coming and going of the celestial luminaries might often be regarded by them with the more composure because of their regularity; but they could never surcease to feel the liveliest interest in those wonderful meteoric changes, so lawless and mysterious in their visitations, which wrought such immediate and palpable effects, for good or ill, upon the lives and fortunes of the beholders. Hence these phenomena were noted and designated with a watchfulness and a wealth of imagery which made them the principal groundwork of all the Indo-European mythologies and superstitions. The thunder was the bellowing of a mighty beast, or the rolling of a wagon. The lightning was a sinuous serpent, or a spear shot straight athwart the sky, or a fish darting in zigzags through the waters of heaven. The stormy winds were howling dogs or wolves; the ravages of the whirlwind that tore up the earth were the work of a wild boar. Light clouds were webs spun and woven by celestial women, who also drew water from the fountains on high, and poured it down as rain. The yellow light gleaming through the clouds was their golden hair. A fast-scudding cloud was a horse flying from its pursuers. Other clouds were cows, whose teeming udders refreshed and replenished the earth; or they were buck goats, or shaggy skins of beasts dripping water. Sometimes they were towering castles, or mountains and caverns, rocks, stones, and crags,[2] or ships sailing over the heavenly waters. In all this, and much more of the same kind, there was not yet an atom of that symbolism which has commonly been assumed as the starting point of all mythology.[3] The mythic animals, for example, were, for those who first gave them their names, no mere images or figments of the mind; they were downright realities, for they were seen by men who were quick to see, and who had not yet learned to suspect any collusion between their eyes and their fancy. These 'natural philosophers'—to speak with Touchstone—had in full perfection the faculty that is given to childhood, of making everything out of anything, and of believing with a large and implicit faith in its own creations.

[1] *Saturday Review*, February 23, 1861.
[2] Nearly all the Sanscrit words for rock, stone, cliff, crag, &c., signify also cloud.
[3] Schwartz, U.M. 12.

[123]

The beings whom they first recognized as gods were those that were visible to them in the sky, and these were for the most part beasts, birds, and reptiles. Some of the latter appeared to combine the flight of birds with the form of creeping things, and then the heavenly fauna was enriched with a new genus, the winged dragon. Glimpses of other human forms besides those of the cloud women were seen from time to time, or their existence was surmised, and gradually the divine abodes became peopled with gods in the likeness of men, to whom were ascribed the same functions as belonged to the bird, beast, and snake-gods. By and by, when all these crude ideas began to shape themselves into something like an orderly system, the surplusage of gods was obviated by blending the two kinds together, or subjecting the one to the other. Thenceforth the story ran that the gods changed themselves from time to time into animal forms, or that each of them had certain animals for his favourites and constant attendants in heaven; and those were sacred to him on earth.

Let us not think too meanly of the intelligence of our simple ancestors because they could regard brutes as gods. It was an error not peculiar to them, but common to all infant races of men. The early traditions of every people point back to a period when man had not yet risen to a clear conception of his own pre-eminence in the scale of created life. The power of discerning differences comes later into play than that of perceiving resemblances, and the primeval man, living in the closest communion with nature, must have begun with a strong feeling of his likeness to the brutes who shared with him so many wants, passions, pleasures, and pains. Hence the attribution of human voice and reason to birds and beasts in fable and story, and the doctrine of the transmigration of souls. To this feeling of fellowship there would afterwards be superadded a sense of a mysterious something inherent in the nature of brutes, which was lacking in that of man. He found himself so vastly surpassed by them in strength, agility, and keenness of sense; they evinced such a marvellous foreknowledge of coming atmospheric changes which he could not surmise; they went so straight to their mark, guided by an instinct to him incomprehensible, that he might well come to look upon them with awe as beings superior to himself, and surmise in their wondrous manifestations the workings of something divine.[1]

The distinction made in historic times between gods of the upper sky, the waters, and the subterranean world, was unknown to the primitive Aryans. The horizon, where earth and sky seem to meet together, was the place in which the supernatural powers were most

[1] Herder, Ideen. Hertz, Der Werwolf.

frequently descried. When they were not there they were beyond the clouds, in their own world, which was common to them all, and which extended indefinitely above and below the surface of the earth. The origin of most water-gods and nymphs of the European Aryans may be traced back to the storm and rain deities of the parent stock; and the greater part of the myths relating to the sea are to be understood as primarily applying not to the earthly, but the cloud-sea, for no other great collection of waters was known to the first Aryans in their inland home. In like manner mythical mountains, rocks, and caverns are generally to be understood as clouds. It was in the clouds that men first beheld the deities of the under-world, whose abode was fixed in later times in the regions from which they might have been supposed to ascend when there was wild work to be done in mid-air.

Although, as we have said, the cloud-sea of the first Aryans has been generally transferred to the earth in the mythologies of the West, nevertheless the existence of an ocean overhead continued to be an article of wide-spread belief in Europe, down at least to the thirteenth century; nor is it quite extinct in some places even at this day. Agobard, Bishop of Lyons, fought hard against it in the ninth century. Many persons, he says, are so insensate as to believe that there is a region called Magonia, whence ships come in the clouds to take on board the fruits of the earth which have been beaten down by storm and hail. The aerial navigators carry on a regular traffic in that way with the storm-making wizards, pay them for the corn they have thrashed with wind and hail, and ship it off to Magonia.[1]

Gervase of Tilbury[2] relates, that as the people were coming out from a church in England, on a dark cloudy day, they saw a ship's anchor fastened in a heap of stones, with its cable reaching up from it to the clouds. Presently they saw the cable strained, as if the crew were trying to haul it up, but it still stuck fast. Voices were then heard above the clouds, apparently in clamorous debate, and a sailor came sliding down the cable. As soon as he touched the ground the crowd gathered round him, and he died, like a man drowned at sea, suffocated by our damp thick atmosphere. An hour afterwards his shipmates cut their cable and sailed away; and the anchor they had left behind was made into fastenings and ornaments for the church door, in memory of the wondrous event. The same author tells another tale to the like effect. A native of Bristol sailed from that port for Ireland, leaving his wife and family at home. His ship was driven far out of its course to the remote parts

[1] D.M. 604.
[2] In his Otia Imperialia, composed about A.D. 1211.

of the ocean, and there it chanced that his knife fell overboard, as he was cleaning it one day after dinner. At that very moment his wife was seated at table with her children in their house at Bristol, and behold! the knife fell through an open skylight, and stuck in the table before her. She recognized it immediately; and when her husband came home long afterwards they compared notes, and found that the time when the knife had fallen from his hand corresponded exactly with that in which it had been so strangely recovered. 'Who, then,' exclaims Gervase, 'after such evidence as this, will doubt the existence of a sea above this earth of ours, situated in the air or over it?' Such a sea is still known to Celtic traditions. 'If our fathers have not lied,' say the peasants of La Vendée, 'there are birds that know the way of the upper sea, and may no doubt carry a message to the blessed in Paradise.'[1]

The elemental nature of the early Aryan gods, however obscured in the monstrous growths of the later Hindu theology, is most transparent in the Rig Veda, the oldest collection of writings extant in any Indo-European tongue. It was put together somewhere about the year 1400 B.C., and consists of the hymns chanted by the southern branch of the Aryans, after they had passed the Indian Caucasus, and descended into the plain of the Seven Rivers (the Indus, the Punjab or Five Rivers, and the Sarasvati), thence to overrun all India. The Sanscrit tongue in which the Vedas are written is the sacred language of India: that is to say, the oldest language, the one which was spoken, as the Hindus believe, by the gods themselves, when gods and men were in frequent fellowship with each other, from the time when Yama descended from heaven to become the first of mortals. This ancient tongue may not be the very one which was spoken by the common ancestors of Hindus and Europeans, but at least it is its nearest and purest derivative, nor is there any reason to believe that it is removed from it by more than a few degrees. Hence the supreme importance of the Sanscrit vocabulary and literature as a key to the languages and the supernatural lore of ancient and modern Europe.

The gods Agni and Soma are described in the Vedas as descending to earth to strengthen the dominion of their own race, the Devas, who are at war with their rivals, the Asuras, and to exalt men to the gods. The story of this great event is variously told. One of its many versions as relates to Agni, the god of fire, is that he had hid himself in a cavern in heaven, and that Mâtarisvan, a god, or demi-

[1] Huber, *Skizzen aus der Vendee*, Berlin (1853), P. 65.

god, brought him out from it and delivered him to Manu, the first man, or to Bhrigu, the father of the mythical family of that name. Mâtarisvan is thus a prototype of Prometheus, and the analogy between them will appear still closer when we come to see in what way both were originally believed to have kindled the heavenly fire which they brought down to earth. The process was the same as that by which Indra kindles the lightning, and which is daily imitated in the Hindu temples in the production of sacred fire. It is so like churning, that both operations are designated by the same word.

'In churning in India, the stick is moved by a rope passed round the handle of it, and round a post planted in the ground as a pivot; the ends of the rope being drawn backwards and forwards by the hands of the churner, gives the stick a rotatory motion amidst the milk, and this produces the separation of its component parts.'— Wilson, *Rig Veda*, I. 28, 4 n.

The process by which fire is obtained from wood is called churning, as it resembles that by which butter in India is separated from milk. The New Hollanders obtain fire by a similar process. It consists in drilling one piece of arani wood into another by pulling a string, tied to it, with a jerk with one hand, while the other is slackened, and so alternately till the wood takes fire. The fire is received on cotton or flax held in the hand of an assistant Brahman.'—Stevenson, *Sâma Veda*, Pref. VII.

Besides the churn, there is another well-known domestic machine to which the 'chark,' or fire generator of India, is nearly related. This is the mangle or instrument for smoothing linen by means of rollers. *Mangle* is a corruption of *mandel* (from the root *mand*, or *manth*, which implies rotatory motion), and as a verb it means properly to roll, in which sense it is still used in provincial German. In North Germany the peasants say, when they hear the low rumbling of distant thunder, *Use Herr Gott mangelt*, 'The Lord is mangling,' or rolling—rolling the thunder. The same verb in Sanscrit is *manthami*, which is always used to denote the process of churning, whether the product sought be butter, or fire, or a mixture of the ingredients for making soma-mead. The drilling, or churning, stick is called mantha, manthara, or, with a prefix, pramantha. The Hindu epics tell how that once upon a time the Devas, or gods, and their opponents, the Asuras, made a truce, and joined together in churning the ocean to procure amrita, the drink of immortality (p. 34). They took Mount Mandara for a churning stick, and wrapping the great serpent Sesha round it for a rope, they made the mountain spin round to and fro, the Devas pulling at the serpent's tail, and the Asuras at its head. Mount Mandara was more anciently written Manthara, and manthara is the Sanscrit name of the churning stick which is used in every dairy in India.

The invention of the chark was an event of immeasurable importance in the history of Aryan civilization. Scattered through the traditions of the race there are glimpses of a time when the progenitors of those who were to 'carry to their fullest growth all the elements of active life with which our nature is endowed,' had not yet acquired the art of kindling fire at will. From that most abject condition of savage life they were partially raised by the discovery that two dry sticks could be set on fire by long rubbing together. But the work of kindling two sticks by parallel friction, effected by the hand alone, was slow and laborious, and at best of but uncertain efficacy. A little mechanical contrivance, of the simplest and rudest kind, completely changed the character of the operation. The chark was invented, and from that moment the destiny of the Aryan race was secured. Never again could the extinction of a solitary fire become an appalling calamity under which a whole tribe might have to sit down helpless, naked, and famishing, until relief was brought them by the eruption of a volcano or the spontaneous combustion of a forest. The most terrible of elements, and yet the kindliest and most genial, had become the submissive servant of man, punctual at his call, and ready to do whatever work he required of it. Abroad it helped him to subdue the earth and have dominion over it; at home it was the minister to his household wants, the centre and the guardian genius of his domestic affections.

Always prompt to explain the ways of nature by their own ways and those of the creatures about them, the Aryans saw in the fire-churn, or chark, a working model of the apparatus by which the fires of heaven were kindled. The lightning was churned out of the sun or the clouds; the sun wheel that had been extinguished at night, was rekindled in the morning with the pramantha of the Asvins. The fire-churn was regarded as a sacred thing by all branches of Indo-Europeans. It is still in daily use in the temples of the Hindus, and among others of the race here and there recourse is had to it on solemn occasions to this day. In Greece it gave birth to the sublime legend of Prometheus. Greek tragedy had its rise in the recital of rude verses in a cart by uncouth actors daubed with lees of wine. The noblest production of the Greek tragic stage was by a transcendant version of the story of a stick twirling in a hole in a block of wood.

To rub fire out of a chark is to get something that does not come to hand of its own accord, and to get it by brisk, if not violent action. Hence we find, along with pramantha, the fire-churning stick, another word of the same stock, *pramatha*, signifying theft; for manthami had come by a very natural transition to be used in the secondary sense of snatching away, appropriating, stealing. In one of these senses it passed into the Greek language, and became the verb *manthanô*, to learn, that is to say, to appropriate knowledge, whence *prometheia*, foreknowledge, forethought. In like manner the French *apprendre*, to learn, means originally to lay hold on, to acquire. Derivatives of pramantha and pramatha are also found in Greek. A Zeus Promantheus is mentioned by Lycophron as having been worshipped by the Thurians, and Prometheus is the glorious Titan who stole fire from heaven. This is the explicit meaning of the name; but, furthermore, it has implicitly the signification of fire-kindler. Prometheus appears distinctly in the latter character when he splits the head of Zeus, and Athene springs forth from it all armed; for this myth undoubtedly imports the birth of the lightning goddess from the cloud. In other versions of the story, Hephaistos takes the place of Prometheus, but this only shows that the latter was, in like manner as the former, a god of fire. At all events in this myth of the birth of Athene, Prometheus figures solely as a fire-kindler, and not at all as a fire-stealer; and since in all the older myths, names were not mere names and nothing more, but had a meaning which served as groundwork for the story, it follows that in this instance the name must have had reference to the Sanscrit *pramantha*. This conclusion is strong enough to stand alone, but it seems also to be corroborated by a name belonging to the later epic times of the Hindus. In the Mahâbhârata and some other works, Siva, who has taken the place of the older fire gods, Agni and Rudra, has a troop of fire-kindling attendants called Pramathas, or Pra-mâthas.

Prometheus is then essentially the same as the Vedic Mâtarisvan. He is the pramantha personified; but his name, like its kindred verb, soon acquired a more abstract and spiritual meaning on Grecian ground. The memory of its old etymon died out, and thenceforth it signified the Prescient, the Foreseeing. Given such a Prometheus, it followed almost as a matter of course that the Greek story-tellers should provide him with a brother, Epimetheus, his mental opposite, one who was wise after the event, and always too late.

With the fire he brought down from heaven, Prometheus gave life to the human bodies which he had formed of clay at Panopeus, in Phocis. Here again his legend is in close coincidence with that of

[129]

Mâtarisvan, for Panopeus was the seat of the Phlegyans, a mythical race, whose name has the same root as that of the Bhrigus,[1] and the same meaning also—fulgent burning. Both races incurred the displeasure of the gods for their presumption and insolence. Phlegyas and others of his blood were condemned to the torments of Tartarus. Bhrigu is of course let off more easily in the Brahmanic legend which tells of his offences, for the Brahmans numbered him among their pious ancestors; but his father, Varuna, sends him on a penitential tour to several hells, that he may see how the wicked are punished, and be warned by their fate.

After what has gone before, the reader will perhaps be prepared to discover a new meaning in the words of Diodorus (v. 67), a meaning not fully comprehended by that writer himself, when he says of Prometheus, that according to the mythographers he stole fire from the gods, but that in reality he was the inventor of the fire-making instrument.

The Aryan method of kindling sacred fire was practised by the Greeks and Romans down to a late period of their respective histories. The Greeks called the instrument used for the purpose *pyreia*, and the drilling stick *trupanon*. The kinds of wood which were fittest to form one or other of the two parts of which the instrument consisted are specified by Theophrastus and Pliny, both of whom agree that the laurel (daphne) made the best trupanon, and next to it thorn and some other kinds of hard wood; whilst ivy, athragene, and Vitis sylvestris, were to be preferred for the lower part of the pyreia. Festus states that when the vestal fire at Rome happened to go out, it was to be rekindled with fire obtained by drilling a flat piece of auspicious wood (tabulam felicis materiae). We gather from Theophrastus and Pliny whence it was that the chosen wood derived its 'auspicious' character, for they both lay particular stress upon the fact, that the three kinds recommended by them were parasites, or—what amounted to the same thing in their eyes—climbers, that attached themselves to trees. The Veda prescribes for the same purpose the wood of an asvattha (religious fig), growing upon a sami (Acacia suma).[2] The idea of a marriage, suggested by such a union of the two trees, is also developed in the Veda with great amplitude and minuteness of detail, and is a very prominent element in the whole cycle of myths connected with the chark.

[1] From the same root as Bhrigu come the German word *blitz*, Old German, *blik*, lightning; Anglo-Saxon, *blican*, and with the nasal, German, *blinken*, English, *blink*, to twinkle, shine, glitter, and also to wink, as the result of a sudden glitter.—See Wedgwood, *Dict. Engl. Etymology*.

[2] The sami sprang from heavenly fire sent down to earth, and the asvattha from the vessel which contained it.

Among the Germans, as Grimm remarks, fire that had long been in human use, and had been propagated from brand to brand, was deemed unfit for holy purposes. As holy water needed to be drawn fresh from the well, in like manner fire which had become common and profane was to be replaced by a new and pure flame, which was called 'wildfire,' in contrast with the tame domesticated element. 'Fire from the flint was no doubt fairly entitled to be called new and fresh, but either this method of procuring it was thought too common, or its production from wood was regarded as more ancient and hallowed.'[1]

The holy fires of the Germanic races are of two classes. To the first class belong those which the Church, finding herself unable to suppress them, took under her own protection, and associated with the memory of Christian saints, or of the Redeemer. These are the Easter fires, and those of St. John's day, Michaelmas, Martinmas, and Christmas. The second class consists of the 'needfires,' which have retained their heathen character unaltered to the present day. With occasional exceptions in the case of the St. John's day fires, those of the first class are never lighted by friction, yet the Church has not quite succeeded in effacing the vestiges of their heathen origin. This is especially evident in the usages of many districts where the purity of the Easter fire (an idea borrowed from pagan tradition) is secured by deriving the kindling flame either from the consecrated Easter candles, or from the new-born and perfectly pure element produced by the priest with flint and steel. Montanus states, but without citing authorities, that in very early times the perpetual lamps in the churches were lighted with fire produced by the friction of dry wood. Formerly, 'throughout England the [house] fires were allowed to go out on Easter Sunday, after which the chimney and fireplace were completely cleaned, and the fire once more lighted.' How it was lighted may be inferred from the corresponding usages in Germany and among the Slavonians. In Carinthia, on Easter Sunday, the fires are extinguished in every house, and fresh ones are kindled from that which the priest has blessed, having lighted it with flint and steel in the churchyard. In the district of Lechrain, in Bavaria, the Easter Saturday fire is lighted in the churchyard with flint and steel, and never with sulphur matches. Every household brings to it a walnut branch, which, after being partially burned, is carried home to be laid on the hearth fire during tempests, as a protection against lightning. Wolf says[2] that the Church began by striking new fire every day; afterwards this was done at least every Saturday, and in the eleventh century the

[1] D.M. 569.          [2] Beiträge, ii, 389.

custom was confined to the Saturday before Easter, on which day fire from the flint is still produced, and blessed throughout the whole Catholic Church. With this new and consecrated fire, says Le Long, a Flemish writer of the sixteenth century, 'every man lighted a good turf fire in his house, and had thereby holy fire in his house throughout the whole year.'

It is otherwise with the needfires, which are for the most part not confined to any particular day. They used to be lighted on the occasion of epidemics occurring among cattle, and the custom is still observed here and there to this day. Wherever it can be traced among people of German or Scandinavian descent, the fire is always kindled by the friction of a wooden axle in the nave of a wagon-wheel, or in holes bored in one or two posts. In either case the axle or roller is worked with a rope, which is wound round it, and pulled to and fro with the greatest possible speed by two opposite groups of able-bodied men. The wheel was, beyond all doubt, an emblem of the sun. In a few instances of late date it is stated that an old wagon-wheel was used, but this was doubtless a departure from orthodox custom, for it was contrary to the very essence of the ceremony. In Marburger official documents of the year 1605 express mention is made of new wheels, new axles, and new ropes; and these we may be assured were universally deemed requisite in earlier times. It was also necessary to the success of the operation that all the fires should be extinguished in the adjacent houses, and not a spark remain in any one of them when the work began. The wood used was generally that of the oak, a tree sacred to the lightning god Thor because of the red colour of its fresh-cut bark. Sometimes, especially in Sweden, nine kinds of wood were used, but their names are nowhere specified. The fuel for the fire was straw, heath, and brushwood, of which each household contributed its portion, and it was laid down over some length of the narrow lane which was usually chosen as the most convenient place for the work. When the fire had burned down sufficiently, the cattle were forcibly driven through it two or three times, in a certain order, beginning with the swine and ending with the horses, or vice versa. In several places in Lower Saxony, according to recent accounts, it is usual for the geese to bring up the rear. When all the cattle have passed through the fire, each householder takes home an extinguished brand, which in some places is laid in the manger. The ashes are scattered to the winds, apparently that their wholesome influence may be spread far abroad, or they are strewed over the fields (as in Appenzell, for instance) that they may preserve the crops from caterpillars and other vermin. In Sweden the smoke of the needfires was believed to have much virtue; it made fruit-trees productive, and nets that had been hung in it were sure to catch much fish.

The earliest account of the needfire in England is that quoted by Kemble[1] from the Chronicle of Lanercost for the year 1268. The writer relates with pious horror how 'certain bestial persons, monks in garb but not in mind, taught the country people to extract fire from wood by friction, and to set up a 'simulacrum Priapi,' as a means of preserving their cattle from an epidemic pneumonia. This 'simulacrum Priapi' was unquestionably an image of the sun-god Fro or Fricco, whom Latin writers of the middle ages commonly designated by the name of the Roman god, and for a manifest reason.[2]

The following account of a Celtic needfire, lighted in the Scottish island of Mull in the year 1767, is cited by Grimm:

In consequence of a disease among the black cattle the people agreed to perform an incantation, though they esteemed it a wicked thing. They carried to the top of Carnmoor a wheel and nine spindles of oak-wood. They extinguished every fire in every house within sight of the hill; the wheel was then turned from east to west over the nine spindles long enough to produce fire by friction. If the fire were not produced before noon, the incantation lost its effect. They failed for several days running. They attributed this failure to the obstinacy of one householder, who would not let his fires be put out for what he considered so wrong a purpose. However, by bribing his servants, they contrived to have them extinguished, and on that morning raised their fire. They then sacrificed a heifer, cutting in pieces and burning, while yet alive, the diseased part. They then lighted their own hearths from the pile, and ended by feasting on the remains. Words of incantation were repeated by an old man from Morven who came over as a master of the ceremonies, and who continued speaking all the time the fire was being raised. This man was living a beggar at Bellochroy. Asked to repeat the spell, he

[1] *The Saxons in England.*
[2] Wolf (Beitr. i. 107) has shown that the worship of Fro in the likeness of Priapus continued down to a late period in Belgium, and quotes, among other pertinent passages, the following from Adam of Bremen: 'Tertius est Fricco pacem voluptatemque largitus mortalibus, cujus etiam simulachrum fingunt ingenti priapo; si nuptiae celebrandae sunt, sacrificia offerunt Fricconi.' Wolf mentions several images of this kind now or till recently extant in Belgium. They are certainly not Roman. The queer little statue which is held in such high honour in Brussels is, according to Wolf, a modernized edition of an image of Fro.

said, the sin of repeating it once had brought him to beggary, and that he dared not say those words again. The whole country believed him accursed.

In the Scottish highlands, especially in Caithness, recourse is still had to the needfire, chiefly for the purpose of counteracting disorders in cattle caused by witchcraft.

To defeat the sorceries, certain persons who have the power to do so are sent for to raise the needfire. Upon any small river, lake, or island, a circular booth of stone or turf is erected, on which a couple or rafter of a birch tree is placed, and the roof covered over. In the centre is set a perpendicular post, fixed by a wooden pin to the couple, the lower end being placed in an oblong groove on the floor; and another pole is placed horizontally, between the upright post and the leg of the couple, into both which the ends, being tapered, are inserted. This horizontal timber is called the auger, being provided with four short arms, or spokes, by which it can be turned round. As many men as can be collected are then set to work, having first divested themselves of all kinds of metal, and two at a time continue to turn the pole by means of the levers, while others keep driving wedges under the upright post so as to press it against the auger; which by the friction soon becomes ignited. From this the needfire is instantly procured, and all other fires being immediately quenched, those that are rekindled in dwelling-houses and offices are accounted sacred and the cattle are successively made to smell them.[1]

The needfire is described under another name by General Stewart, a recent writer on Scottish superstitions, who says that 'the cure for witchcraft, called *Tein Econuch* (or Forlorn Fire), is wrought in the following manner:—

'Notice is previously communicated to all those householders who reside within the nearest of two running streams to extinguish their lights and fires on some appointed morning. On its being ascertained that this notice has been duly observed, a spinning-wheel, or some other convenient instrument calculated to produce fire by friction, is set to work with the most furious earnestness by the unfortunate sufferer and all who wish well to his cause. Relieving each other by turns, they drive on with such persevering diligence that at length the spindle of the wheel, ignited by excessive friction, emits for-

[1] Logan, *The Scottish Gael*, ii, 64.

lorn fire in abundance, which by the application of tow, or some other combustible material, is widely extended over the whole neighbourhood. Communicating the fire to the tow, the tow communicates it to a candle, the candle to a fir torch, the torch to a cartful of peats, which the master of the ceremonies, with pious ejaculations for the success of the experiment, distributes to messengers, who will proceed with portions of it to the different houses within the said two running streams to kindle the different fires. By the influence of this operation the machinations and spells of witchcraft are rendered null and void.'[1]

It appears from the preceding accounts that, both by Celts and Germans, a wheel was often used for kindling the needfire. Jacob Grimm was the first to make it evident that, for the Germans at least, the wheel was an emblem of the sun, and numerous facts which have come to light since he wrote, abundantly verify his conclusion. He mentions, among other evidence, that in the Edda the sun is called *fagrahvel*, 'fair or bright wheel,' and that the same sign ⊙, which in the calendar represents the sun, stands also for the Gothic double consonant HW, the initial of the Gothic word *hvil*, Anglo-Saxon *hveol*, English *wheel*. In the needfire on the island of Mull the wheel was turned, according to Celtic usage, from east to west, like the sun. Grimm has also noticed the use of the wheel in other German usages as well as in the needfire, and he is of opinion that in heathen times it constantly formed the nucleus and centre of the sacred and purifying sacrificial flame. In confirmation of this opinion he mentions the following remarkable custom which was observed on the day when those who held under the lord of a manor came to pay him their yearly dues. A wagon-wheel which had lain in water, or in the pool of a dung-yard, for six weeks and three days, was placed in a fire kindled before the company, and they were entertained with the best of good cheer until the nave, which was neither to be turned nor poked, was consumed to ashes, and then they were to go away. 'I hold this,' says Grimm, 'to have been a relic of a heathen sacrificial repast, and I look upon the wheel as what had served to light the fire, about which indeed nothing further is stated. At all events the fact proves the employment of the wagon-wheel as fuel on occasions of solemnity.'[2]

There was a twofold reason for this use of the emblem of the sun; for that body was regarded not only as a mass of heavenly fire, but also as the immediate source of the lightning. When black clouds

[1] Stewart, *Pop. Superstitions, &c.*, London (1851).
[2] D.M. 578.

concealed the sun, the early Aryans believed that its light was actually extinguished and needed to be rekindled. Then the pramantha was worked by some god in the cold wheel until it glowed again; but before this was finally accomplished, the pramantha often shot out as a thunderbolt from the wheel, or was carried off by some fire-robber. The word thunderbolt itself, like its German equivalents, expresses the cylindrical or conical form of the pramantha.[1] When the bolts had ceased to fly from the nave, and the wheel was once more ablaze, the storm was over. Vishnu undoubtedly figures in the Vedas as a god of the sun, and the great epic of the Hindus relates that when he was armed for the fight, Agni gave him a wheel with 'a thunderbolt nave.' This can only mean a wheel that shoots out thunderbolts from its nave when it is turned. Mithra, the sun-god of the Aryans of Iran, is also armed with a thunderbolt; and the names of Astrape and Bronte, two of the horses of Helios, show plainly that, for the early Greeks also, sun and lightning were associated ideas.[2]

## [ 3  GEORGE  W.  COX ]

No Victorian waved aloft the banner of celestial mythology with greater fervour than George W. Cox (1827–1902), whose heavenly interpretations caused even Müller on occasion to shake his head. In his *Manual of Mythology* (1867), *The Mythology of the Aryan Nations* (two volumes, 1870), and *An Introduction to the Science of Mythology and Folklore* (1881) Cox explained to British adults and youngsters the meaning of mythical stories as early man's view of struggles between day and night, or the clouds scudding before the wind, or the sun toiling in the sky. He indignantly denied any narrow solar bias and opened the gates of symbolism to all the elements. In place of the older allegorical theory that the gods of Olympus represented divinely revealed truths, he would make known the naturalistic explanation that early man developed myths and tales around the sights and sounds of the physical world. For Müller's misleading phrase 'disease of language' he substituted 'failure of memory' as better expressing Müller's point that the Greeks wove stories around Ayran gods after they had forgotten the original meaning of the god-names in their Central Asia homeland. Cox most notably departed from Müller in reducing the philological proofs for Sanskrit roots of Greek deities and plunging

[1] Compare cross-bow bolt.          [2] Kuhn, *Herab.*, p. 66.

straight into the symbolism of natural phenomena. Analogy largely replaced philology in his sweeping claims.

Text from George W. Cox, *An Introduction to the Science of Comparative Mythology and Folklore*. London: C. Kegan Paul and Co., 1881. Pages 27–34, 101–9, 264–76.

The impression that comparative mythology resolves everything into the sun is very widely spread, and maintains itself with singular pertinacity. Few impressions are more thoroughly groundless. The science proves conclusively that the popular traditions which have come down to us in the form whether of myths strictly so called or of folklore generally, embody the whole thought of primitive man on the vast range of physical phenomena.[1] There is scarcely an object of the outward world which has not been described or figured in these popular stories. We have myths and mythological beings belonging to the heavens and the light, to the sun, the moon, and the stars, to the fire and the winds, to the clouds and the waters, to the earth, the underworld, and the darkness. Under all these heads we have a crowd of myths which fall into distinct groups; but the phenomena of the universe do not all leave the same impression on the mind. Some are immeasurably more prominent than others, and more striking. Some are connected immediately and closely with the life and the well-being of man; others scarcely affect them at all. The most important of all are necessarily those of the seasons, and these are dependent directly on the sun, so that of the whole body of myths an immensely large proportion relates to the action of that brilliant orb which even we can seldom mention without running into mythology ourselves. But the myths belonging to other groups are not less marked and distinct, and we shall find in the clouds and water sources of popular stories as rich in thought

[1] Mr. Sayce, in his *Introduction to the Science of Language*, has dealt summarily with the objections commonly urged against the method and results of comparative mythology. These objections fall for the most part under two heads: (1) That there is no warrant for endowing primitive man with the high imagination of a poet; and (2) that the mythopoeic ages must have been marked by dull stupidity, if 'the phenomena of the atmosphere engrossed the whole attention of men who were yet too witless to understand the language in which they were described.' These objections, he remarks, are mutually destructive. The imagination of primitive man was neither too high nor too feeble. 'The gods they worshipped were the gods that brought them food and warmth, and these gods were the bright day and the burning sun. . . . It was not stupidity, but the necessities of his daily existence, the conditions in which his lot was cast, that made man confine his thoughts and care to the powers which gave him the good gifts he desired. Winter, according to the disciples of Zoroaster, was the creation of the evil one, and among the first thanksgivings lisped by our race is praise of the gods as "givers of good things" ' (ii, 268).

[137]

and colouring as any which relate to the bridegroom who comes forth daily from his chamber in the East and rejoices as a giant to run his course.

We can, then, only take these traditions under their several heads, without attempting to determine the exact order in which the conceptions set forth in them arose in the human mind. It is the ethereal heaven, and not the sun, which has been chosen in the language of myths as the abode of the supreme God, the dwelling of the All-father; but it would be rash, perhaps, to assign priority in order of time to myths of the heaven over those of the sun, or to the latter over the former. The Hesiodic Theogony, which gives a long ancestry to Zeus, the supreme god of the Hellenic tribes, and seems to make him younger than Aphroditê, is the growth of a later age which had acquired a love of systematic arrangement; and it is impossible to determine the order in which the ideas of the several beings springing from Chaos and Gaia took shape.[1]

But of the mode in which these ideas were formed we are left in no doubt. The book known as the Rig Veda in the sacred literature of the Hindus exhibits perhaps in their oldest shapes the thoughts of men on the phenomena of the outward world. It contains a multitude of hymns addressed to living powers on the earth and in the heavens; and to these powers the worshipper prays under names denoting what we call natural forces—wind, storm, frost, cold, heat, light and darkness. But for him all these are beings capable of hearing and understanding what he says. They can feel love and hatred; they may be cruel or merciful; and he may win from them by devout service the happiness for which he yearns, or he may ward off with their aid the evils which he dreads. On some he looks with awful fear; to others he can speak almost with affectionate familiarity. He pours out before them all the thoughts of his heart, and the words by which he gives expression to these thoughts describe with

---

[1] We have a parallel case in what are called *roots* in language. We find that many groups of Aryan words can be reduced to a root *mar* or *mal*, this root denoting a gradation of ideas from grinding, crushing, and destroying, to those of languor, decay, softness, and sweetness; and we are apt to suppose that this root was used as a word in something like its naked shape before the several words of which it is regarded as the foundation took shape. The notion is a mere guess, and, it can scarcely be doubted, an erroneous one. The root *mar* or *mal* is found also in the forms *mardh*, *marg*, *mark*, *marp*, *mard*, *smar*. It is thus safe to say that, as 'the vocables that embodied these roots underwent the wear and tear of phonetic decay, many of them passed out of the living speech and were replaced by others, and there was left at last a whole family of nouns and verbs, whose sole common possession was the syllable *mar*. That alone had resisted the attacks of time and change' (Sayce, *Introd.*, ii, 17). Thus the words are necessarily older than the roots contained in them, these being 'due to the reflective analysis of the grammarian' (*ibid.*, p. 18). In the same way it is likely that the attention of primitive men was directed to the objects seen in the heavens before it was fixed on the heaven itself.

marvellous exactness all that they noticed in the world around them.

Thus for him Ushas,[1] the Dawn, is a bright being whom age cannot touch, but who makes men old as she returns day after day and year after year in undiminished beauty. She is full of love, of gentleness, and compassion. She thinks on the dwellings of men, and she smiles on the small and the great. In short, it is impossible to mistake the meaning of the words addressed to her. We see that she is the dawn, and no mere personification of the morning light; but she is as completely a conscious being, moved by the emotions that may stir the human heart, as any woman whom the greatest of epic poets has immortalized in his song. She is bright, fair, and loving—the joy of all who behold her.

'She shines upon us like a young wife, rousing every living being to go to his work.

'She rose up, spreading far and wide, and moving towards everyone. She grew in brightness, wearing her brilliant garment. The mother of the cows, the leader of the days, she shone gold-coloured, lovely to behold.

'She, the fortunate, who brings the eye of the god, who leads the white and lovely steed, the dawn was seen revealed by her rays. With brilliant treasures she follows everyone.

'Shine for us with thy best rays, thou bright dawn, thou who lengthenest our life, who givest us wealth in cows, horses, and chariots.'[2]

Still more exact in its description of the phenomena of the morning and the day is the hymn in which the worshipper addresses her as leading on the sun and going before him, preparing practicable paths and expanding everywhere.

'Lucidly white is she, occupying the two regions[3] and manifesting her power from the east; she traverses the path of the sun, as knowing his course, and harms not the quarters of the horizon.

'Ushas, the daughter of heaven, tending to the west, puts forth her beauty. Bestowing precious treasures on the offerer of adoration, she, ever youthful, brings back the light as of old.'

This is not personification, nor is it allegory. It is simply the language of men who have not learnt to distinguish between subject

---

[1] The name Ushas is in Latin Aurora. In the Graeco-Italian dialects it assumed the form *ausos*. In Latin a secondary noun was formed from the primary one, *ausosa*. But both Greeks and Latins disliked the sound of *s* between vowels; and so with the former Ausos became Auos, Eos, the goddess of the morning; with the latter it became Aurora, the verb appearing in Greek as αὔω, in Latin as *uro*. The Lithuanian form is Ausera. (Peile, *Introduction to Greek and Latin Etymology*, xii.)

[2] R.V. vii. 77.

[3] The upper and middle firmament.

and object, and in it we have the key to expressions with which the hymns of the Rig Veda are filled. Nor need we be surprised if in these hymns the phrases suggested by outward phenomena run into a meaning purely spiritual. This is especially the case with Varuna and Dyaus, the supreme gods of the earliest Vedic ages. The former is simply the heaven which serves to veil or cover Prithivî, the broad or flat earth, which is his bride,[1] and who in the Theogony of Hesiod reappears as Gaia. As such, Varuna is a creation of mythical speech, and is embodied in visible form. He sits on his throne, clothed in golden armour, and dwells in a palace supported on a thousand columns, while his messengers stand round to do his bidding. But in many of the hymns we also find language which is perpetually suggesting the idea of an unseen and almighty Being, who has made all things and upholds them by his will. In these hymns Varuna dwells in all worlds as sovereign. The wind is his breath. It is he who has placed the sun in the heavens, and who guides the stars in their courses. He has hollowed out the channels of the rivers, and so wisely ordered things that, though all the rivers pour their waters into the sea, the sea is never filled. He has a thousand eyes: he knows the flight of birds in the sky, the paths of the ships on the seas, and the course of the far-sweeping wind. Such language may pass easily into that of the purest worship of the One Maker and Father of all men; and thus we have the prayer:

'Let me not yet, O Varuna, enter into the house of clay; have mercy, Almighty, have mercy.

'If I go along trembling like a cloud driven by the wind, have mercy, Almighty, have mercy.

'Through want of strength have I gone to the wrong shore; have mercy, Almighty, have mercy.

'Whenever we men, O Varuna, commit an offence before thy heavenly host, whenever we break thy law through thoughtlessness, have mercy, Almighty, have mercy.'

But although the name of Varuna has a common element with that of Vritra, the dark enemy of Indra, there is no likeness of character between them. Varuna is armed, indeed, with destructive nooses; but these are prepared for the wicked only. They ensnare the men who speak lies, passing by the man who speaks truth. He holds the unrighteous fast in prison, but he does so only as the punisher of iniquity, which cannot be hidden from him who 'num-

---

[1] The name Varuna corresponds to the Greek Ouranos, and is built up on the same root which gives the names of the Hindu Vritra, the veiling demon of darkness, the Greek Orthros, who with Kerberos (Cerberus), the Vedic Çarvara, guards the gates of Hades. Prithivî transliterated into Greek becomes Plateia, our *flat*.

bers the winkings of men's eyes,' and not as the gloomy Hades of the nether world.

The true greatness of Varuna belongs seemingly to one of the earliest stages of Hindu thought. In Greece he reappears as Ouranos; but as there Zeus became the name of the supreme God, Ouranos lost his importance, and almost faded out of sight. The same fate befell Varuna, who gave way first to the correlative of Zeus, the Vedic Dyaus, the god not of the veiling or nightly heaven, but of the bright and gleaming canopy of the day. The name is widely spread among the Aryan tribes. It reappears not only in the Greek Zeus (Zen-os), but in the Latin Juno, answering to a form Zenon, in Diana, Dianus, Janus, and many more. In Teutonic dialects we find it in the form Tiu, the God of light, a name still familiar to us in Tivsdag, or Tuesday. Dyaus was invoked commonly as Dyaus-Pitar, the Zeus Pater, or father Zeus of the Greeks, the Jupiter of the Latins. But although some mythical features entered gradually into the conceptions of this deity, the word retained its original meaning far too clearly to allow it to hold its ground in Hindu mythology. Dyaus, therefore, gave way to his child Indra, who, in a land which under its scorching sun depends wholly on the bounty of the benignant rain-god, was worshipped as the fertilizer of the earth, and was naturally regarded as more powerful than his father.[1] But although his greatness is obscured by that of his son, he still wields the thunderbolt, and is spoken of as the father of the Dawn, who is invincible by all but Indra.

In Mitra, the brother of Varuna, we have another god of the heaven, who, like Dyaus, represents the firmament of noontide. Thus the two represent the phases which pass over the sky by night and by day. Hence it is not strange that in the Zendavesta Mithras should occupy a place between the two powers of light and darkness, of good and evil.

In Indra we have the god whose special office it is to do battle with the demon of drought, and let loose the life-giving waters. He is the son of Dyaus, the gleaming heaven, and he is seen in the dazzling orb which seems to smite the thunder clouds, and compel them to give up their prey. His golden locks flow over his shoulders, and his unerring arrows have a hundred points and are winged with a thousand feathers. In his hand he holds a golden whip, and he is borne across the heaven in a flaming chariot drawn by the tawny or glistening steeds called the Harits. His beard flashes like lightning, and as his eye pierces to every part of the universe, he is

---

[1] The name Indra, which is that of the great stream Indus, denotes moisture or sap.

possessed of an inscrutable and unfathomable wisdom. As the bringer of the rain, and therefore also of the harvest, he is the god whose power is most earnestly invoked by his Hindu worshippers; but no purely spiritual prayer, such as those which were offered to Varuna, was ever addressed to him. The only work for which he was supposed to exist was to do battle with, and to conquer, the demons who were in revolt against him. The chief of these demons is Vritra, the hiding thief; Ahi,[1] the strangling snake; or Pani, the marauder. But he is also known as Namuki, the Greek Amykos, as Sushna, Sambara, Bala, Chumuri. The victory of Indra over these rebels brings plenty of corn, wine, oil; but there is nothing moral or spiritual in the struggle. He is the rescuer of the cows (the clouds), whose milk is to refresh the earth, and which have been hidden away in the caves of the robbers. As driving these before him he is Parjanya, the rain-bringer; and the poet says: 'The winds blow strong, the lightnings flash, the plants spring up, the firmament dissolves. Earth becomes fit for all creatures when Parjanya fertilizes the soil with showers.'[2]


. . . the idea of enforced labour is that which underlies and runs through the whole career of Herakles, the greatest, or at the least the most conspicuous, of all the Hellenic solar heroes.[3] He is said to be a son of Zeus and Alkmene, born according to some in Argos according to others in Thebes. A few hours before his birth, Zeus, we are told, boasted to Hêrê that the child then to be born to the family of Perseus should be the mightiest of men. On hearing this, Hêrê, urged on by Atê, the spirit of mischief, caused Eurystheus to be born before Herakles, who was thus doomed to be the servant of his kinsman. So wroth, it is said, was Zeus when Hêrê told him that Eurystheus must according to his oath be king of Argos, that he seized Atê by the hair of her head, and, swearing that she should never again darken the courts of heaven, hurled her from Olympos. The whole life of Herakles thus became a long servitude to a master meaner and weaker than himself, and one continued self-sacrifice for the good of others, his most marked characteristic being an irresistible bodily strength, which is always used to help the

[1] AHI reappears in the Greek Echis, Echidna, the dragon which crushes its victim with its coil. It is, in short, anything that chokes, whether as *Anhas*, sin, or the Latin *angor*, anguish.

[2] The name Indra is sometimes used as a physical equivalent of Dyaus, the heaven, the clouds being said to move in Indra, as the Maruts, or winds, are described as coursing through Dyaus.

[3] The first part of his name is the same as that of Hêrê, and is, therefore, connected with Helios and the Vedic Surya.

weak and suffering, and for the destruction of all noxious things. The great harvest of myths which has sprung up round his name may be traced to the old phrases which had spoken of the glorious sun as toiling for so poor and weak a creature as man; as born to a life of toil; as entering on his weary tasks after a brief but happy infancy, and as sinking finally to his rest after a fierce battle with the storm clouds which had sought to hinder his journey.

His labours may be said to have begun in his cradle; but the toils known as the twelve labours of Herakles[1] are assigned to later periods of his life. In the Iliad and Odyssey, however, no attempt is made to classify his toils or his exploits. The stories of his infancy tell us that as he lay sleeping in his cradle, two snakes coiled themselves around him, and that the child on waking placed his hands round their necks, and gradually tightened his grasp until they fell dead upon the ground. These snakes are the serpents of the night, on which the sun may be said to lay his hands as he rises, and which he slays as he climbs higher into the heavens.[2] Exposed by his mother Alkmene on a barren plain, he is picked up by the dawn goddess Athênê, who beseeches Hêrê, the queen of the blue heaven, to suckle it. The child bites hard, and Hêrê flings it back to Athênê, who carries him to his mother. The boy grows up in the perfection of human strength and power. His teachers are Autolykos and Eurytos, the harper Linos, Kastor the twin brother of Polydeukes (Pollux), and the wise Centaur Cheiron, who is also the teacher of Asklepios, Iamos, and other heroes.

Thus far we have a time answering to that in which Phoebus is tended by the nymphs in his infancy, when his face is unsoiled and his raiment all white. We can readily understand that the myth may at this point be made to assume the moral aspect of self-denial. The smooth road of indulgence is the easiest for men to travel on, or it may seem to be so at first. But he who takes the rugged path of duty must do so from deliberate choice; and thus Herakles, going forth to his long series of labours, suggests to the sophist Prodikos the beautiful apologue in which Aretê and Kakia, virtue and vice, each claim his obedience. The one promises endless pleasures here and hereafter: the other holds out the prospect of hard days followed by healthful slumbers, and warns him that nothing good was ever won without labour, nothing great ever done without toil. The mind of Herakles is made up at once; and the greatest of all mythical heroes is thus made to enforce the highest lessons

---

[1] The idea of the twelve labours is not improbably Semitic.
[2] These snakes must be distinguished, therefore, from the serpents which impart wisdom to Iamos.

of human duty, and to present the highest standard of human action.

With this high heroic temper Herakles set forth on his great career. His great fight is with the lion of Kithairon (Cithaeron), from whose carcase (or from that of the lion of Nemea) he obtains the skin with which he is commonly represented. In many of the tales which are told of his later career the idea of lofty moral purpose is lost in the notion of constant wanderings in which the toil-worn hero gives himself to any enjoyments of the passing hour, but throughout which he is guarded by invulnerable armour. The coat of mail is brought to him by Athênê, as the armour of Achilles is brought to him by Thetis, and that of Sigurd in the Teutonic epic by his mother Hjordis. His bow and arrows he receives from Phoebus, the lord of the spear-like sunbeams; and from Hermes he obtains his sword, whose stroke may split the forest trees. The arrows, it must be especially noted, are poisoned: and these poisoned barbs are used by Philoktetes, who receives them from Neopto-lemos, the son of Achilles, and also by Odysseus. But we have no historical evidence that poisoned arrows were used by any Hellenic tribes, or that they would not have regarded the employment of such weapons with horror. How then comes it to pass that the Iliad and Odyssey can attribute to any Achaian heroes practices from which their kinsmen would, so far as we can form a judgment, have shrunk with disgust? The mystery is easily solved. The equivocation which turned the violet-tinted rays of morning into spears was inevitable: the change of the spears or arrows into poisoned barbs was, at the least, as natural and necessary, the words Ios and Ion, which furnished a name for the violet hue, for a spear, and for poison, being really homonyms, traceable to two or three roots. Nor are these the only derivatives from these roots which occur in the myths of Herakles. His stoutest ally is Iolaos, the son of Iphikles:[1] his earliest love is Iolê, the daughter of Eurytos, from whom, like Apollo from Daphne, he is parted in the spring-time of life, to see her again once more just when his career is ended.

As the conquest of the lion of Kithairon is the first great exploit, so, according to the later mythographers, who took delight in classi-fying his labours, the bringing up of the dog Kerberos (Cerberus) from Hades is the last. This story is mentioned in the Odyssey, in which Herakles tells Odysseus that his sufferings are but a reflexion of the toils which he had himself undergone through the tyranny of the mean Eurystheus, and that this task of bringing up the

[1] Iphikles is the twin brother of Herakles. He belongs thus to the class of Secondaries, or correlative deities.

hound of Hades had been achieved by the aid of Athênê and Hermes, the dawn and the breeze of the morning.[1] The dog of Yama, the Indian Hades, thus brought back is, of course, carried down again by Herakles to the lowest world.

But the sun, as he rises in the heavens, acquires a fiercer power; and hence Apollon becomes Chrysaor, and Herakles becomes mad. The raging heat burns up the fruits of the earth which the genial warmth had fostered; and so, in accordance with the idea which underlies the myths of Tantalos and Phaethon, Herakles slays his own children by Megara, and two also of the sons of Iphikles. On Laomedon, King of Ilion, who had refused to pay the promised recompense to Poseidon and Phoebus for building the walls of his city, and then cheated Herakles by giving him mortal horses in the place of the deathless steeds for which he had covenanted, the hero takes vengeance in the first Trojan war mentioned in the Iliad, which relates how, coming with six ships and a few men, he shattered its towns, and left its streets desolate.

Of the other exploits of Herakles the greater number explain themselves, although of some it would be rash to venture on an interpretation. The vast mass of tradition which has gathered round his name contains probably a certain amount of Semitic material, and some of the myths seem to reflect the feeling expressed in such legends as those of Pentheus and of Orpheus. The Nemean lion is the offspring of Orthros[2] or Echidna.[3] Another child of the same horrid parents is the Lernaian Hydra, a monster who, like Ahi, Vritra, the Sphinx, or the dragons of Pytho and Thebes, shuts up the waters and causes drought. The stag of Keryneia is, according to some versions, slain, in others only seized by Herakles, who bears it with its golden antlers and brazen feet to Artemis and Phoebus. The story of the Erymanthian boar is in some accounts transferred from Argos to Thessaly or Phrygia; the monster itself, which Herakles chases through the deep snow, being closely akin to the Chimera slain by Bellerophon. In the myth of the stables of Augeias, Herakles appears simply to play the part of Indra when he lets loose the imprisoned waters and sweeps away the filth accumulated on the land. The myth of the Cretan bull brings before us a dark and malignant monster driven mad by Poseidon; but Crete lay within the circle of Phoenician influence, and the bull may be the savage and devouring Moloch of Semitic theology. Although Herakles carries this monster home on his back, he is

[1] *Odyssey*, II, 623.
[2] The Greek form of the Vedic Vritra.
[3] The representative of the Vedic Ahi.

obliged to let it go again; and it reappears as the bull which ravages the fields of Marathon, till it is slain by the hands of Theseus, who is also the slayer of the Minotauros. In the noisome birds which take refuge in the Stymphalian lake because they are afraid of the wolves, we have perhaps a picture of the dark storm clouds dreading the rays of the sun,[1] which can only appear when they themselves have been defeated. The fertilizing rain-clouds appear yet again as the cattle stolen by Geryon, and recovered by Herakles in the story of Cacus. The legend of the golden apples guarded by the Hesperides is only a repetition of a like idea, the same word, Mêla, denoting in Greek both apples and sheep.[2]

The bondage of Apollo connects the story of Herakles with that of Admetos, the chieftain of the Thessalian Pherai, the happy husband of Alkestis, the most beautiful and the most loving of wives, and the lord of a house enriched by the labours of Phoebus, who has brought him health and wealth and all good things. One thing alone is wanting, and this even Apollo cannot grant to him. On the day of his marriage Admetos has made Artemis angry by neglecting her in a sacrifice. The goddess, however, promised that when the hour of his death came, he should escape his doom, if his father, mother, or wife should die for him. Alkestis agreed to do so; and it was her life that he could not win even from Phoebus himself. Thus in the very prime of her beauty she is summoned by Thanatos, death, to leave her home and children, and to cross with him the dark stream which severs the land of the living from the region of the dead; and although Phoebus intercedes for a short respite, the gloomy being whose debtor she is lays his icy hands upon her, and will not let her go until the mighty Herakles grapples with him, and, having by main force rescued her from his grasp, brings her back to her husband. Here, as in the myth of Orpheus, the disaster is brought about or portended by serpents; and when Admetos enters his bridal chamber on the day of his marriage, he sees on the bed a knot of twisted snakes. But although Alkestis may die, Death cannot hold her in his keeping; and the story thus resolves itself into the simple phrases which said that the dawn or twilight, which is the bride of the sun, must die, if she is to live again and stand before her lord in all her ancient beauty.

The narratives of these greater exploits are interspersed with numberless incidents of more or less significance, some of which

[1] The same root or word furnished a name for wolves, λύκοι, and for the rays of the sun. The growth of a myth converting the rays into wolves, would thus be inevitable. The connexion of these ideas is prominent in the story of Lykaon. The comparison of the Myrmidons of Achilles to wolves is especially striking.

[2] We shall see, later on, that a similar equivocation turned the seven stars into seven sages or seven bears.

plainly interpret themselves. Thus in his journey to the land of the Hesperides, he is tormented by the heat of the sun,[1] and shoots his arrows at Helios, who, admiring his bravery, gives him his golden cup wherein to cross the sea. It is a time of many changes, which crowd on each other during the season of his madness, from which he is told that he can be loosed only if he consents to serve for a time as a bondman. He is now sold to Omphalê, and assumes a half-feminine guise. But even with this story of subjection a vast number of exploits are interwoven, among these being the slaying of a serpent on the river Sygaris, and the hunting of the Kalydonian boar. His union with Deianeira, the daughter of the chief of Kalydon, brings us to the closing scenes of his troubled and tumultuous career. He unwittingly slays the boy Eunomos; and refusing to accept the pardon which is freely offered to him, he departs into exile with his wife. At the ford of a river he entrusts her to the charge of the Kentaur (Centaur) Nessos, who acted as ferryman, and who, for attempting to lay hands on Deianeira, is fatally wounded by the hero. In his last moments Nessos bids her preserve his blood, as the sure means of recovering her husband's love if it should be transferred to another.

When at length the evening of his life was come, Deianeira received the tidings that her husband was returning in triumph from Oechalia, not alone, but bringing with him the beautiful Iolê, from whom he had long been parted. Remembering the words of Nessos, Deianeira steeps in his blood the white garment which, at the bidding of Herakles, Lichas comes to fetch from Trachis. The hero is about to offer sacrifice to the Kenaian Zeus, and he wishes to offer it up in peace, clad in a seemly robe of pure white, with Iolê standing by his side. But so it is not to be. Scarcely has he put on the robe, when the poison begins to course through his veins and to rack every limb with agony unspeakable. Once more the suffering hero is lashed into madness, and seizing the luckless Lichas, he hurls him into the sea. Borne at last to the heights of Oeta, he gathers wood, and charges those who are round him to set the pile on fire, when he shall have laid himself down upon it. Only the

---

[1] In reference to such incidents as these, Mr. Paley says: 'A curious but well-known characteristic of solar myths is the identification of the sun both with the agent or patient, and with the thing or object on or by which the act is exercised. Ixion is the sun, and so is Ixion's wheel. . . . Hercules is the sun, who expires in flame on the summit of Mount Oeta; but the fiery robe which scorched him to death is the sun-cloud. Now this, so far from being an objection to the theory, goes far to confirm it. It is the unconscious blending of two modes of representation—the sun as a person, and the sun as a thing. To construct a story, there must be both agents and subject-matter for action; and both, from different points of view, may be the same.' ('On the Origin of Solar Myths,' *Dublin Review*, July 1879, p. 109.)

shepherd Poias ventures to do the hero's will; but when the flame is kindled the thunder crashes through the heaven, and a cloud comes down which bears him away to Olympos, there to dwell in everlasting youth with the radiant Hêbê as his bride. It is the last incident in what has been called the Tragedy of Nature—the battle of the sun with the clouds, which gather round him like mortal enemies at his setting. As he sinks, the fiery mists embrace him, and the purple vapours rush across the sky, like streams of blood gushing from the hero's body, while the violet-coloured evening clouds seem to cheer him in his dying agony.

There is, however, a comic as well as a tragic side to the career of Herakles. The sun may be spoken of as one who toils for us; but he may also be said to enjoy in every land the fruits which he has ripened. Hence in many stories Herakles is a being fond of eating and drinking; and thus when in the house of Admetos he learns that his host has just lost his wife, he regards this as no reason why he should lose his dinner. The same burlesque spirit marks the conflict with Thanatos (death), in which Herakles rescues Alkestis (Alcestis) from his grasp.

After the death of Herakles, his tyrant Eurystheus insisted, it is said, on the surrender of his sons. Hyllos, the son of Deianeira, hastily fled away with his brothers, and after wandering to many places, found a refuge in Athens. This was only saying in other words that on the death of the sun the golden hues of evening are soon banished from the sky, but that after many weary hours they are seen again in the country of the Dawn,[1] as indeed they could be seen nowhere else.

The tale of Troy and Ilion is simply another tale of stolen treasure which is recovered after a fierce struggle from the powers of darkness, which had carried them away from the West. It consists of that series of legends which together make up the mythical history of Paris, Helen, Achilles, and Odysseus. Parts only of this tale—and, indeed, a very small part—are contained in the Iliad and Odyssey, to which almost exclusively we are in the habit of giving the name of Homer; but expressions and hints scattered throughout these poems prove clearly that the poets were acquainted with many incidents and episodes of the story, about which they did not care to speak in detail. The tale begins with the birth of Paris, whose mother Hekabê (Hecuba) dreamt that her son was a torch which would destroy the city of Ilion. Owing to this

[1] Attica, the land of Athênê.

foreboding of evil, the child was exposed, we are told, on the heathy sides of Mount Ida; but, like other Fatal Children, he was rescued by a shepherd, and growing up beautiful, brave, and vigorous, was called Alexandros, the helper of men.[1] Supposing him to be dead, his father Priam ordered a sacrifice to be offered up for his repose in Hades, and his servants chose the favourite bull of Paris, who followed them and was conqueror in his own funeral games. Although no one else knew him, his sister Kasandra, to whom Phoebus had given the power of second sight, under the penalty that her predictions should not be believed, told them who the victor was. Paris, however, refused to stay with those who had treated him so cruelly in his infancy, and in the dells of Ida he won as his bride Oinônê (Oenone), the beautiful daughter of the stream Kebren. With her he remained, until he departed for Sparta with Menelaos, an event brought about by incidents far away in the West, which were to lead to mighty issues.

At the marriage feast of Peleus and Thetis, Eris (strife), who had not been invited with the other deities, cast on the table a golden apple, which was to be given to the fairest of all the guests. It was claimed by Hêrê, Athênê and Aphroditê, and Zeus made Paris the umpire. By him, as we have seen, it was given to Aphroditê, who in return promised him Helen, the fairest of all women as his wife. Some time after this there fell on Sparta a sore famine, from which the Delphian oracle said that they could be delivered only by bringing back the bones of the children of Prometheus. For this purpose Menelaos, the king, came to Ilion, and returned with Paris, who saw the beautiful Helen at Sparta, and carried her away with her treasures to Troy. Resolving to rescue her from Paris, Menelaos invited Agamemnon, king of Mykenai (Mycenae), and other great chieftains to take part in the expedition which was to avenge his wrongs and to recover the wealth of which he had been despoiled. Among these chiefs were the aged Nestor, the wise ruler of Pylos; Aias (Ajax), the son of Telamon; Askalaphos and Ialmenos, sons of Arês; Diomedes, son of Tydeus; and Admetos of Pherai, the husband of Alkestis. But the greatest of all were Achilles, the son of Peleus and the sea-nymph Thetis, and Odysseus, the son of Laertes, chieftain of Ithaca.

The forces thus gathered went to Troy by sea; but the fleet was becalmed in Aulis, and Kalchas, the seer, affirming that this was caused by the anger of Artemis for the slaughter of a stag in her

---

[1] If the first part of the word be taken to mean what it evidently means in Alexikakos, the name is susceptible of another interpretation; but it seems unnecessary to resort to this alternative here.

sacred grove, declared that she could be appeased only by the sacrifice of Iphigeneia, the daughter of Agamemnon. According to the story in the Iliad the sacrifice was made; but there was another version which said that Artemis herself rescued Iphigeneia, while others again said that Artemis and Iphigeneia were one and the same. If, however, her blood was shed, the penalty must be paid; and so in the terrible drama of Aeschylus we find the Atê, whose office it is to exact this penalty to the last farthing, brooding on the house of Agamemnon, until she had brought about the death of the king by the hands of his wife Klytaimnestra (Clytemnestra), and the death of Klytaimnestra and her paramour Aigisthos by the hands of her son Orestes.

The hindrance to the eastward course of the Achaians was now removed, but the achievement of their task was still far distant. Nine years must pass in seemingly hopeless struggle; in the tenth, Ilion would be taken. So mighty was to be the defence of the city, maintained chiefly by Hektor, the son of Priam and brother of Paris, aided by the chiefs of the neighbouring cities, among whom were Aineias (Aeneas), son of Anchises and Aphroditê; Pandaros, son of Lykaon, and bearer of the bow of Apollo; and Sarpêdôn, who with his friend Glaukos led the Lykians from the banks of the eddying Xanthos. The legend of this brilliant hero is, as we have seen, one of the many independent myths which have been introduced into the framework of our Iliad. He is distinctly a being of the same order with Saranyû, Erinys, Iason, Helen, and many more; and the process which made him an ally of Paris is that which separated Odysseus from the eye of the Cyclops, whom he blinded. Another episode of a like kind is that of Memnon, who, like Sarpêdôn, comes from a bright and glistering land; but instead of Lykia it is in this instance Ethiopia. The meaning of the name Sarpêdôn had been so far forgotten that the chief was regarded as a ruler of mortal Lykians, and we are told that his cairn was raised high to keep alive his name amongst his people, although there were versions of the myth which brought him back again to life. But Eôs, the mother of Memnon, is so transparently the morning, that her child must rise again as surely as the sun reappears to run his daily course across the heaven. Like Sarpêdôn, he is doomed to an early death, and when he is smitten by the hand of Achilles, the tears of Eôs are said to fall as morning dew from the sky. To comfort her Zeus makes two flocks of birds meet in the air and fight over his funeral sacrifice, until some of them fall as victims on the altar. But Eôs is not yet satisfied, and she not only demands but wins the return of her child from Hades. The thought of a later age becomes manifest in the tale that when Memnon fell in atonement for the slaughter of Antilochos, his comrades were so plunged in grief that they were changed into birds which yearly visited his tomb to water the ground with their tears.

The story of Achilles himself has many points of marked likeness to the myths of these two heroes; but his guardian Phenix actually recites to him the career of Meleagros as the very counterpart of his own. What the career of Meleagros really signifies we have already seen; and we need only mark what the Iliad tells us, if we would trace the unconscious fidelity of the poet to the types of character sketched out for him in the old mythical phrases. Achilles is pre-eminently the irresistible hero who fights in a quarrel which is not his own. As Herakles served the mean Eurystheus, so Achilles is practially the servant of one on whom he looks down with deserved contempt. But he has his consolation in the love of Briseis, and when he is called upon to surrender the maiden, he breaks out into the passion of wrath which in the opening lines of the Iliad is said to be the subject of the poem. Although the fury of his rage is subdued by the touch of the dawn-goddess Athênê, he yet vows a solemn vow that henceforth in the war the Achaians shall look in vain for his aid. But inasmuch as in many of the books which follow the first the Achaian heroes get on perfectly well without him, winning great victories over the Trojans,[1] and as no reference is made in them to his wrath or to its consequences, the conclusion seems to be forced upon us that these books belong to an independent poem which really was an Iliad, or a history of the struggle of the Achaians for the possession of Ilion or Troy; and that this Iliad, which begins with the second book, has been pieced together with the other poem, which relates to the wrath of Achilles and its results, and is therefore an Achillêis. Thus the poem which we call the Iliad would consist of two poems, into which materials from other poems may or may not also have been worked in. It is, of course, quite possible that these two poems, the Iliad and the Achillêis, may both be the work of one and the same poet, who chose thus to arrange his own compositions; and this is the opinion of some whose judgment on such points is worthy of respect. But although the question is one on which an absolute decision may be unattainable, the balance of likelihood seems to be in favour of the conclusion that these great epic poems grew up in the course of a long series of ages. We have already seen how the germs of a story full of human passion and feeling might be found in epithets, in

[1] *Myth. of Ar. Nat.*, i, 240. Mure, *Critical History of Greek Literature*, i, 256. Grote, *History of Greece*, Part I, ch. xxi.

words, or in phrases, which the forefathers of the Aryan tribes, while yet in their original home, applied consciously to the sights and sounds of the outward world, these sights and sounds being regarded as the work of beings who could feel, and suffer, and toil, and rejoice like ourselves. This language was, strictly, the language of poetry, literally revelling in its boundless powers of creation and development. In almost every word lay the material of some epical incident; and it is the less wonderful, therefore, if each incident was embodied in a separate legend, or even reproduced in the independent tales of separate tribes. A hundred Homers may well have lit their torch from this living fire.[1]

In the ninth book we return to the subject of the wrath of Achilles. The victorious career of the Achaian chieftains is interrupted, and they are made to feel their need of the great hero, who keeps away from the strife. But the embassy which they send to him goes to no purpose, although Phenix holds up to him as a warning the doom of the Kalydonian Meleagros. There must be humble submission, and Briseis must be restored. But Agamemnon cannot yet bring himself to this abasement, and the struggle goes on with varying success and disaster, until their misfortunes so multiply as to excite the compassion of Patroklos, the friend who reflects the character of Achilles without possessing his strength, and who thus belongs to the class of Secondaries. Melted by the tears of this friend, Achilles gave him his own armour, and bade him go forth to aid the Argives, adding a strict caution, which cannot fail to remind us of the story of Phaethon. As Phaethon is charged not to touch the horses of Helios with his whip, so Patroklos must not drive the chariot of Achilles, which is borne by the same undying steeds, on any other path than that which has been pointed out to him. But we are especially told that although Patroklos could wear his friend's armour, he could not wield his spear. The sword and lance of the sun-god may be used by no other hands than his own. As in the story of Phaethon, so here the command was disobeyed; and thus Patroklos, after slaying Sarpêdôn, was himself overpowered and killed by Hektor, who stripped off from his body the glittering armour of his friend. In the heart of that friend the tidings of his death rekindled the fury of the passion which had long been only smouldering. Beneath 'the black cloud of his sorrow' his anguish was preparing an awful vengeance. The beauty of his countenance was marred; but the nymphs rose up from the sea to comfort him. To all consolation he replies that he must have revenge; and when

[1] For a full examination of ¦the question of the composition of the Homeric poems, see *Myth. of Ar. Nat.*, Book I, ch. ix–xi and the works there referred to.

Thetis, his mother, warns him that the death of Hektor must soon be followed by his own, his answer is that even Herakles, the dearest son of Zeus, had submitted to the same hard lot, and that he is ready to face it himself. He has still his unerring spear; and it only remains that he should wait for the glistening armour, wrought on the anvil of the fire-god Hephaistos. But although the hour of his vengeance is not yet come, his countenance still had its terrors, and the very sight of his form filled the Trojans with dismay, as they heard his well-known war cry. His work is in part done. The body of Patroklos is recovered, and Achilles makes a vow that the blood of twelve Trojans shall gush in twelve streams on the altar of sacrifice. But the old phrases which spoke of Herakles as subject to death, still spoke of both as coming forth conquerors of the power which had seemed to subdue them; and true to the ancient speech, the poet makes Thetis assure her son that no hurtful thing shall touch the body of Patroklos, and that, though it should be untended the whole year round, his face should wear at its close a more glorious and touching beauty.

The end now draws nigh. Agamemnon is so far humbled, that he promises to yield to him the maiden whom he had taken away; but with a persistency which except by thinking of the sources of the story we cannot understand, he asserts his own innocence. 'I am not guilty,' he said; 'the blame rests with Zeus and Moira, and Erinys who wanders in the air.' So, again, although on the reappearance of Briseis, Achilles forgives the wrong, he repeats the riddle which lurked in the words of Agamemnon. There was nothing in the son of Atreus, he says, which could really call forth his wrath. 'He could never, in his utter helplessness, have taken the maiden from me against my will; but so Zeus would have it, that the doom of many Achaians might be accomplished.' So he bids them go and eat, and make ready for the fight; but when Agamemnon would have Achilles himself feast with him, he replies that he will touch neither food nor drink until he has won the victory which will give him his revenge.

The same truthfulness to the ideas furnished by the old mythical phrases runs through the magnificent passage which tells us of the arming of Achilles. The picture is more splendidly drawn and coloured; but we are taken back to the imagery of the Vedic hymns, to Indra or to Ushas, as we read that the helmets of the humbler warriors were like the cold snow clouds which gather in the north, but that when Achilles donned his armour, a glorious light flashed up to heaven, and the earth laughed at its dazzling radiance. His shield, we are told, gleamed like the blood-red morn, as it rises from

[153]

the sea; his helmet glittered like a star; each hair on the plume glistened like burnished gold; and when he tried the armour to see whether it fitted him, it bore his limbs like a bird upon the wing. But when, having taken up his spear, he mounts his chariot, and bids his immortal horses bear him safe through the battle, and not leave him to die as they left Patroklos, he hears again the warning of his early death. The horse Xanthos bows his head, and tells him that, though their force is not abated, and their will is only to save the lord whom they serve and love, the will of Zeus is stronger yet, and Achilles must die. But he answers again, as he had answered before, that, whatever may follow, the work of vengeance must be accomplished. Through the wild confusion of the fight which follows, Achilles hastens surely to his victory. His great enemy Hektor appears before him; but although Phoebus has forsaken him, yet Achilles cannot reach him through his own armour, which Hektor had stripped from the body of Patroklos, and which he was now wearing. The death-wound is given where an opening in the plates left the neck bare. The prayer of Hektor for mercy is dismissed with contempt, and in his boundless rage Achilles tramples on the body —a trait of savagery scarcely to be explained by a reference to the manners of the Greeks in any age, but quite intelligible when we compare it with the mythical language of the Eastern Vedic hymns, which speak of the sun as stamping mercilessly on his conquered enemies.

The story of the Iliad is completed with the narrative which tells us how the aged Priam, guided by Hermes, came to Achilles, and embracing his knees, begged for the body of his son, over which Phoebus Apollo had spread his golden shield to keep away all unseemly things, and how it was borne back to Ilion, where his wife, Andromache, bitterly bemoaned her loss, and all the Trojans wept for the hero who had fought for them so bravely.

At this point our Iliad comes to an end; but from the Odyssey we learn that Achilles was slain by Paris and Phoebus Apollo at the Skaian or western gates; that Thetis with her sea-nymphs rose from the water and wrapped his body in shining robes; that after many days the Achaians placed it on the funeral pile, and that his ashes were laid in a golden urn brought by Hephaistos, over which a great cairn was raised, that men might see it afar off as they sailed on the broad Hellespontos, an expression which seems to show that the Hellespont of the Iliad was not merely the narrow strait between Sestos and Abydos, but a wider sea, so-called probably from a people named Helloi or Selloi, who lived on its shores and crossed it in their migration from the east to the west.

[154]

Thus the whole Achilleis seems to be a magnificent solar epic, telling us of a sun rising in radiant majesty, and early separated from the beautiful twilight of the dawn, soon hidden by the clouds, yet abiding his time of vengeance, when from the dark veil he breaks forth at last in more than his early strength, scattering the mists and kindling the rugged clouds which form his funeral pyre nor caring whether the splendour of his victory shall be succeeded by a darker battle as the vapours close again over his dying glory. From other sources we learn that after the death of Achilles the Achaians took Ilion and burnt it, and that Priam and his people were slain. Paris himself, smitten with the poisoned arrows of Philoktetes, fled to Mount Ida, where, as he lay dying, Oenônê appeared before him, beautiful and loving as ever. But though her love might soothe him, it could not heal a wound inflicted by the weapons of Herakles. So Paris died on Ida, and Oenônê also died upon his funeral pile which her own hands kindled.

This wonderful siege of Troy is, it has been well said,[1] simply a repetition of the daily siege of the east by the solar powers that every evening are robbed of their brightest treasures in the west. We have to mark that quite as much stress is laid on the stealing away of the treasures of Helen as on the stealing away of Helen herself, and that we have precisely the same feature in all the great epics of Northern Europe. Of the names of the actors in this great drama some certainly are found in the mythology of the East. The name Helen, we have seen, is that of the Indian Saramâ; and Paris is Pani, the deceiver, who, when Saramâ comes seeking the cows of Indra, beseeches her to remain with him. Although Saramâ refuses to do so, she yet accepts from him a drink of milk; and this passing disobedience to the commands given to her may be the germ of that unfaithfulness of Helen which causes the Trojan war. Whether the name Achilles is that of the solar hero Aharyu, it may be unwise to determine; but it seems more certain that Briseis, who is one of the first captives taken by the Achaians, is the offspring of Brisaya, who in the Veda is conquered by the bright powers before they can recover the treasures stolen by the Panis.

A specially remarkable feature in this story of the Trojan war is the blending of different ideas. A hero may belong to the powers which represent the night and darkness; but the groundwork for the incidents of an heroic career were supplied by phrases which spoke of the toils, the battles, and the victories of the sun and thus regarded, the heroes would reflect a splendour to which, in their relation to their enemies, they would have no right. Thus, as stealing

[1] Max Müller, *Lectures on Language*, Second Series, p. 471.

Helen from the Western Sparta or as abetting in this theft, Paris and all the Trojans represent the dark powers who steal away 'the twilight from the western sky. But in the lives of many of the Trojan chiefs, as perhaps or possibly in that of Paris himself,[1] we have a repetition of the life of Meleagros, Perseus, and other solar heroes. As to Achilles, the points of likeness are beyond question. The key-note of the myth of Herakles, namely, subjection to an inferior, is the key-note of the myth of the great Phthiotic chieftain; and the parting from Briseis is an incident which we look for in all such tales. In the vow which follows his loss we see the veiling of the sun behind the dark clouds; and as the golden rays are no longer seen when his face is hidden, so his followers the Myrmidons no longer appear on the battle-field when their chief hangs up his spear and shield within his tent. These followers are in the Iliad persistently compared with wolves, and we have seen how nearly the Greek name for wolves, given to them, we cannot doubt, from the glossiness of their skin, is allied to words denoting brightness. The rays of the sun would in the old mythical language of poetry be called Lukoi or Lykians; and as the meaning of the phrase became in part forgotten, the Myrmidons, who are simply the sun's rays, would be naturally compared to wolves with gleaming eyes and blood-red jaws. The conflict which precedes the death of Hektor is the mighty battle of the vapours and the sun, who seems to trample on the darkness, as Achilles tramples on the body of Hektor; and as this victory of the sun is gained just when he is sinking into the sea, so the death of Achilles is said to follow very soon after that of Hektor. So again the fight over the dead body of Achilles is the story of a stormy evening, when the clouds fight over the dead sun. The main conclusion is this, that the chief incidents of the story, and even the main features in the character of the chief heroes, were handed down ready-made for the Homeric poets. They might leave out this or that incident; but they were not free to alter the general character of any. Thus they must describe Achilles as fighting in a quarrel which was not his own—as robbed of Briseis—as furious with rage and grief at her loss—as hiding himself in his tent—as sending out Patroklos instead of appearing himself on the battle-field—as shedding the blood of human victims on the funeral pile of his friend,

[1] The beauty of Paris may have been from the first the beauty of the night, cloudless and still. This beauty is evidently signified by the myth of Medousa, as well as by the legends of Kalypso and the fairy queens who tempt Tanhaüser and True Thomas to their caves. Professor Goldziher has shown that in the mythology of the Hebrews the myths of the night are far more important than those of the day, and that they ascribe to the night not only a singular beauty, but a wonderful restorative power. The conditions of the Assyrian climate render this fact easily intelligible.

and as dying early after his bright but troubled career. This necessity seems to explain the whole character of Achilles, which, regarded as that of an Achaian chief, seems untrue not only to their national character but to human nature. His portrait, as drawn in the Iliad, is not only not Achaian; it can scarcely be called human. There is no evidence that Achaian chiefs visited on those who were manifestly innocent the wrong doings of the guilty; that they had no sense of duty, and no sympathy for the sufferings of those had had never injured them; that they offered human sacrifices, or that they fought with poisoned arrows, or that they mangled the corpses of brave enemies whom they had slain. But although we have no evidence that Achaian chiefs ever did such things, it is easy to see that such stories could not fail to spring up, when phrases which had at first denoted the varying action of the sun were regarded as relating to the deeds and sufferings of human beings.

The return of the heroes from Troy is an event answering precisely to the return of Iason (Jason) and his comrades from Kolchis: as they bring back the golden fleece, so Menelaos returns with Helen and her treasures to Sparta. These legends are uniform and consistent only so far as they represent the heroes returning from the east to the west. Otherwise the incidents, and the names of persons and places, are changed almost at will. The tombs of Odysseus, Aineias (Aeneas), and many others, were shown in many places, for it was as easy to take them to one country as to another.

Of these returning chieftains, the most conspicuous is Odysseus, the tale of whose wanderings is given in the Odyssey, and whose story practically reproduces that of Herakles or Perseus, for the simple reason that the return from Ilion to Achaia represents the return journey of the day from east to west. His life, like that of all kindred heroes, is marked by strange changes of happiness and misery, by successes and reverses, ending in complete victory, as the lights and shadows of a stormy and gloomy day are often scattered at sundown by the effulgence of the bright orb whose glory they have so long hidden. Thus Odysseus becomes a counterpart of Achilles, the main difference being that Achilles represents the action of the sun in his strength and his capricious fitfulness, while the character of Odysseus is that of Phoebus, Asklepios, Iamos, and Medeia, the possessors of a marvellous and superhuman wisdom. The desire ever present to his mind is an intense yearning to be united again with his wife, whom he left long ago at eventide in the bloom of her youthful beauty. Thus, although, as he journeys homewards, he is often tempted to tarry or turn aside in his course, he cannot be made to give up his purpose. It is impossible for Helios

[157]

and Surya to deviate from the course marked out for them whether in their daily or their yearly round. The stone which Sisyphos rolls to the top of the hill must roll down again; and the blood of Sisyphos, we must remember, flows in the veins of Odysseus.

## [ 4  ROBERT  BROWN ]

Not all celestial mythologists linked their destiny exclusively with ancient India and the Rig-Veda. Robert Brown, Jr., F.S.A. of Barton-on-Humber (1844–1912) contended strenuously in esoteric studies of Near Eastern deities for Semitic influences on Greek mythology. While ending up with the customary solar, lunar, and stellar readings, he began with the obscured divinities of Egypt, Assyria, Babylonia, Chaldea, and Judaea. Brown suffered from a double grievance: one, because his beloved Near East had been slighted in favour of classical India and Greece, and two, because, he fell outside the intellectual Establishment centred in Oxford, Cambridge, and London. Forced to bear a commonplace name, he seems to have fallen into confusion with other Robert Browns, such as his namesake from Barton-on-Humber who wrote on theological issues. In his presidential address for 1896, Edward Clodd mentioned the death of Robert Brown the preceding year. Yet Brown published his vigorous attack on Lang, *Semitic Influence in Hellenic Mythology*, in 1898, and he is writing *Notes on the Earlier History of Barton-on-Humber* in two volumes produced in 1906 and 1908. There he declares that he alone of his family still lives in Barton, weighted down with 'advancing years and rapidly increasing infirmities,' and that only late in life has he 'turned to local history and topography.' Stung by Lang's barbs, and hungry for praise, Brown found solace in the deference of Prime Minister Gladstone, whom he claims to have converted from an old-fashioned Christian interpretation of Homer to his own thesis of Semitic elements in the Hellenic pantheon (*Mr. Gladstone As I Knew Him, And Other Essays*, 1902).

Brown could not rely on Müller's argument of linguistic identities within a common language family and so resorted to the reasoning that borrowing took place between peoples in close historic contact with each other. Clearly the barbarous Greeks would be the borrowers from their civilized neighbours to the East.

Text from Robert Brown, *Semitic Influence in Hellenic Mythology, with special reference to the recent mythological works of the Rt.*

*Hon. Prof. F. Max Müller and Mr. Andrew Lang* (London: Williams and Norgate, 1898). Pages 81–100, from Part III, 'The Aryo-Semitic School of Hellenic Mythologists.'

## I. Retrospect

In the last century, which is practically removed from us by hundreds of years, it was very generally supposed that Hebrew was the primeval language; and that the gods and stories of mythology were either derived from the circumstances recorded in the Old Testament, or else were events of general history clothed by time in fables, more or less obscure and distorted. The great scholars of the sixteenth and seventeenth centuries, distinguished by their immense erudition and untiring industry, have been of inestimable service in handing down to us the Classical materials for research. As far as their lights permitted, they, as of course, did more than justice to Semitic influence in regions Hellenic; and, after all necessary abatements, such names as *e.g.*, that of Bochart, will ever be held in honour. But they were succeeded by an inferior race, marked by an ever narrowing view, a portentous bigotry, and a philology which, lasting in many instances well into the present century, expired at length in a mere nightmare of absurdities. Says Prof. Skeat:—

'I have had so much to unlearn, during the endeavour to teach myself, owing to the extreme folly and badness of much of the English etymological literature current in my earlier days, that the avoidance of errors [by him] has been impossible'; and he alludes to 'the playful days of Webster's Dictionary . . . when the derivation of native English words from Ethiopic and Coptic was a common thing' (*Principles of Eng. Etymol.*, 2nd series, p. ix).

During the last 150 years England has also produced a curious race of 'Cranks,' by no means yet extinct, who have brought forth various extraordinary works purporting to explain all the history, mystery and belief of the past on philological and general lines purely imaginary. Some of these productions in their day took an honoured place in almost every library; and, from their appearance in booksellers' catalogues, would seem still to command high prices, a touching illustration of the value which mankind almost always puts upon certain peculiar kinds of folly. I do not name any of them, as they are quite unworthy even of such publicity as may be afforded by the pillory.

The follies of Mr. Casubon and his brethren produced in the earlier part of this century a great reaction, in which Germany took the lead. The old-fashioned notions were contemptuously abolished almost *en bloc*. The motto of this new school was 'Greece for the Greeks.' Numerous ancient errors perished forever, but, unfortunately, with them a certain proportion of truth was also thrown overboard. Semitic influence in Greece was scouted as an absurdity; and perhaps the high-water mark in this reaction was reached when 'Kadmos' was declared to be a pure Hellenic name. That time has gone by; and now the schoolboy can read in his Liddell and Scott: 'Κάδμος. The man from the East; cf. Hebr. *Kedem*.' Such is

'Action and reaction
The miserable see-saw of our child-world.'

But the German Classical school were, despite their errors, immeasurably superior to the folly which they overthrew; and such names as *e.g.*, Otfried Müller, will ever remain examples of a superb Classical scholarship, which erred in many details only because it was necessarily ignorant of a mass of knowledge, much of which is a commonplace even to the smatterer of today.

Upon this great scientific advance there followed, its cause being mainly due in the first instance to the British power in India, the gradual rise of a scientific comparative philology, bringing in its train the great truth of the original unity of the Aryan or Indo-European nations, and necessarily producing a study of comparative mythology, which in its logical development, is, as of course, not merely Aryan, but also Semitic, Turanian, and world-wide. The life of Prof. Max Müller, the leading exponent in England of this mighty movement, almost covers its present historical extent. Upon its discoveries and its merits I need not dwell. In this work I am concerned in the endeavour to show that the Aryanists, like the Classical phalanx of Otfried Müller carried away by the splendour of their achievements, have pushed their claims too far, and have not conceded sufficient place to that great historical influence, which, as the years roll, it becomes ever clearer and clearer that the Semitic East exercised upon archaic Hellas. 'The gods will give us some faults to make us men.' The Churches 'of Jerusalem, Alexandria, and Antioch have erred'; and shall the Assemblies of Mythologists altogether escape a similar fate?

Contemporaneous with this last-named movement came that astonishing advance in our knowledge of the ancient and archaic non-Classical world, which we denote by such terms as Egyptology and Assyriology, the latter expression very incorrect indeed, but perhaps too well established in use and general understanding to be altered now. The buried past has risen majestic from the grave of ages, and her train of shadowy kings,—scoffed at by many a great Classical scholar such as Cornewall Lewis,—confronts us as living realities, and even in some instances, like that of a Rameses the Great, actually face to face. Champollion, Lepsius, Birch, Mariette, Maspero, Renouf, Grotefend, Rawlinson, George Smith, what a debt we owe to them, and to their worthy followers and successors in these supremely interesting and important studies.

Lastly, Anthropology has taken the field, represented by many an acute and industrious student and compiler. All honour to them, and success to their efforts! In dealing with the past, skilled assistance from every quarter is most valuable; particularly as the problems to be attacked are almost invariably complex in character, being frequently partly explicable on one line of research and partly on another.

## II. Certain Difficulties of the Student in England

In England the student of the higher and obscurer branches of knowledge, unless he chance to be altogether exceptionally favoured by circumstance and environment, will probably find his lot rather a hard one. He must not expect any of that Government support which France and Germany so carefully and so admirably extend to rising talent. He must renounce all that popularity and the substantial rewards which are bestowed upon the abler of those artists whose themes are morbid piety, prudery, petticoats, or popular demonology. Nor must he expect much sympathy from his more fortunate brethren, until indeed he has become an important personage. Reviewers and critics, should they condescend to notice him, will probably treat him with but scant courtesy, expecially if he chance not to reside in London, Oxford, or Cambridge. And if any well-disposed Nicodemus ventures faintly to ask for a patient hearing for the unfortunate wight, he will be contemptuously told that no profit of any kind arises out of Galilee. I am aware that the reviewer has been much found fault with of late; and we must ever remember that his task is often a very hard one, and that the constant and necessary assumption of a diluted omniscience, whilst all the time he may be but too conscious of a very real and genuine ignorance, will frequently reveal a weary face when the mask is withdrawn. The student, moreover, may often find that unless by some means he can gain the goodwill of certain circles, coteries or cliques, let him write as he may, he will, to a considerable extent, be left out in the cold. I have known several painful instances where men of great powers and great knowledge have dropped sadly and prematurely into the grave, crushed by a grinding poverty and an unjust neglect. But it is not in the nature of the Englishman to yield in such a struggle. And just as our colossal and so deeply envied Empire has been almost entirely built up by the unaided, and even often deeply thwarted, efforts of private individuals, so in the grand fields of research the high-hearted student, even if this great authority be ignorant of him and that important centre acknowledge him not, will yet work on, whilst health and strength permit, content to try to do his duty, however unnoticed and obscure. And I can, from my own experience, assure him of this, that such studies, pursued for their own sake, grow sweeter even as they grow more arduous; and that I for one am deeply grateful to Greeks, Etruscans, Babylonians and others, for the delightful problems which they have bequeathed to us.


*III. General Standpoint of the Aryo-Semitic School*


The Aryo-Semitic school of Hellenic mythologists, whilst fully recognizing the immense services rendered to the cause of knowledge by the old Classical scholars and the Aryanists, and also duly acknowledging the valuable assistance of anthropological research, endeavours, as the special feature of its method, to give the fullest effect to the ever-increasing mass of light which has been thrown by modern discovery upon the archaic history of Egypt and Western Asia in their relation to Hellas. They recognize that for hundreds of years before the commencement of the Olympiads, the Greeks were in close contact with the mixed peoples of Asia Minor, Aryan, and non-Aryan, with the Phoenicians; and, to some extent, even with the Egyptians, who, as early as the Sixth Dynasty, called the Mediterranean 'the Great Circle of the Uinivu,' Sem. Yivâmas (*i.e.*, Javanians) = Ionians. The Aryo-Semitic school gives, which others do not, their legitimate weight to these historical facts. Painting and sculpture, architecture, astronomy, and arithmetic (*vide* Strabo, XVI, ii, 24), the arts of commerce and navigation, weights and measures, the treasures of the forge and the loom, for such gifts

[162]

as these, and for many other features of civilization the Greek, as we know, was indebted to the non-Aryan East. That when he received them, he breathed upon them the splendour and the energy of his own genius is nothing to the present purpose. We know likewise that in the well-known historical period the Greek, like the Roman after him, was ever most willing to receive the foreign divinity and to adopt the foreign ritual. Adônis was the darling of the Athenian matrons of the time of the Peloponnesian war; Alexander accepted Melqârth and Amen, Yahveh and Bel, as fast as he met with their ritual and their votaries (*vide* Hogarth, *Alexander of Macedon*, p. 209); and, when Zeus-Jupiter had long been degraded to a mere planetary genius, Isis, Serapis and Mithras swayed the conservative religionists of the Roman Empire. Apart from evidence, therefore, is it not probable that the archaic Greek, a semi-barbarian with an immense capacity for borrowing, would take somewhat of the religion and ritual of those to whom he owed so much in other ways, and who, from the point of knowledge and civilization, were so greatly his superiors? It would, moreover, be all the easier for him to do this as, to a very great extent, he could do it almost unconsciously. And the cause of this lies in the fact that the Greek was ever prone to find his own divinities in the gods of the nations whom he met. Again and again he speaks of Zeus and Hêra, Athêna and Artemis, when in reality he refers to Semitic divinities entirely distinct. Hêrodotos goes to Egypt, and finds there almost all his Greek gods in full force; just as men since have talked about Juno at Carthage. And this constant habit of the Greek mind, utterly misunderstood, has caused immense confusion in the views and writings of mythologists. Taking such statements as true, *verbatim et literatim*, they have indulged in a vast amount of absolute nonsense. And, although now every scholar understands how these presentments of fact by Hêrodotos and others are to be received, yet, even at the present day, such a giant in scholarship as Prof. Max Müller apparently believes that *e.g.*, the goddess Athêna Onka of Thebes is indeed a variant of his own beloved Ahanâ.

Next, what is the philological aspect of the question? We do not compare the names of Roman and Peruvian divinities because there is neither a linguistic nor an historical connexion between the two nations. And if we find similar customs among them, *e.g.*, each buried their erring vestal virgins alive, we see that such usages spring from causes which operate upon the general mind of mankind, and are independent of any special circumstances. We compare the divinities of Vedic India and of Greece, because there was once an historical connexion between the ancestors of Indians and

[163]

Greeks; and because investigation shows that their languages are in reality but variant dialects of a common original. Now suppose that these two nations had spoken languages philologically unconnected, but had long dwelt side by side; and that India had bestowed upon Greece nearly all the rudiments of civilization, including, as of course, various words and names, it would have been quite legitimate to investigate whether some Vedic divinities might not, under these circumstances, have found an entrance into the Hellenic Pantheon. To give an instance of such a borrowing, and I take it from Prof. Müller, although elsewhere he implies that there are no such cases. Chaïtain ( = Arabic Shaitan, Heb. Satan) appears in the Mordvinian Pantheon (vide C., p. 250), and Christus in the Wotjakian (Ibid., pp. 465, 468). Thus, there may be, and often has been, a borrowing of divinities between nations who dwelt side by side, although their languages have belonged to different families of speech. Such a connexion may be called historical, as opposed to linguistic. Who doubts the equation—Persian Khshayârshâ = Gk. Xerxês? But its truth does not depend upon the fact that Iranian and Greek are two dialects of an original common speech. Its basis is purely historical, viz., that at a certain time the Greeks came in contact with a certain King of Persia, and did their best (such as it was) to reproduce his name in a Greek form. As all scholars admit that the Sk. Dyaus = Gk. Zeus, so are they equally clear that the Ph. Melqârth ('City-King') = Gk. Melikertês (vide C., p. 219); and this latter equation may stand as the corresponding illustrative example in the Aryo-Semitic school. As the one equation logically involves much besides itself, so also does the other. And from the foregoing considerations it will at once be evident that we violate no philological principle when, with due care, we endeavour to explain certain Greek names from Semitic sources.

## IV. Semitic Indications in Greek Mythology

As the Greeks were an Aryan nation, the prior probability is that a Greek divinity is an Aryan divinity. What, then, are the indications of Semitic influence in particular instances? The principal signs which point to the Semitic origin of any particular personage of Hellenic mythology are, (1) When neither his name, nor the chief mythic incidents connected with his legend appear in the other branches of Aryan religious-mythology; (2) When Aryan nature-myths do not supply an easy and appropriate explanation of his

[164]

concept and history; (3) When his cult is found in regions either absolutely non-Aryan, or else permeated with non-Aryan influence; (4) When his form is more or less unanthropomorphic; (5) When his character and story generally are in harmony with those of mythic personages admittedly non-Aryan; and (6) When the resources of Aryan philology are powerless or inadequate to explain his name, and some or many of his principal epithets.

It is to be remembered that the true and original concept of a divinity is best arrived at by the correct interpretation of his name, titles, and epithets; and that almost every real explanation of the Hyponoia of mythology is simple, and by its obvious suitability to the case, justifies itself to an intelligent and unprejudiced mind. Explanation of mythic incident, or any etymon of a divinity-name which is utterly strained and harsh, stands self-condemned. And the same is equally true of an attempted rendering of a cuneiform tablet or of an Etruscan inscription. When Dr. Deecke gave an utterly unnatural, forced, quaint, and in itself improbable rendering of the Etruscan inscription on the leaden plate of Magliano, his effort stood self-condemned. It hardly required to be refuted by a jesting translation of the same inscription by Prof. Pauli, which logically and linguistically was in every way as good or better than the serious attempt; or the severe remark of Prof. Bréal, 'Il y a quelque chose de plus extraordinaire encore que cette traduction: c'est la manière dont elle est justifiée.'


## V. 'The Question of Allies'

Whilst I am alone responsible for many of the applications to detail mentioned in this work, of the general principles of the Aryo-Semitic school, on a 'question of Allies,' as Mr. Lang puts it, we may claim the countenance and support of many great names in the recent past and present. An illustrious adherent was the lamented François Lenormant, whose death at the age of 47, was for the time an almost irreparable loss. It is impossible that the torch of knowledge should, at all events at first, burn with the same brightness in the hand of a disciple who may have caught it as it fell from the dying grasp of the master, as it did when firmly held on high by the latter. Many precious things are sacrificed at the funeral pyre of the illustrious dead. But alike in his Assyriological studies, and in such works as *Les Prèmieres Civilizations* (1874), *Les Origines de L'Histoire* (1880–2), and the *Essai sur la Propagation de L'Alphabet*

*Phénicien,* the master has left us a legacy of the highest value. Another example of sympathetic treatment is furnished by Maury in his well-known *Histoire des Religions de la Grèce Antique.* A crowd of scholars are rallying round the Aryo-Semitic banner, amongst whom I may mention such men as Prof. Max Duncker, author of the *History of Greece*; Canon Isaac Taylor, the well-known historian of the Alphabet; and two other savants whose services to knowledge cannot easily be over-valued, Prof. Sayce and Prof. Fritz Hommel. One of our latest and most powerful recruits is M. Victor Bérard, author of the *De l'Origine des Cultes Arcadiens* (1894).This accomplished writer, who combines an actual and practical knowledge of the locality of which he treats (always a great advantage), with keen acumen and an acquaintance with the latest authorities, bids fair, when his work is carefully weighed and its conclusions duly appreciated, to effect a revolution in many of the current ideas respecting a considerable portion of Greek mythology and legendary history. The vast erudition of Dr. Otto Gruppe, to whose special views on the origin of mythology I do not here refer, is also quite on our side.

There is another name which I can mention here with every respect and with a special pleasure, that of Sir Geo. W. Cox. It will ever remain his special achievement, by working on the analogical principle, to have crystallized into a harmonious whole the general application of the Natural Phenomena Theory to the details of Aryan mythology. The conclusions he has formulated have often been sneered at, seldom or never dealt with 'at grips,' as Mr. Lang would say. In former works I have had at times to criticize his views, and to complain that his attitude respecting Semitic influence in Hellas was too much that of Prof. Max Müller. Mr. Lang commences his Introduction to *M. M.* by observing that 'it may well be doubted whether works of controversy serve any useful purpose.' Therefore, being before all things logical, he naturally proceeds to write a 'work of controversy'; and quotes a saying from Matthew Arnold, foolish, because untrue, that 'on an opponent one never does make any impression.' Apropos of this baseless dogma, let me quote the following passage from the Preface to the second edition of Sir Geo. Cox's *Mythology of the Aryan Nations* (1881):—

During the twelve years which have passed since the publication of the first edition a large amount of solid work has been done within the domain of Comparative Mythology. Of the results so gained probably the most important is the clearer light thrown on the influence of Semitic theology on the

[166]

theology and religion of the Greeks. This momentous question I have striven to treat impartially; and for my treatment of it I have to acknowledge my obligations to Mr. Robert Brown's valuable researches in the field of the great Dionysiak Myth.

I quote the above passage, not at all in my own honour, but simply in that of Sir Geo. Cox. Had he modified his views under the influence of a great man, like Prof. Max Müller, or of a prominent and fashionable man like Mr. Andrew Lang, we might not perhaps have been surprised. But that he, as a fact, did modify his conclusions on the matter, and thereby became, and is, in touch and harmony with the Aryo-Semitic school, simply from a careful consideration of the arguments urged by so humble a student as myself, shows an honesty of purpose and a devotion to truth of a very high order. Human nature is better than Matthew Arnold deemed it.

## VI. *An instance of the results of the Historical Method*

Although our school is specially historical, and we often discover the true meaning of legendary narrative rather in the disputes and contests between hostile tribes and religionists on earth, than in ideas drawn from the successions and discords of the forces of nature, yet it must always be remembered that, as *e.g.*, Prof. Müller has most fully shown, the Natural Phenomena Theory is not merely of Aryan, but of world-wide application. A dawn-myth may be Phoenician, as well as Vedic (*cf.* Gruppe, *Der phoinikische Urtext der Kassiepeialegende*, 1888). But there is one recent instance in which the successful application of the historical method, has so signally put to flight a whole mass of supposed impalpable myth, idle legend and mere invention, an instance so important and so far reaching in its logical consequences, that I cannot leave it here unmentioned. I refer to the complete and most remarkable demonstration of the historical accuracy of the writer of the xivth chapter of the Book of Genesis. Times innumerable have the campaign of Kudur-Lagamar (Chedorlaomer) in the West, his overthrow by Abraham, and the story of Melchizedek been treated as an Oriental romance, incredible, impossible, as baseless as the tale of Judith and Holofernes. Or, again, it has been explained as an elaborate piece of astronomical symbolism, veiling high and wondrous truths. But, thanks to such quiet, patient workers as my friend Mr. T. G.

Pinches of the British Museum, to the labours of Prof. Sayce, and above all, in this instance, to the brilliant results achieved by Prof. Hommel (*The Ancient Hebrew Tradition as illustrated by the Monuments*, Eng. Edit. 1897), the secrets of history, faithfully preserved by the imperishable cuneiform tablets, stand revealed. Now there pass before us the great form of the Elamite conqueror; the mighty Khammurabi-Amraphel, true founder of the grandeur of Babylon; the majestic figure of the Priest-king of Uru-salim ('the-City-of-Peace'); and, lastly, as a necessary corollary, we see in Abraham no eponymous tribal hero, no imaginary personification of the Nocturnal-heaven, but a noble form of flesh and blood consisting, a mighty Shaykh, the terror of the oppressor and the marauder, and the follower, and therefore the friend, of the eternal God.

I do not hesitate to say that the result of the splendid discoveries which have now been made by such men as Hommel, Glaser, Sayce and others, not merely reveals to us the amazingly important part played by archaic Arabia in the history and development of religion, and throws a flood of light upon many a dark and difficult passage in the Old Testament. It does all this indeed, but far more also. It shakes to the foundation the whole vast recent theory and system of the comparatively late origin and composition of the earlier books of the Bible; that huge house of cards reared mainly by Wellhausen with infinite skill and pains, and which, really based chiefly upon nescience and what was for the time being apparent probability, and so eagerly daubed by disciples in Germany and in England with much untempered mortar, now totters to its fall. And these results affect not merely our views about the *Hexateuch*. The whole critical system of the school of Wellhausen stands discredited. Men may attempt to show that such and such a *Psalm* was written in honour of one of the Ptolemies; or, if they like, that the *Song of Songs* was specially composed for Antony and Kleopatra. But the heart has gone out of the business. Khammurabi has dealt the system of Wellhausen its death blow.

## VII. *The Contests of the Gods and Heroes*

The contests of the gods and heroes related in myth and archaic legend are based, wholly or mainly, upon one or more of the three following circumstances:—(1) The apparent succession and conflict of the ordinary phenomena of nature; (2) The actual contests and oppositions of the rival votaries of clashing faiths and cults; and

(3) The fancies of archaic poets and mythographers, these being not wholly arbitrary, but shaped and moulded more or less in accordance with an almost infinite number of pre-existing facts, myths, and floating beliefs.

The Natural Phenomena Theory has made us familiar with an immense number of instances in Aryan mythology of contests based upon the first of these three causes. But it applies in almost equal force elsewhere. Witness in Egypt the contests between Asar (Osiris, probably derived from the Akkadian Marduk-Asari), Râ, and Har (Horus) on the one side; and Set and the monster Tebha (Typhon) on the other. Or witness the Euphratean story of a contest between the Sun-god and the Moon-god (often the Diad of hostile brethren), which centuries after amongst the Persians, took an Euhemeristic character as the rivalry between two opposing satraps Nannaros (Ak. Nannar, a name of the Moon-god) and Parsondês (*vide* Sayce, *Rel. Anct. Babs.*, p. 157 *et seq.*). The *Iliad* furnishes us with the most famous instances of contests of divinities arising from the third of these causes.

But it is with the second of these three underlying sets of circumstances, that the Aryo-Semitic student of Greek mythology is specially concerned. No view of natural phenomena will adequately explain them. No mere poetic fancy called them into being. To take an instance. A well-known, but reverently-regarded, legend told how Hêraklês held a mysterious contest with Apollôn for the possession of the Delphic Tripod; and how the strife between these two mighty personages was only terminated by the direct intervention of Zeus, who severed them by a flash of lightning. (For a good Vase-illustration of this scene, *vide* Walters, *Cat. of the Gk. and Et. Vases in the Brit. Mus.*, Vol. ii (1893), p. 22. As Hêraklês is moving off with the Tripod, Apollôn following, seizes one of its legs; Artemis stands behind him, Athêna behind Hêraklês.) Here the Natural Phenomena Theory is powerless to aid us. We can understand indeed by its assistance how the solar hero Hêraklês can borrow the golden boat-cup of Hêlios, to enable him to sail over the western ocean. For here Hêlios stands confessed as the Sun, pure and simple; and the mythic phrases which tell of the solar hero and the solar barque blend harmoniously. But a personal strife of a great (Aryan) Sun-god against a great (Aryan) Sun-god, and especially against so truly national and revered a figure as Apollôn, who, with Athêna, perhaps best represents the splendour of Hellas at the brief moment of her culmination, is almost inconceivable. No poet or mythographer would ever have dared to excogitate such an idea. Like Hêrodotos, they were all far too *god-fearing*. We know, moreover,

[169]

from various sources and indications that Delphoi was a great centre of rival, and, at times, contending, cults; and this circumstance it is, which constitutes the true Hyponoia of the legend. Mr. Farnell, with whom I am often happy to find myself in agreement, well remarks:—

> No doubt there were physical reasons why Helios and why Poseidon should be worshipped at Corinth; but the Corinthian legend of this strife, the Delphic legend of the contest . . . of Apollo and Heracles for the tripod, the Attic legend of the rivalry of Poseidon and Athena, and many other similar theomachies, probably all contain the same kernel of historical fact, an actual conflict of worships—an earlier cherished by the aboriginal men of the locality, and a later introduced by the new settlers (*Cults*, i. 270).

## VIII. Hêraklês

Hêraklês is not found in the mythology of the other branches of the Aryan nations, and his name, for all its intensely Greek appearance, the Aryanistic philologist is unable to explain (*vide C.*, pp. 612, 632). I am not concerned here to deny that there may perhaps have been a native Hellenic god so called: but it is quite certain that, if such there were, he disappears, like a double star, in the overlapping splendour of his great brother, the Semitic toiling, warring, voyaging, travelling, man-slaying, at times maniacal, Sun-god; whose end is naturally, as Prof. Müller expresses it, 'the sun's death in the fiery clouds.' Prof. Müller excellently illustrates, on the lines of the Natural Phenomena Theory, many incidents in the Hêraklês-myth; but all such illustrations are quite as applicable to a Semitic, as to an Aryan, Sun-god. And, as will be seen, it is just in connexion with some of these exploits of Hêraklês upon which the Aryan mythologist has little or nothing to say, that the Semitic connexion of the hero throws the clearest and most remarkable light. I am quite aware of the ordinary view, one, *e.g.*, usually found in English Dictionaries of Mythology, that the doings of a Semitic Sun-god of the Outer-world were, in comparatively late times, arbitrarily tacked on to a native Hellenic Sun-god of the Inner-world. But this theory altogether collapses under careful examination conducted by the light of modern discoveries. Hêraklês, the dweller at Thebes and at Tiryns; the opponent of such purely Aryan divinities as Hêra, Aïdês, Apollôn, and Arês; the Lion-slayer (*vide* R. B. Jr.,

*Eridinus*, Appendix iii. The Sun-god and the Lion), first worshipped in Greece at the Phoenician Mârath (Marathôn; cf. Paus, I, xxxii, 4); linked by a thousand ties and incidents with Western Asia, and especially with Phoenicia and her colonies, is in all probability Phoenician in name as in nature—Harekhal ('*the* Traveller'; Bérard, *Cultes Arcad.* p. 257). As Prof. Duncker well sums up the matter:—

> Marathon bears the same name as Marathus (Amrit) in Crete, and on the Phoenician coast near Aradus; a fountain springing at Marathon is called Macaria, 'in honour of Heracles'; *i.e.*, it bears the name of Melkarth, which the Greeks modified into Melicertes and Makar; the district of Marathon worshipped Heracles; indeed, it boasted that it had been the first of all the Hellenic countries to worship him. Heracles is Archal, the labouring, striving, fighting Baal Melkarth of the Phoenicians (*Hist. of Greece*, i, 62–3).

And, here, let me remark in passing, that we often meet with much really baseless assertion respecting the alleged comparatively modern date of this or that Greek myth; the reason given generally being that it is not mentioned by earlier writers. As, however, some three-fourths of early Greek literature has perished, such reasons and opinions are generally of very slender value. Moreover, as a rule, the argument from silence must be regarded with very grave suspicion. The altogether undue weight too frequently attributed to it, has again and again led writers into opinions really untenable, and often actually ridiculous.

## [ 5 ABRAM SMYTHE PALMER ]

So persuasive was the theory of heavenly mythology that long after it was supposedly laid to rest, along with its most illustrious spokesmen, it continued to be voiced. Abram Smythe Palmer, doctor of divinity, lecturer at Trinity College, Dublin, and enthusiastic lexicographer, believed he saw signs of 'a reaction taking place in favour of the views advanced by Max Müller' in 1908, the year he reissued 'Comparative Mythology' in book form, with his own extended introduction and additions to the notes. He also included a delicious squib, 'The Oxford Solar Myth,' which had appeared obscurely in *Kottabos*, a magazine of Trinity College, Dublin, No. 5, 1870, written by Dr. R. F. Littledale and 'Dedicated, without permission, to the Rev. G. W. Cox, M.A.' With a wealth of etymological proofs, Littledale demonstrated that Max Müller, a legendary teacher who had travelled from East to West, was himself a solar divinity, preserved even in the children's ditty beginning 'There was a jolly Miller / Lived on the river Dee.'

Palmer made it clear that such levity resulted entirely from the excesses of Cox and cast no reflection on the wisdom of Müller. His own solar commitment and admiration for Müller's mythological method are plainly evident in his book-length interpretation of Samson as a sun-hero.

Text from A. Smythe Palmer, *The Samson-Saga and Its Place in Comparative Religion* (London: Sir Isaac Pitman & Sons, Ltd., 1913). Chapter 14, 'Samson's Blinding and Servitude.' Pages 159–172.

*Samson's Blinding and Servitude*

> The Philistines laid hold on him, and put out his eyes; and they brought him down to Gaza, and bound him with fetters of brass; and he did grind in the prison-house.—xvi. 21.

When Samson, after having been shorn of his locks, awoke out of sleep and thought he would go out, as aforetime he had done 'times upon times,' and 'shake himself,' as does some huge, shaggy animal, this Hebrew Orson discovered that his strength had gone from him (xvi. 19), or, otherwise expressed, that Jahveh had withdrawn His favouring presence. 'The story,' says Gomperz, 'is one of the most transparent of all nature-myths. The Semite explained the weakness of the sun in winter by the story of Samson's—the sun-god's—bewitchment by the seductive goddess of the night, who robbed him of his shining hair; as soon as his long locks, the sun-beams, in which his strength resided, were cut off, it was an easy task to blind him,'[1] or darken his light.

As the hostile powers of cold and darkness gain the upper hand, the former potency of the sun is diminished. Like an old warrior vanquished, he goes to his setting, when Night's

> 'Black contagious breath
> Already smokes about the burning crest
> Of the old feeble and day-wearied Sun.'[2]

As the year advances, vegetation diminishes; and the conclusion was naturally drawn that the sun, on whom vegetation depended, had lost some of his force. This loss of strength was pictured as a

[1] *Greek Thinkers*, i, 35, 525.          [2] Shaks., *K. John*, v, 4, 35.

disease with which the sun was afflicted.[1] In Egyptian legends, the luminary Rā was a king, who grows feeble from old age.

When the Philistines, after no small expenditure of craft and force, had at last got their doughty antagonist in their power, they sang a jubilant song of thanksgiving to Dagon—

'Our god has delivèred
Our foe into our hand,
Who once laid waste our land,
And multiplied our dead.'[2]

Then, in mockery, taking advantage of their captive's well-known bent for jest and humour, they compelled him 'to make sport' for them, after they had reduced him to a state of helpless incapacity by cruelly depriving him of his sight. His physical strength, however, returned with the new growth of his wondrous locks. The Sun, though quenched in darkness, is never vanquished for long, as the dawn of every day and the spring of every year testify.

'Yet shall the agèd sun set forth his hair
To make us live unto our former heat,'[3]

but by, first of all, reviving his own. Samson's foes naturally proceed to turn their captive's magnificent strength to account by giving him some work to do. It is hardly to be supposed that they found no better use to which they could put his mighty thews than setting him—as is often assumed—to turn the handle of a small hand-mill, which in the East can be, and is, customarily worked by a woman. It is far more likely that they forced him to take the place of the horse or ass which plods round and round in the beaten track of the circular area. dragging or pushing the shaft which works a mill of cumbrous size. Bound to this shaft with fetters of brass, the humiliated hero had to tramp round and perform his daily task-work, the grinding-house being his prison-house (compare the Latin *pistrinum*, having both meanings).[4]

The whole of this representation may be due to the primitive conception that the sun, in performing his daily march around the

---

[1] In Latin when the light of the sun or the moon fails or is obscured the luminary is said to grow faint or weak (*languescere, deficere*). The waning sun at sunset, or near the winter solstice, is said to become blind or lame, as he loses strength (M. Müller, *Contributions to Mythology*, 593).

[2] So Lagrange, *Livre des Juges*, xvi, 4.

[3] Marlowe, *Tragedy of Dido*, 1594, Act i.

[4] *E.g.*, 'Ferratus in pistrino ætatem conteras.'—Plautus, *Bacchides*, iv, 5, 11. [Wear out your life in chains in the grinding-house.] 'Molendumst in pistrino, vapulandum, habendæ compedes.'—Terence, *Phormio*, ii, 1, 19. [I must grind in the grinding-house, be beaten, and wear fetters.]

sky, is performing a task of drudgery to which he is compelled by a law ('brazen fetters') imposed upon him by a superior power.

'O Sun, urge rightly thy way along *the fixed road* determined for thee.'—*Assyrian Hymn*.[1]

The sceptical conclusion which led the Peruvian Inca, Yupanqui, to discard his ancient sun-worship is well known. So far from being a god, he said, the sun is like a tied beast who goes ever round and round in the same track. 'He must have a master more powerful than himself who constrains him to his daily circuit without pause or rest.'[2] Obedience to law seemed, to the undisciplined mind, to argue servitude. A similar conception underlies the Eddaic Mundil-föri, the giant who makes the heavens turn round in its daily and yearly revolutions by moving (*foera*) the handle (*mundil, möndull*) of the great world-mill—that being the Teutonic idea of the revolving vault of heaven.[3] Mundilföri, the axis-mover and heaven-turner, is a solar being who has for his children Máni and Sól (*i.e.*, Moon and Sun). As fire-producer by turning, he was identified with Lodhurr, the fire-kindler.[4] We find analogues in Hêraklês, the sun-hero, working the spinning-wheel of Omphalê (? = 'hub' or 'nave' of the circling sky), and in the Vedic, 'twelve-spoked wheel of Rita' (phenomenal law), which 'rolls round the sky' (*Rig-Veda*, I, 164, 11). 'The primitive practices of milling and turning.' says Geiger, 'were symbols of the diurnal revolution of the sun and the firmament.'[5] Indeed, we find a modern writer, who, in his devoted love of Nature, sometimes visualized her phenomena with a boldness almost Oriental, using the same primitive figure when he describes the azure sky in its seeming solidity as—

> A dome turned perfect by the Sun's great wheel,
> 'Whose edges rest upon the hills around.'[6]

A curious reminiscence of Samson as playing the part of a grinder or mill-worker seems to survive in a quarter of Northern Europe where we would least expect it. The Finns, in their national epic, the Kalevala, assign an important role to a mysterious being which bears the name of Sampsa or Sampo. This is a borrowed word

[1] Maspero, *Dawn of Civ.*, 658.
[2] Garcilaso de la Vega. Brinton, *Myths of the New World*, 72; M. Müller, *Chips*, ii, 116.
[3] V. Rydberg, *Teutonic Mythology*, 396–7; M. Müller, *Contributions to Science of Mythology*, 40, 651.
[4] Rydberg, 412; Du Chaillu, *Viking Age*, i, 38; C. F. Keary, *The Vikings*, 65. In the Finnish *Kalevala* the Sun is called 'God's spindle' (Grimm, *T. M.*, 1500).
[5] *Development of the Human Race*, iii.
[6] R. Jefferies, *Field and Hedgerow* (1895), 300.

from the Russian,[1] and, according to Comparetti, is identical with Samson. The exact significance of this conception has been much debated, but many Finnish scholars agree in thinking that Sampsa or Sampo represents the Sun[2] as the source of the blessings of abundance, and that by discharging the functions of a magic mill which grinds out plenty of food, like the Scandinavian Grottemill. Pellervoinen, the god of the fields and agriculture, also has Sampsa as a title. The Sampo. fabricated by the celestial smith Ilmarinen, is the source of prosperity and well-being to the nation. It is a treasure contained in a vari-coloured covering (*Kirjokansi*) or coffer, which is the revolving sky. It is detained imprisoned for a time in the dark Northland, Pohjola, which is Hades. The Kalevala says that Ilmarinen—

> 'Forged with cunning art the Sampo,
> And on one side was a corn-mill,
> On another side a salt-mill,
> And upon the third a coin-mill.
> Now was grinding the new Sampo,
> And revolved the pictured cover,
> Chestfuls did it grind till evening,
> First for food it ground a chestful,
> And another ground for barter,
> And a third it ground for storage.
> Now rejoiced the crone of Pohja (the North),
> And conveyed the bulky Sampo
> To the rocky hills of Pohja,
> And behind nine locks secured it.'[3]

Chakka-vatti, the name which was given to the solarized Buddha in the sense of Universal King, meant, originally, 'the Wheel-Turner' (*Cakra-vartin*), *i.e.*, the Sun as Ruler of the World. Mythical attributes are known to have been attached to Buddha as a sun-hero, just as to Samson. It is recorded of him that his hair shone, rays of light darted from his body, and that he traversed the vault of heaven from East to West.[4]

It is curious to note that notions similar to some of those above mentioned were held by the ancient Babylonians. On a well-known

[1] In Russian Samson is the name of a demon; just as Judas (*Yûdas*) is become an evil spirit, and Andrew (*Antero*) a name for Hell.
[2] So M. O. Donner, *Der Mythus von Sampo*, and Schiefner.
[3] *Kalevala*, ed. Kirby, x, 413–25. See also D. Comparetti, *Trad. Poetry of the Finns*, 188, 194, 253–62.
[4] Kuenen, *Nat. Religions and Universal Religions*, 260–2. Rhys Davids, *Indian Buddhism*, 131.

slab representing the shrine of Shamash, the sun-god of Sippara, the great solar disk is depicted as being held in its place by ropes held in the hands of two small figures, which are, perhaps, the genii who guide the sun along his celestial path.[1]

The solar mythologists, without making any special reference to Samson, have noted that the sun-god is frequently described as 'facing many dangers and many enemies, none of which may arrest his course'; as being 'sullen, capricious, and resentful'; while the constant recurrence of his regular daily work leads to his being regarded as one constrained to toil for others.[2] Gilgamesh, the Babylonian sun-hero, does not rest by day nor by night. Primitive men, who thought that the Sun was a living creature, might, indeed, well marvel at the regularity of his movements, and enquire: 'Why does he go, like a driven beast, in the one invariable round? Has he no freedom of action?' He must be in bondage.

A great master of Aryan learning observes that 'this servitude of solar heroes is a very general feature in ancient mythology.'[3] There is a special reason why it should occur among peoples of Semitic speech where the most ancient word for the sun, Shamash, means 'one who serves,' being derived from *shamash*, to serve or minister.[4] Whatever was the original conception in early times, it was understood later as meaning 'the minister or active servant of the world';[5] or as 'the earliest minister of the Almighty,'[6] at whose commandment 'it runneth hastily' (*Eccles.*, xliii, 5). As an old divine expresses it: 'The sun is His, if He bid it shine, it shineth: at His appointment it runs forward like a giant';[7] which is also a Buddhist idea: 'The Sun is the servant of the Lord and neither by day nor night does he cease from his travelling.'[8] In running his daily course, he was conceived as 'fulfilling his ministry,'[9] as 'executing his Lord's commands';[10] as 'sole ministrante'—Archelaus,[11] and 'lo ministro maggior della natura'—Dante, *Paradiso*,

[1] Ball, *Light from the East*, 156.
[2] G. W. Cox, *Tales of Ancient Greece*, introd.; Grimm, *Household Stories*, vol. i, xxxi (ed. Hunt). The grinding slave was often chained, 'ferratus,'—Plautus, 'habendae compedes'—Terence.
[3] M. Müller, *Contributions*, 618.
[4] In Talmudic Hebrew *Shamash* is to serve or minister (M. Jastrow, *Dict of the Targumim*, etc.); *Idem.*, *Religion of Babylonia*, 68. Compare Egyptian *Shemes*, a servant or attendant (Griffith, *Hieroglyphs*, 62), Heb., *Shemesh*, the Sun.
[5] Hyde, *Rel. Vet. Persarum*, 105.
[6] Byron, *Manfred*, iii, 2.
[7] Thos. Adams, *Sermons*, iii, 160 (1650).
[8] Alabaster, *Wheel of the Law*, 148.
[9] Epictetus, *Enchiridion*, i, 8, 1.
[10] Jerahmeel, *Chron.*, iii, 5; so *Koran*, xvi, *sub. init*; *Ecclus*, xliii, 5.
[11] *Disput. with Manes*, ch. xxii.

x, 28. To this day, the attendant or verger of the Jewish synagogue is called its *shammash*.

This primitive signification of the word would, in later times, readily lend itself to the mythologizing process, and originate stories to the effect that the mighty sun-hero had been brought into servitude and compelled to fulfil menial duties by his enemies.

In the stories which were told in the later mythologies of the sun-god, whether Apollo, Hêraklês, or Sîfrit, being reduced to a position of servitude by his enemies, we may, perhaps, trace a reminiscence of the servile name which was given to the sun-god.

For the binding of the sun-hero, we have, in illustration, the sun in the Teutonic mythology being caught in a noose, so that he cannot continue his journey until he has been ransomed.[1] Here, also, the Day is pictured as a living being who once was tethered with a rope which hindered its dawning,[2] just as very similarly, in myths of the South Pacific, the sun-god Rā, 'with golden locks,' was ensnared with a noose of ropes at his rising, and enslaved by Maui in order to retard his course.[3] The Wyandot Indians have a like myth, which tells of the sun being caught in a trap in the happy hunting-grounds, and, in consequence, not shining for a day.[4] A commonplace among Nature-folk, the idea was also familiar to the nations of antiquity. The Assyrian Hercules, Adar, the solar deity in his might, whose epithet is *dandannu*, 'the very powerful,' is ensnared and held captive by his brother-rival Sin (Nannaros), the lunar god, and he each evening falls into his power, when he sinks into effeminacy, loses his manhood, and is deprived of his strength:[5] just as Samson fares at the hands of Delîlâh. With much the same meaning, 'each evening, when Shamash (the Sun) entered the innermost part of heaven, he was met by Ai, his wife, and he feasted and rested from his exertions in the abode of the gods.'[6] If Timnath, the home of Samson's wife (Judges xiv. 1), is identical wth Timnath-Heres (Judges ii. 9), its meaning would be 'Portion of the Sun'; or (if akin to Têmân, the 'right hand' or 'southern' quarter) it might mean the South or Mid day,[7] to which the young sun directs his course; but we can attach no importance to this identification.

The sun-hero had his eyes put out before he met his tragic death. There is no difficulty in discerning the meaning of this. There is no

---

[1] Grimm, *Teut. Myth.*, 1518.
[2] *Idem.*, 745.
[3] Grey, *Polynesian Myth.*, 35–8; W. W. Gill, *Myths of S. Pacific*, 70, xv, 61–2.
[4] M. C. Judd, *Wigwam Stories*, 165.
[5] See Lenormant, *Beginnings of History*, 166–9.
[6] King, *Bab. Religion*, 33.        [7] Conder, *Syrian Stone-lore*, 34.

image older and more universal than that which regards the round
and brilliant disk as the eye of the sky-god, whether it be of Ahuro-
Mazdâo as with the Persians, or of Horus as with the Egyptians, or
of Zeus as with the Greeks, or of Wuotan as with the Teutons. 'His
eye sendeth forth light from his face when the earth becometh light,'
says the Book of the Dead.[1] The sun is the all-seeing eye of
Varuna, the Vedic sky-god, which surveys the whole earth; *oculus
mundi*, says Ovid;[2] 'the great eye of Heaven,' says Spenser;[3]
'the searching eye of Heaven,' says Shakespeare;[4] *des Tages
Flammenauge*, says Schiller.

'The Sun with one eye vieweth all the world.'[5]

Uncivilized tribes have exactly the same conception; *betuch anuh*
with the Dayaks of Borneo; *màso-andro* with the Malagasy; *mata-ari*
with the Malays, all meaning 'the eye of day.'[6] The natives of
Mangaia, in the South Pacific, say 'the eye of Great Noon (Avatea)
is open' when the sun is in its meridian splendour.[7]

It may be objected that Samson had two eyes put out, whereas
the sun-god has but one.[8] There is, however, an obscure reference,
apparently to some part of the story which has not come down to
us, which shows that the blinded hero was greatly concerned for
only *one* eye, which was much more precious to him than the other.
The literal translation of Judges xvi. 28, says that his prayer to
God in his final throes was that he might be 'avenged on the Philistines *for one of his two eyes*.' To understand this, it is only necessary
to point out that, while a pair of eyes is naturally attributed to the
humanized Sky-god, these were of very unequal importance. They
are the greater and lesser lights of the firmament. The sun was
commonly conceived as being his right eye, and the moon his left.
So it is among the Mangaians of the South Pacific,[9] and so it is in
the Cabala of the Jews.[10] In the ancient Egyptian mythology, the
face of the celestial Horus has two eyes, which he opens in turn,
the right one being the sun and the moon the left.[11] 'The sun-god
enlightens the earth with his two eyeballs' is a frequent expression
in Egyptian texts.[12] A famous hymn to Amon-Ra describes him as

---

[1] Ch. 64; Lady Amherst, *Egyptian Hist.*, 81; Renouf, *Hib. Lect.*, 187.
[2] *Met.*, iv, 228.          [3] *Faerie Queene.*          [4] *Rich. II.*, iii, 2.
[5] *Hen. VI.*, Pt. I., i, 4. So the Greek ὄμμα frequently used of the Sun.
[6] M. Müller, *Contr. to Mythology*, 555; Sibree, *Madagascar*, 556; Keane, *Man: Past
and Present*, 252; Tylor, *P. Cult.*, i, 350; Grimm, *T. Myth.*, 702; Goldziher, 107–10.
[7] W. W. Gill, *Myths. of S. Pacific*, 18.
[8] The Sun-god [Shamash] by a transition easily understood is here confused with
the Sky-god [Anu]. A pair of eyes were, of course, necessary when he was humanized.
[9] Gill, *op. cit.*, 44.          [10] Stehelin, *Rabbin. Literature*, i, 158.
[11] Maspero, *Dawn of Civilization*, 86, 88.          [12] Renouf, *T.S.B.A.*, viii, 229.

the deity, 'Whose right eye each day in heaven is time-controller; . . . From the beginning was his left eye (the moon) in heaven, the meter of time.'[1] When the sun disappears he is said to have lost his sight, but his eyes are restored to him at daybreak.[2] In Orphic poems, the eyes of Zeus are the sun and the moon, and the same idea is found in Buddhist traditions.[3] It has been traced also in the Edda, where Odin is pictured as one-eyed, since he had left the other (the moon) in pledge with Mîmir. The Homeric Cyclops, with his one circular eye, may further be compared.[4]

The loss of his eye by the sun-god occupies a considerable place in the Egyptian mythology. *The Book of the Dead* frequently refers to the conflict of Horus with Set, the power of darkness, in which his eye was destroyed; whence came his names 'the eye-less god,' 'the Prince of Blindness'; Herkhent-an-ma, 'Horus, lord of not-seeing,' with reference to his solar eye being quenched by the hostile power of gloom.[5] Ancient texts speak of him as 'searching for his eyes,' as sitting solitary in 'darkness and blindness,' and having 'his eye restored to him at the dawn of day.' Hence the allusion: 'I make full the eye when it waxeth dim on the day of battle between the two opponents' [Horus and Set].[6] In contrast with this, but based on the same idea, is the Buddhist tradition that in the elemental struggle 'the Bodhisattva keeps his solar eye open, which the storm may darken but cannot close';[7] while, again, we find Cúchulainn, the sun-hero of the ancient Irish, in his war-rage, closing one eye and opening wide the other till it was bigger than the mouth of a meal goblet;[8] just as Lugh, the Irish sun-god, before the battle of Moytura, goes round the host with one eye closed; the allusion being, in either case, to what Dante calls 'the two eyes of the sky.'[9] When the solar hero puts forth his strength, he naturally relies on the eye which makes him invincible. As Ovid expresses it—

'Sol videt e coelo, soli tamen unicus orbis'[10]
[The Sun looks down from heaven, the Sun hath but one eye];

[1] Brugsch, *Oase el Khargeh*, 52. Similarly the Chinese say that 'the eyes are to the body what the sun and moon are to the earth.' (R. K. Douglas, *China*, 283).
[2] Renouf, *T.S.B.A.*, viii, 203.  [3] Grimm, *Teut. Myth.*, 570.
[4] *Idem.*, 702–3.
[5] Wiedemann, *Religion of Anct. Egyptians*, 28. Compare the great one-eyed giant of the Yorubas (W. Africa) which keeps watch where heaven and earth meet, *i.e.*, the horizon on which the sun rises and sets (L. Frobenius, *Childhood of Man*, 381).
[6] Renouf, *Hib. Lect.*, 114; *Proc. Soc. Bib. Arch.*, xiv, 378.
[7] Sénart, *Legende de Bouddha*, 250.
[8] M. Maclean, *Literature of the Celts*, 150.
[9] *Li due occhi del cielo*—*Purg.*, xx, 132.
[10] *Metamorph*, xiii, 853; so 'Omnia qui video . . . mundi oculus'—*Idem.*, iv, 228.

or a later poet, more appositely—

> 'Sunt oculi Phœbus, Phoeboque adversa recurrens
> Cynthia. . . . .
> Lacertorum valido stans robore certus.'[1]

> [His eyes the Sun-god are, and she less bright
> The moon who doth reflect his beams. . . .
> In strength of mighty thews confirmed he stands.]

The above references will enable us probably to understand the meaning of what seems an enigmatical statement; that when the afflicted sun-hero desired to exert all his force in order to wreak vengeance on those who had robbed him of his sight, he bewailed the loss of *one of his eyes* in especial, and thought nothing of the other. We may be certain, I think, that it was his right eye—the sun—that he desiderated. If he could recover that eye as well as his hair—the disk and its beams—the solar Samson could triumph over all his enemies.[2] He would be invincible.

[1] Eusebius, in Tylor, *Prim. Cult.*, i, 350.
[2] It is interesting to note so conservative an exegete as Bishop Wordsworth yielding insensibly to the mythologizing influence, and remarking that when Samson lost his eyes (xvi, 21) 'by his own sin *the sunlight is eclipsed.*'

# III   The Savage Folklorists

WHILE the Natural Phenomena school of mythology was extending its dominion over folklore, following Max Müller's 1856 essay, a rival hypothesis began to marshal its forces. The father of anthropology, Edward B. Tylor, published his *Researches into the Early History of Mankind* in 1865 and his *Primitive Culture* in 1871, now classic works filled with references to and illustrations from collections of peasant folklore and savage myths. At first no sharp break seemed evident between comparative mythology and the new anthropology, for Tylor deferred to Müller's solar analyses of Aryan myths while developing his own thesis of the savage mentality reflected in childlike games, beliefs, sayings, and stories. Savages preceded Aryans and so, according to Tylor's theory of the uniform ascent of all peoples on the ladder of cultural evolution, one stage glided neatly into the next.

Among the host of readers excited by Tylor's new vision was a young scholar at Tylor's own Balliol College in Oxford, Scottish-born Andrew Lang. Reacting quickly to Tylor's portrayal of pre-historic savages eying a jungle populated on all sides with vital spirits, Lang opened a trail leading directly to the modern peasant. In so doing he contrived a new method for folklore, at the same time demolishing the solar, lunar, and stellar mythologists with his facile wit and classical learning. The extension of folklore researches to include the contemporary savage greatly enlarged the sphere of the new subject and gave it a strongly anthropological hue.


## [ 1   EDWARD  B.  TYLOR ]

In *Primitive Culture,* Tylor (1832–1917) introduced a concept which would form the foundation stone for a school of anthropological folklorists. This was the doctrine of survivals, relating the beliefs and practices of long vanished savages to the folklore of the modern

[181]

peasant. In adopting the term 'survival' Tylor replaced the pejorative 'superstition' with a more meaningful and expressive word calling immediately to mind his whole evolutionary position. Now the search for folklore survivals became an exciting and momentous quest, with each new discovery casting its ray of light on the behaviour of prehistoric man. Survivals covered a broader ground than superstitions, including, for instance, the pastimes of children as relics of savage culture. Indeed, all genres of folklore, from games of chance to proverbs and riddles, manners and customs, rhymes and tales, survived in modern society as fragments of primitive culture. After surveying survivals in these forms, Tylor turned to consider 'three remarkable groups of customs.'

Text from Edward B. Tylor, *Primitive Culture, Researches into the Development of Mythology, Philosophy, Religion, Art and Custom.* Two volumes. London: J. Murray, 1871. I, 97–111, from Chapter 3, 'Survival in Culture.'


Let us now put the theory of survival to a somewhat severe test, by seeking from it some explanation of the existence, in practice or memory, within the limits of modern civilized society, of three remarkable groups of customs which civilized ideas totally fail to account for. Though we may not succeed in giving clear and absolute explanations of their motives, at any rate it is a step in advance to be able to refer their origins to savage or barbaric antiquity. Looking at these customs from the modern practical point of view, one is ridiculous, the others are atrocious, and all are senseless. The first is the practice of salutation on sneezing, the second the rite of laying the foundations of a building on a human victim, the third the prejudice against saving a drowning man.

In interpreting the customs connected with sneezing, it is needful to recognize a prevalent doctrine of the lower races, of which a full account will be given in another chapter. As a man's soul is considered to go in and out of his body, so it is with other spirits, particularly such as enter into patients and possess them or afflict them with disease. Among the less cultured races, the connexion of this idea with sneezing is best shown among the Zulus, a people firmly persuaded that kindly or angry spirits of the dead hover about them, do them good or harm, stand visibly before them in dreams, enter into them, and cause diseases in them. The following particulars are abridged from the native statements taken down by Dr. Callaway:—When a Zulu sneezes, he will say, 'I am now blessed. The Idhlozi [ancestral spirit] is with me; it has come to me. Let me hasten and praise it, for it is it which causes me to sneeze!' So he praises the manes of his family, asking for cattle, and wives, and blessings. Sneezing is a sign that a sick person will be restored to health; he returns thanks after sneezing, saying, 'Ye people of ours, I have gained that prosperity which I wanted. Continue to look on me with favour!' Sneezing reminds a man that he should name the Itongo (ancestral spirit) of his people without delay, because it is the Itongo which causes him to sneeze, that he may perceive by sneezing that the Itongo is with him. If a man is ill and does not sneeze, those who come to him ask whether he has sneezed or not; if he has not sneezed, they murmur, saying, 'The disease is great!' If a child sneezes, they say to it, 'Grow!' it is a sign of health. So then, it is said, sneezing among black men gives a man strength to remember that the Itongo has entered into him and abides with him. The Zulu diviners or sorcerers are very apt to sneeze, which they regard as an indication of the presence of the spirits, whom they adore by saying 'Makosi!' (*i.e.* lords or masters). It is a suggestive example of the transition of such customs as these from one religion to another, that the Amakosa, who used to call on their divine ancestor Utixo when they sneezed, since their conversion to Christianity say, 'Preserver, look upon me!' or, 'Creator of heaven and earth!'[1] Elsewhere in Africa, similar ideas are mentioned. Sir Thomas Browne, in his 'Vulgar Errors,' made well known the story that when the King of Monomotapa sneezed, acclamations of blessing passed from mouth to mouth through the city; but he should have mentioned that Godigno, from whom the original account is taken, said that this took place when the king drank, or coughed, or sneezed.[2] A later account from the other side of the continent is more to the purpose. In Guinea, in the last century, when a principal personage sneezed, all present fell on their knees, kissed the earth, clapped their hands, and wished him all happiness and prosperity.[3] With a different idea, the negroes of Old Calabar, when a child sneezes, will sometimes exclaim, 'Far from you!' with an appropriate gesture as if throwing off some evil.[4] Polynesia is another region where the sneezing salutation is well marked. In New Zealand, a charm was said to prevent evil when a child sneezed;[5] if a Samoan sneezed, the bystanders said, 'Life to you!'[6] while in the Tongan group a sneeze on the starting of an expedition

[1] Callaway, *Religion of Amazulu*, pp. 64, 222–45, 263.
[2] Godignus, 'Vita Patris Gonzali Sylveriae,' Col. Agripp, 1616; lib. ii, c. x.
[3] Bosman, 'Guinea,' letter xviii, in Pinkerton, vol. xvi, p. 478.
[4] Burton, *Wit and Wisdom from West Africa*, p. 373.
[5] Shortland, *Trads. of New Zealand*, p. 131.
[6] Turner, *Polynesia*, p. 348; see also Williams, *Fiji*, vol. i, p. 250.

was a most evil presage.[1] A curious American instance dates from Hernando de Soto's famous expedition into Florida, when Guachoya, a native chief, came to pay him a visit. 'While this was going on, the cacique Guachoya gave a great sneeze; the gentlemen who had come with him and were lining the walls of the hall among the Spaniards there all at once bowing their heads, opening their arms and closing them again, and making other gestures of great veneration and respect, saluted him with different words, all directed to one end, saying, "The Sun guard thee, be with thee, enlighten thee, magnify thee, protect thee, favour thee, defend thee, prosper thee, save thee," and other like phrases, as the words came, and for a good space there lingered the murmur of these words among them, whereat the governor wondering said to the gentlemen and captains with him, "Do you not see that all the world is one?" This matter was well noted among the Spaniards, that among so barbarous a people should be used the same ceremonies, or greater, than among those who hold themselves to be very civilized. Whence it may be believed that this manner of salutation is natural among all nations, and not caused by a pestilence, as is vulgarly said,' etc.[2]

In Asia and Europe, the sneezing superstition extends through a wide range of race, age, and country.[3] Among the passages relating to it in the classic ages of Greece and Rome, the following are some of the most characteristic,—the lucky sneeze of Telemachos in the Odyssey;[4] the soldier's sneeze and the shout of adoration to the god which rose along the ranks, and which Xenophon appealed to as a favourable omen;[5] Aristotle's remark that people consider a sneeze as divine ($τόν$ $μὲν$ $πταρμὸν$ $θεὸν$ $ἡγόύμεθα$ $εἶναι$), but not a cough,[6] etc.; the Greek epigram on the man with the long nose, who did not say $Ζεῦ$ $σῶσον$ when he sneezed, for the noise was too far off for him to hear;[7] Petronius Arbiter's mention of the custom of saying 'Salve!' to one who sneezed;[8] and Pliny's question, 'Cur sternutamentis salutamus?' apropos of which he remarks that even Tiberius Caesar, that saddest of men, exacted this observance.[9] Similar

---

[1] Mariner, *Tonga Is.*, vol. i, p. 456.

[2] Garcilaso de la Vega, *Hist. de la Florida*, vol. iii, ch. xli.

[3] Among dissertations on the subject, see especially Sir Thos. Browne, 'Pseudodoxia Epidemica' (Vulgar Errors), book iv, chap. ix.; Brand, *Popular Antiquities*, vol. iii, p. 119, etc.; R. G. Haliburton, *New Materials for the History of Man*, Halifax, N.S. 1863; *Encyclopædia Britannica*, art. 'sneezing'; Wernsdorf, *De Ritu Sternutantibus bene precandi*, Leipzig, 1741; see also Grimm, *D.M.*, p. 1070, note.

[4] Homer, Odyss., xvii, 541.   [5] Xenophon, Anabasis, iii, 2, 9.

[6] Aristot., Problem, xxxiii, 7.

[7] Anthologia Graeca, Brunck, vol. iii, p. 95.   [8] Petron., Arb. Sat., 98.

[9] Plin., xxviii, 5.

rites of sneezing have long been observed in Eastern Asia.[1] When a Hindu sneezes bystanders say, 'Live!' and the sneezer replies, 'With you!' It is an ill omen, to which among others the Thugs paid great regard on starting on an expedition, and which even compelled them to let the travellers with them escape.[2]

The Jewish sneezing formula is, 'Tobim chayim!' *i.e.*, 'Good life!'[3] The Moslem says, 'Praise to Allah!' when he sneezes, and his friends compliment him with proper formulas, a custom which seems to be conveyed from race to race wherever Islam extends.[4] Lastly, the custom ranged through mediaeval into modern Europe. To cite old German examples, 'Die Heiden nicht endorften niesen, dâ man doch sprichet "Nu helfiu Gott!"' 'Wir sprechen, swer niuset, Gott helfe dir.'[5] For a combined English and French example, the following lines (A.D. 1100) may serve, which show our old formula 'waes hael!' ('may you be well!'—'wassail!') used also to avert being taken ill after a sneeze:—

> 'E pur une feyze esternuer
> Tantot quident mal trouer,
> Si *uesheil* ne diez aprez.'[6]

In the 'Rules of Civility' (A.D. 1685, translated from the French) we read:—'If his lordship chances to sneeze, you are not to bawl out, "God bless you, sir," but, pulling off your hat, bow to him handsomely, and make that obsecration to yourself.'[7] It is noticed that Anabaptists and Quakers rejected these with other salutations, but they remained in the code of English good manners among high and low till half a century or so ago, and are so little forgotten now, that most people still see the point of the story of the fiddler and his wife, where his sneeze and her hearty 'God bless you!' brought about the removal of the fiddle case. 'Gott hilf!' may still be heard in Germany, and 'Felicità!' in Italy.

It is not strange that the existence of these absurd customs should have been for ages a puzzle to curious inquirers. Especially the legend-mongers took the matter in hand, and their attempts to devise historical explanations are on record in a group of philosophic

---

[1] Noel, *Dic. des Origines*; Migne, *Dic. des Superstitions*, etc.; Bastian, *Oestl. Asien*, vol. ii, p. 129.

[2] Ward, *Hindoos*, vol. i, p. 142; Dubois, *Peuples de l'Inde*, vol. i, p. 465; Sleeman, *Ramasceana*, p. 120.

[3] Buxtorf, *Lexicon Chaldaicum*; Tendlau, *Sprichwörter, etc. Deutsch-Jüdischer Vorzeit*, Frankf. a. M., 1860, p. 142.

[4] Lane, *Modern Egyptians*, vol. i, p. 282. See Grant, in *Tr. Eth. Soc.*, vol. iii. p. 90.

[5] Grimm, *D. M.*, pp. 1070, 1110.

[6] 'Manuel des Pecchés,' in Wedgwood, *Dic. English Etymology*, s. v. 'wassail.'

[7] Brand, vol. iii, p. 126.

myths,—Greek, Jewish, Christian. Prometheus prays for the preservation of his artificial man, when it gives the first sign of life by a sneeze; Jacob prays that man's soul may not, as heretofore, depart from his body when he sneezes; Pope Gregory prays to avert the pestilence, in those days when the air was so deadly that he who sneezed died of it; and from these imaginary events legend declares that the use of the sneezing formulas was handed down. It is more to our purpose to notice the existence of a corresponding set of ideas and customs connected with gaping. Among the Zulus, repeated yawning and sneezing are classed together as signs of approaching spiritual possession.[1] The Hindu, when he gapes, must snap his thumb and finger, and repeat the name of some God, as Rama: to neglect this is a sin as great as the murder of a Brahman.[2] The Persians ascribe yawning, sneezing, etc., to demoniacal possession. Among the modern Moslems generally, when a man yawns, he puts the back of his left hand to his mouth, saying, 'I seek refuge with Allah from Satan the accursed!' but the act of yawning is to be avoided, for the Devil is in the habit of leaping into a gaping mouth.[3] This may very likely be the meaning of the Jewish proverb, 'Open not thy mouth to Satan!' The other half of this idea shows itself clearly in Josephus' story of his having seen a certain Jew, named Eleazar, cure demoniacs in Vespasian's time, by drawing the demons out through their nostrils, by means of a ring containing a root of mystic virtue mentioned by Solomon.[4] The account of the sect of the Messalians, who used to spit and blow their noses to expel the demons they might have drawn in with their breath,[5] the records of the mediaeval exorcists driving out devils through the patients' nostrils,[6] and the custom, still kept up in the Tyrol, of crossing oneself when one yawns, lest something evil should come into one's mouth,[7] involve similar ideas. In comparing the modern Kafir ideas with those of other districts of the world, we find a distinct notion of a sneeze being due to a spiritual presence. This, which seems indeed the key to the whole matter, has been well brought into view by Mr. Haliburton, as displayed in Keltic folklore, in a group of stories turning on the superstition that any one who sneezes is liable to be carried off by the fairies, unless their power be counteracted by an invocation, as 'God bless you!'[8] The corresponding idea as to yawning is to be

[1] Callaway, p. 263.     [2] Ward, l. c.
[3] *Pend-Nameh*, tr. de Sacy, ch. lxiii.; Maury, *Magie*, etc., p. 302; Lane, l. c.
[4] G. Brecher, *Das Transcendentale im Talmud*, p. 168; Joseph. Ant. Jud., viii, 2, 5.
[5] Migne, *Dic. des Hérésics*, s.v.
[6] Bastian, *Mensch*, vol. ii, pp. 115, 322.
[7] Wuttke, *Deutsche Volksaberglaube*, p. 137.     [8] Haliburton, *op. cit.*

found in an Iceland folklore legend, where the troll, who has transformed herself into the shape of the beautiful queen, says, 'When I yawn a little yawn, I am a neat and tiny maiden; when I yawn a half-yawn, then I am as a half-troll; when I yawn a whole yawn, then am I as a whole troll.'[1] On the whole, though the sneezing superstition makes no approach to universality among mankind, its wide distribution is highly remarkable, and it would be an interesting problem to decide how far this wide distribution is due to independent growth in several regions, how far to conveyance from race to race, and how far to ancestral inheritance. Here it has only to be maintained that it was not originally an arbitrary and meaningless custom, but the working out of a principle.[2] The plain statement by the modern Zulus fits with the hints to be gained from the superstition and folklore of other races, to connect the notions and practices as to sneezing with the ancient and savage doctrine of pervading and invading spirits, considered as good or evil, and treated accordingly. The lingering survivals of the quaint old formulas in modern Europe seem an unconscious record of the time when the explanation of sneezing had not yet been given over to physiology, but was still in the 'theological stage.'

There is current in Scotland the belief that the Picts, to whom local legend attributes buildings of prehistoric antiquity, bathed their foundation-stones with human blood; and legend even tells that St. Columba found it necessary to bury St. Oran alive beneath the foundation of his monastery, in order to propitiate the spirits of the soil who demolished by night what was built during the day. So late as 1843, in Germany, when a new bridge was built at Halle, a notion was abroad among the people that a child was wanted to be built into the foundation. These ideas of church or wall or bridge wanting human blood or an immured victim to make the foundation steadfast, are not only widespread in European folklore, but local chronicle or tradition asserts them as matter of historical fact in district after district. Thus, when the broken dam of the Nogat had to be repaired in 1463, the peasants, on the advice to throw in a living man, are said to have made a beggar drunk and buried him there. Thuringian legend declares that to make the castle of Liebenstein fast and impregnable, a child was bought for hard money of its mother and walled in. It was eating a cake while the masons were at work, the story goes, and it cried out, 'Mother,

---

[1] Powell and Magnussen, *Legends of Iceland*, 2nd ser. p. 448.
[2] The cases in which a sneeze is interpreted under special conditions, as with reference to right and left, early morning, etc. (see Plutarch, De Genio Socratis, etc.), are not considered here, as they belong to ordinary omen-divination.

I see thee still'; then later, 'Mother, I see thee a little still'; and, as they put in the last stone, 'Mother, now I see thee no more.' The wall of Copenhagen, legend says, sank as fast as it was built; so they took an innocent little girl, set her on a chair at a table with toys and eatables, and, as she played and ate, twelve master-masons closed a vault over her; then, with clanging music, the wall was raised, and stood firm ever after. Thus Italian legend tells of the bridge of Arta, that fell in and fell in till they walled in the master-builder's wife, and she spoke her dying curse that the bridge should tremble like a flower-stalk henceforth. The Slavonic chiefs founding Detinez, according to old heathen custom, sent out men to take the first boy they met and bury him in the foundation. Servian legend tells how three brothers combined to build the fortress of Skadra (Scutari); but, year after year, the demon (vila) razed by night what the three hundred masons built by day. The fiend must be appeased by a human sacrifice, the first of the three wives who should come bringing food to the workmen. All three brothers swore to keep the dreadful secret from their wives; but the two eldest gave traitorous warning to theirs, and it was the youngest brother's wife who came unsuspecting, and they built her in. But she entreated that an opening should be left for her to suckle her baby through, and for a twelve-month it was brought. To this day, Servian wives visit the tomb of the good mother, still marked by a stream of water which trickles, milky with lime, down the fortress wall. Lastly, there is our own legend of Vortigern, who could not finish his tower till the foundation-stone was wetted with the blood of a child born of a mother without a father. As is usual in the history of sacrifice, we hear of substitutes for such victims; empty coffins walled up in Germany, a lamb walled in under the altar in Denmark to make the church stand fast, and the churchyard in like manner hanselled by burying a live horse first. In modern Greece an evident relic of the idea survives in the superstition that the first passer-by after a foundation-stone is laid will die within the year, wherefore the masons will compromise the debt by killing a lamb or a black cock on the stone. With much the same idea German legend tells of the bridge-building fiend cheated of his promised fee, a soul, by the device of making a cock run first across; and thus German folklore says it is well, before entering a new house, to let a cat or dog run in.[1] From all this it seems that, with due allow-

---

[1] W. Scott, *Minstrelsy of Scottish Border*; Forbes Leslie, *Early Races of Scotland*, vol. i, pp. 149, 487; Grimm, *Deutsche Mythologie*, p. 972. 1095; Bastian, *Mensch*, vol. ii, p. 92, 407, vol. iii, pp. 105, 112; Bowring, *Servian Popular Poetry*, p. 64. A review of the First Edition of the present work in *Nature*, June 15, 1871, contains the following: —'It is not, for example, many years since the present Lord Leigh was accused of

ance for the idea having passed into an often-repeated and varied mythic theme, yet written and unwritten tradition do preserve the memory of a bloodthirsty barbaric rite, which not only really existed in ancient times, but lingered long in European history. If now we look to less cultured countries, we shall find the rite carried on in our own day with a distinctly religious purpose, either to propitiate the earth-spirits with a victim, or to convert the soul of the victim himself into a protecting demon.

In Africa, in Galam, a boy and girl used to be buried alive before the great gate of the city to make it impregnable, a practice once executed on a large scale by a Bambarra tyrant; while in Great Bassam and Yarriba such sacrifices were usual at the foundation of a house or village.[1] In Polynesia, Ellis heard of the custom, instanced by the fact that the central pillar of one of the temples at Maeva was planted upon the body of a human victim.[2] In Borneo, among the Milanau Dayaks, at the erection of the largest house a deep hole was dug to receive the first post, which was then suspended over it; a slave girl was placed in the excavation; at a signal the lashings were cut, and the enormous timber descended, crushing the girl to death, a sacrifice to the spirits. St. John saw a milder form of the rite performed, when the chief of the Quop Dayaks set up a flagstaff near his house, a chicken being thrown in to be crushed by the descending pole.[3] More cultured nations of Southern Asia have carried on into modern ages the rite of the foundation-sacrifice. A seventeenth-century account of Japan mentions the belief there that a wall laid on the body of a willing human victim would be secure from accident; accordingly, when a great wall was to be built, some wretched slave would offer himself as foundation, lying

---

[1] Waitz, vol. ii, p. 197.
[2] Ellis, *Polyn. Res.*, vol. i, p. 346; Tyerman and Bennet, vol. ii, p. 39.

St. John, *Far East*, vol. i, p. 46; see Bastian, vol. ii, p. 407. I am indebted to Mr. R. K. Douglas for a perfect example of one meaning of the foundation-sacrifice, from the Chinese book, 'Yŭh hea ke' ('Jewelled Casket of Divination'): 'Before beginning to build, the workmen should sacrifice to the gods of the neighbourhood, of the earth and wood. Should the carpenters be very apprehensive of the building falling, they, when fixing a post, should take something living and put it beneath, and lower the post on it, and to liberate [the evil influences] they should strike the post with an axe and repeat—

"It is well, it is well,
May those who live within
Be ever warm and well fed." '

---

having built an obnoxious person—one account, if we remember right, said eight obnoxious persons—into the foundation of a bridge at Stoneleigh. Of course so preposterous a charge carried on its face its own sufficient refutation; but the fact that it was brought at all is a singular instance of the almost incredible vitality of old traditions.'

down in the trench to be crushed by the heavy stones lowered upon him.[1] When the gate of the new city of Tavoy, in Tenasserim, was built, perhaps twenty years ago, Mason was told by an eye-witness that a criminal was put in each post-hole to become a protecting demon. Thus it appears that such stories as that of the human victims buried for spirit-watchers under the gates of Mandalay, of the queen who was drowned in a Birmese reservoir to make the dyke safe, of the hero whose divided body was buried under the fortress of Thatung to make it impregnable, are the records, whether in historical or mythical form, of the actual customs of the land.[2] Within our own dominion, when Rajah Sala Byne was building the fort of Sialkot in the Punjab, the foundation of the southeast bastion gave way so repeatedly that he had recourse to a soothsayer, who assured him that it would never stand until the blood of an only son was shed there, wherefore the only son of a widow was sacrificed.[3] It is thus plain that hideous rites, of which Europe has scarcely kept up more than the dim memory, have held fast their ancient practice and meaning in Africa, Polynesia, and Asia, among races who represent in grade, if not in chronology, earlier stages of civilization.

When Sir Walter Scott, in the 'Pirate,' tells of Bryce the pedlar refusing to help Mordaunt to save the shipwrecked sailor from drowning, and even remonstrating with him on the rashness of such a deed, he states an old superstition of the Shetlanders. 'Are you mad?' says the pedlar; 'you that have lived sae lang in Zetland, to risk the saving of a drowning man? Wot ye not, if you bring him to life again, he will be sure to do you some capital injury?' Were this inhuman thought noticed in this one district alone, it might be fancied to have had its rise in some local idea now no longer to be explained. But when mentions of similar superstitions are collected among the St. Kilda islanders and the boatmen of the Danube, among French and English sailors, and even out of Europe and among less civilized races, we cease to think of local fancies, but look for some widely accepted belief of the lower culture to account for such a state of things. The Hindu does not save a man from drowning in the sacred Ganges, and the islanders of the Malay archipelago share the cruel notion.[4] Of all people the rude Kamchadals have the prohibition in the most remarkable form. They

[1] Caron, *Japan*, in Pinkerton, vol. vii, p. 623.
[2] Bastian, *Oestl. Asien*, vol. i, pp. 193, 214; vol. ii, pp. 91, 270; vol. iii, p. 16. Roberts, *Oriental Illustrations of Scriptures*, p. 283 (Ceylon).
[3] Bastian, *Mensch*, vol. iii, p. 107. A modern Arnaut story is given by Prof. Liebrecht in *Philologus*, vol. xxiii (1865) p. 682.
[4] Bastian, *Mensch*, vol. iii, p. 210. Ward, *Hindoos*, vol. ii, p. 318.

hold it a great fault, says Kracheninnikow, to save a drowning man; he who delivers him will be drowned himself.[1] Steller's account is more extraordinary, and probably applies only to cases where the victim is actually drowning: he says that if a man fell by chance into the water, it was a great sin for him to get out, for as he had been destined to drown he did wrong in not drowning, wherefore no one would let him into his dwelling, nor speak to him, nor give him food or a wife, but he was reckoned for dead; and even when a man fell into the water while others were standing by, far from helping him out, they would drown him by force. Now these savages, it appears, avoided volcanoes because of the spirits who live there and cook their food; for a like reason, they held it a sin to bathe in hot springs; and they believed with fear in a fish-like spirit of the sea, whom they called Mitgk.[2] This spiritualistic belief among the Kamchadals is, no doubt, the key to their superstition as to rescuing drowning men. There is even to be found in modern European superstition, not only the practice, but with it a lingering survival of its ancient spiritualistic significance. In Bohemia, a recent account (1864) says that the fishermen do not venture to snatch a drowning man from the waters. They fear that the 'Waterman' (i.e., water-demon) would take away their luck in fishing, and drown themselves at the first opportunity.[3] This explanation of the prejudice against saving the water-spirit's victim may be confirmed by a mass of evidence from various districts of the world. Thus, in discussing the doctrine of sacrifice, it will appear that the usual manner of making an offering to a well, river, lake, or sea, is simply to cast property, cattle, or men into the water, which personally or by its in-dwelling spirit takes possession of them.[4] That the accidental drowning of a man is held to be such a seizure, savage and civilized folklore show by many examples. Among the Sioux Indians, it is Unk-tahe the water-monster that drowns his victims in flood or rapid;[5] in New Zealand huge supernatural reptile-monsters, called Taniwha, live in river-bends, and those who are drowned are said to be pulled under by them;[6] the Siamese fears the Pnük or water-spirit that seizes bathers and drags them under to his dwelling;[7] in Slavonic lands it is Topielec (the ducker) by whom men are always drowned;[8] when some one is drowned in

[1] Kracheninnikow, *Descr. du Kamchatka, Voy. en Sibérie*, vol. iii, p. 72.
[2] Steller, *Kamtschatka*, pp. 265, 274.
[3] J. V. Grohmann, *Aberglauben und Gebräuche aus Böhmen*, p. 12.
[4] Chap. XVIII.                                    [5] Eastman, *Dacotah*, pp. 118, 125.
[6] R. Taylor, *New Zealand*, p. 48.
[7] Bastian, *Oestl. Asien*, vol. iii, p. 34.
[8] Hanusch, *Wissenschaft des Slawischen Mythus*, p. 299.

Germany, people recollect the religion of their ancestors, and say, 'The river-spirit claims his yearly sacrifice,' or, more simply, 'The nix has taken him:'[1]—

'Ich glaube, die Wellen verschlingen,
Am Ende Fischer und Kahn;
Und das hat mit ihrem Singen
Die Lorelei gethan.'

From this point of view it is obvious that to save a sinking man is to snatch a victim from the very clutches of the water-spirit, a rash defiance of deity which would hardly pass unavenged. In the civilized world the rude old theological conception of drowning has long been superseded by physical explanation; and the prejudice against rescue from such a death may have now almost or altogether disappeared. But archaic ideas, drifted on into modern folklore and poetry, still bring to our view an apparent connexion between the primitive doctrine and the surviving custom.

As the social development of the world goes on, the weightiest thoughts and actions may dwindle to mere survival. Original meaning dies out gradually, each generation leaves fewer and fewer to bear it in mind, till it falls out of popular memory, and in after-days ethnography has to attempt, more or less successfully, to restore it by piecing together lines of isolated or forgotten facts. Children's sports, popular sayings, absurd customs, may be practically unimportant, but are not philosophically insignificant, bearing as they do on some of the most instructive phases of early culture. Ugly and cruel superstitions may prove to be relics of primitive barbarism, for in keeping up such Man is like Shakespeare's fox,

'Who, ne'er so tame, so cherish'd, and lock'd up,
Will have a wild trick of his ancestors.'


## [ 2 ANDREW LANG ]

'Epoch-making' was the adjective used by Joseph Jacobs on belatedly encountering Lang's article in the *Fortnightly Review*, asserting the savage origins of Ayran myths. Jacobs, locked in a vigorous duel with Lang (1844–1912), had assigned priority for the savage origins thesis to James Farrer (see next selection) when the Scot called his attention to the early article. Here Lang first set

[1] Grimm, *Deutsche Myth.*, p. 462.

forth the ideas he was to elaborate for the remainder of his life. Starting with Tylor's theory of evolution and doctrine of survivals, he brought into evidence recent collections of savage and peasant folktales to intensify the shaft of light cast by folklore over the dim past. In one brilliant essay Lang reversed the whole trend of mythological criticism.

Text from Andrew Lang, 'Mythology and Fairy Tales,' *Fortnightly Review*, XIX (May, 1873). Pages 618–31.

In the controversy as to whether Aryan beliefs and customs have been developed out of the lowest stage of savage life, little use has been made of the evidence of *Mährchen*. It is unfortunate that there is nothing in English which corresponds to this word as used by mythologists. Perhaps folks-story is the term that would best suit that strange flower of primitive imagination, the fairy tales that seem the most lawless work of fancy, and yet among Zulus and Samoyeds, in Africa and Germany, in India, Scotland, and modern Greece, are radically and necessarily the same. The remains of the Stone Age are scarcely more broadcast, and more identical in form, than these legends. Tertullian knew the story of Rapünzel, 'Turres Lamiae, Pecten Solis'; an Egyptian papyrus has been unrolled, and found to contain the myth which the Scotch call 'the Milk-white Doo'; an ancestor of Sakya Muni was one of the serpent-girl Melusine's earlier lovers, and she had been Lilith the snake-bride of Adam, and as Echidne had lain by Herakles thousands of years before she wedded the founder of the house of Lusignan.[1]

There are comparatively few places in Europe where the lively oral tradition of *Mährchen* still survives. 'The schoolmaster and the minister come,' as in Barra and Uist, and destroy the old culture of ballad-dance and legendary lore. Thus in Argyll and the Hebrides, Mr. Campbell met a reluctance to tell the tales of the West Highlands, which was not more shyness than a decaying sense of the sacredness of a religious trust. In Russia collectors have to disguise themselves in mean clothing, and haunt the khans and huts of the peasants. In Zulu-land even, the warriors do not like to confess their knowledge of their own fairy tales; and Dr. Callaway found that old women, like 'les bonnes femmes vieilles qui lavent la lexive à la fontaine,' and knew, says Brantôme, the legend of Melusine, were the best repositories of *Mährchen*. In an argument which tries to

[1] See the story of Melusine in Brantôme, in the memoir of the Duc de Montpensier. Three French families are said to have changed their genealogy, that they might trace back to the serpent-ancestress.

prove, and to deduce the consequences of the absolutely primeval character of the lower myths, these facts are worth noting. We must remember, what we are so prone to forget, the quite unbroken nature of peasant-life, and of peasant-faith. The progressive classes had advanced comparatively but a little way in the evolution of creeds and customs when they left the rural people behind. They have turned back on these again and again, in moments of spiritual excitement, have compelled them to put on a semblance of new beliefs, and to call on gods not of their making. But the superstitious instinct has permitted the masses to forget and omit nothing of old cults and old rites. The Nereids in modern Greece still receive offerings of milk and honey, from peasants whose forefathers may have scarcely known the name of Zeus and of the high gods, and whom even the penetrating force of Christianity has hardly won from the practices of the lower culture. If any of the very earliest myths remain in Europe, they must linger in the quiet places where such peasants tell their fairy tales, by the hearth, or in the olive-shade.

More than sixty years have passed since Scott, in a note to 'The Lady of the Lake,' first called attention in England to the scientific importance of these fictions, and at the same time gave what seems a wrong direction to the inquiry. 'A work of great interest,' Scott says, 'might be compiled upon the origin of popular fiction, and the transmission of similar tales from age to age, and from country to country. The mythology of one period would then appear to pass into the romance of the next, and that into the nursery tales of subsequent ages.' Much has been done for the study of 'popular fiction' since Scott wrote this, when the Grimms were even then at work in Germany. Castren has collected the tales that are told around Samoyed hearths, Mr. Campbell has done the same for the West Highlands, Dr. Dasent has translated the Norse stories, Dr. Callaway has made an invaluable contribution from among the Zulus. But Scott's view of the genesis of *Mährchen*, supposing Scott by mythology to have meant the higher mythology, appears still to be the accepted one. Thus, to quote a few instances, Mr. Max Müller says, 'the gods of ancient mythology were changed into the demigods and heroes of ancient epic poetry, and these demigods again became at a later age the principal characters in our nursery tales.'[1] Further, 'in Germany as well as everywhere else, popular fictions are the last remains, the detritus in fact, if we may say so, of an ancient mythology,'[2] Again, Von Hahn, the collector of the modern Greek and Albanian *Mährchen*, founds a comparative table of the higher myths, and of fairy tales—to be examined later—on the theory that

[1] *Chips from a German Workshop*, ii, 243.   [2] *Contemporary Review*, December, 1871.

all myths are imaginative descriptions of the greater elementary powers and changes of nature, that the saga or heroic epic localizes these myths in real places, and attributes the adventures of the gods to supposed ancestral heroes, and that 'the *Mährchen* is the last and youngest form of the saga.'[1]

There is no occasion to multiply instances, but it may be noted that Bernhardi[2] seems to be content when he has shown a German *Mährchen* to have a place in the higher mythology of the north, and that the author of a very able and cautious essay on the subject commits himself to the statement that the popular tale is the latest form of the myth.[3]

The result of this popular theory, if carried out to its consequences, and if all that makes against it is got rid of by an ingenious use of the solar hypothesis, is to support the doctrine that the Aryan religions were not developed out of Fetichism, and that 'the ancestors of the Greeks and Hebrews did not pass through a period of the disgusting customs of savages.' The object of this essay is to demonstrate that the very opposite of Mr. Müller's view is the true one, namely that the *Mährchen*, far from being the detritus of the higher mythology, are the remains of an earlier formation, and that in most cases in which they tally with the higher epic, they preserve an older and more savage form of the same myth, containing more allusions to cannibalism, to magic, or Shamanism, to kinship with the beasts, and to bestial transformations. As *Mährchen* are not peculiar to Indo-European races, but are common to Finns, Samoyeds, Zulus, it will follow that they must be attributed to an epoch prior to the rise of such distinctions as Aryan and Semitic. It will be shown that the supernatural element in these tales is more easily explained as a survival of animal-worship, and of magic, than as a degraded shape of the myths of the elements, and the great vicissitudes of nature. If this be so, the myths of the dawn and of the sun can no longer be considered *primary*, and it will appear that the religious imagination of the Indo-European race must have passed through a stage of Fetichism. Faith will thus be manifest as a continual and rational progress, from the worship of the objects nearest sense, to the adoration of the bodiless forces that strike the loftier imagination, and thence to the higher polytheisms. Thus there will be little room left for degradation through emblems whose purpose has been forgotten; degradation will only take place when the intellectual and priestly

[1] Von Hahn, *Griechische Mährchen*, p. 5.
[2] *Volksmährchen und Epische Dichtung*, T. V. Bernhardi.
[3] Mr. Laurenny, *St. Paul's Magazine*, September, 1871.

aristocracy of a race becomes effete, and falls back on superstitions which now meet it with a new and strange aspect, but which are really the cast-off garments of its spirit, still preserved by the unprogressive classes of the people.

First, then, the *Mährchen* are prior in existence to the heroic sagas. These by their definition are applied mythology, adventures of the gods attributed to heroes, and said to have occurred in definite places. It is obvious that these, as we have them, must have been composed by persons who were acquainted with the names of these places. *Mährchen*, on the other hand, assign no particular locality to the events they record, and seldom any names to the actors, and they are found among non-Aryan nations, where the corresponding higher tradition does not occur. As transmission by copying is out of the question, these nations must either be degenerate, and have forgotten the higher tradition while retaining a lower form identical with that which exists in Aryan countries as *Mährchen*, or the lower form must have been composed prior to the higher, and prior to the separation of races.

Although it is anticipating a more detailed criticism of Von Hahn's comparative tables of legends it may be as well to illustrate this point by a reference to the saga of 'Bertha Broadfoot.' Every one knows Grimm's story of the 'Goose Girl,' the royal bride who has three magical drops of blood in a handkerchief, who possesses a talking horse, and is robbed of these treasures, and of her place as bride, by a wicked bower-maiden. The princess lives in disguise as a servant; she is bound by an oath not to reveal who she is; she is comforted by the head of her horse, which, though slain, yet speaks; and she is restored to her husband. M. Bernhardi has analysed the tale, has brought out its archaic features, and referred the incident of the talking horse to the ancient worship of that animal. Now this very story occurs in a mediaeval epic of the thirteenth century, in which Bertha Broadfoot, the mother of Charles the Great, takes the place, and achieves the adventures, of the bride. At first it is a perfectly natural inference that the higher fiction, with its place in the Carolingian cycle, should be the earlier, and the 'Goose Girl' the lower popular form produced by a distorted recollection of the romance. This, as we have seen, is the opinion of M. Von Hahn. But when we turn to Mr. Campbell's 'Tales from the Gaelic of the West Highlands,' and find this story recurring under the name of 'The Sharp Grey Sheep,' and remember how unlikely it is that the people of Morven borrowed from the French *épopée*, we are puzzled. This is not all. Canon Callaway brings the same legend from among the Zulus, only here the part of the evil maid is played by a cunning beast, who takes the bride's place, and the bridegroom is warned by speaking birds, as in the Scottish 'Rashin-Coatie,' that he is riding off with the wrong love. Is it an accident that the birds' song in Zulu is so like that with which, in a modern Greek ballad, corresponding to 'Lenore's Death-ride,' the birds warn the girl that she is riding with her brother's corpse?[1] Now of three alternatives, one. Either the West Highlanders, and Zulus, and Germans got their story from the old French, or the tale is common property of the tribes before the separation into Aryan and Semitic, or there are necessary forms of the imagination, which in widely separated peoples must produce identical results. The notion of copying is rejected by mythologists, and it follows that either Germans and Celts once dwelt with Kaffirs, and shared their fables and fetichisms, or that the Aryan and the lower races have had to pass through similar conditions of imagination and of society, and therefore of religion.

These conclusions it would be wrong to found upon one instance. We must proceed to analyse the relations of the lower and higher myths, believing that the former will almost invariably turn out to be the elder. It is not unfair to assume, that where the *Mährchen* is common to many distinct races, and the epic use of its theme is peculiar to one race only, or is not found at all, the *Mährchen* is the prior form. It will also be allowed that where the popular tale keeps references to Shamanism, to cannibalism, to kinship with the beasts, which are omitted in the corresponding higher form of the story, these omissions strengthen the belief that the saga is of later date than the tale, and has passed through the refining atmosphere of a higher civilisation. Again, if the epic legends, which do in a certain way correspond in their narrative with *Mährchen*, are the more obscure, wild, and early legends of Greece, those least susceptible of artistic treatment, and if it is just the strangest *Mährchen* that have no corresponding saga, these facts will tend to confirm our hypothesis. We will proceed, then, to analyse the comparative tables of M. Von Hahn, and lastly to criticize a few of the explanations of popular stories which Mr. Max Müller and Mr. Cox have given from their own point of view, and try to show that our theory gives a more natural rendering.

[1] Here are the words of the modern Greek. 'Ah, listen, Constantine, what the birds are saying.' 'They are birds, let them be singing,' says the corpse; 'little birds, let them chatter.' 'The birds sing, the birds say, Lo the fair girl that rides with the dead.' In Zulu the birds say, 'Ukaka, the king's child's gone off with a beast.' He said, 'Haw, my men, you hear what these birds say; did you ever hear birds speak?' They said, 'Oh, sir, the manner of birds of the thorn country, they speak.'—Callaway's *Nursery Tales from the Zulu*; Fauriel's *Chants populaires de la Grèce Moderne*.

M. Von Hahn's formulae are forty in number, but two may be omitted, as they are not worked out. In fourteen of the remaining thirty-eight, the heroic legend which should correspond to the popular tale fails entirely. Twenty-four formulae remain; in these the Greek epic story fails four times, in cases where the German retains some slight resemblance to the *Mährchen*, and the German is absent eight times, where some vestiges of the Greek Saga survive. In two formulae there are sagas with no answering *Mährchen*. The first formula is that of 'Amor and Psyche,' as an epic tale corresponding to the Greek folk-story 'Golden Wand,' our 'Beauty and the Beast,' the Scottish 'Black Bull o' Norroway.' In all these the bride commits an offence against a mystic command of her lover's, loses him, and is reconciled to him after many wanderings.

Now, Mr. Max Müller is undoubtedly right in supposing this to be a myth of the Dawn, the fable of Urväsi, who is lost to the Sun, till Hesperus brings all home; yet as the Dawn is represented in the Indian version as a 'kind of fairy,' not a higher goddess, this must be one of the lower and earlier elementary myths. In fact it is not an epic tradition at all, but must have been current about Thessalian hearths thousands of years before Appuleius took it up, gave it artistic shape, and named hero and heroine Eros and Psyche, in the second century. In Sanscrit, too, the story must have been familiar ages before it was adopted, for a special purpose, into the higher literature of the Brâhmana of the Yagur Veda to explain the ceremony of kindling the sacred fire. Wherever an unbroken peasant class retains the tale, in Scotland, Scandinavia, and modern Greece, the nameless characters are subject to bestial transformation. This primitive feature in Greece leaves a trace in the bride's suspicion that her husband is an enchanted monster; in Sanscrit, the bride and her maidens take the form of birds. So, too, the lost love and her girls, in the Zulu nursery story, are changed into finches.

M. Von Hahn calls his ninth formula 'Orionformel.' Smith's 'Mythological Dictionary' does not contain the legend of Orion's birth in its vulgar shape, but the 'less fastidious Lemprière' may be referred to. All that need be said on the not very delicate theme is, that the wondrous child Orion owes his birth to much the same magic ceremony as that through which the childless Kaffir queen, Ukcombekcantsini, obtains a daughter.[1] When the Finns want to generate a *Paara*, a lubber-fiend like the Scotch 'Brownie,' when an Icelandic wizard would develop the existence of a 'Fetcher,' they have recourse to spells of the same foul magic. This hideous shape of

[1] Callaway, *Nursery Tales from the Zulu*, p. 106; Castren, *Fin. Myth.*, pp. 104, 106.

the lower superstition has, in Hellas, attached itself to the name of Orion, but the belief must, of course, have preceded the legend.

The only resemblance between M. Von Hahn's twelfth formula, the story of Danäe, and the Romaic *Mährchen* of 'The Half-man,' lies in the incident of a mother and her bastard being sent to sea in an ark. The Romaic story is a very singular effort of rude imagination, and is full of talking animals, and of miracles effected by the use of a spell with a primitive sound, 'by the first word of God, and the second of the Fish, let this or that be done.' If the story of Danäe has any connexion at all with this *Mährchen*, it has dropped all its primitive features.

There is no folks-story more widely spread than that of Grimm's 'Machandel-boom.' It occurs in Castren's Samoyedische *Mährchen*; it is the 'Milk-white Doo' of Scotland, the 'Asterinos and Pulja' of modern Greece. Goethe's Marguerite sings a snatch from it in her madness. Mr. Dasent says the Bechuanas have a form of the myth; there is a sort of trace of it in Popol Vuh. Everywhere it relates the adventures of children fleeing from an intolerable horror. Now as copying is impossible, this story must have originated before the heroic tale of 'Phryxus and Hellé,' it cannot be a corrupted later form of 'Phryxus and Hellé.'[1] Moreover, in all the *Mährchen*, the outrage not to be borne is that of cannibalism—cannibalism spoken of in the most familiar matter-of-fact way; and again the adventures include the transformation of one of the children into a bear or a wolf. The Greek poet who turned this early myth into the story of 'Phryxus and Hellé,' and connected it with the Jason cycle, substituted human sacrifice for cannibalism—a change as natural in story as in historical evolution—and suppressed all mention of bestial transformation. In fact, the heroic poets did with the earlier materials of fiction what Mr. Arthur Pendennis did for his characters in 'Walter Lorraine'—raised them in the social scale, and suppressed their vulgar adventures. The myth of the Argonauts supplies another instance. It is incredible that the Scotch should have borrowed the tale of 'Nicht, Nocht, Nothing'; the Russians that of 'Tsar Morskoi'; the Norsemen, 'The Master Maid'; the Finns, part of the feats of Lemminkainen, from the account of the aid which Medea gave to Jason. Jason only represents the highest and latest artistic form of a primeval piece of folklore.

We have said that the wilder *Mährchen* had frequently no epic narrative corresponding to them at all. The seventh of M. Von Hahn's formulae is an instance to the point. There is no Hellenic

[1] It is a curious fact that the Golden Ram of the Greek legend becomes a Beaver in the Samoyed version.

tradition on the subject of a human mother bearing a beast-child, nor is this a thing to be wondered at. But German and Romaic stories on the theme abound. The scandal was current about Bertha, wife of Robert of France; and one has only to open Dr. Callaway's book at random to find instances of a myth so natural to primitive men, and so revolting to later feeling and artistic consciousness. Again, no Greek poem tells of a child dedicated before his birth to a demon; but there are plenty of *Mährchen* on this incident, and the rite itself was actually practised by the Nahuatls in America. Is it strange, too, that no Greek or German epic narrative answers to the folks-story of the men who marry girls whose brothers are animals? The very ties of bestial kinship, a lingering trace of totemism, were half forgotten by, and wholly repellent to, the singers of the heroic ages. These ghastlier tales that Pindar knew, but refused to tell, what are they but echoes from a period of lower cults—memories which the religious instinct dares not resign, and must fashion into some serpentine end of a fair woman's form, some unspeakable horror in the legend of a later and lovelier god?

We need only examine one more formula of M. Von Hahn's—the thirty-second; this he calls the myth of the grateful beasts, and his heroic instance in Greece is the story of Melampus. The myth is that the ears of Melampus were licked by two snakes whom he had rescued, and that he thereon understood the language of birds. This effect was produced, not because the animals were grateful, but because they were serpents. So in the Volsung epic, Sigurd learns the bird's speech after tasting the roasted heart of the serpent Fafnir; and in Scotland Sir James Ramsay, of Bamff, gained similar magic power from tasting the oil of the white serpent of Spain.[1] Is it not plain that these tales go back to the time when our Aryan forefathers were in the mental condition of Dr. Callaway's Kaffir instructor in the Zulu language, who believed that his own brother gained the gift of prophecy, and learned the language of birds, after a day-long battle with a leopard? A Greek ἀοιδός attached to the house of the Melampodidae, might appropriate the current tale to the ancestor of the line, a minstrel of the Ramsays of Bamff might attach it the founder of the house; but the story must have existed in the vague shape of a *Mährchen* prior to any appropriation.

If the conclusions drawn from the evidence which has been examined in some detail be correct, *Mährchen* must be remains from a stage of totemism and belief in magic—must be prior to the myths of the wide forces, the great changes, the universal aspects of nature; to the tales that rise from personifications of sky, and sea,

[1] Chambers' *Popular Rhymes of Scotland.*

and thunder, and fire, winter and summer—all that is most impressive to spirit, and most remote from sense. Men bowed before trees and serpents, bats, 'and sardines, for want of larger gods,' says Garcilasso de la Vega, before they looked up, like Xenophanes, to the blue expanse of heaven and conceived of Zeus.[1] It was only the fourth race of men, says Popol Vuh, that strange fragment of an American cosmogony, whose eyes were purged to see clearly, whose souls were filled with the word of the Creator, who worshipped and waited for the Dawn. Yet it is usual to explain folk-stories as a detritus of these later myths of the elementary forces, and it is time to examine some of these explanations in detail.

Few stories are better known than that of the 'Frog-King,' the German 'Froschkönig.' It occurs in the 'Tales from the West Highlands' and in Mr. Chambers's Lowland collection, and relates how a king's daughter married a frog, who ultimately changed into a handsome young man. 'How came such a story,' says Mr. Max Müller, 'ever to be invented? Human beings were, we may hope, at all times sufficiently enlightened to know that a marriage between a frog and the daughter of a queen was absurd.' Just in the same way, in the Scotch version, 'The lassie didna think that the poor beast could mean onything serious.' Mr. Müller forgets that a Frog, considered as a member of the Frog tribe—the tribe which owned the Frog as totem (there is a Toad tribe in Canada)—must once have been a very marriageable person. Without degrading our ancestors to the rank of mere 'idiots,' we may suppose that when they had left the totem stage of savagery, expressions lingered in language from that period of odd social arrangements, and that as the meaning of these expressions became lost, they gave rise to myths. But to return to the frog. 'It can be shown,' says Mr. Müller, 'that frog was used as a name for the sun. Now at sunrise and sunset, when the sun was squatting on the water, it was called the frog.' Frogs do not, in point of fact, squat on the water, and Mr. Müller quotes no use of this frog-name applied to the sun. Nor does he appear to remember his own statement, that before the Aryans separated 'they could not have known the existence of the sea,'[2] in which the sun-frog ought to have squatted at sunrise and sunset.

But this myth of the frog must have been made before the separation of races; for a quite recognizable form of it occurs among the Zulus.[3] We must suppose, then, that the Sun-frog, as Mr. Cox

[1] Royal Chronicles of the Yncas, 175, 147, 1168; Garcilasso's account of the Totemism of the Collas and other lower tribes of Peru, and of the introduction of Sun-worship by the Yncas, is very minute and instructive.

[2] *Chips*, ii, 46.

[3] Callaway, 241–8. The girl did not marry the frog who came out of the water to her

constantly calls it, must have squatted on the water of a fairly large lake. Some poet or fisherman, to go on with Mr. Müller's explanation, called the sun at dawn a frog, and the remarkable force of this early witticism gave the name the widest popularity, and it became the source of proverbs, such as 'Bheki, the sun, will die at sight of water.' Then it is forgotten that Bheki is a name of the sun, and is supposed to be the name of a girl or of a man, and on this theme a tale is fashioned; 'And so,' says Mr. Müller, 'the change from sun to frog, and from frog to man, which was at first due to the mere spell of language, would in our nursery tales be ascribed to miraculous charms, more familiar to a later age.' Now Castren and Mr. Tylor, and most students of the ways of savages, hold that 'magic belongs to the *lowest* known stages of civilization'; that it is implicit in the very idea of 'miraculous charms'; and that, far from being adopted late into an Aryan myth, its presence is an obvious survival of belief in Shamanism. Mr. Müller's explanation covertly introduces the very thing that needs to be explained. Mr. Cox adopts the same *petitio principii*, when he says of the myth of swan-maidens that 'from the thought which regarded the cloud as an eagle or a swan, it was easy to pass to the idea that these birds were beautiful maidens' (the transition scarcely seems so easy), 'and hence that they could at will, or at the ending of the enchantment, assume human forms.' But to construct this myth, the notion of enchantment or magic, and the absence of our later sense of separation from the beasts, is required as necessary form, and these notions belong to the human mind before it reaches to the personification and worship of the higher and more abstract aspects of the world. Thus we find that among the Laps thunder is a god who slays Shamans and drives them out of heaven, and so Popul Vuh says that 'the gods of the lion, the tiger, and the serpent were petrified at the sight of the sun.'[1] Sabaeism does bring the light, and the cult of thunder and the great free forces of nature clears the air in a manner, and destroys gradually the fear of fetiches nearer to sense. But at the beginning, as at the end of speculation, 'where no gods are, ghosts walk,' and Shamans and spiritualists have their day, or night.

Another instance of explanations by the elementary theory. In criticizing the tale of Eros and Psyche, Mr. Cox speaks of the tasks that have to be accomplished, and of the ministers that aid the

[1] *Cf.*, Philostratus, *Vita. Apoll.*, viii, 7, 2, quoted by Hermann, *Alterthumer der Griechen*, ii, 276. γοήτων δε ξυνουσίαν φεύγουσι μὲν ἱερὰ θεών, ἰχθμὰ γὰρ τῦις παρὰ τὴν τέχνην.

aid, but 'he built a great town, and became a great chief.' There is a Frog tribe among the Brahmins at Munnipore.

heroine. These are bears, wolves, foxes, ducks, swans, eagles, ants, 'all names by which the old mythical language spoke of the clouds, or the winds, or of the light which conquers the darkness. The bear appears in the myth of the "The Seven Shiners," the wolf in the stories of "Phoibos Lukeios," of "Lykaon," and "The Myrmidons." The eagles bear the Surya Bai on their wings through the heavens,' and so on. Something is wanted a great deal more definite and critical than this. Wherever Mr. Cox finds animals playing a part in myth or *Mährchen*, he has recourse to Mr. Müller's interpretation of the bear in the zodiac as the bears, and these as the shiners, and of the wolf-Apollo as the Apollo of light.[1] Thus Mr. Cox writes, 'Probably all the animals selected to perform this office of nourishing exposed children will be found to have names which like the Greek λύκος, a wolf, *denote the glossiness of their coats*.' Even supposing Dr. Müller to be right about the bear, the introduction of every species of animal into human relationship, and into the zodiac, is not thus solved by supposing clouds, stars, and winds received, through a philological accident, beasts' names, on which names myths were founded.[2] The acts of animal-worship and of totemism are too well known for it to be believed that this worship arises from forgetfulness of the meaning of words and symbols. Mr. Cox makes serpent-worship a cult of an emblem of the Phallus, and the Phallus an emblem of the productive life of nature. He takes it for granted that the negroes of Dahomey, for instance, attained to one of the widest of abstract ideas—that of the generative force of the universe—and declined thence into the worship of reptiles and obscene things. For if we find both Aryans and negroes and Mexicans worshipping the serpent, it is absurd to give different reasons, and say that the Aryans had forgotten the meaning of a symbol, while the Africans and Americans are deceived by the devil, or act out of their own superfluous naughtiness. When the Finns and Red Indians venerate the bear, do they do so because they once adored light, and light in some Aryan tongue had a root *ark*, and bears and light got mixed up in an idiom of which Finnish and Choctaw do not retain many traces? Or to return to Eros and Psyche, do birds aid the heroine because clouds are said to be called birds in mythological language, or because the lower races believe, like the Finns today, that sorcerers have *saivos*—familiar birds which do their bidding? The whole question comes to this—are all the wild classical tales of metamorphosis traces of a struggle between the worship

[1] *Aryan Mythology*, i, 231.
[2] The Australian blacks give the constellations the names of animals, not, it is believed, for the glossiness of the fur or feathers of kangaroo or emu.

of animals and the rising anthropomorphic gods, or are we to suppose that after a lovely and blithe adoration of nature's purest powers in human form had been developed, men were driven back to the most disgusting superstitions by the iron necessity of decaying language and forgotten symbols? When Achilles sacrificed his Trojan captives over the tomb of Patroklus, is it more likely that this is a memory of a common savage practice, or that, because the sun's decline is circled by blood-red clouds, a late poet attributed hateful cruelty to a hero whom he had forgotten, *ex hypothesi*, to be a personification of the sun. There can be no miracle so great as what we are asked to believe—that the force of the changed meanings of words compelled the Greeks to construct fictitious traditions exactly tallying with the actual practices of living savages.[1]

All the ingenious devices by which the solar school of comparative mythologists explain away the abundant traces of savage customs and beliefs in Greek traditions, have their root in a false metaphysical conception of the origin of adoration. When scholars insist, with Von Hahn, that the circle of the higher gods was invented first, or with Mr. Cox, declare that 'no real fetich worship could arise while man had not arranged his first conceptions with regard to the nature of all material things, or even to his own,'[2] they forgot that fetichism is part of this very arrangement, is a gradual process which only late attains to the worship of the elements. Mr. Cox goes on to say that the idea of the divinity of outward objects would be an inference, not a sensation, and . . . 'the analysis of language does not show us that the human mind was immediately concerned with any train of connected reasoning.' Mr. Cox seems to suppose that to worship a thing implies on the part of the worshipper a reasoned conception of Godhead, but his statements are best understood by referring to his authority, Mr. Müller. 'All polytheism,' says Mr Müller, 'must have been preceded by a more or less conscious theism, because no human mind could have conceived the idea of Gods, without having conceived the idea of God.'[3] Again, 'If an expression had been given to the primary intuition of the Deity, which is the mainspring of all later religion, it would have been "there is a God," but not yet "there is one God." ' Now, with regard to Mr. Müller's first statement, that no human mind could have conceived the idea of gods, without having conceived the idea of God, it might just as well be said that no human

[1] Is it not more probable that the legends of 'Boots, the Successful Youngest Son,' arose from the custom of making the youngest son the heir, than that they are solar myths of the triumph of the sun over the clouds? cf. Bastian, *Recht's Verhältnisse*, &c.
[2] *Aryan Mythology*, i, 72.
[3] *Chips*, i, 355.

mind could come to the belief in the existence of sensible things, without having previously brought into explicit consciousness the idea of Existence. The mind has forms through which it constructs into existences the presentations of sense, but it only conceives the abstract idea of existence after it has turned itself back on its own creations, and brought into the light that implicit idea which was the unknown condition of its knowing. Just in the same way the mind has a faculty of adoration, but it is only from a later analysis of its own exercise of this faculty, and from reflection on the objects which it adores, that it gets at the idea of Godhead. Man becomes self-conscious, stands in face, as it were, of his own self bowing down to many things, and extracts from all these objects of adoration, and from reflection on the manner in which they impress him, the common feature of Awful Wonder,—and Wonder is the name of Godhead in the language of the Fijians. Meanwhile, as men proceed to apply their new idea of Godhead, the old objects of their half-conscious adoration reassert their existence as gods, and it is slowly that the height and depth of the divine conception is found to be discordant with stocks and stones, and beasts, the

> 'Dogheaded hulks that trod
> Swart necks of the old Egyptians,'

and of all humanity.

When Mr. Müller talks about an 'expression of the primary intuition of the deity,' he might as well ask for an expression of the truth that two straight lines cannot enclose a space, prior to the presentation in intuition of two straight lines. This expression is as unthinkable as form without matter, or matter devoid of form. It is not intended to deny the existence of the higher myths of the elements, nor to refuse them a vast place in the chaotic fairy-land of mythology. Only we do say that to worship the vault of heaven, or the sun, still more that Being 'whose dwelling is the light of setting suns,' demands a training in adoration, and a conception of spirit, whose growth is very gradual. It is not on the purblind savage, but on the soul so educated, as on the moral nature trained in moral practice, that there one day shines the perfect splendour of that Reason which has before been with men, though they knew it not.

If there be any truth in what has been said, it will be impossible to agree with Mr. Herbert Spencer, in making the propitiation of dead ancestors the first germ of religion, for this involves the presence of the conscious conceptions of Ancestors, and of Spirits.[1] Now the idea of ancestors is not primary, for in the savage state,

[1] *Fortnightly Review*, May, 1870.

[205]

preceding the family, ancestors were of course unknown.[1] If there were animal worship before man had the conception of ancestors, then Mr. Spencer's theory of the origin of totemism falls to the ground. This theory, like all that do not begin at the beginning, involves degradation to an extent that really 'makes our ancestors idiots.' On Mr. Spencer's hypothesis, they were worshippers of ancestors, they also had the habit of giving nicknames. They then forgot that the beast-nickname of a certain adored progenitor—say the Crab, applied to a cautious brave—*was* a nickname, supposed the animal to be a real ancestor, and worshipped the shell-fish. To pray to a crab, after being used to praying to the soul of a dead father, is most degenerate; to forget the inference from their own habit of giving nicknames is unworthy of the lower culture. But that inquiring race, the Zulus, are as subversive of the fancy of Mr. Spencer as of the early orthodoxy of Bishop Colenso. In their account of Amatongo, or ancestor-worship, they say that every Kaffir, on coming to years of discretion, learns that he had ancestors, but the odd thing is, that the first Kaffir of all handed down the tradition that the original ancestor was a snake, and that the Kaffirs are serpents. 'We understand if we are told that the Amadhlozi (the ancestral spirits) are in snakes, we don't understand if we are told that the snake is an ancestor.'[2] That is to say, the Zulus have developed the notion of spirits, and of ancestral spirits that survive after death and migrate *into* animals, but they have lost whatever meaning their totemistic forefathers may have had, when they claimed to be, and to be descended from, actual serpents. There was worship before men knew of human ancestors, may there not have been adoration before they knew of spirit? For spirit is not, if Mr. Spencer be right, a primary intuition, but a hypothesis derived from reflection on the phenomena of life, death, sleep, trance, and shadow. As extracted from reflection it is not primary nor given by instinct. What is then primary and instinctive, what but that start, and terrible mingling of attraction and repulsion, with which man is drawn to and driven back by that totally strange thing, which we call the presence of the supernatural? In earliest man almost all that is not I, must have produced this emotion, must have made him bow down *attonitus*, and so we find savages, like those lately

[1] Thus Garcilasso de la Vega (1570), speaking of the Indians before they came under the influence of the solar religion of the Incas, says, 'they knew nothing of living with separate wives,' 'they were not looked on as honourable unless they were descended from a wild animal, such as a bear, lion, tiger, eagle,' 'they only thought of making one differ from another, thus they worshipped herbs, plants, trees,' &c.; in fact appropriated totems before they knew of their human ancestors.
[2] Callaway, *Religion of the Amazulu*, p. 136.

described by Mr. Lyal, who worship anything or everything. This servile attitude towards nature must have lasted long before man, through reflection, attained to the idea of spirit, and gradually invested with spirits his chief, himself, the objects around him, the vault of heaven. He would live in a world where there was no God, but where all things were adorable; and totemism, the selection of one object as the protector of a stock, would be an instance of that appropriation, and 'winning from the vast and formless infinite,' which has created religion, literature, and the family.[1] *Mährchen*, if we are right, are the remains of myths which arose as the notion of the intercommunity and equality of all nature was losing its hold on men. They do not stand to the higher epic traditions as Latin and Greek, or as German and Italian stand to Sanscrit, but as the original agglutinative tongues stand to the developed inflexional languages.

## [ 3  JAMES ANSON FARRER ]

In popularizing the idea of cultural evolution uniformly observable among all the races of mankind, the book of James Anson Farrer (1849–1925) on *Primitive Manners and Customs* especially appealed to the new generation of anthropologically minded folklorists. Farrer, a versatile writer on varied topics, in this his one work of popular anthropology devoted chapters to savage fairy tales, proverbs, and superstitions to show the community of savage with Aryan folklore. His work helped soften the prejudice of Victorian intellectuals toward brutish savages, whom they regarded as degenerate species fallen from a high estate, and promoted Tylor's view that these uncivilized men possessed the rudiments of moral philosophy and religious sentiment. Farrer contended that their proverbs and myths often bore witness to lofty emotions.

Text from James A. Farrer, *Primitive Manners and Customs*. London: Chatto and Windus, 1897. Pages 86–100, from Chapter 3, 'Some Savage Proverbs.'

If now we extend the limits of our comparison, to take in some proverbs of the lower races as well as of the higher, we shall find

[1] Thus, in the earliest traditions of conquest we find a constant struggle between the seed of the serpent and the descendants of the sun, the latter, in Garcilasso's view, being wise enough to appropriate the best possible totem.

therein a strong corroboration of the lesson already learnt in any comparison of the superstitions, myths, and manners of different societies; namely, that differences of race, colour, and even structure, sink into insignificance when compared with the intellectual affinities which unite the families of mankind, and that there is, perhaps, no phase of thought nor shade of feeling belonging to the higher culture of the world to which we may not find an antitype or even an equivalent in the lower. If we take some of the proverbs collected from tribes confessedly low in civilization—those, for instance, of West Africa—and compare them with proverbs still prevalent in Europe, we cannot fail to be struck with the strong likeness between them, as well as impressed with the idea, that many actually existent common sayings may have had their birth in days of the most remote and savage antiquity. The immense number of modern proverbs, drawn from the observation of the natural, and especially of the animal, world (a number which must be nearly one out of five), coupled with the coincidence that the same fact is perhaps the most striking one in the proverbs collected from West Africa, seems to lend some support to such a theory.

As an introductory instance let us take savage and civilized sentiments about poverty, a belief in the misfortune of which is written clearly in every language of Europe. Italian experience says that poverty has no kin, and that poor men do penance for rich men's sins; in Germany the poor have to dance as the rich pipe; whilst in Spain and Denmark the evil is expressed more graphically still, it being matter of observation in the one country that the poor man's crop is destroyed by hail every year; in the other, that the poor man's corn always grows thin. And, in the Oji dialect, spoken by about two millions of people, including the Ashantees, Fantees, and others, it is also proverbial that the poor man has no friend, that poverty makes a man a slave, and that hard words are fit for the poor. And as the Dutch have learnt, that 'poor folks' wisdom goes for little,' or the Italians, that 'the words of the poor go many to the sackful,' so in Oji exactly the same idea is conveyed in the saying, that 'when a poor man makes a proverb it does not spread'; in Yoruba, in the saying, that 'poverty destroys a man's reputation'; and in Accra in the still cleverer proverb, that 'a poor man's pipe does not sound.' [1]

The proverbs of savages are moral and immoral, elevated and base, precisely as are those of more civilized nations. The proverbs

[1] Most of the African proverbs here referred to are taken from Captain Burton's collection from various sources in his *Wit and Wisdom of West Africa*.

of the Yorubas, justly observes the missionary, Mr. Bowen,[1] 'are among the most remarkable of the world'; and indeed the intellectual powers and moral ideas displayed in West African proverbs generally ought largely to modify our conceptions of their originators, and make us sceptical of that extreme dearth of mental wealth which has so frequently been declared to attend a low standard of material advancement. Their wit, terseness, vividness of illustration, and insight into life, are all alike surprising; and acquaintance with them must suggest caution in any estimate of the mental capacities of savages whose languages may have been less investigated and consequently remain less known. 'It has always been passing travellers who have drawn the most doleful pictures of so-called savages, and especially have asserted the poverty of their language.'[2] It may well prove that better acquaintance with the languages of tribes, classed at present for various reasons almost outside the human family, may show them to combine, as Humboldt found was the case with the once depreciated Carib language, 'wealth, grace, strength, and gentleness.' It was said of the Veddahs once that they were utterly destitute of either religion or *language*; and the Samojeds were reported to shriek and chatter like apes.

The Basutos of South Africa are savages, yet the following proverbs are current among them:—

> A good name makes one sleep well.
> Stolen goods do not make one grow.
> Famine dwells in the house of the quarrelsome.
> The thief catches himself.
> A lent knife does not come back alone.
> (*i.e.* a good deed is never thrown away.)[3]

Compare, for elevation of mind, these Yoruban proverbs with those already noticed as current in Italy:—

> He that forgives gains the victory.
> He who injures another injures himself.
> Anger benefits no one.
> We should not treat others with contempt.[4]

On the other hand, 'If a great man should wrong you, smile on him,' may be compared with the Arabic advice about dangerous friends, 'If a serpent love thee, wear him as a necklace'; or with the Pashto

[1] *Central Africa*, p. 289.
[2] Oscar Peschel, *The Races of Mankind*, translation, p. 150.
[3] Casalis, *Les Basutos*, pp. 324–8.
[4] Captain Burton justly calls attention to the possibility of many Yoruban proverbs being relics of the Moslems, who, in the tenth century, overran the Soudan.

proverb of the same intention, 'Though your enemy be a rope of reeds, call him a serpent.'

Here are some more proverbs with whose European equivalents everyone will be familiar:—

### On Faultfinding.

If you can pull out, pull out your own grey hairs. (Oji.)
Before healing others, heal yourself. (Wolof.)

With which we may compare the Chinese:—

Sweep the snow from your own doors without troubling about the frost on your neighbour's tiles.

### On the Value of Experience.

Nobody is twice a fool. (Accra.)
Nobody is twice ashamed. (Accra.)
He is a fool whose sheep run away twice. (Oji.)
He dreads a slowworm who has been bitten by a serpent. (Oji.)

With which we may compare our own—

It's a silly fish that's caught twice with the same bait.

Or the German—

An old fox is not caught twice in the same trap.

To which both Italy and Holland have exactly similar proverbs.

### On Perseverance.

Perseverance always triumphs. (Basuto.)
The moon does not grow full in a day. (Oji.)
Perseverance is everything.
Who has patience has all things. (Yoruba.)
By going and coming a bird builds its nest. (Oji.)

Which latter may be compared with a Dutch proverb—

By slow degrees a bird builds its nest.

And all of them with the Chinese—

A mulberry-leaf becomes satin with time.

### On the Force of Habit.

The thread follows the needle.
Its shell follows the snail wherever it goes. (Yoruba.)
As is the sword so is the scabbard. (Oji.)

To which again China supplies a good parallel in

The growth of the mulberry tree follows its early bent.

### ON CAUSATION.

If nothing touches the palm-leaves they do not rustle. (Oji.)
Nobody hates another without a cause. (Accra.)
A feather does not stick without gum. (A Pashto proverb.)

Again, the Turkish proverb, that curses, like chickens, come
home to roost, or the Italian one that, like processions, they come
back to their starting-point, is well matched by the Yoruba proverb that 'ashes fly back in the face of their thrower.' Or the tendency of travellers to exaggerate or tell lies, impressed as it has been
on all human experience, is also confirmed by the Oji proverb, that
'he who travels alone tells lies.' And the universal belief in the
ultimate exposure of falsehood conveyed in such proverbs as the
Arabian, 'The liar is short-lived'; the Persian, 'Liars have bad
memories'; or the still more expressive Italian saying, that 'the liar
is sooner caught than a cripple,' finds itself corroborated by the
Wolof proverb, that 'lies, though many, will be caught by Truth as
soon as she rises up.' Even in Afghanistan, where it is said that no
disgrace attaches to lying *per se*, and where lying is called an honest
man's wings, while truth can only be spoken by a strong man or a
fool, there is also a proverb with the moral, that the career of falsehood is short.[1]

That 'hope is the pillar of the world,' that 'it is the heart which
carries one to hell or heaven,' or that 'preparation is better than
after-thought'—all experiences of the Kanuri, a Moslem tribe, who
think it a personal adornment to cut each side of their face in
twenty places—shows that there is no necessary connexion between
general savagery and an absence of moral culture. The natives of
New Zealand, with all their barbarity, had in common use a saying
which were a desirable maxim for European diplomacy: 'When you
are on friendly terms, settle your disputes in a friendly way; when
you are at war, redress your injuries by violence.'[2] Even the Fijians
would say that an unimproved day was not to be counted, and that
no food was ever cooked by gay clothes and frivolity.[3] A good
Ashantee proverb warns people not to speak ill of their benefactors,
by forbidding them to call a forest a shrubbery that has once given
them shelter. The proverbs already quoted from Yoruba teach the
same lesson, nor would it be difficult to add many more, all proving

[1] For a collection of Pashto proverbs see Thornburn's *Afghan Frontier*, 1876.
[2] Sir G. Grey, *Polynesian Mythology*, p. 21.          [3] Williams, *Fiji*, p. 97.

[211]

the existence among savages of a morality identical in its main features with that of the higher group of nations to which we ourselves belong, interpenetrated as it has been for ages with the philosophies and religions of the civilized East.

A similar testimony to the intellectual powers of savages is afforded by their proverbs, though of course the argument is only a suggestive one from tribes whose language has been well studied to others not so well known. That the Soudan negroes are on a higher level of general culture than many savages of other islands or continents is proved by the fact that all known Africans are acquainted with the art of smelting iron and converting it into weapons and utensils; so that they may be said to be living in the Iron Age, and thus, materially at least, are more advanced than the Botocudos of Brazil, who are still in the age of polished stone implements. From the fact alone that the Yorubas express their contempt for a stupid man by saying that he cannot count nine times nine, we are enabled at once to place them above tribes whose powers of numeration fall short of such readiness. Hence we should not be justified in expecting to find among Australian or American aborigines proverbs of so high an intellectual order as abound in Africa, of which the following may be selected as samples:—

Were no elephant in the jungle the buffalo would be large;

or—

The dust of the buffalo is lost in that of the elephant.
A crab does not bring forth a bird.
Two small antelopes beat a big one.
Two crocodiles do not live in one hole.
A child can crush a snail, but not a tortoise.
A razor cannot shave itself.
You cannot stop the sun by standing before it.
If you like honey, do not fear the bees.
When a fish is killed its tail is inserted in its own mouth.
    (Said of people who reap the reward of their deeds.)

The Zulus, speaking of the uncertainty of a result, say 'It is not known what calf the cow will have';[1] and when the Fantees tell you to 'cross the river before you abuse the crocodile,'[2] there is no difficulty in translating their meaning into English. In all these proverbs it is obvious how the facts of every-day life have readily served everywhere as the basis of intellectual advancement, and

[1] Callaway, ii, 171.
[2] Burton, *Mission to Dahome*, ii.

how similar lessons have everywhere been drawn from the observation of similar occurrences.

Leaving now the analogy between African and European proverb-lore, which the uniformity of moral experiences and the observation of similar laws of nature sufficiently account for, let us endeavour to find among civilized nations any proverbs which, by the figures involved in them or their likeness to savage maxims, seem to bear a distinct impression of a barbaric coinage. One French proverb may almost certainly be so explained. It is, for instance, well known that the lower races very generally account for eclipses of either sun or moon by supposing them to be the victims of the fury or voracity of some ill-disposed animal, whom they try to divert by every horrible noise they can produce, or by any weapon they have learnt to fashion. A typical instance of this was the belief of the Chiquitos of South America that the moon was hunted across the sky by dogs, who tore her in pieces when they caught her, till driven off by the Indian arrows. It has been suggested that the French proverb, 'Dieu garde la lune des loups,' said in deprecation of a dread of remote danger, is a survival of a similar rude philosophy of nature which is still prevalent in the capital of Turkey, and in the days of St. Augustine was current over Europe.[1]

Another instructive set of proverbs may be adduced to show how the social philosophy current in the savage state may survive in contemporary expressions of modern Europe. In Africa where, speaking generally, a man's wife has no better status in society than that which attaches to his slave or his ox, and a son has been known to wager his own mother against a cow, we cannot be astonished at finding in vogue proverbs strongly depreciatory of the worth of the female sex. Thus a wise Kanuri is cautioned, that if a woman shall speak to him two words, he shall take one and leave the other, nor should he give his heart to a woman, if he would live, for a woman never brings a man into the right way. So, too, Pashto proverbs say contemptuously, that a woman's wisdom is under her heel, and that she is well only in the house or in the grave. The same feeling is endorsed by the Persians, who declare that both women and dragons are best out of the world, classing the former with horses and swords among their by-words of unfaithfulness.

The literatures of all countries are strongly tinged with sentiments of the same unjust nature. Even the French say that a man of straw is worth a woman of gold, though their proverb, 'Ce que femme veut, Dieu le veut,' is as true as it is a witty variation

[1] Tylor, *Primitive Culture*, i, 333.

of the well-known democratic formula. The Italians have made the shrewd observation, that, whilst with men every mortal sin is venial, with women every venial sin is mortal; but no language has anything worse than this, that as both a good horse and a bad horse need the spur, so both a good woman and a bad woman need the stick.

It is, however, in Germany that the character of women has suffered most from the shafts of that other half of the community, which (it might be complained) has as unfair a monopoly of making proverbs as it has of making laws. The humorous saying, that there are only two good women in the world, one of whom is dead and the other not to be found, contains the key to the common national sentiment. A woman is compared to good fortune in her partiality for fools, and to wine in her power to make them. Like a glass, she is in hourly danger; and, like a priest, she never forgets. Her vengeance is boundless, and her mutability find its only parallel in nature in the uncertain skies of April. Her affections change every moment, like luck at cards, the favour of princes, or the leaves of a rose; and though you will never find her wanting in words, there is not a needle-point's difference betwixt her yea and her nay. She only keeps silence where she is ignorant, and it is as fruitless to try to hold a woman at her word as an eel by its tail. Her advice, like corn sown in summer, may perhaps turn out well once in seven years; but wherever there is mischief brewing in the world, rest assured that there is a woman and a priest at the bottom of it. Every daughter of Eve would rather be beautiful than good, and may be caught as surely by gold as a hare by dogs or a gentleman by flattery. Even in the house she should be allowed no power, for where a woman rules the devil is chief servant; whilst two women in the same house will agree together like two cats over a mouse or two dogs over a bone.

Spanish experience on this subject coincides with the Teutonic, but without the expenditure of nearly so much spleen, and with several glimpses of a happier experience. What can be worse than this: 'Beware of a bad woman, nor put any trust in a good one'; or sadder than this: 'What is marriage, mother? Spinning, childbirth, and crying, daughter'? Yet the Spanish woman, as hard to know as a melon, as little to be trusted as a magpie, as fickle as the wind or as fortune, as ready to cry as a dog to limp, in labour as patient as a mule, is not so destitute as the German of any redeeming qualities for her failings. The Spaniard is taught to believe that with a good wife he may bear any adversity, and that he should believe nothing against her unless absolutely proved. It is also in remarkable contrast to the experiences of other countries, that in Spain it should have passed into a proverb, that whilst an unmarried man advocates a daily beating for a wife, as soon as he marries he takes care of his own.

Female talkativeness appears also to be a subject of lament all over the world, from our own island, where a woman's tongue proverbially wags like a lamb's tail, to the Celestial Empire, where it is likened to a sword, never suffered by its owner to rust. Regard not a woman's words, says the Hindoo; and the African also is warned against trusting his secrets even to his wife. The Spaniard believes that he has only to tell a woman what he would wish to have published in the market-place; and all languages have sayings to the same effect. The Scotch divine who, before the Session, defended his heresy that women would find no place in heaven, by the text, 'There was silence in heaven for about the space of half an hour,' only expressed a sentiment of universal currency over the world.

The proverbs collected from the lower races are still very few, when compared with the immense mass of those from nations with whose literature we are more familiar. It is in the nature of things that missionaries and travellers should have been first struck by, and first given us information about, matters more directly challenging their notice than phrases in common use, for a real knowledge of which the most favourable conditions of a prolonged intimacy are obviously requisite. The large collection of such proverbs from West Africa alone, revealing as they do an elevation of feeling and a clearness of intelligence which other facts of their social life would never have led us to suspect, point at the possibility of such collections elsewhere largely modifying our present views concerning other savage tribes. They at least should teach us caution against accepting the conclusions which some writers have drawn from their study of savage languages, when, from the absence or loss in a dialect of such words as 'love' or 'gratitude,' they proceed to explain, on the hypothesis of degradation, that rude state of existence which is denoted by the word 'savage,' and which there are abundant reasons for supposing was really the primitive germ, out of which all subsequent civilization has been unfolded. 'Were,' says Archbishop Trench, 'the savage the primitive man, we should then find savage tribes furnished, scantily enough it might be, with the elements of speech, yet, at the same time, with its fruitful beginnings, its vigorous and healthful germs. But what does their language on close inspection prove? In every case what they are themselves, the remnant and ruin of a better and a nobler past. Fearful indeed is the impress of degradation which is stamped on the language of the savage—more fearful, perhaps, even than that which is stamped upon his form.'[1] Yet, whatever may be the case with some tribes, who may be shown historically to have fallen from a higher state (and such are the exceptions), at least the languages spoken in Africa bear no such 'fearful impress of degradation,' as are declared to be traceable *in every case*, if we may judge of a language by the thoughts which it expresses rather than by the words which it contains.

[1] Trench, *On the Study of Words*, p. 17.

# IV  The Great Team: Definitions and Methods

THE REASONING OF ANDREW LANG appealed irresistibly to a new generation of private scholars who together dedicated their prodigious energies and talents to the cause of folklore science. Joining Lang, the free-lance writer and literary journalist, were George Laurence Gomme, a civil servant, Edwin Sidney Hartland, a lawyer, Alfred Nutt, a publisher, and Edward Clodd, a banker. Meeting regularly in the friendly atmosphere of The Folk-Lore Society, founded in 1878, where each served in turn as president, they moved forward on a common front to advance the serious study of folklore along anthropological lines, disperse the celestial mythologists, ferret out every surviving scrap of folklore from village green and county chronicle, and reconstruct collectively the biography of primitive man. Their endeavours brought to fruition the field baptized by Thoms, who lived to see and help establish the new society. From the energetic five came a torrent of publications, ranging from the incisive note to the multi-volume monograph.

On the first principles of folklore studies the Great Team spoke with one voice. They unanimously affirmed the doctrine of survivals, the need for accurate and systematic fieldwork, the reliance on printed resources of traditions and customs, and the unique value of folklore as a key to understanding the mental growth of man. In their explanatory writings and addresses, they outlined to layman and learned the nature of folklore scholarship in lucid exposition that can stand today among the best answers to the questions framed by Hartland, 'What is Folklore and What is the Good of It?' In the present chapter the Great Team describe the methods of the folklorist.

As they explored ever more intensively the depths and corners of their subject, the fraternal folklorists found themselves developing their own special areas. Chapter V samples these individual investigations. Ultimately they fell to jousting with each other, in

[217]

the give and take of Victorian debate, when their points of view hardened and ran counter to one another. Lang and Hartland disputed over the origins of Australian gods, Gomme and Nutt over ethnic distinctions in folklore, and Clodd and Lang over the relevance of psychical research to folklore studies. Chapter VI portrays these exchanges.


## [ 1    ANDREW    LANG ]


In the opening chapter to one of his most widely read books, *Custom and Myth* (1884), Andrew Lang spelled out 'The Method of Folklore.' Here he expanded the boundaries of folklore materials which Tylor had drawn around the European peasant to embrace the myths of the contemporary savage and even of the educated classes. Anthropology and mythology are brought into the folklore tent to support the contention that men everywhere in all stages exhibit a community of belief and practice and an identity of thought. The method of folklore is to compare the meaningless peasant usage with the fuller savage form and so comprehend its original character in antiquity. This method should be applied not only to superstitions, but also, Lang argued, to myths, which even in their classical garbs display traces of barbarism.

Text from Andrew Lang, *Custom and Myth*. London: Longmans, Green, and Co., 1893. Pages 10–28, Chapter 1, 'The Method of Folklore.'


After the heavy rain of a thuderstorm has washed the soil, it sometimes happens that a child, or a rustic, finds a wedge-shaped piece of metal or a few triangular flints in a field or near a road. There was no such piece of metal, there were no such flints, lying there yesterday, and the finder is puzzled about the origin of the objects on which he has lighted. He carries them home, and the village wisdom determines that the wedge-shaped piece of metal is a 'thunderbolt,' or that the bits of flint are 'elf-shots,' the heads of fairy arrows. Such things are still treasured in remote nooks of England, and the 'thunder-bolt' is applied to cure certain maladies by its touch.

As for the fairy arrows, we know that even in ancient Etruria they were looked on as magical, for we sometimes see their points set, as amulets, in the gold of Etruscan necklaces. In Perugia the

[218]

arrow-heads are still sold as charms. All educated people, of course, have long been aware that the metal wedge is a celt, or ancient bronze axe-head, and that it was not fairies, but the forgotten peoples of this island, who used the arrows with the tips of flint. Thunder is only so far connected with them that the heavy rains loosen the surface soil, and lay bare its long-hidden secrets.

There is a science, Archaeology, which collects and compares the material relics of old races, the axes and arrow-heads. There is a form of study, Folklore, which collects and compares the similar but immaterial relics of old races, the surviving superstitions and stories, the ideas which are in our time but not of it. Properly speaking, folklore is only concerned with the legends, customs, beliefs, of the Folk, of the people, of the classes which have least been altered by education, which have shared least in progress. But the student of folklore soon finds that these unprogressive classes retain many of the beliefs and ways of savages, just as the Hebridean people used spindle-whorls of stone, and bake clay pots without the aid of the wheel, like modern South Sea Islanders, or like their own prehistoric ancestors.[1] The student of folklore is thus led to examine the usages, myths, and ideas of savages, which are still retained, in rude enough shape, by the European peasantry. Lastly, he observes that a few similar customs and ideas survive in the most conservative elements of the life of educated peoples, in ritual, ceremonial, and religious traditions and myths. Though such remains are rare in England, we may note the custom of leading the dead soldier's horse behind his master to the grave, a relic of days when the horse would have been sacrificed.[2] We may observe the persistence of the ceremony by which the monarch, at his coronation, takes his seat on the sacred stone of Scone, probably an ancient fetich stone. Not to speak, here, of our own religious traditions, the old vein of savage rite and belief is found very near the surface of ancient Greek religion. It wants but some stress of circumstance, something answering to the storm shower that reveals the flint arrow-heads, to bring savage ritual to the surface of classical religion. In sore need, a human victim was only too likely to be demanded; while a feast-day, or a mystery, set the Greeks dancing serpent-dances or bear-dances like Red Indians, or swimming with sacred pigs, or leaping about in imitation of wolves, or holding a

---

[1] A study of the contemporary Stone Age in Scotland will be found in Mitchell's *Past and Present*.

[2] About twenty years ago, the widow of an Irish farmer, in Derry, killed her deceased husband's horse. When remonstrated with by her landlord, she said, 'Would you have my man go about on foot in the next world?' She was quite in the savage intellectual stage.

dog-feast, and offering dog's flesh to the gods.[1] Thus the student of folklore soon finds that he must enlarge his field, and examine, not only popular European story and practice, but savage ways and ideas, and the myths and usages of the educated classes in civilized races. In this extended sense the term 'folklore' will frequently be used in the following essays. The idea of the writer is that mythology cannot fruitfully be studied apart from folklore, while some knowledge of anthropology is required in both sciences.

The science of Folklore, if we may call it a science, finds everywhere, close to the surface of civilized life, the remains of ideas as old as the stone elf-shots, older than the celt of bronze. In proverbs and riddles, and nursery tales and superstitions, we detect the relics of a stage of thought, which is dying out in Europe, but which still exists in many parts of the world. Now, just as the flint arrow-heads are scattered everywhere, in all the continents and isles, and everywhere are much alike, and bear no very definite marks of the special influence of race, so it is with the habits and legends investigated by the student of folklore. The stone arrow-head buried in a Scottish cairn is like those which were interred with Algonquin chiefs. The flints found in Egyptian soil, or beside the tumulus on the plain of Marathon, nearly resemble the stones which tip the reed arrow of the modern Samoyed. Perhaps only a skilled experience could discern, in a heap of such arrow-heads, the specimens which are found in America or Africa from those which are unearthed in Europe. Even in the products of more advanced industry, we see early pottery, for example, so closely alike everywhere that, in the British Museum, Mexican vases have, ere now, been mixed up on the same shelf with archaic vessels from Greece. In the same way, if a superstition or a riddle were offered to a student of folklore, he would have much difficulty in guessing its *provenance*, and naming the race from which it was brought. Suppose you tell a folklorist that, in a certain country, when any one sneezes, people say 'Good luck to you,' the student cannot say *a priori* what country you refer to, what race you have in your thoughts. It may be Florida, as Florida was when first discovered; it may be Zululand, or West Africa, or ancient Rome, or Homeric Greece, or Palestine. In all these, and many other regions, the sneeze was welcomed as an auspicious omen. The little superstition is as widely distributed as the flint arrow-heads. Just as the object and use of the arrow-heads became intelligible when we found similar weapons in actual use among savages, so the salutation to the sneezer becomes in-

---

[1] 'At the solemn festival suppers, ordained for the honour of the gods, they forget not to serve up certain dishes of young whelp's flesh' (Pliny, *H. N.*, xxix, 4).

telligible when we learn that the savage has a good reason for it. He thinks the sneeze expels an evil spirit. Proverbs, again, and riddles are as universally scattered, and the Wolufs puzzle over the same *devinettes* as the Scotch schoolboy or the Breton peasant. Thus, for instance, the Wolufs of Senegal ask each other, 'What flies for ever, and rests never?'—Answer, 'The Wind.' 'Who are the comrades that always fight, and never hurt each other?'—'The Teeth.' In France, as we read in the 'Recueil de Calembours,' the people ask, 'What runs faster than a horse, crosses water, and is not wet?'—Answer, 'The Sun.' The Samoans put the riddle, 'A man who stands between two ravenous fishes?'—Answer, 'The tongue between the teeth.' Again, 'There are twenty brothers, each with a hat on his head?'—Answer, 'Fingers and toes, with nails for hats.' This is like the French *'un père a douze fils?'*—*'l'an.'* [1] A comparison of M. Rolland's 'Devinettes' with the Woluf conundrums of Boilat, the Samoan examples in Turner's 'Samoa,' and the Scotch enigmas collected by Chambers, will show the identity of peasant and savage humour.

A few examples, less generally known, may be given to prove that the beliefs of folklore are not peculiar to any one race or stock of men. The first case is remarkable: it occurs in Mexico and Ceylon, and has been found in other regions. In *Macmillan's Magazine* [2] is published a paper by Mrs. Edwards, called 'The Mystery of the Pezazi.' The events described in this narrative occurred on August 28, 1876, in a bungalow some thirty miles from Badiella. The narrator occupied a new house on an estate called Allagalla. Her native servants soon asserted that the place was haunted by a Pezazi. The English visitors saw and heard nothing extraordinary till a certain night: an abridged account of what happened then may be given in the words of Mrs. Edwards:—

> Wrapped in dreams, I lay on the night in question tranquilly sleeping, but gradually roused to a perception that discordant sounds disturbed the serenity of my slumber. Loth to stir, I still dosed on, the sounds, however, becoming, as it seemed, more determined to make themselves heard! and I awoke to the consciousness that they proceeded from a belt of adjacent jungle, and resembled the noise that would be produced by some person felling timber.
>
> Shutting my ears to the disturbance, I made no sign, until, with an expression of impatience, E—— suddenly started up, when I laid a detaining grasp upon his arm, murmuring that

---

[1] Compare Cleobulus, Fr. 2: Bergk, *Lyr. Gr.*, iii, 201. Ed. 4.     [2] Nov., 1880.

there was no need to think of rising at present—it must be quite early, and the kitchen cooly was doubtless cutting firewood in good time. E—— responded, in a tone of slight contempt, that no one could be cutting firewood at that hour, and the sounds were more suggestive of felling jungle; and he then inquired how long I had been listening to them. Now thoroughly aroused I replied that I had heard the sounds for some time, at first confusing them with my dreams, but soon sufficiently awakening to the fact that they were no mere phantoms of my imagination, but a reality. During our conversation the noises became more distinct and loud; blow after blow resounded, as of the axe descending upon the tree, followed by the crash of the falling timber. Renewed blows announced the repetition of the operations on another tree, and continued till several were devastated.

It is unnecessary to tell more of the tale, In spite of minute examinations and close search, no solution of the mystery of the noises, on this or any other occasion, was ever found. The natives, of course, attributed the disturbance to the *Pezazi* or goblin. No one perhaps has asserted that the Aztecs were connected by ties of race with the people of Ceylon. Yet when the Spaniards conquered Mexico, and when Sahagun (one of the earliest missionaries) collected the legends of the people, he found them, like the Cingalese, strong believers in the mystic tree-felling. We translate Sahagun's account of the 'midnight axe':—

When so any man heareth the sound of strokes in the night as if one were felling trees, he reckons it an evil boding. And this sound they call *youaltepuztli* (*youalli*, night; and *tepuztli*, copper), which signifies 'the midnight hatchet.' This noise cometh about the time of the first sleep, when all men slumber soundly, and the night is still. The sound of strokes smitten was first noted by the temple-servants, called *tlamacazque*, at the hour when they go in the night to make their offering of reeds or of boughs of pine, for so was their custom, and this penance they did on the neighbouring hills, and that when the night was far spent. Whenever they heard such a sound as one makes when he splits wood with an axe (a noise that may be heard afar off), they drew thence an omen of evil, and were afraid and said that the sounds were part of the witchery of Tezcatlipoca, that often thus dismayeth men who journey in the night. Now, when tidings of these things came to a certain brave man, one exercised in war, he drew near, being guided

[222]

by the sound, till he came to the very cause of the hubbub. And when he came upon it, with difficulty he caught it, for the thing was hard to catch; natheless at last he overtook that which ran before him; and behold, it was a man without a heart, and, on either side of the chest, two holes that opened and shut, and so made the noise. Then the man put his hand within the breast of the figure and grasped the breast and shook it hard, demanding some grace or gift.

As a rule, the grace demanded was power to make captives in war. The curious coincidence of the 'midnight axe,' occurring in lands so remote as Ceylon and Mexico, and the singular attestation by an English lady of the actual existence of the disturbance, makes this *youaltepuztli* one of the quaintest things in the province of the folklorist. But, whatever the cause of the noise, or of the beliefs connected with the noise, may be, no one would explain them as the result of community of *race* between Cingalese and Aztecs. Nor would this explanation be offered to account for the Aztec and English belief that the creaking of furniture is an omen of death in a house. Obviously, these opinions are the expression of a common state of superstitious fancy, not the signs of an original community of origin.[1]

Let us take another piece of folklore. All North-country English folk know the *Kernababy*. The custom of the 'Kernababy' is commonly observed in England, or, at all events, in Scotland, where the writer has seen many a kernababy. The last gleanings of the last field are bound up in a rude imitation of the human shape, and dressed in some tag-rags of finery. The usage has fallen into the conservative hands of children, but of old 'the Maiden' was a regular image of the harvest goddess, which, with a sickle and sheaves in her arms, attended by a crowd of reapers, and accompanied with music, followed the last carts home to the farm.[2] It is odd enough that 'the Maiden' should exactly translate Κόρη, the old Sicilian name of the daughter of Demeter. 'The Maiden' has dwindled, then, among us to the rudimentary kernababy; but ancient Peru had her own Maiden, her Harvest Goddess. Here it is easy to trace the natural idea at the basis of the superstitious practice which links the shores of the Pacific with our own northern coast. Just as a portion of the yule-log and of the Christmas bread were kept all the

[1] Mr. Leslie Stephen points out to me that De Quincey's brother heard 'the midnight axe' in the Galapagos Islands (*Autobiographical Sketches*, 'My Brother').
[2] 'Ah, once again may I plant the great fan on her corn-heap, while she stands smiling by, Demeter of the threshing floor, with sheaves and poppies in her hands' (Theocritus, vii, 155–7).

year through, a kind of nest-egg of plenteous food and fire, so the kernababy, English or Peruvian, is an earnest that corn will not fail all through the year, till next harvest comes. For this reason the kernababy used to be treasured from autumn's end to autumn's end, though now it commonly disappears very soon after the harvest home. It is thus that Acosta describes in Grimston's old translation (1604) the Peruvian kernababy and the Peruvian harvest home:—

> This feast is made comming from the chacra or farme unto the house, saying certaine songs, and praying that the Mays (maize) may long continue, the which they call *Mama cora*.

What a chance this word offers to etymologists of the old school: how promptly they would recognize, in *mama* mother—μήτηρ, and in *cora*—κόρη, the Mother and the Maiden, the feast of Demeter and Persephone! However, the days of that old school of antiquarianism are numbered. To return to the Peruvian harvest home:—

> They take a certaine portion of the most fruitefull of the Mays that growes in their farmes, the which they put in a certaine granary which they do calle Pirua, with certaine ceremonies, watching three nightes; they put this Mays in the richest garments they have, and, being thus wrapped and dressed, they worship this Pirua, and hold it in great veneration, saying it is the Mother of the Mays of their inheritances, and that by this means the Mays augments and is preserved. In this moneth they make a particular sacrifice, and the witches demand of this Pirua, 'if it hath strength sufficient to continue until the next yeare,' and if it answers 'no,' then they carry this Mays to the farme to burne, whence they brought it, according to every man's power, then they make another Pirua, with the same ceremonies, saying that they renue it, to the ende that the seede of the Mays may not perish.

The idea that the maize can speak need not surprise us; the Mexican held much the same belief, according to Sahagun:—

> It was thought that it some grains of maize fell on the ground he who saw them lying there was bound to lift them, wherein, if he failed, he harmed the maize, which plained itself of him to God, saying, 'Lord, punish this man, who saw me fallen and raised me not again; punish him with famine, that he may learn not to hold me in dishonour.'

Well, in all this affair of the Scotch kernababy, and the Peruvian *Mama cora*, we need no explanation beyond the common simple ideas of human nature. We are not obliged to hold, either that the Peruvians and Scotch are akin by blood, nor that, at some forgotten time, they met each other, and borrowed each other's superstitions.[1] Again, when we find Odysseus sacrificing a black sheep to the dead,[2] and when we read that the Ovahereroes in South Africa also appease with a black sheep the spirits of the departed, we do not feel it necessary to hint that the Ovahereroes are of Greek descent, or have borrowed their ritual from the Greeks. The connexion between the colour black, and mourning for the dead, is natural and almost universal.

Examples like these might be adduced in any number. We might show how, in magic, negroes of Barbadoes make clay effigies of their enemies, and pierce them, just as Greeks did in Plato's time, or the men of Accad in remotest antiquity. We might remark the Australian black putting sharp bits of quartz in the tracks of an enemy who has gone by, that the enemy may be lamed; and we might point to Boris Gudunof forbidding the same practice among the Russians. We might watch Scotch, and Australians, and Jews, and French, and Aztecs spreading dust round the body of a dead man, that the footprints of his ghost, or of other ghosts, may be detected next morning. We might point to a similar device in a modern novel, where the presence of a ghost is suspected, as proof of the similar workings of the Australian mind and of the mind of Mrs. Riddell. We shall later turn to ancient Greece, and show how the serpent-dances, the habit of smearing the body with clay, and other odd rites of the mysteries, were common to Hellenic religion, and to the religion of African, Australian, and American tribes.

Now, with regard to all these strange usages, what is the method of folklore? The method is, when an apparently irrational and anomalous custom is found in any country, to look for a country where a similar practice is found, and where the practice is no longer irrational and anomalous, but in harmony with the manners and ideas of the people among whom it prevails. That Greeks should dance about in their mysteries with harmless serpents in their hands looks quite unintelligible. When a wild tribe of Red Indians does the same thing, as a trial of courage, with real rattlesnakes, we understand the Red Man's motives, and may conjecture that similar motives once existed among the ancestors of the Greeks. Our method, then, is to compare the seemingly meaningless customs or manners of civilized races with the similar customs and manners which exist among the uncivilized and still retain their

[1] In Mr. Frazer's *Golden Bough* is a very large collection of similar harvest rites.
[2] *Odyssey*, xi, 32.

meaning. It is not necessary for comparison of this sort that the uncivilized and the civilized race should be of the same stock, nor need we prove that they were ever in contact with each other. Similar conditions of mind produce similar practices, apart from identity of race, or borrowing of ideas and manners.

Let us return to the example of the flint arrow-heads. Everywhere neolithic arrow-heads are pretty much alike. The cause of the resemblance is no more than this, that men, with the same needs, the same materials, and the same rude instruments, everywhere produced the same kind of arrow-head. No hypothesis of interchange of ideas nor of community of race is needed to explain the resemblance of form in the missiles. Very early pottery in any region is, for the same causes, like very early pottery in any other region. The same sort of similarity was explained by the same resemblances in human nature, when we touched on the identity of magical practices and of superstitious beliefs. This method is fairly well established and orthodox when we deal with usages and superstitious beliefs; but may we apply the same method when we deal with myths?

Here a difficulty occurs. Mythologists, as a rule, are averse to the method of folklore. They think it scientific to compare only the myths of races which speak languages of the same family, and of races which have, in historic times, been actually in proved contact with each other. Thus, most mythologists hold it correct to compare Greek, Slavonic, Celtic, and Indian stories, because Greeks, Slavs, Celts, and Hindoos all speak languages of the same family. Again, they hold it correct to compare Chaldaean and Greek myths, because the Greeks and the Chaldaeans were brought into contact through the Phoenicians, and by other intermediaries, such as the Hittites. But the same mythologists will vow that it is unscientific to compare a Maori or a Hottentot or an Eskimo myth with an Aryan story, because Maoris and Eskimo and Hottentots do not speak languages akin to that of Greece, nor can we show that the ancestors of Greeks, Maoris, Hottentots, and Eskimo were ever in contact with each other in historical times.

Now the peculiarity of the method of folklore is that it will venture to compare (with due caution and due examination of evidence) the myths of the most widely severed races. Holding that myth is a product of the early human fancy, working on the most rudimentary knowledge of the outer world, the student of folklore thinks that differences of race do not much affect the early mythopoeic faculty. He will not be surprised if Greeks and Australian blacks are in the same tale.

[226]

In each case, he holds, all the circumstances of the case must be examined and considered. For instance, when the Australians tell a myth about the Pleiades very like the Greek myth of the Pleiades, we must ask a number of questions. Is the Australian version authentic? Can the people who told it have heard it from a European? If these questions are answered so as to make it apparent that the Australian Pleiad myth is of genuine native origin, we need not fly to the conclusion that the Australians are a lost and forlorn branch of the Aryan race. Two other hypotheses present themselves. First, the human species is of unknown antiquity. In the moderate allowance of 250,000 years, there is time for stories to have wandered all round the world, as the Aggry beads of Ashanti have probably crossed the continent from Egypt, as the Asiatic jade (if Asiatic it be) has arrived in Swiss lake-dwellings, as an African trade-cowry is said to have been found in a Cornish barrow, as an Indian Ocean shell has been discovered in a prehistoric bone-cave in Poland. This slow filtration of tales is not absolutely out of the question. Two causes would especially help to transmit myths. The first is slavery and slave-stealing, the second is the habit of capturing brides from alien stocks, and the law which forbids marriage with a woman of a man's own family. Slaves and captured brides would bring their native legends among alien peoples.

But there is another possible way of explaining the resemblance (granting that it is proved) of the Greek and Australian Pleiad myth. The object of both myths is to account for the grouping and other phenomena of the constellations. May not similar explanatory stories have occurred to the ancestors of the Australians, and to the ancestors of the Greeks, however remote their home, while they were still in the savage condition? The best way to investigate this point is to collect all known savage and civilized stellar myths, and see what points they have in common. If they all agree in character, though the Greek tales are full of grace, while those of the Australians or Brazilians are rude enough, we may plausibly account for the similarity of myths, as we accounted for the similarity of flint arrow-heads. The myths, like the arrow-heads, resemble each other because they were originally framed to meet the same needs out of the same material. In the case of the arrow-heads, the need was for something hard, heavy, and sharp—the material was flint. In the case of the myths, the need was to explain certain phenomena—the material (so to speak) was an early state of the human mind, to which all objects seemed equally endowed with human personality, and to which no metamorphosis appeared impossible.

In the following essays, then, the myths and customs of various

[227]

peoples will be compared, even when these peoples talk languages of alien families, and have never (so far as history shows us) been in actual contact. Our method throughout will be to place the usage, or myth, which is unintelligible when found among a civilized race, beside the similar myth which is intelligible enough when it is found among savages. A mean term will be found in the folklore preserved by the non-progressive classes in a progressive people. This folklore represents, in the midst of a civilized race, the savage ideas out of which civilization has been evolved. The conclusion will usually be that the fact which puzzles us by its presence in civilization is a relic surviving from the time when the ancestors of a civilized race were in the state of savagery. By this method it is not necessary that 'some sort of genealogy should be established' between the Australian and the Greek narrators of a similar myth, nor between the Greek and Australian possessors of a similar usage. The hypothesis will be that the myth, or usage, is common to both races, not because of original community of stock, not because of contact and borrowing, but because the ancestors of the Greeks passed through the savage intellectual condition in which we find the Australians.

The question may be asked, Has race nothing, then, to do with myth? Do peoples never consciously borrow myths from each other? The answer is, that race has a great deal to do with the development of myth, if it be race which confers on a people its national genius, and its capacity of becoming civilized. If race does this, then race affects, in the most powerful manner, the ultimate development of myth. No one is likely to confound a Homeric myth with a myth from the Edda, nor either with a myth from a Brahmana, though in all three cases the substance, the original set of ideas, may be much the same. In all three you have anthropomorphic gods, capable of assuming animal shapes, tricky, capricious, limited in many undivine ways, yet endowed with magical powers. So far the mythical gods of Homer, of the Edda, of any of the Brahmanas, are on a level with each other, and not much above the gods of savage mythology. This stuff of myth is *quod semper, quod ubique, quod ab omnibus*, and is the original gift of the savage intellect. But the final treatment, the ultimate literary form of the myth, varies in each race. Homeric gods, like Red Indian, Thlinkeet, or Australian gods, can assume the shapes of birds. But when we read, in Homer, of the arming of Athene, the hunting of Artemis, the vision of golden Aphrodite, the apparition of Hermes, like a young man when the flower of youth is loveliest, then we recognize the effect of race upon myth, the effect of the Greek genius at work on rude material.

[228]

Between the Olympians and a Thlinkeet god there is all the difference that exists between the Demeter of Cnidos and an image from
Easter Island. Again, the Scandinavian gods, when their tricks are
laid aside, when Odin is neither assuming the shape of worm nor of
raven, have a martial dignity, a noble enduring spirit of their own.
Race comes out in that, as it does in the endless sacrifices, soma
drinking, magical austerities, and puerile follies of Vedic and
Brahmanic gods, the deities of a people fallen early into its sacerdo-
tage and priestly second childhood. Thus race declares itself in the
ultimate literary form and character of mythology, while the common savage basis and stuff of myths may be clearly discerned in
the horned, and cannibal, and shape-shifting, and adulterous gods
of Greece, of India, of the North. They all show their common
savage origin, when the poet neglects Freya's command and tells of
what the gods did 'in the morning of Time.'

As to borrowing, we have already shown that in prehistoric
times there must have been much transmission of myth. The migra-
tions of peoples, the traffic in slaves, the law of exogamy, which
always keeps bringing alien women into the families—all these
things favoured the migration of myth. But the process lies behind
history: we can only guess at it, we can seldom trace a popular
legend on its travels. In the case of the cultivated ancient peoples,
we know that they themselves believed they had borrowed their
religions from each other. When the Greeks first found the Egyptians practising mysteries like their own, they leaped to the conclusion that their own rites had been imported from Egypt. We,
who know that both Greek and Egyptian rites had many points in
common with those of Mandans, Zunis, Bushmen, Australians—
people quite unconnected with Egypt—feel less confident about the
hypothesis of borrowing. We may, indeed, regard Adonis, and Zeus
Bagaeus, and Melicertes, as importations from Phoenicia. In later
times, too, the Greeks, and still more the Romans, extended a free
hospitality to alien gods and legends, to Serapis, Isis, the wilder
Dionysiac revels, and so forth. But this habit of borrowing was
regarded with disfavour by pious conservatives, and was probably,
in the width of its hospitality at least, an innovation. As Tiele remarks, we cannot derive Dionysus from the Assyrian *Daian nisi*
'judge of men,' a name of the solar god Samas, without ascertaining
that the wine-god exercised judicial functions, and was a god of the
sun. These derivations, 'shocking to common-sense,' are to be dis-
trusted as part of the intoxication of new learning. Some Assyrian
scholars actually derive *Hades* from *Bit Edi* or *Bit Hadi*—'though
unluckily,' says Tiele, 'there is no such word in the Assyrian text.'

On the whole topic Tiele's essay[1] deserves to be consulted. Granting, then, that elements in the worship of Dionysus, Aphrodite, and other gods, may have been imported with the strange Aegypto-Assyrian vases and jewels of the Sidonians, we still find the same basis of rude savage ideas. We may push back a god from Greece to Phoenicia, from Phoenicia to Accadia, but, at the end of the end, we reach a legend full of myths like those which Bushmen tell by the camp fire, Eskimo in their dark huts, and Australians in the shade of the *gunyeh*—myths cruel, puerile, obscene, like the fancies of the savage myth-makers from which they sprang.

## [ 2   EDWIN   SIDNEY   HARTLAND ]

In an explicit statement addressed to the layman, Sidney Hartland set forth the laws of tradition as revealed by the science of folklore. This deft discussion of 'Folklore: What Is It and What Is the Good of It?' formed one number in a pamphlet series, *Popular Studies in Mythology, Romance and Folklore*, designed and published by Alfred Nutt to inform the intellectually curious public on these related subjects. In conversational vein Hartland explained how the anthropological approach to the common folklore of everyday life traced curious usages and notions back to their original state in savagery. In this paper he concentrated on beliefs, treating tales in a separate pamphlet (No. 7, *Mythology and Folktales: Their Relation and Interpretation*, 1900). The Gloucester solicitor also brought into the discussion his theory of applied folklore by pointing out the benefits that would accrue to State and Church from a systematic knowledge of the folklore of savages dwelling in colonial possessions.

Text from Edwin Sidney Hartland, 'Folklore: What Is It and What Is the Good of It?' London: David Nutt, 1899. *Popular Studies in Mythology, Romance and Folklore*, No. 2. (Reprint with minor changes of a paper read before the Gloucester Philosophical Society.) Second edition, 1904. Pages 5–47.

I one day met a friend from a neighbouring town, who as soon as he had greeted me inquired whether I had been over to a concert recently given there, about which he was enthusiastic. I was obliged to admit that I had not been, and to excuse myself I floundered into the still more humiliating confession: 'You see, I know very

[1] *Rev. de l'Hist. des Rel.*, vol. ii.

little of music.' He looked at me with a solemn pity in his eyes, and said: 'Ah, yes! it is folklore you are interested in.'

Well, I am interested in folklore; there is no denying it; and I am glad to have an opportunity of telling you why I am interested in it. I hope that when I have done so you will think there is at least no occasion for pitying me.

First, let me try to tell you what folklore is. Euclid, we know upon the unimpeachable authority of Lord Dundreary, is 'all about letting A, B, and C be a triangle—as if I cared what they were.' In the same way, perhaps, many of you may be disposed to think that folklore is all about fairy tales, cures for warts, and so forth— things that no intelligent person would concern himself with. And indeed it must be admitted that, just as one branch of the science of mathematics, usually associated with the great name of Euclid, does teach (among other things) the properties of triangles, so folk- lore does investigate (among other things) the meaning of fairy tales and of cures for warts. But these are only a small part of folk- lore, as folklore itself is but a part—though, as I venture to think, a very important part—of the larger science of Anthropology—the Science of Man. The portion of Anthropology with which folklore deals is the mental and spiritual side of humanity. It is now well established that the most civilized races have all fought their way slowly upwards from a condition of savagery. Now, savages can neither read nor write; yet they manage to collect and store up a considerable amount of knowledge of a certain kind, and to hand on from one generation to another a definite social organization and certain invariable rules of procedure in all the events of life. The knowledge, organization, and rules thus gathered and formu- lated are preserved in the memory, and communicated by word of mouth and by actions of various kinds. To this mode of preserva- tion and communication, as well as to the things thus preserved and communicated, the name of Tradition is given; and Folklore is the science of Tradition.

But here you will tell me: It is impossible to have a science of anything which does not fall into method, and is not capable of being classified and reduced to rule. Tradition is admittedly shift- ing, uncertain, chaotic; and how can you have a science of Tradi- tion? It is a contradiction in terms.

So, indeed, it seems to be; but wait a bit. There is a confusion of thought in the objection. If by Tradition you mean the report of an alleged event not recorded in any contemporaneous writing, but handed down by word of mouth only, then I confess—Tradition is shifting and uncertain.

But even then it obeys *some* laws. Two Gloucestershire legends will illustrate what I mean. The first is recorded by Rudder, who, speaking of Chosen Hill, says: 'There is a silly tradition in this part of the country that the church was begun to be built on a more convenient and accessible spot of ground, but that the materials used in the day were constantly taken away at night, and carried to the top of the hill, which was considered as a supernatural intimation that the church should be built there.'[1] Now, this is a local variant of a very common story, accounting for the sites of churches up and down the country. In every case, of course, the story has arisen long subsequent to the erection of the church, for it professes to account for a situation which is, for some reason, inconvenient or absurd according to the circumstances of the period when the story arose. When the real reason for a given fact is unknown or forgotten in certain stages of culture a story arises (this is the law) attributing to it a supernatural origin. A church is naturally exposed in a special manner to supernatural interference. Hence it is only what we may expect if we find supernatural interference invoked as the reason for the site of the church. The fact forgotten here is that the original village was on the top of the hill. The hilltop was in fact a settlement from very early times, and was fortified by a rampart and ditch, of which the remains are still to be seen. A church must have stood here for many hundred years, since the existing building contains stones carved with what is called Anglo-Saxon work, which have been built into the present fabric in places other than those for which they were designed. The hilltop was, however, practically abandoned during the Middle Ages, for so early as the twelfth century Roger, Archbishop of York, to whose see Churchdown belonged, laid pipes from the well near the top to supply the present village with water, and one of the early miracles credited to Thomas à Becket was performed there during the operation.[2] Hence there has been plenty of time for a tradition like that I have mentioned to grow up.

The laws affecting tradition as a record of historical events have as yet hardly been investigated with scientific accuracy. Theories there have been without number; but these have been, for the most part, little more than guesses. Still, I think I may venture to lay down another law, namely, that when a fact of ancient date is

---

[1] *A New History of Gloucestershire* (1779), p. 339. *Chosen* is apparently a corruption of *Churchdown*.

[2] *Transactions of the Bristol and Gloucestershire Archæological Soc.*, vol. i, p. 167; Abbott, *St. Thomas of Canterbury*, vol. ii, p. 220, quoting in parallel columns the accounts of Benedict (*Materials for the History of Thomas Becket*, Rolls Series, vol. ii, pp. 261–3), and William of Canterbury (*Materials*, vol. i, pp. 253–6).

remembered, the memory of it is not a bare transcript of the event, but is transfigured into some imaginative form, and in some circumstances that transfiguration takes a supernatural shape. Let me illustrate this by the legend of Bisley Church: another instance of the same story of the removal by night of the stones, here definitely said to have been accomplished by the devil. Now, the place pointed out as the intended site of the church is the site of a Roman villa; and when the church was restored, some years ago, portions of the materials of that villa, including an altar of the Penates, were found embedded in the walls.[1] The fact remembered was the removal of the materials from a certain spot; the fact forgotten was that the materials were part of a Roman villa used as a quarry for the church; the supernatural element intruded into the place of the forgotten fact was that the devil for purposes of his own removed them. It is not too much to say that this intrusive supernatural element is the means whereby the memory of the fact has been preserved for 800 or 1000 years. It is like the tannin of the Irish bogs, which, by permeating the substance of the most perishable articles, has preserved for fifteen or twenty centuries the remains of weapons, implements, and household stores, down even to kegs of butter, used by the ancient Irish in their crannogs and fen-fortresses, and so enabled us to reconstruct in a large measure the material civilization of a remote and forgotten period.

I have mentioned these two legends for the purpose of suggesting to you that, even as the record of alleged events, Tradition, however misleading and incorrect, obeys laws as yet imperfectly understood only because imperfectly investigated. But you will observe that when I thus digressed, I was not dealing with Tradition as a witness to specific facts. Nay, not only was I not comparing it with facts, I was using the word Tradition in a much wider sense. Tradition as an object of science means the whole body of the lore of the uneducated. It thus includes customs and institutions, superstitions and medical practice, and many other things beside stories. Stories, too, divide themselves into tales told for amusement, and tales of alleged events intended to be believed. If you put side by side the customs and institutions of different savage races—say of the Australian blackfellows and the Red Indians of North America—amid very considerable divergences you find surprising points of resemblance, And the same thing applies to their beliefs, their medical practice, their witchcraft, their festivals, their stories, and, in short, their way of regarding the world at large and all that is therein, both natural and supernatural. Turning from savage

[1] *Gloucestershire Notes and Queries*, vol. i, p. 390.

nations to the peasantry of civilized Europe, you will be still more astonished to learn that up to the present time the very same conditions of thought are discernible wherever they are untouched by modern education and the industrial and commercial revolution of the last hundred years. There can only be one interpretation of this. The human mind, alike in Europe and in America, in Africa and in the South Seas, works in the same way, according to the same laws. And the aim of the science of Tradition is to discover those laws, by the examination of their products, the customs and beliefs, the stories and superstitions handed down from generation to generation, to ascertain how those products arose and what was the order of their development, and so to co-operate with physical anthropology and archaeology in writing, as it has never yet been written, the history of civilization.

If there be one superstition better known, at all events to educated people, than another, it is the common cure for warts, alluded to just now. Ask a peasant anywhere what you should do to cure your warts, and you will at once be told to take a piece of beef, or a piece of bacon, or a potato, or some such object, and rub the wart with it, and then bury, or throw away, the meat or potato. Sometimes you are advised to tie in a string as many knots as you have warts, touch each of the warts with one of the knots, and then throw away, or bury, the string. The warts will disappear as the meat, or potato, or the string decays. Now, this is a very silly superstition; quite meaningless, you may think, founded on nothing; and you are astonished that anyone can believe it. But there you are too hasty. No belief, no superstition in this world is founded upon nothing. Many of them are founded upon what we deem in the light of science to be insufficient data, and built up by erroneous reasoning; but none of them, not one, is founded upon nothing; while very often the reasoning is accurate, the premises only are insecure. Let us look at this cure for warts. In the first place, warts have an unaccountable way—unaccountable, I believe, even by the most advanced science of the present day—of coming and going. You can never tell whether a wart has come to stay. Consequently, it very often happens that warts do disappear after being treated as the peasant-doctor prescribes. And logicians tell us that there is no commoner blunder in reasoning than that expressed in the phrase '*Post hoc, propter hoc*'—after this, therefore because of it—and that the blunder arises, on the one hand, from not taking into account all the possible causes of an effect; and, on the other hand, from not testing the supposed cause by other evidence. Neither of these logical operations is performed by the peasant. He knows what he has done to the wart; and if the wart disappear, he attributes it without any doubt to his action.

So much for the logical blunder. But what was it that, first of all, caused a wart to be thus treated? Oh, you will say, nobody knows: accident, perhaps. I am not so sure that it was accident; and if nobody knows, perhaps somebody may find out. For, mark this. The essence of the cure for warts is to touch the wart with a substance afterwards allowed to decay, and the wart is expected to vanish just in proportion as the substance which has touched it, and which is now no longer in contact with it, decays. This is a principle of treatment not by any means confined by the peasant-doctor to warts. Take another case. In September 1892, a fashionably dressed young woman was one day seen hovering about a physician's residence in the north of Berlin. When he went out, she met him, and timidly prayed him to take her, when he had an opportunity, to a dead body. He thought she must be suffering from overstrain or mental disorder, and brusquely refused her. In nowise daunted, however, she begged him earnestly to grant her request, explaining that her object was to remove a deformity. As she said this, she laid bare a delicate white hand blemished by a bony outgrowth, known among surgeons as *exostosis*. The medical man became interested; and it was not long before he stood with her in the presence of a corpse. The lady grasped the cold right hand, and with it repeatedly and silently stroked the ugly excrescence. Then, without speaking, she left the room in all haste; nor was the physician able to learn who she was, or what had led her to seek this means of relief.[1]

The cure of superficial diseases, like scrofula, wens, and swollen glands, by the touch of a corpse is well known. And that its virtue lay, not in the cold contact, but in the decay which the dead hand was about to undergo, and which was believed to affect the disease touched by the hand, is shown by a practice in Donegal. There, when you meet a funeral, if you are troubled with warts, you can get rid of them by simply throwing some clay from under your right foot in the path by which the funeral is going, and saying as you do so: 'Corpse of clay, carry my warts away.'[2] In this case the wart is not itself touched by the corpse; but the clay thrown may come in contact with the corpse; and doubtless in older days it was first applied to the warts, and then placed on, or under, the dead body. The ceremony has become mutilated in the process of civilization; but the ritual words, which indicate its intention, remain. So, an

[1] *Berliner Tageblatt*, September 18, 1892.
[2] Professor Haddon in *Folk-lore* (the Transactions of the Folk-lore Soc.), vol. iv, p. 355.

[235]

English cure for boils was to poultice for three days and nights and then to place the poultices, cloths and all, in the coffin of a body about to be buried.[1]

Let us take another example, where the object is not to cause decay and disappearance, but health and new vigour. When children are born with infantile hernia, it is still not a very uncommon remedy in country places to pass the babe at sunrise through a young ash-tree, split open for the purpose. I need not trouble you with the details of the ceremony, except to say that the tree is immediately afterwards bound up again and plastered with mud or clay, in the hope that it will grow together once more, as it generally does. Its recovery is watched with some anxiety, because upon it depends the child's recovery; and it is believed that the child's life and health depend thenceforth upon the life and health of the tree. So far is this belief carried that a friend of mine who caused one such tree to be taken up by the roots and placed in the museum in the county town of a neighbouring county was threatened by the child's father, who declared he would shoot him for it. You will find this remedy mentioned in that delightful English classic, White's *Natural History of Selborne*; and if you go further back you can trace it to Marcellus of Bordeaux, a learned writer on medicine at the beginning of the fifth century, who was physician to no less a personage than the Roman Emperor Theodosius I., and who gravely prescribes it in such cases. In his time a cherry was considered the proper tree for the purpose. The exact kind of tree, however, differs in different countries; and no doubt they are all equally beneficial. For infantile hernia is a condition of body which constantly tends to improve and to cure itself without any treatment, hence the remedy is usually successful.

But what I want you to notice is that, since the child's life and health depend upon the life and health of the tree, the condition of the tree becomes an index of the condition of the child. The mutual contact of the child and the tree has united them so closely that they have become, as it were, parts of one another, like the Siamese twins. Henceforward, separate and distinct as they are to *our* eyes, in the eyes of the peasant neither of them has really an independent existence. This is a belief which, of course, is only implicit in his mind. He is not conscious of it, because he does not reason the matter out. He simply adheres to the traditional rites and opinions of his forefathers; and they have been for ages in a state of decay. Yet it seems probable that there was a time when, strange and impossible as we may think it, nobody was held to have an individual

[1] Thiselton-Dyer, *English Folk-lore*, p. 171.

existence. The idea of individual existence—the notion that every man, woman, and child is a distinct and separate entity, which can be treated by itself, apart from any other—seems to be quite a modern growth in civilization and in thought, however self-evident it may seem to us, and however absurd the contrary. Among savages, the unit of society is not the individual, but the clan. By *the clan* I do not mean the whole tribe to which the individual savage belongs, but his kindred. The *tribe* is a local organization, which may include many kindreds or clans; and, on the other hand, the kindred or clan frequently extends beyond the bounds of the local tribe. But wherever it is found, the clan or kindred is regarded as one single entity: not a corporation, for a corporation is an abstract legal creation of civilized life, though it has perhaps grown up out of the ancient clan. The members of the clan are regarded as members one of another, in a very literal sense, just as you regard your limbs. When a member of the clan has been slain, the others say, not: 'The blood of So-and-so has been spilt,' but '*Our* blood has been spilt.' The injury is felt by the entire kindred; and it is the business of the entire kin to avenge it. And not only so, but every member of the clan is responsible for a wrong committed by any of them. This is the origin of the *vendetta* as practised in the South of Europe, and by savages everywhere. An interesting trial for murder took place nine or ten years ago in Dalmatia. Two brothers, having quarrelled with a neighbour about some goats, threw themselves upon him with their daggers; but he defended himself with his pistol, and having killed one, was tried for murder. The jury properly acquitted him, on the ground that he was only acting in self-defence. Hardly had he left the prison when his surviving assailant, with another brother, hastened to his house. They found there only their foe's wife and daughters; and they waited and watched. Soon they espied his younger brother, a boy of fourteen, carrying a pitcher of water. Crying 'The devil threw thee in our way,' they seized him, and stabbed him so quickly that he had no time even to cry out. They were speedily arrested, tried, found guilty of murder, and condemned, the one to death, and the other to eighteen years' penal servitude. They protested against the sentence, and appealed to the Court of Cassation at Vienna. There their counsel had the assurance to plead that 'in Dalmatia it is every man's duty to take vengeance where blood has been shed; and that the people feel it right to pursue a family, one of whose members has killed a connexion of their own, as long as there is a male descendant.' This was a little more than a civilized court of justice could stand; and the sentences were confirmed, in the hope of teaching the Dalmatian savages that the unity of the kin is not a doctrine of modern jurisprudence.[1] Yet even these Dalmatian savages had progressed a little way towards civilization; for you will have noted that they would not take a woman's life. A little lower down in the scale vengeance is not so choice. In the Fiji islands the theory was thus explained by an old resident to Mr. Fison, in reference to a bloody feud which had lasted for years, and which arose out of the shooting of a dog: 'It's just like this, sir: in a manner o' speakin', say as me and Tom Farrell here has a difficulty, and gets to punchin' one another. If he plugs me in the eye, I don't feel duty bound to hit him back azackly on the same spot. If I can get well in on him anywheres handy, I ain't partickler. And that's how these niggers reckons it.'[2]

I might cite case after case to show you, not only from the *vendetta*, or blood-feud, but also from many other customs and institutions, ay, and ceremonies, practised both by savages and by the uneducated classes of Europe, and even by the educated classes in many parts of the world, how the individual is regarded merely as a portion of the clan, having no rights apart from it, and in fact no separate existence, and how this idea of separate existence and individual rights and responsibilities has been a slow growth in the evolution of human civilization. To treat the subject so as to give you the steps in the argument and to illustrate them by proofs would require volumes. I ventured a year or two ago to write a volume on it, and I don't pretend to have treated the subject fully.[3] If, however, you will for the moment take my word for it, and assume that members of a kin, who perhaps may never have seen one another and never even have heard of one another, are believed to be so closely united, you will not find it difficult to understand that from intimate contact, such as arises when a child is passed through the very vitals of a young tree, there may, in savage and peasant contemplation, spring an union quite as deep and intricate and permanent. When an adventurous traveller goes into the African forests, and desires to form a league of friendship with some powerful chief, he enters into the blood-covenant with him. Blood is drawn from the traveller's arm and from the chief's arm, and mixed and drunk by both parties, or smeared upon one another's flesh. From that moment the traveller becomes akin to the chief; they are bound to one another just as if they were the children of one mother; they become a part of one another; savage

[1] *The Daily News*, July 14, 1894.
[2] Fison and Howitt, *Kamilaroi and Kurnai*, p. 157, note.
[3] *The Legend of Perseus*, vol. ii.

kindred with *all* its consequences is imposed upon them; though the traveller, if he be wise, rarely stays to enter upon many of its duties. The simple contact of the blood has conferred the status of kinship upon both parties and upon all their kindred. This may even be done by accident. Dr. Livingstone was once called in to treat a Balonda woman for a tumour in the arm. In opening the tumour, some of her blood spurted into his eye. She immediately remarked: 'You were a friend before; now you are a blood-relation.' And in saying this she was perfectly serious.[1]

In the same way you may unite yourself to a god. Any portion of your body, such as a lock of your hair, or part of your clothing, or even something which has only touched your hand, suspended upon the object of worship, keeps you, so long as it remains there, in continual union with your god. Greek boys and girls, on arriving at adult life, or before marriage, used to dedicate locks of their hair at the shrines of various gods. Athenian women used to hang up their girdles in the temple of Artemis. This is the origin of the votive offerings you may see by the thousand in churches on the Continent. The wax models of limbs or babies are not merely thank-offerings. They secure the divine influence upon the originals, because they, and through them the originals, are in continual contact with the saint or divine being. I do not mean to say that this notion is always present now to the minds of the people who deposit these offerings. They often do it because it is the customary and proper thing to do; but none the less the origin of the practice is clear.

In West Africa when a man prays to an idol (a fetish, as it is often improperly called) he hammers a nail into it. Not a very reverent way of treating your god; but it only means to keep the god in constant touch with you. You feel safer then. There is a West African god in the British Museum bristling with nails; and Miss Kingsley, the author of *Travels in West Africa,* left to the Pitt-Rivers Museum at Oxford a remarkable specimen, loaded with nails and various other pieces of iron stuck into it in all directions. For the same reason, people drop pins into wishing-wells, or tear shreds from their garments and fasten them on the bushes or trees which overhang the well. The well and the bush are (or were) sacred. They were a god in the olden time, or at least the manifestations of a powerful spirit. *Now* the practice is continued merely from habit. But the habit, like all habits, had once a reason, good or bad; and the reason was the desire for union with a supernatural being.

If, however, it can do you so much good to deposit a part of yourself upon the god; on the other hand, if some such part of you as a

[1] Livingstone, *Missionary Travels*, p. 489.

lock of hair, the paring of your nail, a piece of your food or a rag of your clothes, get into the possession of an evil-disposed person, an enemy or witch, no end of damage can be done to you. For just in the same way as relatives are, in the savage view, parts of one another, affected by everything that is done to either of them, so any part of your person or clothing, or even your property, though to outward appearance detached, is still in union with you, and so much in union, that anything which affects it affects you. In New England a few years since, a man had his foot crushed in a railway accident; and it was necessary to cut it off. His friends held a solemn consultation as to what was to be done with the amputated limb. If it were buried, the stump would continue to be painful, and the unfortunate man would be troubled by disagreeable sensations, until the foot had entirely decayed away. So they resolved to burn it; and burn it they did, to save him from this inconvenience. In Sussex, when a man cuts his hair, the clippings must not be carelessly thrown away, for if a bird were to find any of them and work them into its nest, the man would suffer from headache until it had finished. Or in case a toad got hold of a girl's long back hairs, it would be quite enough to give her a cold in her head.[1]

Witches are more serious still; and all over the world, among peoples in what is called the lower culture, the greatest care is taken to prevent hair, nails, and other portions of the body, or garments and things that have touched the body, from getting into the possession of a conjurer. This is why lovers in their tenderest moments exchange locks of hair. It is the most touching proof of confidence they can give. They are henceforth in the power of one another for good or evil, for the faithless one is so easily punished. In some parts of England a girl forsaken by her lover is advised to boil the lock of his hair, and keep it boiling; for whilst it is simmering in the pot, he is simmering too, and can get no rest. Here let me advise any young lady who has a suitor she does not care for, not on any account to give him a lock of her hair. A tale is told in Corsica of a girl who would not listen to a poor young man. The disconsolate youth prayed her at least to give him a single hair which he might treasure in memory of her. She was, however, too clever for him. She pulled a hair out of a camel-hair sieve which hung on a nail in the kitchen, and sent him that. In the dead of night he worked a charm on the precious hair, and waited, in expectation that the maiden would appear, compelled by his incantation. By-and-by a bumping and fumbling was heard at the door. With beating heart he rushed to open it, when there bounced into his arms not the lady

[1] Hartland, *The Legend of Perseus*, vol. ii, p. 132.

of his love, but the sieve.[1] In Africa the superstition is quite common; and of course the negro has carried it to America. A lady, writing about half a century ago on the island of Antigua, relates that a negro boy had been drowned. One of his kinswomen had had a quarrel with an acquaintance. She contrived to cut off some hair from her acquaintance's head; and this she put in the dead boy's hand, just before his coffin was screwed down, whispering in his ear the word: 'Remember!' The negro who told the tale said: 'De pic'nee jumby [that is, the boy's ghost] trouble he [namely, the lady who had lost the hair] so dat he no know war for do, till at last he go out of he head, an' he neber been no good since.' And a powerful negro conjurer told a friend of mine: 'I could save you, or ruin you, if I could get hold of so much as an eye-winker, or the pealing of one freckle.'[2]

Well, the cure for warts with which we started has led us a long way. But I hope I have succeeded in showing you that it is not entirely foolish; that it is not founded on nothing, but on a philosophy that goes very deep down into savage life, and that crops up in the most unexpected way right in the midst of civilized life, and explains a great variety of practices. I know there are great gaps in my demonstration. That is because the subject is a large one; and they cannot be helped. You cannot put a gallon of beer into a pint pot.

I might go through a long list of beliefs and practices you may still find among the peasantry of the British Islands, and show you how one after another was the decayed representative of some part of the religion or the philosophy of our ancestors far away in those misty prehistoric ages, when they dwelt in caves, or in huts, amid the rocks and the marshes, or in great camps, the remains of which are yet visible on the heights around us. And I think I should be able to make it clear that these beliefs and practices are not arbitrary or capricious, but the logical result of principles accepted by a people in the state of savagery as the explanation of the mystery of the great world in which they found themselves, and which yet puzzles the wisest heads among us. But we pride ourselves on being a practical nation; and I feel that I can hope to excite only a languid interest in the study of folklore, unless I can offer you some suggestions of the way in which it may be turned to useful account. Let me take it as an axiom that there is no science—no branch of methodized knowledge, that is—that has not its practical application. When

---

[1] *Revue des Traditions Populaires*, vol. ix, p. 462.
[2] I have cited these and many other instances of the superstition in *The Legend of Perseus*, vol. ii.

Franklin, playing with his kite in a thunderstorm, brought down sparks from the heavens, he was learning the accidence of that science of Electricity which has given us the Telegraph and Telephone, and which has in store for future generations a power we can hardly as yet conceive. But how many men of his generation were there who did not regard his experiments as mere amusement, unworthy of the attention of serious persons? Priestley, turning from the bewilderments of theology to trifle with 'dephlogisticated air,' was helping to lay the foundations of modern Chemistry, to which we owe so much. So, when Professor Tylor, then unknown to fame, gave himself up to the eccentric study of savage life and savage ideas which issued in those two great works, the *Early History of Mankind* and *Primitive Culture,* nothing would have seemed more unlikely than that his inquiries were to lead to results of value to the maintenance and prosperity of the British Empire. When we consider, however, not merely the vast extent, but the almost infinite diversity of races in all stages of culture, over which we rule—when we recall how impossible it is to govern any people properly unless you understand the ideas and the motives that actuate them, and are able by means of your knowledge to anticipate in some measure their feelings, and to sympathize with them—how important then becomes the effort to grasp the significance of their customs and beliefs, their prejudices and their ideals! Who would have imagined that the obscure and technical details of the land tenure of the aboriginal tribes of India could throw any light upon the condition of Ireland? Yet it is hardly too much to say that, if we had been in possession of India at the time when the conquest and settlements of Ireland in the sixteenth and seventeenth centuries took place, and had then understood as we now understand the land tenures of India, there would have been no Irish Land Question to worry us today. We went in with a rough hand and broke up the fabric of Irish society, imposing upon the land the incongruous feudal theories of English law. We did this, not because we desired to do injustice, but because the Elizabethan lawyers were utterly ignorant of any system of law beside their own. We went to India, and found a state of things in relation to the ownership of land so different from that to which we had been accustomed that at first we were baffled; nor was it without careful and long-continued study, and many mistakes, that we succeeded in comprehending its principles. And then, scholars, turning to the old Irish laws, discovered that on this point the Irish traditions and the traditions of the aborigines of India presented so many traits in common that it might fairly be said the systems were the same. They threw at once

[242]

a flood of light upon one another. Both were systems of customary law; both were rooted in a common philosophy of the essential unity of the kin; and its consequence, the common ownership by the kin, was the same in both. Our own system, although we did not know it, grew up out of similar conditions; but they had been long disturbed and distorted by the vicissitudes of our earlier history and overlaid by our developing civilization. Traces of them, however, are still to be met with up and down the country. Indeed, the open fields of Upton St. Leonard's are a remnant, battered and decayed, of course, of such a state of society and thought; and we cannot fully explain their existence without seeking help from the Brehon laws of Ireland and the folklore, not merely of India, but of other savage races.[1]

Again, what waste of precious human lives might have been avoided in our manifold dealings with tribes in the lower culture if we had been acquainted with their modes of thought! Collisions between white men and savages often occur, and are perhaps unavoidable, from theft and other offences on the part of the savages, and from summary punishment—revenge, rather—on the part of the white men, and from recklessness and sheer cruelty on the part of settlers, traders, and sailors. But these are by no means the only causes. A well-known missionary tells how he and another landed on one of the South Sea Islands, called Aneiteum, and, walking about, came to a hut, which they were about to enter, when half a dozen voices called to them to stop. They then learnt that in the hut was a pig, being fattened for an approaching feast, and the hut was consequently tabooed to strangers. Now *Taboo* is one of the most powerful institutions among the Polynesians; and it has given a word to the English language. Anything on which a taboo is set is thereby rendered sacred, *anathema*. Nobody can touch it or approach it under the severest penalties, often nothing less than death. So it was death for a stranger to go near a pig when it was being fed in anticipation of a feast. And had the missionaries been ignorant of the language, the probability is that they would have violated the taboo and been slain in consequence.'[2]

The blood-feud, or vendetta, which I have already explained, is responsible for the loss of many lives in the intercourse between

[1] The parish of Upton St. Leonard's, near Gloucester, preserved several features of archaic life. Of these the open fields were the most conspicuous; but, alas! an order of the Board of Agriculture has at length permitted their enclosure. The rights of the parties have been settled; many of the open lands have now (1904) been actually enclosed; houses are arising upon them; and in a few months, of a year or two at most, these relics of an earlier state of society will be themselves things of the past. On the subject of the open field system, see *The Village Community*, by G. L. Gomme (Walter Scott, 1890).          [2] Turner, *Nineteen Years in Polynesia*, p. 370.

white men and savages. For, as I have shown you, it is not necessary to retaliate upon the very man who commits the crime. Any of his kindred will do as well. If, therefore, a quarrel arise between white strangers and the natives, and any of the natives be killed, the death of any white man who may be thrown among the survivors is deemed only just and equitable; and this will be repeated until the number of strangers put to death equals the number of the natives killed. Civilized men, not understanding this law, have regarded the natives merely as bloodthirsty savages, and have made not less bloody reprisals, which have only perpetuated the feud and led to more terrible results.

The mention of missionaries leads me to say how lamentable it is that missionaries should be sent out, as they are by all our missionary societies, utterly ignorant of the customs and beliefs of the peoples whom they are going to try to convert to Christianity. At one time there was an excuse for their ignorance, for they only shared it with every one else in Europe. But there is none now, when so much is known about most savage and barbarous races. Let me give you an example of the quandary in which a missionary ignorant on these matters may find himself. One who laboured among the Australian aborigines on the Murray River relates that when he first went among them one of the young men took a fancy to him and adopted him as a brother. It is not quite clear from the narrative whether he went through any ceremony; but probably he did, as he and the young native regarded themselves afterwards as brothers. 'I one day,' he tells us, 'said to his wife: "I am John's brother; you are my sister." The idea was, to her, most ridiculous. With a laugh she said: "No, you are my husband!" '[1] This is an excellent illustration of the length to which the doctrine of the unity of the kin is carried by some savages: even to absolute oneness. The missionary of course had no notion of this: it was one of the things he ought to have known at starting, if he were to avoid needless difficulties; one of the things he had slowly to learn by experience— in this instance ludicrous, but experience that might in easily conceivable circumstances have been tragic. The fact is that such knowledge is not less necessary to Christian enterprise than to good government and successful commercial intercourse.

Again. Theologians trained in civilized life, with the heritage of three thousand years of metaphysical subtleties, forget that the savage mind is unused to their modes of thought, and quite unfitted to grasp their conceptions or to find its way among their distinctions. They start with the notion that all the traditions of the heathen

[1] Fison and Howitt, *op. cit.*, p. 289.

are the suggestions of the devil, or the vile and abominable inventions of fallen human nature, instead of being, as they are, the evidence of the upward strivings of humanity from its primitive condition. Hence, they consider that they have nothing to do with heathen customs but to stamp them out, and to impose their own instead. Not having any common ground of sympathy to base their appeals upon, their work is retarded. They too often succeed only in creating confusion, relaxing the bonds of morality which they find, without effectually substituting any new ones.

In saying this I do not wish to depreciate their noble and self-denying labours. I sympathize profoundly with their efforts. I only want to point out that their methods are not always the wisest because they are ignorant, and therefore clumsy methods. This opinion is supported by a vast mass of evidence, of which I will only quote the latest—that given by Miss Kingsley in her *Travels in West Africa*. 'Taken as a whole,' she says, 'the missionaries must be regarded as superbly brave, noble-minded men who go and risk their own lives, and often those of their wives and children, and definitely sacrifice their personal comfort and safety to do what, from their point of view, is their simple duty; but it is their methods of working that have produced in West Africa the results which all truly interested in West Africa must deplore; and one is bound to make an admission that goes against one's insular prejudice—that the Protestant English missionaries have had most to do with rendering the African useless.' 'The missionary,' she goes on to say, 'to the African has done what my father found them doing to the Polynesians—"regarding the native minds as so many jugs only requiring to be emptied of the stuff that is in them and refilled with the particular form of dogma he is engaged in teaching, in order to make them the equals of the white race." '[1] He forgets that Christianity is, if not the product of, at least inseparably bound up with, a high form of civilization; and the savage is not fitted for it without long years, and perhaps generations, of training, which must begin on the missionary's part by a complete understanding of and sympathy with the native, and by a gradual process must lift the native up out of his abject condition at one and the same time into Christianity and civilization. Of course the better and wiser missionaries fully recognize this. I need only to mention the names of William Ellis, William Wyatt Gill, Duff Macdonald, James Sibree, Dr. Codrington, and Dr. Callaway, as types of a class to which the cause of humanity, as well as that of science, owes a deep debt of gratitude. Would that all were such as these!

[1] Miss Kingsley, *Travels in West Africa*, p. 659.

Here let me say in passing that it is a disgrace to our Government that there is no public institution to which a young man who is going out, either as a Government official in one of our numerous dependencies, or as a missionary, can go to be instructed in Anthropology. Alone, or almost alone, among civilized Governments, ours does nothing to promote the study of savage races. Others have colleges for training in anthropological subjects, or at least a Department of State, like the Bureau of Ethnology at Washington, for the systematic collection and comparison of everything which may throw light on the tribes beneath their sway. Our indifference and contempt, on the other hand, are carried so far, that it is the universal testimony of Government officials that interest in the subject peoples is absolutely discouraged. An official who is known to undertake such inquiries is regarded as a trifler, and is a marked man. He can never look forward to promotion. And yet, ruling as we do over a greater variety of nationalities than any other European people, it is beyond comparison more to our advantage than to that of any other thoroughly to understand the workings of the native mind. It requires but little insight to be assured that we might enormously strengthen our hold upon India if our Government were to take a different line, and were to encourage, instead of discouraging, civil and military officials to inquire systematically into and report upon the ideas and practices of the races of that vast continent. Soldiers in particular have time on their hands, which they too often waste in idleness with all the evils that attend it. How much better it would be if they were given to understand that they were expected to take an intelligent and scientific interest in the humanity about them, and that substantial contributions to our information on the subject would be taken into consideration in reckoning their services to the Empire! Intelligent and scientific interest would lead to sympathy. The natives would be more wisely treated, treated like human beings, instead of, as they too often are, like dogs. And the popularity of our rule and our consequent power would be multiplied a hundredfold.

Of our Colonial Governors, only one has taken up the matter seriously—Sir William MacGregor, lately Governor of British New Guinea. But his testimony is express. 'Ever since the declaration of sovereignty,' he says, 'as much attention as possible has been given to the peculiar usages, customs, and habits of the natives. It has been felt that no man, or body of men, can rule justly and wisely a people with whose customs, usages, and inner life they are unacquainted. In legislation and in executive administration it is imperative that, in a country such as this is, with a mere handful of

Europeans and a numerous savage and semi-savage population, the officers of the Government should not only become acquainted with the hereditary and traditional customs of the natives, but that they should also know their superstitions, their aims, their inter-tribal family and domestic polity, and even their prejudices.'[1] Golden words. We can only hope that Sir William MacGregor's tenure of office continued long enough to impress this principle as a lasting tradition upon the Government of British New Guinea, and that his example may speedily be followed elsewhere.

But you will tell me: 'All this is very remote from us. We are neither Government officials nor missionaries. What is the value of folklore to *us*?'

Well, what I have been saying about Government officials and missionaries applies—in a lesser degree, it is true, but yet applies—to everybody who has to do—and who has not?—with the peasantry and the uneducated classes of our own countrymen. The more perfect your interest in and your sympathy with them, the more completely you can identify yourselves with their modes of thought, the greater your influence for good upon them. The conflict of the classes and the masses about which we hear so much today is all the bitterer because of the chasm which education has opened between high and low. Three hundred years ago the upper classes, as they are called, thought and felt much more nearly like their poorer brethren than now. They accepted the same superstitions; they looked at the world with the same eyes. It is true we are doing our best to diminish the distance that has grown between the educated and uneducated. But it takes time; and depend upon it it is worth while trying to condescend to the lower level, in order the more quickly to raise up those who are there to your own.

Then I have tried to show you that the ideas of 'the folk' have

[1] *Colonial Reports*, No. 131, British New Guinea, p. 34. Since this essay was first published (1899), an attempt has been made by my friend Prof. Haddon to start anthropological classes at Cambridge for intending missionaries and others, with what results it is yet too early to say. Moreover, Lord Curzon has arranged for an Ethnographical Survey of India, which is now proceeding under the direction of Mr. H. H. Risley. The Queensland Government is publishing a most valuable series of researches on the aborigines of that colony by Mr. W. E. Roth, who holds an official position as Protector of Aboriginals in Northern Queensland. It is also continuing the inquiries set on foot by Sir W. MacGregor in British New Guinea. The government of the French Colony of the Ivory Coast W. Africa, has, for the specific purpose of utilizing the native customs in the administration of the colony, obtained and published official returns embodying a quantity of information as to the customs and laws of the tribes under its sway. A commission of inquiry for similar purposes into the laws and customs of the natives of the Transvaal and the Orange River Colony, urged by the Anthropological Institute and the Folk-lore Society supported by a number of distinguished scientific men was *refused* by Mr. Chamberlain.

an interest of their own. Properly studied, they unveil the past of the human race in a way for which we look in vain in the material monuments of antiquity. The legends and practices localized here and there all over the country glorify many a fair hillside, many a majestic building, many a sombre ruin, and lend an additional charm to our holidays and our travels. Amazing to us is the veneration once paid to the body of Edward II in Gloucester Cathedral, amazing are the stories that grew up around it. Not the least amazing is the tradition that he was drawn from Berkeley Castle to his grave by white harts. That was a tradition that grew up in accordance with a law of the human mind revealed by folklore; but it is not for me now to strain your patience by recounting other examples even in this country.

Nor is it only our summer holidays that may be rendered more attractive by the study of folklore. As we sit by the fire in the long winter evenings and read the masterpieces of literature, as I hope some of us sometimes do, we cannot appreciate even these without some knowledge of the ideas current at the time they were written. Take down the mighty Shakespeare, and perhaps you think you can enjoy *A Midsummer Night's Dream* as the audience for whom he wrote it enjoyed it, without concerning yourself about the silly fairy beliefs of our ancestors. But let me ask you What do you know about Robin Goodfellow? Do you imagine that Robin Goodfellow—a mere name to you—conveys anything like the meaning to your mind that it did to those for whom the name represented a still living belief, and who had the stories about him at their fingers' ends? Or let me ask you Why did the fairies dance on moonlight nights? or Have you ever thought why it is that in English literature, and in English literature alone, the fairy realm finds a place in the highest works of imagination? As my predecessor, Mr. Alfred Nutt, in one of his presidential addresses to the Folklore Society, eloquently said:

'We could not blot out from English poetry its visions of the fairyland without a sense of irreparable loss. No other literature save that of Greece alone can vie with ours in its pictures of the land of fantasy and glamour, or has brought back from that mysterious realm of unfading beauty treasures of more exquisite and enduring charm.' What is the reason of this rare distinction? For answers to such questions you must go to folklore.

But there is one literature of more profound and far-reaching influence than even English literature. I refer to the Hebrew literature contained in the Bible. It is full of tales, of allusions to custom, and of descriptions of ritual, which can only be explained by folklore.

More than this, what is called 'the Higher Criticism' has demonstrated by consideration of the internal evidence that many of the books of the Old Testament are of a much later date than they were long supposed to be, though often embodying, revising, and otherwise manipulating earlier materials, either written or oral. All commentators of repute are practically agreed upon this. Even the most orthodox and conservative are too learned and too candid—too judicial, in a word—to deny altogether the force of the destructive criticism that has riddled the old position through and through, or to refuse their assent entirely to its methods and many of its results. It is merely a question of less or more, or this or that particular conclusion. It is generally recognized that theological arguments have no validity against literary and historical evidence. They are not in the same plane; they do not deal with the same subject-matter. If then, for example, we are no longer to accept the Pentateuch as written by Moses, if the narrative be nothing more than a collection of traditions worked up in various ways by various writers, and more than once re-edited, if it be not in the strict sense of the term historical, what are we to say of the laws? Here it is that folklore helps us. The distinction between clean and unclean animals; the ordinance that he who touched a dead body, or even came into the same tent with it, should be impure and unable to go into the sanctuary for seven days, and until the priest had sprinkled him with the water of separation; the decree that, when a man died childless, his brother should take his widow, in the hope of continuing the family of the deceased—these are ancient customs, far more ancient than any date which can be assigned to Moses, world-wide, or based upon ideas that are world-wide; and for them and many others folklore, and folklore alone, has an adequate explanation. In fact, the great mass of Hebrew customs and a considerable proportion of Hebrew stories are neither more nor less than the particular national form assumed by customs and stories and superstitions which are common to mankind and inevitably arise in certain stages of civilization. Science has not yet solved every question in connexion with the history of Hebrew myths and customs; but the late Professor Robertson Smith, in his great fragment on *The Religion of the Semites,* has led the way; and enough has been done to show that we are on the right path. Every new discovery helps us forward; and researches in Hebrew civilization will at no distant day be brought into line with those in other departments of the Science of Man.

I must apologize for detaining you so long. I hope I have not wearied you in trying to show you that the science of Folklore is one of real importance, full of interest, full of surprises to those who are unacquainted with it. It has vast possibilities that will revolutionize our conceptions of human history. Already it has co-operated with prehistoric archaeology to establish beyond cavil that civilization has been evolved through long centuries of struggle from a low form of savagery. What is behind that primitive condition it leaves to other sciences to say. And it has rendered clear that, underlying all differences of race and nationality, we have a common human nature, common to the savage Tasmanian or Bushman and the cultivated Englishman, a common mental constitution which reasons everywhere on the same principles, though it may not attain everywhere to the same results, because it does not start from the same premises. Folklore has lent a new emphasis to the truth enshrined in the ancient declaration that God 'made of one every nation of men for to dwell on all the face of the earth.'

BIBLIOGRAPHY

In case any readers of the foregoing paper may be sufficiently interested to pursue the subject, I append a list of a few books which they will find helpful. This list is not intended to be exhaustive. It only aims at guiding such as wish to obtain a general view of the scope and method of Folklore. Readers who desire more than this will not be long in discovering from the works named below hints for further research.

'The Handbook of Folklore.' Edited by George Laurence Gomme, F.S.A., 1890. Out of print. New edition in preparation.

[One of the publications of the Folk-Lore Society. It affords a general view of the study, with hints on collecting and the scientific work to be done.]

'Researches into the Early History of Mankind and the Development of Civilization,' by Edward B. Tylor, D.C.L., LL.D., F.R.S. London, John Murray, 3rd ed., 1878.

'Primitive Culture; Researches into the Development of Mythology, Philosophy, Religion, Art, and Custom,' by the same. Same publisher. 2 vols., 1st ed., 1871; 4th ed., 1903.

[In these two works Dr. Tylor laid the foundation of the scientific study of the evolution of human ideas and civilization.]

'Custom and Myth,' by Andrew Lang, M.A. London, Longmans, 1884.

'Myth, Ritual, and Religion,' by the same. Same publishers. 2 vols., 1st ed., 1887; 2nd ed., 1899.

[In the latter of these two works Mr. Lang, applying Professor Tylor's method of inquiry, demolished once for all the theories of the philological school of Mythologists, represented in this country primarily by Professor Max Müller. In the new edition, however, he has embodied some hypotheses, expressed first in his recent book on *The Making of Religion*, which do not command unqualified assent.]

[250]

'The Golden Bough: a Study in Magic and Religion,' by J. G. Frazer, M.A. 2 vols. London, Macmillan, 1890. 2nd ed., 3 vols., 1900.

[A study in detail of some profoundly interesting aspects of savage religion.]

'The Blood Covenant: a Primitive Rite and its Bearing on Scripture,' by H. Clay Trumbull, D.D. London, Redway, 1887.

'Lectures on the Religion of the Semites. First Series: The Fundamental Institutions.' By W. Robertson Smith, M.A., LL.D. Edinburgh, A. & C. Black, 1889. 2nd ed., 1894.

[These two books contain the first intelligible account of the theory of the Blood-Covenant and Sacrifice. The relations of the god to his worshippers, holy places and objects are, among other important subjects, treated of in *The Religion of the Semites.*]

'The Legend of Perseus: a Study of Tradition in Story, Custom and Belief.' By Edwin Sidney Hartland F.S.A. 3 vols. London, D. Nutt, 1894–6.

[I venture to include this, because the second volume, dealing with the Life-token, sets out fully the reasoning of the earlier part of the foregoing paper and pursues the subject in directions not touched on above.]

'Ethnology in Folklore,' by George Laurence Gomme, F.S.A. London, Kegan Paul & Co., Limited, 1892.

[The main object of this little book is to determine the value of folklore as evidence of race; but, under the head of the Localisation of Primitive Belief, it includes an account of the worship at sacred wells and trees.]

'An Introduction to Folklore,' by Marian Roalfe Cox. London, D. Nutt, 1895.

[A popular introduction written in a lively and pleasant style.]

Generally, the publications of the Folklore Society, of which 'The Handbook of Folklore' has already been mentioned. Among those bearing on the subject of this paper may be mentioned:

'Folk Medicine: a chapter in the History of Culture,' by William George Black, F.S.A. Scot., 1883.

And numerous articles in

'Folk-Lore' (the Transactions of the Society). Fourteen volumes published, 1890–1903, still proceeding.

It may be added that all the numbers of the series of *Popular Studies,* of which the foregoing paper forms one, bear more or less directly upon the subject of Folklore and attempt to elucidate the principles on which the study of the beliefs, institutions, and literature of peoples in early stages of culture, including those of our own forefathers, should proceed.


# [ 3 ALFRED NUTT ]


In publishing varied books on serious subjects, Alfred Nutt assumed the role of contributor on occasions when he espied an opportunity to further the cause of folklore and comment on matters within his special competence. He saw such an opportunity in issuing a work by Harry Lowerison intended as a naturalist's handbook for children and their parents and teachers. Nutt issued it under the title *Field and Folklore* and added 'A Few Words on Folklore' to acquaint young readers bent on observing flora and fauna with the possibilities of also observing rural rites and ceremonies. In speaking of collecting techniques he quotes at some length from Charlotte Burne, the chief apostle of fieldwork in The Folk-Lore Society, author of the revised *Handbook of Folklore* published by the Society in 1914, editor of Georgina Jackson's *Shropshire Folk-Lore* in 1883, one of the best county collections, and writer of a persuasive exhortation on 'The Collection of English Folklore' (*Folk-Lore*, I, 1880, 313–30).

Text from Harry Lowerison, *Field and Folklore*. London: David Nutt, 1899. Pages 61–76, 'A Few Words on Folklore to the Reader of the Foregoing Pages.'


Mr. Lowerison has told you how you may study the ways of beast, and bird, and plant, in your country rambles, nay, even in the bits of garden and woodland which live on in our towns, surrounded though they be by bricks and mortar. He has told you also somewhat concerning certain classes of man's handiwork, the prehistoric implements which tell almost all we can learn directly respecting his earliest past, and the mediaeval churches which, in so many parts of our land, afford the chief examples of skill used to produce beauty. If you pay attention to what he says, and strive to master his rules, you will have learnt two very precious lessons—to observe closely and accurately, and to observe in a spirit of loving sympathy. You have approved yourself an apt pupil; on foot or cycle you wander far afield, away from rail and high road, glad, townsman as you are, to be rid for a while of endless streets with their never-ceasing rumble and roar, of the scarce ever lifted leaden haze that hangs between you and the open sky. The capacity for sympathetic observation which you have thus acquired in the study of nature will soon reveal to you numberless facts belonging to the world of man, facts of which your school education gives you little if any explanation, and in the interpretation of which your town experience probably leaves you at fault; yet many of them have survived in town life, and may, if you are of an inquiring turn of mind, have already excited your curiosity.

Some of these facts about which I wish to say a few words will appeal to you on what may be called the spectacular or entertainment side. Should you happen to find yourself in the quiet Oxfordshire village of Bampton on Whit Monday, you may chance upon the following procession: Eight Morris dancers dressed in finely pleated white shirts, white moleskin trousers, and top hats decorated with red, white, and blue ribbons; attached to their knees they wear numerous small latten bells, some treble, others tenor, which jingle as they dance; they are accompanied by a fiddler, a clown, and a swordbearer carrying a cake impaled on a sword-blade, which is distributed among the bystanders whilst the dancing is going on.[1] Again, at Haxey, in the Isle of Axholme, Lincolnshire, you might witness the sport known as the Haxey Hood Game. The youth of the town assemble in the afternoon in a field near the churchyard. The hood, a piece of sacking rolled tightly up, well corded, and weighing some six pounds, is thrown into their midst to be scrambled for and carried by the victor to the nearest public-house. Certain players, distinguished by scarlet jackets, and known as plough-bullocks or boggins, are stationed at stated intervals, and if the hood falls into their hands it is dead, and the play begins again.[2] At St. Ives, in Cornwall, a special kind of hockey, known locally as hurling, is played in the streets with a silver-covered ball on the Monday after Quinquagesima Sunday. At Abbot's Bromley, Staffordshire, within the limits of the old Forest of Needwood, the horn-dance is performed on the Monday after September 4, by six men with stags' horns on their heads, a man (known as the Hobby Horse) wearing a wooden horse's head and caparison, and a boy carrying a crossbow and arrow.[3] Throughout the country from Aberdeen to Dorset, even in the immediate neighbourhood of London, shortly before and after Christmas, and also in some places at Eastertide, groups of men may be met, armed with wooden swords and clad in tinselled and beribboned coats; they engage in a series of single combats accompanied by words, in rhyme as a rule, which, though differing considerably in detail, retain everywhere the same substance. This is the so-called Mumming Play.[4]

Here we have a few examples of performances partly spectacular and dramatic in character; in some cases they are strictly local, in

[1] For a full description, with illustrations, see Mr. Manning's paper 'Some Oxfordshire Seasonal Festivals,' *Folk-Lore*, December 1897.
[2] See Miss M. Peacock's paper, 'The Hood Game at Haxey, Lincolnshire,' *Folk-Lore*, December 1896.
[3] See Miss C. S. Burne's paper 'Staffordshire Folk and their Lore,' *Folk-Lore*, December 1896. There are three plates illustrating the Horn-Dance.
[4] There is no independently published monograph on the Mumming Play. Reference should be made to Miss Burne's 'Staffordshire Guisers' Play,' *Folk-Lore Journal*, vol. iv; to Mr. Fairman Ordish's two excellent papers on 'English Folk-Drama,' *Folk-Lore*, 1892 and 1893; and Mr. Rouse's paper, 'Christmas Mummers at Rugby,' with illustrations, *Folk-Lore*, June 1899.' In Sir Walter Scott's notes to 'The Pirate' will be found a highly elaborate literary version.

[253]

nearly all they are associated with a special season; in all cases the players (using the word in the wisest sense) belong to the people and do not form a special class whose sole business it is to perform in this way. There is marked difference in these respects from the kinds of spectacular entertainments town dwellers are familiar with—theatrical and music-hall performances, concerts, cricket and football matches, all of which are carried on by a professional class, and are not tied down in the same way to a particular locality or season. Obviously, the former class of entertainment could not be derived from the latter: it represents a different order of ideas, and testifies to a different state of society.

Besides these performances in which grown-up people take a part, you may often, in your rambles through the countryside, come across groups of children playing games. Many of them have been retained by town children, and will be familiar to you. But many will be new, and those which you do know and have taken part in will, as a rule, be fuller both as regards the words spoken or chanted and the actions represented. If you watch these games closely you will be struck by the fact that their character is not such as you would expect from children of the present day; they abound in obsolete terms and expressions, they do not refer to the manners, customs, or employments of town life. You are vaguely conscious that they belong substantially to 'a long time ago,' and that they reflect the usages of a different state of society from that known to you.[1]

I have so far mentioned customs and practices which are still fairly vigorous, belonging, as they do, to what may be called the recreation side of life. Take another class of practices—those connected with the earning of a livelihood. You may find in the country districts traces of an economic organization differing greatly from anything you know in modern town life, traces, for instance, of special forms of ownership and usage of property, in which each man does not possess a particular *something*—house, garden, shop, tools, or what not—which he uses by himself, and the proceeds of which he keeps for himself, but a number of people have equal rights in the use of a special area of land, or a special stretch of water, or

---

[1] *The* book on Games is Mrs. G. L. Gomme's *Traditional Games of England, Scotland, and Ireland, with Tunes, Singing-Rhymes, and Methods of Playing according to the variants extant, and recorded in different parts of the Kingdom*, 2 vols., large 8vo, £1 5s. net. This work should be in every Free Library in the kingdom, and I trust that readers of these pages will urge the libraries of their own district to purchase a copy if they have not already done so. Mrs. Gomme has reprinted a dozen of the most interesting singing-games in her *Children's Singing-Games*, fully illustrated by Winifred Smith, two series, each 3s. 6d.

a special set of tools (using this word in the widest sense, to take in, for instance, boats or fishing-nets), and are bound by a definite set of rules regulating their use. In one sense practices such as these, though less prominent than the spectacular ones, are better known, and have won an official recognition denied the others: they affected the daily lives and interests of so many people that the general governing and legal system of the country was bound to take note of them. Hence their frequent embodiment in our land laws, thanks to the manorial system, which provided a special court for each manor, and thus stereotyped and gave legal sanction to such local customs of the district comprised within the manor as were allowed to subsist. In many cases, too, local customs were taken over by municipalities. The City of London, a very early municipal body, has retained many early customs, though chiefly as quaint and picturesque survivals, not like the manorial customs in such a form as really to affect the economic and legal status of the citizens. Although, as I have said, these customs have found a resting-place in the general legal system of the country, you will be struck, I think, by their strange, old-world character, by their unlikeness to anything you are likely to meet at vestry or board meetings, in the police or county courts. Even more than the spectacular customs they will impress you as belonging to a different social order from that in which you live.[1]

In ordinary life you are more or less consciously governed by a series of conceptions respecting the management of your body, your mind, and your soul, which you may be said, roughly speaking, to derive from your doctor, your schoolmaster, and your clergyman. Your doctor, I am sure, never told you that a woodlouse rolled up and swallowed alive made a good pill, nor that you could stop bleeding at the nose by wearing round the neck a skein of scarlet tied with nine knots, nor that whooping cough could be banished by putting a live 'dab' on the patient's breast and keeping it there till it died—yet all these and many other remedies even more preposterous and unpleasant according to your ideas, were until recently, and probably still are, firmly believed in by many country folk.[2] Within the memory of living men children supposed

[1] Many manorial customs which struck the older school of antiquaries as curious are recorded in Blount's *Ancient Tenures of Land and Jocular Customs of Manors* (last edition by Hazlitt, 1874), a useful but quite unscientific compilation. Mr. C. J. Elton's *Custom and Tenant Right*, 1882, is admirable as the work of an expert conveyancer and trained archaeologist. See also Prof. Scrutton's *Commons and Common Fields*, 1887. Mr. G. L. Gomme's *Literature of Local Institutions*, 1886, will give the student who wishes to follow up the subject full guidance, and the same author's *Primitive Folk-Moots*, 1880, is a most interesting account of archaic political institutions.
[2] These particular examples are taken from Lady Camilla Gurdon's 'Suffolk' (*County*

to be bewitched or suffering from infantile ailments were 'passed' through the Shrew Ash still standing in Richmond Park near Sheen Gate. Certainly both clergyman and schoolmaster would, had they known it, have frowned at and have striven their utmost to discourage this practice,[1] as they would also such practices as resorting to a wise woman when the butter won't 'come,' in order to remove the spells laid by some malignant person, or as making an image of clay and placing it in running water with a view to injuring an enemy, the idea being that as the image wastes so will the person aimed at. Nor is it likely that clergymen and schoolmasters are responsible for such queer ideas about certain animals as that it is unlucky to meet a hare or a crow, lucky to see a piebald horse, and so on. In any case their intervention could not possibly account for the fact—and a very curious one it is—that ideas such as these vary most remarkably in different localities. Thus at Newport (Shropshire) cats are killed, whilst at Baschurch, only a few miles away, it is unlucky to hurt them, and the fishermen living outside the Claddagh of Galway used, if they could catch a fox, to set it loose and drive it towards the Claddagh, as the fishing population of this quarter of the town deemed it most unlucky to start out fishing if they met this animal.[2] Numberless beliefs and practices of a nature similar to those instances are still in force; not only are they such as could not have originated in schoolroom or church: they are frequently directly opposed to the teaching given there. They do not belong to our modern world.

The word literature calls up in your mind the idea of a book or a newspaper. If you want either to amuse yourself or to get information you turn to one or other of these forms of printed matter. But throughout the country until quite recently numberless folk never thought of reading. All they knew had been told to them: their literature was oral literature. A vast amount of this still survives in the shape of nursery tales, ballads, songs, local rhymes and sayings, proverbs, pithy saws, and the like.[3] A great charm of this oral

[1] See Miss Ffennell's paper, fully illustrated, 'The Shrew Ash in Richmond Park,' *Folk-Lore*, December 1898.

[2] These examples are taken from the *Handbook of Folklore*, edited by G. L. Gomme, No. 20 of the Folk-Lore Society's Publications, price 2s. 6d.

[3] For NURSERY TALES see Mr. Jacobs' *English Fairy Tales*, and *More English Fairy Tales*, the complete editions with notes, parallels and references; Mr. E. S. Hartland's *English Fairy and other Folk Tales* and Mrs. Hunt's translation of Grimm, with introduction by Mr. Lang. In BALLADS get your Free Library to take a copy of Professor Child's *English and Scottish Ballads*, in ten volumes, Boston, 1881–97, one of the most magnificent works ever devoted to any branch of literature, and buy

*Folk-Lore*, Printed Extracts, No. 2), issued by the Folk-Lore Society. The subject is fully treated in Mr. Black's *Folk-Medicine* (Folk-Lore Society's Publications, No. 12).

literature, and one which is likely to at once impress and delight you, is that it varies a great deal locally. Everybody did not go to the same cheap primer or the same snippets periodical. This hill-top or stream has its local legend, it may be of buried treasure, or of a man-devouring, half-supernatural being; that dark lane or copse has its ghost or bogle. Stories cluster round the old houses of the district, stories which profess to be historical, but are, as a rule, remote from any connexion with actual fact. If there are any Megalithic remains (so-called cromlechs, menhirs, druids' altars, and the like) in a district, they usually furnish a good crop of legend. All readers of Scott's 'Kenilworth' are familiar with the legend of Wayland's smithy, a legend, by-the-by, which must most certainly have been brought to England by our Saxon forefathers some fifteen hundred years ago. Districts and villages too are often distinguished by special nicknames, mostly of an uncomplimentary character; local wit exercises itself at the expense of its neighbours in tales and anecdotes handed down often until the original significance has become lost, and a new story has been invented to account for what has become unintelligible. Thus at Stroud in Gloucestershire you may be advised or dissuaded, according as prudence or rashness predominates in your informant, to allude to a dog-pie in the neighbouring village of Painswick. The origin of this prohibition is unknown, but that it is of great antiquity may be surmised from the fact that at a stated season of the year the Painswick villagers bake a special pie in which they insert a china dog.[1] Some of these local *facetiae* have gone into general literature. The reputation of Gotham is known to most readers. But as a rule they have not got into books nor did they come out of books.

Thus, alike in festival and in legal rite, in practices affecting health and the conduct of practical life, in beliefs involving man's attitude towards the supernatural, and in the fiction by which he seeks to hold fast his memory of old time events or to find relaxation from the daily toil of breadwinning, there are still remnants of an older world of belief and custom and fancy to be met with, remnants curiously out of harmony with the dominant conceptions in our attitude towards life, whether on the ethical, the intellectual, the artistic, or the practical side. These remnants are *folklore*, the lore of the folk, 'the unlearned and least advanced portion of the community.'

[1] See Mrs. Gomme's article 'The Painswick Dog-Pie,' *Folk-Lore*, December 1897.

for yourself Mr. Allingham's *Ballad Book* in the Golden Treasury Series. For LOCAL RHYMES, &c., see Northall's *English Folk Rhymes*, 1894, and Chambers' *Popular Rhymes of Scotland*, 1870.

How then does one set about becoming a folklorist, a student of folklore, in the sense that one may set about becoming a naturalist or botanist? If I have succeeded at all in giving you, however briefly, a clear idea of what folklore *is*, I have also indicated how you may become a working folklorist. You must keep eyes and ears open; you must be interested in and sympathetic with people even if they strike you as backward or slow-witted or hopelessly old-fashioned; you must disdain nothing, however meaningless or trivial it may appear at first sight. Accuracy of observation, rigid fidelity of recording you have, I take it, already learnt from your training in 'natural' science; they are as important in studying folklore, nay, more so, precisely because the subject-matter is so fluid, ill-defined, and subject to variation. The complexities are great enough without the introduction of fresh ones due to the carelessness or bias of the observers. For the rest, here is what Miss Burne, the most gifted and successful of collectors of English folklore, has to say:

> The *best* collecting is that which is done *by accident*, by living among the people and garnering up the sayings and stories they let fall from time to time. But one can hardly make a complete collection, even within a limited area, in this way; and deliberate search is therefore necessary, which is often a very uphill task, though to the student of human nature, who 'loves his fellowmen,' it must always be an entertaining and pleasant one, calculated to add to his enjoyment of a country holiday.
>
> When visiting a strange place with the set purpose of personal collecting, the best way of beginning is, perhaps, to get the parish clerk or sexton (if such a person is to be found) to show the church, and then to draw him out on bell-ringing and burying customs, and to obtain from him the names of the 'oldest inhabitants' for further inquiry. Failing the sexton, the village inn-keeper might be a good starting-point. Then a visit may be paid to the school in the mid-day 'recess,' and the children may be bribed to play all the games they know for the instruction of the visitor. Possibly some bits of local legend may be gleaned from them as a foundation for further inquiries. The great value of local legends, especially in England, has already been pointed out, and it is hardly possible to insist too much upon it. These inquiries will often be quite as successful on some points if pursued among the oldest *families* in the place as among the oldest *inhabitants* of the place. Old

household or family customs are best preserved in solitary farmhouses, especially if tenanted by the same family for several generations. But it is a mistake to think that a very remote and thinly populated parish will necessarily yield more folklore of all kinds than another. A scanty stay-at-home population does not preserve legends well, and has not *esprit de corps* sufficient for the celebration of public customs. A large village, or a market-town quite in the country, is generally the best place to find these; and the 'lowest of the people'— the chimney-sweepers, brick-makers, besom-makers, hawkers, tinkers, and other trades in which work is irregular—are those who keep up old games, songs, dances, and dramatic performances.

Most villages have their doctress, generally an intelligent old woman, who, nevertheless, mixes something of superstition with her remedies. But fortune-telling, divination, and sorcery generally, flourish chiefly in the low parts of large towns, where their professors acquire a wide reputation and are resorted to from considerable distances.

Superstitious opinions, though they flourish most, of course, among the lowest classes cannot well be collected direct from them, because they really do not understand what superstition is, and cannot, as they say, 'make out what the gentleman is driving at.' They must be inquired for among the class of small employers, who have a little more cultivation than their work-people, but yet live on terms of sufficient familiarity with them to know their ideas thoroughly and to share a good many of them! A little patient effort will in all probability enable the collector to make the acquaintance of some old grandfather or grandmother of this class, who, sitting in the chimney-corner of an old-fashioned kitchen, loves nothing better than to pour out tales of 'old times.' Here is the collector's opportunity; and from talk of sickles, spinning-wheels, and tinder-boxes he may lead the conversation to matters more purely folk-loric. A list of annual festivals, and the chief customs connected with them, will be found a useful basis for questions. If his witness proves intelligent and comprehending, a list of common superstitions may then be produced and gone through, when a few additions will probably be made to it. A list of proverbs will almost certainly prove a success; the 'old sayings' will be thought extremely interesting, both wise and witty, and the memory ransacked for similar ones. Local legends must, of course, be asked for as local features—hill or well, ruined castle or Roman

[259]

camp—suggest, and will probably vary greatly, ranging from ghost stories to folk-etymology.[1]

And now by way of answer to a question some will think I ought to begin with: What is the good of all this? is it not better to let this old rubbish die out, 'unwept, unhonoured, and unsung'? In the first place, the folk whose lore we collect and study is essentially the portion of mankind which has ever remained in closest contact with Mother Earth, the class upon whose shoulders has been laid the task of making the soil yield food, and of doing the drudgery, the dirty work of humanity. Warriors and lawgivers, saints and philosophers, artists and merchants—the chronicle of their doings is full, but the man with the spade, the man to whom we have to look for the bread lacking which we should starve, history takes no note of him. It is something to recover, in however imperfect, however fragmentary a manner, somewhat of his attitude towards the problems of life and death, to find out under the stress of what conceptions he regulated his conduct, to learn where and how he sought the elements of beauty, and terror, and charm, with which all mankind have essayed to transform, and momentarily transfigure, a life worn down with ceaseless toil. A fragment of folklore has at least the same value as a worked flint or a shard of pre-historic pottery. If investigation of the past be not wholly vain, wholly meaningless, then surely that branch of it which gives us most intimate contact with the minds and hearts and souls of countless generations who otherwise would perish from our ken as utterly as the beasts of the field, may claim some need of recognition and respect.

Apart from this, the scientific, the historic value of folklore, its study has claims even upon the most advanced of modern thinkers. Scarce anything that man has thought, or fancied, or fashioned is so rude and unhandy that it can be utterly rejected as unfit for uses of even the highest culture. In telling you what folklore is I have

[1] This extract is from the Folk-Lore Society's *Handbook of Folklore*. Of this little work, which may be slipped into the coat pocket or into the knapsack, a new and revised edition is coming out in the winter of 1899. It contains, amongst other things, a classified list of some eight hundred questions bearing upon various branches of folklore collecting, and is indispensable to every working folklorist, whether he work among the folk or in the library. The various publications of the Folk-Lore Society are of course full of material. The Society is at present very insufficiently supported by free libraries, archaeological societies and the like, every one of which should join it so as to obtain the publications. No society has printed so large an amount of valuable material in return for so small a subscription (21s. annually), and none deserves better the support of all interested in the study of our national life. Any notes or observations that the collector makes will always be welcome to the Council of the Society, but the collector must not expect to see all his contributions printed, as there is necessarily great overlapping in collections.

emphasized, not unduly nor unfairly, certain features that differ entiate it sharply from our modern *civilization*. That is, as the word indicates, a product of town-life, folklore is a product of the country-side; civilization is dependent upon the written, folklore upon the spoken word; the danger of civilization is over-centralization, a tendency to uniformity, to monotony in our outlook upon life, a tendency which the vigorous 'localism' testified to by folklore may do much to counteract. Another danger is over-specialization, and an increasing tendency to rely upon a professional class to provide beauty or entertainment; here, again, the study of folklore may reveal to us that no small measure of charm and variety may be attained under other conditions. The culture which the study of folklore lays open to our inspection is, of course, meagre and narrow compared with ours, but it had a vitality, an adaptability to the requirements of all, and not merely of a privileged class, an un-forced and spontaneous character which our culture has hardly reached as yet. Primitive and shallow it may have been, but at least, not vulgar, being, as it was, a genuine outgrowth of popular feeling, and not, as is so much of modern culture imitative, alien, and imposed from above. The student of folklore learns not only the lessons of sympathy with all his fellow-men, he also learns that every stage of man's progress has features and merits of its own, and that even the highest advancement cannot afford to cut itself loose from or wholly neglect its past.

## [ 4 G . LAURENCE GOMME ]

As one of his manifold contributions to the resources of the folk-lorist, Gomme edited, with Henry B. Wheatley, a series of chap-books provided with scholarly introductions and notes. His intro-ductory essay to *The History of Thomas Hickathrift* remains a model analysis of the mingling and separation of oral and subliterary streams of tradition in popular legend. At the same time Gomme points out the relationship of the humble chapbook hero and the public-house hero to the renowned champions of myth and com-parative folklore.

Text from *The History of Thomas Hickathrift*. Printed from the Earliest Extant Copies. And edited, with an Introduction, by George Laurence Gomme, London: printed for the Villon Society, 1885. Pages [i]–xix.

There seems to be some considerable reason for believing that the hero of this story was reality. The story tells us that he lived in the marsh of the Isle of Ely, and that he became 'a brewer's man' at Lyn, and traded to Wisbeach. This little piece of geographical evidence enables us to fix the story as belonging to the great Fen District, which occupied the north of Cambridgeshire and Norfolk.

The antiquary Thomas Hearne has gone so far as to identify the hero of tradition with a doughty knight of the Crusaders. Writing in the *Quarterly Review* (vol. xxi, p. 102), Sir Francis Palgrave says:—

> Mr. Thomas Hickathrift, afterwards Sir Thomas Hickathrift, Knight, is praised by Mr. Thomas Hearne as a 'famous champion.' The honest antiquary has identified this well-known knight with the far less celebrated Sir Frederick de Tylney, Baron of Tylney in Norfolk, the ancestor of the Tylney family, who was killed at Acon, in Syria, in the reign of Richard Cœur de Lion. Hycophric, or Hycothrift, as the mister-wight observes, being probably a corruption of Frederick. This happy exertion of etymological acumen is not wholly due to Hearne, who only adopted a hint given by Mr. Philip le Neve, whilome of the College of Arms.

There does not seem to be the slightest evidence for Hearne's identification any more than there is for his philological conclusions, and we may pass over this for other and more reliable information.

We must first of all turn to the story itself, as it has come down to us in its chapbook form. It is divided into two parts. The first part of the story is the earliest; the second part being evidently a printer's or a chapman's addition. Our reprint of the former is taken from the copy in the Pepysian Library at Magdalene College, Cambridge, and which was printed probably about 1660–90; the latter is taken from the British Museum copy, the date of which, according to the Museum authorities, is 1780.

In trying to ascertain something as to the date of the story apart from that of its printed version, it will therefore be necessary to put out of consideration the second portion. This has been written by some one well acquainted with the original first part, and with the spirit of the story; but in spite of this there is undoubted evidence of its literary origin at a date later than the first part. But turning to the first part there are two expressions in this early Pepysian version which have not been repeated in the later editions—those of the eighteenth century; and these two expressions appear to me to indicate a date *after which* the story could not have been originated. On page 1 we read that Tom Hickathrift dwelt 'in the *marsh* of the Isle of Ely.' In the earliest British Museum copy this appears as 'in the *parish* of the Isle of Ely.' Again, on page 11 Tom is described as laying out the giant's estate, 'some of which he gave to the poor for their common, and the rest he made pastures of and divided the most part into *good ground,* to maintain him and his old mother Jane Hickathrift.' In the earliest British Museum copy the expression 'good ground' is displaced by 'tillage.' Now it is clear from these curious transpositions of words in the earliest and latest editions that something had been going on to change the nature of the country. The eighteenth-century people did not know the 'marsh' of Ely, so they read 'parish': they did not know the meaning of 'good ground' so they read 'tillage.' And hence it is clear that at the printing of this earliest version the fen lands of Cambridge and Norfolk had not yet been drained; there was still 'marsh land' which was being made into 'good land.'

But I think there is evidence in this printed chapbook version of the story which tells us that it was taken from a traditional version. Let any one take the trouble to read aloud the first part, and he will at once perceive that there is a ring and a cadence given to the voice by the wording of the story, and particularly by the curious punctuation, which at once reminds us of a narrative from word of mouth. And besides this there is some little evidence of phonetic spelling, just such as might have been expected from the first printer taking the story from the lips of one of the Fen-country peasantry.

Now this internal evidence of the once *viva-voce* existence of the printed legend of Tom Hickathrift has a direct bearing upon the question as to the date of the earliest printed version. The colloquialisms are so few, and the rhythm, though marked and definite, is occasionally so halting and approaches so nearly a literary form, that we are forced to observe that the earliest printed edition now known is certainly not the earliest version printed. There are too few phoneticisms and dialect words to make it probable that the print in the Pepysian collection is the one directly derived from popular tradition. As the various printers in the eighteenth century altered words and sentences here and there, as different editions were issued, so did the seventeenth-century printers; and therefore it is necessary to push the date of the printed version farther back than we can hope to ascertain by direct evidence. There is no reason why there should not have been a sixteenth-century printed version, and to this period I am inclined to allocate the earliest appearance of the story in print.

And then prior to the printed version was the popular version with its almost endless life, perhaps reaching back to that vague period indicated in the opening words of the story, 'in the reign before William the Conqueror.' Already internal evidence has, it is suggested, pointed to a popular unwritten tradition of Tom Hickathrift's life and exploits. But we must ask now, Is there, or was there, any tradition among the peasantry of Lyn and its neighbourhood about Thomas Hickathrift? And, if so, how far does this popular tradition reach back, and how far does it tally with the chapbook version? Again, is this popular tradition independent of the chapbook story, or has it been generated from the printed book? To answer these questions properly we must closely examine all the evidence available as to the existence and form of this popular tradition.

Turning first of all to the historian of Norfolk, Blomefield,[1] writing in 1808, gives us the following account:—

> The town of Tilney gives name to a famous common called Tilney Smeeth, whereon 30,000 or more large Marshland sheep and the great cattle of seven towns to which it belongs are constantly said to feed. Of this plain of Smeeth there is a tradition, *which the common people retain*, that in old time the inhabitants of these towns [Tilney, Terrington, Clenchwarton, Islington, Walpole, West Walton, Walsoken, and Emneth] had a contest with the lords of the manors about the bounds and limits of it, when one *Hickifric*, a person of great stature and courage, assisting the said inhabitants in their rights of common, took an axle-tree from a cart-wheel, instead of a sword, and the wheel for a shield or buckler, and thus armed soon repelled the invaders. And for the proof of this notable exploit they to this day show, says Sir William Dugdale [Dugd. *Hist. of Imbanking,* &c. p. 244; Weever's *Fun. Mon.* p. 866], a large grave-stone near the east end of the chancel in Tilney churchyard, whereon the form of a cross is so cut or carved as that the upper part thereof (wherewith the carver hath adorned it) being circular, they will therefore needs have it to be the grave-stone of *Hickifric*, and to be as a memorial of his gallantry. The stone coffin, which stands now out of the ground in Tilney churchyard, on the north side of the church, will not receive a person above six feet in length, and this is shown as belonging formerly to the giant *Hickifric*. The cross said to be a representation of the cart-wheel is a cross pattée, on the summit of a staff, which staff is styled an axle-tree. Such

[1] Blomefield's *History of Norfolk*, vol. ix. pp. 79–80; the same story is related by Chambers in his *History of Norfolk*, vol. i, p. 370. The parishes of W. and N. Lynn, though lying in marshland, are excluded from any right of pasturage on the Smeth Common.

crosses pattée on the head of a staff were emblems of tokens that some Knight Templar was therein interred, and many such are to be seen at this day in old churches.

Now the reference to Sir William Dugdale is misleading, because, as will be seen by the following quotation, the position of the hero is altered in Dugdale's version of the legend from that of a popular leader to the tyrant lord himself:—'Of this plain I may not omit a tradition which the common people thereabouts have, viz., that in old time the inhabitants of the neighbouring villages had a fierce contest with one Hickifric (the then owner of it) touching the bounds thereof, which grew so hot that at length it came to blows; and that Hickifric, being a person of extraordinary stature and courage, took an axletree from a cart instead of a sword, and the wheel for his buckler, and, being so armed, most stoutly repelled those bold invaders: for further testimony of which notable exploit they to this day show a large gravestone near the east end of the chancel in Tilney churchyard, whereupon the form of a cross is so cut as that the upper part thereof by reason of the flourishes (wherewith the carver hath adorned it) sheweth to be somewhat circular, which they will, therefore, needs have to be the wheel and the shaft the axletree.' This version, taken from Dugdale's *History of Imbanking*, 1772, p. 244, though differing in form, at all events serves to carry us back to 1662, the date when Sir William Dugdale's *History* was first published.

But the local tradition can be carried further back than 1662, because the learned Sir Henry Spelman, in his *Icenia sive Norfolciae Descriptio Topographica*, p. 138, and written about 1640, says, when speaking of Tilney, in Marshland Hundred:

Hic se expandit insignis area quae a planicie nuncupatur tylney-smelth, pinguis adeo et luxurians ut Paduana pascua videatur superasse. . . . Tuentur eam indigenae velut aras et focos, fabellamque recitant longa petitam vetustate de Hikifrico (nescio quo) Haii illius instar in Scotorum Chronicis, qui civium suorum dedignatus fuga, aratrum quod agebat, solvit; arreptoque temone furibundus insiliit in hostes victoriamque ademit exultantibus. Sic cum de agri istius finibus acriter olim dimicatum esset inter fundi dominum et villarum incolas, nec valerent hi adversus eum consistere; redeuntibus occurrit Hikifricus, axemque excutiens a curru quem agebat, eo vice gladii usus; rota, clypei; invasores repulit ad ipsos quibus nunc funguntur terminos. Ostendunt in caemeterio Tilniensi, sepulcrum sui pugilis, axem cum rota insculptum exhibens.

[265]

*Translation*

Here stretches a notable site which is called Tylney-smelth after a [nearby] plain, so fertile and luxuriant that it seems to surpass the Paduan pastures. The natives guard it as if it were their hearth and home and narrate a story of great antiquity concerning Hikifricus (whoever he may be). Like that Haius in the chronicles of the Scots, disgusted with the flight of his fellow citizens, he broke the plough with which he was ploughing and, snatching the shaft, he leapt in fury on the enemies and took away victory from them just as they were rejoicing. Thus while there had been at one time bitter disputes between the lord of the manor and the tenants of the estates, and the latter were not able to withstand him, Hikifricus ran to meet them as they were returning, and wresting an axle from a cart which he was driving and using it as a sword and the wheel as a shield, he drove back the invaders to the boundaries which they now use. People show in the cemetery in Tilney the tomb of its champion where a sculptured axle with a wheel are displayed.

A still earlier version is to be found recorded by Weever in 1631. The full quotation is as follows:

Tylney Smeeth, so called of a smooth plaine or common thereunto adioyning. . . . In the Churchyard is a ridg'd Altar, Tombe, or sepulchre of a wondrous antique fashion, vpon which an axell-tree and a cart wheele are insculped. Vnder this Funerall Monument the Towne dwellers say that one Hikifricke lies interred; of whom (*as it hath gone by tradition from father to the sonne*) they thus likewise report: How that vpon a time (no man knowes how long since) there happened a great quarrell betwixt the Lord of this land or ground and the inhabitants of the foresaid seuen villages, about the meere-marks, limits, or bondaries of this fruitfull feeding place; the matter came to a battell or skirmish, in which the said Inhabitants being not able to resist the landlord and his forces began to giue backe; Hikifricke, driying his cart along and perceiuing that his neighbours were fainthearted, and ready to take flight, he shooke the Axell tree from the cart which he vsed instead of a sword, and tooke one of the cart-wheeles which he held as a buckler; with these weapons he set vpon the Common aduersaries or aduersaries of the Common, encouraged his neighbours to go forward, and fight valiantly in defence of their liberties; who being animated by his manly prowesse, they tooke heart to grasse, as the prouerbe is, insomuch that they chased the Landlord and his companie to the vtmost verge of the said Common; which from that time they haue quietly enjoyed to this very day. The Axell-tree and cart-wheele are cut and figured in diuers places of the Church and Church windowes, which makes the story, you must needs say, more probable. This relation doth in many parts parallell with that of one Hay, a strong braue spirited Scottish Plowman, who vpon a set battell of Scots against the Danes, being working at the same time in the next field, and seeing some of his countrey-men to flie from that hote encounter, caught vp an oxe yoke (Boëthius saith, a Plough-beame), with which (after some exhortation that they should not bee faint-hearted) he beate the said straglers backe againe to the maine Army, where he with his two sonnes (who tooke likewise such weapons as came next to their hands) renewed the charge so furiously that they quite discomfited the enemy, obtaining the glory of the day and victory for their drad Lord and Soueraigne Kenneth the third, King of Scotland; and this happened in the yeare 942, the second of the King's raigne. This you may reade at large in the *History of Scotland*, thus abridged by Camden as followeth,— Weever's *Funerall Monuments*, 1631, pp. 866–67.

And Sir Francis Palgrave, quoting the legend from Spelman, observes,—'From the most remote antiquity the fables and achievements of Hickifric have been obstinately credited by the inhabitants of the township of Tylney. Hickifric is venerated by them as the assertor of the rights and liberties of their ancestors. The "monstrous giant" who guarded the marsh was in truth no other than the tyrannical lord of the manor who attempted to keep his copyholders out of the common field, Tylney Smeeth; but who was driven away with his retainers by the prowess of Tom armed only with his axletree and cart-wheel.'[1] This does not appear to me to put the case too strongly. A tradition told so readily and be-lieved so generally in the middle of the seventeenth century must have had a strong vitality in it only to be obtained by age.

Let us now turn to the other side, namely, the existence of a traditional version in modern days, because it is important to note that the printing of a chapbook version need not have disturbed the full current of traditional thought. In a note Sir Francis Pal-grave seems to imply that the story was still extant without the aid of printed literature. He writes:

[1] *Quarterly Review*, vol. xxi, p. 103.

A Norfolk antiquary has had the goodness to procure for us an authentic report of the present state of Tom's sepulchre. It is a stone soros, of the usual shape and dimensions; the sculptured lid or cover no longer exists. It must have been entire about fifty years ago, for when we were good *Gaffer Crane would rehearse Tom's achievements*, and tell us that he had cut out the moss which filled up the inscription with his penknife, but he could not read the letters.[1]

And Clare, in his *Village Minstrel*, tells us that:—

'Here Lubin listen'd with awestruck surprise,
When Hickathrift's great strength has met his ear;
How he kill'd giants as they were but flies,
And lifted trees as one would a spear,
Though not much bigger than his fellows were;
He knew no troubles waggoners have known,
Of getting stall'd and such disasters drear;
Up he'd chuck sacks as we would hurl a stone,
And draw whole loads of grain unaided and alone.'

And this view as to the existence still of a traditional form of the story is almost borne out by what the country people only recently had to say relative to a monument in that part of the country over which Sir William Dugdale travelled, and of which he has left us such a valuable memorial in his *History of Imbanking*. A writer in the Journal of the Archaeological Association (vol. xxv. p. 11) says:—'A mound close to the Smeeth Road Station, between Lynn and Wisbech, is called the Giant's Grave, and the inhabitants relate that there lie the remains of the great giant slain by Hickathrift with the cart wheel and axletree. A cross was erected upon it, and is to be seen in the neighbouring churchyard of Torrington St. John's, bearing the singular name of Hickathrift's Candlestick.'

It appears, then, that the following may be considered the chief evidence which we have obtained about the existence of the story:—

That a chapbook or literary form of the story has existed from the sixteenth century;

That a traditional story existed quite independently of the literary story in the seventeenth century;

That a traditional story exists at the present time, or until very recently.

And knowing what folklore has to say about the long life of traditions, about their constant repetition age after age, it is not, I

[1] *Quarterly Review*, vol. xxi, p. 102, note.

[268]

venture to think, too much to conclude that a story which can be shown by evidence to have lived on from mouth to mouth for two centuries is capable of going back to an almost endless antiquity for its true original.

Let us now consider what may be the origin of this story. There is one theory as to this which has gained the authority of Sir Francis Palgrave. The pranks which Tom performed 'must be noticed,' says Sir Francis, 'as being correctly Scandinavian.' He then goes on to say, 'Similar were the achievements of the great Northern champion Grettir, when he kept geese upon the common, as told in his Saga. Tom's youth retraces the tales of the prowess of the youthful Siegfried detailed in the Niblunga Saga and in the book of Heroes. It appears from Hearne that the supposed axletree, with the superincumbent wheel, was represented on "Hycothrift's" gravestone in Tylney churchyard in the shape of a cross. This is the form in which all the Runic monuments represent the celebrated hammer or thunderbolt of the son of Odin, which shattered the skulls and scattered the brains of so many luckless giants. How far this surmise may be supported by Tom's skill and strength in throwing the hammer we will not pretend to decide.'[1]

Now this takes the story entirely out of the simple category of local English tradition, and places in at once among those grand mythic tales which belong to the study of comparative mythology and which take us back to the earliest of man's thought and belief. In order to test this theory let us have before us the passages in Tom Hickathrift's history which might be said to bear it out, and then let us compare them with the stories of Grettir.

The analysis of the story based upon the plan laid down by the Folk-Lore Society is as follows:—

(1.) Tom's parents are nobodies, 'a poor man and day labourer' being his father.

(2.) Tom was obstinate as a boy.

(3.) Loses his father, and at first does not help his mother, but sits in the chimney corner.

(4.) Is of great height and size.

(5.) Strength is unknown until he shows it.

(6.) Commits many pranks, among which is the throwing 'a hammer five or six furlongs off into a river.'

(7.) Kills a giant with a club, Tom using axletree and wheel for his shield and buckler.

(8.) Takes possession of the giant's territory and lives there.

[1] *Quarterly Review*, vol. xxi, pp. 102–3.

[269]

(9.) Commits more pranks, 'kicks a football right away.'
(10.) Escapes from four thieves and despoils them.
(11.) Is defeated by a tinker.

It will not be necessary to analyse the whole of the stories to which we are referred for the mythic parallels of Tom Hickathrift; but I will take out the items corresponding to those tabulated above. In the story of 'Grettir the Strong' we have the following incidents:—

(1.) Grettir's father 'had his homestead and farm land.'
(2.) Grettir was obstinate as a boy (does nothing on board ship.)
(3.) Plays pranks upon his father, and returns from attending the horses to the fire-side (Iceland).
(4.) Is short, though strong, and big of body.
(5.) He had not skill to turn his great strength to account.
(6.) He wrestles with other lads, and commits many pranks, flings a rock from its place.
(7.) Wrestles with Karr, the barrow dweller; and
(8.) Takes possession of Karr's weapons and wealth.
(9.) Fights with and conquers robbers.

Now it cannot be denied that there is a great similarity in the thread of these two stories. Norfolk, the colony of the Northmen of old, may well have retained its ancient tradition until the moving incidents of English economic history brought about the weaving of it into the actual life that was pressing round men's thoughts. It would thus leave out the great mass of detail in the old northern tradition, and retain just sufficient to fit in with the new requirements; and in this way it appears to me we have the present form of the story of Tom Hickathrift, its ancient Scandinavian outline, its more modern English application. Now it is curious to note that the cart-wheel plays a not unimportant part in English folklore as a representative of old runic faith. Sir Henry Ellis, in his edition of Brand's *Popular Antiquities* (vol. i. p. 298), has collected together some instances of this; and whatever causes may have led to this survival there is nothing to prevent us from looking upon the wheel and axle in the story of Tom Hickathrift as a part and parcel of the same survival.

There now remains to notice one or two points of interest outside the narrative of the story itself. Of curious expressions we have—

*fitted* (p. 3), to pay any one out, to revenge one's self;
*buttle* of straw (p. 3);

[270]

*shift* (p. 3), to support, to make shift. See Davies's *Supplementary Glossary, sub voce* 'make-shift,' 'shiftful';

*bone-fires* (p. 11). See Ellis's *Brand's Popular Antiquities*, vol. i, p. 300, note;

*cocksure* (p. 14), quite sure.

Of proverbs there are—

to win the horse or lose the saddle (p. 8);

to make hay while the sun did shine (p. 10).

Of games there are mentioned—

cudgells (p. 4);

wrestling (p. 4);

throwing the hammer (p. 4);

football (p. 13);

bear-baiting (p. 13).

It will be observed that the spelling of the name in the Pepysian copy is specially divided thus—Hic-ka-thrift; and though it seems probable that some good reason must be assigned to this, I cannot find out points of importance. But about the dubbing him Mr. (p. 7) or Master, as it would be in full, there is something of great interest to point out. This was formerly a distinct title. In Harrison's *Description of England* we read, 'Who soeuer studieth the lawes of the realme, who so abideth in the vniuersitie, or professeth physicke and the liberall scienccs, or beside his seruice in the roome of a capteine in the warres can liue without manuell labour, and thereto is able and will beare the post, charge, and countenance of a gentleman, he shall be called master, which is the title that men giue to esquiers and gentlemen and reputed for gentlemen.'—Harrison's *Description of England*, 1577 (edited by F. J. Furnivall for the New Shakspere Society, 1877), p. 129.

Of yoemen he says, 'And albeit they be not called master as gentlemen are, or sir as to knights apperteineth, but onelie John and Thomas,' &c. (p. 134): and of 'the third and last sort,' 'named the yeomanrie,' he adds, 'that they be not called masters and gentlemen, but goodmen, as goodman Smith, goodman Coot, goodman Cornell, goodman Mascall, goodman Cockswet,' &c. (p. 137).

Mr. Furnivall's note (p. 123) is as follows:—'*Every Begger almost is called Maister.*—See Lancelot's "MAISTER Launcelet" in the *Merchant of Venice*, II, ii, 51, and the extract illustrating it from Sir Thomas Smith's *Commonwealth of England*, bk. I, ch. 20 (founded on Harrison, i, 133, 137), which I printed in *New Sh. Soc.'s Trans.* 1877-9, pp. 103-4. Also Shakspere getting his "yeoman" father arms, and making him a "gentleman" in 1596.—(Leopold,

*Shakspere,* Introduction, p. ciii.).' We thus get still further indication of the early date of the story, the significance of the title 'Master' having died out during the seventeenth century.

The following is a bibliographical list of some of the editions, many others having been printed from the beginning of this century:—

(1.) The history of Thomas Hickathrift. Printed for the booksellers. London [1790.] 12mo. pp. 24.

Cap. i. Of his birth, parentage, and education. ii. How Thomas Hickathrift's strength came to be known. iii. How Tom came to be a Brewer's man; and how he came to kill a giant, and at last was Mr. Hickathrift. iv. How Tom kept a pack of hounds; his kicking a football quite away; also how he had like to have been robbed by four thieves, and how he escaped.

(2.) The Pleasant and delightful history of Thomas Hickathrift. Whitehaven: printed by Ann Dunn, Market Place (1780], pp. 24.

(3.) The History of Thomas Hickathrift. Printed in Aldermary Churchyard, London. [1790.] 12mo. Part the first, pp. 24.

Similar contents to No. 1, with addition of cap. v. Tom meets with a Tinker, and of the battle they fought.

(4.) The most pleasant and delightful history of Thomas Hickathrift. J. Terraby, printer, Market Place, Hull. [1825.] 2 parts. 12mo. pp. 24; 24.

Same as No. 1. Second part, cap. i. How Tom Hickathrift and the Tinker conquered ten thousand rebels. ii. How Tom Hickathrift and the Tinker were sent for up to court, and of their kind entertainment. iii. How Tom, after his mother's death, went a-wooing, and of the trick he served a gallant who affronted him. iv. How Tom served two troopers whom this spark had hired to beset him. v. Tom, going to be married, was set upon by one and twenty ruffians, and the havock he made. vi. Tom made a feast for all the poor widows in the adjacent houses, and how he served an old woman who stole a silver cup at the same time. vii. How Sir Thomas Hickathrift and his lady were sent for up to court, and of what happened at that time. viii. How Tom was made Governor of the East Angles, now called Thanet, and of the wonderful achievement he performed there. ix. How the Tinker, hearing of Tom's fame, went to be his partner, and how he was unfortunately slain by a lion.

(5.) The history of Thomas Hickathrift. Printed for the Travelling Stationers. 12mo. pp. 24.

Same as No. 3.

[272]

# V   The Great Team:
## Theses and Viewpoints

---

## [ 1   ANDREW   LANG ]

IN HIS ESSAY on 'The Method of Folklore' Lang stated in a general way the new approach to the comparative study of peasant customs and savage myths. Perhaps his most striking application of the method came in his extended essay introducing the standard translation of the Grimms' *Household Tales* rendered by Margaret Hunt in 1884. Here he dealt in detail with the celestial mythological theory, as presented in *Mythology of the Aryan Nations* (2 vols., 1870) by George W. Cox, who applied the principles of Max Müller to the legend cycles of India and Europe. In place of this theory of the origin and diffusion of household tales based on philological reasoning, Lang proposed a wholly different view (first outlined in his *Fortnightly Review* article of 1873; *cf. ante*, pages 193–207). Drawing from anthropological evidence, he elaborated his famous thesis of the savage basis of nursery tales and myths. The Grimms' *Märchen* provided him with story incidents he could tabulate and compare with the ideas of savages. Lang worked hard to cite Tylor on his behalf, although Müller actually held the stronger case since the father of anthropology had accepted solar mythology to explain Aryan myths. On the question of diffusion Lang dragged his feet, preferring to ascribe similarity in tales to the sameness of human imaginations. Later, in his debate with Jacobs, he conceded more to transmission. The following commentary represents the high-water mark of the survival doctrine applied to folktales.

Text from Andrew Lang, 'Introduction' to Grimm's *Household Tales*, translated by Margaret Hunt [1884]. Two volumes. London: G. Bell and Sons, Ltd., 1910. I, xi–lxx.

ARGUMENT

Problems suggested by the study of Household Tales.—The stories consist of few incidents, in many combinations.—The tales are widely distributed.—The incidents are often monstrous and incredible.—The incidents recur in Greek and Indian epics, and in Lives of the Saints.—How are we to explain the *Origin* of Household Tales, their *Diffusion*, their *Relations to Epic Myths?*—Theories of the Diffusion of Tales.—Caution necessary in Examining Tales—Example: 'The Wolf and Kids': explanation of Sir George Cox.—His Theory of the *Diffusion* of Household Tales.—Common heritage of Aryan Race.—His Theory of the *Origin* of the Tales from mental habits and linguistic eccentricities of early man.—Man was 'animistic,' vastly concerned about Phenomena of day and year, and he was oblivious of the meaning of proverbial and popular expressions.—Household Tales are chiefly myths of day, night, summer, winter, dawn, dew, sun, moon, wind, etc. This theory criticized.—Scantiness of Evidence for early man's poetic interest in Nature, and forgetfulness of meaning of language. Sir George Cox's early men really savages.—Contemporary savages have not mental and linguistic habits ascribed to the early men.—Difference between Sir George Cox's and Mr. Max Müller's conception of mythopoeic men.—The evidence of Anthropological science neglected.—Criticism of theory of 'Polyonymy' and 'Oblivion.'—Use of these processes in Sir George Cox's system.—Illustrated by Myth of Jason.—Condemnations of the 'Solar' method quoted.—The criterion of Mr. Max Müller criticized.—The story of 'Frosch-König' as interpreted by Messrs. Cox and Müller.—Sir George Cox's theory that the animals in fairy tales are derived from linguistic confusions criticized.—Relations of *Märchen* to myths examined.—Theory that *Märchen* are *detritus* of myths.—Converse theory that myths are a younger form of *Märchen*.—A Theory of the Origin of Household Tales stated.—The monstrous incidents are survivals from savagery.—The Myths are *Märchen* elaborated.—European *Märchen* hold a mean position between savage tales and heroic myths.—Origin of this theory.—Nature of evidence for savage *Märchen* and for savage ideas.—Defence of trustworthiness of this evidence when carefully handled.—Statement of chief savage ideas.—They reappear in savage and in civilized Tales.—Examples given.—The Myth of Jason criticized according to this Theory.—Summary.—Conclusion.—Notes.

Till shortly before the time of the Brothers Grimm the stories which they gathered (*Kinder- und Hausmärchen*) had been either neglected by men of learning or treated as mere curiosities. Many collections had been made in Sanskrit, Arabic, Italian, French, but they were made for literary, not scientific purposes. The volumes of the Brothers Grimm following on several other scientific collections, and the notes of the Grimms (now for the first time reproduced in English), showed that popular tales deserved scientific study. The book of the Grimms has been succeeded by researches made among all Aryan peoples. We have tales from the Norse, French, Breton, Gaelic, Welsh, Spanish, Scotch, Romaic, Finnish, Italian, in fact, the topic of Household Tales is almost obscured by the abundance of material. Now the least careful reader of these collections must notice certain facts which constitute the problem of this branch of mythology.

In the first place the incidents, plots, and characters of the tales are, in every Aryan country, almost identical. Everywhere we find the legends of the ill-treated, but ultimately successful younger daughter; of the triumphant youngest son; of the false bride substituted for the true; of the giant's wife or daughter who elopes with the adventurer, and of the giant's pursuit; everywhere there is the story about the wife who is forced by some mysterious cause to leave her husband, or of the husband driven from his wife, a story which sometimes ends in the reunion of the pair. The coincidences of this kind are very numerous, and it soon becomes plain that most Aryan Household Tales are the common possession of the peoples which speak an Aryan language. It is also manifest that the tales consist of but few incidents, grouped together in a kaleidoscopic variety of arrangements.

In the second place, it is remarked that the incidents of household tales are of a monstrous, irrational, and unnatural character, answering to nothing in our experience. All animate and inanimate nature is on an intellectual level with man. Not only do beasts, birds, and fishes talk, but they actually intermarry, or propose to intermarry, with human beings.

Queens are accused of giving birth to puppies and the charge is believed. Men and women are changed into beasts. Inanimate objects, drops of blood, drops of spittle, trees, rocks, are capable of speech. Cannibals are as common in the role of the villain as solicitors and baronets are in modern novels. Everything yields to the spell of magical rhymes or incantations. People descend to a very unchristian Hades, or home of the dead. Familiar as these features of the Household Tales have been to us all from childhood, they do

[275]

excite wonder when we reflect on the wide prevalence of ideas so monstrous and crazy.

Thirdly, the student of *Märchen* soon notices that many of the Household Tales have their counterparts in the higher mythologies of the ancient civilized races, in mediaeval romance and saintly legend. The adventure of stealing the giant's daughter, and of the flight, occurs in the myth of Jason and Medea, where the giant becomes a wizard king. The tale of the substituted bride appears in the romance of *Berthe aux grans piès*. The successful younger son was known to the Scythians. *Peau d'Ane* became a saint of the Irish Church, and the 'supplanted bride' developed into St. Tryphine. The smith who made hell too hot for him is Sisyphus in Greek. The bride mysteriously severed from her lord in fairy tales, is Urvasi in the Rig Veda. Thus it is clear that there is some connexion, however it is to be explained, between Aryan household tales and the higher Aryan mythology. The same plots and incidents are common to both myth and *Märchen*.

These three sets of obvious facts introduce us to the three-fold problem of 'storyology,' of the science of nursery tales.

The first discovery—that these tales among the most widely severed Aryan peoples are the same in plot and incident—leads us to inquire into the cause of this community of fable. How are we to explain the *Diffusion* of Household Tales?

The second feature we observed, namely, the crazy 'irrational,' monstrous character of the incidents, leads us to ask, how did such incidents ever come to be invented, and almost exclusively selected for the purpose of popular fiction? What, in fact, is the *Origin* of Household Tales?

The third observation we made on the resemblances between household tales and Greek and Vedic myths, and mediaeval romances, compels us to examine into *the Relations between Märchen and the higher mythologies.*

Taking these three topics in their order, we must first look at what can be said as to the *diffusion* of Household Tales. Why do people so far apart, so long severed by space, and so widely different in language as Russians and Celtic Highlanders, for example, possess the same household stories? There are three, or perhaps we should say four, possible explanations. There is the theory of conscious borrowing. The Celts, it might be averred, read Russian folk tales and acclimatized them. The French took their ideas from the modern Greeks. This hypothesis, thus nakedly stated, may be at once dismissed. The peasant class, which is the guardian of the ancient store of legends, reads little, and travels scarcely at all.

Allied to the theory of borrowing, but not manifestly absurd, is the theory of slow transmission. We may be as convinced as Sir George Cox (*Aryan Mythology*, vol. i, 109), that the Aryan peoples did not borrow consciously from each other. We may agree with Mr. Max Müller that 'nursery tales are generally the last things to be borrowed by one nation from another' (*Chips*, ii, 216). But we cannot deny that 'in the dark backward and abysm of Time,' in the unrecorded wanderings of Man, Household Tales may have drifted from race to race. In the shadowy distance of primitive commerce, amber and jade and slaves were carried half across the world by the old trade-routes and sacred ways. It is said that oriental jade is found in Swiss lake-dwellings, and that an African trade cowry has been discovered deep in a Cornish barrow. Folk tales might well be scattered abroad in the same manner by merchant-men gossiping over their Khan fires, by Sidonian mariners chatting in the sounding *loggia* of an Homeric house, by the slave dragged from his home and passed from owner to owner across Africa or Europe, by the wife who, according to primitive law, had to be chosen from an alien clan. Time past is very long, land has lain where the sea roars now; we know not how the ancestors of existing races may have met and mixed before Memphis was founded, or Babylon. Thus the hypothesis of the transmission of Household Tales cannot absolutely be set aside as in every case without possible foundation.

Before examining theories of the Diffusion and Origin of House-hold Tales, and of their relations to the higher mythologies, something must be said about the materials we possess. A strict criticism of the collections of tales offered to the inquirer, a strict avoidance of theory founded on hasty analogies is needful. We must try to distinguish as far as possible what is ancient and essential, from what is relatively modern and accidental in each tale. We must set apart scientific and exact collections from merely literary collec-tions in which the traditional element is dressed up for the sake of amusement. Grimm's collection of Household Tales or *Märchen* is among the earliest of those which were made for scientific purposes. Sanskrit stories, Arab and Egyptian stories, Italian stories, French stories, had been gathered long before into the garners of Somadeva, *The Thousand and One Nights*, Straparola, the Queen of Navarre, Perrault, and others. But to bring together popular narratives merely to divert the reader is an aim which permits the collector to alter and adorn his materials almost as much as he pleases. Con-sequently the old compilations we have named, however delightful as literature, must be used with great caution for purposes of comparative science. Modern touches, as will be seen, occur freely even in such collections as the Grimms'. Science accepts these narratives (when it can get them unadulterated) as among the oldest productions of the human fancy, as living evidence to the character of the early imaginative faculty. But we must be quite certain that we do not interpret late additions to the tales, as if these incidents were of the primitive essence. An example of this error may be taken from Grimms' Legend (No. 5), 'The Wolf and the Kids.' Here a wolf deceives seven little kids, and eats them all except the youngest, who hides (like the hero of one of M. Fortuné du Boisgobey's novels) 'in the clock-case.' The bereaved old she-goat comes home, finds that only the youngest kid survives, and goes in quest of the wolf. The wolf is found asleep; the old goat cuts him open, and out frisk all the little kids. They then fill the wolf's stomach with stones, and sew up the orifice they had made. When the wolf awakens he is thirsty, and goes to drink, but the heavy stones make him lose his balance, he falls into the well, and is drowned.

Here the essential idea is probably nothing more than the fashioning of a comic story of a weak beast's victory over a strong beast. Similar stories are frequent among the Negroes and Bushmen (see Bleek's *Reynard the Fox in South Africa*, and *Uncle Remus*), among the Red Indians,[1] and, generally, among uncivilized peoples.

A story in some ways like that of the 'Wolf and the Kids,' is common among the negroes of Georgia. In a Kaffir tale (Theal) the arts of the wolf are attributed to a cannibal. Apparently the tale (as negroes tell it) is of African origin, and is not borrowed from the whites. Old Mrs. Sow had five little pigs, whom she warned against the machinations of Brer Wolf. Old Mrs. Sow died, and each little pig built a house for itself. The youngest pig built the strongest house. Brer Wolf, by a series of stratagems, which may be compared to those in Grimms' *Märchen*, entrapped and devoured the four elder pigs. The youngest pig was the wisest, and would not let Brer Wolf come in by the door. He had to enter by way of the chimney, fell into a great fire the youngest pig had lighted, and was burnt to death. Here we have only to note the cunning of the wolf, and his final defeat by the youngest of the pig family, who, as in almost all household tales, is wiser and more successful than his elder brethren. In the same way Grimms' youngest kind was the kid that escaped from the wolf.

The incident on which the revenge turns, the swallowing of the

---

[1] In his *Origine des Romans*, Huet, the learned Bishop of Avranches (1630–1720), mentions the Iroquois Tales of Beavers, Raccoons, and Wolves.

victims and their escape alive, though missing in the negro version is of almost universal occurrence.

It is found in Australia, in Greece it has made its way into the legend of Cronus, in Brittany into the legend of Gargantua. Callaway's collection gives us Zulu examples: in America it is familiar to the Indians of the North, and to those of British Guiana. Grimm gives some German variants in his note; Bleek's *Bushman Folklore* contains several examples of the incident. The Mintiras of Malay have introduced the conception of swallowing and disgorging alive into a myth, which explains the movements of sun, moon, and stars. (Tylor's *Primitive Culture*, i, 338, 356).

In the tale of the Wolf and the Seven Kids, then, the essence is found in the tricks whereby the wolf deceives his victims; in the victory of the goat, in the disgorging of the kids alive, and the punishment of the wolf (as of Cronus in Hesiod) by the stone which he is obliged to admit into his system. In these events there is nothing allegorical or mystical, no reference to sunrise or storms. The crude ideas and incidents are of world-wide range, and suit the fancy of the most backward barbarians. But what is clearly modern in Grimms' tale is the introduction of the clock-case. That, obviously, cannot be older than the common use of tall clocks. If, then, we interpret the tale by regarding the clock-case as its essential feature, surely we mistake a late and civilized accident for the essence of an ancient and barbarous legend. Sir G. W. Cox lays much stress (*Aryan Mythology*, i, 358) on the affair of the clock-case. 'The wolf,' he says, 'is here the Night, or the Darkness, which tries to swallow up the seven days of the week, and actually swallows six. The seventh, the youngest, escapes by hiding herself in the clock-case; in other words, the week is not quite run out, and, before it comes to an end, the mother of the goats unrips the wolf's stomach, and places stones in it in place of the little goats who come trooping out, as the days of the week begin again to run their course.'

This explanation rests on the one obviously modern feature of the story. If the explanation is correct, the state of mind in which Night could be conceived of as a wolf, and as capable of being slit open, loaded with stones, and sewn up again, must have lasted and remained intelligible, till the quite recent invention of clock-cases. The clock-case was then intelligently introduced into the legend. This seems hard to believe, though Mr. Tylor writes (*Primitive Culture*, i, 341) thus, 'We can hardly doubt there is a quaint touch of sun-myth in a tale, which took its present shape since the invention of clocks.'

Surely a clock-case might seem (as to M. Boisgobey's hero, and to the lady freemason in the old story, it did seem) a good hiding-place, even to a mind not occupied at all with the sun. What makes the whole interpretation the more dubious is, that while with Sir George Cox the Wolf is the Night, with M. Husson (in the similar tale of the swallowing of Red Riding Hood) the Wolf is the Sun. And this is proved by the peculiar brilliance of the wolf's fur, a brilliance recognized by Sir G. Cox when he wants the sun to be a wolf.

On the whole, then, the student of *Märchen* must avoid two common errors. He must not regard modern interpolations as part of the mythical essence of a story. He must not hurry to explain every incident as a reference to the natural phenomena of Dawn, Sunset, Wind, Storm, and the like. The points which are so commonly interpreted thus, are sometimes modern interpolations; more frequently they are relics of ancient customs of which the mythologist never heard, or survivals from an archaic mental condition into which he has never inquired. Besides, as Mr. Tylor has pointed out, explanations of the elemental sort, all about storm and dawn, are so easy to find that every guesser can apply them at will to every *Märchen*. In these inquiries we must never forget that 'rash inferences which, on the strength of mere resemblances, derive episodes of myth from episodes of nature, must be regarded with utter distrust, for the student who has no more stringent criterion than this for his myths of sun, and sky, and dawn, will find them wherever it pleases him to seek them' (*Primitive Culture*, i, 319). This sort of student, indeed, finds his myths of sun, and sky, and dawn all through the Grimms' Collection.

We have now set forth the nature of the problems which meet the inquirer into Household Tales, and we have tried to illustrate the necessity of a critical method, and the danger of being carried away by faint or fancied resemblances and analogies. Our next step is to examine the theory of the diffusion and origin of Household Tales set forth by Sir George Cox in his *Mythology of the Aryan Nations* (1870). This theory was suggested by, and, to a certain extent, corresponds with the mythological philosophy of Mr. Max Müller, as published in *Oxford Essays* (1856), and more recently in *Selected Essays* (1881). There are, however, differences of detail and perhaps of principle in the systems of these two scholars. As to the *diffusion* of identical folk tales among peoples of Aryan speech, Sir George Cox (dismissing theories of borrowing or adaptation) writes:

'The real evidence points only to that fountain of mythical language from which have flowed all the streams of Aryan epic poetry, streams so varied in their character yet agreeing so closely in their elements. The substantial identity of stories told in Italy, Norway and India can but prove that the treasure-house of mythology was more abundantly filled before the dispersion of the Aryan tribes than we had taken it to be.' Sir George proceeds to remark on resemblances between German and Hindoo tales, which shew 'the extent to which the folklore of the Aryans was developed while they still lived as a single people' (*Mythol. Aryan*, i, 145). Thus Sir George Cox accounts, on the whole, for the majority of the resemblances among Aryan household tales, by the theory that these tales are the common inheritance of the Aryan race, such narratives the Aryans possessed 'while they still lived as a single people.' The difficulties in which this theory lands the inquirer will afterwards be set forth. Here it may be observed that people who are not Aryans none the less possess the stories.

So much for the *Diffusion* of Aryan Household Tales. They are widely scattered (the theory goes), because the single people which possessed them in its common seat has itself been scattered widely, from Ceylon to Iceland.

Next, what is Sir George Cox's hypothesis as to the *Origin* of Household Tales? We have seen how he supposes they were diffused. We have still to ask how such crazy legends were originally evolved. Why are all things animate and inanimate on a level with man in the tales; why do beasts and trees speak; why are cannibalism, metamorphosis, magic, descents into Hades, and many other impossible incidents so common? What, in short, is the Origin of Household Tales?

Here it is not easy to be brief, as we have to give a summary of Sir George Cox's theory of the intellectual human past, from which he supposes these tales to have been evolved. In the beginning of things, or as near the beginning as he can go, Sir George finds men characterized by 'the selfishness and violence, the cruelty and slavishness of savages.' Yet these cruel and violent savages had the most exquisitely poetical, tender, and sympathetic way of regarding the external world (*Mythol. Ar.*, i, 39), 'Deep is the tenderness with which they describe the deaths of the sun-stricken dew, the brief career of the short-lived sun, and the agony of the Earth-mother mourning for her summer child.' Not only did early man cherish these passionate sympathies with the fortunes of the sun and the dew, but he cherished them almost to the exclusion of emotions perhaps more obvious and natural as we moderns hold. Man did not get used to the dawn; he was always afraid that the sun had sunk to rise no more, "years might pass, or ages, before his rising again

[281]

would establish even the weakest analogy." Early man was apparently much more difficult to satisfy with analogies than modern mythologists are. After the sun had set and risen with his accustomed regularity, 'perhaps for ages,' 'man would mourn for his death as for the loss of one who might never return.'

While man was thus morbidly anxious for the welfare of the sun, and tearfully concerned about the misfortunes of the dew, he had, as we have seen, the moral qualities of the savage. He had also the intellectual confusion, the perplexed philosophy of the contemporary savage. Mr. Tylor, Mr. Im Thurn, Mr. Herbert Spencer, and most scientific writers on the subject, have observed that savages draw no hard and fast line between themselves and the animal or even the inanimate world. To the mind of the savage all things organic or inorganic appear to live and to be capable of conscious movement and even of speech. All the world is made in the savage's own image. Sir George Cox's early man was in this savage intellectual condition, 'He had life, and therefore all things else must have life also. The sun, the moon, the stars, the ground on which he trod, the clouds, storms, and lightnings were all living beings: could he help thinking that, like himself, they were conscious beings also?'

As man thought of all things as living, so he spoke of them all as living. He could not get over the idea that any day living clouds might spring up and choke the living sun, while he had the most unaffected sympathy with the living dawn and the living dew. 'In these spontaneous utterances of thoughts awakened by outward phenomena, we have the source of the myths which must be regarded as primary' (*Myth. Ar.*, i, 42). In all this period, 'there was no bound or limit to the images suggested by the sun in his ever varying aspects.' Man, apparently, was almost absorbed in his interest in the sun, and in speculations about the dew, the cloud, the dawn.

We now approach another influence on mythology, the influence of language. While man was in the conditions of mind already described by Sir George Cox, he would use 'a thousand phrases to describe the actions of the beneficent or consuming sun, of the gentle or awful night, of the playful or furious wind, and every word or phrase became the germ of a new story, *as soon as the mind lost its hold on the original force of the name.*' Now the mind was always losing its hold on the original force of the name, and the result would be a constant metamorphosis of the remark made about a natural phenomenon, into a myth about something denoted by a term which had ceased to possess any meaning. These myths, caused by forgetfulness of the meaning of words (as we understand our author), were of the *secondary* class, and a third class came into existence through folk-etymologies, as they are called, popular guesses at the derivations of words. We have now briefly stated Sir George Cox's theory of the origins of myths, and of the mental condition and habits through which myths were evolved. But how does this theory explain the origin of Household Tales?

This question ought to lead us to our third problem, what are the relations of Household Tales to the higher mythologies? But it may suffice to say here that in Sir George Cox's opinion, most of the Household Tales are, in origin, myths of the phenomena of day and night. They are versions of the myths about the dark Night-powers stealing the golden treasure of Day; about Dawn loving the Dew; about the Birth and Death of the Sun; about the fortune of the Clouds, and so forth. Briefly, to illustrate the theory, we have a primary myth when early man says the (living) sun (Kephalos) loves the (living) dew (Prokris), and slays her by his arrows (that is, his rays).

We have a secondary myth where it is forgotten that Kephalos only meant the sun, and Prokris only meant the dew, and when Kephalos is taken for a shepherd swain, and Prokris for a pretty nymph. Lastly, we have a tertiary myth when Apollo Lycaeus (whose name meant Apollo of the Light) is supposed—by a folk-etymology—to be Apollo the Wolf, and is said to have been born from a were-wolf.[1]

Household Tales are these myths in the making, or these myths filtered down through the memories and lips of uncounted generations (*Myth. Ar.*, 165). It is on these principles that Sir George seeks to explain the irrational and unnatural element so powerful in folk tales.

We must now briefly criticize Sir George's system as a whole. Next we must see how the system is applied by him, and, lastly, we must approach the theory which we propose to substitute for that set forth in *Mythology of the Aryan Peoples*.

The point most open to criticism in Sir George Cox's statement of his views, and in the similar views of Husson, De Gubernatis, and many other mythologists, is the very inadequate evidence. The farmers of Primary Myths, in Sir George Cox's system are (apparently) savages. Of savages they have the moral qualities and the intellectual habits. 'The prominent characteristics of that early time were the selfishness, the violence, the cruelty and harshness of savages.' So much for morality. As for intellect, of the several

[1] In these examples Sir G. Cox's theories are only accepted for the sake of argument and illustration.

objects which met his eye, says our author, mythopoeic man had no positive knowledge, whether of their origin, their nature, or their properties. But he had life, and therefore all things else must have life also. This mental stage 'Animism,' 'personalism,' or whatever we may call it, is also characteristic of savages. Now when we come in our turn to advance a theory of the origin of Household Tales, many points in these tales will be deduced from the cruelty and from the 'Animism' of men like the framers of Sir George Cox's 'Primary Myths.' But Sir George's evidence for the savage estate of early myth-making man is mainly derived from the study of language.[1] This study has led him to views of the barbarism of the myth-makers with which we are glad to agree, yet he dissents here from his own chief authority, Mr. Max Müller. In the third chapter of the first volume of *Mythology of the Aryan Races*, the chapter which contains evidence for the intellectual condition of early humanity, Sir George Cox quotes scarcely any testimony except that of Mr. Max Müller.

The most important result of the whole examination, as conducted by Sir George Cox, is that mythopoeic man, knowing nothing of the conditions of his own life or of any other, 'invested' all things on the earth or in the heavens with the same vague idea of existence. But while Sir George Cox makes this 'Animism'—this investing of all things with life—the natural result of man's *thought*, Mr. Max Müller ascribes the habit to the reflex action on thought of man's *language*. Man found himself, according to Mr. Müller (*Selected Essays*, i, 360), speaking of all objects in words which had 'a termination expressive of gender, and this naturally produced in the mind the corresponding idea of sex,' and, as a consequence, people gave 'something of an individual, active, sexual, and at last personal character' to the objects of which they spoke. Mr. Müller is aware that the 'sexual character of words reflects only the quality of the child's minds' but none the less he attributes the 'animism' of mythopoeic man to the reflex influence of man's language, whereas Sir George Cox attributes it to the direct influence of man's thought. Thus Sir George deserts the authority from which he derives his evidence, and it is not here alone that he differs from Mr. Müller. Sir George's framers of 'primary myths' are savages, morally and intellectually; Mr. Müller's mythopoeic men, on the other hand, are

[1] When *The Mythology of the Aryan Nations* was written, philologists were inclined to believe that their analysis of language was the true, perhaps the only key, to knowledge of what men had been in the pre-historic past. It is now generally recognized (though some scholars hold out against the opinion) that the sciences of Anthropology and Archaeology also throw much light on the human past, which has left no literary documents. Compare Schrader's *Sprach-Vergleichung und Urgeschichte*. (Jena, 1883.)

practically civilized. Man, in Mr. Müller's 'mythopoeic age,' had the modern form of the Family, had domesticated animals, was familiar with the use of the plough, was a dweller in cities, a constructor of roads, he was acquainted with the use of iron as well as of the earlier metals. (*Selected Essays*, vol. i, 'Comparative Mythology.'[1]) There is thus no escaping from the conclusion that, though Mr. Müller's evidence is nearly the sole basis of Sir George Cox's theories, yet from that evidence Sir George draws inferences almost the reverse of those attained by Mr. Müller. Yet starting from the same evidence, and from different inferences, the two authors arrive at much the same conclusion in the long run.

We have complained of the inadequate evidence for Sir George Cox's system. It is, as we have seen, derived from Mr. Max Müller's analysis of the facts of language. But there is another sort of evidence which was germane to Sir George's purpose, and which he has almost absolutely neglected. That evidence is drawn from the study of the manners and customs of men, and is collected and arranged by the science of Anthropology. The materials of that science are found in the whole of human records, in history, in books of travel, in law, customs, superstition. A summary of the results so far attained by anthropology and ethnology is to be studied by English readers in Mr. Tylor's *Primitive Culture* and *Early History of Man*. These works deal with the evolution of human institutions of every kind from their earliest extant forms found among savages. We are thus enabled, by the science of students like Mr. Tylor, to understand what the ideas and institutions of savages are, and how far they survive, more or less modified, in civilization. Now Sir George Cox's makers of primary myths were in the savage state of culture, or, as he himself puts it, 'The examination of our language carries us back to a condition of thought not many degrees higher than that of tribes which we regard as sunk in hopeless barbarism' (*Myth. Ar.*, i, 35). But his description of the intellectual and moral condition of the primary myth-makers (*Myth. Ar.*, i 39–41) shows that really Sir George's mythopoeic men were in no higher degree of 'culture' than Red Indians and Maoris. As this is the case, it would surely have been well to investigate what history has to say about the mental habits of savages. As the makers of primary myths were savages, it would have been scientific to ask, 'How do contemporary savages, and how did the savages of history, regard the world in which they find themselves, and of what character are their myths?' Sir George

---

[1] Mr. Müller has stated this proposition, but a note in *Selected Essays* proves that he now admits the uncertainty of the early use of iron.

Cox, however, leaves on one side and practically unnoticed all evidence except philological evidence as to the general habits of men in the same intellectual condition as his own makers of primary myths. Herein lies, we think, the original error of his system.

Instead of examining the natural history of savages to see how men like his primary myth-makers regard the universe, Sir George Cox describes the prevalence among mythopoeic men of what we must regard as a purely fanciful mental attitude. Sir George's myth-makers, as we have seen, lived in a tremulous and passionate sympathy with nature, and with the fortunes of the day and the year, of the dawn and the dew. 'Perhaps for ages they could not believe that the sun would rise again in the morning.' From every stage in the sun's progress the myth-makers derived thrilling excitement. They threw themselves with their whole souls into the love affairs and distresses of the dew. They mourned for the setting sun, 'as for the loss of one who might never return.'

Now does Sir George give any evidence, drawn from the natural history of man, for all this sentimental, yet sincere, primitive excitement about the processes of nature. None, or next to none. We do find summer-feasts and winter-fasts, rituals of regret and rejoicing for the coming and departing of summer among many races. Here and there (as in the *Popol Vuh*, an enigmatic, Quichua record) we see traces of anxious interest in the sun. Again, all savage races have nature-myths explanatory of the motions of the heavenly bodies—a rude sort of science. But as to this all absorbing, all-pervading tender and poetic habit of primitive sympathy with natural phenomena, we find no proof of it anywhere. Savages, like civilized people, are much more interested in making love, making war, making fun, and providing dinner, than in the phenomena of nature.[1] But in Sir George Cox's system of mythology the enormous majority of myths and of household tales are simply the reflections of the supposed absorbing and passionate early sympathy of savages with the processes of nature. For the existence to the necessary extent of that sympathy we find no evidence. In all ages men must have been more concerned about earthly gold and mortal young women than about the 'dawn gold' or 'the dawn maiden,' yet in myths where gold or girls occur, Sir George sees the treasures of the light, or the radiant maiden of the morn. This is natural, while he is convinced that the makers of primary myths were so intensely absorbed in sympathy with clouds, and dew, and sunshine. But we

---

[1] Inferences drawn from the Vedas are not to the point, as the Vedas contain the elaborate hymns of an advanced society, not (except by way of survival) the ideas of early myth-makers.

ask again for sufficient evidence that these sentiments existed in a degree capable of exercising an exclusive influence on myths.

Turning from the theory of the primary to that of the secondary myths, we again note the absence of convincing testimony, or indeed of any valid testimony at all.

Primary myths arose, Sir George says, from thought; secondary myths from language. They came into existence because 'a thousand phrases would be used to describe the action of the beneficent or consuming sun,' and so forth, 'and every word or phrase became the germ of a new story, as soon as the mind lost its hold on the original force of the name' (*Myth. Ar.*, i, 42). This application of dozens of names and phrases to the same object is called *polyonymy* by Mr. Max Müller, and the converse use one name for a vast variety of objects (which become '*homonyms*') he calls *synonymy*. It is Mr. Müller's opinion that, in the mythopoeic age, people might call the sun (let us say) by some fifty names expressive of different qualities (this is *polyonymy*), while some of these names would be applicable to other objects also. These other objects would then be *homonyms* of the sun, would be called by the same names as the sun was called by. (This is *synonymy*.) The meaning of all these names would be lost in perhaps three generations, but the names and the phrases in which the names occurred would survive after their significance was lost. It is clear that if ever such a state of language prevailed, the endless consequent misunderstandings might well blossom into myths. For example, the grandfather (in the mythopoeic age) observes the rush of the ascending sun, and calls him 'the lion.' The father, being accustomed to the old man's poetic way, understands his meaning perfectly well, and the family style the sun 'the lion,' as they also, *ex hypothesi*, call him by forty-nine other names, most of which they moreover apply to other objects, say to the tide, the wind, the clouds. But the grandson finds this kind of talk hopelessly puzzling (and no wonder), and he, forgetting the original meanings, comes to believe that the sun *is* a lion, and the night (perhaps) a wolf, and so he tells stories about the night-wolf, the sun-lion, and so on. (Here the examples are our own, but the theory is Mr. Müller's. *Selected Essays*, i, 376–8.)

No marvel if myths arose in an age when people spoke in this fashion, and when the grandson retained the grandsire's phrase, though he had helplessly forgotten the grandsire's meaning. Mr. Müller protests against degrading our ancestors into 'mere idiots.' but if they escaped becoming hopeless imbeciles during this 'mythopoeic age' it is highly to their credit.

But where is the evidence for *polyonymy, synonymy* and rapid oblivion, the three factors in secondary myth-making? As far as we have been able to discover, we are offered no convincing evidence at all. Mr. Müller gives cases of *polynonymy* and *synonymy* from the Veda (*Selected Essays*, i, 377).[1] But (1.) The Vedic age is, *ex hypothesi*, long subsequent to the mythopoeic age. (2.) The necessary and indispensable process of forgetfulness of the meaning of phrases does not occur in the age of the Veda. People in the Veda call the earth wide, broad, great (*polynonymy*). They also apply the term 'broad' to a river, sky, and dawn. But did their grandchildren on this account mistake the Earth for the Dawn, or the Sky for the Earth? Thus Mr. Müller is apparently unable to give examples of his causes of myth from the age in which myths proceeded from these causes, and when he does produce examples of the causes, they result in no myths. Where he finds the effects he does not demonstrate the existence of the causes; when he has evidence for the existence of the causes, he shews no effects (*Selected Essays*, i, 377, 378). When Mr. Müller does attempt to adduce a term which originally was a mere name, and later became a proper name, and so indicated a person, the process can be accounted for by another explanation (*Selected Essays*, i, 378). '*Ζεύς* being originally a name for the sky, like the Sanskrit Dyáus, became gradually a proper name.' But if the sky was in the mind of the makers of primary myths, a *person* inevitably and from the first (as we think, in agreement with Sir George Cox), then the name of the sky was from the first a proper name. When all things were persons (as they are to the minds of savages and primary myth-makers) all names may be regarded as proper names. It is the ascertained condition of the savage intellect (as stated by Sir George Cox and by anthropologists) which invests all things with personal character. Forgetfulness of meaning of words is not the cause. The processes of *polynonymy, synonymy,* and oblivion are superfluous as means of accounting for the personal aspect of all things in mythology. They are also (as far as we have been able to discover) processes for which no good evidence is produced.

Sir George Cox has borrowed *polyonymy* and its effects from Mr. Müller, though he gives no evidence to prove that it was ever a large factor in mythology. At first the processes of *polyonymy* and oblivion seem superfluous in Sir George's system, because he has already (in the intellectual condition of his primary myth-makers) sufficient myth-making power. While his early men regarded all things as

---

[1] Kuhn also brings forward the Vedic language as proof of the existence of polyonymy and synonymy. *Ueber Entwicklungsstufen der Mythenbildung*, p. 1.

living and personal, they would account for all natural processes on that hypothesis, and the explanations thus given would be nature-myths of the class current among savages. For example, if Sir George's early men thought (as they did) that the sun was alive, they might well marvel at the regularity of his movements; why did he not run about the sky at random as a brute runs about the woods? Why did he go, like a driven beast, in a regular round? To answer this question the New Zealanders and North American Indians have evolved a story that Maui or Tcha-ka-betch once set traps for the sun, caught him, beat him, and made him move for the future with orderly propriety. This is an undeniable nature-myth, and savage mythology, like that of Greece and of the Veda, is full of similar mythic explanations of natural phenomena. To explain such myths no processes of *polyonymy, synonymy*, and oblivion are needed. Why then are those processes required in the system of Sir George Cox? For this reason; he is not content with the myths which declare themselves to be nature-myths. He wishes to prove that epic and romantic legends, which say nothing about sun, moon, stars, and wind, are nature-myths in disguise. Here the processes of *polyonymy* and oblivion become useful.

For example, we have the myth which tells how Jason sought the golden fleece in an eastern land, how he won the treasure and the daughter of its owner, how he returned home, deserted Medea, wedded Glauce, and died. Now nothing is openly said in this legend about natural phenomena, except that the Colchian Royal House belongs to the solar race as the royal family did in India and Peru, and as the Totem tribe or *gens* of suns (Natchez and Aurelii) did in North America and in Rome. How, then, can the Jason legend be explained on a nature-myth? By the aid of *polyonymy*, thus: The sun had countless names. The names for sun, and dawn, and cloud, lost (in Sir George's opinion) their original sense, and became names of heroes, ladies, gods and goddesses. The original sense of the names was half remembered and half forgotten. Athene is 'the dawn goddess' (*Myth. Ar.* ii. 119). Phrixus, the child of Nephele, is the son of the cloud. Hellê, the drowned girl of the fable, is 'the bright clear air illuminated by the rays of the sun.' When we are told that she was drowned, no more was originally meant than that 'before the dawn can come the evening light must die out utterly' (*Ar. Myth.*, ii, 273). Here let us pause and reflect. In the myth, Phrixus and Hellê, children of Nephele, escaped being sacrificed by flying away on a winged ram with a golden fleece. Hellê fell off and was drowned. How does Sir George Cox explain all this? Nephele is the cloud, so far all is plain sailing. The cloud has two children, one

[289]

'the frigid Phrixus'; the other, 'the bright clear air illuminated by the rays of the sun'; or again, 'the evening light.' Early men, we are to suppose, said that the cloud produced cold, and also bore the warm evening air. Why do the warm air and the cold air go off together eastward on a golden flying ram? This we do not see that Sir George explains, but the fleece of the ram (after that animal has been slain) becomes the treasure of the light, which is sought in the east by Jason. But who is Jason? His name 'must be classed with the many others, Jasion, Janus, Iolaos, Iaso, belonging to the same root' (*Myth. Ar.* i, 150, *note* 1). And what is the root? Well (ii, 81) Iamus, from the same root, means 'the violet child'; he was found among violets. Now 'ιον (violet) applies to the *violet* coloured sunset clouds, and ιός also means a spear, and 'represents the far-darting rays of the sun.' 'The word as applied to colour is traced by Prof. Max Müller to the root *i*, as denoting a crying hue, that is, a loud colour.'[1] Thus, whether we take ιός to mean a spear, or violet, or what you please, Jason's name connects him with the sun. The brain reels in the attempt to make sense of the cold air and the hot air, children of the cloud, going eastward, on a ram covered with the treasures of the light, and when we come to the warm air dying, and the light, being stripped (in the east) from the ram, and being sought for by a man whose name more or less means violet, and who comes from the west, and when all this is only the beginning of the tale, we are absolutely perplexed. Whoever told such tales? Yes, we say, if ever men were deep in the perplexing processes of polyonymy, synonymy and oblivion, if ever the grandfather used countless allegorical phrases, which the grandchild piously retained, while he quite forgot their sense, then, indeed, this kind of muddled and senseless nature-myth may have been evolved. But we vainly asked for evidence of the existence and activity of polyonymy, synonymy, and oblivion. The first and last of the three factors are useful, however, to Sir George Cox, when he tries to show that myths which do not give themselves out for nature-myths are nature-myths in disguise after all. But we have observed no evidence (except the opinion of some philologists) for the theory on which the whole demonstration depends. Again, M. Decharme, with just as much reason, makes Phrixus 'the demon of thunder,' and Hellê, 'a goddess of lightning!' This kind of philosophy is too facile. To opinions like those which Sir George Cox has advanced with so much earnestness, and in such a captivating style of eloquence, it has always been objected that there is an improbable monotony in the theory which resolves most of old romance into a series of

[1] The 'violet shrinking meanly' of Miss Bunion's poem, has a 'loud,' or 'crying' colour!

remarks about the weather. This objection has not been made by uncritical writers only. M. Meyer complains, almost petulantly, of that 'eternal lay-figure,' the sun in all his mythological disguises. (*Romania.*) No historical hero, no custom, no belief, M. Meyer vows, is out of danger from the solar mythologists.

Mr. Tylor again writes (*Primitive Culture*, i, 319), 'No legend, no allegory, no nursery rhyme is safe from the hermeneutics of a thorough-going mythologic theorist. Should he, for instance, demand as his property the nursery "Song of Sixpence," his claim would be easily established: obviously the four-and-twenty blackbirds are the four-and-twenty hours, and the pie that holds them is the underlying earth covered with the over-arching sky: how true a touch of nature is it that "when the pie is opened," that is, when day breaks, "the birds begin to sing," the King is the Sun, and his "counting out his money," is pouring out the sunshine, the golden shower of Danae; the Queen is the Moon, and her transparent honey the moonlight. The maid is the "rosy-fingered" Dawn, who rises before the Sun, her master, and "hangs out the clothes" (the clouds) across the sky; the particular blackbird who so tragically ends the tale by "snipping off her nose," is the hour of sunrise. The time-honoured rhyme really wants but one thing to prove it a sun-myth, that one thing being a proof by some argument more valid than analogy.' Mr. Tylor easily shows that historical persons may be disposed of no less readily than the characters of Nursery Rhymes as solar-myths. Analogy is usually the one argument advanced for this scheme, and the analogies (as will be shown) are often so faint as to be practically non-existent. What 'false analogies' can be made to prove, Mr. Max Müller has demonstrated (*Selected Essays*, ii, p. 449). Mr. Müller has also gently censured (*Selected Essays*, i, 564, 565) the ready way in which M. Husson shows that Red Riding Hood was the Dawn: 'It would be a bold assertion to say that the story of Red Riding Hood was really a metamorphosis of an ancient story of the rosy-fingered Eos, or the Vedic Ushas with her red horses.' In Mr. Müller's opinion 'there is but one safe path to follow in these researches into the origin of words or stories. . . . In addition to the coincidences in character-istic events, we have the evidence of language. Names are stubborn things,' and more to the same purpose. Here we touch one of the differences between Sir George Cox and Mr. Max Müller. Mr. Müller, like Sir George Cox, is of opinion that all the stories of princesses imprisoned, and delivered by young bright heroes, 'can be traced back to mythological tradition about the spring being released from the bonds of winter.' But in each case Mr. Müller asks

for names of characters in the story, names capable of being analysed into some equivalent for powers of nature, sun, wind, night, or
what not. Now, we have elsewhere tried to show that, in mythological interpretation, scarcely any reliance can be placed on
analysis of the names of the characters.[1] It seems more than probable that in most cases the stories are older than the names. Again,
the custom of giving to real persons names derived from forces and
phenomena of nature is widely prevalent in early society. Men and
women are styled 'cloud,' 'sun,' 'wind,' and so forth. These names,
then, even when they can be traced in myths, offer no surer ground
for a theory than the analysis of such names as Jones and Thompson
would do in a novel. Having to name the characters in his tale, the
early story-teller might naturally give such personal titles as were
common in his own tribe, such terms as 'Wind,' 'Cloud,' 'Sun,' and
so forth. Thirdly, the best philologists differ widely from each other
as to the roots from which the names spring, and as to the sense of
the names. But feeble as is the method which relies on analysis of
mythical names, it is at all events less casual than the method
which is satisfied with mere 'coincidence in characteristic events.'
The simple argument of many mythologists may be stated thus.
'The dawn is a maiden, therefore all maidens in myths are the
dawn.' 'The sun is golden, therefore all gold in myths must be
solar.' These opinions are derived, in the long run, from the belief
that the savage primary myth-makers were so much pre-occupied
with the daily phenomena of nature, and again from belief in the
action of polyonymy and oblivion. We have attempted to show that
there is no evidence given to prove either that early man was in
passionate, ceaseless anxiety about nature, or that 'polyonymy'
and oblivion ever existed in such strength as to produce the required effects on myths. As a rule, a real nature-myth avows itself
for what it is, and attempts to give a reason (unscientific of course)
for this or that fact, or assumed fact, in nature. Such tales though
wild, and based on misconception, are intelligible and coherent. We
have already seen how far from coherent or intelligible is Sir
George Cox's explanation of part of the Jason legend as nature-
myth.

We promised that, after criticizing Sir George Cox's theory of
the Origin of Myths and Household Tales, we would examine his
method of interpreting individual stories. Let us see how Mr.
Müller, followed by Sir George, handles a tale with which we are all
familiar. In Grimm's *Frosch König* (vol. i, Tale i.), a frog (who in
Grimm turns out to be a disguised prince) is betrothed to a princess.

[1] Fraser's Magazine, *Mythological Philosophy of Mr. Max Müller.*

'How came such a story,' asks Mr. Max Müller, 'ever to be invented? Human beings were, we may hope, at all times sufficiently enlightened to know that a marriage between a frog and the daughter of a Queen was absurd. . . . We may ascribe to our ancestors any amount of childlike simplicity, but we must take care not to degrade them to the rank of mere idiots.'

Mr. Müller thus explains the frog who would a-wooing go. As our ancestors were not mere idiots, the frog story must have had a meaning which would now seem rational. In old times (Mr. Müller says) the sun had many names. 'It can be shown that "frog" was an ancient name for the sun.' But though it can be shown, Mr. Müller never shows it. He observes 'this feminine Bheki (frog) must at one time have been used as a name for the sun.' But though he himself asks for 'chapter and verse from the Veda,' he gives us no verse and no chapter for his assertions (*Chips*, ii, 201, 247). His theory is that tales were told of the sun, under his frog name, that people forgot that the frog meant the sun, and that they ended by possessing an irrational tale about the frog going a-wooing.

The Frog-sun[1] whose existence is established on this scanty testimony, is a great favourite with Sir George Cox, and occurs no fewer than seven times in his *Mythology of the Aryan Peoples*. Nay, this frog is made to explain the presence of many of the wonderful talking animals in Myth and Household Tale. 'The frog prince or princess is only one of the thousand personifications of names denoting originally the phenomena of day and night. As carrying the morning light from the east to the west the sun is the Bull bearing Eurôpê from the purple land (Phoinikia), and the same changes which converted the Seven Shiners into the Seven Sleepers of Ephesus, or the "Seven Sages" (of Greece?), or the Seven Champions of Christendom, or the Seven Bears, transformed the sun into a wolf, a bear, a lion, a swan.' (*Ar. Myth.*, i, 105.)

Here we have the old use of analogies. Because of a theory (probably incorrect) that the Seven Bears of Indian stellar myth were originally even shiners, several sorts of people in sets of seven twinkle off as 'shiners' also, stellar or solar shiners. In the same way the theory of the sun-frog (without chapter or verse as it is) proves that some animals in Household Tales are the sun.

As the appearance of beasts with human qualities and accomplishments is one of the most remarkable features of Household Tales, we may look at another statement of Sir George Cox's views on this subject. Metamorphosis of men into animals and of animals into men is as common in Household Tales as a sprained ankle is in

[1] See note, *ad fin*, and 'Cupid and Psyche' in the author's *Custom and Myth*.

modern novels. Sir George Dasent (*Popular Tales*, p. cxix) pointed out that the belief in such metamorphoses 'is primeval, and the traditions of every race tell of such transformations.' Sir George Cox takes one of Sir George Dasent's numerous examples, and remarks 'if this be an illustration, it accounts for all such transformations, but it does so in a way which is completely subversive of any hypothesis of nature-worship. *Such myths may all be traced to mere forgetfulness of the original meaning of words.*' As proof, Sir George Cox adduces the well worn 'seven shiners,' and the supposed confusion between λευκός, *shining*, and λύκος, *a wolf*, 'so named from the glossiness of his "coat," ' as if wolves had coats so peculiarly glossy. By these examples alone (omitting the frog-sun) Sir George Cox contests the plain straight-forward theory of Sir George Dasent, that men everywhere naturally believe in metamorphosis and lykanthropy. Sir George Cox wishes to trace lykanthropy to a confusion between λύκος, and λευκός. On this point Sir Alfred Lyall, after long observation of Indian beliefs, says, 'To those who live in a country where wicked people and witches are constantly taking the form of wild beasts, the explanation of lykanthropy by a confusion between *Leukos* and *Lukos* seems wanton.' (*Fortnightly Review*.)

Wantonly or not, Sir George Cox traces 'all such myths to mere forgetfulness of the original meaning of words.' For this prodigiously sweeping generalization no evidence except evidence like that of the supposed frog-sun and 'seven shiners' and *Leukos* and *Lukos* is afforded. (*Ar. Myth.*, i, 140–1, *note* 1.) 'Bears, wolves, foxes, ducks, swans, eagles, ants, all these are names under which the old mythical language spoke of the clouds, or the wind, or of the light which conquers the darkness.' Here again we have, by way of supporting evidence, the 'seven shiners,' and 'the wolf in the stories of Phoibos Lykeios.' As the belief in metamorphosis, and in beasts which are rational and loquacious, is world wide, and is the natural result of the ideas of 'primary myth-makers,' or savages, Sir George Cox's theory, that such notions are all to be traced to forgetfulness of the meaning of words demoting natural phenomena, is too narrow, and is too devoid of evidence. Another explanation will presently be offered.

We may now leave Sir George's theories of the diffusion and origin of Household Tales. They are widely diffused, he thinks, because the race which originally evolved them is also scattered far and wide, and has carried them everywhere in its wanderings. The stories originated, again, in man's early habit of imaginatively endowing all things with life, in his almost exclusive preoccupation with the changes of the day and the year, and in 'polyonymy,' and forgetfulness of the meaning of language. The third problem, as we saw, is to explain the relations between Household Tales and the higher mythologies. Are children's *Märchen* the *detritus*, the last worn relics of the higher myths, as these reached the peasant class, and passed through the fancy of nurses and grandmothers? Or do the Household Tales rather represent the oldest forms of the Romantic myths, and are the heroic legends of Greece, India, Finland, Scandinavia, Wales, merely the old nursery stories elaborated and adorned by the arts of minstrels and priests? On the former hypothesis, *Märchen* are a *detritus*; on the latter *Märchen* are rather the surviving shapes of the original germs of myths. On this topic Sir George Cox, as far as we have ascertained his meaning, appears to hold what is perhaps the most probable opinion, that in certain cases the Household Tale is the decaying remnant of the half-forgotten myths, while in other cases it rather represents the original *näif* form out of which the higher myth has been elaborated (*Ar. Myth.*, i, 123). Possibly we have not succeeded here in apprehending the learned author's sense. As a rule, however, writers on these subjects believe in the former hypothesis, namely, that Household Tales are the *detritus* of the higher myths; are the old heroic coins defaced and battered by long service. Thus, about the time when the Grimms were collecting their stories, Scott wrote (in a note to the *Lady of the Lake*), 'The mythology of one period would appear to pass into the romance of the next, and that into the nursery tales of subsequent ages.' Mr. Max Müller expresses the same idea (*Chips*, xi, 243), 'The gods of ancient mythology were changed into the demigods and heroes of ancient epic poetry, and these demigods again became at a later age the principal characters in our nursery tales.' The opposite of this theory might be expressed thus, 'Stories originally told about the characters of savage tales were finally attracted into the legends of the gods of ancient mythology, or were attributed to demigods and heroes.' The reasons for preferring this view (the converse of Mr. Müller's) will presently be explained. In the meantime Mr. Müller's hypothesis 'has great allies' in Scott; and in Von Hahn, who holds that myths are imaginative descriptions of the greater elementary powers and changes of nature; that the *Saga* or heroic epic localizes the myths in real places, and attributes the adventures to supposed ancestral heroes, and, finally, 'that the *Märchen*, or Household Tale is the last and youngest form of the *saga*' (*Griechische Märchen*, p. 5).

Starting from this point, namely, from the doubt as to whether *Märchen* are the youngest (Von Hahn. Max Müller), or rather, as we shall attempt to show, the oldest extant form of the higher myths, we will endeavour to explain our theory of the whole subject. That theory must first be stated as briefly and clearly as possible.

With regard (1) to the *Origin* of the peculiar and irrational features of myth and *Märchen* we believe them to be derived and inherited from the savage state of man, from the savage conditions of life, and the savage way of regarding the world. (2) As to the *Diffusion* of the tales, we think it impossible at present to determine how far they may have been transmitted from people to people, and wafted from place to place, in the obscure and immeasurable past of human antiquity, or how far they may be due to identity of human fancy everywhere. (3) As to the relations between Household Tales and Greek or other civilized myths, we prefer the following theory, which leaves room for many exceptions. The essence both of *Märchen* and myths is a number of impossible and very peculiar incidents. These incidents are due to the natural qualities of the savage imagination. Again, the incidents are combined into various romantic arrangements, each of these arrangements being a *Märchen*. The *Märchen* were originally told among untutored peoples, about anonymous heroes,—a boy, a girl, a lion, a bear,—such were the leading characters of the earliest tales. As tribes became settled, these old stories were localized. The adventures (originally anonymous) were attributed to real or imaginary named persons or gods, and were finally adorned by the fancy of poets like the early singers of Greece. Thus, while a savage race has its *Märchen* (in which the characters are usually beasts or anonymous persons), the civilized race (or the race in a state of higher barbarism) has the same tale, developed and elaborated into a localized myth, with heroes rejoicing in such noble names as Perseus, Odysseus, Jason, Leminkainen, or Maui. But while the progressive classes in civilized countries are acquainted with the named heroes, and the elaborate forms of the legends, the comparatively stationary and uneducated classes of shepherds, husbandmen, wood-men, and fishers, retain a version but little advanced from the old savage story. They have not purified away the old ferocious and irrational elements of the tale, or at most they have substituted for the nameless heroes, characters derived from history or from Christian records. Thus the Household Tales of the European peasantry occupy a mean position between the savage story, as we find it among African tribes, and the elaborate myth which, according to our theory, poets and priests have evolved out of the original savage *data*.

To sum up the theory thus briefly stated:

1. The origin of the irrational element in myth and tale is to be found in the qualities of the uncivilized imagination.

2. The process of *Diffusion* remains uncertain. Much may be due to the identity everywhere of early fancy: something to transmission.

3. Household Tales occupy a middle place between the stories of savages and the myths of early civilizations.

There are probably *Märchen*, however, especially among the tales of modern Greece, which are really the *detritus*, or worn and battered relics of the old mythologies.

Nothing is easier than to advance new theories. The difficulty begins when we try to support them by argument and evidence. It may be as well to show how the system which we have just explained occurred to the mind of the writer. It was first suggested, years ago, by the study of savage *Märchen*. If Bushmen and Samoyeds, and Zulus, and Maoris, and Eskimo, and Odjibwas, and Basutos have household tales essentially identical with European *Märchen*, how, we asked, is this to be explained? Mr. Max Müller and Sir G. W. Cox had scouted the idea of borrowing. Then, was it to be supposed that all the races with Household Tales had once shared the capacious 'cradle of the Aryan Race'? That seemed hard to demonstrate.[1] To account for the identity of savage and Indo-European *Märchen*, there remained the process of slow filtration and transmission on one hand, and the similarity of the workings of the human mind (especially in its earlier stages) on the other hand. But Mr. Max Müller had already discredited the hypothesis that *Märchen* 'might have been invented more than once' (*Chips*, ii, 233). 'It has been said,' writes Mr. Müller, 'that there is something so natural in most of the tales, that they might well have been invented more than once. This is a sneaking argument, but has nevertheless a certain weight. It does not apply, however, to our fairy tales. They surely cannot be called "natural." They are full of the most unnatural conceptions. . . .' Among these unnatural conceptions, Mr. Müller noted the instance of a frog wooing a maiden; and he went on, as we have already seen, to explain such ideas on the hypothesis that they resulted from 'a disease of language,' from forgetfulness of the meaning of words. Now some little anthropological study had shown us that the ideas (so frequent in Household Tales), which Mr. Müller calls *unnatural*, were exactly the ideas

[1] This appears, however, to be the theory by which Sir George Cox would prefer to account for the diffusion of myths possessed by the Aryan race among the Indians of Labrador (cf. Hind's *Explorations in Labrador*).

most *natural* to savages. So common and so natural is the idea of animal kinship and matrimonial alliance with animals to the savage mind, that stories turning on these *data* are, of all stories, the most likely to have been invented in several places.[1] We do not say that they were thus separately invented, but only that the belief on which they turn is, of all beliefs, the most widely diffused. Having once attained this point, we soon discovered that other essential incidents in *Märchen*, incidents which seem unnatural to civilized men, are common and accredited parts of the savage conception of the world he lives in. When this was once ascertained, the rest of our theory followed on the ordinary lines of the evolution of human institutions. To take an example in another province. Savages of a certain degree of culture make hand-turned pots of clay. Civilized races use the wheel. Peasants in remote districts of civilized countries make hand-turned pots of clay much like those of savages. The savage tale answers to the savage pipkin. The vase from Vallauris answers to the civilized myth. The hand-turned pot from Uist or Barra, answers to the peasant *Märchen*; pot and *Märchen* both surviving, with modifications, from the savage state, among the non-progressive class in civilized countries.

Such pipkins from the Hebrides (where Mr. Campbell collected his *Tales*) resemble much more the pre-historic and savage pot than they resemble our Vallauris vase, with its classic shape, ornament, and balance. Just in the same way, the West Highland or Russian *Märchen* is much more akin to the Zulu story than to the civilized myth of Greece, which turns on the same ideas. In both the material and the imaginative product, you have the same process of evolution. You have the rude stuff, clay and small flints and shells for the savage pot, savage ideas for the savage tale. You have the refined, selected clay for the civilized vase, the ingenious process of fabrication, the graceful form and ornament. In the realm of imagination these answer to the plastic fancy of old minstrels, and of Homer or Apollonius Rhodius, refining and modifying the rude stuff of savage legend. Finally, among the non-progressive crofters of the Hebrides you have (in manufacture) the rude clay, the artless *façon*, the ornament incised with the nails; and you have, in the imaginative province, tales almost as wild as the working of Bushman or Zulu imagination. (Campbell's *Tales of the West Highlands*).

Here then is an example, and dozens might be given of the process of evolution, which is the mainspring of our system. Another

---

[1] Ὁμοίως που ἀνέμιξαν θηρία καὶ ἀνθρώπους, says Porphyry, speaking of the founders of the old Religions; 'they mixed up men and beasts indiscriminately.' Porph. ap. Euseb. *Praep. ev*, iii, 4.

example may be taken from the realm of magic. All over the world savages practise spells, divinations, superstitious rites; they maim images to hurt the person whom the image resembles; they call up the dead; they track the foot-prints of ghosts in ashes; they tie 'witch-knots'; they use incantations; they put sharp objects in the dust where a man has trodden that the man may be lamed. Precisely the same usages survive everywhere in the peasant class, and are studied by amateurs of folklore. But among the progressive classes of civilization those practices do not occur at all; or if they do occur, it is by way of revival and recrudescence. On the other hand, the magical ideas are found much elaborated, in the old myths of civilization, in the saga of Medea and Circe, of Odin and Loki. Probably it will now be admitted that we have established the existence of the process of evolution on which our theory depends. It is a *vera causa*, a verifiable working process. If more examples are demanded, they may be found in any ethnological museum. In General Pitt Rivers's anthropological collection, the development may be traced. Given stone, clay, the tube, or blow-pipe, and the throwing-stick, and you advance along the whole line of weapons and projectiles, reaching the boomerang, the bow, the stone-headed arrow, the metal arrow-head, the dagger, the spear, the sword, and, finally, the rifle and bayonet. The force which works in the evolution of manufactured objects works also in the transmutation of custom into law, of belief into tale, and of tale into myth, with constant minute modification, and purification, degradation, and survival.

If we have established the character of our theory, as one of a nature acknowledged and accepted by science, we have still to give evidence for our facts. The main purpose of our earlier pages was to show that the popular mythological theory of Sir G. W. Cox had either no evidence, or scanty evidence, or evidence capable of a more correct interpretation than it receives from its friends. The evidence for our own theory will be closely scrutinized: let us examine its nature and extent. First, have savages Household Tales, and do they correspond with those of the Aryan race?

The questions raised by the similarity between Aryan folk-tales on the one hand, and African folktales on the other, have not yet been seriously considered by mythologists.[1] When Mr. Max Müller

---

[1] Dr. Reinhold Köhler informs the author that he has written nothing on the *Märchen* of savages. Felix Liebrecht has used a few Zulu and Maori examples in *Zur Volkskunde* (Heilbronn, 1879). Some remarks on these topics, disavowing the theory that any one single source of myth can be discovered, will be found in Mr. Max Müller's preface to Mr. Gill's *Myths and Songs from the South Pacific.* Mr. Ralston (*Nineteenth Century*, Nov. 1879) says that 'the popular tales which are best known

wrote (*Chips*, ii, 211) on Dr. Callaway's Zulu *Märchen*, he had only the first part of the collection before him. As the learned writer observed, much more material was required; we wanted more Zulu tales, and other tales from members of the same great South African race, for purposes of comparison. We still need, for comparative purposes, much larger collections of savage instances than we possess. But these collections are amassed slowly, and it has seemed well, for our present end, to make use of the materials at hand. If comparatively scanty in quantity, they are very remarkable in character. From Africa we have 'Nursery Tales, Traditions, and Histories of the Zulus, in their own words, with a translation into English, and notes,' by the Rev. Canon Callaway, M.D. (Trübner, London, 1868.) We have also Dr. Bleek's *Bushman Folklore* (Trübner, 1875), and his *Reynard the Fox in Africa*, and Steere's *Swahili Tales*. Madagascar is represented by the collections of the Rev. James Sibree published in the *Folk-Lore Record* (1883). Some Basuto tales are given by Casalis (*Les Bassoutos, ou 23 ans de séjour au sud de l'Afrique*, 1860). Some Ananzi stories from West Africa are printed in Sir George Dasent's *Tales from the Norse* (1859). From the Kaffirs we derive Theal's *Kaffir Folk-lore* (Sonnenschein, London, *n.d.*). Mr. Gill has given us some South Sea examples in his *Myths and Songs from the South Pacific*. (London, 1876.[1]) The Folk-Lore Society of South Africa, in a little periodical now extinct, gave other African examples. Jülg's *Kalmückische Märchen* are Indian in origin. Schoolcraft and his associates collected North American Indian examples in *Algic Researches*. Samoyed *Märchen* have been published by Castren (*Ethnologische Vorlesungen*, St. Petersburg, 1857); and examples of *Märchen*, magnified and elaborated, occur in Japanese mythology (*Transactions of Asiatic Society of Japan*, vol. x.); in New Zealand Myths (Taylor's *New Zealand*); and in the accounts of Melanesian and Andaman myth, by Mr. Codrington and other writers, in the *Journal of the Anthropological Institute*. While Mr. Mitford has given us *Tales of Old Japan*, Prof. Hartt has collected the *Märchen* of the Indians on the Amazon. Rink has published those of the Eskimo; and scattered examples are to be found in Bancroft's large compilation on the *Native Races of the Pacific*, and in the old *Relations* of the Jesuit fathers and other missionaries. Thus there are gleanings

[1] Turner's *Samoa* (1884) also contains some South Sea *Märchen*.

to us possess but few counterparts in genuine savage folk-lore,' though he admits that some incidents are common both to European and uncivilized *Märchen*. We trust to show, however, that the common incidents, and even plots, are unexpectedly numerous.

which may be provisionally used as samples of a large harvest of savage children's tales. The facts already in our possession are important enough to demand attention, particularly as the savage tales (in Africa especially) correspond, as will be shown, so closely with the European and Aryan examples.

Here then, in the volumes named, we have a gleaning at least, from the harvest of savage *Märchen*. The names of most of the collectors will be to anthropologists, if not to all etymologists, a guarantee of their accuracy. Here, too, it may be observed, that a race so non-Aryan as the ancient Egyptians possessed Household Tales identical (in 'unnatural' incident, and to a great extent in plot) with our own (Maspero, *Contes Egyptiens*).

It will be shown later that the ideas, stock incidents and even several of the plots of savage and other non-Aryan Household Tales are identical with the ideas, incidents, and plots of Aryan *Märchen*. It will also be shown that in the savage *Märchen*, the ideas and incidents are the inevitable result of the mental habits and beliefs of savages. The inference will be that the similar features in European tales are also derived from the savage conditions of the intellect. By 'savages' we here mean all races from the Australians and Bushmen to such American tribes as the Algonquins, and such people as the Maoris. In this recent multitude of stocks there are found many shades of nascent civilization, many degrees of 'culture.' But the races to whom we refer are all so far savage, that they display the characteristic feature of the savage intellect.

Before taking another step, we must settle the question of evidence as to savage ideas. We have ourselves criticized severely the evidence offered by certain mythologists, without, however denying that they may possess more than they offer. It is natural and necessary that we, in turn, should be asked for trustworthy testimony. How do we know anything about the ideas of savages? How can we pretend to understand anything about the nature of the savage imagination? The philological school of mythologists, about whose scanty show of proof we have complained, are conscientiously desirous that our evidence should be full and trustworthy. Now, according to Mr. Max Müller, the materials which we possess for the study of savage races 'are often extremely untrustworthy' (*India and what it can teach us*). This remark, or its equivalent, is constantly repeated, when any attempt is made to study the natural history of man. M. Reville, on the other hand, declares with truth that our evidence is chiefly embarrassing by the very wealth of documents. (*Les religions des Peuples non Civilisés*). We naturally side with M. Reville.

Consider for a moment what our evidence as to the life and ideas of savages is; our evidence, in the first place, from the lips of civilized eyewitnesses. It begins with the Bible, which is rich in accounts of early religious ideas, animal worship, stone worship, ritual, taboos on articles of food, marriage customs and the like. Then we have Herodotus, with his descriptions of savage manners, myths, and customs. Next come all the innumerable Greek and Roman geographers, and many of the historians and general writers, Aristotle, Strabo, Pliny, Plutarch, Ptolemy, and dozens of others. For the New World, for Asia, for Africa, we have the accounts of voyagers, merchants, missionaries, from the Arab travellers in the East to Marco Polo, to Sahagun, to Bernal Diaz, to Garcilasso de la Vega, to Hawkins, to all the Spanish travellers, and the Portuguese, to Hakluyt's men; we have the Jesuits, with their *Relations Edifiantes*; we have evangelists of every Christian church and sect; we have travellers of every grade of learning and ignorance, from shipwrecked beachcombers to Nordenskiöld and Moseley. Now from *Leviticus* to the *Cruise of the Challenger*, from Herodotus to Mariner, nay, from the Rig-Veda to Fison and Howitt, we possess a series of independent documents on savage customs and belief, whether found among actual savages or left as survivals in civilization. These documents all coincide on certain points, and establish, we venture to say, with evidence that would satisfy any jury, the ancient existence of certain extraordinary savage customs, myths, ideas, and rites of worship. These ideas and rites are still held and practised by savages, and seem natural to their state of mind. Thus the coincident testimony of a cloud of witnesses, through three thousand years, establishes the existence of certain savage beliefs and rites, in every quarter of the globe. Doubtless in each instance the evidence must be carefully scrutinized. In matters of religion, missionaries may be witnesses biassed in various ways, they may want to make out that the savage has no religion at all, or that he is a primitive methodist.[1] The scientific explorer may have a sceptical bias: the shipwrecked mariner who passes years with a savage tribe, may be sceptical or orthodox, or may have his report tinged by the questions put to him on his return to civilization. Again, savages take pleasure in hoaxing their catechists, and once more, the questions put by the European may suggest answers appropriate but wholly false. Therefore in examining the reports as

[1] Compare the monotheism of Mr. Ridley's *Kamilaroi* (*Kamilaroi and other Australian Languages*, p. 135), with Mr. Howitt's remarks (*Kamilaroi and Kurnai*, p. 254). Mr. Howitt thinks that the Missionaries have connected the idea of a God with the Australian Trinity of mere demons, Brewin, Ballamdut, and Baukan.

to savage character, we must deal cautiously with the evidence. If our witness be as candid, logical, and fair as Dr. Bleek, Mr. Codrington, Mr. Orpen, Mr. Gill, Egede, Dr. Rink, Dobrizhoffer, or a score of other learned missionaries and explorers, we may yield him some confidence. If he be tinged and biassed more or less by scientific theories, philological or anthropological, let us allow somewhat for the bias; probably we must allow still more in our own case. If the witness be unlearned, we have, at least, the probability that he is not transplanting to Otaheite or to Queensland ideas and customs which he has read about in Herodotus or Strabo, or theories of Müller or McLennan.[1] Lastly, if all evidence from all quarters and all ages, evidence learned and unlearned, ancient, mediaeval, and modern agrees in certain points, and if many of the witnesses express surprise at the occurrence of customs and notions, which our reading shows to be almost universal, then let the undesigned coincidence itself stand for confirmation. To our mind this kind of treatment of evidence is not unscientific. It is permitted to investigators, like Darwin and Romanes. Mr. Max Müller, however, is so far from being satisfied with the method (as we have stated it) that he draws a line between what will content the scholar, and what the ethnologist will put up with. Mr. Müller's criticism deserves quotation in full (*Nineteenth Century*, January 1882): 'Comparative mythology is chiefly studied by two classes—by scholars and by anthropologists. Now the true scholar who knows the intricacies of a few languages, who is aware of the traps he has to avoid in exploring their history, who in fact has burnt his fingers again and again when dealing with Greek, and Latin, and Sanskrit, shrinks by a kind of instinct from materials which crumble away as soon as critical scholarship attempts to impart to them a certain cohesion and polish. These materials are often supplied by travellers ignorant of the language, by missionaries strongly biassed in one direction or the other, or by natives who hardly understood the questions they were asked to answer. A very useful collection was made some time ago by Mr. Tylor to show the untrustworthiness of the accounts of most travellers and missionaries, when they give us their impressions of the languages, religions, and traditions of races among whom they lived for a longer or shorter time. The same people who by one missionary are said to worship either one or

---

[1] 'Illiterate men, ignorant of the writings of each other, bring the same reports from various quarters of the globe.' So the author of the *Origin of Rank* (Prof. Millar, of Glasgow) wrote in the last century. This argument from undesigned coincidence, or recurrence, must be faced by people who deny the adequateness of anthropological evidence.

[303]

many gods, are declared by another to have no idea and no name of a Divine Being. But, what is stranger still, even the same person sometimes makes two equally confident assertions which flatly contradict each other.' Several examples of these inconsistencies are quoted.

Any reader of this passage might naturally suppose that Mr. Tylor thought our materials for the study of savage religions, language, and traditions quite untrustworthy. If Mr. Tylor really thought thus, we might abandon any attempt to explain mythology and customs by the study of savages. But as Mr. Tylor has devoted several chapters of *Primitive Culture* to examining the savage origins of mythology and religion, he apparently does not think our evidence so very hopeless after all. The passage in Mr. Tylor's work to which Mr. Müller refers is (probably), *Primitive Culture*, i, 418, 419. Mr. Tylor there remarks, 'It is not unusual for the very writer who declares in general terms the absence of religious phenomena among some savage people, himself to give evidence that shows his expressions to be misleading.' But, far from dismissing the whole topic as one on which no anthropological reports can be trusted, Mr. Tylor goes on to show that the inconsistencies of evidence have chiefly arisen from want of a definition of religion. The missionary says, 'the savage has no religion,' meaning nothing like what the missionary understands by religion. He then proceeds to describe practices which, in the eyes of the anthropologist, are religious enough. Mr. Tylor then discounts reports which are hasty, or made in ignorance, and finds that there is still left that enormous body of testimony on which he bases his theory of savage philosophies, religions, and mythologies. Mr. Tylor, to be brief, judges evidence by the tests we have already proposed. The inquirer 'is bound to use his best judgment as to the trustworthiness of all the authors he quotes . . . but it is over and above these measures of precautions that the test of recurrence comes in.' By 'recurrence' Mr. Tylor means what we have called 'undesigned coincidence.' Thus, 'if two independent visitors to different countries, say a mediaeval Mahommedan Tartary, and a modern Englishman in Dahome, or a Jesuit missionary in Brazil, and a Wesleyan in the Fijian Islands, agree in describing some analogous art or rite or myth among the people they have visited, it becomes difficult or impossible to set down such correspondence to accident or wilful fraud' (*Primitive Culture*, i, 9).

Such, then, are our tests of reported evidence. Both the quantity and the quality of the testimony seem to justify an anthropological examination of the origin of myths and *Märchen*. As to the savage ideas from which we believe these *Märchen* to spring we have yet stronger evidence.[1]

We have the evidence of institutions. It may be hard to understand what the savage *thinks*, but it is comparatively easy to know what he does. Now the whole of savage existence, roughly speaking, is based on and swayed by two great institutions. The first is the division of society into a number of clans or stocks. The marriage laws of savages depend on the conception that these stocks descend from certain plants, animals, or inorganic objects. As a rule no man and woman believed to be connected by descent and blood kinship with the same animal, plant, stone, natural phenomenon, or what not, can intermarry. This law is sanctioned by severe, sometimes by capital, punishment. Now about the evidence for this institution there can be no mistake. It has been observed by travellers in North and South America, in Australia, Samoa, India, Arabia, in Northern Asia, and in West and South Africa. The observations were obviously made without collusion or intention to support a scientific theory, for the scientific importance of the institution was not perceived till about 1870.[2]

The second institution of savage life, from which the nature of savage ideas may be deduced, is the belief in magic and in 'medicine-men.' Everywhere we find Australians, Maoris, Eskimo, old Irish, Fuegians, Brazilians, Samoyeds, Iroquois, and the rest, showing faith in certain jugglers or wizards of their own tribe. They believe that these men can turn themselves or their neighbours into animal shapes;[3] that they can go down into the abodes of the dead; that they can move inanimate objects by incantations; that they can converse with spirits, and magically cure or inflict diseases. This belief declares itself in the institutions of untutored races; the sorcerer has a considerable share in what may be called political and priestly power.

We have now unfolded the character of our evidence. It is based, first on the testimony of innumerable reports corroborated by recurrence or coincidence; next on the testimony of institutions.

[1] Mr. Ralston (*Nineteenth Century*, November 1879) seems to think that the historical interpreters of *Märchen* wish to resolve all incidents into traces of actual customs. But traces of customs are few, compared with survivals of ideas, or states of opinion, or 'wild beliefs' of which Mr. Ralston (p. 852, *loc. cit.*) himself contributes an example.
[2] The first writer who collected examples of these facts was Mr. McLennan ('The Worship of Plants and Animals,' *Fortnightly Review*, 1869).
[3] Mr. Ralston writes ('Beauty and the Beast,' *Nineteenth Century*, December 1878), 'The were-wolf stands alone.' But a reference to the article on *Lykanthropy* (*Encyclop. Britann.*) will show that sorcerers are believed to be capable of transforming either themselves or their neighbours into all manner of animals. The wolf is only the beast most commonly selected for purposes of transformation in Europe. Lions, tigers, crocodiles, birds, are quite as frequent in other parts of the world.

If this evidence seems inadequate, what have we to fall back upon? Merely the conjectures of philologists; we must follow the star of etymological guesses after which our fathers, the old antiquaries, went wandering. It may be said, with truth, that modern philology has a method far more scientific and patient than the random practice of old etymology. Granted, but a glance at the various philological interpretations, for example, of Greek mythical names, will show that philologists still differ on most mythical points where difference is possible. When applied to the interpretation of the past of human thought and human history, philology is a most uncertain guide. Thus, Schrader observes (*Sprachvergleichung und Urgeschichte*, p. 431), that comparative philology has as yet contributed very little certain knowledge to the study of mythology. In the region of history, as he shows, the best philologists contradict each other and themselves, as to the metals possessed by the early Aryans. Yet philology is the science which claims possession of 'the only method that can lead to scientific results,' results which differ with the views of each individual scholar.

We are now able to prove, from the social and political institutions of savages, their belief in human descent from animals, in kinship with animals, in powers of metamorphosis, in the efficacy of incantations, and in the possibility of communion with the dead. Savages also believe in the possibility of 'personal intercourse between man and animal,' 'the savage man's idea of the nature of those lower animals is very different from the civilized man's' (Tylor, *Primitive Culture*, i, 467; ii, 230). Mr. Tylor gives many curious observances, as proofs of the existence of these wild conceptions. We may add that savages believe the human soul passes into animal shapes at death, and that women may bear animal children.

Similar views prevail about inanimate nature. 'To the savage all nature seems animated, all things are persons.' We have already seen that Sir George Cox assumed this state of thought in the makers of his 'primary' myths. 'To the Indian all objects animate and inanimate seem exactly of the same nature, except that they differ in the accident of bodily form.' (Im Thurn, *Indians of Guiana*, p. 350).

Other savage ideas may be briefly explained. Among savages many harmless and necessary acts are 'taboo'd' or forbidden for some mystic or ceremonial reason.

Again, the youngest child in polygamous families is apt to be the favourite and heir. Animals of miraculous power are supposed to

[306]

protect men and women. Cannibalism is not unknown in practice, and, as savages seldom eat members of their own tribe, alien tribes are regarded as cannibals. Further, various simple moral ideas are inculcated in savage tales. We may now offer a short list of savage ideas, and compare each idea with an incident in a savage and in a civilized Household Tale.[1]

## 1. SAVAGE IDEA.

### Belief in kinship with Animals.

| Savage Tale. | European Tale. |
| --- | --- |
| Woman marries an elephant. | Man weds girl whose brothers |
| Woman marries a whale. | are ravens. |
| Woman gives birth to crows. | Queen accused of bearing pup- |
| Man marries a beaver. | pies or cats. |
| Girl wooed by frog. | Girl marries a frog. |
| Girl marries serpent. | Girl marries a tick. |
| | Man marries a frog. |

## 2. SAVAGE IDEA.

### Belief in Metamorphosis.

| Savage Tale. | European Tale. |
| --- | --- |
| Hero becomes insect. | Hero becomes worm. |
| Hero becomes bird. | Heroes become birds. |
| Hero becomes mouse. | Hero becomes roebuck. |
| Girls become birds. | Girls become birds. |

## 3. SAVAGE IDEA.

### A. Inanimate objects obey incantations, and speak.

| Savage Tale. | European Tale. |
| --- | --- |
| Hero uses incantations with success. | Hero uses incantations with success. |

### B. Inanimate objects may speak.

| Savage Tale. | European Tale. |
| --- | --- |
| Drops of spittle speak. | Drops of spittle speak. |

---

[1] The authorities for the existence of these ideas, customs, and beliefs, with references for the tales based on the beliefs and customs, will be found at the end of this Introduction.  [See original edition, pp. lxxi–lxxv.—R.M.D.]

## 4. SAVAGE IDEA.

*Animals help favoured Men and Women.*

| *Savage Tale.* | *European Tale.* |
|---|---|
| Hero is helped by ox. | Heroine is helped by bull. |
| Heroes helped by wolf. | Heroine is helped by sheep. |
| | Hero is helped by various beasts. |

## 5. SAVAGE IDEA.

*Cannibals are a constant danger.*

| *Savage Tale.* | *European Tale.* |
|---|---|
| Hero and heroine are captured by cannibals. | Hero and heroine are captured by cannibals. |
| Hero or heroine flees from home to avoid being eaten. | Hero or heroine flees from home to avoid being eaten. |

## 6. SAVAGE IDEA.

*The belief in possible descents into Hades, a place guarded by strange beasts, and where living men must not eat.*

| *Savage Tale.* | *European Tale.* |
|---|---|
| Descent by a Melanesian. | Descent of Psyche. |
| His adventures. | Her similar adventures. |
| Descent by an Odjibwa. | |
| His adventures. | |

## 7. SAVAGE CUSTOM.

*Husband and wife are forbidden to see each other, or to name each other's names.*

| *Savage Tale.* | *European Tale.* |
|---|---|
| Wife disappears (but not apparently because of infringement of taboo). | Husband or wife disappear when seen, or when the name is named. (These acts being prohibited by savage custom.) |
| Wife disappears after infringement of taboo. | |

## 8. SAVAGE CUSTOM.

*The youngest son in the Polygamous family is the heir.*

| *Savage Tale.* | *European Tale.* |
|---|---|
| King's youngest son, as heir, | Youngest son or daughter suc- |

| | |
|---|---|
| is envied and ill-treated by his brothers. | ceeds where the elders fail, and is betrayed by jealousy of the elders. |

## 9. SAVAGE IDEA.

*A. Human strength, or soul, resides in this or that part of the body, and the strength of one man may be acquired by another who secures this part.*

| *Savage Tale.* | *European Tale.* |
|---|---|
| Certain giants take out their hearts when they sleep, and are overcome by men who secure the hearts. | The giant who has no heart in his body. |
| | The man whose life or force depends on a lock of hair, and is lost when the hair is lost. |

## SAVAGE IDEA.

*B. Souls of dead enter animal forms.*

| *Savage Tale.* | *European Tale.* |
|---|---|
| Dead boy becomes a bird. | Dead boy becomes a bird. |

The lists now furnished exhibit several of the leading and most 'unnatural' ideas in European Household Tales. It has been shown that these ideas are also found in savage Household Tales. It has further been demonstrated that the notions on which these incidents are based are as natural to, and as common among, savages as they seem 'unnatural' to the modern civilized student of Aryan dialects. The conclusion appears to follow inevitably, that the incidents of savage stories are derived from the beliefs and ideas of savages, while the identical incidents in civilized tales are an inheritance, a survival from a past of savagery. If we are not to believe this, we must first reject the evidence offered as untrustworthy and next explain the phenomena as the result of forgetfulness of the meaning of words, and of other linguistic processes for which, as we have shown, the evidence is neither copious, nor unimpeachable, nor to the point.

At the beginning of this essay we remarked that Household Tales consist of but few incidents, in an immense variety of combinations. To the incidents already enumerated, we may add such as spring from a few simple moral conceptions. Thus, among savages as in Europe, *the duty of good temper and courtesy is illustrated* by the tale

[309]

of the good girl, or boy, who succeeded in enterprises where the bad girl or boy failed as a punishment of churlishness or disobedience. Again, in savage as well as civilized tales, *curiosity in forbidden matters is punished,* as in all the stories of opening a taboo'd door, or tampering with matters taboo'd. Once more *the impossibility of avoiding Fate is demonstrated* in such tales as 'The Sleeping Beauty,' the unborn child who is exposed to make of no effect an evil prophecy, and so forth. Again, *the folly of hasty words* is set forth in stories of the type of Jeptha's foolish vow. By help of such simple moral conceptions as these, and of supernatural incidents which appear natural to the savage, the web of Household Tales is woven.

There remain, however, features in Household Tales, savage or civilized, which we do not even pretend to explain. Why does the supplanted bride, whose place is taken by a false bride, appear so often? What superstition is at the bottom of the incident of the lover who forgets his beloved after he has been kissed by his mother or his hound? Why does the incident of the deserted girl, who hides in a tree, and whose beautiful face is seen reflected in a well beneath, occur so frequently in countries as far apart as Scotland and Madagascar? These are among the real difficulties of the subject. Again, while most of the incidents of Household Tales are, as we have seen, easily accounted for, the tissue of plot into which they are woven is by no means so readily explained.

We may now examine, as briefly as possible, a famous myth of the classical world, and point out its component parts and stock ideas, which are scattered through the Household Tales of the civilized and barbarous races. For our present purpose the myth of Jason is as well suited as any other.[1]

If our system be correct, the Jason myth is a heroic legend, with a plot composed of incidents now localized, and with characters now named, but the events were originally told as happening in no particular place, and the characters were originally mere 'somebodies.' The Jason myth starts from the familiar situation common in Household Tales. A Boeotian king (Athamas) has a wife, Nephele, and two children, a boy and a girl, named Phrixus (or Phryxus) and Helle. But Athamas takes a new wife or mistress, Ino, and she conspires against her step-children. By intrigues, which it is needless to explain, Ino procures a decree that Phrixus and Helle shall be sacrificed to Zeus, this feature being a survival from the age of human sacrifice in Greece. As Phrixus stood at the altar, Nephele brought forward a golden ram which could speak. Phrixus and Helle mounted on the ram; the beast flew eastwards; Helle fell off,

[1] See 'A Far Travelled Tale' in the author's *Custom and Myth.*

and was drowned in the Hellespont; Phrixus reached Colchis, sacrificed the ram, dedicated the golden fleece in a temple, and became the eponymous, or name-giving hero of Phrygia (Apollodorus, 1. ix, 1). The Scholiast, on *Iliad*, vii., 86, quotes the story, with some unimportant variations from Philostephanus. He says that the ram met Phrixus and revealed to him the plot against his life. The Scholiast on *Apoll. Rhod.*, 1., 256, gives Hecataeus as authority for the ram's power of conversation. Apollonius writes,

$$\dot{\alpha}\lambda\lambda\dot{\alpha} \; \varkappa\alpha\dot{\iota} \; \alpha\dot{\upsilon}\delta\dot{\eta}\nu$$
$$\dot{\alpha}\nu\delta\varrho o\mu\acute{e}\eta\nu \; \pi\varrho o\acute{e}\eta\varkappa\varepsilon \; \varkappa\alpha\varkappa\grave{o}\nu \; \tau\acute{e}\varrho\alpha\varsigma.$$

The classical writers were puzzled by the talkative ram, but to students of Household Tales the surprise would be if the ram did *not* speak. According to De Gubernatis, the ram is the cloud or the sun, or a mixture; 'the sun in the cloud butts with its rays until it opens the stable and its horns come out.' And so forth.

We may now compare Household Tales which contain *unlocalized* versions of the early incidents in the Jason myth. The idea of the earlier incidents is that children, oppressed or threatened at home, escape by aid of an animal, or otherwise, and begin a series of adventures. The peculiar wrong from which the children escape, in the classic and heroic myth, is human sacrifice. In the Household Tales, on the other hand, they usually run away to escape being eaten. As human sacrifice is generally a survival of cannibalism, and is often found clinging to religion after cannibalism has died out of custom, it is only natural that the religious rite should be found in the classic myth, the savage custom in savage tales, and in the household stories which we regard as survivals of savagery. In the following Household Tales, the children flee from home like Phrixus and Helle, to escape being eaten, sometimes by a step-mother, sometimes by a mother, while in the most civilized version they only run away from a step-mother's ill-treatment.

Our first example is from *Samojedische Märchen* (Castren, p. 164). Here the childless wife intends to devour the daughters of her rival, whom she has slain. The daughters escape, and when they reach the sea, they are carried across not by a golden ram, but by a beaver. The Epirote version of the story is given by Von Hahn (*Gr. Mär.*, i, 65). A man brings home a pigeon for dinner, the cat eats it; the wife, to conceal the loss of the pigeon, cooks one of her own breasts; the husband relishes the food, and proposes to kill his own two children and eat them. Exactly as the ram warned Phrixus, according to Philostephanus, so the dog warns the boy hero of the Epirote *Märchen*, and he and his sister make their escape. The tale then shades off into one of the *Märchen* of escape by magical devices, which are the most widely diffused of all stories. But these incidents recur later in the Jason legend. Turning from the Samoyeds and the Epirotes to Africa, we find the *motif* (escape of brother and sister) in a Kaffir tale, 'Story of the Bird that made Milk.' Here the children flee into the desert to avoid the anger of their father, who had 'hung them on a tree that projected over a river.' The children escape in a magical manner, and intermarry with animals (Theal's *Kaffir Folk Lore*, p. 36). Finally, among the Kaffirs, we find a combination of the form of the stories as they occur in Grimm (ii, 15). Grimm's version opens thus, 'Little brother took his little sister by the hand and said, "Since our mother died our step-mother beats us every day . . . come, we will go forth into the wide world." ' The Kaffir tale (Demane and Demazana) tells how a brother and sister who were twins and orphans were obliged on account of ill-usage to run away from their relatives. Like Hänsel and Grethel they fall into the hands of cannibals, and escape by a ruse. In their flight they are carried over the water, neither by a ram nor a beaver, but by a white duck.

Here, then, we see how widely diffused are the early ideas and incidents of the Jason cycle. We see, too that they are consistent with the theory of a savage origin, if cannibalism be a savage practice, and if belief in talking and protective animals be a savage belief.

The Jason myth proceeds from the incidents of the flight of the children, and enters a new cycle of ideas and events. We come to incidents which may be arranged thus:

1. The attempt to evade prophecy. (Compare *Zulu Tales*, p. 41).
2. The arrival of the true heir.
3. Endeavour to get rid of the heir by setting him upon a difficult or impossible adventure. (Callaway's *Zulu Tales*, p. 170).
4. The hero starts on the adventure, accompanied by friends possessed of miraculous powers. (Compare *Kalewala*).

In the Jason Legend the true heir is Jason himself. His uncle, Pelias, the usurper of his kingdom, has been warned by prophecy to guard against a one-shoe'd man. Jason has lost one shoe crossing the river. His uncle, to get rid of him, sends him to seek, in far-away Colchis, the golden fleece of the talking ram. He sets forth in a boat with a talking figure-head, and accompanied by heroes of supernatural strength, and with magical powers of seeing, hearing, and flying.

All these inventions are natural, and require no comment. The companions of the hero, 'Quick Sight,' 'Fine Ear' and the rest, are well known in European Household Tales, where their places are occasionally taken by gifted beasts. The incident of the expedition, the companions, and the quest in general, recurs in the *Kalewala*, the national poem of the Finns. When Jason with his company arrive in Colchis, we enter on a set of incidents perhaps more widely diffused than any others in the whole of folklore. Briefly speaking, the situation is this: an adventurer comes to the home of a powerful and malevolent being. He either is the brother of the wife of this being, or he becomes the lover of his daughter. In the latter case, the daughter helps the adventurer to accomplish the impossible tasks set him by her father. Afterwards the pair escape, throwing behind them, in their flight, various objects which detain the pursuer. When the adventurer is the brother of the wife of the malevolent being the story usually introduces the 'fee fo, fum' formula,—the husband smells the flesh of the stranger. In this variant, tasks are not usually set to the brother as they are to the lover. The incidents of the flight are much the same everywhere, even when, as in the Japanese and Lithuanian myths a brother is fleeing from the demon-ghost of his sister in Hades, or when, as in the Samoyed tale, two sisters are evading the pursuit of a cannibal step-mother. The fugitives always throw small objects behind them, such as a comb, which magically turns into a forest, and so forth.

We have already alluded to the wide diffusion of these incidents, which recur, in an epic and humanized form, in the Jason myth. By way of tracing the incidents from their least civilized to their Greek shape, we may begin with the Nama version. It is a pretty general rule that in the myths of the lower races, animals fill the roles which, in civilized story, are taken by human beings. In Bleek's *Hottentot Fables and Tales*, p. 60, the incidents turn on the visit of brothers to a sister, not on the coming of an adventurous lover. The sister has married, not a wizard king, nor even a giant, but an elephant. The woman hides her brothers, the elephant 'smells something.' In the night, the woman escapes, with all the elephant's herds except three kine, which she instructs to low as loud as if they were whole flocks. These beasts then act like the 'talking spittle,' in Gaelic and Zulu, and like the chattering dolls in the Russian tale. The woman bids a rock open, she and her brothers enter, and when the elephant comes the rock closes on him, like the 'Rocks Wandering,' or clashing rocks, in the Odyssey, and he is killed. In the Eskimo Tale (Rink, 7) two brothers visit a sister married to a cannibal, but she has become a cannibal too. A tale much more like the Hottentot story of the Nama woman is the Eskimo 'Two Girls' (Rink, 8). One of the girls married, not an elephant, but a whale. To visit her, her two brothers built a boat of magical speed. In their company the woman fled from the whale. But instead of leaving magical objects, or obediently lowing animals behind her, she merely tied the rope by which the whale usually fastened her round a stone. The whale discovered her absence, pursued her, and was detained by various articles which she threw at him. Finally she and her brothers escaped, and the whale was transformed into a piece of whale-bone. In the Samoyed story (Castren, 11) the pursuit of the cannibal is delayed by a comb which the girl throws behind her, and which becomes 'a thick wood'; other objects tossed behind become rivers and mountains. The same kind of feats are performed during the flight, in a story from Madagascar (*Folk-lore Record*, August 1883), a story which, in most minute and curious detail of plot, resembles the Scotch 'Nicht, Nocht, Nothing,' the Russian 'Tsar Morskoi,' and the Gaelic 'Battle of the Birds.' In Japan, as among the Samoyeds, the hero (when followed by the Loathly Lady of Hades) throws down his comb, and it turns into bamboo sprouts, which naturally check her in her approach (*Trans. Asiat. Soc. of Japan*, vol. x., p. 36). The Zulu versions will be found in Callaway, pp. 51, 90, 145. In the Russian Tale (Ralston, p. 120), we find that the adventurer is not the brother of the wife of an animal, but the lover of the daughter of the Water King. By her aid he accomplishes the hard tasks set him, and he escapes with her, not by throwing objects behind, but by her magical gift of shape-shifting. The story takes the same form in the old Indian collection of Somadeva (cf. Köhler, *Orient und Occident*, ii., pp. 107–14. Ralston, pp. 132, 133). The father of the maiden in the Indian version is both animal and giant, a Rakshasa, who can fly about as a crane. In Grimm (51) the girl and her lover flee, by the aid of talking drops of blood, from a cruel witch step-mother. The best German parallel to the incidents of the adventurer's success in love, success in performing the hard tasks, and flight with the girl, is Grimm's 'Two Kings' Children' (110). The Scotch version is defective in the details of the flight. (*Nicht, Nought, Nothing,* collected by the present writer, and published, with notes by Dr. Köhler, in *Revue Celtique*, vol. iii, 3, 4.)

It is scarcely necessary to show how the incidents which we have been tracing are used in the epic of Jason. He himself is the adventurer; the powerful and malevolent being is the Colchian King Aeetes, the daughter of the king, who falls in love with the adventurer, is Medea. Hard tasks, as usual, are set the hero; just as in the *Kalewala*, Ilmarinen is compelled to plough the adder-close with a plough of gold, to bridle the wolf and the bear of Hades, and to catch the pike that swims in the waters of forgetfulness. The hard tasks in the Highlands and in South Africa may be compared (Campbell, ii, 328; Callaway, 470). Instead of sowing dragons' teeth, the Zulu boy has to 'fetch the liver of an Ingogo,' a fabulous monster. When the tasks have been accomplished, the adventurer and the king's daughter, Jason and Medea, flee, as usual, from the wrath of the king, being aided (again as usual) by the magic of the king's daughter. And what did the king's daughter throw behind her in her flight, to delay her father's pursuit? Nothing less than the mangled remains of her own brothers. Other versions are given; that of Apollonius Rhodius (iv, 476, cf. *Scholia*) contains a curious account of a savage expiatory rite performed by Jason. But Grote (ed. 1869, i, 232) says, 'So revolting a story as that of the cutting up of the little boy cannot have been imagined in later times.' Perhaps, however, the tale, though as old as Pherecydes, is derived from a Folk-etymology of the place called Tomi (τέμνω). While the wizard king mourned over the castaway fragments of his boy, the adventurer and the king's daughter made their escape. The remainder of the Jason legend is chiefly Greek, though some of the wilder incidents (as Medea's chaldron) have their parallels in South Africa.

We have now examined a specimen of the epic legends of Greece. We have shown that it is an arrangement, with local and semi-historical features, of a number of incidents, common in both savage and European Household Tales. Some moments in the process of the arrangement, for example, the localizing of the scene in Colchis, and the attachment of the conclusion to the fortunes of the Corinthian House, are discussed by Grote (i, 244). Grote tries to show that the poetic elaboration and arrangement were finished between 600 and 500 B.C. Whatever the date may have been, we think it probable that the incidents of the Jason legend, as preserved in *Märchen*, are much older than the legend in its epic Greek form. We have also shown that the incidents for the most part occur in the tales of savages, and we believe that they are the natural expressions of the savage imagination. We have not thought it necessary to explain (with Sir George Cox) the mutilation of the son of Aeetes as a myth of sunset (*Ar. Myth.*, i, 153) 'a vivid image of the young sun as torn to pieces among the vapours that surround him, while the light, falling in isolated patches on the sea, seems to set bounds to the encroaching darkness.' Is the 'encroaching darkness' Aeetes? But Aeetes, in myth, was the son of the Sun, while Sir George Cox recognizes him as 'the breath or motion of the air.'[1]

[1] While Aeetes is the 'breath or motion of the air' with Sir George Cox, in the opinion of Mr. Brown (*The Myth of Kirke*), Aeetes is Lunus, and forms with Circe 'an andro-

Well, Jason was (apparently) the Sun, and Apsyrtus is the young Sun, and Medea is the Dawn, and Helle is the evening Air, and Phryxus is the cold Air, and the fleece is the Sunlight, and Aeetes is the breath of the Air, and the child of the Sun, and why they all behave as they do in the legend is a puzzle which we cannot pretend to unravel.

Did space permit, we might offer analyses of other myths. The Odyssey we have dealt with in the introduction to our prose translation (Butcher and Lang ed. 1883). The myths of Perseus and of Urvasi and Pururavas may be treated in a similar way.[1] As to the relations between the higher myths and *Märchen*, civilized or savage, there is this to be said: where the *Märchen* is diffused among many distinct races, while the epic use of the same theme is found only among one or two cultivated peoples, it is probable that the *Märchen* is older than the cultivated epic. Again, when the popular tale retains references to the feats of medicine men, to cannibalism, to metamorphosis, and to kinship with beasts, all of which are suppressed or smoothed down in the epic form of the story, these omissions strengthen the belief that the epic is later than the tale, and has passed through the refining atmosphere of a higher civilization.

As to the origin of the wild incidents in Household Tales, let any one ask himself this question: Is there anything in the frequent appearance of cannibals, in kinship with animals, in magic, in abominable cruelty, that would seem unnatural to a savage? Certainly not; all these things are familiar in his world. Do all these things occur on almost every page of Grimm? Certainly they do. Have they been natural and familiar incidents to the educated German mind during the historic age? No one will venture to say so. These notions, then, have survived in peasant tales from the time when the ancestors of the Germans were like Zulus or Maoris or Australians.

Finally, as to the *diffusion* of similar *incidents* in countries widely severed, that may be, perhaps, ascribed to the identical beliefs of early man all over the world. But the diffusion of *plots* is much more hard to explain, nor do we venture to explain it, except by the

---

[1] See 'Cupid, Psyche, and the Sun-Frog' in the author's *Custom and Myth*.

gynous Moon, *i.e.*, the ascription of both male and female potentialities to the lunar power.' Medea is the Moon, too, with Mr. Brown, while Sir George Cox writes, 'Medeia herself appears in benignant guise in the legend of the Goose-girl at the Well (the *Dawn-maiden* with her snow-white clouds)' (*Ar. Myth.*, i, 429). Where incidents may be explained by fanciful guesses at the etymology of words, every scholar has an equal right to his own interpretations. Each may see the moon, where another finds the sun, or the wind, or the cloud. But the conflicting guesses destroy each other.

chances of transmission in the long past of human existence. As to the 'roots' or 'radicals' of stories, the reader who has followed us will probably say, with Mr. Farrer (*Primitive Manners*, p. 257), 'We should look, not in the clouds, but upon the earth; not in the various aspects of nature, but in the daily occurrences and surroundings,' he might have added, in the current opinions and ideas, 'of savage life.'

## [ 2  GEORGE  LAURENCE  GOMME (*a*) ]

As longtime director of The Folk-Lore Society, Gomme conceived various bibliographical and co-operative projects designed to enhance the resources of the folklorist, while as a research scholar he tenaciously pursued an independent line. In particular he espoused the folkloristic study of early village and tribal institutions, such as open-air assemblies, customarily passed by for tales, superstitions, and festivals. As his pet thesis he rode hard the argument that the folklorist could distinguish ethnic layers of tradition in the mass of peasant survivals and so reconstruct the historical sequence of aboriginal and Aryan social institutions. While Lang and Hartland and Clodd traced the ideas of the European peasant back to the savages of Australia and Africa, Gomme, the historian of London, sought to recreate the savages of Britain. When he looked abroad, it was usually to India, also an agrarian land with mixed Aryan and non-Aryan peoples.

Text from George Laurence Gomme, *Ethnology in Folklore*. London: Kegan Paul, Trench, Trubner and Co., 1892. Chapter 5, 'The Ethnic Genealogy of Folklore,' pages 109–34.

The analogies which exist between savage custom and European folklore suggested the first stage of the argument for the existence of ethnic elements in folklore. What is this folklore, which can be traced to nothing, outside of folklore, in the habitual beliefs and customs of civilized countries, and which is parallel only to the habitual beliefs and customs of savages? A key to the answer was supplied when it was pointed out that there is an equation which consists, on the one side, of Indian religious rites, in which Aryan and non-Aryan races take their respective parts, and, on the other side, of custom in survival among European peasantry. From this it was argued that the appearance of the factor of race on one side of the equation made it necessary that it should also be inserted on the other side, and it was therefore urged that the items of folklore thus earmarked should be separated off into groups of non-Aryan and Aryan origins.

It follows from this, then, that relics of *different* races are to be found in the folklore of countries whose chief characteristics have up to the present been identified by scholars as belonging to *one* race. So important a conclusion necessitates some further inquiry into those items of folklore on the European side of the equation which are thus allocated to different race origins, and it may be urged that they should contain some quality which of itself, now that we have the key, will help to identify them as of non-Aryan or Aryan origin. We must not, in short, rely upon the comparative method for everything. Aryan belief and custom, though doubtless not easily distinguishable in some cases from non-Aryan belief and custom, is in other cases definitely and distinctly marked off from it both in theory and practice. In folklore, therefore, this difference would also appear if the hypothesis as to origin is true. There must at least exist some beliefs and some usages which are inconsistent with the corresponding Aryan beliefs and usages—an inconsistency which in the last stages of survival does not perhaps present a very important consideration to the peasantry among whom the folklore obtains, but which, if traced back to the originals, may be shown to have been an important factor in the development of primitive Aryan thought and custom.

Hence, in attempting to trace out the originals of modern folklore, it is clear that its inconsistencies must be carefully observed. For the purpose of the problem now under discussion we must note these inconsistencies, in order to see if they may be identified with two distinct lines of primitive custom and belief. On the one hand there would be the line of parallel to modern savagery, where the folklore, that is, is at the same level of development in human culture as the savage custom or belief; on the other hand, there would be the line of parallel to a much higher culture than savagery. If these two inconsistent lines of development are both represented in folklore, though in spirit antagonistic to each other, the point is gained that in folklore is discoverable at least two separate lines of descent. They must have been produced by the presence within the country where they now survive of different races living together in the relationship of conquered and conquerors; they must have been subsequently handed on by generation after generation of the same races; they must finally have been preserved by the peasantry, long after distinction of race in Europe had ceased to exist, as mere

[318]

observance of custom, because as such they were part and parcel of their stock of life-action, not pushed out of existence by anything higher in religion or culture, but retaining their old place year after year, decade after decade, simply because their dislodgment, without adequate replacement from other sources, would have created a vacuum as foreign to nature in man as to nature in the world surrounding man.

We have thus two distinct lines of parallel to trace out—a parallel with savagery and a parallel with a higher culture. The work before us is not one that can be accomplished off-hand. Folklore has a genealogy, so to speak, where the links are represented by the various changes which the condition of survival inevitably brings about. I have said that there is no development in folklore. All chances of development had been crushed out when the original elements of what is now classed as folklore were pushed back from the condition of tribal or national custom and belief to that of tolerated peasant superstition. But this does not mean that no change of any sort has taken place. The changes of decay, degradation, and misapplication have taken the place of change by development.

The marked features of these changes are capable of some classification, and I shall term them symbolism, substitution, and amalgamation. A practice originally in one particular form assumes another form, but still symbolical of the original; or it is transferred to another object or set of objects; or it becomes joined on to other practices and beliefs, and produces in this way a new amalgamation. All these processes indicate the change of decay incidental to survivals, not the change of development, and in tracing out the genealogy of folklore it is the changes of decay which mark the steps of the descent. When children are made to jump through the midsummer fires for luck, human sacrifice has in folklore become symbolized; when the blood of the cock is sprinkled, as in France, over the stones of a new building the animal object of the sacrifice has been substituted for the human object; when the wise man of the Yorkshire villages has assumed the character of part wizard or witch, part sorcerer, magician, or enchanter, and part conjurer, there has been an amalgamation of the characters and credentials of three or four entities in pagan priesthood. And so through all these changes we must endeavour to carefully work back step by step to the original form. That form as restored will represent the true survival enshrined in folklore, and according to its equation with savage, or with an ascertained development from savage originals, will it be possible to decide to what early race it is to be attributed—the highly organized Aryan, capable of a culture equal to his language, or the ruder and more savage predecessors of the Aryan people.

I will now give some examples of the ethnic genealogy of folklore on the lines just traced out. They are examples chosen not for the special object of endeavouring to prove a point, but as evidence of what a careful examination of folklore in detail and in relation to its several component elements might produce if it were systematically and carefully pursued in this manner. The study is laborious, but the results are correspondingly valuable, particularly when it appears that from no other branch of knowledge can we hope to obtain information as to what our ancestors thought and believed.

1. As an act of sorcery the mould from the churchyard known as the 'meels,' was in north-eastern Scotland used for throwing into the mill-race in order to stop the mill-wheel.[1] That the mould is not used because it is a consecrated element of the churchyard is suggested by the harmful result expected, and its connexion with the dead is the only alternative cause for its use; so that our examination of this superstitious practice points to some as yet unexplained use of products closely connected with the dead. The importance of this conclusion is shown by an Irish usage—people taking the clay or mould from the graves of priests and boiling it with milk as a decoction for the cure of disease.[2] Again, in Shetland a stitch in the side was cured by applying to the part some mould dug from a grave and heated, it being an essential of the ceremony that the mould must be taken from and returned to the grave before sunset.[3] In the first of these cases the grave mould is used as food, and it is this circumstance more than the supposed cures effected by it which must be taken as the lowest point in the genealogy of this item of folklore.

The next link in the genealogy shows that the use of grave-mould is only a substitution for the use of the corpse itself. The Irish have a superstition that to dip the left hand of a corpse in the milk-pail has the effect of making the milk produce considerably more cream and of a richer and better kind.[4] A new element presented by the analysis of this form of the custom is that the result is not connected with the cure of disease but with the increase of dairy produce. The limitation to a particular part of the dead body, the left hand, dis-

[1] Gregor, *Folklore*, p. 216.
[2] Wilde's *Beauties of the Boyne*, p. 45; Croker, *Researches in South of Ireland*, p. 170; cf. *Rev. Celt.*, v., 358. The dew collected from the grave of the last man buried in the churchyard as an application for the cure of goitre may perhaps be a remnant of this class of belief. It occurs at Launceston.—Dyer, *English Folklore*, p. 150.
[3] Rogers, *Social Life in Scotland*, iii, 226.
[4] Croker, *op. cit.*, p. 234.

appears in a custom once obtaining at Oran in Roscommon. There a child was disinterred and its arms cut off, to be employed in the performance of certain mystic rights, the nature of which unfortunately are not stated by my authority.[1] Scottish witches are credited with opening graves for the purpose of taking out joints of the fingers and toes of dead bodies, with some of the winding sheet, in order to prepare a powder for their magical purposes.[2] In Lincolnshire a small portion of the human skull was taken from the graveyard and grated, to be used in a mixture and eaten for the cure of fits.[3] For the cure of epilepsy near Kirkwall a similar practice was resorted to, while in Caithness and the western isles the patient was made to drink from a suicide's skull.[4]

Fresh light is thrown upon the nature of the magical practices alluded to in these examples by the evidence afforded by Scottish trials for witchcraft. From the trial of John Brugh, November 24, 1643, it appears that he went to the churchyard of Glendovan on three several occasions, and each time took up a corpse. 'The flesch of the quhilk corps was put aboue the byre and stable-dure headis' of certain individuals to destroy their cattle.[5] This practice, when subjected to analysis, becomes divided into two heads:

(1) The distribution of human flesh among owners of cattle.

(2) The object of such distribution to do harm to these cattle-owners.

We have thus arrived step by step at the bodies of the dead being used for some undetermined purposes. Another group of such practices surviving in folklore represents by symbolization a still further step in the genealogy. A note by Bishop White Kennet speaks of a 'custom which lately obtained at Amersden in the county of Oxford, where at the burial of every corps one cake and one flaggon of ale just after the interment were brought to the minister in the church porch.'[6] This, in the opinion of the writer, seems 'a remainder' of the custom of sin-eating, and it is probable he is right. The sin-eating custom is thus given by Aubrey: 'In the county of Hereford was an old custome at funeralls to have poor people who were to take upon them all the sinnes of the party deceased. The manner was that when the corps was brought out of the house and layd on the biere, a loafe of bread was brought out and delivered to the sinne-eater over the corps, as also a mazar bowle of maple (gossips

[1] Wilde, *Irish Popular Superstitions*, p. 28.
[2] Brand, *Pop. Antiq.*, iii, 10.
[3] Dyer, *English Folklore*, p. 147.
[4] Rogers, *Social Life in Scotland*, iii, 225.
[5] Dalyell, *Darker Superstitions of Scotland*, p. 379.
[6] Aubrey's *Remaines of Gentilisme*, p. 24.

bowle) full of beer, which he was to drinke up, and sixpence in money, in consideration whereof he tooke upon him (*ipso facto*) all the sinnes of the defunct, and freed him or her from walking after they were dead.'[1] Aubrey specifically mentions Hereford, Ross, Dynder ('*volens nolens* the parson of ye Parish'), and 'in other places in this countie,' as also in Breconshire, at Llangors, 'where Mr. Gwin, the minister, about 1640, could no hinder ye performing of this ancient custome,' and in North Wales, where, instead of a 'bowle of beere they have a bowle of milke.'

This account is circumstantial enough. Bagford, in his well-known letter to Hearne (1715), mentions the same custom as obtaining in Shropshire, 'in those villages adjoyning to Wales.' His account is: 'When a person dyed there was notice given to an old sire (for so they called him), who presently repaired to the place where the deceased lay and stood before the door of the house, when some of the family came out and furnished him with a cricket, on which he sat down facing the door. Then they gave him a groat which he put in his pocket; a crust of bread which he ate; and a full bowle of ale which he drank off at a draught. After this he got up from the circket and pronounced with a composed gesture the ease and rest of the soul departed, for which he would pawn his own soul.'[2] There seems some evidence of this custom being in vogue at Llandebie, near Swansea, until about 1850,[3] where the ceremony was not unlike that described as having been practised in the west of Scotland. 'There were persons,' says Mr. Napier, 'calling themselves sin-eaters, who when a person died were sent for to come and eat the sins of the deceased. When they came their *modus operandi* was to place a plate of salt and a plate of bread on the breast of the corpse and repeat a series of incantations, after which they ate the contents of the plates and so relieved the dead person of such sins as would have kept him hovering around his relations, haunting them with his imperfectly purified spirit, to their great annoyance and without satisfaction to himself.'[4] The Welsh custom, as des-

[1] Aubrey's *Remaines of Gentilisme*, pp. 35, 36.
[2] Leland's *Collectanca*, i, lxxvi.
[3] *Archæologia Cambrensis*, iii, 330; *Journ. Anthrop. Inst.*, v, 423; Wirt Sikes, *British Goblins*, pp. 326, 327. The Welsh practice of the relatives of the deceased distributing bread and cheese to the poor *over the coffin* seems to me to confirm the evidence for the Welsh sin-eater. One of Elfric's canons says, *inter alia*, 'Do not eat and drink over the body in the heathenish manner.'—Wilkins, *Cvncilia*, i, 255.
[4] Napier, *Folklore of the West of Scotland*, p. 60. I am not quite satisfied with this example. Mr. Napier evidently is not minutely describing an actual observance, and in his book he frequently refers to customs elsewhere. In this instance he does not appear to be alluding to any other than Scottish customs, and it is to be noted that his details differ from Aubrey's and Bagford's, nor can I trace any authority for his details except his own observation, unless it be from Mr. Moggridge's account in

cribed by Mr. Moggridge, adds one important detail not noted with reference to the other customs—namely, that after the ceremony the sin-eater 'vanished as quickly as possible from the general gaze.'

The chief points in these remarkable customs are:

(1) The action of passing the food over the corpse, as if thereby to signify some connexion with the corpse;

(2) The immediate disappearance of the sin-eater; and

(3) The object of the ceremony to prevent the spirit of the deceased from annoying the living.

In these customs clearly something is symbolized by the supposed eating up of the sins of the deceased.[1] As Mr. Frazer has observed in reference to these practices, 'the idea of sin is not primitive.'[2] I do not think with Mr. Frazer that the older idea was that death was carried away from the survivors. Something much less subtle than this must have originated all these practices, or they could not have been kept up in so materialistic a form. Folklore tends to become less material as it decays; it goes off into almost shadowy conceptions, not into practices which of themselves are horrid and revolting. These practices, then, must be the indicator which will help us to translate the symbolism of folklore into the usage of primitive life. The various forms of the survival seem to indicate that we have here a group of customs and beliefs relating to some unknown cult of the dead—a cult which, when it was relegated to the position of a survival by some foreign force which arrested development and only brought decay and change, showed no tendency towards any high conception of future bliss for the deceased in spirit-land; a cult which was savage in conception, savage in the methods of carrying out the central idea which promoted it, savage, too, in the results which must have flowed from it and affected the minds and associations of its actors.

What is the savage idea connected with the dead which underlies these gloomy and disgusting practices preserved in folklore? Let me recall a passage in Strabo relating to the practices of early British savages. The inhabitants of Ireland were cannibals, but they also 'deemed it honourable to eat the bodies of their deceased

---

[1] I must acknowledge my indebtedness to Mr. Hartland for the use I make of the custom of sin-eating. He was good enough to draw my attention to a study of the subject he was preparing, and which since the above passage was written he has read before the Folklore Society.

[2] Frazer, *Golden Bough*, ii, 152, *note*; Miss Burne also seems to suggest this idea (*Shropshire Folklore*, p. 202).

---

*Arch. Cambrensis*, which, however, it does not follow exactly. He is so reliable in respect of all his own notes that I should not doubt this if it were not for the certain amount of vagueness about the language.

[323]

parents.'[1] Now, the eating of dead kindred is a rite practised by savages in many parts of the world, and it is founded primarily on the fear which savage man had for the spirits of the dead.

The conception of fear in connexion with the dead is still retained in folklore. Miss Burne, with great reason, attributes the popular objection to carrying a corpse along a private road to the dread lest the dead should come back by the road the corpse travelled.[2] In Scotland the same dread is expressed by the curious practice of turning upside down all the chairs in the room from which the corpse has just been taken;[3] in England by the practice of unhinging the gate and placing it across the entrance, and of carrying the corpse to the grave by a roundabout way.[4] There is also the practice in Scotland of keeping up a dance all night after a funeral,[5] which by the analogous practice among the Nagas of India must be attributed to the desire to get rid of the spirit of the deceased.[6] The Caithness Scots, too, share with some South African tribes a deep-rooted reluctance to speak of a man as dead.[7] The point of these practices is that the returning ghosts are not friendly to their earthly kindred, do not represent the idea of friendly ancestral spirits who, in their newly-assumed character of spirits, will help their kindred on earth to get through the troubles of life. The mere fear of ghosts, which is the outcome of modern superstition, does not account for these practices, because it does not cover the wide area occupied by them in savage life which Mr. Frazer has so skilfully travelled over. In this connexion, too, I would mention that, associated with the outcast and the criminal, the same idea of fear for the ghosts of the dead is perfectly obvious, which introduces the further suggestion that in this case we have evidence of a certain degraded class of the modern population becoming identified in the peasant mind—in the minds of those, that is, who have kept alive the oldest instincts of prehistoric times—with the ideas and practices which once belonged to a fallen and degraded race existing in their midst. For my present purpose I will quote from Mr. Atkinson the following passage: 'There is no doubt that the self-murderer or the doer of some atrocious deed of violence, murder, or lust was buried by some lonely roadside, in a road-crossing, or by the wild

---

[1] Strabo, lib. iv, cap. v, sect. 4.
[2] *Shropshire Folklore*, p. 303.  [3] *Folklore Record*, ii, 214.
[4] Frazer, in *Journ. Anthrop. Inst.*, xv, 72.
[5] Napier, *Folklore of West of Scotland*, p. 66; *Folklore Journal*, iii, 281; Pococke's *Tour through Scotland*, 1760, p. 88.
[6] Owen's *Notes on the Naga Tribes*, p. 23.
[7] *Journ. Anthrop. Inst.*, xx, 121; Lubbock, *Prehistoric Times*, p. 471; it is also an Australian belief.—*Trans. Ethnol. Soc.*, i, 299; iii, 40.

woodside, and that the oak, or oftener thorn stake was driven through his breast. These characters could not rest in their graves. They had to wander about the scenes of their crimes or the places where their unhallowed carcases were deposited, unless they were prevented, and as they wanted the semblance, the *simulacrum*, the shadow substance of their bodies, for that purpose, the body was made secure by pinning it to the bottom of the grave by aid of the driven stake. And there were other means adopted with the same end in view. The head was severed from the body and laid between the legs or placed under the arm—between the side and the arm, that is—or the feet and legs were bound together with a strong rope; or the corpse might be cut up into some hollow vessel capable of containing the pieces, and carried away quite beyond the precincts of the village and deposited in some bog or morass.'[1] These ghastly ceremonies throw much light on the old folk-belief as to the dead. What is now confined to the suicide or criminal in parts of England is identical with ceremonies performed by savage tribes for all their dead, and it is impossible to put on one side the suggestion that we have in this partial survival relics of a conception of the dead which once belonged to an ethnic division of the people, and not to a caste created by the laws of crime.

I am anxious in this first attempt at definitely tracing out the genealogy of a particular element in folklore to show clearly that the process is a justifiable one. It will not be possible in all instances to do this, partly on account of space and partly on account of the singular diversity of the evidence. But in this instance the attempt may perhaps be made, and I will first proceed to set down, in the usual manner of a genealogy, the various stages already noted in this case, and I will then set down the parallel genealogy supplied from savagery. (See page 326.)

This genealogy seems to me clear and definite, and its construction is singularly free from any process of forced restoration. Looked at from the point of view of geographical distribution, it has to be pointed out that this group of folklore is found in isolation in the outer parts of the country. The significance of its distribution in certain localities must be taken into account, and it is important to draw attention to the isolation of the several examples. It clearly does not represent a cult of the dead generally present in the minds of the peasantry. A totally different set of beliefs has to be examined for this, and to these beliefs I now turn for evidence of that inconsistency in folklore which I have urged shows distinct ethnic origins.

[1] Atkinson, *Forty Years in a Moorland Parish*, pp. 217, 218. The modern reason for these doings is the idea of 'ignominy, abhorrence, execration, or what not.'

Eating of dead kindred

British savagery | Modern savagery

Inhabitants of Ireland

Development or change

Survival in folklore

Dead body = food eaten out of the hand[2]

Relics of the dead treated in revolting manner

[Practice arrested]

Dead body = distributed among community[3]

Dead body = food taken from to eat the sin of the deceased

Pounded bones or ashes = eaten by kinsmen[4]

Dead body = cut up and placed over cattle byres

Water in which body is placed = drank by kinsmen[5]

Corpse hand = dipped in milk for increase of supply

Corpse fingers and toes = magic rites of witches, harmful (?)

Practice still continued by many races[1]

Corpse arms and legs = magic rites unknown

Grave mould [of priest] = cure of disease

Grave mould = harm to mill

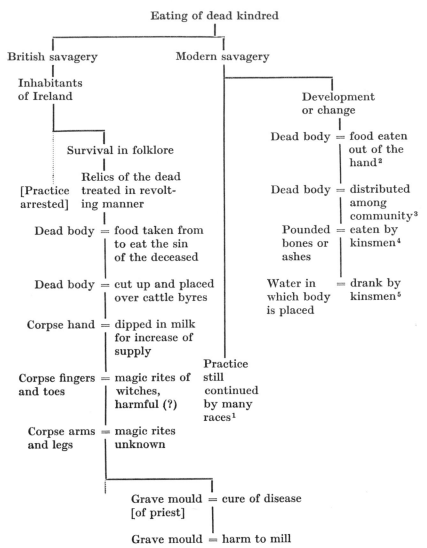

[1] Ancient Peruvians (Dormer, *Origin of Primitive Superstitions*, p. 151; Hakluyt, *Rites of the Incas*, p. 94); Battahs of Sumatra (Featherman, *Soc. Hist.*, 2nd div., 336; *Journ. Ind. Arch.*, ii, 241; Marsden, *Sumatra*, p. 390); Philippine Islanders (Featherman, *op. cit.*, p. 496); Gonds and Kookies of India (Rowney, *Wild Tribes of India*, p. 7; *Journ. As. Soc. Bengal*, xvi, 14); Queensland (*Journ. Anthrop. Inst.*, ii, 179; viii, 254; J. D. Lang's *Queensland*, pp. 333, 355–7); Victoria (Smythe's *Aborigines of Victoria*, i, pp. xxix, 120); Maoris (Taylor's *New Zealand*, p. 221). All these examples are not, it should be stated, attributed to fear of dead kindred; but the whole point as to the origin of the practice is one for argument and more evidence. These examples do not exhaust the list; they are the most typical.

[2] The Kangras of India.—*Punjab N. & Q.*, i, 86.

[3] The Koniagas (Spencer, *Principles of Sociology*, p. 262. It is remarkable that this custom is the alternative to immersing the dead body and drinking the water); Australians (Smythe's *Aborigines of Victoria*, i, 121; Featherman, *op. cit.*, pp. 157, 161).

[4] Tarianas and Tucanos.—Spencer, *op. cit.*, p. 262.        [5] Koniagas (see note 3).

The facts will then stand as follows: On the one hand there is a definite representation of a cult of the dead based on the fear of dead kindred and found in isolated patches of the country; on the other hand there is a definite representation of a cult of the dead based on the love of dead kindred and found generally prevalent over the country.

The survivals of this cult in folklore are numerous. As soon as death has taken place doors and windows are opened to allow the spirit to join the home of departed ancestors;[1] the domestic animals are removed from the house;[2] the bees are given some of the funeral food and are solemnly told of the master's death by the nearest of kin;[3] the fire at the domestic hearth is put out;[4] careful watch is made of the corpse until its burial;[5] soul-mass cakes are prepared and eaten.[6]

A singular unanimity prevails as to the reasons for these customs, which may be summed up as indicating the one desire to procure a safe and speedy passage of the soul to spirit-land, or, as it is put in modern folklore, 'lest the devil should gain power over the dead person.'[7]

In the removal of the domestic animals we can trace the old rite of funeral sacrifice. Originally, says Napier, the reason for the exclusion of dogs and cats arose from the belief that if either of these animals should chance to leap over the corpse and be permitted to live the devil would gain power over the dead person. In Northumberland this negative way of putting the case is replaced by a positive record of the sacrifice of the animals that leapt over the coffin.[8] But probably human sacrifice, that pitiable kindness to the dead, is symbolized in the Highland custom at funerals, where friends of the deceased person fought until blood was drawn—the drawing of blood being held essential.[9] The real nature of the soul-mass cakes as the last vestiges of the old rite of funeral sacrifice to the manes of the deceased has been proved by Dr. Tylor.[10] The striking custom of putting out the fire is to be interpreted as a desire

[1] Brand, ii, 231; Henderson, *Folklore of Northern Countries*, pp. 53, 56; Dyer, *English Folklore*, p. 230.    [2] Napier, p. 60.
[3] The examples of this custom are very numerous. I have summarized the principal of them in *Folk-Lore*, iii, 12.
[4] Pennant, *Tour in Scotland*, i, 44.
[5] Napier, *Folklore of West Scotland*, p. 62.
[6] Brand, i, 392; ii, 289.
[7] Napier, pp. 60, 62.
[8] Henderson, p. 59. Cats are locked up while the corpse remains in the house in Orkney (Gough's *Sepulchral Monuments*, vol. i, p. lxxv); and in Devonshire (Dyer's *English Folklore*, p. 109).    [9] *Folklore Journal*, iii, 281.
[10] *Primitive Culture*, ii, 38.

not to detain the soul at the altar of the domestic god, where the spirits of deified ancestors were worshipped. And the message to the bees is clearly best explained, I think, as being given to these winged messengers of the gods[1] so that they may carry the news to spirit-land of the speedy arrival of a new-comer.

All these solemnities betoken very plainly that we are dealing with the survivals in folklore of the Aryan worship of deceased ancestors, one of the most generally accepted conclusions of comparative culture.[2] I need scarcely point out how far removed it is, as a matter of development in culture, from the more primitive fear of dead kindred. Manes worship, based upon the fear of the dead, is found in many parts of the primitive world;[3] the worship of a domestic god, based upon his helpfulness, is found also.[4] But, except among the Aryan peoples, these two cults do not seem to have coalesced into a family religion. In this family religion, centred round the domestic hearth where the ancestral god resided, the fear of dead kindred has given way before the conception of the dead ancestor who had 'passed into a deity [and] simply goes on protecting his own family and receiving suit and service from them as of old; the dead chief [who] still watches over his own tribe, still holds his authority by helping friends and harming enemies, still rewards the right and sharply punishes the wrong.'[5] And, in the meantime, the horrid practices and theories of savagery which we have previously examined are contrasted, in Aryan culture, with the funeral ceremony whereby the kinsmen of the deceased perform the last rites, and with the theory that these rites are necessary to ensure that the ghosts of the dead take their place in the bright home of deified ancestors,[6] both practice and theory being represented in

[1] The bees supplied the sacred mead and were therefore in direct contact with the gods. Cf. Schrader, *Prehistoric Antiquities of the Aryans*, p. 321.
[2] Hearn, *Aryan Household*, p. 54; Maine, *Ancient Law*, p. 191; Spencer, *Principles of Sociology*, pp. 314–16; De Coulanges, *Cité Antique*, pp. 33, 71; Kelly, *Indo-European Folklore*, p. 45; *Revue Celtique*, ii, 486; Cox, *Introd. to Myth. and Folklore*, p. 168; Elton, *Origins of Engl. Hist.*, p. 211, are the most accessible authorities, to which I may perhaps add my *Folklore Relics of Early Village Life*, pp. 90–123. Rogers, in his *Social Life in Scotland*, iii, 340, 341, has a curious note on the *lares familiares* or wraiths of the Highlanders, connecting them with the ghosts of departed ancestors. I note Schrader's objection in *Prehistoric Antiquities of the Aryan Peoples*, p. 425, that the unsatisfactory state of the Greek evidence prevents him from accepting the general view, but I think the weight of evidence on the other side tells against this objection.
[3] Tylor, *Primitive Culture*, ii, 103–9; Spencer, *Principles of Sociology*, pp. 304–13.
[4] Cf. my *Folklore Relics*, pp. 85–90.
[5] Tylor, *Primitive Culture*, ii, 103.
[6] This is a common Greek and Hindu conception.—*Odyss.*, xi, 54; *Iliad*, xxiii, 72; Monier Williams, *Indian Wisdom*, pp. 206, 255.

folklore by the absolute veto upon disturbing the graves of the dead.[1]

These facts of Aryan life, indeed, bring us to that sharp contrast which it presents to savage life in its conception of the family. If ancestors are revered and this reverence finds expression in the nature of the funeral customs, so are children brought into the pale of the family by customs indicative of some sacred ceremony connecting the new house inmates with the gods of the race. I agree with Kelly in his interpretation of the stories of the feeding the infant Zeus with the honey from the sacred ash and from bees. 'Among the ancient Germans,' says Kelly, 'that sacred food was the first that was put to the lips of the new-born babe. So it was among the Hindus, as appears from a passage in one of their sacred books. The father puts his mouth to the right ear of the new-born babe, and murmurs three times, 'Speech! Speech!' Then he gives it a name. Then he mixes clotted milk, honey, and butter, and feeds the babe with it out of pure gold. It is found in a surprising shape among one Celtic people. Lightfoot says that in the Highlands of Scotland, at the birth of an infant, the nurse takes a green stick of ash, one end of which she puts into the fire, and while it is burning receives in a spoon the sap that oozes from the other, which she administers to the child as its first food. Some thousands of years ago the ancestors of this Highland nurse had known the *fraxinus ornus* in Arya, and now their descendant, imitating their practice in the cold North, but totally ignorant of its true meaning, puts the nauseous sap of her native ash into the mouth of her hapless charge.'[2] I have quoted this long passage because it shows, as Kelly expresses it, 'the amazing toughness of popular tradition,' and because it brings into contrast the savage practice of the Irish mothers who dedicated their children to the sword. Solinus tells us that the mother put the first food of her new-born son on the sword of her husband, and, lightly introducing it into his mouth, expressed a wish that he might never meet death otherwise than in war and amid arms. Even after the introduction of Christianity the terrible rites of war were kept up at the ceremonials of infancy. Train says that a custom identical with that just quoted from Solinus was kept up, prior to the Union, in Annandale and other places along the Scottish border,[3] and Camden records that the right arm of children was kept unchristened so that it might deal a more deadly blow.[4] The same usage obtained in the borderland of England and Scotland,[5] and it is no

[1] *Choice Notes, Folklore*, p. 8.     [2] Kelly, *Indo-European Folklore*, pp. 145, 146.
[3] *History of Isle of Man*, ii, 84, *note* 1.
[4] *Britannia*, s.v., 'Ireland.'      [5] Guthrie, *Old Scottish Customs*, p. 144.

doubt the parent of the more general custom in the north of England not to wash the right arm of the new-born infant, so that it could the better obtain riches.[1]

Not only are these savage rites in direct contrast to the food rites of the early Aryan birth ceremony, but they also stand out against the relics of Aryan house-birth preserved in folklore, and which are centred round the domestic hearth.[2] The child, put on a cloth spread over a basket containing provisions, was conveyed thrice round the crook of the chimney, or was handed across the fire in those places where the hearth was still in the centre of the room.[3] In Shropshire the first food is a spoonful of butter and sugar.[4]

But, again, there is another contrast to be drawn. It is the father who, according to Pennant, prepares the basket of food and places it across the fire, and it is the father, in more primitive Aryan custom, who mixes the sacred food and first feeds the child. In the Irish rites just noticed it is the mother who acts the part of domestic priest. This contrast is a very significant one. The principle of matriarchy is more primitive than that of patriarchy, and it may point to a distinction of race. The position of the mother in Irish birth rites is not an accidental one. It is of permanent moment as an element in folklore. Mothers in many places retain to this day their maiden names,[5] and this in former days, if not at present, suggests that children followed their mother's rather than their father's name and kindred. The importance of these considerations in connexion with birth ceremonies is clearly shown by the fact of the survival of the singular custom of the 'couvade,' where the husband takes to his bed at the birth of a child and goes through the pretence of being ill. 'The strange custom of the couvade,' says Professor Rhys, 'was known in Ireland, at least in Ulster, and when the great invasion of that province took place under the leadership of Ailill and Medb, with their Firbolg and other forces, they found that all the adult males of the kingdom of Conchobar Mac Nessa were laid up, so that none of them could stir hand or foot to defend his country against invasion excepting Cúchulainn and his father alone.'[6] No doubt this legend takes us into the realms of mythology, to the battles and doings of gods rather than of men; but Professor

---

[1] Henderson, *Folklore of Northern Counties*, p. 16.
[2] Hearn, *Aryan Household*, p. 73.
[3] Gordon Cumming, *In the Hebrides*, p. 101; Dalyell, *Darker Superstitions of Scotland*, p. 176; Pennant, *Tour in the Highlands*, iii, 46.
[4] Burne, *Shropshire Folklore*, p. 284.
[5] Athlone (Mason's *Stat. Acc. of Ireland*, iii, 72); Knockando, Elginshire (*New Stat. Acc. of Scotland*, xiii, 72).
[6] *Celtic Heathendom*, p. 627; *cf.* pp. 140, 363, 471, 482, 627, 646, *Rev. Celt.*, vii, 227.

Rhys has shown good cause for believing that the mythological reason for the death or inactivity of the Ultonian heroes had ceased to be intelligible at an early date, 'long, probably, before any Aryan wanderer had landed in these islands,' and so the persistence of the myth of the Ultonian inactivity naturally came to be interpreted sooner or later in the light of the only custom that seemed to make it intelligible—namely, that of the couvade. Without concerning ourselves about the mythology connected with this particular episode, here is the custom itself standing out clearly and distinctly, and its duration of 'four days and five nights' may be the period allotted to the primitive formula. It is to be traced also in Scotland. A man who had incurred the resentment of Margaret Hutchesone 'that same night took sicknes: and had panes as a woman in chyld-birth.'[1] On the borders of Scotland, as lately as the year 1772, there was pointed out to Mr. Pennant the offspring of a woman whose pains had been transferred to her husband by the midwife. The legends of the saints relate that Merinus, a future bishop, having been refused access to the castle of some Irish potentate whose spouse was then in labour, and treated with contempt, prayed for the transference of her sufferings to him, which ensued immediately.[2] In Yorkshire, too, a custom exists, or existed, which seems without doubt to be a survival of this peculiar custom. 'When an illegitimate child is born it is a point of honour with the girl not to reveal the father, but the mother of the girl goes out to look for him, and the first man she finds keeping his bed is he.'[3] These are the last remnants in custom, as well as in tradition, of a singularly symbolical practice, which had to do with some aspect of society when motherhood, not fatherhood, was the initial point of birth-right, and which, in the opinion of most writers who have investigated the subject, is to be classed as non-Aryan in origin—an opinion which is fortified by its prevalence among the Basque people of today, while elsewhere in Europe it is found only by digging amongst the mass of folklore, and then only in such isolation as to suggest that it does not belong to the main current of traditional peasant life.

Alike, then, in customs relating to the dead and in customs relating to birth there are two streams of thought, not one. The one is savage, the other is Aryan. That both are represented in folklore indicates that they were arrested in their development by some

---

[1] Quoted in Dalyell's *Darker Superstitions*, p. 133.
[2] Pennant, *Tour* 1772, p. 79.
[3] *Academy*, xxv, p. 112. Unfortunately the exact place in Yorkshire where this custom obtains is not stated.

[331]

forces hostile to them, and pushed back to exist as survivals if they were to exist at all. At the moment of this arrest the one must have been practised by savages, and we may postulate that the arresting force was the incoming Aryan culture; the other must have been practised by Aryans, and we may postulate that the arresting force was Christianity. Thus the presence of savage culture and Aryan culture, represented by savages and Aryans, is proved by the evidence of folklore.[1]

## [ 2  GEORGE  LAURENCE  GOMME (b) ]

Gomme's concern with English village institutions dominated his books and can be appreciated in the following address he made to the 1891 folklore congress. He strove to replace the conventional treatment of community history from the perspective of the manor with the view of pre-Aryan tribesmen and Aryan tenants, whose inconspicuous records must be found largely through folklore survivals.

Text from George Laurence Gomme, 'The Non-Aryan Origin of Agricultural Institutions,' *The International Folk-Lore Congress, 1891, Papers and Transactions*. Edited by Joseph Jacobs and Alfred Nutt. London: David Nutt, 1892. Pages 348–56.

It would almost seem as if the comparative method of studying institutions were still on its trial. In other branches of study, philology, mythology, and even archaeology, there is little disposition to dispute the right which this method claims towards elucidating the problems which beset the inquirer. In institutions, however, there has always been a latent notion that the comparative method is not quite satisfactory, and in some quarters it is ignored altogether, while in others its efficacy is openly disputed. It would be profitless, I think, to inquire as to the causes of this objection to the comparative method when applied to the study of institutions, and so I pass on to a consideration of its effect upon one division of the subject which has greatly interested me, namely, agricultural institutions. I shall draw my illustrations from one particular area, namely, the British Isles, because it is only by

---

[1] Mr. Elton declares for the pre-Celtic origin of the sin-eating, among other customs. They 'can hardly be referred to any other origin than the persistence of ancient habits among the descendants of the Silvrian tribes.'——*Origins of English History,* p. 179.

fixing upon some definite area that one can properly test the position which various scholars have taken up.

I put my facts in this way:—(1) In all parts of Great Britain there exist rites, customs, and usages connected with agriculture which are obviously and admittedly not of legislative or political origin, and which present details exactly similar to each other in *character*, but differing from each other in *status*. (2) That the difference in status is to be accounted for by the effects of successive conquests. (3) That the identity in character is not to be accounted for by reference to manorial history, because the area of manorial institutions is not coincident with the area of these rites, customs, and usages. (4) That exact parallels to them exist in India as integral portions of village institutions. (5) That the Indian parallels carry the subject a step further than the European examples because they are stamped with the mark of difference in race-origin, one portion belonging to the Aryan people and the other to the non-Aryan.

I shall now pick out some examples, and explain from them the evidence which seems to me to prove that race-distinction is the key for the origin of these agricultural rites and usages in Europe as in India.

I have dealt with these examples at some length in my recent little book on the village community, though, I fear, very imperfectly. But I venture to think that the opposition to my theory in some quarters is due as much to objection against the principles of the comparative method as against my particular application of them.

My first point is that to get at the survivals of the village community in Britain it is not necessary to approach it through the medium of manorial history. Extremely ancient as I am inclined to think manorial history is, it is unquestionably loaded with an artificial terminology and with the chains so deftly forged by lawyers.

In the table on the next page I give an analysis of the chief features in the types of the English village community, and it will be seen that the manorial element is by no means a common factor in the series.

This clearly shows us the types marking a transition from the tribal form to the village form. In Harris we have the chief with his free tribesmen around him, connected by blood kinship, living in scattered homesteads, just like the German tribes described by Tacitus. Under this tribal community is the embryo of the village community, consisting of smaller tenantry and cottar serfs, who live together in minute villages, holding their land in common and

[333]

yearly distributing the holdings by lot. In this type the tribal constitution is the real factor, and the village constitution the subordinated factor as yet wholly undeveloped, scarcely indeed discernible except by very close scrutiny.

At Kilmorie the tribal community is represented merely by the scattered homesteads. These are occupied by a joint farm-tenantry, who hold their lands upon the system of the village community. Here the village constitution has gradually entered into, so to speak, the tribal constitution, and has almost absorbed it.

| Type | Status | Tribal Constitution | | | | Village Constitution | | | | | Land Rights | |
|---|---|---|---|---|---|---|---|---|---|---|---|---|
| | | Chief | Free tribesmen | Scattered homesteads | Free comial | Tenantry in joint farms | Cottar serfs attached to farmstead | Villeins under manorial system | Municipal evolution | Homesteads grouped in villages | Periodical allotment | Shifting of arable mark |
| Harris | Tribal | + | + | + | | | | | | | | |
| | Village | | | | | + | + | | | | + | |
| Kilmorie | Tribal | | | + | | | | | | | | |
| | Village | | | | | + | + | | | | ⊥ | |
| Heisgeir | Tribal | | | | + | | | | | | | + |
| | Village | | | | | + | | | | + | + | |
| Lauder | Tribal | | | | + | | | | | | | + |
| | Village | | | | | | | | + | + | + | |
| Aston | Tribal | | + | | + | | | | | | | |
| | Manorial | | | | | | | + | | + | + | |
| Rothwell | Tribal | | | | | | | | | | | |
| | Village | | | | | + | | | | + | + | |
| Malmesbury | Tribal | | + | | + | | | | | | | |
| | Municipal | | | | | | | | + | + | + | |
| Hitchin | Tribal | | | | | | | | | | | |
| | Manorial | | | | | | | | + | + | + | |

At Heisgeir and Lauder the tribal community is represented by the last link under the process of dissolution, namely, the free council of the community by which the village rights are governed, while the village community has developed to a considerable extent.

[334]

GEORGE LAURENCE GOMME

At Aston and at Malmesbury the old tribal constitution is still kept alive in a remarkable manner, and I will venture to quote from my book the account of the evolution at Aston of a tenantry from the older tribal constitution, because in this case we are actually dealing with a manor, and the evidence is unique so far as England is concerned.

It will be seen that the village organization, the rights of assembly, the free open-air meetings, and the corporate action incident to the manor of Aston and Cote, attach themselves to the land divisions of sixteen hides, because although these hides had grown in 1657 into a considerable tenancy, fortunately as a tenancy they kept their original unity in full force and so obstinately clung to their old system of government as to keep up by *representation* the once undivided holding of the hide. If the organization of the hide had itself disappeared, it still formed the basis of the village government, the sixteen hides sending up their sixteen *elected* representatives.

How the tenancy grew out of the original sixteen homesteads may perhaps be conjecturally set forth. In the first plan the owners of the yard-lands succeeded to the place originally occupied by the owners of the sixteen hides. Instead of the original sixteen group-owners we have therefore sixty-four individual owners, each yard-land having remained in possession of an owner. And then at succeeding stages of this dissolution we find the yard-lands broken up, until in 1848 'some farmers of Aston have only half or even a quarter of a yard-land, while some have as many as ten or eleven yard-lands in their single occupation.' Then disintegration would proceed to the other proprietary rights, which, originally appendant to the homestead only, became appendant to the person and not to the residence, and are consequently 'brought and sold as separate property, by which means it results that persons resident at Bampton, or even at great distance, have rights on Aston and Cote Common.' And finally we lose all traces of the system, as described by Mr. Horde and as depicted by the representative character of the Sixteens, and in its place find that 'there are some tenants who have rights in the common field and not in the pasture, and *vice versa* several occupiers have the right of pasture who do not possess any portion of arable land in the common field,' so that both yard-lands and hides have now disappeared, and absolute ownership of land has taken their place. Mr. Horde's ms. enables us to proceed back from modern tenancy-holding to the holding by yard-lands; the rights of election in the yard-lands enables us to proceed back to the original holding of the sixteen hides.

[335]

At Hitchin, which is Mr. Seebohm's famous example, we meet with the manorial type. But its features are in no way peculiar. There is nothing which has not its counterpart, in more or less well-defined degree, in the other types which are not manorial. In short, the manorial framework within which it is enclosed does little more than fix the details into an immovable setting, accentuating some at the expense of others, legalizing everything so as to bring it all under the iron sovereignty which was inaugurated by the Angevin kings.

My suggestion is that these examples are but varying types of one original. The Teutonic people, their Celtic predecessors, came to Britain with a tribal, not an agricultural, constitution. In the outlying parts of the land this tribal constitution settled down, and was only slightly affected by the economical conditions of the people they found there; in the more thickly populated parts this tribal constitution was superimposed upon an already existing village constitution in full vigour. We, therefore, find the tribal constitution everywhere—in almost perfect condition in the north, in Wales, and in Ireland, in less perfect condition in England. We also find the village constitution everywhere—in almost embryo form in the north, Wales, and in Ireland; in full vigour and force in England, especially in that area which Professor Rhys has identified as the constant occupation-ground of all the races who have settled in Britain.

Now the factor which is most apparent in all these cases is the singular dual constitution which I have called tribal and village. It is only when we get to such cases as Rothwell and Hitchin that almost all traces of the tribal element are lost, the village element only remaining. But inasmuch as this village element is identical in *kind*, if not in degree, with the village element in the other types, and inasmuch as topographically they are closely connected, we are, I contend, justified in concluding that it is derived from the same original—an original which was composed of a tribal community with a village community in serfdom under it.

This dual element should, I think, be translated into terms of ethnology by appealing to the parallel evidence of India. There the types of the village community are not, as was thought by Sir Henry Maine and others, homogeneous. There the dual element appears, the tribal community at the top of the system, the village community at the bottom of the system. But in India a new factor is introduced by the equation of the two elements with two different races—the tribal element being Aryan, and the village element non-Aryan. Race-origins are there still kept up and rigidly adhered

[336]

to. They have not been crushed out, as in Europe, by politcal or economical activity.

But if crushed out of prominent recognition in Europe, are we, therefore, to conclude that their relics do not exist in peasant custom? My argument is that we cannot have such close parallels in India and in England without seeing that they virtually tell the same story in both countries. It would require a lot of proof to establish that customs, which in India belong now to non-Aryan aborigines and are rejected by the Aryans, are in Europe the heritage of the Aryan race.

The objections to my theory have been formulated recently by Mr. Ashley, who follows Mr. Seebohm and M. Fustel de Coulanges as an adherent of the chronological method of studying institutions. Like the old school of antiquaries, this new school of investigators into the history of institutions get back to the period of Roman history, and there stop. Mr. Ashley suggests that because Caesar describes the Celtic Britons as pastoral, that therefore agriculture in Britain must be post-Celtic. I will not stop to raise the question as to who were the tribes from which Caesar obtained his evidence. But it will suffice to point out that if Caesar is speaking of the Aryan Celts of Britain—and this much seems certain—he only proves of them what Tacitus proves of the Aryan Teutons, what the sagas prove of the Aryan Scandinavians, what the Vedas prove of the Aryan Indians, what philology, in short, proves of the primitive Aryans generally, namely, that they were distinctly hunters and warriors and hated and despised the tillers of the soil.

It does not, in point of fact, then, help the question as to the origin of agricultural rites and usages to turn to Aryan history at all. In this emergency Roman history is appealed to. But this is just one of those cases where a small portion of the facts are squeezed in to do duty for the whole.

Both Fustel de Coulanges and Mr. Seebohm think that if a Roman origin can be *prima facie* shown for the economical side of agricultural institutions, that there is nothing more to be said. But they leave out of consideration a whole set of connected institutions. Readers of Mr. Frazer's *Golden Bough* are now in possession of facts which it would take a very long time to explain. They see that side by side with agricultural economics is an agricultural religion, of great rudeness and barbarity, of considerable complexity, and bearing the stamp of immense antiquity. The same villagers who were the observers of those rules of economics which are thought to be due to Roman origin were also observers of ritual and usages which are known to be savage in theory and practice. Must we, then, say

[337]

that all this ritual and usage is Roman? or must we go on ignoring it as an element in the argument as to origin of agricultural institutions? One or the other of these alternatives must, I contend, be accepted by the inquirer.

At all events, I enter, on behalf of the science of folklore, an earnest protest against this latter 'method of research.' Because the State has chosen or been compelled for political reasons to lift up peasant economics into manorial legal rules, thus forcibly divorcing this portion of peasant life from its natural associations, there is no reason why students should fix upon this arbitrary proceeding as the point to begin their examination into the origin of village agriculture. Manorial tenants pay their dues to the lord, lot out their lands in intermixed strips, cultivate in common, and perform generally all those interesting functions of village life with which Mr. Seebohm has made us all familiar. But, in close and intimate connexion with these selfsame agricultural economical proceedings, it is the same body of manorial tenants who perform irrational and rude customs, who carry the last sheaf of corn represented in human or animal form, who sacrifice animals to their earth deities, who carry fire round fields and crops, who, in a scarcely disguised ritual, still worship deities which there is little difficulty in recognizing as the counterparts of those village goddesses of India who are worshipped and venerated by non-Aryan votaries. Christianity has not followed the lead of politics, and lifted all this portion of peasant agricultural life into something that is religious and definite. And because it remains sanctioned by tradition, we must, in considering origins, take it into account in conjunction with those economic practices which have been unduly emphasized in the history of village institutions. In India, primitive economics and religion go hand in hand as part of the village life of the people; in England, primitive economics and *survivals* of old religions, which we call folklore, go hand in hand as part of the village life of the people. And it is not in the province of students to separate one from the other when they are considering the question of origin.

This is practically the whole of my argument from the folklore point of view. But it is not the whole of the argument against the theory of the Roman origin of the village community. I cannot on this occasion re-state what this argument is, as it is set forth at some length in my book. But I should like to point out that it is in reality supported by arguments to be drawn from ethnological facts. Mr. Ashley surrenders to my view of the question the important point that ethnological data, derived from craniological investigation, fit in 'very readily with the supposition that under the

Celtic, and therefore under the Roman rule, the cultivating class was largely composed of the pre-Celtic race; and allows us to believe that the agricultural population was but little disturbed.' Economically it was certainly not disturbed by the Romans. If the important art of brick-making carried on by Romans in Britain was absolutely lost after their departure; if the agricultural implements known to and used by the Romans were never used in Britain after their departure; if the old methods of land-surveying under the *agrimensores* is not to be traced in Britain as a continuing system; if wattle and daub, rude uncarpentered trees turned root upwards to form roofs, were the leading principies of house-architecture, it cannot be alleged that the Romans left behind any permanent marks of their economical standard upon the 'little disturbed agricultural population.' Why, then, should they be credited with the introduction of a system of lordship and serf-bound tenants, when both lordship and serfdom are to be traced in lands where Roman power has never penetrated, under almost exactly similar conditions to the feudal elements in Europe? It it be accepted that the early agricultural population of Britain was non-Aryan; if we find non-Aryan agricultural rites and festivals surviving as folklore among the peasants of to-day; why should it be necessary, why should it be accepted as a reasonable hypothesis, to go to the imperial and advanced economics of Rome to account for those other elements in the composition of the village community which, equally with the rites and festivals, are to be found paralleled among the non-Aryan population living under an Aryan lordship in India? The only argument for such a process is one of expediency. It does so happen that the Roman theory *may* account for some of the English phenomena. But, then, the Celtic and Teutonic, or Aryan theory, also accounts for the same English phenomena, and, what is more, it accounts for other phenomena not reckoned by the Roman theory. My proposition is that the history of the village community in Britain is the history of the economical condition of the non-Aryan aborigines; that the history of the tribal community is the history of the Aryan conquerors, who appear as overlords; and that the Romans, except as another wave of Aryan conquerors at an advanced stage of civilization, had very little to do with shaping the village institutions of Britain.

## [ 3  ALFRED NUTT ]

The overriding interest of Alfred Nutt lay in the continuities between medieval Celtic literature and modern Gaelic folklore which the folklorist could make manifest. This interest is plainly evinced in one number of the *Popular Studies in Mythology, Romance and Folklore* which he ostensibly devoted to 'The Fairy Mythology of Shakespeare.' This essay synopsized the ideas he had set forth in the second volume of *The Voyage of Bran*. Shakespeare's fairies had from the first attracted England's antiquaries and folklorists, eliciting commentaries by John Brand, Francis Douce, Thomas Keightley, James Orchard Halliwell-Phillips, Thomas Wright, and William John Thoms. Nutt too used the Bard as a springboard and ascribed to Shakespeare's Puck a Celtic basis transmitted through the Arthurian romances. In his Celtic domain the publisher enjoyed a splendid proving ground to test the doctrine of survivals.

Text from Alfred Nutt, *The Fairy Mythology of Shakespeare*. London: David Nutt, 1900. Pages 1–37. *Popular Studies in Mythology, Romance and Folklore*, No. 6 (This text was reprinted with slight changes from Nutt's presidential address of 1897 to The Folk-Lore Society on 'The Fairy Mythology of English Literature: Its Origin and Nature,' printed in *Folk-Lore*, VIII, 1897, pp. 29–53.)

Few things are more marvellous in the marvellous English poetic literature of the last three centuries than the persistence of the fairy note throughout the whole of its evolution. As we pass on from Shakespeare and his immediate followers to Herrick and Milton, through the last ballad writers to Thomson and Gray, and then note in Percy and Chatterton the beginnings of the romantic revival which culminated in Keats and Coleridge, was continued by Tennyson, the Rossettis, and Mr. Swinburne, until in our own days it has received a fresh accession of life alike from Ireland and from Gaelic Scotland, we are never for long without hearing the horns of Elfland faintly winding, never for long are we denied access to

> Charmed magic casements opening on the foam
> Of perilous seas in faery lands forlorn.

We could not blot out from English poetry its visions of the fairyland without a sense of irreparable loss. No other literature save that of Greece alone can vie with ours in its pictures of the land of phantasy and glamour, or has brought back from that mysterious

[340]

realm of unfading beauty treasures of more exquisite and enduring charm.

There is no phenomenon without a cause; but in the immense complexity of historical record it is not always easy to detect the true cause, and to trace its growth and working until the result delight us. Why does the fairy note ring so perfectly throughout that literature of modern England which has its roots in and which derives the best of its life's blood from the wonderful half-century: 1580–1630? Reasons, causes must exist, nor—let me here forestall a possible objection—do we wrong genius by seeking to discover them. Rather, I hope, may individual genius, however pre-eminent, acquire fresh claims to our love and gratitude when we note that it is no arbitrary and isolated phenomenon, but stands in necessary relation to the totality of causes and circumstances which have shaped the national character. And, should we find these causes and circumstances still potent for influence, may we not look forward with better confidence to the future of our poetic literature?

Early in the half-century of which I have just spoken, some time between 1590 and 1595, appeared the *Midsummer Night's Dream*, the crown and glory of English delineation of the fairy world. Scarce any one of Shakespeare's plays has had a literary influence so immediate, so widespread, and so enduring. As pictured by Shakespeare, the fairy realm became, almost at once, a convention of literature in which numberless poets sought inspiration and material. I need only mention Drayton, Ben Jonson, Herrick, Randolph, and Milton himself. Apart from any question of its relation to popular belief, of any grounding in popular fancy, Shakespeare's vision stood by itself, and was accepted as the ideal presentment of fairydom which, for two centuries at least, has signified to the average Englishman of culture the world depicted in the *Midsummer Night's Dream*. To this day, works are being produced deriving form and circumstance and inspiration (such as it is) wholly from Shakespeare.

Now if we compare these literary presentations of Faery, based upon Shakespeare, with living folklore, where the latter has retained the fairy belief with any distinctness, we find almost complete disagreement; and if, here and there, a trait seems common, it is either of so general a character as to yield no assured warrant of kinship, or there is reason to suspect contamination of the popular form by the literary ideal derived from and built up out of Shakespeare. Yet if we turn back to the originator of literary fairyland, to the poet of the *Midsummer Night's Dream*, we can detect in *his* picture all the essentials of the fairy creed as it has appealed, and

[341]

still appeals, to the faith and fancy of generations more countless than ever acknowledged the sway of any of the great world-religions, we can recover from it the elements of a conception of life and nature older than the most ancient recorded utterance of earth's most ancient races.

Whence, then, did Shakespeare draw his account of the fairy world? As modern commentators have pointed out, from at least two sources: the folk-belief of his day and the romance literature of the previous four centuries. This or that trait has been referred to one or the other source; the differences between these two have been dwelt upon, and there, as a rule, the discussion has been allowed to rest. What I shall essay to prove is that in reality sixteenth-century folk-belief and mediaeval fairy romance have their ultimate origin in one and the same set of beliefs and rites; that the differences between them are due to historical and psychological causes, the working of which we can trace; that their reunion, after ages of separation, in the England of the late sixteenth century, is due to the continued working of those same causes; and that, as a result of this reunion, which took place in England because in England alone it could take place, English poetry became free of Fairydom, and has thus been enabled to preserve for the modern world a source of joy and beauty which must otherwise have perished.

I observed just now that the modern literary presentation of Faery (which is almost wholly dependent upon Shakespeare) differed essentially from the popular one still living in various districts of Europe, nowhere, perhaps, more tenaciously than in some of the Celtic-speaking portions of these isles. I may here note, according to the latest, and in this respect the best, editor of the *Midsummer Night's Dream*, Mr. Chambers, what are the characteristics of the Shakespearian fairies. He ranges them as follows:—

(*a*) They form a community under a king and queen. (*b*) They are exceedingly small. (*c*) They move with extreme swiftness. (*d*) They are elemental *airy* spirits; their brawls incense the wind and moon, and cause tempests; they take a share in the life of nature; live on fruit; deck the cowslips with dewdrops; war with noxious insects and reptiles; overcast the sky with fog, &c. (*e*) They dance in orbs upon the green. (*f*) They sing hymns and carols to the moon. (*g*) They are invisible and apparently immortal. (*h*) They come forth mainly at night. (*i*) They fall in love with mortals. (*j*) They steal babies and leave changelings. (*k*) They come to bless the best bride-bed and make the increase thereof fortunate.

[342]

This order of characteristics is, I make little doubt, what would occur to most well-read Englishmen, and denotes what impressed the fancy of Shakespeare's contemporaries and of the after-world. The fairy community, with its quaintly fantastic parody of human circumstance; the minute size and extreme swiftness of the fairies, which insensibly assimilate them in our mind to the winged insect world—these traits would strike us at first blush, and these have been insisted upon and developed by the imitators of Shakespeare; only on second thoughts should we note their share in the life of nature, should we recall their sway over its benign and malign manifestations, and this side of fairy activity is wholly ignored by later fairy literature.

Yet a moment's reflection will convince us that the characteristics upon which Shakespeare seems to lay most stress, which have influenced later poets and story-tellers, and to which his latest editor assigns the first place, are only secondary, and can in no way explain either how the fairy belief arose nor what was its real hold upon popular imagination. The peasant stooping over his spade, toilfully winning his bread from Mother Earth, was scarce so enamoured with the little he knew of kings and queens that he must feign the existence of an invisible realm; nor would the contrast, which touches alike our fantasy and our sense of the ludicrous, between minute size and superhuman power appeal to him. The peasant had far other cause to fear and reverence the fairy world. In his daily struggle with nature he could count upon fairy aid if he performed with due ceremony the ancient ritual handed down to him by his forefathers; but woe betide him if, through carelessness or sluttish neglect of these rites, he aroused fairy wrath—not help, but hindrance and punishment would be his lot. And if neglect was hateful to these mysterious powers of nature, still more so was prying interference—they work as they list, and when man essays to change and, in his own conceit, to better the old order, the fairy vanishes. All this the peasant knows; it is part of that antique religion of the soil which means so much more to him than our religions do to us, because upon it, as he conceives, depend his and his children's sustenance. But be he as attentive as he may to the rites by which the fairy world may be placated and with which it must be worshipped, there come times and seasons of mysterious calamity, convulsions in the invisible world, and then—

> The ox hath therefore stretch'd his yoke in vain,
> The ploughman lost his sweat, and the green corn
> Hath rotted ere his youth attain'd a beard;

> The fold stands empty in the drowned field,
> And crows are fatted with the murrion flock.
>
> . . . . . . . . . . . . . .
>
> No night is now with hymn or carol blest;
> Therefore the moon, the governess of floods,
> Pale in her anger, washes all the air,
> That rheumatic diseases do abound:
> And thorough this distemperature we see
> The seasons alter.

Such calamities are luckily rare, though, as the peasant full well knows, the powers he dreads and believes in can—

> . . . overcast the night,
> The starry welkin cover up anon
> With drooping fog as black as Acheron.

But as a rule, they are kindlier disposed; not alone do they war with blight, and fog, and flood, and all powers hostile to the growth of vegetation, but increase of flock and herd, of mankind also, seems good in their eyes—it may be because they know their tithes will be duly paid, and that their own interests are inextricably bound up with that of the mortals whom they aid and mock at, whom they counsel and reprove and befool.

Here let me note that not until the peasant belief has come into the hands of the cultured man do we find the conception of an essential incompatibility between the fairy and the human worlds— of the necessary disappearance of the one before the advance of the other. Chaucer, if I mistake not, first voiced this conception in English literature. In words to be quoted presently, he relegates the fairies to a far backward of time, and assigns their disappearance, satirically it is true, to the progress of Christianity. To the peasant, fairydom is part of the necessary machinery by which the scheme of things, as known to him, is ordered and governed; he may wish for less uncanny deities, but he could not conceive the world without them; their absence is no cause of rejoicing, rather of anxiety as due to his own neglect of the observances which they expect and which are the price of their favour.

I do not, of course, claim that the foregoing brief sketch of the psychological basis of the fairy creed, as exemplified in still living beliefs of the peasantry throughout Europe, represents the view of it taken by Shakespeare and his literary contemporaries, but yet it is based wholly upon evidence they furnish. And if we turn to the bald and scanty notes of English fairy mythology, to which we can

[344]

with certainty assign a date earlier than the *Midsummer Night's Dream*, we shall find what may be called the rustic element of the fairy creed insisted upon, proportionately, to a far greater extent than in Shakespeare. Reginald Scot and the few writers who allude to the subject at all, ignore entirely the delicate fantastic traits that characterize Shakespeare's elves; they are wanting precisely in what we, with an ideal derived from Shakespeare in our mind, should call the 'fairylike' touch; they are rude and coarse and earthy. And, not implicitly, but explicitly, a conception of the true nature of these peasant deities found expression in Shakespeare's own days. At the very time the *Midsummer Night's Dream* was being composed or played, Nash wrote as follows: 'The Robin-good-fellows, elfs, fairies, hobgoblins of our latter age, which idolatrous former days and the fantastical world of Greece ycleped Fauns, Satyrs, Dryads, Hamadryads, did most of their pranks in the night'—a passage in which the parallel suggested is far closer and weightier in import than its author imagined.

The popular element in Shakespeare's fairy mythology is, then, the same as that testified to by somewhat earlier writers, but touched with the finest spirit alike of grace and humour, and presented in a form exquisitely poetical. Naturally enough it is accidental and secondary characteristics of the fairy world which are emphasized by the poet, who is solely concerned with what may heighten the beauty or enliven the humour of his picture. But with his unerring instinct for what is vital and permanent in that older world of legend and fancy, to which he so often turned for inspiration, he has yet retained enough to enable us to detect the essence of the fairy conception, in which we must needs recognize a series of peasant beliefs and rites of a singularly archaic character. If we further note that, so far as the outward guise and figure of his fairies is concerned, Shakespeare is borne out by a series of testimonies reaching back to the twelfth-century Gervase of Tilbury and Gerald the Welshman, who give us glimpses of a world of diminutive and tricky sprites—we need not dwell longer at present upon this aspect of Elfland, but can turn to the fay of romance.

It is evident that Shakespeare derived both the idea of a fairy realm reproducing the external aspect of a mediaeval court, and also the name of his fairy king from mediaeval romance, that is, from the Arthurian cycle, from those secondary works of the Charlemagne cycle, which, like Huon of Bordeaux, were modelled upon the Arthur romances, and from the still later purely literary imitations alike of the Arthur and the Charlemagne stories. But the Oberon of romance has been regarded as a being totally different in essence and origin from the Robin Goodfellow, the Puck of peasant belief, and their bringing together in the *Midsummer Night's Dream* as an inspiration of individual genius. I hope to show that the two strands of fiction have a common source, and that their union, or rather reunion, is due to deeper causes than any manifestation, however potent, of genius.

What has hitherto been overlooked, or all too insufficiently noted, is the standing association of the fairy world of mediaeval romantic literature with Arthur. Chaucer, in a passage to which I have already alluded, proclaims this unhesitatingly:—

> In the olde daies of the King Arthoure,
> Of which that Bretons speken grete honoure,
> Al was this land fulfild of fayerye;
> The elf-queen with hyr jolly companye
> Danced ful oft in many a greene mede.

We first meet the mediaeval fairy in works of the Arthur cycle as ladies of the lake and fountain, as dwellers in the far-off island paradise of Avalon, as mistresses of or captives in mysterious castles, the enchantments of which may be raised by the dauntless knight whose guerdon is their love and never-ending bliss, these fantastic beings play a most important part in the world of dream and magic haze peopled by Arthur and his knights and their lady-loves. If an instance be needed how vital is the connexion between Arthur and Faery, it is furnished by the romance of Huon of Bordeaux. As far as place and circumstance and personages are concerned, this romance belongs wholly to the Charlemagne cycle; in it Oberon makes his first appearance as king of Faery, and it is his role to protect and sustain the hero, Huon, with the ceaseless indefatigable indulgence which the supernatural counsellor so often displays towards his mortal protégé alike in heroic legend and in popular tale. He finally leaves him his kingdom; but before Huon can enjoy it Oberon must make peace between him and Arthur. 'Sir, you know well that your realme and dignity you gave me after your decease,' says the British king. In spite of the Carolingian setting, Huon of Bordeaux is at heart an Arthurian hero; and the teller of his fortunes knew full well that Arthur was the claimant to the throne of Faery, the rightful heir to the lord of fantasy and glamour and illusion.

Dismissing for a while consideration of the Arthurian fay, we may ask what is the Arthurian romance, and whence comes it? For ample discussion of these points I must refer to Nos. 1 and 4 of these Studies. To put it briefly, the Arthurian romance is the Norman-

French and Anglo-Norman re-telling of a mass of Celtic fairy tales partly mythic, partly heroic in the shape under which they became known to the French-speaking world, tales which reached the latter alike from Brittany and from Wales in the course of the eleventh and twelfth centuries. Some of these fairy tales have come down to us in Welsh in a form entirely unaffected by French influence, others more or less affected, whilst some of the Welsh versions are simple translations from the French. The nearest analogues to these Welsh-Breton fairy tales, preserved to us partly in a Welsh, but mostly in a French dress, are to be found in Ireland. That country possesses a romantic literature which, so far as interest and antiquity of record are concerned, surpasses that of Wales, and which, in the majority of cases where comparison is possible, is obviously and undoubtedly more archaic in character. The relation between these two bodies of romantic fiction, Irish and Welsh, has not yet been satisfactorily determined. It seems most likely either that the Welsh tales represent the mythology and heroic legend of a Gaelic race akin to the Irish conquered by the Brythons (Welsh), but, as happens at times, passing their traditions on to their conquerors; or else that the Irish story-tellers, the dominant literary class in the Celtic world throughout the sixth, seventh, and eighth centuries, imposed their literature upon Wales. It is not necessary to discuss which of these two explanations has the most in its favour; in either case we must quit Britain and the woodland glades of Shakespeare's Arden and turn for a while to Ireland.

Examining the fairy belief of modern Ireland or of Gaelic Scotland, we detect at once a great similarity between it and English folklore, whether recoverable from living tradition or from the testimony of Shakespeare and other literature. Many stories and incidents are common to both, many traits and characteristics of the fairy folk are similar. This is especially the case if we rely upon Irish writers, like Crofton Croker, for instance, who were familiar with the English literary tradition, and may possibly have been influenced by it. But closer examination and reference to more genuinely popular sources reveal important differences. To cite one marked trait, the Irish fairies are by no means necessarily or universally regarded as minute in stature. Two thoroughly competent observers, one, Mr. Leland Duncan, working in North Ireland,[1] the other, Mr. Jeremiah Curtin, in South Ireland,[2] agree decisively as to this; fairy and mortal are not thought of as differing in size.

[1] *Folk-Lore*, June 1896.
[2] *Cf. Tales of the Fairies and of the Ghost World, collected from Oral Tradition in South-West Munster*, London, 1895.

But what chiefly impresses the student of Irish fairy tradition is the fact that the fairy folk are far more definitely associated with special districts and localities and tribes and families than is the case in England.

We can detect among them a social organization in many respects akin to that of mankind; we can draw up a map of fairy Ireland and say—Here rules this chieftain, there that chieftainess has sway— nay more, these potentates of the invisible realm are named; we are informed as to their alliances and relationships; we note that their territory and interests seem at times to tally with those of the great septs which represent the tribal organization of ancient Ireland. O'Brien is not more definitely connected with Munster, O'Connor with Connaught, than is this or that fairy clan.

If we turn from tradition as still recoverable from the lips of the Irish-speaking population of today, and investigate the extremely rich store of romantic narratives which, preserved in Irish MSS. dating from 1100 A.D. to fifty years ago, represent an evolution of romance extending over fully 1000 years (for the oldest MSS. carry us back some 200 to 300 years from the date of their transcription), we meet the same supernatural personages as figure in contemporary folklore, playing often the same part, endowed with traits and characteristics of a similar kind. Century by century we can trace them back, their attributes varying in detail, but the essence of their being persisting the same, until at last the very oldest texts present them under an aspect so obviously mythological that every unprejudiced and competent student of Irish tradition has recognized in them the dispossessed inmates of an Irish Pantheon. This mysterious race is known in Irish mythic literature as the Tuatha de Danann, the folk of the goddess Danu, and in some of the very oldest Irish tales, tales certainly 900, perhaps 1100 years old, they are designated by the same term applied to them by the Irish peasant of today, *aes sidhe*, the folk of the *sidhe* or fairy hillocks.

The tales in which this wizard race figures fall into two well-defined classes. By far the larger portion are heroic sagas, tales, that is, which describe and exalt the prowess, valour, and cunning of famous champions or chiefs. There are several well-defined cycles of heroic saga in Irish tradition, and their personages are assigned to periods centuries apart. Yet the Tuatha de Danann figure equally in the various cycles—chiefs and champions die and pass away, not they. Undying, unfading, masters and mistresses of inexhaustible delight, supreme in craft and counsel, they appear again and again as opponents and protectors of mortal heroes, as wooers of mortal maidens, as lady-loves of valiant champions. The part they play in these sagas may be more or less prominent, but its character is always secondary; they exist in the story for the convenience of the mortal hero or heroine, to aid in the accomplishment of the humanly impossible, to act as a foil to mortal valour or beauty, to bestow upon mortal champions or princesses the boon of immortal love.

Such is, all too briefly sketched, the nature of this body of romantic fiction. Whoso is familiar with Arthurian romance detects at once an underlying similarity of conception, plot, and incident. In both, specially, does the woman of the immortal race stand before us in clearer outline and more vivid colouring than the man. Nor is the reason far to seek: the mortal hero is the centre of attraction; the love of the fairy maiden, who comes from her wonderland of eternal joys lured by his fame, is the most striking token and the highest guerdon of his prowess. To depict her in the most brilliant colours is the most effectual way to heighten his glory.

Both these bodies of romantic fiction, Irish and Arthurian, are in the main variations upon one set of themes—the love of immortal for mortal, the strife or friendly comradeship between hero and god or fairy.

If we now turn back to the living folk-belief of the Irish peasant after our survey of the mediaeval romantic literature, we are seemingly at fault. The fairies are the lineal descendants of the Tuatha de Danann; name and attributes and story can be traced, and yet the outcome is so different. The Irish peasant belief of today is agricultural in its scope and intent, as is the English—the Irish fairies are bestowers of increase in flock and herd, protectors and fosterers of vegetation, jealous guardians of ancient country rites. In spite of identity of name and attribute, can these beings be really the same as the courtly, amorous wizard-knights and princesses of the romances? The difference is as great as between the Oberon and Puck of Shakespeare. And yet, as we have seen, the historical connexion is undeniable; in Ireland, the unity of the fairy world has never been lost sight of, as it has in England.

Hitherto I have brought before you stories in which the Tuatha de Danann play a subordinate part because the mortal hero or heroine has to be glorified. But there exists also a group of stories in which these beings are the sole actors, which are wholly concerned with their fortunes. We are in a position to demonstrate that these stories belong to a very early stratum of Irish mythic literature. After the introduction of Christianity into Ireland, the tales told of the Tuatha de Danann, the old gods, seem to have considerably exercised the minds of the literary and priestly classes. They were too widely popular to be discarded—how then should they be dealt with? One way was to minimize the fantastic supernatural element and to present the residuum as the sober history of kings and heroes who had lived in the dim ages before Christ. This way was taken, and a large body of resulting literature has come down to us. But a certain number of fragmentary stories, and one long one, to which this minimizing, rationalizing process has been applied scarcely if at all, have also been preserved; and these must obviously be older than the rationalized versions. And as the latter can be traced back to the eighth and ninth centuries of our era, the former must belong to the earliest stages of Irish fiction.

Now if we examine these few remains of Irish mythology as contradistinguished from Irish heroic legend, we no longer find the Tuatha de Danann, as in the latter, figuring mainly as amorous wizards and love-lorn princesses whose chief occupation is to intrigue with or against some mortal hero or heroine—they come before us as the divine *dramatis personae* of a series of myths the theme of which is largely the agricultural prosperity of Ireland; they are associated with the origin and regulation of agriculture, to them are ascribed the institution of festivals and ceremonies which are certainly of an agricultural character. I cannot here give the evidence in any detail, but I may quote one or two instances. The mythology told of the struggles of the Tuatha de Danann against other clans of supernatural beings; in one of these struggles they overcome their adversaries and capture their king; about to be slain, he seeks to save his life; he offers that the kine of Ireland shall always be in milk, but this does not avail him; then that the men of Ireland should reap a harvest every quarter of the year, but his foes are inexorable; finally, he names the lucky days for ploughing and sowing and reaping, and for this he is spared. The mythology which relates the triumph of the Tuatha de Danann also chronicles their discomfiture at the hands of the sons of Mil; but even after these have established their sway over the whole of visible Ireland and driven the Tuatha de Danann into the shelter of the hollow hill, they still have to make terms with them. The chief of the Tuatha de Danann is the Dagda, and this is what an early story-teller says of him: 'Great was the power of the Dagda over the sons of Mil, even after the conquest of Ireland; for his subjects destroyed their corn and milk, so that they must needs make a treaty of peace with the Dagda. Not until then, and thanks to his goodwill, were they able to harvest corn and drink the milk of their cows.'

There runs, moreover, throughout these stories a vein of rude and gross buffoonery which contrasts strongly with the character assigned to the Tuatha de Danann in the heroic sagas.

The true character of this mysterious race may now seem evident, and their substantial identity with the fairy of living peasant lore require no further demonstration. But I must quote one passage which shows that the ancient Irish not only possessed a mythology, but also an organized ritual, and that this ritual was of an agricultural sacrificial nature. A tradition, which is at least as old as the eighth century of our era, ascribes to Patrick the destruction of Cromm Cruaich and his twelve fellow-idols which stood on the plains of Mag Slecht. Here is what Irish mythic legend has to tell of the worship paid to the Cromm:—

He was their god.

. . . . . . . . . . . .

To him without glory
They would kill their piteous wretched offspring,
With much wailing and peril,
To pour their blood around Cromm Cruaich.
Milk and corn
They would ask from him
In return for one-third of their healthy issue.

Such then are the Irish Tuatha de Danann, beings worshipped at the outset with bloody sacrifices in return for the increase of flock and herd and vegetable growth; associated in the oldest mythological tales with the origin and welfare of agriculture; figuring in the oldest heroic tales as lords of a wonderland of inexhaustible delights, unfading youth, and insatiable love; still the objects of peasant reverence and dread; called to this very day, as they were called centuries ago, and still retaining much of the hierarchical organization and material equipment due to their incorporation in the higher imaginative literature of the race.

The chain of development which can be followed in Ireland can only be surmised in England; but the Irish analogy allows, I think, the conclusion that the fairy of English romance has the same origin as the Tuatha de Danann wizard hero or princess of Irish romance—in other words, the same ultimate origin as the elf or Puck of peasant belief. Oberon and Puck would thus be members of one clan of supernatural beings, and not arbitrarily associated by the genius of Shakespeare.

Here let me forestall a possible objection. Shakespeare's fairies are, it may be said, Teutonic, and only Celtic evidence has been

[351]

adduced in favour of my thesis. I would answer that, so far as the matter in hand is concerned, the antithesis of Celtic and Teutonic is an imaginary one. I use Celtic evidence because, owing to historical causes I shall touch upon presently, Celtic evidence alone is available. That evidence carries us back to a period long antedating the rise of Christianity; and at that period there was, I believe, substantial agreement between Teuton and Celt in their conception of the processes of nature and in the rites and practices by which the relations between man and nature were regulated. The fairy belief of the modern German peasant is closely akin to that of the modern Irish peasant, as indeed to that of the Slavonic or Southern peasant, not because one has borrowed from the other, but because all go back to a common creed expressing itself in similar ceremonies. The attempt to discriminate modern national characteristics in the older stratum of European folklore is not only idle but mischievous, because it is based upon the unscientific assumption that existing differences, which are the outcome of comparatively recent historical conditions, have always existed. I will only say that, possibly, the diminutive size of the fairy race belongs more especially to Teutonic tradition as developed within the last 2,000 years, and that in so far the popular element in Shakespeare's fairy world may be Teutonic rather than Celtic.

No, the fairy creed the characteristics of which I have essayed to indicate, and which I have brought into organic connexion with the oldest remains of Celtic mythology, was, I hold, common to all the Aryan-speaking people of Europe, to the ancestors of Greek and Roman and Slav, as well as to the ancestors of Celt and Teuton. I leave aside the question of its origin: the Aryans may, as some hold, have taken over and developed the ruder faith of the soil-tilling races whom they subjugated and upon whom they imposed their speech. I content myself with noting that it was the common faith of Aryan-speaking Europeans, and further, that Greeks and Celts have preserved its earliest forms, and have embodied it most largely in the completed fabric of their mythology. Let us hark back to Nash's parallel of elves and Robin Goodfellows with the fauns and satyrs of the fantastical world of Greece. The parallel is a valid and illuminating one, for the fauns and satyrs are of the train of Dionysus, and Dionysus in his oldest aspect is a divinity of growth, vegetable and animal, worshipped, placated, and strengthened for his task, upon the due performance of which depends the material welfare of mankind, by ritual sacrifice.

Dionysus was thus at first a god of much the same nature, and standing on the same plane of development, as, by assumption, the

Irish Tuatha de Danann. But in his case the accounts are at once fairly early and extensive, in theirs late and scanty. I have quoted, for instance, almost the only direct piece of information we have concerning the ritual of the Irish gods; that of the Greek god, on the other hand, which survived, in a modified and attenuated form, far down into historic times, is known to us in detail. It undoubtedly consisted originally in an act of sacrifice, animal or human, shared in by all the members of a community, who likewise shared the flesh of the victim, which was applied to invigorate alike the indwelling spirit of vegetation and the participating worshippers, who thus entered into communion with their god. The circumstances of these sacrificial rites were originally of savage horror, and the participants were wrought up to a pitch of the wildest frenzy in which they passed beyond the ordinary limits of sense and effort.

Greek evidence not only allows us to reconstitute this ancient ritual, shared in at one time by all Aryan-speaking Europeans; it also enables us to establish a psychological basis upon which the complex and often apparently inconsistent beliefs connected with the fairy world can be reared and built into an orderly structure of thought and imagination. The object of the sacrifice is to reinforce the life alike of nature and of the worshipper; but this implies a conception, however crude, of unending and ever-changing vital essence persisting under the most diverse manifestations: hence the powers worshipped and appealed to, as they slowly crystallize into definite individualities, are necessarily immortal and as necessarily masters of all shapes—the fairy and his realm are unchanging and unfading, the fairy can assume all forms at will. Again, bestower of life and increase as he is, he must by definition, be liberal and amorous— alike in romance and popular belief, the fairy clan is characterized by inexhaustible wealth and by an amiable readiness to woo and be wooed. The connexion of the fairy world with the rites of rustic agriculture is so natural on this hypothesis as to need no further demonstration; but on any other hypothesis it is difficult if not impossible to explain.

I would only note that the practice of actual sacrifice has but recently become extinct, even if it be extinct; and where actually extinct it is represented by survivals, such as passing an animal through the smoke of the bonfire. I would also urge that the love of neatness and orderly method so characteristic of the fairy world is easily referable to a time when all the operations of rural life formed part of a definite religious ritual, every jot and tittle of which must be carried out with minute precision. Similarly, the practice of carrying off human children has its roots in the conception of the fairy as the lord and giver of life. For, reasoned early man, life is not an inexhaustible product, the fairy must be fed as well as the mortal; hence the necessity for sacrifice, for renewing the stock of vitality which the fairy doled out to his devotee. But this source of supply might be insufficient, and the lords of life might, from the outset, be regarded as on the look-out for fresh supplies; or else, when the practice of sacrifice fell into disuse, the toll levied regularly in the old days upon human life might come to wear in the popular mind the aspect of raids upon human by an unhuman society.

Whilst many of the phenomena of fairydom thus find a reasonable—nay, inevitable—interpretation in the conceptions inherent to the cult, others are referable to the ritual in which it found expression. The participants in these rites met by night; by rapid motion prolonged to exhaustion, by the monotonous repetition of music maddening to the senses, by sudden change from the blackness of night to the fierce flare of torch and bonfire—in short, by all the accompaniments of the midnight worship which we know to have characterized the cult of Dionysus among the mountains of Thrace, and which we may surmise to have characterized similar cults elsewhere, they provoked the god-possessed ecstasy in which Maenad and Bassarid, with senses exacerbated to insensibility, rent asunder the living victim and devoured his quivering flesh. The devotees were straightway justified in their faith; for in this state of ecstasy they became one with the object of their worship; his powers and attributes were theirs for the time; they passed to and were free of his wonderland, full of every delight that could allure and gratify their senses.

Have we not in rites such as these the source of tales found everywhere in the peasant fairy lore of Europe and represented with special vividness in Celtic folklore? At night the belated wanderer sees the fairy host dancing their rounds on many a green mead; allured by the strange enchantment of the scene he draws near, he enters the round. If he ever reappears, months, years, or even centuries have passed, seeming but minutes to him, so keen and allabsorbing has been the joy of that fairy-dance. But oftener he never returns, and is known to be living on in Faery, in the land of undeath and unalloyed bliss.

Here, if I am right, living tradition has preserved the memory of a cult which the Greek of two thousand years back held to be of immemorial antiquity. Historical mythology and current tradition confirm and interpret each other. Yet it would, I think, be an error to regard the persistence and wide spread of the story as due solely to the impression made upon the popular mind by the fierce and dark rites of which it is an echo. Rather has it survived because it sums up in one vivid symbol so many aspects of the fairy world. It not only kept alive a memory, it satisfied a psychological demand.

Indeed, when an incident has become an organic portion of a myth—and to do this it must fulfil logical and psychological requirements which are none the less real because they differ from those which civilized men would frame—the connexion persists so long as the myth retains a spark of life. We saw that the deities which were gradually elaborated out of the primitive spirits of vegetation are essentially amorous and endowed with the power of transformation or reincarnation. A vivid form of expressing this idea is to represent the god amorous of a mortal maiden, and father by her of a semi-divine son whose nature partakes of his own, and who is at times a simple incarnation of himself. What further contributed to the vogue and persistence of this incident was that it lent itself admirably to the purposes of heroic legend; the eponymous founder, the hero *par excellence* of a race, could always be connected in this way with the clan of the immortals. We meet the incident at all stages of development. At times, as in the case of Arthur, or of Cuchulinn, son of the Irish Apollo-Dionysus, Lug, it has become wholly heroicized, and the semi-divine child has to conform to the heroic standard; at other times, as in the case of Merlin, or of Mongan, son of the Irish sea-god, Manannan mac Lir, the wonder-child manifests his divine origin by craft and guile rather than by strength and valour; in especial, he possesses the art of shape-shifting, which early man seems to have regarded as the most valuable attribute of godhead. We should not at first blush associate merry Puck with these semi-divine heroes and wizards. Yet consider the tract entitled *Robin Goodfellow; His Mad Pranks and Merry Jests, &c.*, the only known edition of which bears the date 1628; it has been much debated if it was composed before or after the *Midsummer Night's Dream*. Mr. Chambers inclines to the latter opinion. In this tract, Robin Goodfellow is son of the fairy king by a maiden whom he came nightly to visit, 'but early in the morning he would go his way, whither she knew not, he went on suddainly.' Later, the son has a vision, in which he beholds the dances and hears the strains of fairyland, and when he awakes he finds lying by his side a scroll, beginning with these words:

Robin, my only sonne and heire,

in which the father promises, amongst other gifts:

[355]

> Thou hast the power to change thy shape
> To horse, to hog, to dog, to ape;

and assures him:

> If thou observe my just command
> One day thou shalt see Fayry Land.

I believe that in this doggrel chapbook we have the worn-down form of the same incident found in the legends of Arthur and Merlin, of Cuchulinn and Mongan, told also in Greek mythology of no less a person than Dionysus, son of Zeus and Semele, the mischievous youth who, as we learn from the Homeric Hymn, amused himself in frightening Greek sailors by transformation tricks of much the same nature as those dear to Puck.

We may now revert to our starting-point, to the question why should the fairy world be specially prominent in English literature, a question which, if asked before, has doubtless been answered by unmeaning generalities about national temperament. But national temperament is the outcome of historic conditions and circumstances which exist none the less though we cannot always trace them. In essaying an answer I will pick up the various dropped threads of the investigation and endeavour to weave them into one connected strand.

Mythology presupposes beliefs, and also rites in which those beliefs find practical expression. Rites comprise forms of words and symbolic acts. The form of words, the liturgic chant, may develop into a narrative, the symbolic act may require explanation and give rise to another narrative. As the intellectual and religious horizon of the worshipping race widens, these narratives are amplified, are differentiated, are enriched with new fancies and conceptions. In course of time the narratives crystallize around special divine beings; and as these latter develop and acquire fresh attributes, so their attendant narrative groups, their myths, may come to transcend the germ whence they have sprung, and to symbolize conceptions of such far wider scope as to obscure the connexion between origin and completed growth. This happened in Greece with the Dionysus myths, but not until they had been noted at such a stage as to allow recognition of their true nature. Greek mythology in its later forms conquered Rome, entirely driving out the old Roman myths (many of which had probably progressed little beyond the agricultural stage), although the religious conservatism of Rome maintained the rites themselves in an archaic form. Rome conquered Southern and much of Western Europe and imposed late

[356]

Greek mythology in Latin dress upon these lands. But in Western Europe, Ireland wholly, and Britain partly, escaped Roman influence. Celtic mythology, starting from the same basis as Greek Dionysus mythology, was left at liberty to develop upon its own lines. The Greek Dionysiac myths, expanding with the marvellous expansion of the Hellenic genius, grew away from their primitive rustic basis, and connexion was broken between the peasant creed and the highest imaginative literature. Celtic mythology developed likewise, but to an extent as far less as the Celt had lagged behind the Greek in the race of civilization. The old Irish gods, themselves an outcome of the primitive agricultural creed, were worked into the heroic legends of the race, and suffered transformation into the wizard champions and enchantresses of the romances, but they never lost touch with their earliest forms; the link between the fairy of the peasant and the fairy of literature (for heroic saga *is* literature although traditional literature) was never wholly snapped; and when the time came for the highest imagination of mankind to turn to the old pre-Christian world for inspiration, in these islands alone was there a literary convention which still led back to the wealth of incident and symbol preserved by the folk. In these islands alone, I say, and why? Because the Arthurian romance, that form of imaginative literature which revealed Celtic mythology to the world, although it entered English literature later than it did that of France or Germany, although France first gave it to all mankind, and Germany bestowed upon it its noblest mediaeval form, yet was at home here, whilst on the Continent it was an alien. When the destined hour struck, and the slumbering princess of Faery should awake, it was the youngest quester who gave the releasing kiss and won her to be his bride; if we seek their offspring, we may find it in the English poetry of the last three centuries.

When the destined hour had struck! for the princess might not be roused from her slumber before the appointed time. We all know the sixteenth century as the age of Renaissance and Reformation. But what precisely is implied by these words? For over a thousand years the compromise come to between Christianity and the pre-Christian world had subsisted, subject, as are all things, to fluctuation and modification, but retaining substantially its outline and animating spirit. At last it yielded before the onslaught of two different forces—one, sympathetic knowledge of the pre-Christian classic world, resulting in the Renaissance, and the other, desire to revert to the earliest form of Christianity before the latter had effected its compromise with classic civilization, resulting in the Reformation. The men who had passed through the impact of these

[357]

forces upon their hearts and brains could no longer look upon the pre-Christian world, under whatever form it appeared to them, with the same eyes as the men of the Middle Ages. It stimulated their curiosity, it touched their imagination, it was fraught to them with problems and possibilities their predecessors never dreamt of. Throughout the literature of the sixteenth century we may note the same pre-occupation with romantic themes which are older than, and outside, Christianity. In Italy, as was but natural, the purely classic side of the revival predominated, and the romantic poems of Pulci, Berni, and Ariosto are only brilliant examples of conscious literary art; in France, peasant folklore and romance formed the groundwork of the great realistic burlesque in which the chief master of French prose satirized the society of his day and sketched the society of his dreams; in Germany, no supreme literary genius arose to voice the tendency of the age, but there was developed the last of the great impersonal legends of the world, the story of Faustus, ready to the hands of Germany's master-poet when he should come, and reminding us that wizardcraft has the same ultimate origin as, and is but the unholy and malign side of, the fairy belief. In England, where Celtic mythology had lived on as the Arthurian romance, where the latter, although a late comer, was at home, where alone literature had not been wholly divorced from folk-belief, Shakespeare created his fairy world.

Since his days, fairydom has become, chiefly owing to the perfection of his embodiment, a mere literary convention, and has gradually lost life and savour. Instead of the simpering puppets—stock properties of a machine-made children's literature—to which the fairies have been degraded, I have endeavoured to show them as they really appeared to the men and women who believed in them,—beings of ancient and awful aspect, elemental powers, mighty, capricious, cruel, and benignant, as in Nature herself. I believe that the fairy creed, this ancient source of inspiration, of symbolic interpretation of man's relation to nature, is not yet dried up, and that English literature, with its mixed strain of Teutonic and Celtic blood, with its share in the mythologies of both these races, and in especial with its claim to the sole body of mythology and romance, the Celtic, which grew up wholly unaffected by classic culture, is destined to drink deeply of it in the future as in the past, and to find in it the material for new creations of undying beauty.

BIBLIOGRAPHICAL APPENDIX

There are only two good accounts of the fairy belief, studied as a whole and with a view to determining its origin, nature, and growth:—(1) The essay prefixed to *Irische Elfenmärchen*, a translation by the Brothers Grimm of Crofton Croker's *Fairy Legends and Traditions of the South of Ireland*, published at Berlin in 1826. Croker translated this essay into English and affixed it to the second edition of his *Legends* (1827–8), where it occupies pages 1–154 of vol. iii. (2) *Les Fées du Moyen Age, recherches sur leur origine, leur histoire et leurs attributs*, by Alfred Maury, Paris, 1843; reprinted, Paris, 1896, in the volume entitled *Croyances et Legendes du Moyen Age* (12 francs). The Grimms' essay is, like all their work, absolutely good as far as it goes, and only needs amplification in the light of the fuller knowledge derived from the researches of the last seventy-five years. Halliwell's *Illustrations of Shakespeare's Fairy Mythology* (London, 1845; reprinted with additions by Hazlitt, 1875) is a useful collection of materials. The best edition of the *Midsummer Night's Dream*, as far as the objects of this study are concerned, is that by Mr. E. K. Chambers, 1897. An immense amount of out-of-the-way material is gathered together in *Shakespeare's Puck and his Folklore illustrated from the superstitions of all nations, but more especially from the earliest religion and rites of Northern Europe and the Wends*, 3 vols., 1852, by Mr. Bell; but the writer's perverse fantasticality and his utter lack of true critical spirit make his work dangerous for any but a trained scholar. Mr. Hartland's *The Science of Fairy Tales; an Inquiry into Fairy Mythology*, 1891 (3s. 6d.), is a most valuable study of several fundamental themes of fairy romance as exemplified in traditional literature. Dyer's *Folk Lore of Shakespeare*, 1884 (14s.), must also be mentioned, but cannot be recommended.

### REGINALD SCOT'S 'DISCOVERY OF WITCHCRAFT'

originally published 1584, is accessible in Nicholson's reprint, 1886 (£2 5s.). The quotation from Nash is taken from Halliwell's *Illustrations*.

### SHAKESPEARE AND LEGEND

Shakespeare's three greatest tragedies—Hamlet, Lear, Macbeth—are all founded upon heroic-legendary themes, and in each case the vital element in the legend is disentangled and emphasized with unerring skill. Indeed, wherever he handles legendary romance, he obtains the maximum of artistic effect without, as the artist so frequently does, offering violence to the spirit of the legend.

### GERVASE OF TILBURY AND GERALD THE WELSHMAN

Compare Mr. Hartland's *Science of Fairy Tales* (ch. vi.), 'Robberies from Fairyland.' Gervase's *Otia Imperialia*, a mine of wealth to the student of mediaeval folklore, is accessible in Liebrecht's admirable edition, 1856 (about 12s. 6d.).

### FAIRYDOM AND THE ARTHURIAN ROMANCE

Compare Nos. 1 and 4 of the present series of *Popular Studies*.

### GAELIC FAIRY LORE

No really good general survey of the subject exists, save the Grimms' essay already mentioned. This was substantially based upon the information brought together by Crofton Croker in the work quoted above; by Mrs. Grant, *Essays on the Superstitions of the Highlanders of Scotland*, 2 vols., 1811; and by Sir Walter Scott in his *Demonology and Witchcraft*, 1831, and *Minstrelsy of the Scottish Border*, 4 vols., 1802–03. Since then, a considerable amount of Irish material has been brought together by Carleton (*Traits and Stories of the Irish Peasantry*, 1830–2), by Lady Wilde (*Ancient Legends, Charms, and Superstitions of Ireland*, 1887 (6s.)), by P. Kennedy, *Legendary Fictions of the Irish Celts*, 1866, reprinted 1891 (3s. 6d.), and *Fireside Stories of Ireland*, 1871, chiefly with a view to illustrating the tales and legends collected by them. Mr. Curtin's *Tales of the Fairies and of the Ghost World*, 1893 (3s. 6d.), is more directly illustrative of the fairy belief as such, and is most valuable. Mr. Yeats' articles in the *Nineteenth Century* (January 1898, *Prisoners of the Gods*) and the *Contemporary Review* (September 1899, *Ireland Bewitched*) deserve the closest attention, though it may be thought that he sometimes reads into the information he has collected a poetic significance it does not really possess. Mr. Leland Duncan's article in *Folklore* (June 1896, *Fairy Beliefs from County Leitrim*) is of great value, and the *Transactions* generally of the Folklore Society are full of material.

In Scotland, Campbell of Islay's *Popular Tales of the West Highlands*, 4 vols., 1860–2, reprinted 1893, are of course indispensable. Vols. i–v of *Waifs and Strays of Celtic Tradition*, especially vols. i and v, contain much fairy lore. The oldest and perhaps most valuable account of the Scotch Gaelic fairy world, the Rev. Robert Kirk's *Secret Commonwealth of Elves, Fauns, and Fairies*, written in 1696, has been printed by Mr. Lang, with an admirable Introduction, 1893 (7s. 6d.). Martin's *Description of the Western Islands of Scotland*, written 1695, reprinted 1884, may likewise be consulted.

### The Tuatha de Danann

For a full development, with citation and discussion of authorities, of the argument set forth in these four pages, *cf.* my *Voyage of Bran* (ch. xvii).

### The Agricultural Base of Fairy Lore

These pages are practically a summary of Chaps. xvi–xviii of the *Voyage of Bran*, to which I refer for a full presentment of the theories here urged.

### Robin Goodfellow, &c.

Reprinted in Halliwell-Hazlitt's *Illustrations of Shakespeare's Fairy Mythology*.

# [ 4  EDWIN  SIDNEY  HARTLAND ]

As the Great Team began to parcel out their respective provinces, the mantle of the folktale specialist fell to Hartland. From 1890 on he prepared multiple reviews in *Folk-Lore* of the folktale publications issued during the year, commenting always with firm and astute judgment. His two major early studies, *The Science of Fairy Tales* (1891) and *The Legend of Perseus* (1894–6), delved deeply into the savage elements detectable in *Märchen* and classical myths. Hartland remained faithful to the strict Tylorian creed of evolutionism after Lang faced about to support the idea of high gods among primitive peoples. Tradition followed consistent laws dependent on the primitive ideas they embodied, Hartland stoutly maintained, and in his scientific analysis of fairy tales, legends, and sagas he illustrated the symmetry and regularity of those laws. Because his position required a faith in the trustworthiness of tradition, he commenced *The Science of Fairy Tales* with a skilful chapter affirming his confidence in oral narratives as reservoirs of primitive ideas. This chapter also reveals his intimacy with the settings and styles of storytelling.

Text from E. S. Hartland, *The Science of Fairy Tales*. London: Walter Scott, 1891. Chapter One, 'The Art of Story-telling,' pages 1–21.

The art of story-telling has been cultivated in all ages and among all nations of which we have any record; it is the outcome of an instinct implanted universally in the human mind. By means of a story the savage philosopher accounts for his own existence and that of all the phenomena which surround him. With a story the mothers of the wildest tribes awe their little ones into silence, or rouse them into delight. And the weary hunters beguile the long silence of a desert night with the mirth and wonders of a tale. The imagination is not less fruitful in the higher races; and, passing through forms sometimes more, sometimes less, serious, the art of story-telling unites with the kindred arts of dance and song to form the epic or the drama, or develops under the complex influences of modern life into the prose romance and the novel. These in their various ways are its ultimate expression; and the loftiest genius has found no fitter vehicle to convey its lessons of truth and beauty.

But even in the most refined products of the imagination the same substances are found which compose the rudest. Something has, of course, been dropped in the process; and where we can examine the process stage by stage, we can discern the point whereat each successive portion has been purged away. But much has also been gained. To change the figure, it is like the continuous development of living things, amorphous at first, by and by shooting out into monstrous growths, unwieldy and half-organized, anon settling into compact and beautiful shapes of subtlest power and most divine suggestion. But the last state contains nothing more than was either obvious or latent in the first. Man's imagination, like

[361]

every other known power, works by fixed laws, the existence and operation of which it is possible to trace; and it works upon the same material,—the external universe, the mental and moral constitution of man and his social relations. Hence, diverse as may seem at first sight the results among the cultured Europeans and the debased Hottentots, the philosophical Hindoos and the Red Indians of the Far West, they present, on a close examination, features absolutely identical. The outlines of a story-plot among savage races are wilder and more unconfined; they are often a vast unhidebound corpse, but one that bears no distant resemblance to forms we think more reasonable only because we find it difficult to let ourselves down to the level of savage ignorance, and to lay aside the data of thought which have been won for us by the painful efforts of civilization. The incidents, making all due allowance for these differences and those of climate and physical surroundings, are not merely alike; they are often indistinguishable. It cannot, of course, be expected that the characters of the actors in these stories will be drawn with skill, or indeed that any attention will be paid to them. Character-study is a late development. True: we ought not to overlook the fact that we have to do with barbarous ideals. In a rudimentary state of civilization the passions, like the arts, are distinguished not by subtlety and complexity, but by simplicity and violence of contrast. This may account to some extent for what seems to us repulsive, inconsistent or impossible. But we must above all things beware of crediting the story-teller with that degree of conscious art which is only possible in an advanced culture and under literary influences. Indeed, the researches which are constantly extending the history of human civilization into a remoter and remoter past, go everywhere to show that story-telling is an inevitable and wholly unconscious growth, probably arising, as we shall see in the next chapter, out of narratives believed to record actual events.

I need not stop now to illustrate this position, which is no new one, and the main lines of which I hope will be rendered apparent in the course of this volume. But it is necessary, perhaps, to point out that, although these are the premises from which I start, the limitations imposed by a work of the size and pretensions of this one will not allow me to traverse more than a very small corner of the field here opened to view. It is, therefore, not my intention to attempt any formal proof of the foregoing generalizations. Rather I hope that if any reader deem it proper to require the complete evidence on which they rest, he will be led to further investigations on his own behalf. His feet, I can promise him, will wander along flowery paths, where every winding will bring him fresh surprises, and every step discover new sources of enjoyment.

The stories with which we shall deal in the following pages are vaguely called Fairy Tales. These we may define to be: Traditionary narratives not in their present form relating to beings held to be divine, nor to cosmological or national events, but in which the supernatural plays an essential part. It will be seen that literary tales, such as those of Hans Andersen and Lord Brabourne, based though they often are upon tradition, are excluded from Fairy Tales as thus defined. Much no doubt might be said both interesting and instructive concerning these brilliant works. But it would be literary criticism, a thing widely different from the scientific treatment of Fairy Tales. The Science of Fairy Tales is concerned with tradition, and not with literature. It finds its subjects in the stories which have descended from mouth to mouth from an unknown past; and if reference be occasionally made to works of conscious literary art, the value of such works is not in the art they display, but the evidence they yield of the existence of given tales in certain forms at periods and places approximately capable of determination: evidence, in a word, which appropriates and fixes a pre-existing tradition. But even in this they are inferior in importance to historical or topographical works, where we frequently meet with records of the utmost importance in considering the origin and meaning of Folk-tales.

Literature, in short, of whatever kind, is of no value to the student of Fairy Tales, as that phrase is here used, save as a witness to Tradition. Tradition itself, however, is variable in value, if regard be had alone to purity and originality. For a tribe may conceivably be so isolated that it is improbable that any outside influence can have affected its traditions for a long series of generations; or on the other hand it may be in the highway of nations. It may be physically of a type unique and unalloyed by foreign blood; or it may be the progeny of a mingling of all the races on the earth. Now it is obvious that if we desire to reason concerning the wide distribution, or the innate and necessary character of any idea, or of any story, the testimony of a given tribe or class of men will vary in proportion to its segregation from other tribes and classes: where we can with most probability exclude outside influence as a factor in its mental evolution, there we shall gather evidence of the greatest value for the purpose of our argument.

Again: some nations have developed the art of story-telling more highly than others, since some stages of civilization are more favourable to this development than others, and all nations are not in the same stage. The further question may, therefore, be put whether these various stages of development may not produce differences of manner in story-telling—differences which may indicate, if they do not cause, deep-seated differences in the value of the traditions themselves. To make my meaning clear: a people which requires its story-tellers to relate their stories in the very words in which they have been conveyed from time immemorial, and allows no deviation, will preserve its traditions with the least possible blemish and the least possible change. In proportion as latitude in repetition is permitted and invention is allowed to atone for want of memory, tradition will change and become uncertain. Such latitude may be differently encouraged by different social states. A social state is part of, and inseparable from the sum total of arts, knowledge, organization and customs which we call the *civilization*, or the *stage of civilization*, of a people. It may be worth while to spend a short time in examining the mode of story-telling and the requirements of a story-teller among nations in different stages of civilization. We shall thus endeavour to appreciate the differences in the manner of telling, and to ascertain in general terms how far these differences affect the value of the traditions.

If we turn first to some of the Celtic nations, we find a social state in which the art of story-telling has received a high degree of attention. The late Mr. J. F. Campbell, to whom the science of Folklore owes an incalculable debt, describes a condition of things in the Western Highlands extremely favourable to the cultivation of folk-tales. Quoting from one of his most assiduous collectors, he says that most of the inhabitants of Barra and South Uist are Roman Catholics, unable to speak English or to read or write. Hence it is improbable that they can have borrowed much from the literature of other nations. Among these people in the long winter nights the recitation of tales is very common. They gather in crowds at the houses of those who are reputed to be good tale-tellers. Their stories frequently relate to the exploits of the Ossianic heroes, of whose existence they are as much convinced as ordinary English folk are of the existence and deeds of the British army in its most recent wars. During the tales 'the emotions of the reciters are occasionally very strongly excited, and so also are those of the listeners, almost shedding tears at one time, and giving way to loud laughter at another. A good many of them firmly believe in all the extravagance of these stories.' Another of his collectors, a self-educated workman in the employ of the Duke of Argyll, writing more than thirty years ago to him, speaks of what used to take place about Loch Lomond upwards of fifty years before—that is to

say, about the beginning of the present century. The old people
then would pass the winter evenings telling each other traditional
stories. These chiefly concerned freebooters, and tribal raids and
quarrels, and included descriptions of the manners, dress and
weapons of their ancestors and the hardships they had to endure.
The youngsters also would gather, and amuse themselves with
games or the telling of tales of a more romantic cast. But the chief
story-tellers appear to have been the tailors and shoemakers, who
were literally journeymen, going from house to house in search of
work. As they travelled about, they picked up great numbers of
tales, which they repeated; 'and as the country people made the
telling of these tales, and listening to hear them, their winter night's
amusement, scarcely any part of them would be lost.' In these tales
Gaelic words were often used which had dropped out of ordinary
parlance, giving proof of careful adherence to the ancient forms;
and the writer records that the previous year he had heard a story
told identical with one he had heard forty years before from a different man thirty miles away; and this story contained old Gaelic
words the meaning of which the teller did not know. A gamekeeper
from Ross-shire also testified to similar customs at his native place:
the assemblies of the young to hear their elders repeat, on winter
nights, the tales they had learned from their fathers before them,
and the renown of the travelling tailor and shoemaker. When a
stranger came to the village it was the signal for a general gathering
at the house where he stayed, to listen to his tales. The good-man
of the house usually began with some favourite tale, and the
stranger was expected to do the rest. It was a common saying: 'The
first tale by the goodman, and tales to daylight by the guest.' The
minister, however, came to the village in 1830, and the schoolmaster
soon followed, with the inevitable result of putting an end to these
delightful times.[1]

Not very different is the account given by M. Luzel of the *Veillées*
in which he has often taken part in Brittany. In the lonely farmhouse after the evening meal prayers are said, and the life in Breton
of the saint of the day read, all the family assemble with the servants and labourers around the old-fashioned hearth, where the fire
of oaken logs spirts and blazes, defying the wind and the rain or
snow without. The talk is of the oxen and the horses and the work
of the season. The women are at their wheels; and while they spin
they sing love ditties, or ballads of more tragic or martial tone. The
children running about grow tired of their games, and of the tedious

[1] Campbell, vol. i, pp. xii, xiv, lvii.

conversation of their elders, and demand a tale, it matters not what, of giants, or goblins, or witches—nay, even of ghosts. They are soon gratified; and if an old man, as frequently happens, be the narrator, he is fortified and rewarded for the toil by a mug of cider constantly replenished. One such depositary of tradition is described as a blind beggar, a veritable Homer in wooden shoon, with an inexhaustible memory of songs and tales of every kind. He was welcome everywhere, in the well-to-do farmhouse as in the humble cottage. He stayed as long as he pleased, sometimes for whole weeks; and it was with reluctance that he was allowed to leave in order to become for a time the charm of another fireside, where he was always awaited with impatience.[1]

M. Braga, the Portuguese scholar, quotes an old French writer, Jean de Chapelain, as recording a custom in Normandy similar to that of Ross-shire, that the guest was always expected to repay hospitality by telling tales or singing songs to his host. And he states that the emigrants from Portugal to Brazil took this custom with them. In Gascony M. Arnaudin formed his collection of tales a few years ago by assisting at gatherings like those just described in Brittany, as well as at marriages and at various agricultural festivals.[2]

Similar customs existed in Wales within living memory, and in remote districts they probably exist today. If they do not now continue in England, it is at least certain that our forefathers did not differ in this respect from their neighbours. A writer of the seventeenth century, in enumerating the causes of upholding 'the damnable doctrine of witchcraft,' mentions: 'Old wives' fables, who sit talking and chatting of many false old stories of Witches and Fairies and Robin Goodfellow, and walking spirits and the dead walking again; all of which lying fancies people are more naturally inclined to listen after than to the Scriptures.' And if we go further back we find in chapter clv of the printed editions of the 'Gesta Romanorum' an interesting picture of domestic life. The whole family is portrayed gathering round the fire in the winter evenings and beguiling the time by telling stories. Such we are informed was the custom among the higher classes. It was, indeed, the custom among all classes, not only in England but on the Continent, throughout the Middle Ages. The eminent French antiquary, Paul Lacroix, speaks of wakes, or evening parties, where fairy tales and other superstitions were propagated, as having a very ancient origin. He states that they are still (as we have already seen in Brittany and Gascony) the custom

[1] Luzel, *Veillées, passim.*
[2] Introduction to Romero, p. x.; Arnaudin, p. 5.

in most of the French provinces, and that they formed important events in the private lives of the peasants.[1]

It is difficult to sever the occasion and mode of the tale-telling from the character of the teller; nor would it be wise to do so. And in this connexion it is interesting to pause for a moment on Dr. Pitré's description of Agatuzza Messia, the old woman from whom he derived so large a number of the stories in his magnificent collection, and whom he regarded as a model story-teller. I am tempted to quote his account at length. 'Anything but beautiful,' he says, 'she has facile speech, efficacious phrases, an attractive manner of telling, whence you divine her extraordinary memory and the sallies of her natural wit. Messia already reckons her seventy years, and is a mother, grandmother, and great grandmother. As a child, she was told by her grandmother an infinity of tales which she had learned from her mother, and *she* in turn from her grandfather; she had a good memory and never forgot them. There are women who have heard hundreds of tales and remember none; and there are others who, though they remember them, have not the grace of narration. Among her companions of the Borgo, a quarter of Palermo, Messia enjoyed the reputation of a fine story-teller; and the more one heard her, the more one desired to hear. Almost half a century ago she was obliged to go with her husband to Messina, and lived there some time: a circumstance, this, worthy of note, since our countrywomen never go away from their own district save from the gravest necessity. Returning to her native home, she spoke of things of which the gossips of the neighbourhood could not speak: she spoke of the Citadel, a fortress which no one could take, not even the Turks themselves; she spoke of the Pharos of Messina, which was beautiful, but dangerous for sailors; she spoke of Reggio in Calabria, which, facing the walls of Messina, seemed to wish to touch hands with them; and she remembered and mimicked the pronunciation of the Milazzesi, who spoke, Messia said, so curiously as to make one laugh. All these reminiscences have remained most vivid in her memory. She cannot read, but she knows so many things that no one else knows, and repeats them with a propriety of tongue that is a pleasure to hear. This is a characteristic to which I call my readers' attention. If the tale turns upon a vessel which has to make a voyage, she utters, without remarking it, or without seeming to do so, sailors' phrases, and words which only seamen and those who have to do with seamen are acquainted with. If the heroine arrives, poor and desolate, at a baker's and takes a place there, Messia's

---

[1] Thomas Ady, *A Candle in the Dark* (1656) (*Cf.* Aubrey, *Remaines*, p. 67); *Gesta Romanorum*, Introd., p. xxv (E.E.T.S.); Lacroix, p. 100.

[367]

language is so completely that of the trade that you would believe that the baking of bread had been her business, whereas at Palermo this occupation, an ordinary one in the families of the large and small communes of the island, is that of professional bakers alone. . . . As a young woman Messia was a tailoress; when through toil her sight became weakened, she turned to sewing winter quilts. But in the midst of this work, whereby she earns her living, she finds time for the fulfilment of her religious duties; every day, winter and summer, in rain or snow, in the gloaming she goes to her prayers. Whatever feast is celebrated in the church, she is solicitous to attend: Monday, she is at the Ponte dell' Ammiraglio praying for the Souls of the Beheaded; Wednesday, you find her at San Giuseppe keeping the festival of the Madonna della Providenza; every Friday she goes to San Francesco di Paola, reciting by the way her accustomed beads; and if one Saturday pass when she ought to go to the Madonna dei Cappuccini, another does not; and there she prays with a devotion which none can understand who has not experienced it. Messia witnessed my birth and held me in her arms: hence I have been able to collect from her mouth the many and beautiful traditions to which her name is appended. She has repeated to the grown man the tales she had told to the child thirty years before; nor has her narration lost a shade of the old sincerity, vivacity, and grace. The reader will only find the cold and naked words; but Messia's narration consists, more than in words, in the restless movement of the eyes, in the waving of the arms, in the gestures of the whole person, which rises, walks around the room, bends, and is again uplifted, making her voice now soft, now excited, now fearful, now sweet, now hoarse, as it portrays the voices of the various personages, and the action which these are performing.'[1]

Such a woman as is here described is a born story-teller; and her art, as exhibited in the tales attributed to her in Dr. Pitré's collection, reaches perhaps the highest point possible in tradition. Women are usually the best narrators of nursery tales. Most of the modern collections, from that of the brothers Grimm downwards, owe their choicest treasures to women. In the Panjab, however, Captain Temple ascribes to children marvellous power of telling tales, which he states they are not slow to exercise after sunset, when the scanty evening meal is done and they huddle together in their little beds beneath the twinkling stars, while the hot air cools, the mosquito sings, and the village dogs bark at imaginary foes. The Rev. Hinton Knowles' collection was gathered in Cashmere apparently from men and boys only; but all classes contributed, from the

[1] Pitré, vol. iv, p. xvii.

governor and the pandit down to the barber and the day-labourer, the only qualification being that they should be entirely free from European influence.[1]

But nursery tales told simply for amusement are far from being the only kind of traditional narrative. Savage and barbarous races, to whom the art of writing is unknown, are dependent upon memory for such records as they have of their past; and sometimes a professional class arises to preserve and repeat the stories believed to embody these records. Among the Maoris and their Polynesian kinsmen the priests are the great depositaries of tradition. It is principally from them that Mr. White and the Rev. W. W. Gill have obtained their collections. But the orators and chiefs are also fully conversant with the narratives; and their speeches are filled with allusions to them, and with quotations from ancient poems relating the deeds of their forefathers. The difficulty of following such allusions, and consequently of understanding the meaning of the chiefs when addressing him on behalf of their fellow-countrymen, first induced, or compelled, Sir George Grey, when Governor of New Zealand, to make the inquiries whose results are embodied in his work on Polynesian Mythology. The Eskimo of Greenland, at the other end of the world, divide their tales into two classes: the ancient and the modern. The former may be considered, Dr. Rink says, as more or less the property of the whole nation, while the latter are limited to certain parts of the country, or even to certain people who claim to be akin to one another. The art of telling these tales is 'practised by certain persons specially gifted in this respect; and among a hundred people there may generally be found one or two particularly favoured with the art of the *raconteur*, besides several tolerable narrators.' It is the narrators of the ancient tales 'who compose the more recent stories by picking up the occurrences and adventures of their latest ancestors, handed down occasionally by some old members of the family, and connecting and embellishing them by a large addition of the supernatural, for which purpose resort is always had to the same traditional and mystic elements of the ancient folklore.'[2]

But the art of story-telling has not everywhere given rise to a professional class. When the Malagasy receive friends at their houses, they themselves recount the deeds of their ancestors, which are handed down from father to son, and form the principal topic of conversation. So, too, the savage Ahts of Vancouver Island sit round their fires singing and chatting; 'and the older men, we are

[1] *Wide-awake Stories*, p. 1; Knowles, p. ix.
[2] White, vol. i, p. vi; Sir G. Grey, p. vi; Gill, p. xx; Rink, pp. 83, 85.

[369]

told, lying and bragging after the manner of story-tellers, recount their feats in war, or the chase, to a listening group.' Mr. Im Thurn has drawn an interesting picture of the habits at night of the Indian tribes of Guiana. The men, if at home, spend the greater part of the day in their hammocks, smoking, 'and leisurely fashioning arrow-heads, or some such articles of use or of ornament. . . . When the day has at last come to an end, and the women have gathered together enough wood for the fires during the night, they, too, throw themselves into their hammocks; and all talk together. Till far into the night the men tell endless stories, sometimes droning them out in a sort of monotonous chant, sometimes delivering them with a startling amount of emphasis and gesticulation. The boys and younger men add to the noise by marching round the houses, blowing horns and playing on flutes. There is but little rest to be obtained in an Indian settlement by night. These people sleep, as dogs do, without difficulty, for brief periods, but frequently and indifferently by day or night as may be convenient. The men, having slept at intervals during the day, do not need night-rest; the women are not considered in the matter. At last, in the very middle of their stories, the party drops off to sleep; and all is quiet for a short while. Presently some woman gets up to renew the fires, or to see to some other domestic work. Roused by the noise which she makes, all the dogs of the settlement break into a chorus of barks and yelps. This wakes the children, who begin to scream. The men turn in their hammocks, and immediately resume their stories, apparently from the point at which they left off, and as if they had never ceased. This time it is but a short interruption to the silence of the night; and before long everything again becomes quiet, till some new outbreak is caused, much as was the last. In the very middle of the night there are perhaps some hours of quiet. But about an hour before dawn, some of the men having to go out to hunt, effectually wake everybody about them by playing flutes, or beating drums, as they go to bathe before leaving the settlement.'[1]

But the folktale cannot be separated in this inquiry from the folksong with which, in its origin and development, it is so closely connected. In India there are, or were until recent years, everywhere professional bards; and the stories told in Indian villages are frequently the substance of the chants of these bards. More than this, the line between singing and narration is so faintly drawn, that the bards themselves often interpose great patches of prose between

[1] Ellis, *History of Madagascar*, vol. i, p. 264; Sproat, *Scenes and Studies of Savage Life*, p. 51; Im Thurn, pp. 215, 216.

the metrical portions of their recitations. Fairs, festivals, and marriages all over India are attended by the bards, who are always ready to perform for pay and drink. Mr. Leland believes the stories he obtained from the Christian Algonkins of New England, concerning the ancient heroes of the race and other mythical personages, to have once been delivered as poems from generation to generation and always chanted. The deeds of Maori warriors are handed down in song; just as we find in Beowulf, the story of Hrothgar's ancestors was sung before his own companions-in-arms by his gleemen to the accompaniment of some instrument after the mead cup had gone round. The Roman historian attests the prevalence among the German tribes of ancient songs, which he expressly mentions as their only kind of memory or record,—thus showing that all their tales, whether mythologic or heroic, were for better preservation cast into metrical form. Some of these, enshrining the deeds of their heroes, were chanted on going into battle, in order to arouse the warriors' courage. And as far back as the light of history, or of literature, penetrates, not only the Teutonic, but also the Celtic nations loved to have their actions celebrated thus. To a Welsh king his household bard was as necessary as his domestic chaplain, or his court physician, and in the ancient laws his duties, his precedence, his perquisites, and even the songs he was expected to sing, are minutely prescribed. The bards were organized into a regular order, or college, with an official chief. They were not merely singers or poets, but also tale-tellers; and from the Mabinogion we gather that listening to songs and tales was one of the habitual, if not daily pastimes, of a court.[1]

It is needless to follow through the Middle Ages the history of the troubadour, the minstrel and the jongleur, who played so large a part in the social life of those times. Many of them were retainers o noblemen and kings; but others roamed about from place to place, singing their lays and reciting their stories (for they dealt in prose as well as verse), very much in the manner of the Indian bards just mentioned. Their stock-in-trade must have been partly traditional and partly of their own composition. In this respect they were probably less hide-bound than their Indian brethren are. For the latter, whether retainers of the native grandees, as many of them are, or members of the humbler class of wandering minstrels, are expected to repeat their lays as they have received them. But, although in the main these professional gentlemen adhere to the traditional

---

[1] Temple, *Legends of the Panjab*, vol. i, p.-v; Thorburn, p. 172; Leland, p. 12; Taylor, p. 306; *Beowulf*, lay 16; Tacitus, *Germania*, cc., 2, 3; *Ancient Laws and Institutions of Wales* (Public Record Commission, 1841), pp. 15, 35, &c.

words which they know by heart, the temptation must be very strong to foist at suitable pauses into their tales impromptu passages—best described in stage language as 'gag'—which they think will be acceptable to their audience. And whether or not this be actually the case with the Indian bards, we are expressly told that it is so with the Arab story-teller, and that it accounts for much of the ribaldry and filth which have become embedded in the immortal 'Nights.' A viol having only one string accompanies the passages in verse with which the stories are interlarded; and a similar instrument seems to be used for the like purpose among the orthodox Guslars of Bosnia and Herzegovina.[1] A description given by Sir Richard Burton of a story-teller at the bazaar at Tangier may stand, except as to the external details, for that of an Arab reciter throughout Northern Africa and the Moslem East. 'The market people,' he says, 'form a ring about the reciter, a stalwart man, affecting little raiment besides a broad waist-belt into which his lower chiffons are tucked, and noticeable only for his shock hair, wild eyes, broad grin, and generally disreputable aspect. He usually handles a short stick; and, when drummer and piper are absent, he carries a tiny tomtom shaped like an hour-glass, upon which he taps the periods. This Scealuidhe, as the Irish call him, opens the drama with an extempore prayer, proving that he and the audience are good Moslems; he speaks slowly and with emphasis, varying the diction with breaks of animation, abundant action and the most comical grimace: he advances, retires, and wheels about, illustrating every point with pantomime; and his features, voice and gestures are so expressive that even Europeans who cannot understand a word of Arabic, divine the meaning of his tale. The audience stands breathless and motionless, surprising strangers by the ingenuousness and freshness of feeling hidden under their hard and savage exterior. The performance usually ends with the embryo actor going round for alms, and flourishing in the air every silver bit, the usual honorarium being a few *f'lús*, that marvellous money of Barbary, big coppers worth one-twelfth of a penny.' Another writer, who has published modern Arab folk-tales, obtained eleven out of twelve from his cook, a man who could neither read nor write, but possessed an excellent memory. His stories were derived from his mother and aunts, and from old women who frequented his early home. The remaining tale was dictated by a sheikh with some, though small, pretensions to education, and this tale, though at

---

[1] Burton, *Nights*, vol. x, p. 163; *Revue des Trad. Pop.*, vol. iv, p. 6. In Greece and Albania, however, the viol would seem not to be used. Women are the chief reciters. Von Hahn, vol. i, p. ix.

bottom a genuine folk-tale, presented traces of literary manipulation.[1]

The literary touches here spoken of were probably not impromptu. But it must be admitted that the tendency to insert local colouring and 'gag' is almost irresistible amongst the Arabs. Dr. Steere notices it as a characteristic of the story-tellers of the Swahili, a people of mixed Arab and Negro descent at Zanzibar;[2] and it is perhaps inevitable in a professional reciter whose audience, like himself, is restless and vivacious in so high a degree. The only case in which any restraint would be certain to be felt is where a narrative believed to be of religious import is given. Under the influence of religious feeling the most mobile of races become conservative; and traditions of a sacred character are the most likely of all to be handed down unchanged from father to son. Directly we get outside the charmed circle of religious custom, precept, and story, the awe which has the most powerful effect in preserving tradition intact ceases to work; and we are left to a somewhat less conservative force of habit to retain the old form of words and the time-honoured ceremonies. Still this force is powerful; the dislike of voluntary change forbids amendment even of formularies which have long ceased to be understood, and have often become ridiculous because their meaning has been lost. It is by no means an uncommon thing for the rustic story-teller to be unable to explain expressions, and indeed whole episodes, in any other way than Uncle Remus, when called upon to say who Miss Meadows was: 'She wuz in de tale, Miss Meadows en de gals wuz, en de tale I give you like hi't wer' gun ter me.' Dr. Steere, speaking of a collection of Swahili tales by M. Jablonsky which I think has never been published, tells us that almost all of the tales had 'sung parts,' and of some of these even they who sang them could scarcely explain the meaning. Here we may observe the connexion with the folksong; and it is a strong evidence of adherence to ancient tradition. Frequently in Dr. Steere's own experience the skeleton of the story seemed to be contained in these snatches of song, which were connected together by an account, apparently extemporized, of the intervening history. In these latter portions, if the hypothesis of extemporization were correct, the words of course would be different, but the substance might remain untouched. I suspect, however, that the extemporization was nothing like so complete as the learned writer imagined, but rather that the tale, as told with song and narrative mingled, was in a state of gradual decay or transition from verse to prose,

[1] Spitta Bey, p. viii.
[2] Steere, pp. v, vii.

and that the prose portions were, to almost as great an extent as the verse, traditional.

Be this as it may, the tenacity with which the illiterate story-teller generally adheres to the substance and to the very words of his narrative is remarkable—and this in spite of the freedom sometimes taken of dramatic illustration, and the license to introduce occasional local and personal allusions and 'gag.' These are easily separable from the genuine tale. What Dr. Rink says of the Eskimo story-telling holds good, more or less, all over the world. 'The art,' he states, 'requires the ancient tales to be related as nearly as possible in the very words of the original version, with only a few arbitrary reiterations, and otherwise only varied according to the individual talents of the narrator, as to the mode of recitation, gesture, &c. The only real discretionary power allowed by the audience to the narrator is the insertion of a few peculiar passages from other traditions; but even in that case no alteration of these original or elementary materials used in the composition of tales is admissible. Generally, even the smallest deviation from the original version will be taken notice of and corrected, if any intelligent person happens to be present. This circumstance,' he adds, 'accounts for their existence in an unaltered shape through ages; for had there been the slightest tendency to variation on the part of the narrator, or relish for it on that of the audience, every similarity of these tales, told in such widely-separated countries, would certainly have been lost in the course of centuries.' Here the audience, wedded to the accustomed formularies, is represented as controlling any inclination to variation on the reciter's part. How far such an attitude of mind may have been produced by previous repetitions in the same words we need not inquire. Certain it is that accuracy would be likely to generate the love of accuracy, and *that* again to react so as to compel adherence to the form of words which the ear had been led to expect. Readers of Grimm will remember the anxiety betrayed by a peasant woman of Niederzwehr, near Cassel, that her very words and expressions should be taken down. They who have studied the records collectors have made of the methods they have adopted, and the assistance they have received from narrators who have understood and sympathized with their purpose, will not find anything exceptional in this woman's conduct.[1]

Nor must we overlook the effect of dramatic and pantomimic action. At first sight action, like that of Messia or the Arab reciter, might seem to make for freedom in narration. But it may well be questioned if this be so to any great extent. For in a short time

[1] Rink, p. 85; Grimm, *Märchen*, p. vii.

certain attitudes, looks, and gestures become inseparably wedded, not only in the actor's mind, but also in the minds of the audience who have grown accustomed to them, with the passages and the very words to which they are appropriate. The eye as well as the ear learns what to expect, with results proportioned to the comparative values of those two senses as avenues of knowledge. The history of the stage, the observation of our own nurseries, will show with how much suspicion any innovation on the mode of interpreting an old favourite is viewed.

To sum up: it would appear that national differences in the manner of story-telling are for the most part superficial. Whether told by men to men in the bazaar or the coffee-house of the East, or by old men or women to children in the sacred recesses of the European home, or by men to a mixed assembly during the endless nights of the Arctic Circle, or in the huts of the tropical forest, and notwithstanding the license often taken by a professional reciter, the endeavour to render to the audience just that which the speaker has himself received from his predecessors is paramount. The faithful delivery of the tradition is the principle underlying all variation of manner; and it is not confined to any one race or people. It is not denied that changes do take place as the story passes from one to another. This indeed is the inevitable result of the play of the two counteracting forces just described—the conservative tendency and the tendency to variation. It is the condition of development; it is what makes a science of Folktales both necessary and possible. Nor can it be denied that some changes are voluntary. But the voluntary changes are rare; and the involuntary changes are only such as are natural and unavoidable if the story is to continue its existence in the midst of the ever-shifting social organism of humanity. The student must, therefore, know something of the habits, the natural and social surroundings, and the modes of the thought of the people whose stories he examines. But this known, it is not difficult to decipher the documents.

There is, however, one caution—namely, to be assured that the documents are gathered direct from the lips of the illiterate storyteller, and set down with accuracy and good faith. Every turn of phrase, awkward or coarse though it may seem to cultured ears, must be unrelentingly reported; and every grotesquery, each strange word, or incomprehensible or silly incident, must be given without flinching. Any attempt to soften down inconsistencies, vulgarities or stupidities, detracts from the value of the text, and may hide or destroy something from which the student may be able to make a discovery of importance to science. Happily the collectors of the present day are fully alive to this need. The pains they take to ensure correctness are great, and their experiences in so doing are often very interesting. Happily, too, the student soon learns to distinguish the collections whose sincerity is certain from those furbished up by literary art. The latter may have purposes of amusement to serve, but beyond that they are of comparatively little use.

## [ 5  EDWARD  CLODD (*a*) ]

Starting from the same evolutionary premises as his associates, Edward Clodd (1840–1930) found himself pursuing the idea of magic held by savages and surviving among civilized nations. Magic, he wrote, rules the life of the savage, and from magic stems every practice of occult power. An excellently preserved version of the folktale 'Tom Tit Tot'—the Grimms' 'Rumpelstiltskin'—recovered in his own Suffolk County led Clodd to probe behind the tale's central incident, hinging on the power over the demon possessed by the knower of his name. The exploration resulted in *Tom Tit Tot, An Essay on Savage Philosophy in Folk-Tale* (1898), parts of which Clodd incorporated into a subsequent study, *Magic in Names and in Other Things* (1920). In *Myths and Dreams* (1885) he had considered the same class of phenomena, pointing out the savage's inability to distinguish between waking and sleeping perceptions. In these works he accumulated a mass of examples illustrating the tendency of uncivilized men to associate magical power or 'mana' with inanimate objects and intangible things like shadows, reflections, and names.

Text from Edward Clodd, *Tom Tit Tot, An Essay on Savage Philosophy in Folk-Tale*. London: Duckworth and Co., 1898. Chapter 5, 'Barbaric Ideas About Names,' pages 53–6; Chapter 6, 'Magic Through Tangible Things,' pages 57–78.

Before the discovery of iron; before the invention of the art of spinning; before the formulation of the theory of spirits, against whose wiles mortals might successfully plot,—men had found the necessity of inventing signs or symbols wherewith to distinguish one another. Among these was the choice of personal names, and it is in this that the justification exists for assuming the name-incident in 'Tom Tit Tot' to be probably the most archaic element

[376]

in the story. Barbaric man believes that his name is a vital part of himself, and therefore that the names of other men and of superhuman beings are also vital parts of themselves. He further believes that to know the name is to put its owner, whether he be deity, ghost, or mortal, in the power of another, involving risk of harm or destruction to the named. He therefore takes all kinds of precautions to conceal his name, often from his friend, and always from his foe. This belief, and the resulting acts, as will be shown presently, are a part of that general confusion between the objective and the subjective—in other words, between names and things or between symbols and realities—which is a universal feature of barbaric modes of thought. This confusion attributes the qualities of living things to things not living; it lies at the root of all fetishism and idolatry; of all witchcraft, shamanism, and other instruments which are as keys to the invisible kingdom of the dreaded. Where such ideas prevail, everything becomes a vehicle of magic, and magic, be it remembered, rules the life of the savage. It is, as Adolf Bastian aptly remarks, 'the physics of mankind in a state of nature,' because in the perception, however blurred or dim, of some relation between things, science is born. To look for any consistency in barbaric philosophy is to disqualify ourselves for understanding it, and the theories of it which aim at symmetry are their own condemnation. Yet that philosophy, within its own irregular confines, works not illogically. Ignorant of the properties of things, but ruled by the superficial likenesses which many exhibit, the barbaric mind regards them as vehicles of good or evil, chiefly evil, because things are feared in the degree that they are unknown, and because, where life is mainly struggle, man is ever on the watch against malice-working agencies, wizards, medicine-men, and all their kin. That he should envisage the intangible—that his name should be an entity, an integral part of himself, may the less surprise us when it is remembered that language, from the simple phrases of common life to the highest abstract terms, rests on the concrete. To 'apprehend' a thing is to 'seize' or 'lay hold' of it; to 'possess' a thing is to 'sit by' or 'beset' it. To call one man a 'sycophant' is to borrow the term 'fig-blabber,' applied by the Greeks to the informer against those who broke the Attic law prohibiting the export of figs; to call another man 'supercilious' is to speak of him as 'raising his eyebrows'; while, as we all know, the terms 'disaster' and 'lunatic' preserve the old belief in the influence of the heavenly bodies on human life. Even the substantive verb 'to be,' the 'most bodiless and colourless of all our words,' is made up of the relics of several verbs which once had a distinct physical significance. 'Be' contained the

[377]

idea of 'growing'; 'am, art, is,' and 'are,' the idea of 'sitting'; 'was' and 'were,' that of 'dwelling' or 'abiding.'

The dread of being harmed through so intangible a thing as his name, which haunts the savage, is the extreme and more subtle form of the same dread which, for a like reason, makes him adopt precautions against cuttings of his hair, parings of his nails, his saliva, excreta, and the water in which his clothes—when he wears any—are washed, falling under the control of the sorcerer. Miss Mary Kingsley says that 'the fear of nail and hair clippings getting into the hands of evilly disposed persons is ever present to the West African. The Igalwa and other tribes will allow no one but a trusted friend to do their hair, and bits of nails or hair are carefully burnt or thrown away into a river. Blood, even that from a small cut on the finger, or from a fit of nose-bleeding, is most carefully covered up and stamped out if it has fallen on the earth. Blood is the life, and life in Africa means a spirit, hence the liberated blood is the liberated spirit, and liberated spirits are always whipping into people who don't want them.[1] Crammed with Pagan superstitions, the Italian who is reluctant to trust a lock of his hair to another stands on the same plane as the barbarian. Sometimes, as was the custom among the Incas, and as is still the custom among Turks and Esthonians, the refuse of hair and nails is preserved so that the owner may have them at the resurrection of the body.[2] In connexion with this, one of my sons tells me that his Jamaican negro housekeeper speaks of the old-time blacks keeping their hair-cuttings to be put in a pillow in their coffins, and preserving the parings of their nails, because they would need them in the next world. It is a common superstition among ourselves that when children's teeth come out they should not be thrown away, lest the child has to seek for the lost tooth after death. On the other hand, it is an equally common practice to throw the teeth in the fire 'out of harm's way.'

But the larger number of practices give expression to the belief in what is known as 'sympathetic magic'; as we say, 'like cures like,' or more appositely, in barbaric theory, 'kills like.' Things outwardly resembling one another are believed to possess the same qualities, effects being thereby brought about in the man himself by the production of like effects in things belonging to him, or in images or effigies of him. The Zulu sorcerers, when they have secured a portion of their victim's dress, will bury it in some secret

[1] *Travels in West Africa*, p. 447.    [2] *The Golden Bough*, vol. i, p. 203.

place, so that, as it rots away, his life may decay. In the New Hebrides it was the common practice to hide nail-parings and cuttings of hair, and to give the remains of food carefully to the pigs. 'When the *mac* snake carried away a fragment of food into the place sacred to a spirit, the man who had eaten of the food would sicken as the fragment decayed.'[1] Brand tells that in a witchcraft trial in the seventeenth century, the accused confessed 'having buried a glove of the said Lord Henry in the ground, so that as the glove did rot and waste, the liver of the said lord might rot and waste'; and the New Britain sorcerer of today will burn a castaway banana skin, so that the man who carelessly left it unburied may die a tormenting death. A fever-stricken Australian native girl told the doctor who attended her that 'some moons back, when the Goulburn blacks were encamped near Melbourne, a young man named Gibberook came behind her and cut off a lock of her hair, and that she was sure he had buried it, and that it was rotting somewhere. Her marn-bu-la (kidney fat) was wasting away, and when the stolen hair had completely rotted she would die.' She added that her name had been lately cut on a tree by some wild black, and that was another sign of death. Her name was Murran, which means 'a leaf,' and the doctor afterwards found that the figure of leaves had been carved on a gum-tree as described by the girl. The sorceress said that the spirit of a black fellow had cut the figure on the tree.[2] The putting of sharp stones in the foot-tracks of an enemy is believed to maim him, as a nail is driven into a horse's footprint to lame him,[3] while the chewing of a piece of wood is thought to soften the heart of a man with whom a bargain is being driven. Folk-medicine, the wide world through, is full of prescriptions based on sympathetic or antipathetic magic. Its doctrine of 'seals' or 'signatures' is expressed in the use of yellow flowers for jaundice, and of eyebright for ophthalmia, while among the wonder-working roots there is the familar mandrake of human shape, credited, in virtue of that resemblance, with magic power. In Umbria, where the peasants seek to nourish the consumptive on rosebuds and dew, the mothers take their children, wasted by sickness, to some boundary stone, perchance once sacred to Hermes, and pray to God to stay the illness or end the sufferer's life. The Cheroki make a decoction of the cone-flower for weak eyes because of the fancied resemblance of that plant to the strong-sighted eye of the deer; and they also drink an infusion of the tenacious burrs of the common beggars' lice,

[1] Codrington, *Melanesians*, p. 203.
[2] Brough Smyth, *Aborigines of Victoria*, vol. i, p. 468.
[3] Grimm, *Teutonic Mythology*, p. 1093.

[379]

an American species of the genus *Desmodium*, to strengthen the memory. To ensure a fine voice, they boil crickets, and drink the liquor. In Suffolk and other parts of these islands, a common remedy for warts is to secretly pierce a snail or 'dodman' with a gooseberry-bush thorn, rub the snail on the wart, and then bury it, so that, as it decays, the wart may wither away.

Chinese doctors administer the head, middle, or roots of plants, as the case may be, to cure the complaints of their patients in the head, body, or legs. And with the practice of the Zulu medicine-man, who takes the bones of the oldest bull or dog of the tribe, giving scrapings of these to the sick, so that their lives may be prolonged to old age,[1] we may compare that of doctors in the seventeenth century, who with less logic, but perchance unconscious humour, gave their patients pulverized mummy to prolong their years.[2] 'Mummie,' says Sir Thomas Browne, 'is become merchandise. Mizraim cures wounds, and Pharaoh is sold for balsams.'[3]

In Plutarch's *Roman Questions*, which Dr. Jevons, in his valuable preface to the reprint of Philemon Holland's translation,[4] remarks 'may fairly be said to be the earliest formal treatise written on the subject of folk-lore,' reference is made to the Roman customs of not completely clearing the table of food, and 'never putting foorth the light of a lampe, but suffering it to goe out of the owne accord.' These obviously come under the head of sympathetic magic, 'being safeguards against starvation and darkness.' In Melanesia, if a man wounds another with an arrow, he will drink hot juices and chew irritating leaves to bring about agony to the wounded, and he will keep his bow taut, pulling it at intervals to cause nerve-tension and tetanus in his victim. Here, though wide seas between them roll, we may compare the same philosophy of things at work. The 'sympathetic powder' used by Sir Kenelm Digby in the seventeenth century was believed to cure a wound if applied to the sword that inflicted it; and, today, the Suffolk farmer keeps the sickle with which he has cut himself free from rust, so that the wound may not fester. Here, too, lies the answer to the question that puzzled Plutarch. 'What is the reason that of all those things which be dedicated and consecrated to the gods, the custome is at Rome, that onely the spoiles of enemies conquered in the warres are neglected and suffered to run to decay in processe of time: neither is there any

[1] Bishop Callaway, *Zulu Nursery Tales*, p. 175.
[2] Lang's *Myth, Ritual, and Religion*, vol. i, p. 96. The inclusion of mummy in the old pharmacopoeias was perhaps due to certain virtues in the aromatics used in embalming.
[3] *Urn-Burial*, iii, p. 46 (collected works).
[4] *Bibliothèque de Carabas*, vol. vii (Nutt, 1892).

reverence done unto them, nor repaired be they at any time when they wax olde?' Of course the custom is the outcome of the belief that the enemy's power waned as his armour rusted away.

Equally puzzling to Plutarch was the custom among Roman women 'of the most noble and auncient houses' to carry 'little moones upon their shoes.' These were of the nature of amulets, designed to deceive the lunacy-bringing moon-spirit, so that it might enter the crescent charm instead of the wearer. 'The Chaldeans diverted the spirit of disease from the sick man by providing an image in the likeness of the spirit to attract the plague.'[1] 'Make of it an image in his likeness (*i.e.*, of Namtar, the plague); apply it to the living flesh of his body (*i.e.*, of the sick man), may the malevolent Namtar who possesses him pass into the image.'[2] But the reverse effect was more frequently the aim. A Chaldean tablet records the complaint of some victim, that 'he who enchants images has charmed away my life by image'; and Ibn Khaldun, an Arabian writer of the fourteenth century, describes how the Nabathean scorcerers of the Lower Euphrates made an image of the person whom they plotted to destroy. They transcribed his name on his effigy, uttered magic curses over it, and then, after divers other ceremonies, left the evil spirits to complete the fell work.[3] In ancient Egyptian belief the *ka* of a living person could be transferred to a wax image by the repetition of formulae; and there is no break in the long centuries between Accadian magic, which so profoundly influenced the West, and the practice of injuring a man through his image, which flourishes today. The Ojibways believe that by drawing the figure of any person in sand or clay, or by considering any object as the figure of a person, and then pricking it with a sharp stick or other weapon, or doing anything that would be done to the living body to cause pain or death, the person thus represented will suffer likewise.[4] King James I, in his *Daemonologie*, Book II. ch. v, speaks of 'the devil teaching how to make pictures of wax or clay, that by roasting thereof the persons that they bear the name of may be continually melted or dried away by sickness,' and, as showing the continuity of the idea, there are exhibited in the Pitt Rivers Museum at Oxford, besides similar objects from the Straits Settlements, a 'Corp Creidh' or 'clay body' from the Highlands, and a pig's heart from Devonshire, with pins stuck in them.

The assumed correspondence between physical phenomena and

[1] Jevons, Plutarch's *Romane Questions*, p. 79.
[2] Lenormant, *Chaldean Magic*, p. 51.     [3] *Ibid.*, p. 63.
[4] Dorman, *Primitive Superstitions*, p. 139.

human actions is further shown in Dr. Johnson's observation, when describing his visit to the Hebrides, that the peasants expect better crops by sowing their seed at the new moon; and he recalls from memory a precept annually given in the almanack, 'to kill hogs when the moon is waxing, that the bacon may prove the better in boiling.' With the ancient Roman custom of throwing images of the corn-spirit (doubtless substitutes of actual human offerings) into the river, so that the crops might be drenched with rain, we may compare the practice of the modern Servians and Thessalians, who strip a little girl naked, but wrap her completely in leaves and flowers, and then dance and sing round her, while bowls of water are poured over her to make the rain come. The life of man pulsates with the great heart of nature in many a touching superstition, as in the belief in the dependence of the earth's fertility on the vigour of the tree-spirit incarnated in the priest-king; in the group which connects the waning of the days with the decline of human years; and, pathetically enough, in the widespread notion, of which Dickens makes use in *David Copperfield*, that life goes out with the ebb-tide.

> I was on the point of asking him if he knew me, when he tried to stretch out his arm, and said to me, distinctly, with a pleasant smile, 'Barkis is willin'.'
> And, it being low water, he went out with the tide.

The general idea has only to be decked in another garb to fit the frame of mind which still reserves some pet sphere of nature for the operation of the special and the arbitrary. 'The narrower the range of man's knowledge of physical causes, the wider is the field which he has to fill up with hypothetical causes of a metaphysical or supernatural character.'[1]

We must not pass from these examples of belief in sympathetic connexion, drawn from home as well as foreign sources, without reference to its significance in connexion with food outside the prohibitions which are usually explained by the totem, that is, abstinence from the plant or animal which is regarded as the tribal ancestor.

Captain Wells, who was killed near Chicago in 1812, and who was celebrated for his valour among the Indians, was cut up into many parts, which were distributed among the allied tribes, so that all might have the opportunity of getting a taste of the courageous soldier. For it is a common belief among barbaric folk that by eating the flesh of a brave man a portion of his courage is absorbed. The Botecudos sucked the blood of living victims that they might

[1] Lang, *Myth, Ritual, and Religion*, vol. i, p. 88.

imbibe spiritual force, and among the Brazilian natives the first food given to a child, when weaning it, was the flesh of an enemy.[1] Cannibalism, the origin of which is probably due to a scarcity of animal food, therefore acquires this superadded motive, in which also lies the explanation of the eating of, or abstaining from, the flesh of certain animals. The lion's flesh gives courage, the deer's flesh causes timidity; and in more subtle form of the same idea, barbaric hunters will abstain from oil lest the game slip through their fingers. Contrariwise, the Hessian lad thinks that he may escape the conscription by carrying a baby-girl's cap in his pocket: a symbolic way of repudiating manhood.[2]

Most suggestive of all is the extension of the idea to the eating of the slain god, whereby his spirit is imbibed, and communion with the unseen secured. To quote Mr. Frazer, the savage believes that 'by eating the body of the god he shares in the god's attributes and powers; and when the god is a corn-god, the corn is his proper body; when he is a vine-god, the juice of the grape is his blood; and so, by eating the bread and drinking the wine, the worshipper partakes of the real body and blood of his god. Thus the drinking of wine in the rite of a vine-god, like Dionysus, is not an act of revelry; it is a solemn sacrament.'[3] Experience shows that people possessing intelligence above the ordinary often fail to see the bearing of one set of facts upon another set, especially if the application can be made to their traditional beliefs, whether these are only mechanically held, or ardently defended. It is, therefore, not wholly needless to point out that Mr. Frazer's explanation is to be extended to the rites attaching to Christianity, transubstantiation being, laterally[4] or lineally, the descendant of the barbaric idea of eating the god, whereby the communicant becomes a 'partaker of the divine nature.' In connexion with this we may cite Professor Robertson Smith's remark, that a notable application of the idea of eating the flesh or drinking the blood of another being, so that a man absorbs its nature or life into his own, is the rite of blood-brotherhood, the simplest form of which is in two men opening their veins and sucking one another's blood. 'Thenceforth their lives are not two, but one.'[5] Among the Unyamuezi the ceremony is performed by cutting incisions in each other's legs and letting the blood trickle together.[6] Fuller reference to this widely diffused rite will, however,

[1] Dorman, *Primitive Superstitions*, p. 149.
[2] Tylor, *Primitive Culture*, vol. i, p. 107.        [3] *Golden Bough*, vol. i, p. 89.
[4] See, on this matter, Professor Percy Gardner's tract on the *Origin of the Lord's Supper*, pp. 18–20 (Macmillan and Co.).
[5] *Religion of the Semites*, p. 296.
[6] Speke, *Journal of Discovery of the Source of the Nile*, p. 96.

have more fitting place later on, when treating of the custom of the exchange of names which, as will be seen, often goes with it. Belief in virtue inhering in the dead man's body involves belief in virtue in his belongings, in which is the key to the belief in the efficacy of relics as vehicles of supernatural power. Here the continuity is clearly traceable. There is no fundamental difference between the savage who carries about with him the skull-bones of his ancestor as a charm or seat of oracle, and the Buddhist who places the relics of holy men beneath the tope, or the Catholic who deposits the fragments of saints or martyrs within the altar which their presence sanctifies; while the mother, treasuring her dead child's lock of hair, witnesses to the vitality of feelings drawn from perennial springs in human nature. Well-nigh every relic which the Church safeguards beneath her shrines, or exhibits, at stated seasons, for the adoration of the crowd, is spurious,[1] yet no amount of ridicule thrown on these has impaired the credulity whose strength lies in the dominance of the wish to believe over the desire to know.[2]

In 'Whuppity Stoorie' the widow and the witch 'watted thooms' over their bargain. Man's saliva plays a smaller, but by no means inactive, part in his superstitions. A goodly-sized book might be written on the history and ethnic distribution of the customs connected with it. Employed as vehicle of blessing or cursing, of injury or cure, by peoples intellectually as far apart as the Jews, the South Sea Islanders, the mediaeval Christians, and the Central Africans of today, the potencies of this normally harmless secretion have been most widely credited.[3] Among ourselves it is a vehicle of one of the coarsest forms of assault, or the degenerate representative of the old luck-charm in the spitting on money by the cabman or the costermonger. Among certain barbaric races, however, the act expresses the kindliest feeling and the highest compliment. Consul Petherick says that a Sudanese chief, after grasping his hand, spat on it, and then did the like to his face, a form of salute which the consul returned with interest, to the delight of the recipient. Among the Masai the same custom is universal; and while it is bad form to kiss a lady, it is *comme il faut* to spit on her.[4] The authority who

[1] On the manufacture of and traffic in relics, see Froude, *Erasmus*, p. 128; Gregorovius, *Hist. of Rome in the Middle Ages*, vol. ii, pp. 73–7; iii, pp. 72–5.
[2] In John Heywood's *Enterlude of the Four P's* (a Palmer, a Pardoner, a 'Poticary, and a Pedlar), the author, a sixteenth-century writer of Morality Plays, did not allow his staunch Catholicism to hinder his flinging some coarse satire at the relicmongers. He represents the Pardoner as exhibiting, among other curios, the jaw-bone of All Saints, a buttock-bone of the Holy Ghost, and the great toe of the Trinity.
[3] Art. on 'Saliva Superstitions,' by Fanny D. Bergen, *American Folk-Lore Soc. Journal*, vol. iii, p. 52.
[4] Joseph Thomson, *Through Masai Land*, p. 166.

reports this adds an account of certain generative virtues with which saliva, especially if administered by a white man, is accredited.[1] But it is as a prophylactic, notably in the form of fasting spittle, and as a protection against sorcery and all forms of black magic, that we meet with frequent references to it in ancient writers, and in modern books of travel. 'Spittle,' says Brand, 'was esteemed a charm against all kinds of fascination,'[2] notably against the evil eye, the remedy for which, still in vogue among the Italians, is to spit three times upon the breast, as did the urban maiden in Theocritus when she refused her rustic wooer. It came out in the course of a murder trial at Philippopolis, that the Bulgarians believe that spitting gives immunity from the consequences of perjury.[3] An example of its use in benediction occurs, as when the Abomel of Alzpirn spat on his clergy and laity; but more familiar are the cases of its application in baptism and name-giving. Seward says that 'the custom of nurses lustrating the children by spittle was one of the ceremonies used on the Dies Nominalis, the day the child was named; so that there can be no doubt of the Papists deriving this custom from the heathen nurses and grandmothers. They have indeed christened it, as it were, by flinging in some Scriptural expressions; but then they have carried it to a more filthy extravagance by daubing it on the nostrils of adults as well as of children.'[4] Ockley tells that when Hasan was born, his grandfather, Mohammed, spat in his mouth as he named him; and Mungo Park thus describes the name-giving ceremony among the Mandingo people. 'A child is named when it is seven or eight days old. The ceremony commences by shaving the head. The priest offers a prayer, in which he solicits the blessing of God upon the child and all the company, and then whispering a few sentences in the child's ear, spits three times in his face, after which, pronouncing his name aloud, he returns the child to its mother.'

All which, of course, has vital connexion with the belief in inherent virtue in saliva, and therefore with the widespread group of customs which have for their object the prevention of its falling within the power of the sorcerer. Suabian folk-medicine prescribes that the saliva should at once be trodden into the ground lest some evil-disposed person use it for sorcery. As the result of extensive acquaintance with the North American Indians, Captain Bourke says that all of them are careful to spit into their cloaks or blankets;

---

[1] *Ibid.*, p. 165.
[2] *Popular Antiquities*, iii, p. 228 (Hazlitt's edition).
[3] *Westminster Gazette*, July 28, 1897.
[4] *Conformity between Popery and Paganism*, p. 14; Brand, iii, p. 229.

and Kane adds his testimony that the natives of Columbia River are never seen to spit without carefully stamping out the saliva. This they do lest an enemy should find it, and work injury through it. The chief officer of the 'king' of Congo receives the royal saliva in a rag, which he doubles up and kisses; while in Hawaii the guardianship of the monarch's expectorations was intrusted only to a chief of high rank, who held the dignified office of spittoon-bearer to the king, and who, like his fellow-holders of the same trust under other Polynesian rulers, buried the saliva beyond the reach of malicious medicine-men. Finally, as bearing on the absence of any delimiting lines between a man's belongings, there may be cited Brand's reference to Debrio. He 'portrays the manners and ideas of the continent, and mentions that upon those hairs which come out of the head in combing they spit thrice before they throw them away.'[1]

The reluctance of savages to have their portraits taken is explicable when brought into relation with the group of confused ideas under review. Naturally, the man thinks that virtue has gone out of him, that some part of his vulnerable self is put at the mercy of his fellows, when he sees his 'counterfeit presentment' on a sheet of paper, or peering from out magic glass. The reluctance of unlettered people among ourselves to have their likenesses taken is not uncommon. From Scotland to Somerset[2] there comes evidence about the ill-health or ill-luck which followed the camera, of folks who 'took bad and died' after being 'a-tookt.' These facts will remove any surprise at Catlin's well-known story of the accusation brought against him by the Yukons that he had made buffaloes scarce by putting so many pictures of them in his book.[3]

## [ 5  EDWARD  CLODD (b) ]

Clodd did not rest content with his examination of savage conceptions of magic but, according to the anthropological method of folklore, eyed the continuation and persistence of magical ideas in the upper levels of civilization. Himself an uncompromising freethinker, the banker boldly followed the evidence to its logical climax, the incorporation of barbaric magic in sacred Christian ritual. The researches of his fellows had thrown long shadows in this direction, but it remained for Clodd in 1897, in his second

[1] *Pop. Antiq.*, iii, p. 231.
[2] Napier, *Folklore of West Scotland*, p. 142; Elworthy, *Evil Eye*, p. 86.
[3] Dorman, p. 140.

presidential address to The Folk-Lore Society, to shock Victorian Anglicans by saying that the evolutionary climb of man extended not only from savages to peasants but even to wearers of the old school tie. This is the address that led to former prime minister Gladstone's resignation from the Society.

Text from Edward Clodd, 'Presidential Address,' *Folk-Lore*, VII (1896). Pages 40–60.

Comparative anatomy has not more completely demonstrated the common descent of man and ape, and the consequent classification of man in the order Primates, than comparative anthropology has demonstrated his advance from the animal stage to civilization. That work can never be undone. And one momentous effect of it is the disproof of traditional theories about man's paradisaical state, and his fall therefrom. Yet how slow is the perception of so complete a revolution in our ideas has illustration in the following paragraph, which occurs in a recent book on prehistoric archaeology.

> The school of amalgamated Pagan and Christian thought, amongst other absurdities, traces the pedigree of the first settlers in Ireland up to Adam. Now that part of the assertion is correct, namely, that Adam was the first man for we possess a higher authority than Irish pedigrees for the assertion.[1]

One can only exclaim: 'If they do these things in a green tree, what shall be done in the dry?' An example of this kind at least brings home the fact that if in many ways the work of the older scientific societies is well advanced in its emancipation of the mind from obsolete ideas, the work of our Society has scarcely begun. We start, be it remembered, where physical anthropology leaves off; since to folklore is allotted the high task of tracing the course of man's mental development. Justification of this claim is supplied by the materials which come within our province. They are to be included under the broad term 'superstitions,' all of which are, or have been, operative upon conduct. The history of superstitions is included in the history of beliefs; the superstitions being the germ plasm of which all beliefs above the lowest are the modified products. Belief incarnates itself in word or act. In the one we have the charm, the invocation, and the dogma; in the other the ritual and ceremony. 'A ritual system,' Professor Robertson Smith remarks, 'must always remain materialistic, even if its materialism is disguised under the cloak of mysticism.'[2] And it is with the incarnated

[1] *Pagan Ireland*, p. 28. By W. G. Wood Martin. Longmans, 1895.
[2] *Religion of the Semites*, p. 419.

ideas, uninfluenced by the particular creed in connexion with which it finds them, that the folklorist deals. His method is that of the biologist. Without bias, without assumptions of relative truth or falsity, he searches into origins, traces variations, compares and classifies, and relates the several families to one ordinal group. He must be what was said of Dante, 'a theologian to whom no dogma is foreign.' Unfortunately, this method, whose application to the physical sciences is unchallenged, is, when applied to beliefs, regarded as one of attack, instead of being one of explanation. But this should not deter; and if in analysing a belief we kill a superstition, this does but show what mortality lay at its core. For error cannot survive dissection. Moreover, as John Morley puts it, 'to tamper with veracity is to tamper with the vital force of human progress.'[1]

Now, up to the present, we have not faced this question of the larger significance of folklore. We have only 'cast a sheep's eye' at it. Our treatment has been allusive; never quite direct. We meet and discuss groups of interesting facts; facts whose humour tickles us, or whose pathos moves us. And, as Omar Khayyám says, we have 'talked about it and about.' There has been hesitation to approach the ultimate conclusions to which the facts point; partly from the wholesome influence of the scientific spirit which bids us make sure that the fact will bear the weight of the inference; partly, too, from the tremendous power of the *taboo* which would limit the scope of inquiry by artificial threats to trespassers.

To bring home my meaning, let us look at the general attitude towards a couple of books whose subjects are of momentous import, and which may be bracketed together as complementary to each other. I refer to Mr. Frazer's *Golden Bough* and Mr. Hartland's *Legend of Perseus*. I was specially careful to follow the numerous reviews of Mr. Frazer's book, and in none that came under my eye was the far-reaching significance of the materials hinted at. The connexion of the Arician custom of killing the priest-god with groups of allied customs was discussed; there was much discursive talk about tree-spirits, separable souls, and taboos, about survivals of tree-worship in 'stinking ydols,' as old Stubbs calls the May-poles in his *Anatomie of Abuses*—in fine, a great deal of dancing round them by the critics. Now the full title of Mr. Frazer's book is, *The Golden Bough: a Study in Comparative Religion.* In the preface he says that its 'central idea is the conception of the slain god.' In the last sentence he reminds us that 'the king of the wood no longer stands sentinel over the Golden Bough. But Nemi's woods are still

[1] *Compromise*, p. 141.

green, and at evening you may hear the church bells of Albano, and, perhaps, if the air be still, of Rome itself, ringing the Angelus. *Le roi est mort; vive le roi.*'[1]

Could Mr. Frazer have pointed in more suggestive language the moral of all the *folklore* that he has crammed between his title page and these concluding words? And the sum of it is this. The god becomes incarnate in man, animal, or plant, and is slain; both the incarnation and the death being for the benefit of mankind. The god is his own sacrifice, and in perhaps the most striking form, as insisted upon by Mr. Frazer, he is, as corn-spirit, killed in the person of his representative; the passage in this mode of incarnation to the custom of eating bread sacramentally being obvious.[2] The fundamental idea of this sacramental act, as the mass of examples collected by Mr. Frazer further goes to show, is that by eating a thing its physical and mental qualities are acquired. So the barbaric mind reasons, and extends the notion to all beings. To quote Mr. Frazer: 'By eating the body of the god he shares in the god's attributes and powers. And when the god is a corn-god, the corn is his proper body; when he is a vine-god, the juice of the grape is his blood; and so by eating the bread and drinking the wine the worshipper partakes of the real body and blood of his god. Thus the drinking of wine in the rites of a vine-god like Dionysus is not an act of revelry; it is a solemn sacrament.[3] It is, perhaps, needless to point out that the same explanation applies to the rites attaching to Demeter, or to add what further parallels are suggested in the belief that Dionysus (who appears in hagiology as St. Denis[4]) was slain, rose again, and descended into Hades to bring up his mother Semele from the dead. This, however, by the way. What has to be emphasized is, that in the quotation just given we have transubstantiation clearly defined as the barbaric idea of eating the god. In proof of the unbroken continuity of that idea two witnesses—Catholic and Protestant— may be cited.

The Church of Rome, and in this the Greek Church is at one therewith, thus defines the term transubstantiation in the Canon of the Council of Trent:—

If any one shall say that in the most holy sacrament of the Eucharist there remains the substance of bread and wine together with the body and blood of our Lord Jesus Christ, and shall deny that wonderful and singular conversion of the whole substance of the bread into the body, and of the whole

---

[1] Vol. ii, p. 371.　　　　[2] *Ibid.*, p. 78.　　　　[3] Vol. i, p. 89.
[4] M. Jean Reville in *Revue de l'Histoire des Religions*, vol. xiii, 1886.

substance of the wine into the blood, the species of bread and wine alone remaining—which conversion the Catholic Church most fittingly calls Transubstantiation—let him be anathema.

Professor Haddon has kindly furnished me with the most apposite evidence from the Protestant side that one has seen for many a day. It is culled from a Nonconformist organ, the *British Weekly*, of August 29 last. A correspondent writes:—

A few Sundays ago—8 o'clock celebration of Holy Communion. Rector, officiating minister (Hawarden Church).

When the point was reached for the communicants to partake, cards containing a hymn to be sung after Communion were distributed among the congregation. This hymn opened with the following couplet:—

Jesu, mighty Saviour,
Thou art *in* us now.

And my attention was arrested by an asterisk referring to a footnote. The word 'in,' in the second line, was printed in italics, and the note intimated that those who had *not* communicated should sing '*with*' instead of '*in*,' *i.e.*, those who had taken the consecrated elements to sing 'Thou art *in* us now.' and those who had not, to sing 'Thou art *with* us now.'

Whether, therefore, the cult be barbaric or civilized, we find theory and practice identical. The god is eaten so that the communicant thereby becomes a 'partaker of the divine nature.' Upon this, even did time permit, there is no need to enlarge. There is only the need to point out that the inclusion of the rite within the province of folklore is warranted by its identity with barbaric rites.

Turning to Mr. Hartland's book, although the concluding section has not yet appeared, the drift of the work is clear, and, in fact, has been indicated in the preface. 'The figure of Perseus, the god-begotten, the dragon-slayer, became very early a type of the Saviour of the world, while the conception underlying the Life-token obtained its ultimate expression in the most sacred rite of Christian worship.' It is thus evident that Mr. Hartland's survey overlaps the ground taken by Mr. Frazer. He has collected a large number of variants of legends of miraculous conceptions and virgin births, the existence of which demands, for purposes of inquiry and comparison, the inclusion of every story of corresponding character. *Credo quia ineptum*, the barbarian may say with his betters, for the examples cited by Mr. Hartland show that, certain savage creation-myths perhaps excepted, into no other group do the grotesque and fantastic so largely enter. Fecundation is believed to be caused by eating and drinking certain things; by the scent of flowers, or by touching them or anything else which is thought to have magic properties; by holy water, or the unconsecrated rain; by sunrays and the wind; by a glance; by helpful beasts and birds; and so forth. The agency of the flower is probably an explanation of the lily held towards the Virgin by the angel in pictures of the Annunciation, although a later and loftier idea sees in the white blossom the symbol of purity. But that the grosser notions obtained for centuries is shown in the mediaeval belief in conception by the ear. 'In a hymn ascribed to St. Thomas à Becket occur the lines:—

> "Gaude Virgo mater Christi,
> Quae per aurem concepisti,
> Gabriele nuntio."

and in an old glass window, now, I believe, in one of the museums of Paris, the Holy Ghost is represented hovering over the Virgin in the form of a dove, while a ray of light passes from his beak to her ear, along which ray an infant Christ is descending.'[1] No discontinuity is traceable between these ideas and the general belief at the time when the Synoptic Gospels took shape,

that superhuman personages and great religious leaders were born of virgin mothers through divine agency. So was Apollonius of Tyana; and Origen himself tells us (in *Celsum* 129), how Plato was said to have been born of Amphiktione, 'her husband Ariston having been restrained from coming together with her (συνελθεῖν) until she should bring forth the child begotten by Apollo.' In this and similar tales we make acquaintance with the intellectual atmosphere in the midst of which the Christian doctrine of the miraculous conception originated and grew up.[2]

The folklorist takes up the quest where the historian lays it down, and brings his cumulative evidence to prove that the belief is of no special time or people, but the offspring of barbaric confusion about life generally, and about birth specifically. David Hume anticipated modern theories of animism in the remark that 'there is a universal tendency among mankind to conceive all beings like themselves, and to transfer to every object those

---

[1] Langlois, *Peinture sur Verre*, p. 147. Quoted in Lecky's *Hist. of Rationalism*, i, 212 (1875 edition).
[2] F. C. Conybeare. Letter on the recently discovered 'Old Syriac Palimpsest of the Gospels,' *Academy*, December 22, 1894, p. 535.

[391]

qualities with which they are familiarly acquainted, and of which they are intimately conscious.'[1]

Add to this attribution of life corresponding to our own to everything, the belief that death is a non-natural event; add, too, the rough inferences which the untutored mind draws from the mystery of origins and growth, from the seeming unrelation between the seed and the plant, the egg and the animal, the pupa and the insect; and herein there lie the sufficing materials for the belief in human descent from trees and stones of which totemism is an outcome; in the passage of life from one body to another of which metempsychosis is an outcome; and in the varied possible modes of generation, of which the highest outcome is belief in incarnate deities.

To those who are familiar with Dr. Tylor's *Primitive Culture* it is obvious that both Mr. Frazer and Mr. Hartland are but following the lines laid down in that great book. But their merit is to have advanced folklore still further from the empirical stage, and to show how it alone supplies the explanation of beliefs and customs, and of rites and ceremonies, all the world over and through every grade of culture. They who would deny the fundamental unity of these phenomena, and justify the exclusion of any portion of them from comparative treatment, will, if successful in their contention, at least be grateful to those whose challenge has secured them that desired result.

It is because folklore appeals to me as a subject freighted with human interest that I would thus press upon you plain dealing with the materials whose meaning it is our duty to seek to reach. And if books of the type of the *Golden Bough* and the *Legend of Perseus* have some higher purpose than entertainment, it must follow that they drive home the evidence as to the persistence of barbaric ideas and their outward expression throughout the higher culture.

Excavations have shown that the church of St. Peter in the Vatican was founded near a seat of worship of Cybele, the Magna Mater, whose image in the shape of a rough field-stone had been given by the Phrygian priests and was welcomed at Rome 204 B.C., with unusual pomp;[2] while the basilica of St. Clement, perhaps, after the Pantheon, the most interesting ecclesiastical relic in that city, is built over a temple dedicated to Mithra. In his *Customs and Lore of Modern Greece*,[3] Mr. Rennell Rodd tells us that a church dedicated to the Virgin of Fecundity has been shown to occupy the site of a temple of Eilythuia, the deity who presided over childbirth,

[1] *The Natural Hist. of Religion* (Works, vol. iv, p. 446, ed. 1826).
[2] Gregorovius: *Hist. of Rome*, i, 90; Mommsen, iii, 115.     [3] Ch. v.

while the Twelve Apostles have succeeded to the altar of the Twelve Gods. Professor Rhys and other authorities assert with good reason that our own cathedral of St. Paul stands on the same high ground where a temple to the Celtic god Lud was raised; and so one might go on quoting examples, wherein are more than allegories; even unbroken evidences of the pagan foundation which, itself resting on barbaric bedrock, upholds the structures of classic and christian faiths.

In my former address some examples of survivals of superstition among the uncultured, both here and abroad, were given. They were drawn from newspaper reports, as best verifying what one sought to maintain in proof of the living power of folklore. Did time allow, and did the subject demand it, there would be no difficulty in presenting a fresh selection gathered from the same popular source during the current year. There was the incident at Long Sutton where a farmer's wife assaulted an old woman named Perkins for bewitching her cream and her hens, so that the one couldn't be churned, and the others wouldn't lay.[1] That was settled by a payment of £4 to the injured bewitcher. There was the curious evidence at the inquest on a drowned woman at Spalding that the device of floating a loaf of bread containing quicksilver was resorted to for the purpose of finding the body. There was the odd remark of the mother of Gamble, the half-witted youth charged with the recent boy-murder at Islington, that he was always worse when the moon is at the full.[2] There was the excitement in the churchyard of St. John's, Hackney, last August, on the report that a sheeted ghost had been seen, when there collected as many thousands, led by curiosity or belief in the possibility of the thing, as gathered in Bohemia last January on the news that the Virgin Mary had appeared in a wood near Braunau.[3]

These, however, by the way. And while it is well to keep on the lookout for like examples at like levels, let us not forget the monition, to 'first cast out the beam' from our 'own eye,' that we may 'see clearly to cast out the mote' from our 'brother's eye.' This counsel may be heeded by choosing from the newspapers a few examples of survivals among the intelligent; examples, as one may call them, of 'spiritual wickedness in high places.' Let it be noted that they derive their chief value, at least for the present purpose, from the ideas at the core of each which connect them with barbaric ideas. It is these that survive the changes in the pantheon of every

[1] *Daily Chronicle*, June 8, 1895.
[2] *Weekly Sun*, December 8, 1895.
[3] *Times*, January 3, 1895. *Westminster Gazette*, August 21, 1895.

[393]

race. Of the Greek peasant of today Mr. Rodd testifies that, 'much as he would shudder at the accusation of any taint of paganism, the ruling of the Fates is more immediately real to him than divine omnipotence.' Mr. Tozer confirms this in his *Highlands of Turkey*. He says: 'It is rather the minor deities and those associated with man's ordinary life that have escaped the brunt of the storm, and returned to live in a dim twilight of popular belief.'[1] In India, Sir Alfred Lyall tells us that, 'even the supreme triad of Hindu allegory, which represent the almighty powers of creation, preservation, and destruction, have long ceased to preside actively over any such corresponding distribution of functions.'[2] Like limited monarchs, they reign, but do not govern. They are superseded by the ever-increasing crowd of godlings whose influence is personal and special, as shown by Mr. Crooke in his instructive *Introduction to the Popular Religion and Folklore of Northern India*.[3] In this island the Celtic and pre-Celtic paganism remained unleavened by the old Roman religion. The gods whom the legions brought followed them when they withdrew. The names of Mithra and Serapis occur on numerous tablets, the worship of the one—that 'Sol invictus' whose birthday at the winter solstice became the anniversary of the birth of Christ—had ranged as far west as South Wales and Northumberland, while the foundations of a temple to the other have been unearthed at York. The chief Celtic gods were, in virtue of common attributes as elemental nature-deities, identified with certain *dii majores* of the Roman pantheon, and the *deae matres* equated with the gracious or malevolent spirits of the indigenous faith. But the old names were not displaced. Neither did the earlier Christian missionaries effect any organic change in popular beliefs, while, during the submergence of Christianity under waves of barbaric invasion, there was infused into the old religion kindred elements from oversea which gave it yet more vigorous life. The gist of these remarks is to show that all changes in popular belief have been and practically remain superficial; that the old animism still informs the higher creeds.

Of this I proceed to take four examples: (1) Exorcism; (2) Water-worship; (3) Orientation; (4) Divine Judgments.

1. *Exorcism.*—In the *Services of Holy Week from the Sarum Missal* issued by members of the Church of England forming the society of St. Osmund, the 'Clerks' are directed to 'venerate the Cross, with feet unshod,' and to perform other ceremonies, which are preceded

[1] Vol. ii, p. 307.
[2] *Asiatic Studies*, p. 28.
[3] Allahabad, the Government Press, 1894.

by that of driving the devil out of flowers. This is the formula to be used:

> I exorcise thee, creature of flowers or branches; in the Name of God + the Father Almighty, and in the name of Jesus Christ + His son, our Lord, and in the Power of the + Holy Ghost; and henceforth let all strength of the adversary, all the host of the devil, every power of the enemy, every assault of fiends, be expelled and utterly driven away from this creature of flowers or branches, etc. (p. 3).

Here the flowers and leaves *shall be sprinkled* with HOLY WATER, and *censed* (p. 5).

Recognizing that this is part of a movement by a minority of people to re-introduce a discarded ritual, the difference between those who support and those who repudiate it is one of degree. For both believe in the existence and ceaseless activity of Satan and his myrmidons. One Gulielmus Parisiensis made a computation as to the number of these, and found it to be 44, 435, 556.[1] The data on which he arrived at this are not forthcoming, but the estimate strikes us as too small. There are not enough to go round. The arithmetic of the subject is, however, of no consequence; the folklorist is concerned only with the ceremony of exorcism as putting the savage and the civilized on a common plane. For the ceremony is based upon the belief in the association of magic with plants as the habitats of evil spirits. And so the fragrant flowers come to be regarded as laboratories where demons prepare the baleful draughts which the 'hatefull hag' dispenses to the doomed, and the continuity of barbaric ritual is maintained by the sprinkling of the exorcized water and the swinging of the censer over the lilies and the roses.

2. *Water-worship.*—The Bishop of Cashel is reported to have said in a recent charge 'that as an infant is incapable of the exercise of faith and repentance, so spiritual grace is imparted in infant baptism.'[2] Whoever thus argues that the combined gases whose symbol is $H_2O$, or that any other materials, are a vehicle of supernatural efficacy, writes himself the lineal descendant of the 'medicine man.' For what else have we in this episcopal utterance but the barbaric conception of water as a living thing; as a god, call we it Poseidon, Neptune, Manannan Mac Lir, or Nodens; or as the dwelling-place of godlings, demons, or of the quasi-human beings of the mermaid or kelpie type? None can quarrel with the Church

[1] 'The Christian Hell,' by James Mew, *Nineteenth Century*, November, 1891, p. 727.
[2] *Illustrated London News*, August 10, 1895.

which, in bygone days, adopting what it could not abolish, consecrated to saint or Madonna the springs and wells dedicated to pagan deities. They who made that change made a wise concession, not to perpetuate the old ideas, but to invest them with a beautiful symbolism; whereas these modern materialists who advocate the doctrine of the regeneration of a human soul by water are heathens in thin disguise, offering the folklorist excellent subject for analysis and comparison.

Passing from font to healing spring, those who are curious to see how water which perhaps has medicinal virtue is assumed to be an agent of miraculous recovery can travel in a few hours to the shrine of St. Winifred in Flintshire. Pennant the antiquary, describing the well in the last century, tells of the votive offerings, in the shape of crutches and other objects, which were hung about it, and to this day the store is receiving additions. The sick crowd thither as of old they crowded into the temples of Aesculapius and Serapis; mothers bring their sick children as in Imperial Rome they took them to the Temple of Romulus and Remus. A draught of water from the basin near the bath, or a plunge in the bath itself, is followed by prayers at the altar of the chapel which encloses the well. When the saint's feast-day is held, the afflicted gather to kiss the reliquary that holds her bones. There is nothing new under the sun. Horace tells of the shipwrecked sailor who hung up his clothes as a thankoffering in the temple of the sea-god who had preserved him; Polydorus Vergilius, who lived in the early part of the sixteenth century, that is, some 1,500 years after Horace, describes the classic custom of *ex voto* offerings at length, while Conyers Middleton, in his *Letter from Rome*, first published in 1729, speaks of it as 'a practice so common among the *Heathens*, that no one *custom of antiquity* is so frequently mentioned by all their writers' . . . 'but the most common of all *offerings* were *pictures* representing the history of the miraculous cure or deliverance vouchsafed upon the vow of the donor.'[1] Of which offerings, the *blessed Virgin* is so sure always to carry off the greatest share, that it may be truly said of her what *Juvenal* says of the *Goddess Isis*, whose religion was at that time in the greatest vogue in *Rome*, that the *painters got their livelihood out of her*.[2] Middleton tells the story from Cicero which, not without covert sympathy, Montaigne quotes in his Essay on 'Prognostications.' Diagoras, surnamed the Atheist, being found one day in a temple, was thus addressed by a friend: 'You, who think the gods take no care of human affairs, do not you see here by this number of pictures how many people, for the sake of

[1] P. 146 (fourth edition, 1741).  [2] *Ibid.*, p. 151.

their vows, have been saved in storms at sea, and got safe into harbour?' 'Yes,' answered Diagoras, 'I see how it is; for those are never painted who happen to be drowned.'

As for St. Winifred's Well, the newspapers now and again report a 'miracle'[1] which the medical journals explain away;[2] the repute of this Welsh Bethesda increases, so that a new wing to house the growing number of pilgrims is being added; and every night about two hundredweight of water is sent off to various parts of the country, and even to America and the colonies.[3]

3. *Orientation.*—'When Bishop Thorold was buried in Winchester Cathedral last week the coffin was placed in the grave with the feet to the west instead of to the east. A few hours after the funeral had taken place, and after all the company had dispersed, the coffin was lifted from the grave and placed in the usual eastward position which has been adopted with every Bishop of Winchester who is buried in the cathedral.'[4]

The writer's implication of a special custom in regard to those prelates shows that the barbaric origin of orientation is not familiar to him. But although it is bringing 'owls to Athens' to enlarge on the matter in your presence, it may refresh some impaired memory to hear what Dr. Tylor says about the history of the rite in Christendom.

It is not to late and isolated fancy, but to the carrying on of ancient and widespread solar ideas, that we trace the well-known tradition that the body of Christ was laid with the head towards the west, thus looking eastward, and the Christian usage of digging graves east and west, which prevailed through mediaeval times, and is not yet forgotten.[5]

To this may be added an extract from a letter by Dr. Tylor, which appeared in *The Times* of July 15, 1875:—

English theologians argue about the Eastward Position without a hint of its being a pre-Christian rite as wide as the world and almost as old as the hills. In their controversies we find not a word of what can be learnt of its origin from Lucian and Vitruvius, from the Brahman standing on one leg to perform his devotions towards the East, or the medicine-man of the

---

[1] *Westminster Gazette,* May 23, 1894.
[2] *Brit. Medical Journal,* October 12, 1894.
[3] *Daily News,* March 18, 1895.
[4] *Westminster Gazette,* August 9, 1895.
[5] *Primitive Culture,* vol. ii, p. 383. *Cf.* Brand's *Pop. Antiquities,* vol. ii, p. 217 (Hazlitt's edition).

American prairie setting out the weapons in the East of the lodge to catch the earliest rays of the rising sun.

4. *Divine Judgments.*—During the last general election the Rev. Thomas Cockram, Rector of Adstock, in a circular asking his parishioners to vote for 'Church and Queen,' reminded them of sundry warnings from God to the Liberal party. Of one of these Mr. Labouchere was the strange and, of course, unwitting instrument.

'But,' adds the reverend politician, 'not content with that, they must needs this session introduce a Bill which was to deprive the Church in Wales of the bulk of her endowments— to rob God directly. The day before the Bill was introduced, the Prime Minister was seized with a violent attack of influenza, from which he scarcely recovered, only to harden his heart, as did the Pharaoh of Moses' day,' etc.[1]

Here again, speaks the lineal descendant of the medicine-man; providing another subject for dissection by the folklorist. For this theory of divine interference in petty human affairs is of the essence of barbaric belief in gods who behave as spiteful men, who strike at offenders in indirect, underhand ways, and hurl their judgments abroad so recklessly that when, as happened a year or two ago, the tower of Shrewsbury Church was struck by lightning, some sapient teleologists saw in this an outburst of divine anger on the town for its erection of a statue to Darwin. But upon this matter it is needless to dwell; it suffices to note an example of what doubtless represents an opinion more often felt than expressed. It shows with what tenacity the old belief in portents, omens, and all their kin, resists the extension of that modern conception of the imperturbable course of nature under which, as Matthew Arnold sings in *Empedocles*:—

Streams will not check their pride
The just man not to entomb,
Nor lightnings go aside
To give his virtues room.
Nor is that wind less rough which blows a good man's barge.

Let it be noted that this general line of inquiry on which we are travelling was laid down many years ago by successful shrewd observers of the relation between past and present, among whom limits permit reference only to Burton, Hobbes, and Conyers Middleton.

[1] *Westminster Gazette*, July 24, 1895.

Burton's various allusions in his *Anatomy of Melancholy*[1] indicate that he looks on pagan practices with much the same eyes that the early Roman Catholic missionaries looked on the shaven Buddhist monks of Tibet, when they saw in their rosaries, bells, holy water, and worship of relics, the wiles of the arch-deceiver who had tempted those men to mock the solemn rites of Catholicism. For he speaks of the Devil's devices in 'the strange Sacraments, the goodly Temples, the Priests and Sacrifices,' and 'imitation of the Ark.' But Hobbes, in the *Leviathan*, recognizes the continuity of ideas under change of names; *mutato nominem tantum.*

> Venus and Cupid appearing as 'the Virgin Mary and her Sonne,' and the 'Αποθ'εωσις of the Heathen surviving in the Canonization of Saints. The carrying of the Popes 'by Switzers under a Canopie' is a 'Relique of the Divine Honours given to Caesar'; the carriage of Images in *Procession* 'a Relique of the Greeks and Romans.' . . . 'The Heathen had also their *Aqua Lustralis*, that is to say, *Holy Water*. The Church of Rome imitates them also in their *Holy Dayes*. They had their *Bacchanalia*, and we have our *Wakes* answering to them; They their *Saturnalia*, and we our Carnevalls and Shrove-tuesdays liberty of Servants; They their Procession of Priapus, we our fetching-in, erection, and dancing about *May-Poles*; and Dancing is one kind of worship; They had their Procession called *Ambarvalia*, and we our Procession about the Fields in the *Rogation week*.'[2]

To this may be added, as one of the most striking examples, the transformation of the *Lupercalia* into the feast of the Purification of Mary. But the subject cannot be further pursued here; enough that what Hobbes has written concerning the Kingdom of the Fairies, and what Conyers Middleton has elaborated in his parallels or, as he calls it in the sub-title of his book, 'an exact CONFORMITY between POPERY and PAGANISM,' may be commended to such as have not read their works. Enough has been said, I hope, to indicate what strata of human history await that fuller explanation which lies within the province of folklore. Until our time that work has extended but a little way down. The old labourers thought that they were near primary formations when they struck on classical or so-called pagan ideas. In truth, they had probed but a comparatively recent layer, since far beneath lay the unsuspected prehistoric deposits of barbaric ideas which are coincident with, and composed

[1] Chiefly in Part III, sect. iv, sub-sect. ii, iii.
[2] Pp. 530, 532, 533. Oxford reprint of the first edition (Thornton, 1881).

of, man's earliest speculations about himself and his surroundings.

But, like the divisions of the strata of the globe itself, ours are artificial. There is no real detachment.

The rite of *baptism* cannot be satisfactorily explained without reference to barbaric lustrations and water-worship generally;[1] nor that of the *eucharist* without reference to sacrificial feasts in honour of the gods; feasts at which they were held to be both the eaters and the eaten. In the gestures denoting *sacerdotal benediction* we have probably an old form of averting the evil eye; in the act of *breathing*, the survival of belief in transference of spiritual qualities, the soul being, as language evidences, well-nigh universally identified with breath. The modern spiritualist who describes apparitions as having the 'consistency of cigar-smoke,'[2] is one with the Congo negroes who leave the house of the dead unswept for a time lest the dust should injure the delicate substance of the ghost; and the inhaling of the last breath of the dying Roman by his nearest kinsman has parallel in the breathing of the risen Jesus on his disciples that they might receive the Holy Ghost.[3] In the offering of *prayers for the dead*; in the *canonization* and *intercession* of *saints*; in the *prayers* and *offerings* at the *shrines of the Virgin* and *saints*, and at the *graves of martyrs*; there are the manifold forms of that great cult of the departed which is found throughout the world. To this may be linked the *belief in angels*, whether good or bad, or guardian, because the element common to the whole is animistic, the peopling of the heavens above, as well as the earth beneath, with an innumerable company of spiritual beings influencing the destinies of men. Well might Jews and Moslems reproach the Christians, as they did down to the eighth century, with having filled the world with more gods than they had overthrown in the Pagan temples; thus echoing a complaint which Petronius, who lived in the reign of Nero, puts into the mouth of Quartilla, that 'the place is so densely peopled with gods that there is hardly room for the men,'[4] while we have Erasmus, in his *Encomium Moriae*, when reciting the names and functions of saints, adding that 'as many things as we wish, so many gods have we made.' Closely related to this group of beliefs is the *adoration of relics*, the vitality of which has springs

[1] Since this Address was in type, I find Dr. Whitley Stokes suggesting, in a letter to the *Academy*, February 15, 1896, 'that the source of Christian infant baptism, like the source of Christian parthenogenesis, etc., is to be found in folklore.'
[2] 'There formed on the side where I was sitting a dwarfish figure, which seemed about the consistency of cigar-smoke,—the proper attenuated form for a ghost to assume.'—*The Great Secret*, p. 225. By a Church of England Clergyman.
[3] John xx, 22.
[4] 'Utique nostra regio tam præsentibus plena est numinibus ut facilius possis deum quam hominem invenire.'—*Satyricon*, ch. xvii.

too deep in human nature to be wholly abolished, and whose inclusion within the province of folklore has warrant, whether we examine the fragments of saints or martyrs which lie beneath every Catholic altar, or the skull-bones of his ancestor which the savage carries about with him as a charm. Then there is the long list of *church festivals*, the reference of which to pagan prototypes is but one step towards their ultimate explanation in nature-worship; there are the *processions* which are the successors of Corybantic frenzies, and, more remotely, of savage dances and other forms of excitation; there is that active belief in the *Second Advent* which is a member of the widespread group wherein human hopes fix eyes on the return of long-sleeping heroes; of Arthur and Olgar Dansk, of Väinämöinen and Quetzalcoatl, of Charlemagne and Barbarossa, of the lost Marko of Servia and the lost King Sebastian.

And so the list of subjects charged with material for the folklorist might run on, but that an end must be made of it here.

Suffice it, that when the origin of these several groups of beliefs and customs is made clear—as made clear it will be—there will be given further evidence of the unity of man psychically as well as physically; further evidence of the impossibility of excluding him from the operation of the great law of development, of descent with modification, which rules throughout the organic world. Long banished from the inorganic realm and from the sphere which includes all lower life, the forces of the spirit of caprice and disorder retreated within the citadel of Mansoul. But folklore, in alliance with the Determinist philosophy, will drive them thence, because it is the agent of order, and not of confusion. Its high mission is to contribute to the freedom of the spirit, to deliver those who, being children of superstition, are therefore the prisoners of fear.

You will, I hope, agree with me that the volume and variety of the materials which are in hand warrant us not only in showing their significance, but in attempting some definite conclusions. Those which I have ventured to draw you will please take for what they are worth as being only the expression of individual opinion.

Since passing the proof of this address, I have read Dr. Frank Granger's recently-published work on the *Worship of the Romans*. As further evidence of the persistence and significance of Pagan ideas, of which it is crammed with illustrations, the book is invaluable.

[Observation having been made as to certain references to matters of controversy in the President's Address, the Editor is authorized by the Council to explain that, in accordance with the general rule in all scientific societies, that Address is not open to criticism or alteration by the Council or by the Editor. It is the expression of the views of the President, and is listened to by the members with the respect due to his position. It does not necessarily express the opinions of the Council or of the members at large.]

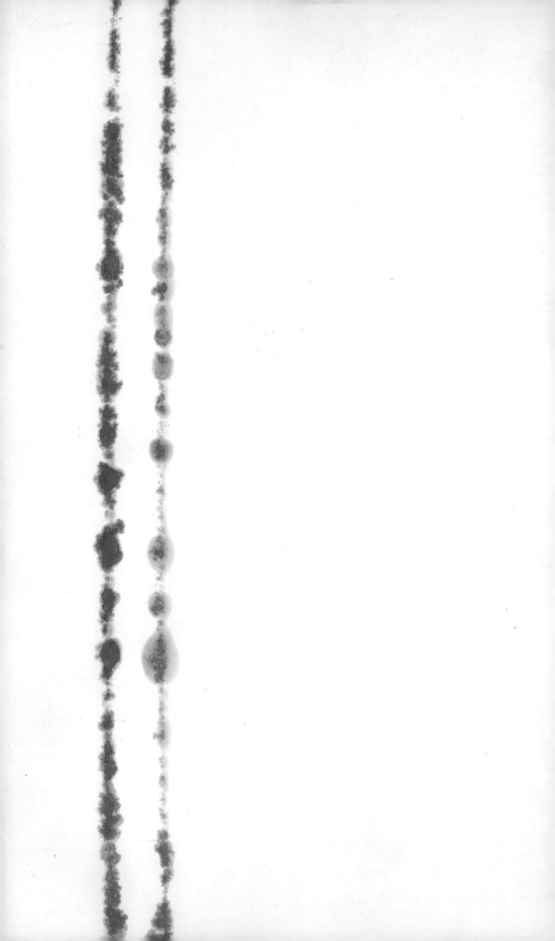

-C. NOV. 1977

£1·50

9/12

**Hertfordshire**
COUNTY COUNCIL
Community Information

17 AuG 2002
7 SEPT 2002
OCT 14· 02

– 5 NOV 2002
Nov 23rd.

1 0 APR 2002
29 APR 2002
20 MAY

1 1 SEP 2003

7 JUN 2002

1 3 JUL 2002

31 AUG 2002

Please renew/return this item by the last date shown.

So that your telephone call is charged at local rate, please call the numbers as set out below:

|  | From Area codes 01923 or 0208: | From the rest of Herts: |
|---|---|---|
| Renewals: | 01923 471373 | 01438 737373 |
| Enquiries: | 01923 471333 | 01438 737333 |
| Minicom: | 01923 471599 | 01438 737599 |

L32b